Shaykh Yūsuf al-Qaraḍāwī

Modern Intellectual and Political History of the Middle East
Fred H. Lawson, *Series Editor*

Select titles in Modern Intellectual and Political History of the Middle East

Emirate, Egyptian, Ethiopian: Colonial Experiences in Late Nineteenth-Century Harar
Avishai Ben-Dror

The Iranian Constitutional Revolution and the Clerical Leadership of Khurasani
Mateo Mohammad Farzaneh

Jurji Zaidan and the Foundations of Arab Nationalism
Thomas Philipp

Mirror for the Muslim Prince: Islam and the Theory of Statecraft
Mehrzad Boroujerdi, ed.

Mohammad Mosaddeq and the 1953 Coup in Iran
Mark J. Gasiorowski and Malcolm Byrne, eds.

Ottoman Rule of Law and the Modern Political Trial: The Yıldız Case
Avi Rubin

The Revolt of the Young: Essays by Tawfiq al-Hakim
Mona Radwan, trans.

Why Alliances Fail: Islamist and Leftist Coalitions in North Africa
Matt Buehler

Shaykh Yūsuf al-Qaraḍāwī

Spiritual Mentor of Wasaṭī *Salafism*

Sagi Polka

Syracuse University Press

First Edition 2019

19 20 21 22 23 24 6 5 4 3 2 1

∞ The paper used in this publication meets the minimum requirements of the American National Standard for Information Sciences—Permanence of Paper for Printed Library Materials, ANSI Z39.48-1992.

For a listing of books published and distributed by Syracuse University Press, visit www.press.syr.edu.

ISBN: 978-0-8156-3634-2 (hardcover)
978-0-8156-3652-6 (paperback)
978-0-8156-5480-3 (e-book)

Library of Congress Cataloging-in-Publication Data

Names: Polka, Sagi, author.
Title: Shaykh Yūsuf al-Qaraḍāwī: spiritual mentor of Wasaṭī Salafism / Sagi Polka.
Description: Syracuse, N.Y. : Syracuse University Press, [2019] | Series: Modern intellectual and political history of the Middle East | Includes bibliographical references and index.
Identifiers: LCCN 2019002574 (print) | LCCN 2019004672 (ebook) | ISBN 9780815654803 (E-book) | ISBN 9780815636342 (hardcover : alk. paper) | ISBN 9780815636526 (pbk. : alk. paper)
Subjects: LCSH: Qaraḍāwī, Yūsuf. | Muslim scholars—Biography. | Salafīyah. | Salafīyah—History.
Classification: LCC BP80.Q357 (ebook) | LCC BP80.Q357 P655 2019 (print) | DDC 297.8/1092 [B] —dc23
LC record available at https://lccn.loc.gov/2019002574

Manufactured in the United States of America

In loving memory of my devoted mother, Hasida,
my guide and mentor

Contents

Illustrations

Acknowledgments

This book is the fruit of years of inquiry into the discourse in contemporary Islam, focusing in particular on the *wasaṭiyya* movement and its head, Shaykh Yūsuf al-Qaraḍāwī. After completing my PhD dissertation on the *wasaṭiyya* movement under the supervision of Michael Winter, I taught text-based courses on various aspects of al-Qaraḍāwī's teachings for many years. The students of these courses, many of them Muslims, provided the inspiration for the present book. Throughout the years of research, many people helped me, and I would like to take this opportunity to thank them. First and foremost, I thank the Nehemiah Levtzion Center for Islamic Studies, which has provided me with a research fellowship for the past two years, made possible thanks to the efforts of Meir Hatina, chairman of the Department of Middle Eastern History at the Hebrew University, and of Liat Kuzma, head of the Levtzion Center.

I also thank all of the friends who agreed to read a preliminary version of the book's chapters and made very useful comments: Meir. M. Bar-Asher, Ella Landau-Tasseron, Aharon Layish, Binyamin Abrahamov, Isaac Hasson, Yoram Meital, and Vardit Rispler-Haim. Each of them read one chapter dealing with a topic in his or her respective field of specialization. Their comments were illuminating and helpful. I also express my heartfelt thanks to the two anonymous readers of the manuscript, who made a crucial contribution to the book by highlighting important aspects of the various currents of Islamic thought. I learned much from these readers, but, of course, whatever errors the book may contain are my own.

A special word of appreciation goes to Michael Winter, the devoted supervisor of my dissertation. It was in his courses on contemporary Islamic thought that I first became exposed to the fascinating intellectual world of the *wasaṭiyya* movement.

My research necessitated the acquisition of numerous Muslim publications. My trusted friend Yaacov Setty helped me to purchase them in Cairo. Without the help of the Israeli ambassador in Cairo, David Govrin, the books could not have been dispatched to me.

A special thanks to the two translators, Hagit Migron and Michael Guggenheimer, who translated the Hebrew manuscript into English with professionalism and dedication and while understanding the intricacies of the text.

I extend my gratitude to Syracuse University Press for its willingness to take on the task of publication. Special thanks go to Alison M. Shay, the acquisitions editor, who accompanied the manuscript from its first stages and worked tirelessly to bring it to publication. My thanks also to the series editor, Fred Lawson, who together with Alison helped develop the manuscript and gave useful advice, and to Kelly Balenske, the assistant editor, who was very helpful in the last stages of editing. Without the publisher's efforts and commitment, the book would not have seen the light of day.

My thanks and appreciation to Annie Barva for her professional and thorough editing of the manuscript, which greatly improved the text.

Last but not least, I offer my heartfelt gratitude to my dear wife, Ariella, and my two charming daughters, Oshrit and Noga, who made so many sacrifices over such a long time so that I would be able to devote my time to this research.

Abbreviations

ECFR	European Council for Fatwā and Research
IS	Islamic State
IUMS	International Union of Muslim Scholars
MB	Muslim Brotherhood
UAE	United Arab Emirates
UN	United Nations

Note on Transliteration and Translations

Arabic words and terms are spelled in accordance with the transcription rules of the *International Journal of Middle East Studies* (*IJMES*). However, I also transliterated words in common use that according to the *IJMES* rules should not be transliterated—for example, *sharīʿa*, *muftī*. The same goes for proper nouns such as "Qur'ān," "Qur'ānic," and "al-Qaraḍāwī." I spelled well-known names without transliteration—for example, "Osama bin Laden" and "al-Qaʿida" (the latter should have been transliterated "al-Qāʿida"). A *tāʾ marbūṭa* that is not in the construct state is transliterated as *h* in words that are preceded by *ā*—for example, *ḥayāh*, *duʿāh*.

Islamic terms that possess religious and cultural connotations that a literal English translation cannot fully convey—for example, *ḥākimiyya*—are, when first mentioned, given a literal translation and accompanied by an explanation and the original term in transliteration, and they subsequently appear only in transliteration.

The plural form of a number of words—for example, *ḥadīth* and *fatwā*—is given with a suffixed *-s* instead of with the proper denotation of the plural in Arabic (which, in these examples, would be *aḥādīth* and *fatāwā*).

The Translations

Translations of various Arabic writings, especially those of Shaykh Yūsuf al-Qaraḍāwī, the Salafist jihadists, and liberal intellectuals, are my own. However, the translated Qur'ānic verses are taken in part from the translation by M. A. S. Abdel Haleem, *The Qur'an: A New Translation*,[1] and in part from the Sahih International website. I have sometimes inserted my own comments (within square brackets) based on Islamic Qur'ānic exegesis into translations of Qur'ānic verses.

For translating *ḥadīth* traditions, I used mainly the Sunnah.com website, to which I added my own comments (within square brackets) based on Islamic *ḥadīth* exegesis.

The Clash within Islam

A Sampling of Representative Quotes

"Istanbul (*al-Qusṭanṭīniyya*) has been conquered, and now Rome is left to be conquered.[1] This means that Islam will return to Europe once again, after it was expelled from it. . . . I think that this time it will conquer it through preaching (*da'wa*) . . . , through thought, because Europe today thirsts for a religion that will extricate it from its worry, its confusion at the suffering it experiences because of materialism and permissiveness, and it will not find this remedy except in Islam."

—Shaykh Yūsuf al-Qaraḍāwī[2]

"I think that this conquest of Europe will be by means of the pen and the tongue rather than the sword and tip, and that the world will open its arms and heart to Islam after it had been made miserable by materialistic man-made philosophies (ideologies) and awaits divine help and guidance from Allah. Only in Islam will it find its life buoy."

—Shaykh Yūsuf al-Qaraḍāwī[3]

"This religion [Islam] arrived with the sword, arose with the sword, and will persist with the sword. If the sword will be lost, the faith will be lost. This religion is one of awe [*hayba*] . . . , a religion of fear [*rahba*], power, attack, heroism; it considers weakness a crime whose perpetrator deserves hellfire. . . . We shall not stutter or be ashamed when we present our religion to mankind; it is a religion whose aim is to save humanity as a whole . . . on the entire earth. It aims to save man . . . the human species on earth, the entire earth."

—'Abdallah 'Azzām[4]

"Military action aims first and foremost to hit the head of global unbelief America and its ally Israel. Second, to hit its local allies who rule in our countries. The assault on America aims at weakening and exhausting it so that it becomes like the Soviet Union and shuts itself up within itself following its military defeats, its losses in lives, and its economic losses. As a result, its hold on our countries will be loosened, and then its allies will fall one by one."

—Ayman al-Ẓawāhirī[5]

"O Muslims! Islam never was a religion of peace. Islam is a religion of warfare. Your Prophet was sent with the sword, as a mercy to the worlds, and commanded to fight until Allah alone would be worshipped. [The Prophet], may Allah pray for him and give him peace, said to the polytheists [*mushrikūn*] in his tribe: 'I have come to slaughter you.'"

—Abū Bakr al-Baghdādī[6]

"Religious Salafiyya/*uṣūliyya* is the warm breast that feeds the ideas of the soldiers of the jihadi Salafī militias. When secularism [*'ilmāniyya*] will prevail in the Arab world, terrorism will cease as a matter of course. We are aware that the reality at the end of the twentieth and the beginning of the twenty-first century is such that the incidence of terrorism has increased with the emergence of religious Salafism/fundamentalism. We also note that it is religious Salafism/fundamentalism, terrorism's second line, that nourishes the terrorist militias conceptually and religiously."

—Shākir al-Nābulsī[7]

"While the laws of minor jihad—that is, of fighting or war—are restricted to certain times and circumstances, the permanent laws are those of major jihad, the jihad against the soul's [lusts]. But politics and Islamic jurisprudence [*fiqh*] have pushed major jihad aside and raised high the flag of minor jihad because this jihad serves and implements their objectives. The temporary law [war] in Islam has become a permanent state at the expense of the faith and of humanity."

—Muḥammad Sa'īd al-'Ashmāwī[8]

"One of the most important challenges facing our Arab societies with respect to Islam is the ideological and utilitarian use of Islam for the realization of collective, political, or personal benefits and objectives. Whether this use is made by the political groups themselves or by political regimes and authorities that lack social, political, and legal legitimacy, the result is the same: it turns Islam into a tool and restricts it to worldly functions and purposes."

—Naṣr Ḥāmid Abū Zayd[9]

Shaykh Yūsuf al-Qaraḍāwī

Introduction

Wasaṭī *Islamism*

A Clash within Islam: The *Wasaṭī* Interpretation versus the Jihadi Salafī Interpretation

In an age when beheadings of those whom the Islamic State (IS) considers to be infidels fill the screens and when a captured Jordanian soldier is burned alive (January 2015), a number of Muslim clerics (*'ulamā'*, sing. *'ālim*), some belonging to the establishment and others working independently, have been making an attempt to present an alternative to the way IS interprets Islam. They accuse the Islamists of distorting what they, the clerics, perceive as the real and true Islam. To delegitimize the Islamism of the kind espoused by members of IS, these clerics use various insulting epithets when speaking of them, such as "the new Tatars," "contemporary Khawārij,"[1] and "the dogs of hell," a title given them in a statement attributed to the Prophet.[2]

As an alternative to this interpretation of Islam and in order to cope with what these *'ulamā'* consider "intellectual extremism" (*al-taṭarruf al-fikrī*) and "terrorism" (*irhāb*), the *'ulamā'* stress the need for a "balanced religious discourse" that will preserve the immutable principles of Qur'ānic law (*sharī'a*) but at the same time offer practical solutions to the challenges that Muslim society faces.[3] Such a discourse should be based on *wasaṭiyya* (literally "centrism") and moderation (*i'tidāl*) as the essential traits of Islam and as the means for coping with religious exaggeration (*ghulū*) and extremism. But Muslim liberals, such as Shākir al-Nābulsī (d. 2014), one of the foremost representatives of the neoliberal stream, accuse these clerics, in particular Shaykh Yūsuf al-Qaraḍāwī, the subject of this book, of helping terrorism take root in the Muslim world through their rulings on jihad and *istishhād* (martyrdom).[4] Furthermore, according to al-Nābulsī, one of the factors that led to the creation of the "bin Laden phenomenon" was the creation by clerics such as al-Qaraḍāwī of a class of *'ulamā'* who claim to possess the only true religious knowledge. This class has monopolized religious knowledge and accuses anyone who disagrees with it of heresy.[5]

Egyptian president 'Abd al-Fattah al-Sisi (b. 1954), to cope with what he perceived as the Islamist threat to his regime posed by the Muslim Brotherhood (MB, Jamā'at al-Ikhwān al-Muslimīn) and IS, called on his country's religious establishment to carry out a "religious revolution" and bring about a *tajdīd* (renewal) of religious discourse to bring Islam back to its original tolerant form rather than retain the extremists' distorted form. As part of this effort, a number of institutions and forums were established, and the al-Azhar Institute announced that it would foster *wasaṭiyya* and moderation and disseminate the *wasaṭī* (literally "centrist") philosophy throughout the Muslim world as well as in the West.[6] The Egyptian Ministry of Religious Endowments began to publish letters translated into numerous languages in which the "correct religious discourse" is presented to make it possible, the ministry hopes, for all people to live peacefully in justice, equality, and liberty.[7]

The Muslim cleric most closely identified with the idea of *wasaṭiyya* is Shaykh Yūsuf al-Qaraḍāwī (b. 1926), who transformed the idea into a school (madrasa) with its own clear features and established several institutions—for example, the International Union of Muslim Scholars (IUMS, al-Ittiḥād al-'ālamī li-'ulamā' al-Muslimīn)—to disseminate it and to constitute an alternative to a "juridical flaw" from which, in al-Qaraḍāwī's opinion, the violent groups in Islam suffer. His students, who have organized into an active body, call him "the *imām* of *wasaṭiyya*."[8] Shaykh 'Abdallah Yūsuf al-Qaraḍāwī was born on September 9, 1926 (Rabī' al-Awwal, AH 1345) in the village of Ṣafṭ Turāb in Egypt's al-Gharbiyya governorate, some twenty kilometers northeast of Ṭantā.[9] He is named "al-Qaraḍāwī" after the village of al-Qaraḍa,[10] from which the family originally came. His father died when he was two years old, and he was raised by his mother. His uncle Aḥmad acted as his guardian, and Yūsuf even called him "father."[11] At the age of five, he started memorizing the Qur'ān at the Qur'ān school (*kuttāb*), and at the age of seven he began attending elementary school as well, going there in the afternoons while continuing to attend the *kuttāb* in the mornings. Before the age of ten, he had learned the Qur'ān by heart. At age twelve, he enrolled in the al-Azhar Religious Institute (al-Maʿhad al-Dīnī) and chose to follow the Ḥanafī school, quite at random, he says, even though the people of his village were followers of the Shāfiʿī school.[12] In his childhood, he was also exposed to Ṣūfism because there were several Ṣūfī orders in his village, chief among them al-Ṭarīqa al-Khalīliyya. Thus, as a boy he became familiar with the works of Abū Ḥāmid al-Ghazālī (d. 1111), which had a profound influence on him.[13]

Al-Qaraḍāwī views himself as the renewer (*mujaddid*) of Islam in our age and as the successor of the reformers (*muṣliḥūn*), in particular Muḥammad Rashīd Riḍā (d. 1935), whose ideas greatly influenced the MB. Al-Qaraḍāwī grew up in the combined melting pot of al-Azhar University, where he studied and received his PhD in the early 1970s, and the MB, of which he was officially a member until the mid-1960s. Although he withdrew his membership, he has since remained an important guide for the MB and is to this day a source of authority and inspiration for its intermediate generation. He has striven to create a "*wasaṭī* culture" using a combination of rulings (*fatwā*s) based on the principles of *wasaṭiyya*, most importantly that of facilitation (*taysīr*) in applying the law and preaching (*daʿwa*) in the *wasaṭī* spirit. In fact, al-Qaraḍāwī has become so identified with both activities that he has been called "the jurist of the preachers and the preacher of the jurists" (*faqīh al-duʿāh wa-dāʿiyat al-fuqahā'*). By maneuvering with more flexibility in the law, using independent reasoning (*ijtihād*) in issuing *fatwā*s and renewal of jurisprudence (*tajdīd al-fiqh*) and taking the goals (*maqāṣid*) of the *sharīʿa* into account, he has striven to provide creative solutions in Islamic law to the problems of the changing times. The legal creativity he has shown in developing solutions to problems has captivated contemporary Muslims, with whom he communicates using all the media that modern technology has made available.

Al-Qaraḍāwī has stated that it is his hope that the nation's future leaders will come from among his students, whom he urges to adopt the "way of renewing *wasaṭiyya*" (*minhaj al-wasaṭiyya al-mujaddida*).[14] In the 1970s, he proposed *wasaṭiyya* as a method for guiding (*tarshīd*) the phenomenon of the Islamic awakening (*al-saḥwa al-Islāmiyya*), especially the Islamic movements in Egypt that rebelled against Gamal ʿAbd al-Nasir's (d. 1970) regime and eventually assassinated Anwar Sadat in 1981. Today, especially in the wake of the attacks in the United States on September 11, 2001 (9/11), al-Qaraḍāwī presents *wasaṭiyya* as a response and an alternative to the jihadi Salafism espoused by groups such as al-Qaʿida and IS. *Wasaṭī* Islam perceives itself as the true Islam that is based on the words of the Qur'ān and the Sunna and views the jihadi Salafī version of Islam as a distortion that generated Islamophobia in the West, which in turn gave rise to the identification of Islam with terrorism.

Al-Qaraḍāwī insists on presenting himself and his *wasaṭiyya* philosophy as the epitome of moderation and tolerance, the opposite of extremism displayed by jihadi Salafism. However, a liberal and fearless critic of religious discourse, Naṣr Ḥāmid Abū Zayd (d. 2010), has argued that in the religious discourse there is no significant difference between "moderates" (*muʿtadilūn*) and "extremists" (*mutaṭarrifūn*). The difference is one of degree rather than of kind; both "moderate" and "extremist" legists and preachers, he argues, use the same devices—first and foremost the device of presenting their own ideas and interpretation of the holy texts as synonymous with the faith itself. In this way, they present their own ideological stance as necessarily true and accordingly reject any opposing interpretation. In such ideological disputes, these clerics, including al-Qaraḍāwī, delegitimize their opponents by accusing them of heresy (*takfīr*). On the latter issue, Abū Zayd notes, there is no tangible difference in the Muslim religious discourse of moderates and extremists: they may disagree on the boundaries of the principle's implementation but not on the principle itself, as shown throughout this volume.[15]

One of al-Qaraḍāwī's sharpest critics, ʿAbd al-Razzāq ʿĪd (b. 1950), a Syrian liberal, argues in *Yūsuf al-Qaraḍāwī between Tolerance and Terrorism* that the "*wasaṭiyya*" that al-Qaraḍāwī falsely claims to follow has nothing whatsoever to do with religious toleration (*tasāmuḥ*) or moderation (*iʿtidāl*). Rather, it involves, so ʿĪd claims, moving between moderation and extremism according to one's momentary tactical interests.[16] ʿĪd accuses al-Qaraḍāwī of acting out two different but interchanging roles, depending on circumstance. On the one hand, he takes on a role like Osama bin Laden's and insists that Muslims who refuse to follow his version of Islam deserve the death penalty for apostasy (*ḥadd al-ridda*). 'Īd explains that al-Qaraḍāwī would impose the death penalty not only on secularists but also on pan-Arab nationalists, who may be assumed to be secular, as well as liberals, Communists, socialists, democrats, and the like. On the other hand, al-Qaraḍāwī assumes the mantle of "Westernism" (*ifranjiyya*). In this role, he declares that democracy is the spirit of Islam. 'Īd explains: "Since the 'satellite station shaykh' has the spiritual authority of the prophets and the material authority of the rich and powerful, he enjoys every kind of immunity in order to sew them a democracy 'made to order' according to their specific measure. It is enough if something is published in the name of his 'holiness' for it to be perceived as legitimate."[17]

To elucidate the interpretation and ideology of *wasaṭī* Islam, we must first define four fundamental principles pivotal to contemporary Muslim discourse: *wasaṭiyya*, Salafism, Islamism, and liberalism. *Wasaṭiyya* and the Salafī stream share the basic aspiration of returning to the "pure and original faith" of Islam's first three generations. At the same time, *wasaṭiyya* seeks to distance itself from some of the ideas of Salafism and especially of jihadi Salafism, which forms the ideological infrastructure of global jihad. This study explores the similarities and differences between *wasaṭiyya* and Salafism, in particular jihadi Salafism. Islamism is crucial to this study as well: *wasaṭiyya*, the MB, and jihadi Salafism all belong to the Islamist stream, despite some ideological differences between them. This study argues that *wasaṭiyya* occupies a place between the MB and jihadi Salafism, which requires an examination of the concept of Islamism. Liberalism is also pivotal to this study because *wasaṭiyya* regards itself as an answer to liberal secularism. So this introduction reviews the *wasaṭī*/liberal-secular polemic, examining it from a historical perspective.

Wasaṭiyya

In her article on *wasaṭīyya*, Bettina Gräf argues that the term was coined in the twentieth century. She is unable to determine precisely when it made its first appearance but notes that clerics at al-Azhar, such as Shaykh Muḥammad al-Madanī (d. 1968), used it in the 1960s.[18] However, it should be pointed out that there is a very rich contemporary Islamic literature on the roots of the *wasaṭī* approach in the Qur'ān,[19] the Sunna, the Prophet's biography, and the principles of the faith.[20] Because the term is perceived as positive, Muslim scholars have naturally sought to find its roots in classical Muslim sources, where it and its meaning as defined by al-Qaraḍāwī do not appear, but the root *w s ṭ* and its basic idea do.

Al-Qaraḍāwī calls the approach that he developed and that he believes should guide the Islamic awakening *wasaṭiyya*.[21] Even before he gave his approach this name, he defined the term as one of the unique features of Islam in general. He explained the principle of *wasaṭiyya* as constituting a balance (*tawāzun* or *ta'ādul*) between two conflicting positions, with no inclination by one to deny the right of the other. As examples of parallel or contradictory extremes, he gives the following: materialism and spirituality, individualism and communalism, ideals and reality, continuity and change, and so on. Each of the extremes, he claims, has its just share, not too little but also not too much, as stated in Qur'ān (Q) 55:7–9: "He has raised up the sky. He has set the balance. So that you may not exceed in the balance. Weigh with justice and don't fall short in the balance."[22]

Al-Qaraḍāwī defines *wasaṭiyya* as a balance between two opposing poles, taking a third position between the two extremes. This middle position combines elements from both poles—those elements that are compatible and can be merged—and that is why Muḥammad 'Imāra (b. 1931), an Egyptian *wasaṭī* thinker who in the 1980s abandoned Marxism in favor of Islamic thought, described it as an ideology of "merging" (*jāmi'a*).[23] Based on this definition, Uriya Shavit translates *wasaṭiyya* as "the harmonizing middle-ground" approach.[24] However, an examination of the *wasaṭī* positions on major issues shows that these positions do not in fact find a harmony between two opposing views. Rather, as discussed in this book, *wasaṭiyya* largely challenges and rejects both poles, offering a new position as an answer to its opponents from both sides.

To better portray itself as the ideal middle way, *wasaṭiyya* characterizes the two poles in a very radical, simplified, and negative way. For example, in discussing the *tajdīd al-fiqh*, al-Qaraḍāwī says that at one pole are the "enemies of renewal," such as the Salafīs, who cleave fanatically to a particular school of jurisprudence and accept *ijtihād* only within the confines of that school; these people advocate the freezing (*tajmīd*) rather than the renewal (*tajdīd*) of Islam. At the other pole, he says, are those who advocate excessive renewal and seek to eliminate anything that is ancient, even if it is central to the identity of society. He accuses them of blindly emulating the West: "For them, ancient Western [ideas] are new, [so] they call to adopt them, the good along with the bad and the sweet along with the bitter." He adds that "between these two poles there exists a conspicuous middle way that rejects the rigidity of the former approach as well as the negativity [*juḥūd*] of the latter and seeks wisdom wherever it is found." *Wasaṭiyya*, he claims, preaches *tajdīd* as long as it is within the boundaries of Islam's original framework, thus combining all the good of the past with all the good of the modern age. He argues that this is the position of all genuine Islamic preachers, who advocate "openness to the world but not assimilation" and believe not only in the permanent goals of Islam but also in flexible means of achieving them.[25] However, in contrast to al-Qaraḍāwī's claims, this study shows that on many issues, first and foremost women's issues, al-Qaraḍāwī's legal approach has much in common with the Salafī approach: both rely on a literal reading of the Qur'ān and Sunna texts. Chapter 6 shows that the difference between the *wasaṭī* and liberal approaches hinges precisely on their differing interpretations of the Qur'ānic text.

It may be justly claimed that the *wasaṭī* movement's slogan and its ultimate source of inspiration is Q2:143: "We have made you [believers] into a just community [*umma wasaṭ*], so that you may bear witness [to the truth] before others and so that the Messenger may bear witness [to it] before you." This verse declares that *wasaṭ* is a trait of the Muslim nation. Exegetes of the Qur'ān have given this expression various interpretations, which greatly influenced al-Qaraḍāwī's decision to choose the word *wasaṭiyya* as the name of his philosophical approach.[26]

It should be noted that this Qur'ānic verse alludes to the changing of the direction of prayer (*qibla*). The verse that precedes it mentions the fools (*sufahā'*)—an appellation that, according to exegetes, refers to the Jews, the polytheists, and the hypocrites—who wonder why the direction has changed. Verse 143 states that Muslims are tasked with testifying that the previous generations had received Allah's Word from the messengers who had been sent to them, whereas the Prophet Muḥammad is tasked with testifying that the Muslims believe in him. In other words, the verse does not present the Muslims as a moderate or tolerant nation but as the nation that has received the correct guidance from Allah and the Messenger and that therefore serves as the standard to which all other nations are compared. The verse reflects the Qur'ānic perception (stated explicitly in Q3:110) that Muslims are the best of nations. Al-Qaraḍāwī does admit that the word *wasaṭ* in this verse can also mean "good," but he prefers to interpret it as meaning "taking the middle way" because this interpretation allows him to argue that the notion of *wasaṭiyya* is rooted in the Qur'ān. In his critique of al-Qaraḍāwī's ideology, however, Mu'tazz al-Khaṭīb, a Syrian researcher who authored a biography of al-Qaraḍāwī, asserts that the Qur'ān contains no allusion to *wasaṭiyya* in the sense of the middle way. The Qur'ān, he says, presents Islam as the one and only truth from which all other faiths deviate, as stated in Q48:28.[27]

How, therefore, should the term *wasaṭiyya* be translated? Bettina Gräf argues that al-Qaraḍāwī uses the term *wasaṭiyya* as one of a series of synonyms, among them *i'tidāl* (moderation), *ta'ādul* (equilibrium), *tawassuṭ* (intermediacy), *tawāzun* (balance), and even *wasaṭ* (middle). Taking these synonyms into account, the term *wasaṭiyya* has usually been translated as "mainstream." However, in Gräf's opinion, this translation ignores the element of resistance and defiance the term connotes, so she proposes that it be translated as "counterbalance," at least in its use by al-Qaraḍāwī after 2001.[28]

The term *wasaṭiyya* as used in this book refers to the movement of that name. It implies all of that movement's unique features, as defined by al-Qaraḍāwī and analyzed in this introduction and throughout the book. Because of the term's heavy semantic load and because any attempt to translate it will of necessity reflect some of its aspects but ignore others, it is better to use it as given.

Salafī and Salafism

The word *Salafiyya* is derived from the root *s l f*, "past" (see, for example, Q2:275).[29] Salafīs are Muslims who wish to emulate the pious forefathers in all aspects of their lives. Traditions quote the Prophet to the effect that the best generations of Islam are the first three: "The best people are my generation [*qarnī*—that is, the Prophet's Companions], then those who come after them, and then those who come after them." The transmitter adds, "I do not know if [the Prophet counted up] to the third or fourth [generation]. [The Prophet] said: After them [people] will come, some of whom will testify before they take their oath and take an oath before they testify [that is, whose words are not trusted; therefore one should take an oath at the same time as giving testimony]."[30] The *salaf*, or founding fathers, are deemed to embody Islam in its purest and most original form, its golden age, before the appearance of the various schools and approaches that entered Islam following the conquests and introduced non-Muslim philosophies into it.[31]

As Bernard Haykel has noted, "The term *salafī*, and those it designates, remains ill-defined and often misunderstood in the literature on this movement, and in studies on Islamism more generally."[32] In a revolutionary study, Henri Lauzière shows that the term *Salafiyya*, in the sense of "a method" and "a way" (*minhaj*) is a product of the twentieth century. He argues that from the Middle Ages until the beginning of the twentieth century Muslim scholars and activists referred to themselves as "Salafī" only as a mark of their adherence to the theology of the Ḥanbalī school of jurisprudence. In other words, before the twentieth century, "Muslims did not use the term *salafī* to signal their adherence to a movement or multifaceted religious orientation called Salafism (Salafiyya)."[33] His study refutes a view that was common among scholars—namely, that the Islamic reform movement at the end of the nineteenth century and the beginning of the twentieth century was Salafī.[34] Lauzière shows that it was not until the 1970s that Salafism underwent a process of *ideologization*—that is, transformed into a complete and total ideology. The term *minhaj*, denoting a way and a method, reflects this process.[35] Haykel notes that this use of the term *minhaj* is a modern development and is due to Nāṣir al-Dīn al-Albānī (d. 1999), the founder of puristic Salafism, whose use of it was inspired by its appearance in the Qur'ān (Q5:48).[36]

According to Haykel, the Salafīs are a group that defines its reform plan first and foremost through its creedal tenets—that is, through theology.

Legal rulings and forms of "sociability and politics" are only secondary elements of this self-definition, which is based on the Salafis' views on the nature of faith, how they define God's oneness (*tawḥīd*), and their approach to understanding God's attributes (*ṣifāt Allah*). Haykel enumerates the Salafis' main tenets: (1) a return to the authentic beliefs and practices of the first three generations of Muslims (the pious forefathers), from the time of Muḥammad until the time of Aḥmad b. Ḥanbal (d. 855 CE); (2) emphasis on a specific, unique understanding of the principle of the duty to profess God's oneness; (3) duty to fight heresy, especially all forms of association (*shirk*) of other beings or things with God; (4) acknowledgment that the valid sources of authority are the Qur'ān, the Sunna, and the consensus of opinion (*ijmāʿ*) among the Prophet's Companions; (5) the need to purify Islam of forbidden innovations (*bidʿa*, pl. *bidaʿ*) in creed and religious practice; and (6) a strict constructionist interpretation of the Qur'ān and the Sunna is sufficient to guide Muslims everywhere, now and in the future.[37]

Salafī Heterogeneity: Factions

Salafis today belong to numerous schools that differ considerably from each other, in particular with respect to the method (*minhaj*) in which the faith's main doctrines (*ʿaqīda*) should be implemented, especially that of God's oneness.[38] Quintan Wiktorowicz has identified three main groups of Salafis: purists, politicos, and jihadis. He points out that the various factions share a common creed, based on the idea of God's oneness, adding that "divisions have emerged as a result of the inherently subjective nature of applying religion to new issues and problems."[39] The purists' approach is to cleanse Islam so that it reverts to how it is represented in the Qur'ān, the Sunna, and the consensus of opinion among the Prophet's Companions. They believe that emphasis should be placed on the promotion of the Salafī creed and on the struggle against deviant practices. They compare this struggle to the Prophet's fight against idolatry. Until Islam is purified, they believe, political activity will lead to corruption and injustice because society does not understand the tenets of the creed. According to this approach, the right way to implement the faith is through proselytizing, cleansing and purifying (*tazkiya*), and educating.[40]

The political approach in Salafism was born, according to Wiktorowicz, in the 1980s and 1990s among MB members who were persecuted in their homeland and immigrated to Saudi Arabia during the 1960s. In Saudi Arabia, they spread a political version of Islam mainly in the form of an "awakening" (*Ṣaḥwa*) movement and Sururism, named after its founder, Shaykh Muḥammad Surūr Zayn al-ʿĀbidīn (d. 2016). The two main figures of the Ṣaḥwa movement were Salmān al-ʿAwda (b. 1956) and Safar al-Ḥawālī (b. 1955).[41] They combined Wahhābism with the MB's political activism and criticized the Saudi regime. The Ṣaḥwa movement provided the main impetus for the antiregime protests that broke out in the wake of the Saudi government's decision to allow US troops to enter the country and help the Persian Gulf states against Iraq following the latter's invasion of Kuwait in 1990.[42] Sururism differs from both the MB and traditional Salafism, showing the influence of both Ibn Taymiyya (d. 1328) and Sayyid Quṭb (who was executed in 1966). It adopted Ibn Taymiyya's extreme hostility toward the Shīʿīs and other non-Sunnī groups and Sayyid Quṭb's principle of God's sovereignty (*ḥākimiyya*) (for more on the term *ḥākimiyya*, see chapter 4). Muḥammad Surūr condemned the absolute loyalty of some Wahhābī clerics to the Saudi state but also expressed his opposition to attempted coups against Muslim regimes because of his concern that such coups would lead to internecine fighting among Muslims.[43]

Jihadi Salafism

Thomas Hegghammer notes that the term *jihadi Salafism* has become increasingly popular in recent years but that its origins are unclear.[44] Abū Muḥammad al-Maqdisī (b. 1959), a Jordanian thinker who has had an important influence on the shaping of jihadi Salafism, makes the following significant distinction concerning this term: "The term *jihadi Salafism* was not what we called ourselves, but what others called this current. We did not condemn [the term] or reject it because whoever called us thus did so because they viewed the reality of those who belonged to this current and tried to do it justice by using this title, which, they thought, [reflects] their reality and their situation."[45] Al-Maqdisī stresses that those who use the term *jihadi Salafism* are treating the movement fairly, in contrast to governments and their mobilized media, which use such insulting terms or names as *takfīriyyūn*, referring to those who exaggerate in accusing other Muslims of heresy (i.e., accuse them of heresy without sufficient justification); "Khawārij"; "the group that has gone astray" (*al-fi'a al-ḍālla*); *bughāh*, "the rebels"; and the like.[46] He maintains that what defines jihadi Salafism and what sets it apart from other *da'wa* and jihad movements is that it strives to realize *tawḥīd* by means of jihad against the idols (*ṭawāghīt*).[47]

There exist among researchers of jihadi Salafism a number of theses concerning the movement's history and origin. According to Wiktorowicz, jihadi Salafism is a movement that urges the use of violence to establish a Muslim state. He identifies its origins in the war against the Soviets in Afghanistan (1979–89), where Saudi Salafīs were exposed to the political ideas of the MB but also to those of Sayyid Quṭb and other Islamists, such as the Egyptian Islamic Jihad. Toward the mid-1990s, the Saudi government began a campaign of harsh repression against the regime's opponents among the political Salafīs, thus creating a vacuum that was subsequently filled by the jihadi Salafīs.[48]

Shiraz Maher argues that the emergence of jihadi Salafism as an idea was prompted by the decline of political Islam at the beginning of the 1990s. He identifies a number of events that he believes were indicative of the beginnings of post-Islamism, the era that followed the failure of political Islam: the civil war in Algeria (1991–2002), the fierce repression of the MB in Egypt and Syria and of the Nahḍa movement in Tunisia, and the sentencing of the Ṣaḥwa movement leaders in Saudi Arabia to long prison terms. Maher perceives the beginnings of jihadi Salafism in the course of the Algerian civil war but adds that the movement took on a concrete and identifiable shape only in the wake of the Iraqi invasion of Kuwait (1990) and especially during the Iraq War (2003–11). This was a period in which jihadi groups led by al-Qa'ida in Iraq produced a spate of publications that explained the ideas behind their activity.[49]

Daniel Lav, in contrast, argues that jihadi Salafism was the product of the encounter between Quṭbism, on the one hand, and Salafism and Wahhabism, on the other. According to Lav, contemporary jihadi Salafīs have adopted Quṭb's emphasis on the concept of *tawḥīd* as the main pivot of Islam and of *ḥākimiyya* as the central aspect of true *tawḥīd*.[50]

The view subscribed to here is that the seeds of jihadi Salafism were sown in Egyptian prisons already by the 1950s. Sayyid Quṭb can therefore be considered the father of contemporary jihadi Salafism even if he did not define himself as a Salafī and despite the fact that in his day jihadi Salafism had yet to emerge. In his comprehensive encyclopedia *The Global Islamic Resistance Call*, Abū Muṣʿab al-Sūrī (b. 1958), a Syrian al-Qaʿida theorist and strategist,[51] describes jihadi Salafism as a mixture of Quṭb's jihadi philosophy, the Salafī creed, and the Wahhābī method of *daʿwa*. He argues that the political, legal, and movement dimensions in contemporary jihadi thought were born of a combination of the MB's way, which is political and educational in nature, and "Quṭbī movementalism [*al-ḥarakiyya al-Quṭbiyya*]," based on the principles of God's sovereignty.[52] Because, as al-Sūrī points out, the MB's ideology constitutes one of the sources of influence on jihadi Salafism, it is no wonder that al-Qaraḍāwī, a Brotherhood ideologue, and jihadi Salafists agree on certain points, despite the significant differences between them on important issues, as shown in chapter 4.

The Intellectual Genealogy of Jihadi Salafism

Here the term *intellectual genealogy* is used to denote a collection of ideas with components and layers from the Islamic reformist generation of the end of the nineteenth century and the beginning of the twentieth century to the establishment of the IS in June 2014. These ideas underwent modification from one stage to another, but all constitute attempts at formulating an original Islamic response to the challenge posed by Western culture. Let us try, for example, to locate elements in MB movement founder Ḥasan al-Bannā's thinking that, mutatis mutandis, constitute the basic building blocks of the jihadi Salafīs' ideological framework.

1. The principle that Islam is all-encompassing. Among the things it encompasses are "jihad and *daʿwā*, or army and idea."[53]

2. The objective that the MB should withstand the dominant wave of materialism and the culture of pleasure and desire that constitute Western civilization. This wave, al-Bannā claimed, swept over the Muslim nations and moved them far away from the path of Islam. The MB should

pursue the ugly Western wave on its own territory: "We shall pursue it [the materialist culture of the West] into the midst of its own house until the entire world shall cheer in the Prophet's name, the entire world shall know for certain the Qur'ān's instructions and the Qur'ān's shadow, the light spreading over the earth shall be disseminated. Then that for which Muslims strive shall be realized; there will no longer be any temptation [*fitna*], and all faith shall be to God alone."[54]

3. The dissemination of Islamic *da'wa* and the protection of Islam's holy sites (*muqaddasāt al-Islām*). These are a duty upon Muslims just as it is their duty to fast, pray, perform the pilgrimage, give to charity, do good, and refrain from evil. For this reason, the Prophet's Companions, the "chosen generation," were called "monks at night, horsemen by day" (*ruhbān bil-layl, fursān bil-nahār*).

4. The MB should undertake to achieve reform in stages, from the bottom up—from the Muslim individual to family, society, and homeland. One of the objectives of the reform was "to bring back the Muslim nation's international nature, by liberating its homelands, reviving its glory, and bringing close its culture and unity, until all this will bring about the return of the absent caliphate and the yearned-for unification."[55] Ḥasan al-Bannā noted that the Brotherhood should place at the head of its program the idea of the caliphate and its revival but realized that this program requires preparation.[56]

5. The slogan for the MB includes the phrase "jihad is our way" (*al-jihād sabīlunā*); al-Bannā explained that jihad will continue until the Day of Resurrection. He defined a number of levels of jihad, the lowest being "condemnation in the heart" and the highest "fighting for God." Between these two levels, there is jihad with the tongue, the pen, and the hand and the saying of truth to a despotic ruler. The relationship between *da'wa* and jihad is clear: "There can be no *da'wa* except through jihad. The loftier and the broader *da'wa*'s horizon, the more powerful will be the jihad on its behalf, the price required to support it and the recompense to those who implement it."[57]

In al-Qaraḍāwī's view, one of the achievements of the Islamic awakening in general and of the MB in particular was the revival of the concept of jihad not only in the spiritual sense of the struggle against one's own desires

1. The Muslim Brotherhood emblem: two swords with the Qur'ān between them and underneath them the first word of Q8:60, *prepare* ("Prepare whatever forces you [believers] can muster"). Encircling the swords, Qur'ān, and word is the MB's slogan, formulated by Ḥasan al-Bannā (*read from the top, counterclockwise*): "Allah is our objective, the Messenger is our leader, the Qur'ān is our constitution, jihad is our way, death for the sake of Allah is our highest hope."

and the devil's intrigues but also in the sense of the struggle against imperialism outside the nation and despotism inside the nation. He describes the MB's jihad as focused on two objectives: realization of the Muslim idea and liberation of Muslim soil. The former consists of living a full Muslim life, guided by the faith, and the latter means, according to al-Qaraḍāwī, the liberation "of every land into which Islam has entered and governed and in which minarets rose high. It is a duty to liberate [such land] from every unbelieving, foreign rule, from every despotic, sinful rule. This is an individual duty of every inhabitant [of this land] and then on all those around them, according to their distance and according to the needs, burdens, and requirements of the jihad, until it encompasses all Muslims."[58] This statement, in which al-Qaraḍāwī explains the Brotherhood's view of jihad, contains the seeds from which would emerge the Salafī conception of jihad, according to which the Muslim nation faces two enemies: the far enemy—namely the "unbelievers," headed by the Jews and Christians or, to use the global jihadi reference, the "Zionist-Crusader alliance"—and the near enemy in the form of despotic Muslim regimes. The dispute between al-Qaraḍāwī and some jihadi Salafī thinkers on this issue is focused on the question of whether Muslim regimes that do not govern according to *sharīʿa* should be accused of unbelief and on the status of Muslim countries in which *sharīʿa* is not the law of the land (see chapters 3 and 4).

Another significant element in the ideological mosaic that constitutes jihadi Salafism is the Quṭbist ideology. Sayyid Quṭb, like the leaders and thinkers of jihadi Salafism, was a member of the Brotherhood from the early 1950s.[59] He was greatly enamored of al-Bannā's epistles, but after having learned them, he developed his own unique approach. He planted the seeds of jihadi Salafism not by uprooting what al-Bannā had sown but by adding to it. Quṭb's ideas have been a source of inspiration for and influence on jihadi Salafīs. Thus, for example, Ayman al-Ẓawāhirī (b. 1951), the leader of al-Qaʿida, wrote in his book *Horsemen under the Prophet's Banner*: "Sayyid Quṭb's call for a pure profession of God's *tawḥīd* and for absolute submission to Allah's *ḥākimiyya* and to the sovereignty of the Lord of the World's path was and remains the spark that lit the flame of the Islamic revolution against the enemies of Islam inside and outside and whose blood-soaked chapters are still being written every day."[60]

Quṭb's great influence on jihadi Salafism can be seen in ʿAbdallah ʿAzzām's short composition commemorating the twentieth anniversary of Quṭb's death. In this work, ʿAzzām describes Quṭb's unique traits, adding that his untimely death prevented him from seeing the blessed fruit that Allah had raised from his, Quṭb's, writings.[61] ʿAzzām admits that Quṭb influenced his own thinking about Islam more than anyone else. He adds that Quṭb left an enormous legacy in Islamic thought and clarified concepts that had disappeared from Muslims' minds for a long time, such as idolatrous rulers (*ṭāghūt*, pl. *ṭawāghīt*); unbelief or pre-Islamic paganism (literally, ignorance) (*jāhiliyya*); God's sovereignty (*ḥākimiyya*); loyalty and disavowal (*al-walā' wal-barā'*); God's oneness (*tawḥīd*); and more. 'Azzām describes Quṭb's influence on the jihadi Salafī fighters as follows: "Those who entered Afghanistan understood the profound influence of Sayyid Quṭb's ideas on jihad in Islam and on the entire generation throughout the world. Some of them [the jihadi fighters] did not ask you for a garment even if they were naked or food even if they were hungry or weapons if they were unarmed; rather, they asked for Sayyid Quṭb's books."[62]

Quṭb's Innovative Ideas

The clash between the MB and the Egyptian regime in 1965 formed the backdrop for Quṭb's extremist ideas.[63] Quṭb laid out his revolutionary ideas in texts he wrote between 1955 and 1964 during his imprisonment by the 'Abd al-Nasir regime. The most important work he penned during this period was *In the Shade of the Qur'ān*, a thirty-volume commentary on the Qur'ān, and his ideas became fully formed in the book *Milestones* (1964). In both of these works, he discusses two related concepts borrowed from the teachings of prominent Indian scholar Abū al-A'lā al-Mawdūdī (d. 1979):[64] "new *jāhiliyya*" and "the sovereignty of Allah" (*ḥākimiyyat Allah*; for a discussion of this concept, see chapter 4). Quṭb derived his knowledge of al-Mawdūdī's use of these terms from the book *What Did the World Lose Owing to the Decline of Islam?*, by Indian scholar Abū al-Ḥasan al-Nadwī (d. 1999), an important Muslim thinker in his own right. Following al-Mawdūdī and al-Nadwī, Quṭb used the term *jāhiliyya* (originally referring to the pre-Islamic period) to describe a non-Islamic state of affairs in which men are ruled and enslaved by their fellow men—that is, in which they renounce the sovereignty of Allah and instead deify and worship human rulers.[65] Quṭb regarded all societies of his day to be ignorant and without the right belief (*jāhilī*), including those who purported to be Muslim, on the grounds that they ascribed sovereignty not only to Allah but also to others besides Allah.[66] He presented a dichotomous view that precluded any compromise: a society could either accept Allah's exclusive sovereignty and thus exist in a state of belief or else be in a state of *jāhiliyya*, unbelief. As John Calvert points out, Quṭb directed the concept of divine sovereignty against the nationalist regime that had imprisoned him and outlawed the organization to which he belonged. By constructing the individual Muslim as a juridical subject beholden to the exigencies of the *sharīʿa* alone, he sought to delegitimize the legislative and executive authority held by the Free Officers and all other systems of government based on worldly interests and ties.[67]

The solution Quṭb proposed to this problematic state of affairs was to renounce *jāhiliyya* and embrace Islam, as Muslims did in the first days of the religion, under the Prophet Muḥammad. In the Muslim society that would replace the *jāhilī* one, he said, faith would be the basis for citizenship.[68] The first step in creating such a society was to establish a small group of true believers. According to Quṭb, he wrote *Milestones* as a guide for this pioneering group. He stressed that this group would have to constitute "an exceptional Qur'ānic generation," comparable to the generation of the Prophet and his Companions, and, like the founding generation of Islam, they would have to disassociate themselves from all aspects of *jāhilī* life—namely, all perceptions and beliefs, customs and habits, culture, art, and laws that do not originate in the Qur'ān. He clarified that *jāhilī* life includes not only non-Muslim perceptions and customs but also many elements regarded as part of Muslim culture and philosophy but not in fact derived from the Qur'ān.[69]

Quṭb's ideas were a source of inspiration for many Islamic groups that emerged in the late 1960s and the 1970s, such as the Egyptian Islamic Jihad (al-Jamāʿa al-Islāmiyya, sometimes referred to in the West as the Egyptian Islamic Group), led by ʿUmar ʿAbd al-Raḥmān (d. 2017, known as the Blind Shaykh), and another group called Egyptian Islamic Jihad, one of whose members in the late 1960s was Ayman al-Ẓawāhirī, the current leader of al-Qaʿida. In fact, in his trial for his role in the Anwar Sadat assassination, ʿAbd al-Raḥmān echoed Quṭb when he accused the Egyptian regime and society of being *jāhilī* and went further than Quṭb by saying explicitly that "the rulers who replace Allah's laws with their own laws or the laws of some other [human] are heretical; there is no doubt of that."[70] As Fawaz Gerges writes, "It would not be an exaggeration to say that jihadis look up to Quṭb as a founding, spiritual father, if not the *muftī*, or theoretician, of their contemporary movement."[71]

It should be noted that liberal writers such as Shākir al-Nābulsī likewise regard jihadi Salafism, which they call "terrorist," as the natural offspring of Quṭbism. Al-Nābulsī considers Quṭb to be the main ideologue of both jihadi Salafism, represented by al-Qaʿida, and political Islam, represented by the MB and Hamas.[72] This approach is endorsed in this study, as shown in chapter 4.

Quṭb's legacy to jihadi Salafīs consists of the following ideas:

1. Islam means first and foremost acceptance of the creed "there is no God but Allah" in its true meaning—namely, reasserting *ḥākimiyya* in everything and expelling those who attack and encroach on God's rule and who claim the right of sovereignty for themselves. Quṭb here refers to Muslim rulers who, in his view, violate *ḥākimiyyat Allah* and take some of His prerogatives for themselves.[73] The testimony "there is no God but Allah" means that God is the one and only deity, Lord of the World, with full responsibility (*qiwāma*), government, and sovereignty. For Quṭb, this testimony is a full way of life in every domain.

2. Quṭb argued that the nature of Islam implies the necessity of jihad by the sword in addition to jihad through *daʿwa*. He changed the meaning of "defensive jihad" to mean protection of persons and not only of the land. In his own words, the objective of jihad is "a general declaration of man's liberation from enslavement to other men and acceptance of God's divinity and his being the sovereign of the worlds; destruction of the kingdom of human desire on earth and establishment of the kingdom of divine *sharīʿa* in the world of mankind."[74] Like al-Bannā, Quṭb insisted that jihad was necessary for *daʿwa*.

3. Quṭb declared that there is only one abode of Islam, *dār al-Islām*—namely, the place where the Islamic state has been established, *sharīʿa* reigns supreme, God's punishments are imposed, and the Muslims are loyal to each other. All other places are *dār al-ḥarb*, the abode of war. The relationship between the two abodes is either war or truce (*hudna*) under Muslim protection. According to Quṭb, "a Muslim has no homeland except where Allah's *sharīʿa* is implemented and where his ties with the other

inhabitants of the homeland are based on the tie to Allah. A Muslim has no citizenship except his faith, which makes him a member of the Muslim nation in *dār al-Islām*."[75]

Al-Qaraḍāwī's View of Sayyid Quṭb and Quṭbism

Al-Qaraḍāwī's attitude toward Quṭb exemplifies the ambivalent attitude among members of the Brotherhood, who greatly admired Quṭb as a scholar but at the same time objected to aspects of his basic concepts, such as God's sovereignty, the "new *jāhiliyya*," *takfīr*, and jihad. Al-Qaraḍāwī expresses his admiration for Quṭb in the following words:

> No honest student or fair examiner will doubt that Quṭb is a grand Muslim, a great man of *da'wa*, an appreciated writer, and a special intellectual. He is a man who has committed himself to his religion immaculately, who has devoted himself exclusively to Allah. His prayer, his works, his life and death [a phrase that alludes to Q6:162] he gave to the Lord of the World, without any associate. There can be no doubt of Sayyid Quṭb's loyalty to the thought in which he believed, nor can there be any doubt of his enthusiasm for his thought and his self-obliteration for it. He risked his life and sacrificed himself for Islam as he believed in it.[76]

For al-Qaraḍāwī, the most pernicious aspect of Quṭb's philosophy is his broad use of the idea of *takfīr*, which he expanded to such an extent that readers of his Qur'ānic commentary *In the Shadow of the Qur'ān* and *Milestones* are given to understand that all Muslim societies have become *jāhiliyya*. Al-Qaraḍāwī explains that Quṭb does not merely mean that these societies are behaving and acting in a *jāhiliyya* way but that they are also *jāhilī* in their faith (*jāhiliyyat al-'aqīda*)—that is, they do not believe in God or associate others with Him, do not recognize God's sovereignty, and add partners to God in the form of imported laws, values, and conceptions that replace those of *sharī'a*. When Quṭb came to this conclusion, he decided, according to al-Qaraḍāwī, not to offer Islam as a social, economic, political, or legal system to Muslims at this time because such an offer can be usefully made only to believers, but today's Muslims have not yet reached this stage. Therefore, Islam should today be presented mainly as a faith, so that Muslims will come to believe in Allah as sovereign, Islam as the right faith, Muḥammad as God's Messenger, and *sharīʿa* as the law. Al-Qaraḍāwī adds that Quṭb compared contemporary Muslim societies to Meccan society in the Prophet's days; he notes that the Prophet, too, did not present Islam to the people of Mecca as a legislative system and a political regime, but only as belief in one God.[77]

Al-Qaraḍāwī has also stated that he does not share Quṭb's view of jihad.[78] The latter, according to al-Qaraḍāwī, called on the Muslims to prepare for war against the entire world, a war that would be waged until everyone converted to Islam or paid the poll tax (*jizya*) if they did not convert.[79] Jihad, in this view, is not something temporary or limited to certain circumstances, and its objective is not to protect the state's borders. Rather, jihad has its own justification, derived from the character of the Muslim religion, whose essence is both the destruction of *jāhilī* regimes and governments that are based on the principle of "sovereignty of man over man" (*ḥākimiyyat al-bashar lil-bashar*) and the establishment of the kingdom of divine *sharīʿa*.[80] Quṭb justified his position with the Verse of the Sword (Āyat al-Sayf, Q9:5; for a discussion of this verse, see chapter 5), in which Muslims are urged to kill the polytheists everywhere, as well as with Qur'ān 8:39, which calls upon them to "fight [the unbelievers] until there is no more persecution [of Muslims and of those who preach Islam]."

Al-Qaraḍāwī classifies al-Mawdūdī and Sayyid Quṭb as supporters of "offensive jihad" (see chapter 6).[81] He counters that Quṭb ignored the many Qur'ānic verses that call for peace and for defensive jihad—that is, for waging war only against those who fight the Muslims.[82] Al-Qaraḍāwī concludes that Quṭb's approach is based on hostility toward the entire world, friend and foe alike. In taking this stand, Quṭb provokes everyone and mobilizes the world against the Muslims, who are perceived as a threat. It is this fear of Islam (Islamophobia) that al-Qaraḍāwī has been trying to fight, especially since the 9/11 attacks, as reflected in his writings.[83]

Although al-Qaraḍāwī tries to present himself as advocating defensive jihad, as opposed to Quṭb, who advocates offensive jihad, both of them evidently share the belief that the world culture is ill and that Islam is the cure for this malady. A comparison between a passage in Quṭb's book *Milestones* and a passage in al-Qaraḍāwī's book *Islam: The Culture of Tomorrow* clearly reflects that these two thinkers share this view. Quṭb wrote:

> The leadership of Western man in the world is coming to an end, not because Western civilization is materially bankrupt or has lost its economic or military might, but because the Western order has played its part and no longer possesses that stock of values that gave it its predominance. Now there is need for a leadership that can maintain and cultivate the material culture that mankind has attained thanks to Europe's material creative genius, while also providing mankind with completely new values that it has not yet known, through a combination of tradition, activism, and pragmatism. Only Islam possesses these values, and Islam is the way.[84]

Al-Qaraḍāwī has written very similarly:

> Today mankind needs a civilization with a philosophy and mission different from those of Western civilization, with its two streams, capitalist and communist. Both these streams are the fruit of the same tree, a tree that the Qur'ān, the Torah, and the New Testament all curse—the tree of utilitarian materialism. . . . Mankind needs a culture that forms a tight bond between heaven and earth, combining divine meaning with human benefit, merging the reasoning mind with the faithful heart. . . . The only such culture is that of Islam, in which balance and perfection are revealed in a way that only the All Knowing and All Wise [Allah] can attain.[85]

Al-Qaraḍāwī believes that the Muslim nation's mission is reflected in the words of Rib'ī b. 'Āmir, one of the Prophet's Companions, to Rustum, the leader of the Persian forces in the Battle of al-Qādisiyya (657 CE): "Allah sent us in order to lift the people out of worshipping creatures to the worship of Allah alone, from this world's troubles to its breadth, and from the oppression of [other] religions to the justice of Islam."[86] This definition of Islam's mission reflects the considerable similarity between al-Qaraḍāwī and Sayyid Quṭb.

Liberalism and Secularism

Wasaṭiyya presents itself as the answer to two trends that emerged in the Islamic world in the twentieth century and that al-Qaraḍāwī regards as "the enemies of the Islamic solution": secularism in general and extremism in the name of Islam. Hence, it is pertinent to examine the concepts of liberalism and secularism, on the one hand, and Islamism, on the other, which occupy a central place in both *wasaṭī* discourse and Islamic discourse at large.

The concept of secularism entered the intellectual discourse in the Arab world in the mid-nineteenth century as part of Europe's growing cultural influence on the Arab countries. Although the colonialist European powers, such as France and Great Britain, were seen as imperialist invaders seeking to take over the Arab region, certain elites, especially Western-educated intellectuals, looked up to them and adopted European ideas. The debate about secularism in the Arab world initially focused on the issue of state-religion relations and on secularism as a possible source of Europe's superiority in science, technology, and administration.[87] In fact, the term *secularism* was rendered into Arabic as *'ilmāniyya*, from the word *'ilm* (science), or as *'almāniyya*, from the word *'ālam* (world). Al-Qaraḍāwī and other opponents of secularism sometimes translate *secularism* as *lādīniyya* or *dunyawiyya*, signifying "unrelated to religion" or even "opposed to religion" and connoting an addiction to the hollow pleasures of this world.[88]

It should be noted that in the Middle East the term *liberalism* does not have the same range of meanings it has in the West, where it was coined. In Egypt in the 1920s, liberalism was associated with a number of values: loyalty to the state, human rights, and a reliance on human reasoning (*ra'y*) in all spheres, including religion. It denoted an overall commitment to reshaping society based on universal humanistic values and a secular perception of the state.[89]

The Three Generations of the Liberal Movement

This study claims that *wasaṭiyya* emerged mainly in response to the liberal stream in the Muslim world, which, according to *wasaṭiyya*, advocated the separation of religion and state. Within the liberal movement, it is possible to discern three separate generations whose claims *wasaṭiyya* confronts.[90]

The first generation was active in Egypt from the 1920s until the Free Officers revolution of 1952. This period was marked by a dominance of liberal-secular thinking in Egypt, but the revolution in 1952 and the transition from monarchy to republic spelled the defeat of this liberal trend. During this initial phase, the Islamic counterweight to the liberal-secular stream was provided mainly by the MB movement, founded by al-Qaraḍāwī's mentor, Ḥasan al-Bannā, in 1929.

The second generation of liberals emerged in Egypt in the 1980s in response to the violent Islamist movements that arose in the country in the 1970s and 1980s and that accused the regime of apostasy (*ridda*). Those involved in the *wasaṭiyya* movement claim that they confronted both the violent movements' radical ideas and the liberals' ideas in an attempt to find a "middle road" between them.

The third generation of liberals are the "neoliberals," as they call themselves. The neoliberals are a group of secular intellectuals and thinkers who are not associated with any particular political party but nevertheless have formed a movement whose members share certain ideas.[91] This movement began to coalesce in the early 1990s following a number of global developments, including the decline and ultimate collapse of the Communist regimes in eastern Europe and the end of the Cold War between the Western and Eastern blocs, the emergence of the United States as a single superpower, and the spread of globalization.[92] In the wake of the 9/11 attacks, the neoliberals became involved in ideological debates on issues such as the meaning of jihad in Islam and the roots of terrorism, including the relationship between terror and school curricula in the Muslim world. Neoliberal thinker Shākir al-Nābulsī, a prominent critic of al-Qaraḍāwī, contends that despite the disagreements between the various liberal writers, the common denominator among them is that they all advocate complete freedom of thought and freedom of religion as well as freedom and full equality for women. They hold that political pluralism and political, religious, and educational reform (*iṣlāḥ*) are the top priority in the current stage, and they share a belief that in the modern era there must be separation of religion and state, that religion and heritage must be subjected to scientific scrutiny, and that democratic values must be implemented.[93] A comparison of the neoliberals' ideological platform as set out by al-Nābulsī[94] (given in appendix B) and the *wasaṭiyya* platform as set out by al-Qaraḍāwī[95] (given in appendix A), in particular regarding such issues as the perception of jihad and the status of women, affords a broader perspective on the nature of *wasaṭiyya*.

The Confrontation between Wasaṭiyya *and Secular Liberalism*

Even the terms used to describe the two sides in this clash are in dispute. According to al-Nābulsī, it is a confrontation between fundamentalism (*uṣūliyya*), on the one side—which he regards as synonymous with political Islam as represented by the MB and by its spiritual mentor, al-Qaraḍāwī—and liberalism, enlightenment (*tanwīr*), and secularism, on the other. He defines fundamentalism in negative terms as an intellectual tendency to resist change and to take a rigid position on every issue.[96] Abū Zayd prefers to call the side represented by intellectuals like him "enlighteners" (*tanwīriyyūn*) rather than "secularists" (*ʿilmāniyyūn*) because, he claims, the latter was coined by their detractors as a term that implies heresy and betrayal.[97] Evidence for his point is provided by al-Qaraḍāwī's own explanation of the term *ʿilmāniyya*, which, he contends, means the detachment of religion from the state and from society, leaving it a "prisoner" of the individual's conscience. To al-Qaraḍāwī's mind, this attitude is foreign to Islamic tradition and will be rejected by the Muslim nation's defense mechanisms as an intrusive "Western product" that did not grow out of Muslim soil.[98] In a sermon on June 13, 1997, in his mosque in Qatar, he said: "The most important ideological campaign in which our *umma* is engaged, in both the East and the West, is the campaign between Islam and secularism."[99]

In his polemic on secularism, al-Qaraḍāwī defines it as

> the disassociation of religion from the life of man, as an individual and as a society, so that religion has no power in guiding, informing, and educating or in legislating for mankind. [According to the secularists], man's point of departure in life is solely his own reason, instincts, and

> psychological motivations. In other words, secularism means divesting Allah of control over his creatures. He has no power over them; they are their own masters and therefore do as they please, rule as they please, and are not held accountable for their actions.[100]

This definition presents secularism as completely incompatible with *sharīʿa* because the role of *sharīʿa*, as defined in the Qur'ān (45:18), is to ensure that people do not follow their own instincts but rather the guidance of Allah.

The liberals, however, do not accept al-Qaraḍāwī's claim that the goal of secularism is to remove religion from the public sphere and confine it to the private sphere. Al-Nābulsī states that secularism does not advocate separating religion from society and everyday life. It only advocates separating religion from politics and preventing clerics from interfering in people's lives through a multitude of directives and prohibitions. He argues that the Muslim religious establishment derives significant social, economic, and political benefits from the association of religion and the state, which allows this establishment to be part of the regime. He and his fellow liberals therefore wish to distance the clerics from the state and the government for the good of the religion itself, he says.[101] According to the liberal Naṣr Ḥāmid Abū Zayd, clerics such as al-Qaraḍāwī falsely accuse the secularists of advocating the uprooting of religion from everyday life and from society so they can proclaim secularism heretical.[102]

Abū Zayd describes the dispute between Islamists such as al-Qaraḍāwī and secularists such as himself as a dispute between two diametrically opposed approaches: the secularists' modern, enlightened, and unfettered understanding of Islam versus the Islamists' narrow and rigid understanding, which relies on a literal interpretation of the Islamic sources. The former approach is critical and rational; it does not regard the Islamic heritage as divine but as the product of human reasoning, and it takes a critical view of history. Conversely, the latter approach, which Abū Zayd attributes to al-Qaraḍāwī, among others, sanctifies the past and its values, producing a distorted perception of the present and blocking the path to the future. Abū Zayd contends that scholars of al-Qaraḍāwī's ilk exploit the Islamic heritage for pragmatic and political ends and abhor criticism because it undermines the legitimacy of their claims.[103] Al-Nābulsī accurately describes the liberals' perception of the past in the neoliberals' platform: "There is no absolute loyalty to the past as such or any rigid adherence to it. An understanding of the present impels us to reevaluate past values and [highlights] the need to create the future, which is the heart of modernism."[104] Al-Qaraḍāwī's very different attitude to the past is evident from his characterization of the Islam he preaches. He describes it either as the "first Islam [*al-Islām al-awwal*]," prior to the introduction of various innovations, or as the "pure Islam," as understood by the very best generations of the Islamic nation: the Prophet's generation and the generation immediately following that one. These generations, he says, had the best understanding of Islam's spirit and intentions, so Muslims who seek enlightenment should turn to them for guidance.[105]

Al-Qaraḍāwī accuses the secularists of heresy. He states that a secular person who disagrees in principle with the idea of government through *sharīʿa* (*taḥkīm al-sharīʿa*) is a Muslim in name only and must be considered an apostate (*murtadd*). Furthermore, al-Qaraḍāwī has ruled that a Muslim who accepts or preaches secularism is likely to become a heretic even if he does not deny God's existence. This is the case if such a secularist rejects the prohibition on usury, the prohibition on drinking wine, and the like because such prohibitions are, to use al-Qaraḍāwī's words, "things known necessarily in religion [*maʿlūm min al-dīn bil-ḍarūra*]" that have been accepted by the Muslim nation's consensus.[106] In equating secularism with apostasy, al-Qaraḍāwī rejects it categorically and makes any need for intellectual debate with it superfluous. Islam, he insists, is a comprehensive system of life and as such cannot accept that any "ideology" (such as secularism) be given a share in how life is to be directed.[107] He accuses the secularists of calling for the rule of *jāhiliyya*—that is, of man-made instead of divine laws.[108] By adopting such a dichotomous view, *jāhiliyya* rule versus Islamic rule, and accusing his secularist rivals of *jāhiliyya*, al-Qaraḍāwī the *wasaṭī* to all intents and purposes adopts the views of Sayyid Quṭb, an important source of inspiration for global jihad.

We should note that al-Qaraḍāwī's accusations of heresy against secularists and secularism constitute extremism even according to his own definition. He has argued that one form of religious extremism is to condemn others, to dismiss their virtues, and to exaggerate their negative features: "For the extremist, the fundamental principle is to accuse, and the basic feature of accusation is condemnation, in contradiction to divine constitutions and [human] laws, which consider a person to be innocent until their guilt has been established."[109] In fact, however, al-Qaraḍāwī declared that accusations of unbelief (*takfīr*) are the epitome of extremism because they cause the accused's life and property to be forfeit. In blatant disagreement with his own ruling that secularists should be considered unbelievers if they reject prohibitions such as engaging in usury and drinking alcohol, he formulates the following principle in his discussion of *takfīr*: "Whoever has entered Islam with certitude cannot be expelled from it without the same certitude. For certitude cannot be removed through doubt. Sins [*maʿāṣī*] do not remove a Muslim from Islam, not even major sins [*kabāʾir*] such as murder, adultery [*zinā*], and wine drinking, as long as [the sinner] does not express disrespect toward God's laws on such matters and does not reject them."[110]

Wasaṭiyya *versus Liberalism/Secularism on the State and Religion*

As part of his debate with the secularists, al-Qaraḍāwī seeks to refute one of their basic claims: that the Islamists aim to transform the Muslim countries into theocracies and that secularism is the best defense against this threat. The secularists describe the Islamic state as one that governs in the name of Allah, in contrast to the secular state, which is committed to human rights and freedoms. Al-Qaraḍāwī challenges this claim by drawing a distinction between a theocracy and an Islamic state and by arguing that *wasaṭiyya* flatly rejects the former and seeks to establish the latter. Based on an innovative interpretation of the Qurʾān and the Sunna, he argues that an Islamic state is in fact a civil state (*dawla madaniyya*) whose source of authority is Islam. In such a state, he says, the Muslim *umma* elects the leader and pledges an oath of loyalty to him, and the ruler makes decisions based on the principle of consultation (*shūrā*). In other words, al-Qaraḍāwī argues that the state, as defined by the Islamic sources, is essentially democratic. He calls it a "democratic theocracy" or "divinely inspired democratic government"[111] and argues that it differs from the ecclesiastic theocracy of the Middle Ages in several crucial ways.

First, the status of clerics in Islam is completely different from that of the priesthood in the Christian theocracy, for in Islam clerics have no monopoly over religious affairs and are not required to mediate between an individual and God. Second, according to al-Qaraḍāwī, the function of the ecclesiastic theocracy is to control the people and their conscience and to govern their spiritual and material lives, without allowing the people to challenge this authority (in fact, defying it is seen as tantamount to defying God). Conversely, the function of the Islamic state is to care for the people as a father cares for his children and to establish justice and strengthen the religion. Third, a theocracy enforces its authority through intimidation and coercion, whereas an Islamic state avoids these practices and in fact encourages criticism of the ruler.[112]

It should be noted that secularist liberals reject al-Qaraḍāwī's claim regarding the place of clerics in the Islamic state. According to Abū Zayd, the representatives of political Islam, among them al-Qaraḍāwī, deny that Islam has a priesthood in the Christian sense, yet Islamic clerics act like a priesthood when they level accusations of heresy against critical liberals such as himself.[113] Moreover, Abū Zayd believes that the association of Islam with terrorism is the fault of these selfsame clerics, who in the name of Islam assume sponsorship (*wiṣāya*) over people's hearts and minds; it is also the fault of those who in response to this sponsorship minimize the importance of faith and religion in social and political life.[114] The liberals accuse clerics such as al-Qaraḍāwī of seeking to control both religion and politics. They condemn this goal based on their assumption that Islam, like Christianity, should have two separate authorities—religious and political.[115]

As far as al-Qaraḍāwī is concerned, the *wasaṭī* vision of the ideal Islamic state is meant to be an answer to the liberal-secular vision as reflected, for example, in the approach taken by Muḥammad Saʿīd al-ʿAshmāwī (d. 2013). Al-ʿAshmāwī contends that Islam does not mandate any particular type of government; moreover, Islam rejects the notion of a theocracy that attributes infallibility or sanctity to the ruler. He writes:

"Islam is concerned with man rather than regime, with conscience rather than laws, with spirit rather than words. A true Islamic government, which corresponds to the Islamic writings and the spirit of the faith, is a government based on justice and humanity. It is described as a civil government that emanates from the people and serves the people."[116]

'Alī 'Abd al-Rāziq and the Question of the Caliphate: A Historical-Ideological Perspective

According to al-Qaraḍāwī, the most dangerous aspect of the Western secularism that arose in Egypt under the influence of British imperialism was that it penetrated not only the state education facilities but also the very bastion of Islamic scholarship, al-Azhar. As an example, he points to the book *Islam and the Foundations of Governance* (1925) by al-Azhar shaykh 'Alī 'Abd al-Rāziq (d. 1966),[117] which drew a sharp distinction between Islam and the governing of the state and argued that Islam does not advocate a specific form of government. Years later, in 1950, another al-Azhar scholar, Khālid Muḥammad Khālid (d. 1996), repeated this claim in his book *From Here We Begin*, in which he attacked the notion of Islamic government and called to adopt a national (*qawmī*) form of governance.[118] Criticizing these shaykhs, al-Qaraḍāwī says that they "wore the hat" of an Islamic scholar, but in their heads was a secularist ideology that did not regard life, history, and events through an Islamic lens of adherence to the Qur'ān and the Sunna. He claims that shaykhs like them are tools in the hands of liberal and socialist rulers in the Muslim world, who use them to deceive the Muslim people and attack the "wise, sober, and correct Islamic trends"—namely, the MB and his *wasaṭī* school.[119]

It goes without saying that al-Qaraḍāwī wholly rejects 'Abd al-Rāziq's claim that Islam is divorced from issues of politics and state. In fact, for al-Qaraḍāwī, 'Abd al-Rāziq's book was part of the West's successful "cultural invasion" (*ghazw thaqāfī*) of Egypt: it demonstrated that in Egypt in the 1920s Islam was no longer the basis of identity and that the *sharī'a* had been superseded by the British legacy of man-made law. This invasion was thus part of the reality that mandated the establishment of the MB and the launching of its *da'wa* in 1929.

The liberals, in contrast, regard ʿAbd al-Rāziq as a leading representative of the liberal-secularist approach. ʿAbd al-Rāziq is well versed in Islam, which the liberals regard as important ammunition in their war with the Islamists. Al-Nābulsī, for example, contends that secularism cannot be imposed from without but must emerge from within the religion, and he attempts to show that Islam is compatible—more so than any other religion—with the secularist approach.[120] However, he complains that ʿAbd al-Rāziq went too far in *Islam and the Foundations of Governance* in that he not only called for the separation of religion and state but rejected any connection between religion and politics, a position that placed him in a position of weakness vis-à-vis his rivals and critics. A more logical stance, argues al-Nābulsī, is to acknowledge the connection between Islam and politics and the fact that Islam became a state even before it was fully consolidated as a religion in that Muḥammad founded his state in Medina immediately after the immigration (*hijra*) (and thus even before the Qur'ān had descended in its entirety). According to al-Nābulsī, the secularists should argue that the model of Muḥammad's state in Medina and the model of the Righteous Caliphate are not suited to the modern world. The model suited to today's world is a secular state in the spirit of Muʿāwiya, the founder of the Umayyad dynasty (661–750 CE), but with a new character.[121]

The "Islamic Solution" (al-Ḥall al-Islāmī)

In response to ʿAbd al-Nasir's National Charter (Al-Mīthāq al-Waṭanī, 1962),[122] one of whose principles was the "inevitability of the socialist solution," al-Qaraḍāwī published a book series titled "The Inevitability [Ḥatmiyya] of the Islamic Solution" in the late 1960s and early 1970s.[123] In these books, he explained that whereas ʿAbd al-Nasir used the term *inevitability* in the sense of Marxist determinism—that is, to convey the inevitability of socialism—he (al-Qaraḍāwī) uses it to convey the idea that the circumstances in the Muslim world, especially the Arab world, mandate the adoption of an Islamic solution (*al-ḥall al-Islāmī*) because all of the imported solutions have failed.[124] Al-Qaraḍāwī describes the Islamic solution as a situation in which Islam will guide and lead society in all spheres and domains, both material and spiritual. In other words, the Islamic solution will create a society that is Islamic in every aspect and component. He stresses that the Islamic solution does not involve just legislation and laws—that is, the application of the Qur'ānic punishments (*ḥudūd Allāh*)[125]—as some of its opponents believe, especially the secularists in the Muslim world. Because the formation of a genuinely Islamic society is the ultimate goal of the Islamic solution, the solution requires the establishment of a pure Islamic rule in some geographical territory, which will guide society according to Allah's directives. Whoever thinks that an Islamic society can exist without Islamic rule, says al-Qaraḍāwī, is making two mistakes: first, he misunderstands the essence of an Islamic society, which regards the establishment of Islamic rule as a religious duty and does not recognize the separation of religion and state; second, he erroneously believes that an Islamic society can exist under a rule that is not Islamic but rather secular, national, socialist, or liberal.[126]

The Islamist-Secularist Debate of the 1980s

The 1980s saw the emergence of a new generation of liberals in Egypt as a counterweight to the fundamentalists or Islamists. These new thinkers had much in common with the liberals of the 1920s, but they also had unique characteristics of their own—hence, the application of the term *neoliberals* to them in the academic literature.[127] Prominent among them were Faraj Fūda (assassinated in 1992 by the Egyptian Islamic Jihad), Ḥusayn Aḥmad Amīn (d. 2014), and Muḥammad Sa'īd al-'Ashmāwī.[128] Like the liberals of the 1980s, Egyptian intellectuals associated with the political Left also took part in the struggle against religious extremism in this period; chief among these intellectuals was the Egyptian philosopher Fu'ād Zakariyyā (d. 2010), a veteran left-wing thinker and lecturer on philosophy at Ain Shams University.[129]

The terms al-Qaraḍāwī uses to describe his argument with Zakariyyā are very telling. He refers to a debate between them in 1986, organized by the Medical Association, as a dispute between truth, represented by Islam, and falsehood, represented by secularism, and as an illustration of Q17:81: "Truth has come, and falsehood has departed."[130] It should be stressed that

Muḥammad was instructed to speak this verse as he arrived to smash the idols at the Kaʿba (630 CE). In other words, the falsehood invoked in the verse is the falsehood of polytheism, whereas the truth is that of Islam. In quoting this verse in the context of the debate with the secularists, al-Qaraḍāwī implied that he regards secularism as falsehood and heresy.

It is also instructive to examine the criteria al-Qaraḍāwī uses for how the controversy with the secularists should be decided. The shaykh states that the secularists claim the right to interpret Islam from their own perspective but that in actual fact Islam is not malleable or open to every interpretation. The way to settle any dispute about it, he says, is to turn to the Qur'ān and the Sunna, as stated in Q4:59; if these texts provide no definite answer, the solution must be derived through jurisprudence (*fiqh*) and its principles for deriving rulings. Any dispute between the Islamic scholars and the secularists must be referred to the experts, or *ahl al-dhikr*, "those who have knowledge," as they are called in the Qur'ān (16:43)—in other words, the expert scholars and jurisprudents. Interestingly, al-Qaraḍāwī notes that if both sides possess knowledge and the dispute between them cannot be resolved on that basis, the deciding criterion must be that of piety, for a pious scholar will never sell out his religion for the sake of material gain.[131] Clearly, these criteria for deciding disagreements between the Islamists and secularists tip the scale in favor of the former and preclude any possibility of the secularists proving their case.

9/11 as a Crucial Milestone in the Debate between *Wasaṭiyya*, Jihadi Salafism, and Liberalism

The Wasaṭī *Condemnation of the Attacks*

In the wake of the 9/11 attacks, al-Qaraḍāwī published a condemnation on September 12, 2001,[132] which he repeated in a Friday sermon on September 21, 2001.[133] He also devoted his weekly program on the al-Jazeera network, *Sharīʿa and Life,* on September 16, 2001, to a discussion of the attack and its significance.[134] Al-Qaraḍāwī began his condemnation with expressions of sorrow for what happened, although he took care to stress that he was opposed to the pro-Israel US policy. He insisted that the Muslim religion respects the lives of all human beings and forbids taking a life, considered as the worst of sins in Islam (in this context he quotes Q5:32). Al-Qaraḍāwī declared that what happened on 9/11 was a terrible crime according to Islam because Islam, he claimed, fights only against those who fight it and does not harm the innocent. As proof, he mentioned a story about the Prophet, who in one of his wars saw a woman who had been killed and condemned his Companions: "[This woman] was not a fighter [*mā kānat hādhihi li-tuqātila*; i.e., she posed no threat]."[135] Al-Qaraḍāwi used this anecdote to argue that war in Islam is a defensive measure only and that Islam respects the lives of the innocent (on this issue, see chapter 6).

However, despite his condemnation of the attacks, al-Qaraḍāwī expressed his hope that the attack would cause the US government to search its conscience concerning its foreign policy, especially its pro-Israel stance, and to consider the Palestinian people's tragedy honestly and justly.[136] However, he added that this criticism of US policy does not mean that innocent American citizens should be attacked, as happened on 9/11. Rather, America should be punished, if possible, by an attack against its armed forces and, if that is not possible, by economic and political warfare—for example, with a boycott.[137] In this context, he argued that American leadership is conditional on its acting with justice (*ʿadl*), not with oppression and aggression, because despotic and corrupt nations are punished by God.[138] So, in fact, al-Qaraḍāwī justified the Muslims' war against America but opposed the killing of innocent civilians. His justification for the war against America uses the same argument al-Qaʿida used to justify the 9/11 attacks. According to Osama bin Laden, the Israeli-Palestinian conflict and American support for Israel were evidence of a Zionist-Crusader alliance and a new Christian-Jewish crusade against Islam.[139]

Although al-Qaraḍāwī defined the 9/11 attacks as terrorism (for a discussion of the meaning of the term *irhāb* [terrorism], see chapter 6), he maintained that the right way to fight terrorism is by attacking its causes, the most important of which is oppression, mainly by the United States, which supports the Zionists instead of truth and justice—that is, the Palestinian side. He believes that the war against terror takes place mostly at the level of ideas and that therefore the United States must study the terrorist's mind and motivations. In one of his sermons, al-Qaraḍāwī said that bin

Laden was not a single person only, but a manifestation of the resistance of the oppressed on earth against their oppressors, in which the weak use methods that the strong consider unacceptable, such as the 9/11 attacks.[140]

The *wasaṭī* reaction to 9/11 evoked criticism from both the liberals and the jihadi Salafīs—even though *wasaṭiyya* and jihadi Salafism are similar in that both rationalize and excuse the attacks. It is worth noting that Abū Muḥammad al-Maqdisī, an important Jordanian jihadi Salafī thinker, stated in a ruling that gave *sharʿī* legitimacy to the 9/11 attacks that al-Qaraḍāwī's call on Muslims to donate blood and money to the victims was null and void because a Muslim's blood and property are forbidden to the infidel. Al-Maqdisī declared that it is forbidden to restore American "blood" (i.e., one is allowed to shed it) with Muslim blood, which one is forbidden to shed. He criticized al-Qaraḍāwī and continued: "Do the 'clerics of evil' [*ʿulamāʾ al-sūʾ*] want the Muslims to support God's enemies with money, nay, even with blood, so that they [God's enemies, in this case the Americans] will spend this money and be strengthened by it in order to impede God's religion [Islam] [*al-ṣadd ʿan dīn Allāh*] and to fight God's rightful guardians [*awliyāʾ Allāh*]?"[141] In al-Maqdisī's view, the clerics who condemned the 9/11 attacks, including al-Qaraḍāwī, served the rulers and were willing to give opinions that fit their interests or the interests of the government, even if such opinions were contrary to Muslim law. He called them "shaykhs of the satellite stations" and pointed to the ostensible contradiction between al-Qaraḍāwī's call to boycott American products and his call on American Muslims to donate blood to the 9/11 victims.[142] Despite al-Maqdisī's criticism of al-Qaraḍāwī's so-called condemnation of the attack, both consider it a punishment that God brought on America because of its actions in and policy toward the Muslim world, to which it has brought much destruction, and because of its support for Israel's deeds in Palestine.[143]

The liberal Qatari academic ʿAbd al-Ḥamīd al-Anṣārī, a former dean of Islamic law at the University of Qatar, rejects al-Qaraḍāwī's explanation of the causes of Islamic terrorism. He argues that terrorism cannot be explained as a reaction to political circumstances, local or global, because the Muslims are not the only nation that has suffered and is still suffering from Western injustice. All nations feel oppression by America and the West, for that is the nature of international conflicts between the strong and the weak and has been since the dawn of time. Yet other nations that have suffered at the hands of the West do not raise their children to abhor it.[144]

The 9/11 Attacks: The Wasaṭī*-Liberal Debate about the Roots of Islamic Terrorism*

The events of 9/11 and each group's distinct perception of these events brought the differences between the liberal and *wasaṭī* streams into sharp focus. Liberals such as al-Nābulsī regarded 9/11 as a critical new test for Islamic religious thought and Arab political thought. According to him, the Arab way of thinking failed to change following this catastrophe (*kāritha*): Arabs continued to believe that there is a clash between the Muslim and Western cultures and that the West seeks to destroy Islam, a goal that the Muslims must thwart.[145] The neoliberals, whose platform al-Nābulsī laid out, responded to 9/11 by engaging in self-scrutiny and efforts to reform Islam. They claimed that Islam had been "hijacked and distorted, becoming a bloodthirsty and armed ideology," and so they demanded a reform in religious education, for example. In their platform, they asserted that reform may be sourced from the non-Muslim world as long as this is done diplomatically. "The main thing," they wrote, "is that it should come, whether it arrives on an Arab camel, a British tank, an American ship, or a French submarine."[146] The neoliberals saw nothing wrong in using the help of external forces to defeat what they call "the germ of tyranny" and to implement democracy in the Arab world. They argue, in fact, that outside help is necessary owing to the Arab elites' and political parties' impotence to achieve this aim on their own. They pointed out that the Europeans vanquished Nazism only with American aid and that America also helped to liberate Kuwait from the Iraqi occupation in 1990.[147]

The liberals, then, sought to diagnose the internal reasons for the 9/11 attacks and the emergence of the bin Laden phenomenon. Al-Qaraḍāwī, in contrast, blamed 9/11 on external forces while avoiding any kind of self-criticism. His explanation contrasts with that of the Tunisian liberal writer al-ʿAfīf al-Akhḍar (d. 2013), who stated that the religious sources of terror must be dried up by criminalizing all *fatwās* that incite to kill Muslims or non-Muslims and by recognizing the rights of Muslim and non-Muslim women, which, he said, are enshrined in international conventions but are not recognized by the *sharīʿa*. He also spoke of the need to respect the rights of minorities; give hope to young people, whose current outlook on the future is bleak; and rebuild the education system, especially the religious one.[148]

ʿAbd al-Ḥamīd al-Anṣārī ascribes terrorism to a deeply entrenched culture of hatred going back to the time of the Khawārij and the Battle of Ṣiffīn (657 CE). In other words, in diagnosing the roots of terrorism, al-Anṣārī employs self-criticism, a critical assessment of Islamic thought, rather than evoking conspiracy theories or external causes, as al-Qaraḍāwī does. He writes further: "Acts of terrorism grow out of our own environment and our own society. [Terror] has a familiar and well-known ideological structure and clear, albeit mistaken, religious perceptions. The terrorists are faithful disciples of a cultural discourse that is filled with deep hatred for Western civilization, its values, its norms, and its perceptions. They [the terrorists] are the result of this discourse." The hallmark of this discourse, he stresses, is an "arrogant [*istiʿlāʾī*]" and fanatical outlook that claims to have a monopoly over the absolute truth; its main aim is to malign Western culture by presenting it as aggressive, materialistic, and promiscuous in order to cause Muslim youth to despise it and to "inoculate" them against its cultural and religious influence. At the same time, this religious discourse presents the Muslim past as magnificent and glorious by focusing only on its heroic moments and ignoring more than a thousand years of darkness, wars, bloodshed, and backwardness.[149]

The remedy for this illness, al-Anṣārī proposes, is to reform the religious discourse by adapting it to the spirit of the age and purging it of complexes and delusions, manifested in the belief that the world's one and only concern is to conspire against the Muslims. Out of responsibility for the youth, preachers must not incite them to die and to hate life and society. Instead, "the mosques must be platforms for right guidance; they must not be used to promote political agendas, as the leaders of political Islam do, especially the MB, which entices the youth and pushes them toward places of death in the name of jihad and martyrdom [*istishhād*]."[150]

Al-Qaraḍāwī's sermons provide good examples of the discourse al-Anṣārī criticizes so sharply. In one of these sermons, apparently delivered during the Bosnia War (1992–95), al-Qaraḍāwī claimed that "heretical groups" were waging a war against the Muslim nation with the aim of exterminating it on every level: physical, spiritual, material, religious, creedal, ideological, and cultural. He noted that the Prophet had predicted in a *ḥadīth* that the nations of the world would attack the Muslims, but the Muslims would be weak owing to their excessive "love for this world and hatred of death [*ḥubb al-dunyā wa-karāhiyat al-mawt*]." The Prophet, he explained, was referring to Muslims who refused to sacrifice themselves for the sake of their faith. He then quoted a line from al-Bannā's *Treatise on Jihad* that exhorts Muslims to "love death for the sake of Allah and pursue it, and it will give you life." In these statements, the shaykh essentially urged Muslim youths to prefer death over life because the Muslims will achieve victory not thanks to their numbers but thanks to their willingness to sacrifice themselves (as implied in the *ḥadīth* he quoted).[151]

One recurrent theme in Muslim discourse after 9/11 is the connection between the curricula in the schools throughout the Muslim world and terrorism in the name of Islam. The West and the Muslim liberals claimed that religious education led to terrorism, but al-Qaraḍāwī viewed the demand by the United States after 9/11 that Muslim countries modify their curricula as part of an American cultural war against Islam and as an attempt by "the strong" (America) to force "the weak" (Islam) to reshape its curricula in order to please the former.[152] Clearly, al-Qaraḍāwī viewed this demand as a kind of cultural imperialism. In contrast, liberal intellectuals such as the Tunisian writer al-ʿAfīf al-Akhḍar saw a direct connection between Islamic education and terrorism. Al-Akhḍar called for removing from religious instruction all representations of non-Muslims as devils and to refrain from calling them "infidels."[153]

The 9/11 Attacks: A Turning Point in Relations between Muslims and the West

The 9/11 attacks marked a significant turning point in the history of the Islamic awakening and Islam-West relations. After the attacks, al-Qaraḍāwī set out a course for the awakening movement designed to lead it from the stage of adolescence (*murāhaqa*), as he called it, to the stage of maturity (*rushd*)—that is, from emotionality to rationality and from rage and violence to moderation and compassion.[154] The *wasaṭiyya* movement was at the forefront of the fight against the Islamophobia that erupted in the West after 9/11 and wished to change the negative attitude toward Islam and its mission that had become prevalent there. To this end, it took on an apologetic tone characteristic of the Islamic modernism of the late nineteenth and early twentieth centuries. To demonstrate to the West that Islam is a peace-loving religion and has been so since its inception, *wasaṭiyya* had to deal with significant historical and textual evidence that does not necessarily support this assertion. To achieve this, it either removed from its lexicon or reinterpreted certain Islamic terms originating in classical Muslim legal literature that were in conflict with the message that *wasaṭiyya* presented as the "true Islam." For example, *wasaṭīs* have replaced the term *ahl al-dhimma*, "protected people," with *muwāṭinūn*, "citizens" of the Muslim state, who have rights as such, although they do not belong to the Muslim faith. Following the 9/11 attacks, *wasaṭīs* were increasingly prepared to replace terms such as *infidel* with *non-Muslims*.[155] They were even willing to give up such a deeply rooted term as *jizya* (poll tax) and replace it with *zakāh* (charity) or the like. The discarding of terms such as *infidel* and *protected people* was meant for Westerners, who find them offensive. But the change of terminology does not change the essence of the attitude toward non-Muslims, especially considering that al-Qaraḍāwī believes that essence counts more than words. As shown in this study, *wasaṭiyya*'s essential attitude toward the Islamic perception of non-Muslims remains largely apologetic.

Though critical of al-Qaʿida, al-Qaraḍāwī holds that the West used 9/11 as a pretext to launch a massive campaign against Islam in general. He wrote: "After September 11, a huge media offensive was launched against Islam, in addition to the military campaign. Islam came to be considered the source of terror and violence in the world. Muslims began to face questions by the people of the West everywhere, baseless accusations against Islam, its Book, its Prophet, its *sharīʿa*, Muslim civilization and history, and the Muslim nation." He pointed out that although America declared "global war" against terrorism, evidence showed that this was a war against Islam and the Muslim nation, whose aim was to take control of the Muslims' treasures and to subjugate the Muslims. He accused America of trying to dictate to the Muslim nation how it should think and even of trying to reshape its religion, to create an "American Islam" to replace "Qur'ānic" or "Muḥammadan" Islam.[156] In fact, like al-Qa'ida and IS, al-Qaraḍāwī was of the opinion that after the 9/11 attacks America launched a crusade against Islam. All three believed that President George W. Bush's use of the word *crusade* on September 17, 2001,[157] was not a slip of the tongue but a reflection of his innermost thoughts. However, they differed on the best way to cope with this crusade: global jihad declared war on America, whereas al-Qaraḍāwī chose *da'wa* and proposed economic jihad against America.

The Term *Islamism*

The term *Islamism* is used in Western research to describe the Islamic movements—whether political or jihadi—that arose in the 1960s and 1970s in Egypt and other Muslim countries, such as Sudan. These movements, which transformed Islam into an ideology, emerged as a social and political force and as a major expression of the opposition to the world order that prevailed at the time. They are one manifestation among many of the phenomenon of Islamic awakening, a concept that many Islamic thinkers, including al-Qaraḍāwī, frequently evoke. On the political plane, one of its characteristics is transforming Islam into a major political tool and engaging in activism in the name of Islam. Hence, some Western researchers call this phenomenon "political Islam." In a *fatwā* on the term *political Islam*, however, al-Qaraḍāwī says that it is unacceptable because it is based on a plan hatched by the enemies of the faith to divide Islam into various distinct types, such as revolutionary, reactionary, radical, right wing, left wing, and so on, while in fact there is only one original Islam, that of the Qur'ān and the Sunna. He insists that "true Islam" must be political in nature and that if one removes politics from Islam, it becomes something different.[158]

It should be noted that the term *Islamists* (*Islāmiyyūn*) is used both by Western academics and by the members of the Islamic movements. The latter use it to imply that they are the exclusive representatives of the "correct" or "true" Islam, whereas Western academics use it to indicate that the Islamic movements have transformed Islam from a religion into a political ideology that seeks to reform society. As Olivier Roy notes, Islamists see Islam not merely as a religion, but as a political ideology that should reshape all aspects of society.[159] In Western research, the term *Islamism* often co-occurs with the term *fundamentalism*. This co-occurrence provokes opposition from some Muslims because in the West the term *fundamentalism* generally denotes religious extremism.[160]

In the context of these definitions of *liberalism* and *Islamism*, it is illuminating to note how Shākir al-Nābulsī regards the ideological conflict in today's Muslim world. He characterizes it in terms of a conflict between fundamentalism (*uṣūliyya*), on the one hand, and enlightenment (*tanwīr*) and secularism, on the other. Al-Nābulsī defines *uṣūliyya* as "a mentality and ideological approach that [opts for] rigidity and stagnation in every domain it addresses, a defensive psychological mechanism that justifies self-isolation and condemns the changing world around it."[161] According to him, *uṣūliyya* emerged along with political Islam—that is, along with the MB in the late 1920s. This approach, he contends, differs greatly from the true Islam, for the latter emanates from Allah and His Messenger, the Qur'ān, and the Sunna, whereas *uṣūliyya* is of human provenance, created by scholars and jurisprudents. Al-Nābulsī stresses that the secularists direct their criticism at *uṣūliyya*, not at the religion itself.[162] He states further that *uṣūliyya*, including the *wasaṭī* stream, provides ideological and religious sustenance to the terrorist militias in the Arab world and played a central role in enabling the events of 9/11.[163] This study demonstrates that his claim certainly has substance; however, it is also important to note the differences between *wasaṭiyya* and jihadi Salafism, which are outlined in this book.

Al-Nābulsī argues that the proponents of *uṣūliyya* seek to attain power and that once they do, they will use it to condemn the rationalists, who propose scriptural interpretations different from their own. He therefore holds that the *uṣūliyya* movements, such as the MB, are not genuine religious movements at all but rather political movements in a religious guise. This, he says, is why the secularists demand that clerics keep away from the sphere of politics.[164] Like other secularists, he regards *'ilmāniyya* (secularism) as the proper counterweight to *uṣūliyya* because it aims to keep religion away from politics and away from scientific and artistic endeavor.[165]

Wasaṭiyya and Its View of Extremism in the Name of Islam

Wasaṭiyya's main role in the age of awakening is to diagnose the reasons for the emergence of extremism and to present itself as the cure for this phenomenon. Whereas *wasaṭiyya* regards itself as a remedy for extremism in Islam, the liberals regard political Islam—or *uṣūliyya*, to use al-Nābulsī's term—as the ideological and religious wellspring of the terrorist militias. Analyzing the term *taṭarruf* (extremism), al-Qaraḍāwī notes that its literal meaning is "to be on the edge, far from the middle" but, he argues, Islam takes the middle road. Islam's texts preach moderation and warn against extremism, which they refer to as exaggeration (*ghulū*), excess (*tanaṭṭu'*), and strictness (*tashdīd*).[166] According to al-Qaraḍāwī, one of the main sources of extremism in Islam is a superficial understanding of the religion and its tenets, which stems not from complete ignorance but from partial and unsystematic knowledge. The extremists, he says, possess a partial knowledge of the religion but do not realize this fact—a situation more dangerous than absolute ignorance. One manifestation of partial knowledge is a tendency to adopt a literal understanding of the Qur'ān and the Sunna, the two main textual sources of Islam. As stated, al-Qaraḍāwī attributes this tendency to the Salafīs. The *wasaṭī* cure for this illness is to draw a distinction between the texts pertaining to ritual, which a Muslim must follow verbatim, and the texts pertaining to interpersonal relationships and social behavior, which must not be understood literally but rather interpreted according to their intention and their spirit. The Salafīs, says al-Qaraḍāwī, follow the principle of blind obedience in both domains, which leads to excessive strictness in jurisprudence (see chapter 6).[167] However, as shown in chapter 6, a comparison between the *wasaṭī* and liberal approaches to the issues of the veil (*ḥijāb*) and the dress code for women as well as to the issue of homosexuality reveals that al-Qaraḍāwī, too, espouses a literal interpretation of the text rather than one that is based on the text's intention. For example, he states that the punishment for homosexuality should be identical to the punishment for *zinā*, adultery: stoning to death if the perpetrator is married and flogging if he is not. The liberals, in contrast, argue that as part of human rights that are enshrined in the Qur'ān, individuals are entitled to freedom, including sexual freedom.

According to al-Nābulsī, both Salafism and *uṣūliyya* reject the historical interpretation (*al-tafsīr al-tārīkhī*) of the Islamic sources in favor of a rigidly literal interpretation. He and other liberals reason that because societies evolve and change over time but religious texts do not, the latter must be periodically reassessed and reinterpreted to adapt them to changing norms and lifestyles. When religious texts are wholly incompatible with contemporary societal norms, they must be discarded in favor of civil texts (*nuṣūṣ madaniyya*) that are compatible with them. They point out that some Islamic countries, such as Egypt and Jordan, adopted this approach when they stopped applying Qur'ānic punishments (*ḥudūd Allāh*) such as the amputation of a thief's hand (Q5:38) and the stoning of adulterers (Q24:2). The liberals find evidence for the validity of the historical approach in Qur'ānic verses pertaining to the adherents of other religions, such as the Jews and Christians. They point out that the Qur'ānic attitude to these non-Muslims changed according to the period and the circumstances in which the verses were revealed (as discussed in chapter 5). Al-Nābulsī notes that the "ignoramuses of *uṣūliyya*" falsely present this liberal approach as evidence that the liberals seek to revoke certain religious texts.[168] He presents this accusation as false (although in actual fact it is not unfounded, for, as shown earlier, the liberals indeed argue that the circumstances of the modern world render certain Qur'ānic texts irrelevant).

Although al-Qaraḍāwī, too, ascribes importance to the circumstances in which verses were revealed (*asbāb al-nuzūl*), he contends that the liberals go too far in this respect, limiting the Qur'ān's applicability to the time of the Prophet and thereby casting doubt on its eternal validity.[169] Conversely, liberals such as al-'Ashmāwī contend that the clerics who politicize Islam, such as al-Qaraḍāwī, prohibit regarding any law as relative or temporary and therefore forbid making any change to a divine law or suspending it.[170] In his neoliberal platform, al-Nabulsī advocates "treating [certain] *sharīʿa* laws—such as the laws pertaining to women's *ḥijāb*, inheritance, testimony, and [right to] hold high office—as suitable for the time and place [in which they were revealed] and not as eternal, as some clerics claim."[171]

Another reason for extremism, in al-Qaraḍāwī's estimation, is unqualified persons' attempt to derive knowledge directly from the religious texts without the mediation of expert scholars. Many extremists, he observes, are self-taught: they are not graduates of religious schools but have degrees in medicine or science.[172] In this context, he writes: "One who swims in this sea [of religious knowledge] by himself and is not a proficient swimmer is in danger of being buffeted to and fro by the waves or swept by the currents in directions he did not intend. Often he may be swallowed up by the sea and never arrive at the shore or find anyone to save him, for he continued on his own without helper or guide."[173] Al-Qaraḍāwī observes that some young people turn directly to the Qur'ān and Sunna because they distrust the expert scholars, especially those who are affiliated with the rulers. Sympathetic to this position, he stresses that *wasaṭiyya* defies the Islamic establishments that serve the regimes and that, as a *wasaṭī* scholar, he is committed to deserving the trust of his followers. He calls upon the religious establishments to reform themselves, to avoid becoming embroiled in local politics, and instead to produce pious scholars with a clear-headed perspective on their era and reality. He advises them to adopt the *wasaṭī* interpretation, which is objective and has not been politically recruited. This study demonstrates, however, that *wasaṭī* exegesis is not in fact free of political and sectarian agendas. It is these agendas that motivate liberals to accuse al-Qaraḍāwī of making ideological use of religion for worldly, nonreligious ends, as exemplified by rulings tailored to the needs of the MB and Hamas, which are discussed later.[174] The liberal secularist al-ʿAshmāwī argues that the representatives of political Islam, including al-Qaraḍāwī, rely on terror and violence, which result from the exploitation of religion for political or partisan aims. When Islam is free of such tendencies, al-'Ashmāwī claims, the Muslim nation will be a paragon of tolerance and freedom of expression.[175]

Al-Qaraḍāwī's claim that exegesis of the Qur'ān and the Sunna is the exclusive prerogative of the *'ulamā'* contradicts another of his rulings, that every Muslim is "the master of his own faith [*rajul li-dīnihi*]" and that the *'ulamā'* (*rijāl al-dīn*) are merely experts in the Islamic sciences, comparable to experts on ethics, philosophy, and law in other societies.[176] Liberal critics of the contemporary religious discourse, such as Abū Zayd, criticize *'ulamā'* such as al-Qaraḍāwī for claiming the exclusive right to interpret the religious texts. Abū Zayd asserts that these *'ulamā'* draw a false identity between their interpretation of the texts and the texts themselves and thus conceal from the Muslims that the Qur'ān is multifaceted (*al-Qur'ān ḥammāl awjuh*), as 'Alī b. Abī Ṭālib stated: "The Qur'ān is a written text. It does not speak; it is men who speak [on its behalf]." Abū Zayd stresses that it is this aspect of the Qur'ān that allows for pluralism and thereby lends Islamic culture its unique character. But the *'ulamā'*, he says, deny this pluralism by trying to monopolize Qur'ānic exegesis.[177]

The Academic Literature on al-Qaraḍāwī and *Wasaṭiyya*

This book is the first devoted specifically to the *wasaṭī* school of Islam as shaped by al-Qaraḍāwī. The shaykh himself, despite his central role and innovative approach as an Islamic cleric, is the topic of only two books in English, both published in 2009. The first is an anthology of essays edited by Bettina Gräf and Jakob Skovgaard-Petersen dealing with various aspects of the "al-Qaraḍāwī phenomenon," including one essay focusing on *wasaṭiyya*.[178] In the preface to this anthology, Gudrun Krämer writes: "The idea of moderate Islam, or the Islam of the middle ground, *al-wasaṭiyya*, invites further study, not least to highlight even more forcefully that moderation can mean different things in different contexts."[179] The present book fills this gap in the research. The second book, by Samuel Helfont, is devoted to al-Qaraḍāwī and modernity.[180] It examines how modernity shaped Yūsuf al-Qaraḍāwī's outlook and analyzes his approach to modernity and his views on four topics: jihad, relations with non-Muslims, democracy, and women and feminism. Helfont argues that al-Qaraḍāwī's writings are filled with modern conceptions—with respect to democracy and feminism, for example—and that his approach to defining the relationship between those conceptions and Islam is what makes him unique.

Muhammad Qasim Zaman has published an important book that examines al-Qaraḍāwī as a religious authority who criticizes Islam from within.[181] It discusses the contents, rhetoric, and ambiguities of the critiques by modern Muslim *'ulamā'* of the crises in Muslim societies, in particular after the events of 9/11. The analysis in the book focuses on criticism enunciated by Rashīd Riḍā, al-Qaraḍāwī, and a number of clerics belonging to the Deobandi school in southern Asia on a number of issues that have preoccupied the Muslim world since the nineteenth century. Zaman's book is unique in the comparative perspective it provides in that he not only deals with Riḍā and al-Qaraḍāwī, both Arabs from the Middle East, but also compares them with the Deobandi of southern Asia.

Raymond William Baker has studied the phenomenon of the "New Islamists" (another name for the proponents of *wasaṭiyya*).[182] He describes them as Islamic activists who do not advocate violence and have formed themselves loosely into a school of thought in order to provide guidance to various bodies and Islamic groups, including the trade unions in Egypt. Baker locates the *wasaṭī*s between the quietists, who focus on personal faith and worship, and the radicals, who seek to reshape their societies along religious lines using violent methods. Examining the thought of al-Qaraḍāwī alongside that of the Egyptian writer Fahmī Huwaydī (b. 1937) and the jurists Muḥammad Salīm al-'Awwā (b. 1942) and Ṭāriq al-Bishrī (b. 1933), Baker's research focuses on three topics: culture, especially educational reform and attitudes toward the arts; society, in particular nation building and the creation of an economy; and politics, in particular the struggle for the *tajdīd* of Islam and international relations.

In the literature on the phenomenon of Islamism, the *wasaṭī* Islamist stream is often claimed to lack any distinct unifying characteristics. In his book *Sharī'a and Muslim Minorities*, Uriya Shavit discusses the *fiqh* of Muslim minorities in the West and the rulings issued with respect to them, with emphasis on the differences between the *wasaṭī* and Salafī approaches. Of *wasaṭiyya*, Shavit writes: "*Wasaṭiyya* is not a political party. Neither is it a social movement. There exists no foundational canonical text that represents it. Rather, it is an approach to Islamic law and, more broadly, a call to reform Muslim societies. This approach has been led, systemized, institutionalized, and popularized by the Egyptian-born Yūsuf al-Qaraḍāwī."[183]

However, some researchers have attempted to outline the characteristics shared by all proponents of *wasaṭiyya*. R. Hrair Dekmejian, for example, points to several such characteristics: (1) the combination of the major tenets of Salafism with the concept of renewal; (2) the giving of priority to *da'wa* in order to Islamize the Muslim *umma* as a prelude to establishing an Islamic state; (3) advocation of a gradual rather than immediate implementation of political objectives, in opposition to the position taken by the radical Islamists; (4) pragmatism; (5) cooperation with nationalistic and quasi-democratic regimes until Islam supplants nationalism as the dominant ideology; and (6) universalism—that is, involvement in national political affairs as a means first to Islamize individual regimes as a prelude to building the universal nation.[184]

In fact, an in-depth study of al-Qaraḍāwī's writings, as is undertaken in this book, reveals that *wasaṭiyya* can indeed be regarded as a systematic school of thought and jurisprudence anchored in a set of specific principles—the thirty basic principles analyzed in chapter 3 (see the translation of the *wasaṭiyya* principles in appendix A)—and that Yūsuf al-Qaraḍāwī can be regarded as its leader, or *imām*. In setting out the principles of *wasaṭiyya*, the shaykh himself did not call it a school of thought but rather a "method" or "way" (*manhaj*); however, a passage in which he explains the need for clear-cut principles demonstrates that he indeed sought to outline a consistent ideology. In this passage, he states that "in order to keep *wasaṭiyya* from being falsely embraced by people who neither know it or understand it and by anyone without knowledge, guidance, and a clarifying text, I felt the need to set out for the Muslim reader the characteristics, guidelines, and rules that define the *shar'ī* and ideological roots of this stream or this way so that these [characteristics and guidelines] will serve as a beacon for those who wish to be guided by this way and to follow its path."[185] The principles of the *wasaṭī* stream are described in al-Qaraḍāwī's book *The Fiqh of Islamic Wasaṭiyya: Characteristics and Beacons.*[186] *Wasaṭiyya*'s status as a religious school is also reflected in the existence of the al-Qaraḍāwī Students Forum (Multaqā Talāmīdh al-Qaraḍāwī), which meets regularly and whose purpose, as articulated by Libyan preacher Shaykh Salām al-Shaykhī, is to inculcate the fundamentals of al-Qaraḍāwī's religious methodology (*manhajiyya*) and to preserve the vitality of this path of renewal. Moreover, al-Shaykhī refers to al-Qaraḍāwī as *imām*, the title borne by leaders of Islamic legal schools.[187] The ideological platform of the *wasaṭī* stream can also be found in the charter of the IUMS, founded by al-Qaraḍāwī in 2004. This charter states explicitly that the IUMS espouses the *fiqh* of the *wasaṭī* school (*al-madrasa al-wasaṭiyya*).

Presenting the principles of *wasaṭiyya* became especially important after the attacks of 9/11, which prompted many in the Muslim world and the West to call for reexamining the Muslim religious discourse, in particular the attitude to non-Muslims. This book shows that al-Qaraḍāwī has sought, especially since the 9/11 terrorist attacks, to present the *wasaṭī* stream as a response to the terrorism perpetrated in the name of Islam; however, unlike liberal Muslim thinkers such as the Tunisian intellectual al-ʿAfīf al-Akhḍar, he does not find the roots of Islamic terrorism in the school curricula taught in the Muslim world, in the content of mosque sermons, or in the mixing of religion and politics. In contrast to the liberals' self-critical approach, he sees this terrorism as a reaction to Western injustice toward Islam and to the Zionist occupation of Palestine. In this manner, he essentially justifies and rationalizes the terror perpetrated by Muslims against the West. According to the *wasaṭī* view, the West has placed Islam in the dock, especially since 9/11, and *wasaṭiyya* seeks to defend Islam's good name. The only changes it proposes to solve the conflict with the West are cosmetic, such as using the term *non-Muslims* instead of *infidels* and referring to Jews and Christians living in Muslim countries as "citizens" rather than "protected persons" (*ahl al-dhimma*). This change in terminology does not run deep, for *wasaṭiyya*, like jihadi Salafism, regards Islam as the one true faith and all other religions as false and believes that the entire world will eventually be Islamic. The *wasaṭiyya* vision is not one of religious and ideological pluralism, but of global Islamic hegemony. This study therefore shows that the difference between *wasaṭiyya* and jihadi Salafism does not lie in their vision but in the means they propose to realize it. The jihadi Salafīs advocate violent jihad as the way to implement the vision, whereas *wasaṭiyya* advocates slow and gradual change through the extensive use of *da'wa*, preaching, in combination with jihad.[188]

This book provides an in-depth analysis of the alternative interpretation proposed by *wasaṭiyya* and shaped by Yūsuf al-Qaraḍāwī. The analysis is based on a careful reading of the many and varied texts produced by this school; an examination of the exegetical, philosophical, and conceptual disputes it has with the Salafīs, especially those of the jihadi variety; and discussion of Qaraḍāwī's intellectual confrontations with liberals as well as with *'ulamā'* whose rulings differ from his own. The book presents the main elements of *wasaṭiyya* as defined by al-Qaraḍāwī, some of which derive from the twenty fundamentals al-Bannā lists in "Message of Teachings";[189] it also examines the main points of dispute as well as the points of similarity between the *wasaṭī*, Salafī, and liberal interpretations on three cardinal issues: the concept of jihad; the vision of the Islamic state; and principles of legal rulings, in particular on social issues, with a focus on women's issues.

This Book's Contribution

The major original conclusions derived from the research reported in this book include:

1. *Wasaṭiyya* developed out of the basic principles that al-Bannā formulated in the 1920s and 1930s for what he called the "Islam of the MB." Al-Qaraḍāwī felt that such a development was needed to meet two significant challenges facing the Muslim world: westernization and Islamism. *Wasaṭiyya*'s main contribution was the interpretation of Islam that it developed as part of the Islamic awakening that began at the end of the 1960s and intensified in the course of the 1970s. Al-Qaraḍāwī took al-Bannā's principles and his own, adapted them to the changing times, and sought to promote them as universal, detaching them from their association with the MB.

2. *Wasaṭiyya* had a profound effect on the MB's intermediate generation, as can clearly be seen in the views of such figures as 'Abd al-Mun'im Abū al-Futūḥ (b. 1951) and 'Iṣām al-'Aryān (b. 1954). This generation looked to al-Qaraḍāwī as an authoritative source of religious law. Al-Qaraḍāwī's *wasaṭiyya* philosophy influenced the emergence of a reformist camp within the MB, which challenged the Brotherhood's old guard. The shaykh's influence on the reformist camp could be seen, for example, in the platform of the Freedom and Justice Party (Ḥizb al-Ḥurriyya wal-'Adāla, founded in June 2011).

3. An examination of the *wasaṭī* position on the two issues of jihad and the attitude toward non-Muslims in comparison to the jihadi Salafī position may lead to the mistaken conclusion that the former represents a more moderate approach. However, when its approach is compared to that of the Muslim liberals, it becomes clear that on a continuum with the liberals at one end and the jihadi Salafīs at the other, the *wasaṭī* position is closer to the latter, in contrast to the image that *wasaṭiyya* wishes to project of itself.

Wasaṭiyya can be regarded as a brand of Salafism and called "*wasaṭī* Salafism." It is Salafī in that it purports to return to the Qur'ān and the Sunna; in fact, it can even be regarded as a type of jihadist Salafism in that it shares the vision of the ultimate victory of Islam over all other religions. It is *wasaṭī* in that it advocates pragmatism, realism, and gradualness in choosing a path toward attaining its goals.

4. The *wasaṭī* approach to the challenge that the West poses to Islam consists of an attempt to formulate what al-Qaraḍāwī characterizes as a middle position between the emulation of the West espoused by the secularists of the Muslim world and the total war against the West declared by global jihad.

Wasaṭiyya presents itself as being open to global cultures, especially to the West. But an analysis of its views on the West, especially when compared to the liberal position, reveals that the only thing *wasaṭiyya* is prepared to borrow from the West is its science and technology; in fact, *wasaṭiyya* warns against the adoption of Western thought, philosophy, and culture. According to al-Qaraḍāwī, whatever is borrowed from the West must be imbued with the Muslim spirit. *Wasaṭiyya*, like jihadi Salafism, considers the West as lacking in ethics and values; Muslim culture is thus perceived as the appropriate alternative to Western culture.[190]

Al-Qaraḍāwī's point of departure from the West is that he views Islam as a universal mission and that the people of the West are part of the "worlds" to which Muḥammad was sent. He believes that the negative opinion of Islam that he discerns among many Westerners is owing to the heritage of the Crusades. He demands that the West free itself of its long-time hostility toward Islam and of its imperialist desire to take control of Islamic lands and their resources.[191]

Wasaṭiyya presents itself as a contemporary "middle way" in Islam also with respect to globalization. It puts at one end the "westernizers," who accept globalization, and at the other the "isolationists," who fear the West and reject globalization, but places itself in the middle. It promotes the exploitation of globalization's benefits, such as the communication revolution, while keeping its distance from its more negative aspects, such as Western domination, which *wasaṭī*s perceive as synonymous with Americanization. However, a closer look at the *wasaṭī* position on globalization, especially when compared to the liberal view, reveals that it considers globalization a new type of Western—nay, American—imperialism, which must be resisted, especially in its cultural aspects, through which, according to al-Qaraḍāwī, the West attempts to change the Muslim identity.

5. The present study shows that the *wasaṭī* approach is basically both apologetic and dogmatic. This becomes especially clear when one considers al-Qaraḍāwī's rulings on women's issues, such as the Islamic laws that discriminate against women in matters of inheritance and testimony. A comparison of al-Qaraḍāwī's *wasaṭī* position with that of liberals such as Muḥammad Sa'īd al-'Ashmāwī on the issue of the *ḥijāb*, for instance, reveals that concepts such as "women's liberation," "women's human rights," and "women's equality" are perceived very differently by the two groups. Although al-Qaraḍāwī wishes to present himself as a champion of women's liberation who advocates liberating Muslim women from the shackles of ancient social traditions as well as from Western influences, he remains very dogmatic in his approach, which he bases on the old religious texts. He insists that women's traditional role of raising children and seeing to

their husbands' needs is paramount and affects their possible participation in social and political affairs, which must therefore remain relegated to second place. The liberals, in contrast, insist that women be treated first and foremost as human beings, not just as women, and that it is clerics' interpretation of religious texts rather than the texts themselves that are the obstacle to women's liberation. Al-Qaraḍāwī's dogmatism can also be clearly seen in his rulings on homosexuality, which he regards as a disease and a deviation from the natural, divinely ordained human inclination to be attracted to the opposite sex.

6. *Wasaṭiyya* developed a school of jurisprudence after it formulated a method of making legal decisions, whose core principle is to exploit the leeway provided by two mechanisms of *sharīʿa*: *maṣlaḥa* as an independent legal principle and the tools of *sharʿī* politics (*siyāsa sharʿiyya*). In addition, *wasaṭiyya* adopted the principle that it will not fanatically adhere to any one legal school of jurisprudence (*madhhab*) as well as the principle of facilitation as a basic objective of *sharīʿa*. This approach to legal decision making enables *wasaṭiyya* to implement its view that *sharīʿa* is valid for all times and all places, and that the *fatwā*s based on it can change in accordance with changing times, places, and circumstances.

The present study compares al-Qaraḍāwī's rulings on a number of key issues with the rulings of those whom he calls "the *ʿulamāʾ* of the rulers" (i.e., clerics employed by the regime). One confrontation between them concerned the right to rebel against the ruler, which took place in the wake of al-Qaraḍāwī's announcement of his *fiqh al-thawra* (jurisprudence of revolution), in which he gave his rulings concerning the revolutions of the "Arab Spring." In these rulings, he is revealed as the *muftī* of the MB movement.

Two other issues on which al-Qaraḍāwī disputed the views of the official clerics are the peace treaty with Israel and the legitimacy of martyrdom attacks (*istishhād*). On both issues, his views are quite close to those of jihadi Salafism.

Al-Qaraḍāwī presents himself as a "divinity scholar" (*ʿālim rabbānī*), whose only guide is God and who does not allow himself to be influenced by any political or ideological considerations. However, the present study shows that his legal decisions are in line with the MB's positions.

Al-Qaraḍāwī is thus first and foremost an adherent of the MB (*ikhwānī*), who has striven to universalize al-Bannā's narrow group ideology.

Al-Qaraḍāwī wishes to promote *wasaṭīyya* as the Muslim response to both jihadi Salafism and secular liberalism. However, as this study shows, the *wasaṭīs*' claim that their way constitutes a golden mean between the two extremes is incompatible with its actual positions and views. To the contrary, *wasaṭīyya* refuses to countenance liberalism, which it accuses of unbelief, while it shares the vision of jihadi Salafism, even though it claims that the latter holds a mistaken view on a core issue in Islamic discourse, as we shall see in chapter 5 on jihad.

7. Both *wasaṭīyya* and the liberals have called for the rejuvenation of religious thought and religious reform. But al-Qaraḍāwī interprets *tajdīd* (literally "renewal") as going back to the "pure" Islam of the *salaf*, whereas the liberals view it as a product of human knowledge and not just of expertise in Islamic law. For the liberals, *tajdīd* involves primarily the use of human intelligence and knowledge about reality, without denying the principles of the faith. The liberals reject al-Qaraḍāwī's basic premise that the *salaf* knew better because they lived in the times of the Prophet and his Companions and therefore deserve to be imitated. They insist not only that modern Muslims are unable to emulate the *salaf*'s mentality, but that Muslims today possess knowledge that the *salaf* did not. For this reason, the liberals, in contrast to al-Qaraḍāwī's dogmatism, are in favor of innovative thinking, especially with respect to the religious texts.

The Structure of the Book

The book consists of two parts. Part one (chapters 1–3) focuses on the historical, cultural, and intellectual background against which the *wasaṭiyya* movement emerged; the basic principles of *wasaṭiyya* as formulated by al-Qaraḍāwī (which are, to a large extent, developments of al-Bannā's principles); and al-Qaraḍāwī's biography and his development as a Muslim scholar. Part two (chapters 4–6) compares *wasaṭiyya* to its two rivals in contemporary Islamic discourse: jihadi Salafism and liberalism. Chapter 4 examines the basic principles of jihadi Salafism as well as the *wasaṭīs*' and the liberals' positions on these principles. Chapter 5 focuses on the conception of jihad espoused by *wasaṭiyya*, jihadi Salafism, and liberalism. Chapter 6 discusses the *wasaṭī* juridical methodology, as demonstrated through rulings on social issues in general and on women's issues in particular, which are compared to both the Salafī rulings on and the liberal approach to these issues.

Part One

The Emergence of *Wasaṭiyya*

1

Wasaṭiyya, an Innovating Salafism

*Reform (*Iṣlāḥ*) and Renewal (*Tajdīd*)*

This chapter examines *wasaṭiyya* as a stream that advocates reform (*iṣlāḥ*) and renewal (*tajdīd*). As a reformist stream, *wasaṭiyya* grew out of the Islamic modernism of the late nineteenth and early twentieth centuries. Like Islamic modernism, it emerged as an answer to the challenge of Western imperialism and especially the challenge of ideological-cultural imperialism. Hence, this chapter discusses *wasaṭiyya* as part of the Islamic Awakening of the 1970s and 1980s, which is likewise perceived—by the Islamists who have made Islam into an ideology, both political and jihadi—as an Islamic answer to the Western challenge. The chapter examines the remedy proposed by *wasaṭiyya* for the Islamic nation's malady: Salafism combined with renewal. To accurately assess the change proposed by al-Qaraḍāwī's *wasaṭiyya*, it compares the *wasaṭī* perception of both *tajdīd* and *iṣlāḥ* to the liberal perception of these principles.

Wasaṭiyya as a Stream of *Iṣlāḥ* and *Tajdīd*

Shaykh Yūsuf al-Qaraḍāwī can definitely be referred to as one of the "makers of contemporary Islam," as John Esposito and John Voll call such individuals in their book by this title.[1] Esposito and Voll describe these thinkers as "modern Muslim activist intellectuals" who shaped the conceptual world and set the terms for most debates in the Muslim countries in the twentieth century and whose modes of thinking were at the heart of the Islamic Awakening of the 1970s.[2] These activist intellectuals emerged in the second half of the twentieth century as a result of several important developments in the Muslim world. The first was the rise, beginning in the late nineteenth century, of secular Muslim intellectuals as part of the interaction of the Muslim world with the West and as a result of the westernization and modernization of many sectors in Muslim societies. These secular intellectuals wielded much influence; however, they also evoked opposition because their vision was felt to be disconnected from the Islamic heritage. Moreover, in the late nineteenth century the West was associated not only with modernity but also with imperialism and the foreign domination of Arab societies. Hence, Muslim intellectuals who were considered "too secular" or "too westernized" were frequently seen as agents of imperialism. At the same time, because Muslim societies recognized the need for reform and modernization, the traditional Muslim *'ulamā'* were no longer seen as a viable alternative for these Western intellectuals, and so their status in Muslim society declined. This state of affairs led to the advent in the late nineteenth century of a new kind of Muslim intellectual who combined many of the characteristics of the secular intellectual with the characteristics of a traditional Islamic scholar. These reformist intellectuals, often referred to in the academic literature as the "Islamic modernists," are to a large extent the precursors of the modern Muslim activist intellectuals of the late twentieth century, including al-Qaraḍāwī. The latter, too, are committed to *tajdīd* and *iṣlāḥ* in contemporary Muslim societies and represent a fascinating combination of the traditional role of the Islamic scholar (*'ālim*) as understood in Muslim societies and the role of the intellectual as understood in modern Western societies.[3]

Al-Qaraḍāwī: An Heir to the Legacy of *Iṣlāḥ*

Al-Qaraḍāwī's *wasaṭī* thought owes much to the reformist ideologies of Jamāl al-Dīn al-Afghānī (d. 1897),[4] Muḥammad 'Abduh (d. 1905),[5] and Muḥammad Rashīd Riḍā, all of whom, like him, sought to reform Muslim society by means of Islam.[6] For these fathers of the reformist stream in the late nineteenth and early twentieth centuries, the main impetus was to prove that Islam is not incompatible with the needs and demands of the modern age and thus to uphold it in the face of the challenge posed by

Western culture and ideas. To this end, they cultivated the perception that the key to *tajdīd* lay in the Muslim tradition itself.

In Western academic literature, the reformist current of the late nineteenth and early twentieth centuries is called "Islamic modernism" or the "Salafī current," though its ideologues did not use the term *Salafī* in its contemporary sense.[7] These thinkers generally used the term *iṣlāḥ* to describe their philosophy and activity. Despite the diversity of this current, one can identify a number of basic principles that were accepted by all of its members and that today inspire the ideologies of the MB and al-Qaraḍāwī's *wasaṭī* stream. One of these principles is a longing for the "pure Islam" of Islam's first generations (*salaf*), prior to the introduction of forbidden innovations (*bida*ʿ). An important juristic principle that guided the reformists was the rejection of the blind imitation (*taqlīd*) of previous jurists and of blind compliance with any legal school.[8] They instead called not only for *tajdīd* but also for *ijtihād*—independent human reasoning in juristic effort based on the primary sources of Islam, the Qur'ān and the Sunna.[9] The purpose of *ijtihād* was to adapt Islam to contemporary circumstances in accordance with the *maṣlaḥa* of the Muslim *umma*. The modernist reformists advocated applying *ijtihād* to social and pecuniary issues (*muʿāmalāt*), while relying exclusively on the Qur'ān and the Sunna in matters of worship (*ʿibādāt*).[10] They criticized the *ʿulamā'* for refusing to adapt Islam to the modern age, but at the same time they also criticized westernized Muslims who championed secularism.[11]

Al-Qaraḍāwī believes that the Islamic scholars have a pivotal role in enacting reform, and in this context he wrote in the IUMS charter:

> The Islamic scholars throughout the Muslim world are called upon today to raise the banner of comprehensive reform, enhance the nation's awareness of this reform, and encourage it to follow the path of reform. This will not come to be unless the scholars address the concerns of the [Muslim] nation as a whole, identify its most pressing problems, and provide solutions in the spirit of Islam—as part of jurisprudential and ideological *ijtihād* that is open to the spirit of the age, benefits from the experience of others, and is compatible with the principles, laws, and goals of the *sharīʿa*.[12]

Muhammad Qasim Zaman regards al-Qaraḍāwī and Rashīd Riḍā, who greatly influenced al-Qaraḍāwī, as "reformist scholars" who criticize certain aspects of Islamic tradition from within and who made an important contribution to the reformist discourse in Muslim societies. According to Zaman, the reformist scholars should not be regarded as systematic thinkers who set out a uniform and monolithic philosophy, but as activist intellectuals who responded over the years to important controversies, both old and new.[13]

The *Wasaṭī* and Liberal Perceptions of Reform

For al-Qaraḍāwī, reform involves "treating our various illnesses [with medications] from our own pharmacy and not that of others, by our own diagnosis and not that of foreign physicians, with prescriptions of our own and not of others; the reform that we promote has aims, conditions, and boundaries."[14] He rejects the kind of reform proposed by the secularists and the admirers of the Americans, whose objective, so he states, is to make the Muslim nation, in the words of the *ḥadīth*, "go in the footsteps of others, a handbreadth at a time, a pace at a time, [so that] if [others] entered the lizards' den, they would also enter." The reform that westernizing secularists want to promote, al-Qaraḍāwī maintains, aims at "drying up the springs [*tajfīf al-yanābī'*]" of the Muslim nation's religion in education, *da'wa*, and culture in general. The reform proposed by the *wasaṭīs*, in contrast, constitutes a call to preach *ijtihād* and *tajdīd* as well as to fight against paralysis and blind imitation of Islam's founding generation and its schools of jurisprudence.

Wasaṭiyya considers *ijtihād* and *tajdīd* religious duties and practical necessities. It views its proposed reform as the right way to revive the Muslim nation so that the nation can realize its purpose as divinely ordained in the Qur'ān (3:110)—in other words, to command good and prohibit evil. *Wasaṭiyya* insists that *tajdīd* is to be applied only to the means of achieving this purpose, but that the objectives do not change, contrary to the westernizers and the admirers of America within the Muslim nation, who wish "to renew the Ka'ba by bringing a stone for it from Europe," in the words of Muḥammad Iqbāl (d. 1938), an Indian poet and philosopher, considered Pakistan's spiritual father.[15] Or, in the words of the Egyptian writer Muṣṭafā Ṣādiq al-Rāfiʿī (d. 1937), "They [the westernizers and the admirers of America] want to renew religion and language, the sun and the moon."[16] *Wasaṭiyya*'s objective, in contrast, is that the nation renew itself from within, fulfill its mission, and realize its aims, becoming a "just community," as God willed it, that will testify for the people (Q2:143) and reign supreme among humankind. For al-Qaraḍāwī, the crux of *iṣlāḥ* and *tajdīd* in Islam is a return to the original religion of the first Muslim generations, a vision that he shares with the Salafīs.

Today a rift can be discerned in Islam between Salafism—whether al-Qaraḍāwī's *wasaṭī* Salafism, traditional Salafism, or jihadi Salafism—and secularist liberalism. The liberal perception of the reform and its format is clearly summed up in the following principles, drafted by the Tunisian thinker al-ʿAfīf al-Akhḍar:

1. The texts of the Qur'ān, the Sunna, and the *ḥadīth* must be studied and taught through the lens of comparative religion. This approach will help the Muslim to understand the religion in all of its dimensions, freeing him from what al-Akhḍar calls "religious irrationality" and endowing him instead with a rational religious outlook that does not accept what contradicts human rights and the sciences.

2. The principle of *ijtihād*, which Muslim scholars limit to matters that are not explicitly addressed by the Qur'ān and the Sunna, must be replaced with the principle of abrogation (*naskh*), which is accepted in the exegesis of Islamic scripture. The liberals seek to apply this principle to Qur'ānic verses and to *ḥadīth*s that are incompatible with the spirit of our times. Arguing that the literal interpretation of the Qur'ān and the Sunna is the source of extremism and terror, they suggest that these texts be interpreted according to the historic circumstances in which they descended and to abrogate all verses and traditions that are at odds with the good of humanity and of Muslims today. (For a fuller discussion of the *wasaṭī* and liberal interpretations of the Qur'ān and the Sunna, see chapter 6.)

3. Religion and state as well as believer and citizen must be distinguished. In the spirit of modernity, this separation will be based on specialization: clerics will lead believers in matters of their faith, and politicians will lead them in their everyday worldly affairs.

4. Reform will give priority to "the birth of a new form of individual," who does not dissolve into his nation but is

> the sole possessor of his head and his private parts. The latter he uses just as he wishes within the framework of a rational objective law that does not forbid love between consenting adults. He also has full freedom in his head to think as he wishes, free from censorship or self-censorship, free of all punishments or threat of punishment. He is an independent, free individual who thinks for himself, who determines his own fate in his daily life; he chooses for himself his own personal religiosity and does not hesitate to question his belief or cast doubts upon it. This individual henceforth is fit to be the object of any reform that is conscious of its aims and its priorities.

Al-Akhḍar adds that "the individual that dissolves into the 'nation' constitutes the solid kernel of the ideology of Islamic terrorism," whereas "this [new] individual—a believer as a person but a secularist as a citizen—is the only one who is qualified to effect a reconciliation with the world he lives in, divested of any hysterical fears or delirious denunciations of others as 'infidel.'"

5. The reform of Islam will be an integral part of a comprehensive reform in all domains, including education, in particular religious education. Like other liberals, al-Akhḍar holds that the essence of the reform in religious education must consist of replacing the Salafī education, whose graduates are "unemployable semiclerics," with rationalist education that will produce twenty-first century professionals: technicians, engineers, researchers, scientists, and doctors.[17]

In stark contrast to the liberals, who as the basis for reform seek to create a free individual who does not "dissolve" into his nation, al-Qaraḍāwī seeks to create a global Islamic nation. Common sense, Muslim interests, and the character of our age, he says, obligate the Muslims to form a large nation that all of them can join and that will ensure their growth and protect them. Forming a large bloc is necessary from a military point of view to ensure that enemies will not defeat the Muslim countries one by one as well as from an economic point of view to ensure that the Muslims do not enter the technological age while in a state of division.[18]

ʿAbd al-Ḥamīd al-Anṣārī, too, described the liberal perspective on the *iṣlāḥ* and *tajdīd* of Islam. He stated that the key to reform is respect for all human beings, in accordance with Q17:70: "And We have certainly honored the children of Adam." This, he said, means respecting Muslims and non-Muslims, men and women, Salafīs and Ṣūfīs. From the liberal perspective, reform is not possible without openness to other cultures, which will remove the hatred felt by many Muslims toward non-Muslims and allow them to be fair and just in their dealings with the other, as they are instructed in Q60:8: "Allah does not forbid you from those who do not fight you because of religion and do not expel you from your homes—from being righteous toward them and acting justly toward them."[19] Al-Qaraḍāwī, too, regards this verse as the basis for relations between Muslims and non-Muslims. But he also points to the verse that follows it (60:9), which stresses that Muslims must not make allies of non-Muslims who fight them or expel them from their homes or who aid in their expulsion. From this verse, he concludes that a fundamental distinction must be made between non-Muslims (including polytheists) who fight the Muslims and those who don't.[20]

The liberals recognize a need for far-reaching change in the Arab and Muslim world, change that should be led by enlightened preachers, clerics, and intellectuals. These reformists, says Shākir al-Nābulsī, must be alert to the era in which they live, its demands and its challenges. They must be armed with courage and clear-eyed political vision so as to draft a program for reforming the nation. According to al-Nābulsī, this program must involve several aspects:

1. *The granting of freedoms.* According to the liberals, Islam heralded the values of freedom of thought, belief, and expression as well as personal and political freedoms—for they all follow from Q2:256, "There shall be no coercion in the religion."

2. *The establishment of civil rights, rule of law, and equality before the law.* These aspects of the polity, the liberals say, are insufficiently respected by the peoples and the rulers of the Muslim world, which has often resulted in a state of anarchy.

3. *The enacting of democracy.* The liberals hold that the current controversy in the Muslim world between the advocates of the principle of

consultation (*shūrā*) and the advocates of democracy is a barren and pointless one because *shūrā* is just a step on the way to democracy, not an end in itself, as al-Nābulsī argues. Political freedoms are possible only as part of democracy, he says.

4. *A reexamination of women's status in society.* The limitations imposed on women do not originate in the Prophet's Islam or in the texts of the Qur'ān and the Sunna, but in the rulings of Muslim jurists and in entrenched tribal customs.

5. *Development of civil society.* Change in the Arab and Muslim world cannot happen without building a civil society and abolishing the military and dictatorial regimes.[21]

Al-'Afīf al-Akhḍar writes that reform should involve two stages: first, formal legislation and, second, the inculcation of the reformist values in the Muslim's collective consciousness. The second stage largely falls to the media, the education system, and the enlightened religious discourse. Moreover, only partnership between the secularists and enlightened Muslims can accelerate the successful implementation of this reform, he contends.[22] It seems that both *wasaṭī* Islam and jihadi Salafism are an obstacle to the comprehensive reform that the liberals envision.

The Western Challenge and the Muslim Responses

From the late eighteenth century on, the Muslim world was directly confronted with the West, whose power was steadily growing and whose military, economic, and technological might far exceeded its own. The weakness of the Muslim world in comparison to Europe led Muslims to ponder the source of this inferiority—namely, what went wrong in Islam that caused it to deviate from the historical path that Allah had ordained for it, which was supposed to lead to Muslim superiority over other civilizations.[23] The decline of the Muslim world and the rise of Europe led many Arab intellectuals, especially those who were exposed to European culture and were impressed by its achievements, to call for reform. The intellectual debate that arose in the Muslim world drew a contrast between religion and state, between religion and reason or science, and between purity of origin (*aṣāla*) and modernity (*mu'āṣara*).[24] As discussed later, *wasaṭiyya* holds that in Islam no contradiction exists between these purported opposites.

Al-Qaraḍāwī traces several stages and trends in the Muslim world's reaction to the West.

First came the stage of complete capitulation to the Western culture that infiltrated the Muslim countries. As evidence of this capitulation, the shaykh points out that in the early twentieth century educated Muslims in the Middle East espoused one of two imported foreign ideologies: either liberalism or Marxism. In this period, he says, Islamic thought was absent, with the exception of the work of some isolated figures who opposed westernization, such as Rashīd Riḍā, who published his views in his journal *The Lighthouse* (*al-Manār*). An example of this espousal of Western thought can be found in Ṭaha Ḥusayn's (d. 1973) book *The Future of Culture in Egypt* (1938). Ḥusayn wrote that Egyptians must discard the notion that certain peoples were born to rule Egypt, whereas other peoples were born to be ruled by the Egyptians. The way to eliminate this mode of thinking, he said, was "to follow in the footsteps of the Europeans in order to be their equals and their partners in civilization."[25]

Next came the stage of justification or apologetics, marked by an adoption of Western norms while attempting to find Islamic justifications for them. One example is the adoption of the capitalistic practice of usury while trying to argue that the *sharī'a* does not in fact ban it. Another example is Muḥammad 'Abduh's ruling in favor of polygamy in Islam. In his ruling, he stresses that the Qur'ānic verses that permit polygamy (4:3 and 4:129) charge a Muslim to treat his wives equally, without showing preference for one over the others. However, he says, Q4:129 proclaims that complete fairness is in fact impossible, which means that the Qur'ān actually forbids polygamy.[26] (For a discussion of the polygamy issue, see chapter 6.)

The third stage was one of defending Islam. At this stage, says al-Qaraḍāwī, the religion was seen as being "in the dock"; that is, any custom or norm that differed from the Western ones had to be justified and defended, such as the ban on usury or the Muslim woman's right to wear a veil. An example of this defensive approach can be found in some of al-Qaraḍāwī's own rulings, such as his approach to polygamy. He defends the Islamic practice of polygamy by saying,

> Though it is preferable for the man to suffice with a single wife in order to steer clear of pitfalls and avoid difficulties in this world and punishment in the world to come, certain human considerations, both individual and social, motivated Islam to allow a Muslim to marry more than one wife, for Islam is a religion that suits man's inborn characteristics [*fiṭra*] and addresses reality without underestimating it, exaggerating it, or harboring delusions.[27]

Finally, there came the stage of pride and the confrontation with Western norms, in particular its culture of materialism, whether capitalist or communist. According to al-Qaraḍāwī, the pioneers of this struggle were Abū al-Aʿlā al-Mawdūdī (d. 1979) in Pakistan; Ḥasan al-Bannā, Sayyid Quṭb, and Muḥammad al-Ghazālī (d. 1996) in Egypt; and Muṣṭafā al-Ṣibāʿī (d. 1964), founder of the Syrian MB, and Saʿīd Ḥawwā (d. 1989), al-Bannā's student who brought the MB's ideas to Syria. In this roster, al-Qaraḍāwī also includes some Shīʿī thinkers, such as Muḥammad Bāqir al-Ṣadr (d. 1980) in Iraq and ʿAlī Sharīʿatī (d. 1977), who inspired the Islamic Revolution of 1979 in Iran. The shaykh writes that this stage, which is also the stage of *wasaṭiyya*, "was characterized not only by pride and by confronting [the West] but also by [other factors, including] openness, flexibility of thought, tolerance toward the other who differs in ideology or faith, a call for dialogue, the triumph of the *wasaṭī* stream that preaches moderation, a [clear] understanding of the religion and the adaptation of religion to reality, and interaction with others."[28] He claims that at this stage some thinkers who had espoused Marxism, such as Khālid Muḥammad Khālid, or liberalism, such as ʿAlī ʿAbd al-Rāziq, abandoned them in favor of Islam. According to al-Qaraḍāwī, the Islamic Awakening is the resounding answer to Western imperialism and indicates that imperialism failed to attain its goal, which was to distance the Muslim *umma* from its religion and change its very essence.[29] However, it should be noted that, despite al-Qaraḍāwī's claim that *wasaṭiyya* confronts Western norms, an examination of his writings and rulings reveals that he takes an apologetic and defensive approach on many issues. For example, in his ruling on democracy he defends Islam by stating that the Qur'ān and the Sunna denounce tyranny and actually laid down the foundations of democracy long before the West did. At the same time, he adds that there is nothing to prevent Muslims from borrowing democratic institutions and methods from the West, such as elections and voting.[30] (For al-Qaraḍāwī's approach to democracy, see chapter 4.)

The conditions al-Qaraḍāwī lays out for borrowing mechanisms from Western democracy shed light on the sophistication and duality of *wasaṭiyya*: superficially it appears to display openness to the West, but in essence it is dogmatic. *Wasaṭiyya* sanctions the borrowing of ideas and methods, but only as long as they do not contradict any definite text (*naṣṣ muḥkam*) or *sharī'a* law. Furthermore, it contends that Muslims must adapt any borrowed element to the spirit of Islam, so that this element becomes part of Islam and sheds its foreign character. The shaykh emphasizes that it is permissible to borrow technical methods from Western democracy, but not its philosophy, for this philosophy may allow what the religion forbids, forbid what the religion allows, or revoke the commandments.[31]

Wasaṭiyya: The Stream of the Islamic Awakening

Al-Qaraḍāwī defines the current era, from the 1970s to today, as "the age of awakening,"[32] in which the Islamic solution has taken root as an alternative to the two "imported" solutions that, according to him, failed in all domains of life: the liberal-democratic solution and the socialist-revolutionary one.[33] According to al-Qaraḍāwī, the emergence of this Awakening movement—which he calls the movement of *iḥyā'* (revitalization), *ba'th* (revival), or *yaqẓa* (awakening)—is one of the greatest achievements of the Muslims in the twentieth century, for it has renewed the Muslims' confidence in Islam's ability to govern all areas of life. Writing at the turn of the twenty-first century, al-Qaraḍāwī stated that the most important actions and accomplishments of this movement were calling for the enactment of the *sharī'a* across the Muslim world; precipitating two Islamic revolutions, a Shī'ī one in Iran in 1979 and a Sunnī one in Sudan in 1989, both of which led to the establishment of Islamic states;

reviving jihad; bringing Muslim youth back to Islam; reviving the custom of donning the *ḥijāb* among Muslim women; and realizing the vision of an Islamic economy.[34]

In mapping and characterizing the various streams of the Awakening movement, al-Qaraḍāwī claims that *wasaṭiyya*, which is based on facilitation and renewal, is the stream with the widest support base. This stream, he says, is best able to address the Muslims in contemporary terms and conduct a dialogue with its opponents; therefore, it represents the true Islam, and the future belongs to it.[35] In enumerating the groups within the Awakening movement that he criticizes and denounces, al-Qaraḍāwī distinguishes the following categories:

1. The *takfīrī* groups (those that accuse Muslims of unbelief), such as Excommunication and Emigration (al-Takfīr Wal-Hijra), which—as evident from its name—accuses of apostasy (*ridda*) all society with the exception of those Muslims who agree with it. Al-Qaraḍāwī maintains that these groups emerged out of Gamal ʿAbd al-Nasir's prisons in Egypt during the 1950s and that their ideology is based on a literal reading of Sayyid Quṭb's writings. They believe that they are the only true Muslims, whereas all others have excluded themselves from the fold of Islam (*murtaddūn*). As stated, the shaykh calls these *takfīrī* groups ideological offspring of the ancient Khawārij, who broke away from ʿAlī's camp in the Battle of Ṣiffīn (657 CE), and he states that the *takfīrī*s are dangerous because in accusing other Muslims of *ridda*, they essentially sanction the killing of these Muslims.[36]

2. The violent groups whose hostility is directed mainly at Muslim rulers who do not govern according to the *sharīʿa*. The members of this stream accuse the rulers of *ridda* based on Ibn Taymiyya's *fatwā* regarding the Mongols and fight them on the grounds that it is a Muslim's duty to forcefully put right what is wrong. Challenging their view, al-Qaraḍāwī argues that the authority to put right what is wrong is the ruler's sole prerogative. If the ruler is the one responsible for the reprehensible practices or the violations of Islam, then he must be opposed in a wise and prudent manner and only if fighting him does not yield results that are even more reprehensible, such as anarchy and bloodshed among Muslims.[37]

3. "The stream of strictness and stagnation"—that is, the (nonjihadi) Salafīs, whom he also calls the "new Ẓāhirīs," after a medieval school of Islamic thought that advocated a literal interpretation of the Islamic sources. He describes this stream as the antithesis of *wasaṭiyya* because it is characterized by rigid thinking, strict rulings based on a literal readings, and a brand of *da'wa* that repels people instead of attracting them. He denounces it for focusing on marginal religious issues, such as men's beards and women's veils, instead of on issues crucial for the future of the *umma*. He is also critical of its strict prohibitions, such as the ban on Muslims living in the West and attaining Western citizenship, on women leaving their homes in case this incites temptation among men, and on women voting and running in parliamentary elections.[38]

Naturally, al-Qaraḍāwī wants *wasaṭiyya* to supersede all other streams in the Awakening movement, and he believes that its influence is indeed growing steadily. As evidence of this growth, he notes that in the early 1970s the young members of Islamist groups in Egypt's universities mostly espoused extremist views, but after they encountered *wasaṭī* preachers, they abandoned these views in favor of *wasaṭiyya*.[39] However, this study shows that, in contrast to these claims, al-Qaraḍāwī's *wasaṭiyya* actually combines al-Bannā's *ikhwānī* ideology with elements from Sayyid Quṭb's ideology and even levels accusations of heresy at its opponents, chief among them the secularist liberals. This study also shows that, despite his claim that *wasaṭiyya* fights against the use of violence, al-Qaraḍāwī actually preaches violence, including against Muslim rulers who do not implement the *sharī'a*.

The Global Jihad Groups

According to al-Qaraḍāwī, one of the welcome fruits of the Islamic Awakening that started in the 1970s was the revival of jihad for the sake of Allah. As an example, he mentions the jihad against the Soviets in Afghanistan (1979–89), saying that the fighters who came to that land from all over the Muslim world "found an opportunity to achieve 'one of the two best things' [an allusion to Q9:52], either victory over the invading atheist infidels or *istishhād* [martyrdom] and Paradise." As another example, he mentions the Palestinian intifada in 1987, which he calls "the revolution of the mosques" because, according to him, the first calls for it were made in Gaza mosques. He also mentions the founding of Hamas in late 1987 and of Palestinian Islamic Jihad, which emerged in Gaza in the early 1980s, as part of the Awakening and adds: "Each one [of these movements] carried out courageous *istishhād* operations in Jerusalem, Tel Aviv, and elsewhere, operations that struck fear in the hearts of the usurping enemies of Allah and disturbed Israel's tranquility."[40] According to al-Qaraḍāwī, the revival of jihad, which is a fruit of the Awakening, proves that faith is the source of the *umma*'s strength and that when the *umma* cleaves to Islam, its enemies are powerless to defeat it.

In light of these views, it might be assumed that al-Qaraḍāwī also regards the movements of global jihad as part of the Islamic Awakening. Indeed, he does regard them as such; moreover, he shares part of their vision, as shown in chapters 4 and 5. However, he also harshly criticizes them and contends that their ideology—like that of the Islamic groups that were active in Egypt during Anwar Sadat's administration and were ultimately responsible for his murder—is rooted in the thought of the ancient Khārijī extremists (*ghulāh*). In the introduction to his two-volume work *The Jurisprudence of Jihad*, in which he seeks to refute the arguments of these groups, he writes:

> The al-Qaʿida organization and the jihadi Salafism[,] . . . just like the jihadi groups that preceded them, developed a *fiqh* that they spread and an ideology that they marketed. They acquired disciples and followers who want to declare war on anyone and everyone. Hence, there is no choice but to answer them and refute their questionable views, by means of which they have captivated youths who do not possess the religious knowledge that would inoculate them against easily falling prey to [the Salafī-jihadis].[41]

During the most recent wave of the Awakening, which began after 9/11, two major fronts of confrontation have emerged: *wasaṭiyya* versus jihad Salafism and *wasaṭiyya* versus secular liberalism. Regarding the first front, this study shows that *wasaṭiyya* shares the basic vision of the jihadi Salafīs but differs from them on the correct way to actualize this vision. Regarding the second front, this study shows that *wasaṭiyya* rejects the liberal secular outlook and accuses its proponents of heresy.

The *Wasaṭī* Solution: Combining Salafism and *Tajdīd*

As part of his effort to present *wasaṭiyya* as the ideological answer to both jihadi Salafism and liberal secularism, al-Qaraḍāwī describes it as an innovative type of Salafism. He does not believe that Salafism is inconsistent with *tajdīd* and modernity (*mu'āṣara*).[42] In his words, "I never see a contradiction between Salafism and renewal or between Salafism and modernism. I am a modern Salafī. There is nothing wrong with a person living in his own times; whoever reads books but does not read reality, lives in the past, and forgets his own times is not a scholar."[43] He considers the *wasaṭī* movement a continuation of the innovational Salafī school founded by Ibn Taymiyya and his disciples, especially Ibn Qayyim al-Jawziyya (d. 1350).[44] The same combination is also represented in the modern Salafī movement, most particularly by Muḥammad 'Abduh and his disciple Muḥammad Rashīd Riḍā. Al-Qaraḍāwī considers Rashīd Riḍā a truer representative of Salafism than 'Abduh and was clearly more influenced by the former.[45]

*Wasaṭī*s Claim to Be *Salafī*s, and *Salafī*s Claim to be *Wasaṭī*s

Uriya Shavit argues that *wasaṭī*s consider their movement to be Salafī, and Salafīs claim that their school is *wasaṭī*.[46] Although this is indeed the case, as is shown in the two parties' polemical writings, each group has its own quite distinct views on what constitutes *wasaṭiyya* and how the term *Salafiyya* is to be defined. The term *Salafī* is commonly used by Islamists of different schools as a mark of piety and religious legitimacy.[47] Small wonder, then, that both sides depict themselves as Salafīs.

Al-Qaraḍāwī defines himself as a "true Salafī" and complains that the term *Salafism* has been distorted by both its supporters and its detractors. He therefore undertook the task of redefining what he calls "the true Salafī way." He accuses supporters of Salafism of having distorted the meaning of Salafism and having reduced it to formalities instead of focusing on essential issues in theology, religious jurisprudence, and mysticism. He complains that the *salaf* method has become for its supporters merely a method of polemics instead of a constructive path of action, and its opponents describe it as a reactionary method that looks only to the past and has no interest in the present or the future. It has been accused of engaging in fanaticism, of refusing to listen to other opinions, and of opposing *tajdīd* and *ijtihād*—in short, of not recognizing the middle road, or *wasaṭ*.[48] *Wasaṭīs* thus maintain that their approach, *wasaṭiyya*, returns Salafism to its original roots—that, in fact, *wasaṭiyya* is the true Salafism.[49]

Both Salafīs and *wasaṭīs* accept the legal principle of *wasaṭiyya*, but each group claims that its interpretation is the right one. The Salafīs claim that they are *wasaṭīs* and that the heads of the *wasaṭī* movement, especially al-Qaraḍāwī, are guilty of the "theft of *wasaṭiyya*." The Salafīs admit that *wasaṭiyya* is a characteristic of the Muslim nation according to the Qur'ān (Q2:143), but Salafī writers, of both the jihadi and the nonjihadi variety, accuse al-Qaraḍāwī's movement of misusing the term *wasaṭiyya*. Thus, for example, Shaykh Abū Baṣīr al-Ṭarṭūsī (b. 1959), an important theoretician of jihadi Salafism, accuses this movement of using the *wasaṭī* principle in order to become free of the restrictions of *sharīʿa* law or perhaps even to abolish the *sharīʿa* under the pretext that Islam calls for *wasaṭiyya* rather than strictness (*tashaddud*) in the application of religious law.[50] *Salafī* thinkers stress that *wasaṭiyya* is a characteristic of the "victorious community" of Muslims, who, according to one of the traditions concerning the Day of Judgment, will bring about the victory of Islam and will not be harmed by those who abandon it. This community, according to tradition, will retain the ember of faith and continue in the Prophet's footsteps; therefore, the Salafīs call themselves "the victorious community."[51] Although al-Ṭarṭūsī agrees that a moderate interpretation of religious law is a characteristic of *wasaṭiyya*, he insists that the principle must not be used to violate the law as presented in the Sunna, as do those whom he calls "possessors of sick souls [*aṣḥāb al-nufūs al-marīḍa*]," an indirect allusion to al-Qaraḍāwī, whom he also accuses of unbelief.[52] Al-Ṭarṭūsī argues that those who interpret *wasaṭiyya* as taking a position in the middle between truth and falsehood are wrong because by doing so they bring unbelief closer to faith. He calls such people "defeatists who are lax [in their faith]" and use *wasaṭiyya* as an excuse to avoid anything in the *sharīʿa* they do not like.[53]

Wasaṭiyya as Renewing (*Mujaddida*): *Tajdīd*

Al-Qaraḍāwī stresses that by "renewal" he does not mean the creation of a new version of Islam; rather, he wishes that Islam be returned to its state during the Prophet's lifetime and during the life of his Companions and the subsequent generation (*tābiʿūn*). His aim is to return the faith to its original facilitation rather than to strictness (*taʿsīr*) in order to spread good tidings (*tabshīr*) rather than aversion (*tanfīr*) toward religion, and to focus on major issues rather than on trivialities. He argues that the *fatwās* issued during the first two generations after the founding of Islam reflect a good understanding of the spirit and goals of Islam without insisting on a literal interpretation of the texts of the Qur'ān and the Sunna but rather by applying *ijtihād* to real-life issues. The first two generations' *muftīs* assumed as given that God created religion for the benefit of His servants and therefore intended it as a favor rather than an onus. In other words, when giving *fatwās*, the two first generations of Islam used the *wasaṭī* method.[54] Al-Qaraḍāwī thus sees no contradiction between Salafism and "renewal": true Salafism renews, and true *tajdīd* is Salafī. He therefore regards the ideology that the Islamist movement should adopt as both renewing and Salafī.[55]

Laying the Groundwork for *Wasaṭī* Innovations: The *Ḥadīth* of *Tajdīd*

The idea of cycles of *tajdīd* never became a significant element in mainstream Islam. It was always restricted to very small groups that consisted mainly of disciples of Islamic scholars who considered their mentors to be renewers (*mujaddidūn*) in the sense that they revived learning and dissemination of the Muslim heritage. The original intent behind expressions such as "renewal of the faith" (*tajdīd al-dīn*) and "revival of tradition" (*iḥyāʾ al-sunna*) was the dissemination and study of existing traditions in order to bring them alive, as they were in the past, but in the very same form as they had before, with no changes, modifications, or reforms. The famous *ḥadīth* about the *tajdīd* of religion in one-hundred-year cycles—"God will send to this community at the turn of every century someone [or people] who will restore religion"—first appeared in the ninth century CE in an eschatological context in Abū Dāwud's (d. 888) *ḥadīth* collection. It remained rare in Muslim literature until the tenth century CE and later appeared only infrequently.[56]

However, according to al-Qaraḍāwī, the idea of *tajdīd* is inherent already in the Qur'ān and Sunna. True, the word itself does not appear in the Qur'ān, but the principle does, he claims. He broadens the concept's definition to include not only making something old new again but also causing a transition from a certain state to a better one. The latter idea, he argues, can already be discerned in the Qur'ān, where Muslims are urged to progress and strive to improve, as in Q16:125, where the Prophet is called upon to argue with his opponents "in the most gracious way [*bi-llatī hiya aḥsan*]," and Q41:34, where Muslims are told to "repel evil with what is better."[57]

Muslim scholars have given various answers to the question of the purpose of this famous *ḥadīth* about the *tajdīd* of religion. One answer, which may also explain why al-Qaraḍāwī makes frequent use of it, is that its basic message is that the religious renewer provides the means whereby Islam's continued existence is assured even after the Prophet's death and the cessation of revelation. The list of *mujaddidūn* given in Muslim sources includes clerics whose function it was, according to a famous tradition, to serve as "the prophets' inheritors." In the classical Muslim literature, the "*ḥadīth* of renewal" is closely associated with *ijtihād*; in fact, the *ḥadīth* is quoted as proof that *ijtihād* will never cease, thanks to the appearance of a "renewer" every century.[58]

In his commentary on this *ḥadīth*, al-Qaraḍāwī focuses on the question of the identity of the referent of the word *man*, "whoever" or "someone," in the *ḥadīth*. He answers that although most commentators have interpreted the word as referring to a single person,[59] he believes that in this case it refers to a group of people, whether religious scholars, leaders, or educators. *Mujaddidūn* can thus exist in one or more countries and can operate on their own or in cooperation with each other.[60] It is worth noting here that long before al-Qaraḍāwī gave this interpretation, some classical *ḥadīth* exegetes had already determined that the word *man* could be plural in meaning rather than singular. These exegetes argued that protection of the faith was the purview not only of Muslim jurists but also of transmitters of traditions, reciters of the Qur'ān, preachers, and even rulers.[61]

Al-Qaraḍāwī clearly uses the "*ḥadīth* of renewal" to give legitimacy to the idea of innovation in *fatwā*s handed down in the spirit of *wasaṭiyya*. For this purpose, he greatly expands the meaning of the concept of *tajdīd* and grants it pride of place in his *wasaṭī* philosophy, in contrast to its marginal position in the classical Muslim literature. One of the keys to renewal, in his view, is "insight" (*fiqh*)[62] of two types: insight into God's ways (*sunan Allāh*) in the world and insight into religion—that is, into God's laws. *Tajdīd* in this context is a profound mental and cultural process that will bring about a revival of active *ijtihād* for the purpose of finding solutions to contemporary problems within *sharī'a*. (For more on al-Qaraḍāwī's views on *ijtihād*, see chapter 6.)

The Liberal Understanding of *Tajdīd*

The issue of *tajdīd* is central to the ideological conflict between al-Qaraḍāwī's *wasaṭiyya* and the liberal stream. As mentioned, al-Qaraḍāwī defines *tajdīd* as a return to the original form of Islam. He explains that the *tajdīd* of religion is like the *tajdīd* of an ancient building: it does not mean demolishing the old structure and erecting a new one.[63] This approach contrasts with that of Abū Zayd, a critic of the religious discourse in general. Abū Zayd regards *tajdīd* as vital in light of the Islamic world's social, political, economic, cultural, and ideological crisis. He rejects al-Qaraḍāwī's basic assumption that *tajdīd* means a return to the past, noting that contemporary Muslims are just as capable of thinking and reasoning as the ancient Muslims and, moreover, have access to knowledge that was unavailable to the forefathers of Islam. Accusing the Islamist movements of fearing innovation and fresh interpretations of the religious texts, he calls for an ideological revolution (*tathwīr*) that goes beyond mere enlightenment (*tanwīr*). He also argues that the rejection of thought (*tafkīr*), which in his opinion characterizes religious discourse, is responsible for the phenomenon of accusations of heresy (*takfīr*)—not only in the religious sense, which he describes as the most dangerous kind, but also in the political, racial, or cultural sense—that is, any kind of rejection of the other.[64]

The Kuwaiti liberal writer Aḥmad al-Baghdādī (d. 2010) claims that the *mujaddidūn* who are mentioned in Islamic commentaries on the *ḥadīth* of *tajdīd* played no vital or significant role in advancing innovation because they did not introduce any real change that affected people's lives. All their innovations remained within the confines of the traditional heritage of a Muslim society that knew nothing beyond the *sharīʿa*. "These *mujaddidūn*," he wrote, "did not pursue anything that can be termed research that rejects existing [ideas] or critical research."[65]

Al-Baghdādī asserts that the efforts to renew religious thought—including al-Qaraḍāwī's—focus on *ijtihād* while ignoring the principle of freedom of opinion. Explicating the difference between the two terms, he noted that *ijtihād* is the exclusive province of religious experts and results in their monopolizing religious knowledge, whereas *freedom of opinion* applies to everyone. In addition, *ijtihād* applies only to particular fields of expertise, whereas opinion can be expressed in any domain. He suggests replacing the term *ijtihād* with the term *ḥurriyyat al-ra'y* (freedom of opinion):

> Since nobody has a monopoly over religion, anyone is entitled to express his opinion, providing that he presents religious and logical evidence for it. This depends on one important and crucial condition: that the jurists [*fuqahā'*] be deprived of the authority to accuse others of *ridda* or threaten them with *ḥisba* lawsuits alleging un-Islamic behavior[66]—lawsuits that have no place in intellectual [debates]. Simply put, each side must conform to the norms of civilized discourse and refrain from inciting people against its rivals.[67]

Al-Baghdādī contends that religious thinking—including that of al-Qaraḍāwī—is helpless to tackle the truths of life because it is unable to propose solutions to the core issues faced by Islam today, including the following, some of which are discussed in greater detail in part two of this book, which compares al-Qaraḍāwī's views on these issues with the jihadi Salafīs' and the liberals' views:

1. *Religious freedom.* Al-Baghdādī notes that this value has been widely accepted by the international community since the United Nations' (UN) adoption of the Universal Declaration of Human Rights in 1948, yet Islamic *fuqahā'* and exegetes still understand this principle in a very limited way. That is, they interpret Q2:256 ("there is no coercion in religion") to mean that nobody can be forced to convert to Islam, yet they employ coercion in prohibiting apostasy in that they rule that apostates (*murtaddūn*) are deserving of death. This interpretation, says al-Baghdādī, constitutes "ideological paralysis that contravenes any call for renewal" because it precludes any reform in the domain of individual freedoms and especially religious freedom.

2. *The laws of the Islamic* sharīʿa. In al-Baghdādī's opinion, some of these laws are no longer applicable, such as those pertaining to slavery, spoils of war, and the taking of hostages as well as other laws that infringe on human rights and especially women's rights. He contends that Islamic thought rejects most of the human rights that are mentioned in the Declaration of Human Rights.

3. *Equality.* Al-Baghdādī notes that equality is a fundamental principle in modern societies, yet the Islamic religious discourse still regards some aspects of it as controversial, including the principle of equality among citizens and the unacceptability of laws that prohibit non-Muslims from holding certain high-level positions. The *fuqahā'* are unable to reform their thinking on these issues, as evidenced by rulings, for example, that prohibit participating in non-Muslim holiday celebrations.[68] The *fuqahā'* also deny political equality to women, as is shown in chapter 6 on jurisprudence. Al-Baghdādī accuses them of refusing to adapt their thinking on these issues to the changing times.

4. *Democracy.* A debate is still ongoing in Islamic circles regarding the religious legitimacy of democratic regimes. According to al-Baghdādī, conservative Islamists have not been able to resolve this dilemma; they are helpless to propose any feasible alternative to democracy, yet they refuse to reform their way of thinking about it.

5. *The arts.* Al-Baghdādī notes that religious thinkers have largely remained silent about the arts except to pronounce that some of them are incompatible with the *sharīʿa* and that they refuse to reform their views on the arts. Jurists who still prohibit the making of sculptures, for example, are simply following the lead of their predecessors without considering that the world has completely changed, he stated.[69]

For al-Baghdādī, renewing the religious thinking means reforming its position on these core issues. Western civilization, he notes, is now besieging Islamic thought from every direction—not because there is a Western conspiracy against Islam, but because Islam is no longer able to meet the ideological challenges posed by the West. International law, for example, is now dominated by Western thinking. This renders irrelevant many traditional Islamic notions, including those pertaining to relations between Muslims and non-Muslims, such as the Islamic jurists' distinction between *dār al-Islām* and *dār al-ḥarb.* The notion that ancient books of *fiqh* can provide the "ideological reinforcement" needed to contend with the West is nothing but arrogance, claims al-Baghdādī; moreover, it is the reason for Islam's inability to renew itself. "How can we contend with [Western] civilization, which relies on reason in every aspect, using a mentality that keeps the mind shackled in the chains of the past?!" he asks.[70]

Conclusion

In this chapter, we saw that *wasaṭiyya* presents itself as a stream of reform and renewal and that it associates both of these concepts with a return to the original Islam or the Islam of the *salaf.* Believing that the Muslim nation in the twentieth and twenty-first centuries suffers from a malady whose essence is imitation of the West and loss of identity, *wasaṭiyya* proposes a remedy that is a blend of Salafism and renewal. Followers of *wasaṭiyya* see it as a unique current within the Islamic Awakening movement and regard the Awakening movement as another link in the chain of Muslim responses to the challenge posed by the West. Al-Qaraḍāwī holds that one of the signs of the Islamic Awakening in the twentieth century was the revival of jihad in its military sense. Accordingly, he regards jihadi Salafism as part of the Awakening movement, although he has juridical reservations about some of its ideas and therefore maintains that one of the roles of *wasaṭiyya* is to guide and correct the perceptions of the Salafī current. *Wasaṭiyya*, then, emerged as a response to the currents in the Awakening movement with which it disagrees—in particular the current that accuses other Muslims of heresy, especially the Muslim regimes that do not implement the *sharīʿa*—and also as a response to secular liberalism, which it regards as an agent of the West's "ideological imperialism."

2

The *Wasaṭiyya* School as Shaped by Yūsuf al-Qaraḍāwī

From the Muslim Brotherhood to Wasaṭiyya

In December 2014, an international conference under the banner "The al-Azhar Conference for Coping with Extremism and Terror" took place at al-Azhar University in Egypt. The conference's closing statement declared that armed groups that use violence and terror against their fellow Muslims ostensibly in the name of the faith are "sinful gangs [*jamāʿāt āthima*]" in thought and behavior and that the killing of innocents is a crime against humanity that Islam condemns in the strongest terms: "These crimes are not only inconsistent with the True Faith [i.e., Islam] but also harm the Faith, which is a faith of peace and unity, justice, benevolence, and human fraternity."[1] Conferences of this kind are often convened in the Muslim world in order to combat global jihad organizations' interpretations of the Qur'ān and the Sunna, based on which they carry out acts that they perceive as legitimate jihad but that their opponents consider terrorism, forbidden by Islam.[2] To deal with this interpretation, which many consider a mistaken distortion of Islam, its opponents have established numerous bodies whose purpose is to promote a balanced religious and educational discourse in which stress is placed on the *wasaṭī* culture in Islam.

The term *wasaṭiyya* appears even in the names of some of these bodies that are expected to generate a renewal (*tajdīd*) of religious discourse in Islam. Thus, for example, Egypt's minister of endowments, Muḥammad Mukhtār Gumʿa (b. 1966), inaugurated the World Forum for Tolerance and *Wasaṭiyya* in February 2015, which convened a conference in May that recommended that school curricula be reexamined with the aim of disseminating moderation and condemning excess.[3] Such official bodies, founded by the religious establishment and the regime, present *wasaṭiyya* as the proper response to radical Islam as represented by al-Qaʿida and IS.[4]

Al-Azhar University presents itself as the answer to those who promote accusations of heresy (*takfīr*; see chapter 4), a bastion of moderation and *wasaṭiyya*, and takes it upon itself to disseminate this message. In keeping with this aim, the senate of al-Azhar approved the introduction of a course titled "The Culture of *Wasaṭiyya* in Islam" as part of the curriculum of all the university's faculties.[5] However, al-Qaraḍāwī, who has been called "the *imām* of *wasaṭiyya*,"[6] has criticized al-Azhar as an organ of the regime, a status that, he believes, detracts from the credibility of that institution's message. Furthermore, al-Qaraḍāwī transformed the meaning of the term *wasaṭiyya* from a generalized antonym of *extremism* to the name of a distinct philosophical and juridical school. This change in the concept of *wasaṭiyya* under al-Qaraḍāwī's leadership is the subject of this chapter.

The chapter examines how al-Qaraḍāwī formulated and shaped *wasaṭiyya* as an ideological stream using Ḥasan al-Bannā's doctrine as his point of departure. This issue is explored by analyzing al-Qaraḍāwī's interpretation of al-Bannā's principles. The chapter also outlines the gradual evolution of al-Qaraḍāwī's *wasaṭī* platform, whose principles are meant to provide an answer to the changes that occurred in the Islamic discourse between the 1980s and the 2000s.

The Evolution of al-Qaraḍāwī's *Wasaṭiyya*

Bettina Gräf describes how the meaning of the term *wasaṭiyya* evolved in al-Qaraḍāwī's thought in terms of the historical context in which it was used. She is clearly right in that the concept's meanings did evolve gradually. She states that at the beginning of the 1970s al-Qaraḍāwī used the term in the context of a proposed "Islamic solution" that would serve as an alternative to both capitalism and socialism. In the 1980s, he added a new dimension in the wake of his desire to distance himself from the radical Islamist movements whose rapid rise had produced the assassination of President Anwar Sadat in 1981. He rejected both secularism and religious extremism and presented *wasaṭiyya* as the path to which the Islamic Awakening should be guided.[7] At the turn of the 1990s, al-Qaraḍāwī was forced to face the fact that following the end of the Cold War, Islam was being presented by politicians, the media, and academia all over the world as a dangerous religion. In Egypt, acts of violence and even murder were committed in the name of Islam—for example, the assassination of the secular liberal Egyptian thinker Faraj Fūda in 1992 by Egyptian Islamic Jihad.[8] Al-Qaraḍāwī's response was to stress the importance of the *wasaṭī* approach at all levels, including that of Islamic jurisprudence.[9]

Gräf finds that the meaning and function of the term *wasaṭiyya* have changed over time in al-Qaraḍāwī's writings, assuming particular importance since the 1990s owing to the twin factors of the emergence of the New Islamists and the dynamics of their discourse as well as the growth of the new media and novel means of dissemination. She stresses al-Qaraḍāwī's status as "shaykh of the media," imposing the need for messages that are simple and convey complex ideas in easily comprehensible language. This need took the form of the slogan "*al-wasaṭiyya wal-i'tidāl*," which Gräf translates as "balance and moderation."[10]

However, an examination of al-Qaraḍāwī's own words on his motives for adopting the *wasaṭī* method reveals that he views the term *wasaṭiyya* as a profound principle rather than merely as an easily assimilated slogan, as Gräf claims. In the program *Jurisprudence for Life* (*Fiqh al-ḥayāh*) broadcast on the Anā satellite channel on September, 15, 2009, al-Qaraḍāwī was asked why he chose to pursue the *wasaṭiyya* path. In his reply, he mentioned three reasons.[11] First, in his view, this is the approach that best expresses true Islam, the Islam of the Qur'ān and the Sunna of the Prophet and his Companions. In other words, *wasaṭiyya* reflects the spirit of Islam,[12] the way that the Qur'ān calls "the straight path" (*al-ṣirāṭ al-mustaqīm* [Q1:6 and elsewhere]). Second, a more personal reason, *wasaṭiyya* is inherent in his character, and he therefore viewed it as a gift from God.[13] Al-Qaraḍāwī also admitted to having been greatly influenced by religious thinkers of the past who, although they did not use the term *wasaṭiyya*, held and discussed *wasaṭī* views. He mentioned Abū Ḥāmid al-Ghazālī (d. 1111),[14] Ibn Taymiyya (d. 1328)[15] and his student Ibn Qayyim al-Jawziyya (d. 1350),[16] and Abū Isḥāq al-Shāṭibī (d. 1388)[17] as having helped shape his views.

According to his testimony, he became an adherent of *wasaṭiyya* in the mid-twentieth century. The first book in which he promotes the *wasaṭī* approach is *The Lawful and the Prohibited in Islam*.[18] In the introduction to the book's first edition (1960), he prepared the ground for the adoption of the *wasaṭī* method. He discussed two views that were common among Muslims at the time. One group was so blinded by the brilliance of Western civilization that it treated the latter's principles and traditions as axiomatically true and believed that Islam must give way before them. For this group, what is permissible is whatever the West regards as such and whatever is forbidden is whatever the West considers as such. These people, al-Qaraḍāwī argued, forgot that Islam is Allah's word, which always prevails. The second view belonged to those who adhered to certain positions regarding what is permitted and what is forbidden based on the texts of a given school of jurisprudence and claimed that their views were the only true Islam. They refused to budge from their positions or to examine the evidence for those positions. If asked, this group did not hesitate to declare that music or singing or playing the game of backgammon is forbidden in Islam. Al-Qaraḍāwī accused this group of having forgotten the ways of the pious forefathers (*al-salaf al-ṣāliḥ*), who ruled that something should be forbidden only if it has been declared so in the Qur'ān and the Sunna.[19]

Al-Qaraḍāwī stated that he did not wish to belong to either of these groups—that is, he wanted neither to submit himself to the West nor to follow any single school of Islamic jurisprudence blindly in every matter because no single school is in sole possession of the truth. He added that in fact the founders of these schools never laid claims to infallibility but rather saw themselves as independent legists (*mujtahidūn*) who, according to one famous *ḥadīth*, deserved recompense if they made a mistaken ruling and double the recompense if they ruled correctly.[20] In this choice, al-Qaraḍāwī followed in the footsteps of the *imām* al-Shāfiʿī (d. 820): "My opinion is correct [but] could be mistaken; the opinion of another is mistaken [but] could be correct." According to al-Qaraḍāwī, Muslim religious scholars have the means to find a balance between different views and to come to a proper decision; instead of blindly following a single school of jurisprudence, they should follow only arguments and a legal indicant.[21]

A perusal of al-Qaraḍāwī's writings reveals that during the 1960s and 1970s he did not use the term *wasaṭī school*. In the introduction to his important legal book *The Laws of Alms* (1969), he states that he takes "a just, balancing, middle approach [*mawqif wasaṭ 'adl*]: I welcome anything new and useful and adhere to everything old and good. Thus I have benefited from the old and the new, with no excessive sternness or looseness."[22]

At the beginning of the 1980s, al-Qaraḍāwi published a book devoted to religious extremism, its causes, and how to combat it. In this book, *The Islamic Awakening between Stagnation and Extremism*, he did not yet use the term *wasaṭī school*;[23] instead, what he would later call "*wasaṭī*," he referred to as "comprehensive (*shāmil*) or true Islam."[24] One remedy for religious extremism he proposed in this book was that young people should be taught about their religion from clerics who are, in his words, "the middle and balance between the 'exaggerators' [*ghulāh*] and the 'overly free' [*mutasayyibūn*]."[25]

Al-Qaraḍāwī first used the phrase *Islamic wasaṭī stream* in 1985 in the context of the debate between secularists and Islamists in Egypt. In his refutation of the arguments made by Fu'ād Zakariyyā (on this issue, see the introduction), a leader of the secularist camp, al-Qaraḍāwī defined his own kind of Islam as "the Islam represented by the enlightened, balanced [or proportionate, *mu'tadil*], committed [to Islam and its commandments, *multazim*]."[26] Here he elucidated for the first time the characteristic features of *wasaṭiyya* that, as he noted, went beyond the twenty fundamentals that al-Bannā had formulated in 1940 for the MB in "Message of the Teachings."[27] One characteristic of *wasaṭiyya*, as al-Qaraḍāwī presented it to the secularists in the 1980s, is that in this approach Islam "represents a positive balance in all domains: faith and deeds, the material and the spiritual. It operates in the life of the individual to create a balance between matter and spirit, between mind and heart, between this world and the next, and between rights and obligations."[28] This was al-Qaraḍāwī's first representation of the fundamentals of *wasaṭiyya*; he repeated them later in 2004 and 2008[29] and eventually formulated *wasaṭiyya*'s thirty principles in 2010.

At the end of the 1980s, in his book *The Islamic Awakening and the Concerns of the Arab and Islamic Homeland* al-Qaraḍāwī defined Islamic *wasaṭiyya* as the largest and most important component of the Islamic Awakening.[30] He enumerated four characteristics of *wasaṭiyya* in the context of the Islamic Awakening: it provides a balance between Salafism and renewal; it provides a balance between permanent and changing aspects of religion; it warns against rigidity in Islam, dilution of Islam, and adoption of only parts of Islam; it provides a comprehensive understanding of Islam via al-Bannā's principle "Islam is all-encompassing" (*shumūl al-Islām*).[31]

The Evolution of al-Qaraḍāwī's Thirty *Wasaṭī* Principles

The thirty principles of *wasaṭī* Islam evolved in several stages. The first version was published in the mid-1980s in the course of al-Qaraḍāwī's debate with the most prominent representative of the secularists, Fu'ād Zakariyyā.[32] In early 2004, the shaykh presented in brief outline a different version of twenty of the principles at the twelfth session of the European Council for Fatwā and Research (ECFR, al-Majlis al-Ūrūbī lil-Iftā' wal-Buḥūth), which he headed then and still heads.[33] Yet another version was published in 2008,[34] and the latest version to date was published in 2010.[35] (See appendix A for a full translation of the latest version.)

The differences between the versions clearly reflect the historical circumstances in which the principles were formulated. For example, the version of the 1980s, set out by al-Qaraḍāwī during his debate with the secularists, included the following principle:

> [*Wasaṭī*] Islam counters [one] idea with another and counters doubts with evidence. There is no coercion in religion [Q2:256] and no coercion in thought. It [*wasaṭī* Islam] rejects violence as a method and terror as a means, whether it is [terror] by the rulers or by the ruled. It believes in purposeful and constructive dialogue that allows each side to express itself clearly and is committed to the objectivity and civilized discourse advocated in Q16:125: "Argue with them in a way that is best."[36]

As part of the debate with the secularists, this principle highlights the contrast between *wasaṭiyya* and the violent groups that were active in Egypt in the 1970s and 1980s, which targeted the "apostate" regime and whose violence peaked with the assassination of Anwar Sadat in October 1981. However, this principle also expresses criticism toward the regime for responding to the Islamist groups' violence with violence of its own instead of engaging them in dialogue and confronting their ideology.

In the wake of 9/11, *wasaṭiyya* sought to define Islam's attitude toward non-Muslims and to highlight the tolerant aspects of the religion and the defensive nature of its jihad. Hence, in the abbreviated version of the principles written in 2004, Principle 10 speaks of "jihad and preparation [for war] against the aggressors and an inclination to peace [*musālama*] toward those [non-Muslims] who are inclined to peace."[37] In the version developed in 2008, Principle 13 calls for "peace with anyone who extends his hand in peace, alongside commitment to the duty of [waging] jihad for the sake of Allah in order to defend the sanctity [*ḥurma*] of the religion, the holy places, and the oppressed upon the earth and in order to confront the arrogant pharaohs upon the earth [Muslim tyrants who do not rule according to the *sharīʿa*]." It also speaks of "the need to explain the different types of jihad: spiritual jihad, jihad through *daʿwa*, civil [*madanī*] jihad,[38] and other types."[39] In this version, al-Qaraḍāwī thus defines two legitimate targets for jihad: foreign enemies who have conquered Muslim lands, and tyrannical Muslim rulers whom he pejoratively refers to as "pharaohs." What he writes in his extensive, two-volume work *The Jurisprudence of Jihad* suggests that the jihad against the foreign enemy is meant to be military, whereas the jihad against the Muslim rulers is meant to be civil jihad or jihad by means of *daʿwa*.[40]

In the 2000s, the main challenge to *wasaṭiyya* was not posed by the secularists but by the global jihad organizations and their vision of the caliphate and of Islamic governance. Hence, in the version of 2010, Principle 15 emphasizes the just and virtuous nature of the Islamic state that *wasaṭīyya* seeks to establish, describing it as "a just state that engages in *daʿwa* and leads the *umma* to truth and virtue, establishes Allah's justice upon the earth, and governs [according to] what Allah sent down: the Scripture and the Balance [Q57:25]."[41] This wording seeks to assure the West, following 9/11, that the Islamic state envisioned by *wasaṭiyya* is not one that fights the entire world but a state that engages in *daʿwa*, is based on justice, and is essentially democratic.

Following 9/11 and the emergence of the jihadi Salafī stream, the shaykh wished to present a *wasaṭī* discourse both to the West and to the Islamic world as well as to develop a *wasaṭī* mode of *da'wa*.[42] The version of the thirty principles published in 2010 reflects clearly the objective of shaping the *wasaṭī* discourse in the wake of the 9/11 attacks. Many of the principles (eleven out of thirty) delineate the *wasaṭī* vision of the Islamic society and state, including in the realm of international relations, especially relations between Muslims and non-Muslims. Principle 7 speaks of "deepening human and social values such as justice, consultation [*shūrā*], freedom, dignity [*karāma*], and human rights."[43] This statement reflects the influence of Muḥammad al-Ghazālī, specifically his interpretation of the twenty principles in al-Bannā's "Message of Teachings" (1940). Al-Ghazālī complemented al-Bannā's principles with ten principles of his own, one of which states, "Man has material and spiritual rights as befitting the honorable [standing] bestowed upon him by Allah [an allusion to Q17:70] and his exalted status upon the earth. Islam clarifies these rights and preaches to respect them."[44]

As part of the effort to present *wasaṭiyya* as an alternative to the jihadi Salafī ideology and to mend the reputation of Islam, especially in the eyes of the West, Principle 18 (2010) highlights "the belief in the need for pluralism, mutual recognition, and tolerance [*tasāmuḥ*] among the peoples, the belief that humanity is a single family and civilizations should coexist, fertilize one another, interact, and borrow from one another without isolating themselves and without [harboring a sense of] superiority."[45] This language, too, is influenced by the principles al-Ghazālī articulated in the late 1980s, one of which informs al-Qaraḍāwī's perception of international relations in the post-9/11 era states as follows: "The Muslims' relations with the global community is based on the belief in pure human brotherhood; Muslims preach their faith by [presenting] evidence and through persuasion alone and do not plot to harm Allah's servants [i.e., other human beings]."[46]

This *wasaṭī* perspective contrasts with the perspective of jihadi Salafīs such as Shaykh Abū Baṣīr al-Ṭarṭūsī. For al-Ṭarṭūsī, a universalist approach that advocates brotherhood and cooperation among all peoples, regardless of religion, is heresy. In this regard, he has written: "When 'humanity' becomes a slogan to which one anchors one's loyalty and disavowal [*al-walā' wal-barā'*], to which one makes offerings, and for the sake of which one sacrifices one's soul, and when [humanity] is the basis for declaring war and peace—then it becomes an idol [*ṭāghūt*] that is worshipped instead of Allah."[47]

The statements al-Qaraḍāwī made after 9/11, favoring pluralism and treating all of humanity as a single family, are completely at odds with what he wrote before the attacks. For example, in his book *The Signs Heralding the Victory of Islam*, he wrote that the Qur'ān promises the triumph of Islam "whether the infidels like it or not." He also found signs of this victory in *ḥadīth*s, such as the *ḥadīth* predicting Islam's eventual conquest of Rome.[48] This *ḥadīth*, wrote the shaykh, means that Europe will one day be Islamic—although this time the conquest will be a peaceful one by means of the pen and the tongue rather than the sword, for "the world will open its arms and its heart to Islam. After suffering the torture of materialistic, man-made philosophies, [the world now] craves heavenly aid and the guidance of Allah, and only Islam can offer it a lifeline."[49]

In 2000, al-Qaraḍāwī wrote that "Islam poses a danger only to promiscuity and atheism, oppression and enslavement," and offers the world nothing but good, love, peace, and Allah's compassion.[50] Yet elsewhere he envisions the coming of a "victorious generation": a Muslim generation of *da'wa* and jihad similar to the generation of the Prophet and his companions, which will not lay down its sword "until there is no more *fitna* and the religion, all of it, is for Allah" (Q8:39). Upon the coming of this generation, he says, "all of Allah's land [i.e., the entire world] will be a battlefield" in which Muslims from across the globe, regardless of ethnicity or nationality, will fight the Muslims' enemies everywhere. For example, Arabs will fight the Communist invaders in Afghanistan, and Pakistanis will fight the Jewish invaders in Palestine and Lebanon—for unbelief is a single nation (*al-kufr milla wāḥida*).[51] Belying his call for pluralism, he also states in his volumes on jihad that the Muslims are responsible for spreading Islam's mission throughout the world and that Allah, history, and their conscience will hold them accountable if the nations remain ignorant of the light of Islam. On this basis, al-Qaraḍāwī proclaims that the goal of jihad in our era is to "make Allah's word supreme," clarifying that "Allah's word" means first and foremost the true faith, Islam. Moreover, he stresses that spreading the word of Islam may require the recruitment of Muslim armies to ensure the safety of those engaged in *daʿwa*.[52]

Wasaṭī Thought as Formulated by al-Qaraḍāwī

Principles of Wasaṭiyya *and al-Bannā's Twenty Fundamental Principles*

Uriya Shavit claims that second-generation Islamist thinkers of the MB's mainstream, those who follow in the footsteps of al-Bannā, especially al-Qaraḍāwī, share al-Bannā's vision that Islam must be revived as a comprehensive system, that the Muslim nation must be revived as well, that an end must be put to Western physical and cultural dominance of the lands of Islam, and that the revolution will come about through education and cultural activity. Shavit points to one aspect in which al-Bannā differs from his disciples of the second generation. Al-Bannā, as a political philosopher as well as a political leader, focused his efforts on the national level, on Egypt, although ideologically he fostered a universal belief in the revival of Islam. The following generation, however, at some point ceased their involvement in efforts to foment revolution against the regimes in their respective states and adopted a pan-Islamic view. Some ceased their political activity entirely, and others refrained only from involvement in the politics of their own states.[53]

A perusal of *wasaṭiyya*'s main principles reveals that al-Bannā's heritage served as a fundamental inspiration for al-Qaraḍāwī's thinking, even beyond those aspects Shavit mentions. We may thus maintain that al-Qaraḍāwī elaborates al-Bannā's philosophy and sheds light on practical applications of the latter's twenty tenets. *Wasaṭiyya* identifies three unique elements that it shares with the MB: a comprehensive view of Islam, unity among all Muslims around al-Bannā's twenty tenets,[54] and the importance of creating a pioneering avant-garde after the MB provides an Islamic education to all. The avant-garde will have absorbed the three values stressed by both al-Bannā and al-Qaraḍāwī: a religious as well as a rationalist education, spiritual awakening, and fraternity.[55]

Al-Qaraḍāwī follows in al-Bannā's footsteps.[56] It is therefore no wonder that his *wasaṭī* principles bear similarities to the twenty fundamental tenets enunciated in al-Bannā's "Message of Teachings."[57] Al-Qaraḍāwī in his writings further developed and elaborated *wasaṭī* principles, which have their roots in al-Bannā's tenets:

1. Islam as a comprehensive system for every aspect of life is a principle enunciated by Rashīd Riḍā, even before al-Bannā.[58]
2. The Qur'ān and the Sunna are the sources of Islamic law.
3. Mind and thought are to be respected alongside inspiration (*waḥy*). True traditions and common sense cannot contradict each other, as Ibn Taymiyya argued.[59]
4. Excommunication of fellow Muslims (*takfīr*) should be avoided whenever possible.
5. Priorities exist in one's religious obligations: acts of the heart are more important than acts of the limbs, and creed takes precedence over deeds (*'amal*).
6. Gradualness is the rule in *da'wa*, issuing legal rulings (*iftā'*) and bringing about change.

Wasaṭiyya accepts al-Bannā's view that society should be Islamized from the bottom up. First, the individual must change himself or herself and then establish a domestic environment in which the rules of Islam are obeyed. The next stage is to show society as a whole the path of Islam by *da'wa*. In the fourth stage, according to al-Bannā, the homeland must be liberated from foreign rule, and, finally, the government must be reformed so that it acts in accordance with the laws of Islam.[60] In line with al-Bannā's view, al-Qaraḍāwī stresses in his explanation of *wasaṭī* thought the family's importance as the basis for society and therefore the importance of building the family on true Muslim foundations. Society must subsequently be shaped in accordance with the principles of brotherhood and mutual responsibility, like the society that the Prophet Muḥammad built in Medina after the immigration (622 CE).[61] As its final goal, *wasaṭiyya* wishes to establish a "just state" (*al-dawla al-ṣāliḥa*), one that leads the Muslim nation to truth and goodness and establishes justice on earth. In such a state, al-Qaraḍāwī insists, people have the right to choose their own "strong and trustworthy" leaders (based on Q28:26).[62]

Al-Qaraḍāwī's Interpretation of al-Bannā's Twenty Principles

To understand the changes al-Qaraḍāwī made to the MB's fundamental ideas—changes that eventually coalesced into his *wasaṭī* ideology—it is crucial to examine his interpretation of al-Bannā's twenty principles, which al-Bannā set out in his most important work, "Message of Teachings." Al-Bannā addresses this epistle to the members of his movement, "the jihad-fighting Muslim Brothers who believe in the exalted nature of their *da'wa* and the sanctity of their idea, [and who,] based on their faith, decided to live in [their *da'wa*] or else die for its sake." He also clarifies that the messages in the treatise are not lessons to be learned but rather instructions to be implemented. "Message of Teachings" includes ten fundamental principles for Islamic action that al-Bannā calls "the foundations of the pledge [*arkān al-bay'a*]," to which every MB member has to pledge his commitment in order to advance from the status of a "participant member" to that of an "active member." Al-Bannā's twenty fundamentals emanate from the first of these principles—namely, "understanding" (*fahm*). Al-Qaraḍāwī explains that al-Bannā put this fundamental first because he understood the "*fiqh* of priorities" and realized that "thought precedes movement" and "knowledge precedes action."[63]

Several commentaries on al-Bannā's "Message of Teachings" have been written; according to al-Qaraḍāwī, the most important of them is the one by Muḥammad al-Ghazālī. The shaykh explains that he began writing his own commentary in the 1970s but did not hasten to complete it because he believed that al-Ghazālī's was sufficient, but then "Allah opened my heart [i.e., made me receptive to the idea of] finishing what I had started because there is no harm in a plurality of commentaries, and each shaykh has his own way, as the saying goes."[64] Al-Qaraḍāwī asserts that his commentary is unique in presenting the jurisprudential roots (*ta'ṣīl*) of al-Bannā's principles and the evidence for them in the Muslim sources.

Al-Qaraḍāwī does not regard al-Bannā's principles as intended for the MB alone and therefore dedicates his commentary to "all those devoted to Islam and concerned with its *umma* and with exalting its word and enacting its *sharī'a*."[65] In fact, al-Qaraḍāwī's stated objective in writing his commentary is to bring Islamic groups (*jamā'āt*) closer together and to remove the reasons for hostility between them. He believes that al-Bannā's ideas can form a basis for cooperation among various groups by creating a consensus on fundamental issues. There are many impediments to establishing a single global Islamic movement, he says, but the adoption of al-Bannā's principles can ensure that the plurality of groups becomes a source of variety and richness, not a source of disputes and struggles.[66]

An examination of the shaykh's commentary shows how he developed al-Bannā's principles, which underpin the MB's ideology, and forged them into an exegetic methodology and a consolidated ideological system. I demonstrate this development by presenting al-Qaraḍāwī's commentary on two of al-Bannā's principles, pertaining to (1) the Qur'ān and Sunna as Islam's sources of authority and (2) the settling of jurisprudential disputes.

The Wasaṭī *Interpretation of al-Bannā's Principle of the Qur'ān and Sunna as Islam's Sources of Authority*

Al-Bannā's second principle states: "The honorable Qur'ān and the purified Sunna are the source of every Muslim's knowledge of the laws of Islam. The Qur'ān is to be understood according to the rules of the Arabic language without forced or arbitrary [interpretations], and the Sunna must be understood based on the trustworthy transmitters of *ḥadīth*."[67] This principle is the foundation of al-Qaraḍāwī's *wasaṭī* exegesis of the Qur'ān and the Sunna,[68] which he utilizes in his debate with rival streams, including the secularists and especially the jihadi Salafīs. For example, *wasaṭiyya* presents an alternative interpretation of the Verse of the Sword (Q9:5), as discussed further in chapter 5. Because this exegetical method is al-Qaraḍāwī's main contribution to contemporary Islamic discourse, it is important to outline some of its basic assumptions. At the heart of this exegetic method are several principles that can be summarized as follows:

1. In interpreting texts from the Qur'ān and the Sunna, one must determine the true *goals* of the text.
2. To accomplish this, the interpretation must consider the textual and extratextual *context*:

2a. The interpretation of Qur'ānic verses and even of single words in the Qur'ān must consider the textual context—that is, the immediate context in which they appear as well as other Qur'ānic verses pertaining to the same topic. An interpretation of a verse cannot be valid if it contradicts what is said in another Qur'ānic verse.[69]

2b. The interpretation of Qur'ānic verses and *ḥadīth*s must consider the historical circumstances in which the verse descended or the *ḥadīth* was uttered because some verses and *ḥadīth*s are meant to address a specific incident or problem.

2c. The Sunna must be interpreted in light of the Qur'ān.

2d. The interpretation of the Sunna must consider the Sunna's general goals, which are unchanging, whereas the means to accomplish these goals may be subject to change.

Al-Qaraḍāwī uses some of these principles in his interpretation of the verse on the poll tax (*jizya*, Q9:29), which commands the Muslims to "fight those of the People of the Book who do not [truly] believe in God and the Last Day, who do not forbid what God and His Messenger have forbidden, [and] who do not obey the rule of justice until they pay the *jizya* according to their financial ability and while in a state of humiliation." This verse poses a problem for *wasaṭiyya* because it implies that the purpose of fighting the Jews and Christians is to force them to convert, and therefore it appears to contradict the *wasaṭī* claim that jihad in Islam is purely defensive. To overcome this problem, al-Qaraḍāwī notes that this verse, judging by the context in which it appears, descended after the Battle of Tabūk (630 CE) between the Prophet's forces and the Byzantines. The Byzantines, he explains, were completely unwilling to accept Islam and its global mission and killed Islamic preachers, so war against them was unavoidable. Moreover, although they purported to be Christians—that is, People of the Book—in actuality they distorted Christianity by embellishing it with elements from their earlier pagan religion. The *jizya* verse therefore had a specific purpose: it was meant to instruct the Muslims to persist in their war against the Byzantines. Al-Qaraḍāwī notes further that the verse must be interpreted in conjunction with other Qur'ānic verses, such as 4:90, which, according to him, refers to the polytheists and states that if the latter wish to live in peace with the Muslims, the Muslims must not fight them. He then argues that if the Qur'ān instructs the Muslims to refrain from fighting even the polytheists when the latter refrain from fighting the Muslims, then surely the Qur'ān would not command the Muslims to fight the People of the Book when they offer the Muslims peace.[70] Ḥasan al-Bannā's younger brother, Gamāl al-Bannā (d. 2013), proposed a similar interpretation of this verse, but his writings on some of the issues discussed in this book are liberal in their approach. According to him, the *jizya* verse does not refer to all the People of the Book, but only to a deviant group among them that does not believe in Allah or in the Day of Judgment and permits what Allah and His Messenger forbade. This group, he says, was apparently hostile to Islam, which required fighting it and imposing the *jizya* on it.[71]

It should be noted that both al-Qaraḍāwī and liberal writers such as Gamāl al-Bannā, a prolific writer who offers some liberal opinions, and Muḥammad Sa'īd al-'Ashmāwī take an apologetic approach to the issue of the *jizya*, stating that the *jizya* verse does not contradict the principle of freedom of belief in Islam and the statement that "there is no coercion in religion" (Q2:256). Both al-Qaraḍāwī and al-'Ashmāwī claim that the *jizya* was paid in lieu of military service and expressed the protected status that the Jews and Christians enjoyed in the Islamic state in return for their loyalty to this state. According to al-Qaraḍāwī, the payment of the *jizya* constitutes "active participation in bearing the burden of the state and in placing resources at the disposal of the public, both Muslim and non-Muslim."[72] Gamāl al-Bannā writes in a similar vein that the *jizya* was a way for the Jews and Christians to keep their faith and that it ensured their freedom from religious coercion. He, too, argues that the tax was in return for the protection granted to the Jews and Christians and adds that it benefited them more than it benefited the state.[73] A topic of particular controversy is the part of the *jizya* verse that states that the People of the Book must pay the tax "while they are humbled." Classical exegetes contended that the reference is to physical humiliation or even violence of some kind. Al-Qaraḍāwī adopts Rashīd Riḍā's opinion that the word *ṣāghirūn* in this verse does not mean "humbled" but rather expresses that the Jews accept the authority of the Islamic state over non-religious matters.[74]

The exegetical principles listed earlier—especially principle 2b—also come into play in al-Qaraḍāwī's interpretation of the *ḥadīth* presented by the jihadi Salafī Abū Muḥammad al-Maqdisī as evidence for his claim that Muslims may not reside in an original *dār al-kufr*, "abode of unbelief," such as the West: "I am not responsible for any Muslim who stays among polytheists. They asked: Why, Messenger of Allah? He said: Their fires should not be visible to one another [i.e., you should live as far as possible from them]." Al-Qaraḍāwī considers this *ḥadīth*'s chain of transmission to be weak because it does not contain the name of a Companion of the Prophet. He explains that its content must be understood in the context in which it was said;[75] the Prophet uttered his statement to people who had converted to Islam and still lived in Mecca among the idolaters and had not immigrated to the *dār al-Islām* of those days, Medina. During the confrontation between the Muslims and the idolaters in Mecca, the Muslim force did not identify the new converts to Islam and killed them. So the Prophet commanded that the families of the dead Muslims should be paid half the ransom because the victims were also at fault for residing among the idolaters. The Prophet's intention in this *ḥadīth*, according to al-Qaraḍāwī, was to declare that Muslims are not responsible for the deaths of Muslims who live among the polytheists because the latter Muslims put their own lives at risk by living where they do. He adds that when the circumstances in which the *ḥadīth* was uttered changed and the reasoning behind it was no longer valid, so that no benefit resulted from it and it did not prevent any harm, then the rule mentioned in it was no longer in effect.[76] Al-Qaraḍāwī, in complete contrast to al-Maqdisī, rules that Muslims belong to a nation with a universal message and that it is therefore their duty to be present in the countries of the West and to influence these leaders of the world. He concludes that the question of whether a Muslim may reside in a non-Muslim country or in *dār al-kufr* or not does not even arise because if there could be no Muslims outside *dār al-Islām*, proselytizing for the faith would become impossible.[77]

Principle 2c states that the Sunna must be interpreted in light of the Qur'ān. This principle entails that no *ḥadīth* can be considered reliable if it contradicts explicit Qur'ānic verses (*muḥkamāt*). Al-Qaraḍāwī employs this principle in interpreting the *ḥadīth* of the sword, frequently quoted by jihadi Salafīs: "I was sent with the sword just before the Day of Judgment so that Allah is worshipped alone without partners" (for a detailed discussion of this *ḥadīth*, see chapter 5). To deal with this *ḥadīth*—another text that potentially belies the *wasaṭī* claims that Islam is a peaceful religion and that all jihad is defensive—al-Qaraḍāwī argues that it contradicts what is said in the Qur'ān regarding the purpose of the Prophet's mission. The Qur'ān never says, in any verse, that Allah sent Muḥammad with a sword. Rather, al-Qaraḍāwī says, Allah sent Muḥammad upon his mission armed with "guidance to the right path, the true religion, mercy, a remedy [for sinful thoughts], and *da'wa*," as evident from several verses, which al-Qaraḍāwī quotes.[78]

Finally, principle 2d states that the interpretation of the Sunna must consider the Sunna's general goals, which are unchanging, whereas the means to accomplish these goals may change from era to era. As an example, al-Qaraḍāwī presents the *ḥadīth* about the new moon as a sign for the start of the Ramaḍān fast: "Fast *when you see it [the new moon] and break your fast when you see it again*. Should it be overcast, allow [the moon] to complete [its thirty-day cycle]." The goal of this *ḥadīth*, says the shaykh, is to make sure the believers fast for the correct number of days. It employs the means of sighting the moon because this was the only means to track the days that was available to people at the time this *ḥadīth* was transmitted. However, in later periods, scientific advances provided other ways to calculate the date on which the fast should start. These methods are more reliable, states al-Qaraḍāwī, and can promote Muslim unity by ending the controversies regarding the start of Ramaḍān. "The Sunna, which allowed us to use a less efficient means [i.e., the sighting of the moon] . . . would [surely] not reject a better means," he reasons.[79]

Al-Bannā's Eighth Principle: The Handling of Jurisprudential Controversies among Muslims

Al-Bannā's eighth principle says: "Differences in subsidiary matters of Islamic jurisprudence should not cause division, contention, or hatred among Muslims. To every independent legist [*mujtahid*] is a reward. In cases of disagreement, there is no harm in objective scientific investigation in an atmosphere of love for the sake of Allah and cooperation with the aim of determining the truth, as long as this does not lead to objectionable controversy or fanaticism."[80] This principle forms the basis for al-Qaraḍāwī's jurisprudence of controversy (*fiqh al-ikhtilāf*) for handling controversy among Muslims.[81] This *fiqh* comprises several guidelines, two of which are worth considering here.

The first, borrowed from Rashīd Riḍā, states: "Let us cooperate in matters on which we agree and excuse [*ʿudhr*] each other in matters on which we disagree."[82] This guideline includes two components: (1) cooperation in agreed-upon matters and (2) the seeking of religious grounds for excusing opinions differing from one's own—in other words, for being tolerant of controversy. Al-Qaraḍāwī interprets the first component to mean that it is possible to cooperate even with "innovators" (*mubtadiʿūn*) and "those who stray from the right path"—possibly referring to the Shīʿa—as long as their innovations are within the boundaries of Islam's most basic agreed-upon principles, the Six Articles of the Faith: belief in Allah, in the angels, in the revealed books, in Muḥammad and the other prophets, in the Day of Judgement, and in predestination by Allah.[83]

This pragmatic interpretation of Rashīd Riḍā's guideline is one of the "magic formulas" of *wasaṭiyya* that differentiate it from the jihadi Salafism. Al-Qaraḍāwī employs it in the cause of rapprochement between the Sunna and the Shīʿa, for example. He advocates focusing on the points of agreement between the two sects, such as the belief in the Qur'ān and in its divine origin, while ignoring the claim made by some Shīʿīs regarding omissions in the present Qur'ānic codex. The latter is a "subsidiary matter" that can be put aside, he says; it is best to concentrate on the practical political, economic, social, and cultural issues on which the Sunnī and Shīʿī can agree.[84] This approach contrasts sharply with that of the jihadi Salafīs, who reject out of hand any possibility of rapprochement with the Shīʿa. Al-Ṭarṭūsī ruled that Twelver Shīʿa (whom he, like other jihadi Salafīs, calls *Rāfiḍa*) is "a sect of polytheism, or attributing partners to Allah [*shirk*] and apostasy [*ridda*] that is outside the fold of Islam."[85] Similarly, Abū Muṣʿab al-Zarqāwī (d. 2006), the former head of al-Qaʿida in Iraq, stated that "there cannot be even the most minimal doctrinal or ideological rapprochement between the Sunnīs and the Rawāfiḍ [i.e., the Shīʿa]."[86]

Al-Qaraḍāwī, despite his call for a Sunnī–Shīʿī rapprochement, caused an uproar in the Muslim world when he said in 2008, "The Shīʿīs are Muslims, but they are introducers of forbidden religious innovations [*mubtadiʿūn*]. The danger they pose stems from their attempt to infiltrate [*ghazw*] Sunnī society. They are able to do this thanks to the great sums of money at their disposal and thanks to their missionaries, who are adept at preaching the Shīʿī way to Sunnī society. Moreover, this society lacks the cultural immunity [required to resist this] Shīʿī infiltration."[87] After this statement provoked protests in Iran, the shaykh issued a response in which he reiterated his position, asserting that only the Sunnī sect follows the true path, while all other sects, including the Shīʿīs, are misguided. He referred to the Sunnīs as "the saved sect" (*al-firqa al-nājiya*), a term originating in a well-known *ḥadīth* stating that Islam will split into seventy-three sects, all of which except one will be doomed. The shaykh did stress in this response that he regards the Shīʿīs as innovators rather than as infidels, but he accused them of pagan behaviors, such as visiting the tombs of saints and asking for their intercedence instead of praying directly to Allah.[88]

The shift in al-Qaraḍāwī's attitude toward the Shīʿīs in 2008 was a response to the spreading phenomenon of *tashayyuʿ*, sympathy toward Shīʿīsm, in the Sunnī world, especially following the Hizbullah–Israel war of 2006 and as a result of Iranian religious proselytizing in Sunnī countries. His malleable stance on Shīʿīsm, shifting along with the political climate, was also evident in his changing attitude toward the Shīʿī Hizbullah. In 2006, during the Hizbullah–Israel war, al-Qaraḍāwī defended this organization: he opposed a *fatwā* issued by the Salafī Saudi shaykh ʿAbdallah ibn Jabrīn (d. 2009), who forbade Sunnīs to aid Hizbullah or pray for its victory on the grounds that Shīʿīs are infidels.[89] In a *fatwā* al-Qaraḍāwī issued in response, he denied that the Shīʿīs are infidels and argued that Muslims must indeed aid Hizbullah against Israel because "anyone who opposes and fights Israel is our ally to some extent." However, he also warned the Shīʿīs not to use their "victory" over Israel in the war as evidence of the rightness of Shī'ism or as an excuse to infiltrate Sunnī societies and spread their faith.[90]

But following Iran's and Hizbullah's involvement in the Syria war in collaboration with the Bashar al-Asad (b. 1965) regime, al-Qaraḍāwī again changed his tune. In a sermon in Qatar in May 2013, he stated that Hizbullah could no longer be seen as "the party of Allah" (which is the meaning of the name "Hizbullah" and an expression appearing, for instance, in Q58:22) but rather must been seen as "the party of Satan [*ḥizb al-Shayṭān*]," an expression taken from Q58:19. If Hizbullah were really the party of Allah, he said, it would aid truth against falsehood and justice against oppression—that is, aid the Syrian people against their regime rather than the opposite. He accused Hizbullah secretary-general Ḥasan Naṣrallah (b. 1960) of fighting for an idol-ruler (*ṭāghūt*) rather than for Allah, quoting a verse (Q4:76) that states that those who fight in the cause of *ṭāghūt* are unbelievers.[91]

Muslim liberals present these *fatwā*s by al-Qaraḍāwī as proof that he and others like him exploit Islam to promote "sectarian, political, and personal interests and objectives"[92] or to "politicize Islam by [promoting] extremism, violence, and terror," as al-'Ashmāwī puts it, and mix political objectives with religious ones. Especially interesting is al-'Ashmāwī's insight that those who politicize Islam—a group that, according to the liberals, includes al-Qaraḍāwī and is perhaps even led by him—divide Muslims into two categories: the people of Allah (*ḥizb Allāh*, not in the sense of the Lebanese movement but in the broad sense of Q5:56—that is, the true believers) and the people of Satan (*ḥizb al-Shayṭān*). Furthermore, they believe that the people of Allah (a group that obviously includes themselves) must wage jihad against the people of Satan (a group that includes all of their opponents) until the latter are completely eliminated.[93] Al-Qaraḍāwī's branding of the Lebanese Hizbullah as "the party of Satan," which delegitimizes this organization while implying that al-Qaraḍāwī and his followers are "the party of Allah," is an example of this approach.

The second guideline in al-Qaraḍāwī's *fiqh al-ikhtilāf*, borrowed from Ibn Taymiyya,[94] distinguishes between "controversy of multiple opinions" (*ikhtilāf tanawwu'*) and "controversy of opposition" (*ikhtilāf taḍādd*).[95] The first type involves multiple opinions, all of which are religiously valid, in which case the choice between them is up to every individual Muslim. An example is the precise form of the supplication (*du'ā'*) at the beginning of the prayer. Both al-Qaraḍāwī and al-Ṭarṭūsī regard this type of controversy to be legitimate and acceptable. The second type involves contrasting opinions, whether on the basic tenets of the faith or on subsidiary issues, but only one of these opinions is correct.[96] Al-Qaraḍāwī contends that this type of controversy is unacceptable (*mardūd*) and must be avoided. Al-Ṭarṭūsī states that this type of controversy cannot be religiously justified when it pertains to roots and beliefs and especially to *tawḥīd* because such justification would destroy the religion and its roots, creating a new religion with new roots.[97] As mentioned earlier, al-Qaraḍāwī stresses that the controversy between the various groups of the Islamic Awakening must be "controversy of multiple opinions" rather than "controversy of opposition." That is, it must involve variety rather than conflict and mutual contradiction. Each group may devote itself to a different domain, but on crucial issues all sects must agree and form a single rank "like a structure joined firmly" (Q61:4).[98]

Conclusion

This chapter has examined the development of the *wasaṭī* stream under al-Qaraḍāwī's leadership. It shows that al-Qaraḍāwī did not begin using the term *wasaṭī stream* on a regular basis until the mid-1980s. Furthermore, the ideological principles of *wasaṭiyya* developed in stages, aiming to meet the challenges of the times—first, the challenge of secularism, which was raised against the "Islamic solution" presented by the Islamic movement in the 1980s, and later the challenge of the Salafī movement, especially the jihadi Salafī one, in the 1990s. As a result of this development in stages, the *wasaṭī* principles have appeared in a number of different versions over the years.

This study shows that *wasaṭiyya* is anchored in the principles of the MB movement as presented by Ḥasan al-Bannā in the 1940s but that al-Qaraḍāwī significantly broadened and embellished these principles to create a basis for an elaborate system of *wasaṭī* exegesis. As clarified in the chapter, this system has two major characteristics: it affords greater flexibility and maneuverability in interpreting the Qur'ān and the Sunna, and it outlines basic parameters for a "*fiqh* of controversy" among different Islamic streams.

It should be noted that although al-Qaraḍāwī has set out principles for civilized debate with rivals, he does not always abide by these principles, as evidenced by many of his statements on the liberal secularists and the Shīʿa.

3

Al-Qaraḍāwī, al-Azhar, and the Muslim Brotherhood

In this chapter, I examine al-Qaraḍāwī's biography to gain an understanding of the soil from which the *wasaṭī* idea grew and took shape.[1] The first part of the chapter focuses on the two institutions that had the greatest influence on al-Qaraḍāwī's development into an *ʿālim*: al-Azhar and the MB. The chapter analyzes al-Qaraḍāwī's unique relationship with the Brotherhood: he withdrew his membership in the organization in the mid-1960s yet remained a religious authority and guide of both the mother organization in Egypt and its offshoot, Hamas. The second part of the chapter focuses on two issues. First, there is a discrepancy between al-Qaraḍāwī's self-presentation and reality: al-Qaraḍāwī presents himself as an unbiased scholar and therefore as an alternative to the establishment shaykhs, but an examination of his rulings reveals that he is in fact a very political scholar. The second issue is the causes that have made al-Qaraḍāwī such an influential *ʿālim* throughout the Muslim world. I argue that his influence cannot be explained as due only to the means used for the dissemination of his message, especially the various communications media; rather, that influence comes first and foremost from the *wasaṭī* message itself and from al-Qaraḍāwī's unique style of *daʿwa*, whose objective is the creation of a "*wasaṭī* culture."

Al-Azhar and the Muslim Brotherhood: The Forges That Shaped al-Qaraḍāwī's Thought

Al-Qaraḍāwī and al-Azhar

Two major institutions were responsible for shaping al-Qaraḍāwī's worldview and path: al-Azhar University and the MB, although the MB scholars

2. Shaykh Yūsuf al-Qaraḍāwī at the Third Annual Doha Educational Conference in February 2006. Photograph by Nmkuttiady. (From "Qardawi," Wikimedia Commons, n.d., at https://commons.wikimedia.org/wiki/File:Qardawi.JPG.)

apparently had a greater impact on him than the formal education he received at al-Azhar.[2] Al-Qaraḍāwī belongs to the first generation of al-Azhar students and graduates who joined the MB and were active in it, yet he differs from other scholars that belonged simultaneously to both institutions. Upon joining the MB, some of the latter gradually lost their independent Azhari identity and thus had little or no impact beyond the confines of the MB. An example is Shaykh Muḥammad 'Abdallah al-Khaṭīb (b. 1929), a member of the MB's Guidance Bureau (Maktab al-Irshād), who was called the "MB *muftī*." Others, such as Shaykh Muḥammad al-Ghazālī,[3] continued to regard themselves as al-Azhar scholars. Because al-Azhar advocated taking an appeasing stance toward the Egyptian regime, these figures found themselves in a problematic position during the MB's intense clashes with the al-Nasir regime in 1954, and some of them were eventually expelled from the movement.[4] Al-Qaraḍāwī, however, managed to strike a unique balance between his Azhari identity and his membership in the MB, a movement that combines *da'wa* and politics.[5]

Al-Qaraḍāwī is an al-Azhar scholar and has expressed great reverence for this institution. For example, in his book on al-Azhar's mission, he wrote that "al-Azhar's scholars are heirs of the prophets [based on a famous *ḥadīth*[6]] who guide God's creatures on the right path and preach truth. They are envoys of good, keys to the righteous way, and illuminators of the darkness."[7] However, even as a student at al-Azhar, al-Qaraḍāwī called for reforming this institution. Over the years, he criticized it mainly for its subservience to the regime and its lack of independence, both of which became especially apparent after 1961 when a law placed al-Azhar's budget under state control.[8] It was al-Qaraḍāwī's dissatisfaction with this aspect of al-Azhar that led him to found the IUMS in 2004, an institution that would serve as an alternative source of authority for Muslims.[9]

Al-Qaraḍāwī's criticism of al-Azhar, whose scholars he accuses of being servants of the regime, is pointedly expressed in his letter of resignation from al-Azhar's Council of Senior Scholars (Hay'at Kibār al-'Ulamā'), sent in December 2013 after the shaykh of al-Azhar at the time, Aḥmad al-Ṭayyib (b. 1946; the shaykh of al-Azhar from 2010), supported 'Abd al-Fattah al-Sisi's ouster of president of Egypt Muhammad Mursi (b. 1951). In his letter, al-Qaraḍāwī wrote that al-Azhar had long fulfilled its duty of giving good advice to Muslim leaders and Muslims at large (giving advice is mandated by the well-known *ḥadīth* "*al-dīn al-naṣīḥa*" [religion is advice]).[10] It had fulfilled this duty in the period of the Mamluks, the Turks, and the monarchy and had also led the revolutions against the French and the English. Al-Azhar continued to lead the people steadfastly until 1952, when the Free Officers revolution made it subordinate to the regime. According to al-Qaraḍāwī, after this revolution al-Azhar began following every sinful and lying ruler. In other words, it betrayed the role of the free scholars, to whom al-Qaraḍāwī purports to belong, which is to take a stand based on the Qur'ān and the Sunna alone.[11]

Especially revealing are statements the shaykh made in his historic Friday sermon in al-Azhar on November 16, 2012. Having been banned for decades from preaching in al-Azhar and praying in Egypt's mosques, he was once again able to mount the pulpit at al-Azhar following Mursi's election. He said:

> Is it strange that an al-Azhar cleric should come to preach at the al-Azhar mosque? It is not strange at all. . . . Today we speak from this spot, this al-Azhar pulpit that has become the pulpit of the entire Sunnī world. For years this pulpit was monopolized by whoever monopolized it [i.e., the various Egyptian regimes], but it did not [remain monopolized] forever, for it is the pulpit of Islam, of the Qur'ān and of Muḥammad, God's prayers and peace be upon him, and therefore it must return to its [real] owners and people.[12]

Al-Qaraḍāwī is also critical of al-Azhar's curriculum, its teachers, and its teaching methods, all of which he experienced firsthand when he studied there. He states that in order to fulfill its mission—which he believes is to preach the true Islam, awaken the believing Egyptian public, guide the Arab and Muslim peoples, and produce reformist preachers—al-Azhar must provide its students with an in-depth understanding of both Islam and the contemporary world. In other words, it must preserve the Muslim past without isolating itself from the present. The shaykh states further that an al-Azhar scholar must be virtuous of character, a paragon not only of religious knowledge but also of good deeds. As part of this virtuosity, an al-Azhar scholar must have the courage to tell the truth and insist on it even if it is not to the ruler's liking. He mentions as an example of such a scholar Aḥmad b. Ḥanbal (d. 855), the founder of the Ḥanbalī school of jurisprudence, who was persecuted by the Islamic inquisition (*miḥna*) for insisting that the Qur'ān was uncreated, contra the position of the Abbasid caliph al-Ma'mūn (reigned 813–55 CE), but did not recant his views.[13]

Accordingly, al-Qaraḍāwī believes that al-Azhar must be more scrupulous in selecting its students in order to produce graduates who possess the mind of a scholar, the heart and the moral conscience of a believer, the wisdom of a preacher, the vigor of a jihad fighter, and the civilized and cultured nature of a Muslim who is part of the modern world. Furthermore, it must be equally scrupulous in choosing its teachers. The key to success, al-Qaraḍāwī says, is to select teachers who are also educators, mentors, and role models and who will imbue their students not only with knowledge but also with piety, good conduct, and asceticism. An al-Azhar teacher must be a father figure and spiritual leader for his students, he stresses.[14]

Criticizing the education he received at al-Azhar,[15] al-Qaraḍāwī complains that the elementary and high school curricula did not include foreign languages. He also writes that the lessons lacked "a spirit of *da'wa*" and were "spiritually dry."[16] He states that al-Azhar classes on faith and theology often focus on obsolete issues deriving from historical disagreements between the various Islamic schools or from the influence of Greek philosophy, which are irrelevant to today's world. Each era is confronted with different logical dilemmas and has its own methods of addressing them, he says, so al-Azhar must update the curriculum on the fundamentals of monotheism and focus on evidence in the Qur'ān and the Sunna rather than sink into arcane theological disputes.[17] In this context, the shaykh advocates a comprehensive reform of the study of Islamic jurisprudence (*fiqh*) at al-Azhar. The guidelines he suggests for training scholars in this field are in the spirit of his *wasaṭī* ideology (on the principles of *wasaṭī* jurisprudence, see chapter 6).[18]

Al-Qaraḍāwī and the Muslim Brotherhood

Al-Qaraḍāwī, like other students of Ḥasan al-Bannā who belong to what Uriya Shavit calls the "second-generation mainstream Islamist intellectuals,"[19] considers al-Bannā to have been "a rare personality or, more exactly, several people in one: scholar, preacher, educator, reformer, jihadi, and politician."[20]

Al-Qaraḍāwī first encountered his spiritual mentor in 1938, when al-Bannā visited the local MB branch in Ṭanṭa to deliver a New Year sermon. Al-Qaraḍāwī was captivated by al-Bannā; in his memoirs he describes this first encounter thus: "From the age I developed some awareness, I used to attend the New Year sermons delivered each year by the village clerics. The sermons were about the [Prophet's] *hijra* [immigration]. They were always the same, dealing with the story of the spider and the dove and so on. But that night [in al-Bannā's sermon] I heard something new and original, the like of which I had never heard before. I understood it, digested it, and learned almost all of it by heart because it was so clear, concise, and eloquent."[21] Elsewhere in his memoirs he writes of the same day: "If in the world of romantic love they speak of 'love at first sight,' in the world of *da'wa* we may speak of 'love from the first word.' My heart became bound to al-Bannā; it was [like] the bond between a [Ṣūfī] disciple and his master, a student and his teacher, a soldier and his commander—though I did not become a soldier in his group [i.e., an MB member] until three years later."[22] From that day forward, al-Qaraḍāwī made sure to attend every sermon that al-Bannā delivered in Ṭanṭa. The shaykh writes that he was also deeply affected by the members of the MB youth movement who marched through the streets of Ṭanṭa carrying copies of the Qur'ān, waving MB banners, and calling out MB slogans.

Al-Qaraḍāwī officially joined the MB in 1941, though he says that he felt part of the movement from the day he heard al-Bannā's New Year sermon three years earlier.[23] According to al-Qaraḍāwī, joining the MB was a significant turning point for him. It widened his horizons and enhanced his understanding of Islam as a comprehensive system, for al-Bannā championed the principle of an all-inclusive Islam that encompasses religion and this world; *da'wa* and state; creed and law; worship and leadership; the Qur'ān and the sword (the last two are the main elements in MB's emblem; see figure 1 in the introduction).[24] The shaykh adds that as a result of his activity in the MB, he also developed an interest in the needs of the Islamic *umma* as a whole so that he no longer focused on just his own personal aspirations and ambitions. For instance, he embraced the aspiration to liberate the Islamic lands from any foreign rule and to replace foreign ideas and imported man-made laws with the laws of Islam. Al-Qaraḍāwī's association with the MB also contributed to his Ṣūfī perceptions, for al-Bannā had originally been a member of a Ṣūfī order,[25] which was reflected in some of the MB's methods of teaching and guidance. Al-Bannā described the MB's *da'wa* as both Salafist and Ṣūfist: Salafist because the MB aspires to return Islam to its pure sources, the Qur'ān and the Sunna, and Ṣūfist because the movement recognizes that the basis of good is purity of heart and of soul, a persistence in worship, love for the sake of Allah, and cooperation in righteousness (the last expression is inspired by Q5:2).[26]

Al-Qaraḍāwī combined his high school studies with activism in the MB, working with the MB's student department and *da'wa* department. As part of this activity, he visited villages and cities across Egypt to spread the MB message. Reading the MB's weekly, *Al-Ikhwān al-Muslimūn*, he became familiar with Shaykh Muḥammad al-Ghazālī, who greatly influenced his thinking and his way.[27] He also composed poems celebrating Muslim and national events. However, al-Qaraḍāwī later became critical of the MB's methods of training for placing too much emphasis on the practical at the expense of educating its members, cultivating their talents, and shaping their ideological and cultural identity. He notes, for example, that the MB could have guided a preacher like himself toward writing, not just toward oral preaching, and it also could have arranged for him to learn English.[28]

The Ordeals of an MB Member: The Experience of Prison

In 1948, the MB was outlawed in Egypt, and many of its members were arrested, among them al-Qaraḍāwī.[29] He was still in prison when he heard that al-Bannā had been assassinated on February 13, 1949.[30] (Al-Bannā was killed in revenge for the assassination of Egyptian prime minister Maḥmūd Fahmī Bāshā al-Nuqrāshī, who had been shot in December 1948 by an MB member, a veterinary student named 'Abd al-Majīd Aḥmad Ḥasan.[31]) While in prison, al-Qaraḍāwī wrote a play titled *A Scholar and a Tyrant*, about the medieval scholar Sa'īd b. Jubayr (assassinated in 714 CE), who opposed al-Hajjāj b. Yūsuf, the ruthless Umayyad governor of Iraq who was known as "the shedder of blood" (*saffāḥ*). By means of this play, the shaykh sought to draw a parallel between the tyrannical Egyptian regime at the time, which imprisoned MB members like himself, and al-Hajjāj's brutal rule. He also wished to extol the courage of religious scholars, such as Sa'īd b. Jubayr, who stood up against tyranny.[32] Among al-Qaraḍāwī's fellow prisoners at the time was Shaykh Muḥammad al-Ghazālī, who served as prayer leader for the MB prisoners.[33]

Al-Qaraḍāwī was freed in the first wave of releases after the fall of Ibrahīm ʻAbd al-Hādī's government in the summer of 1949. The MB welcomed the ouster of al-Hādī, who was prime minister between December 1948 and July 1949 and whose government was responsible for imprisoning many of its members. Upon his release from prison, al-Qaraḍāwī began to study in the Theology Faculty (Kulliyyat Uṣūl al-Dīn) at al-Azhar University. He notes in his autobiography that, beyond the required books on the syllabus, he was also provided with other books, among them the works of Ibn Taymiyya and his student Ibn Qayyim al-Jawziyya, which contributed greatly to the consolidation of his ideas. During his studies, he attended not only al-Azhar lectures but also those given by MB shaykhs, chief among them Muḥammad al-Ghazālī; al-Sayyid Sābiq (d. 2000), author of the well-known book *Jurisprudence of the Sunna*; and Shaykh al-Bahī al-Khūlī (d. 1977), an MB founder and a member of the movement's Guidance Bureau.[34]

In 1954, following clashes between the MB and the al-Nasir regime, there was another wave of arrests of MB activists (the period from the late 1940s until the mid-1960s would come to be known in MB circles as the time of *miḥan*, "difficult trials, ordeals"). Al-Qaraḍāwī was arrested in January but was freed only six weeks later, after the Free Officers regime signed an agreement with the MB in March and released MB prisoners.[35] However, later that year, following the assassination attempt against Gamal ʻAbd al-Nasir in Alexandria on October 26, 1954, al-Qaraḍāwī was arrested again,[36] and this time he remained in prison until June 1956. This period of incarceration was accompanied by brutal torture, which he described in an ode (*qaṣīda*) that came to be known as his "*qaṣīda nūniyya*" (i.e., *qaṣīda* rhyming in *nūn*).[37] In prison, the shaykh became a sort of teacher for other incarcerated MB members, clarifying Islamic principles for them, especially the twenty fundamentals (*usūl*) of al-Banna's "Message of Teachings." Later in life al-Qaraḍāwī would write commentary on some of these fundamentals, which became the kernel of his principles of *wasaṭiyya* (see chapter 2).[38]

Upon his release from prison this time, the shaykh decided to resume his higher studies, and in 1957 he enrolled in the Department of Qur'ān and Sunna Sciences at al-Azhar's Faculty of Islamic Fundamentals. In 1960, he submitted a research proposal on alms or charitable giving (*zakāh*) in Islam and its impact on social problems, and in 1973 he completed his PhD on this topic. Even earlier, in late 1970, he had published his book *The Laws of Alms*, a comprehensive two-volume study that is part of his considerable writings on Muslim economics.[39] Because of his knowledge in economics and banking, al-Qaraḍāwī was appointed religious adviser to the world's first Islamic bank, established in Dubai in 1975.

Al-Qaraḍāwī's Immigration to Qatar

In the mid-1950s, for security reasons the authorities banned al-Qaraḍāwī from work involving direct contact with the public (i.e., teaching and preaching). However, thanks to the patronage of then minister of religious endowments Aḥmad Ḥasan al-Bāqūrī (d. 1985), who had been an MB member and who had begun his service as minister in 1952,[40] and of Muḥammad al-Bahī (d. 1982), who later became minister of religious endowments in 1962, al-Qaraḍāwī was employed at this ministry and later at al-Azhar's Islamic Culture Department, which al-Bahī headed. Al-Bahī asked him to write for the ministry's journal *Minbar al-Islam* and also to issue rulings in the journal's feature "Yastaftūnaka" (They Request from You [a Religious Ruling]) in response to readers' questions.[41] Al-Qaraḍāwī notes that those who wrote the responses in this feature before him had used archaic language and had often issued strict rulings at odds with the spirit of the times. He, however, followed the juristic principle of facilitation (*taysīr*) and the *da'wa* principle of bringing good tidings (*tabshīr*).[42]

Al-Bahī involved al-Qaraḍāwī in writing religious guides that answered questions by Muslims living in America and Britain. This project led him to write his well-known and important book *The Lawful and the Prohibited in Islam*,[43] published in 1960. He states that this book took a *wasaṭī* path, which naturally angered extremists on both the left and the right. Furthermore, it did not follow any particular Islamic legal school, which upset devout adherents of the various schools. The shaykh also notes that the book, like his rulings in the ministry journal, followed the juristic principle of facilitation. As a consequence, some advocates of strictness naturally opposed it; some even quipped that the book should have been entitled *The Lawful and the Lawful in Islam* because it allowed much more than it forbade. Al-Qaraḍāwī responded to these critics by advising them to author their own book and entitle it *The Forbidden and the Forbidden in Islam*.[44] The Salafī Saudi shaykh Sāliḥ al-Fawzān (b. 1935) devoted an entire book to critiquing *The Lawful and the Prohibited in Islam*.[45] (For the differences between the Salafī and *wasaṭī* legal approaches, see chapter 6.) This book was among the first products of al-Qaraḍāwī's extensive interest in the Muslim minorities living outside *dār al-Islām*. He issued many rulings regarding them, laying the foundations for what would be known as "the jurisprudence of the minorities" (*fiqh al-aqalliyyāt*). In 1997, he established the ECFR, which specializes in this kind of *fiqh*.[46]

In September 1961, al-Qaraḍāwī left Egypt for Qatar after passing the test that qualifies an al-Azhar scholar to be lent to one of the university's institutes abroad that has a need for teachers. This move was an important turning point in his life. Al-Qaraḍāwī stresses that when he immigrated to Qatar, he left the MB "in body but not in spirit"[47] and kept in touch with the movement in various ways. Though he could no longer meet with its members on a regular basis, he did meet them occasionally during his summer visits to Egypt, while on pilgrimage to Mecca, and when Egyptian MB members visited him in Qatar. Muḥammad al-Ghazālī, for example, visited the shaykh during his three-year sojourn in that country beginning in 1981.[48] Moreover, some MB members who were imprisoned in Egypt during the Nasserist period joined al-Qaraḍāwī in Qatar after their release, and together they formed a group of MB members in Qatar. Al-Qaraḍāwī represented this group in the MB's International Organization (al-Tanẓīm al-Duwalī), which he helped to found. This body began to coalesce in the 1960s; the International Organization was meant to constitute a center for MB members outside Egypt and to help in raising funds and promoting the MB's *da'wa*.[49]

Al-Qaraḍāwī in Qatar: Disseminating *Wasaṭiyya*

Allen Fromherz claims in his modern history of Qatar that al-Qaraḍāwī used Qatar and the al-Jazeera television station (founded there in 1996) as a base from which he could disseminate his conservative interpretation of Islam. Fromherz adds that al-Qaraḍāwī's views on Islam do not match those of Qatar's elite, nor are they consistent with the interests of the United States, the main guardian of Qatar's security. Fromherz notes that the ruling Āl Thānī family may have had an interest in benefiting from al-Qaraḍāwī's reputation, and, in turn, al-Qaraḍāwī benefited from being hosted in Qatar. He adds that the Muslim world has a long history of religious scholars who have used the faith as an efficient tool for supervision over the state and that "even if al-Qaraḍāwī has never criticized Qatar directly[,] his neo-traditionalist discourse consumed so readily by Muslims around the world, including Qataris, implicitly seeks to limit the scope and nature of Qatar's own, largely Westernized development and to question the rationale behind it."[50]

Al-Qaraḍāwī's activities in Qatar have focused mainly on education; *da'wa* in mosques; promotion of Islamic banking in the Persian Gulf region; preaching in the media, since the mid-1990s mainly through the al-Jazeera network; and MB activities in Qatar. A prominent feature of al-Qaraḍāwī's life in the years he has resided in Qatar is his numerous trips to other countries for the promotion of his *da'wa* and to attend the many conferences at which the *wasaṭī* position have taken shape. His educational projects in Qatar are worth mentioning, in particular his reform of the Religious Institute (al-Ma'had al-Dīnī) upon his arrival in the country in 1961 and the founding of a *sharī'a* faculty at Qatar University in 1976.

Qatar under Emir Ḥamad b. Khalīfa Āl Thānī (b. 1952, ruled 1995–2013) celebrated al-Qaraḍāwī as a national asset and viewed him as one of its vehicles of power and influence in the Arab world. A former Qatari minister expressed this view very clearly when he said in 2002 at a conference on US relations with the Arab world, "Saudi Arabia has Mecca and Medina, and we [in Qatar] have al-Qaraḍāwī."[51] After Emir Ḥamad b. Khalīfa passed the throne to his son Tamīm b. Ḥamad (b. 1980) in 2013, rumors appeared in the media that the new emir, fearing the MB's influence, had given al-Qaraḍāwī one month to leave the country and that he planned to revoke the Qatari citizenship that his father had granted the shaykh. Al-Qaraḍāwī's office was quick to deny these rumors, stating that they had been spread by the Syrian media because of the shaykh's harsh criticism of the Bashar al-Asad regime. The statement underscored the strong ties between al-Qaraḍāwī and the Qatari royal family, both father and son, and stressed the shaykh's great appreciation of Qatar's position in support of the "Arab Spring" revolutions in 2011. It also underscored al-Qaraḍāwī's important role in Qatar, manifested, for example, in his educational enterprises, his representation of Qatar at international conferences, and his appearance on influential television programs.[52] The very vehemence of the denials suggests that there was indeed some tension between al-Qaraḍāwī and the new emir. Nevertheless, al-Qaraḍāwī continues to live and work in Qatar, and the rumors regarding the revocation of his citizenship seem to be unfounded.

Al-Qaraḍāwī emphasizes that nobody in Qatar has ever tried to limit what he has said in his sermons and classes or to intervene in their content, even though he often has addressed sensitive issues and has not minced his words. He denies claims that following several of these sermons the Qatari authorities punished him by silencing him for a period; rather, if he was away from the mosque, it was due to other, unrelated reasons.[53] Summarizing forty years of living in Qatar, he reiterates that he has always felt completely at liberty to speak his mind there. He states that foreign ambassadors would occasionally complain to the former Qatari emir, Ḥamad b. Khalīfa Āl Thānī, about some of al-Qaraḍāwī's sermons or rulings, but that the emir always replied that he did not intervene in the affairs of clerics.[54]

The accuracy of these statements seems questionable, however. Al-Qaraḍāwī's sermons have often addressed political issues related to Qatar's foreign relations, and when his statements contravened Qatar's policies, it appears that the authorities did not refrain from acting. For example, the shaykh was apparently punished after a sermon he delivered on January 24, 2014, was dedicated to the Arab Spring revolutions, in particular the revolution in Egypt. In the sermon, al-Qaraḍāwī heaped praise upon Qatar for supporting the revolutions while so many others in the Arab world conspired against them, and he condemned the United Arab Emirates (UAE) for opposing every Islamic regime, for imprisoning the Arab Spring's proponents, and especially for sheltering Egyptian politician Aḥmad Shafīq (b. 1941), an associate of Egyptian president Husni Mubarak (b. 1928, president 1981–2011).[55] The shaykh also accused the Gulf Arabs of conspiring against "Islamic regimes" (presumably meaning the MB-associated regimes that emerged in several Arab countries following the Arab Spring).[56]

Following this sermon, al-Qaraḍāwī was absent from the mosque for three weeks. Upon his return, on February 21, he explained that he had fallen ill due to weather changes and his advanced age and condemned the "liars" and "hypocrites" who claimed the authorities had suspended him from preaching: "As long as I live and have a thinking mind, a speaking tongue, and a functioning body, I shall continue to preach and to tell the truth, no matter whom I please and whom I anger. I do not care about anyone's pleasure or anger; I care only about pleasing Allah."[57] Al-Qaraḍāwī's vehement and lengthy remarks suggest that there had indeed been some tension with the Qatari regime over his criticism of the UAE. Qatar's foreign minister at the time, Khālid b. Muḥammad al-ʿAtiyya (b. 1967), confirmed this when he clarified that al-Qaraḍāwī's statements in his sermon on January 24 did not reflect Qatar's foreign policy and that Qatar's relations with the UAE were strategic.[58]

It should be noted that although al-Qaraḍāwī has spent decades in Qatar and plays an important role there, he has remained Egyptian in essence. He still speaks in the Egyptian dialect (which is apparent even when he speaks in classical Arabic), and he constantly stresses that despite the hostility of the Egyptian regime toward him, he has never severed his ties with his homeland and its people, for they are an integral part of him and he of them. In this context, he wrote: "It is Egypt that frowns at me whenever I smile at it and bites my hand whenever I extend it in greeting. [But] when I say 'Egypt,' I mean the state, not the people. For, praise Allah, I am loved by the people of my homeland just as I am [loved] by other Muslims, [a love that] I sense and feel wherever I go in the Muslim lands. This is a divine boon for which I cannot be grateful enough."[59]

Al-Qaraḍāwī's Unique Relationship with the Muslim Brotherhood

According to al-Qaraḍāwī, after the ordeal of 1965 he asked that he be excused from his official duties within the MB in order to devote his time to serving all Muslims, of all schools, and in every country. Since then, he has repeatedly stressed that he remains loyal to the MB and its *da'wa* and has never stopped spreading the MB's message, for spreading this message is the objective he lives for and is willing to die for: "I am a son, a brother, and a father of the [MB's] *da'wa*; it is [part] of me, and I am [part] of it."[60] The shaykh notes that because he remained loyal to the MB and its *da'wa* even after withdrawing from the movement, many of its members consider him part of the MB. Some regard him as their primary *muftī* and rely on his rulings, and others regard him as the chief theoretician of the MB's *da'wa*, who formulates its foundations and develops its ideology. Al-Qaraḍāwī's book series "Toward a Unified Ideology for Those Promoting Islam," which are essentially his interpretation of al-Bannā's twenty fundamentals (discussed in chapter 2), reflect his latter role.[61]

Al-Qaraḍāwī's claim that he remained a prominent figure and a source of authority for the MB even after his official withdrawal from the movement is supported by the repeated requests he received to serve as the MB's supreme guide (*al-murshid al-'āmm*). According to the shaykh, he was offered this position on several occasions: after the death of Ḥasan al-Huḍaybī in 1973, the MB's second supreme guide, who fulfilled this position from 1951 until 1973;[62] after the appointment of al-Huḍaybī's successor, 'Umar al-Tilmisānī (d. 1986), who was supreme guide from 1973 to 1986 but insisted that his identity remain a secret and so was known as "the secret guide";[63] when al-Tilmisānī fell ill;[64] and finally after the appointment of Ma'mūn al-Huḍaybī (d. 2004), who was supreme guide from 2002 until his death but, according to al-Qaraḍāwī, was willing to step aside in al-Qaraḍāwī's favor.[65] The shaykh says, however, that he declined all the offers, preferring to be the guide of the Islamic *umma* as a whole.[66] The era of 'Umar al-Tilmisānī's leadership of the MB, during the Anwar Sadat presidency, provides further evidence of al-Qaraḍāwī's high standing in the movement despite his official withdrawal from it. When Anwar Sadat permitted the MB in Egypt to renew the publication of its journal *Al-Da'wa*, al-Tilmisānī, who was the journal's chief editor,[67] asked al-Qaraḍāwī to write for it, and he indeed contributed articles on issues such as jihad and al-Bannā's fundamentals as well as chapters from his book *The Education of a Preacher*.[68]

Describing one of the occasions on which he was offered the position of MB's supreme guide, al-Qaraḍāwī recounts that in 1976 he attended the first international conference on Muslim economics in Mecca. During this conference, he says, three senior MB figures approached him and asked him to serve as supreme guide in place of al-Tilmisānī, who was ill at the time. These figures explained that what the movement needed in that period, the mid-1970s, was a young, clever, and pious leader who combined jurisprudence and *sharīʿa*, understood the spirit of the age, remained loyal to the MB's *daʿwa*, and could be someone around whom the movement could unite. The shaykh, they said, possessed all these qualities and was therefore eminently suitable for the position. According to al-Qaraḍāwī, he declined the offer on the grounds that Allah had blessed him with religious knowledge but not with political acumen. He stressed this point in a letter he later wrote to Maḥmūd Abū al-Saʿūd (d. 1993), one of the figures who had made him the offer. In the letter, he explained that one had to know, like the Prophet Muḥammad, the unique qualities of one's companions and offer them the roles to which they were best suited. The MB *daʿwa*, he said, was religious in its character and objective but was realized by political means; therefore, it required a leader with a deep knowledge not only of the Islamic sources but also of politics, but he did not possess the latter knowledge. Al-Qaraḍāwī also mentioned that the slogan of the MB's *daʿwa* is "Allah is our objective" (*Allāh ghāyatunā*), so the movement needed a leader of surpassing spirituality and piety, whose purity of heart was such that it illuminated his surroundings, but he did not regard himself as being at that spiritual level.[69]

In this letter, the shaykh presented two arguments against his serving as supreme guide. The first, that he was insufficiently familiar with politics, seems like an excuse, considering his stated belief that the *sharīʿa* encompasses all domains of life, including politics, and that a *muftī* must therefore answer any question put to him, including on politics, after taking some time to study the matter.[70] In fact, al-Qaraḍāwī deals extensively with political jurisprudence (*al-fiqh al-siyāsī*), both on the theoretical level by laying down guidelines for it (see chapter 6) and on the practical level by issuing many rulings in this domain. The second argument—that he had not yet attained the appropriate spiritual level—may seem like an empty show of humility, but the shaykh took great pains to stress that it was not. He noted that good opinion of others is not always objective and that he knows himself better than anyone else.[71]

It seems, however, that the true reason behind al-Qaraḍāwī's rejection of the role was his stated desire to be an asset for all Muslims. This aspiration is rooted deep in his perception of the *umma*. The shaykh considers the Muslim *umma* and its unity to be a reality rather than a construct or an illusion,[72] and he wants this *umma*—which the Qur'ān (2:143) describes as "the nation of *wasaṭ*" (i.e., of the middle road)—to espouse *wasaṭiyya* and thereby gain its rightful place among the peoples of the world. Al-Qaraḍāwī believes that he can help attain this goal only if he serves as an ideologue for all Muslims, not just for a particular movement. He stresses that in today's world there is no place for small entities, but only for large and united ones, such as the European Union. Through *wasaṭiyya*, al-Qaraḍāwī aims to realize what he sees as the vast potential of Muslim culture and to free the Muslim nation of its sense of inferiority vis-à-vis the culture of the West. In this context, he told the worshippers at his Qatar mosque on November 19, 2000, "No, by Allah, we are not tails, for Allah created us to be heads. We are not slaves, for our mothers bore us to be free."[73] Al-Qaraḍāwī aspires to utilize the mass media capabilities of the globalized era, which have transformed the world into a "global village," to spread the *wasaṭī* message among Muslims and to champion it as the Muslim answer to the West. In pursuing both goals, he wishes to lead the Muslim nation as a whole and not just the MB.

The research literature offers some interesting explanations for the intriguing fact that al-Qaraḍāwī remained a spiritual leader and authority for the MB even after he ceased to be an official movement member. Husam Tammam attributes the shaykh's and his *wasaṭī* thinking's abiding influence on the MB to the fact that he is a very versatile Islamic scholar who deals with many different facets of Islamic philosophy.[74] He is at once a jurist, a preacher, an educator, and a commentator on Islamic current affairs who formulates the *wasaṭī* response to events affecting the Muslim nation. In addition, he is also the MB's poet and has composed many inspirational anthems aimed at imbuing the movement's youth with a spirit of fighting and rebellion.[75]

Tammam notes further that throughout the years al-Qaraḍāwī has remained loyal and committed to the MB's legitimate and unanimously selected leadership and has refrained from entering into direct conflict with it, despite his criticism of certain currents within the MB. As a faithful disciple of Ḥasan al-Bannā's *wasaṭī* current in the MB, the shaykh, as we saw, was certainly critical of Sayyid Quṭb's current, which was developed against al-Bannā's ideas. In fact, apart from the MB's second supreme guide, Ḥasan al-Huḍaybī, whose book *Preachers Not Judges* criticizes Quṭb's ideas, al-Qaraḍāwī was the most prominent MB figure who criticized some of Quṭb's ideas (see the introduction).[76]

Accordingly, the shaykh refrained from associating himself with factions that split off from the MB movement. This was particularly noticeable during the crisis of the Wasaṭ Party's (Ḥizb al-Wasaṭ) withdrawal from the MB in 1996. Al-Qaraḍāwī certainly identified with the party's program and was close to the MB members who founded it, all of them members of the MB's middle generation.[77] In fact, the party's founders were no doubt influenced by his political ideas, such as his ruling that sanctioned party pluralism (*taʿaddudiyya ḥizbiyya*), his concept of cultural Islam (*al-Islām al-ḥaḍārī*),[78] and, more broadly, the principles of *wasaṭiyya* that gradually took shape in the 1980s. The influence of these principles can be discerned in the party's platform.[79] However, in spite of this connection, al-Qaraḍāwī did not join the party, especially after its members withdrew from the MB.[80] Al-Qaraḍāwī's loyalty to the MB, says Tammam, explains why his writings continue to be an important source of authority for the movement.[81]

Tammam's explanations are convincing, but an examination of al-Qaraḍāwī's writings and rulings reveals three additional interesting factors that have a direct bearing on his unique relationship with the MB: the first has to do precisely with his considerable influence on the MB's middle generation, whose members are sometimes called the "New Brothers"; the second is al-Qaraḍāwī's vast esteem for and identification with the ideology of the MB and its founder al-Bannā; and the third is that al-Qaraḍāwī was first and foremost a legal authority for the MB (particularly for the mother organization in Egypt and for Hamas) and only later became a "global *muftī*." Al-Qaraḍāwī's position as a legal authority for the MB is reflected very clearly in his rulings that pertain to the Arab Spring and especially to the revolution in Egypt (the shaykh's so-called "*fiqh* of the revolution") (points that I discuss further later in this chapter).

Al-Qaraḍāwī's Influence on the Muslim Brotherhood's Middle Generation

The MB's middle generation is younger than the movement's founders but older than its youngest generation. At its core are Islamist student leaders who joined the MB in the 1970s and early 1980s and brought a new dynamism to the movement. The first role entrusted to them as leaders in the early 1980s was to promote the MB in the universities. With the encouragement of then supreme guide 'Umar al-Tilmisānī, they also put their energy into attaining prominent positions in Egypt's professional unions, and upon succeeding they launched many initiatives that far exceeded the unions' official role. To promote their goals, they formed ties with a wide range of professionals, regime officials, political parties, and civil society organizations, including ones that were not part of the Islamic current. Over time, because of their ongoing dialogue with figures outside the movement, including Copts, liberated and unveiled Muslim women, and representatives of humanitarian and human rights organizations around the globe, many of their principles and values began to change. This change caused tension and eventually a rift between the second-generation activists and the MB's veteran leadership.[82]

This tension increased over time. The senior leaders on the Guidance Bureau blocked the advancement of second-generation leaders to decision-making positions, and the second generation criticized the old guard's demand for blind obedience and loyalty. They complained that the veteran leaders, because of the long periods they had spent in jail or in exile, were out of touch with the great changes that were occurring in Egyptian society at the time. They also complained about the old guard's "victim complex" and its tendency toward secretiveness in managing the movement's affairs—traits that they said led to a troubled relationship with the state. They claimed that the old guard's behavior bore the mark of the MB's Secret Apparatus,[83] from which some of the Guidance

Bureau members had emerged. As the middle generation's ideas began to take shape, its members began calling themselves "the reformist group" or "the reformist current," and their reformist ideas began gaining traction within the MB among the older and younger generations alike.[84]

The middle generation's calls for change within the MB led to intense internal arguments in the movement. One point of contention concerned the values of liberty, pluralism, and human rights and their compatibility with the *sharīʿa*. The reformists claimed that these values can be found in the Qur'ān and the Sunna and in the example set by the Prophet. They returned to al-Bannā's treatises, placing emphasis on those that describe the Western parliamentary system as close to the Islamic ideal. They also criticized the MB's traditional position on the status of women, including the claim that a woman's role in society should be confined to the home and to her position as a wife and a mother (see chapter 6). These positions, they said, were backward and at odds with the egalitarian spirit of Islam and with the Prophet's own treatment of women.[85]

It should be borne in mind, however, that the leaders of the reformist current in the MB were professionals and political activists, not Islamic scholars. According to Carrie Rosefsky Wickham, the religious and religious-legal basis for their ideas was provided by independent scholars and intellectuals who during the 1980s and 1990s began to present more progressive interpretations of Islam as part of what was called "the new Islamic discourse." Chief among the proponents of this new line of thought were al-Qaraḍāwī and Muḥammad al-Ghazālī. Others were independent Egyptian thinkers, such as Muḥammad Salīm al-ʿAwwā, the former secretary of the IUMS; Ṭāriq al-Bishrī; Muḥammad ʿImāra; ʿAbd al-Wahhāb al-Masīrī (d. 2008); ʿĀdil Ḥusayn (b. 1932); and Fahmī Huwaydī. These thinkers presented significant arguments in favor of pluralism, democracy, and the civil rights of women and non-Muslims. They found proof for their ideas in classical Muslim texts and pretexts for them in Islamic history, thereby providing the ideas with religious-legal legitimacy. These "new Islamist intellectuals" found a receptive audience in the activists of the MB's middle generation, who read their writings, invited them to conferences, and sought their guidance and advice. Wickham writes that it was thanks to the MB reformists' efforts that these thinkers and intellectuals' ideas were translated into practical initiatives and plans.[86]

The influence of al-Qaraḍāwī's *wasaṭī* ideas can clearly be seen among the members of the MB's middle generation, which Gilles Kepel calls "the Neo-MB"[87] and whose most typical representatives are figures such as 'Abd al-Mun'im Abū al-Futūḥ, who was a member of the MB Guidance Bureau until 2011 and ran for president in Egypt in 2012, and 'Iṣām al-'Aryān, who would later become the deputy chairman of the MB's Freedom and Justice Party established following Egypt's revolution in 2011. Al-Qaraḍāwī's influence on this generation has been especially noticeable since the mid-1980s, when they began expressing a commitment to Islamic democracy as a form of government.[88] These figures stress that they do not aspire to establish a religious state in Egypt—that is, a theocracy—but rather wish to form a civil state whose source of authority is Islam.[89] They envision a state in which all citizens enjoy equal rights and duties by virtue of their Egyptian citizenship (*muwāṭana*), a principle that al-Qaraḍāwī claims derives from the Islamic sources.[90] According to this approach, Islam is the source of authority for the state in that it outlines the state's cultural, social, and political framework and dictates its fundamental principles; however, non-Muslim citizens, such as Egypt's Copts, are entitled to every civil right by virtue of their Egyptian citizenship—except the right to serve as the head of the state (in other words, the position of president is reserved for a Muslim, as al-Qaraḍāwī indicates in one of his rulings).[91]

One of this generation's most typical representatives, 'Abd al-Mun'im Abū al-Futūḥ, acknowledged al-Qaraḍāwī's considerable influence on the middle generation of the Egyptian MB. Al-Futūḥ describes al-Qaraḍāwī as the "correct thinker [*al-nānẓir al-qawīm*]" of the MB school of thought.[92] Furthermore, in the course of a meeting between al-Qaraḍāwī and his disciples in July 2007, Abū al-Futūḥ told him,

> The second generation of the revival [*iḥyā'*] of the Muslim Brotherhood, those called "the generation of the Islamic Awakening of the 1970s," recognize the grace that Allah has bestowed upon you, [which has enabled

> you] to clarify what was blurred, explain what was unclear, and make what was difficult easy . . . as you asked guidance from the words of Allah, may He be blessed and glorified: "Say [God here addresses the Prophet Muḥammad], 'This is my way: based on clear evidence, I, and all who follow me [those who believe in my mission and are guided by me], call [people] to God [convince the people on the basis of clear and certain evidence]' [Q12:108]."[93]

Al-Qaraḍāwī's Vast Esteem for the Muslim Brotherhood and Its Founder, Ḥasan al-Bannā

Al-Qaraḍāwī regards the MB as a movement of renewal (*tajdīd*) and reform (*iṣlāḥ*) that forms a significant part of the Islamic Awakening and whose uniqueness lies in several factors: the perception of Islam as a comprehensive system encompassing all domains of life; the call for unity and concord; the rejection of all factors that distance people from Islam and blacken its image; and the emphasis on building and shaping consciousness through education.[94] In his wide-ranging and multidimensional activity, al-Qaraḍāwī has worked to promote the MB enterprise, transforming it from a sectoral goal into a pan-Muslim goal while working to forge a culture of *wasaṭiyya*.

Listing the MB's achievements over the years, al-Qaraḍāwī states that on the ideological level this movement managed to oppose the West's "cultural invasion" and to restore the Muslims' faith in Islam and its mission; on the emotional level, it succeeded in enhancing Muslim engagement with the problems of the *umma*, especially the Palestinian problem; on the educational level, it raised generations of Muslims with a deep understanding of Islam as an inclusive and comprehensive system; in the domain of jihad, it managed to revive not only spiritual jihad (*jihād al-nafs*)—individuals' struggle against their evil inclinations—but also physical jihad against the imperialist forces and the tyrannical regimes in Muslim countries; on the economic level, it succeeded in outlining a Muslim economy as an alternative to both capitalism and socialism; and on the social level, it provided many necessary social services to the populace.[95] Al-Qaraḍāwī adds that all these goals and achievements are also shared by the *wasaṭī* stream, which managed to form itself into an ideological school in the spirit of al-Bannā and the MB but at the same time adapted its messages to the changing reality. The shaykh holds that many of the challenges that prompted the founding of the MB in the late 1920s still face Islam today. In order to cope with such challenges inside and outside the Muslim world, he says, he developed the *wasaṭī* movement and combined in himself the roles of preacher and jurist.

The figure al-Qaraḍāwī most admires is his spiritual mentor, Ḥasan al-Bannā, as expressed in a poem he wrote in al-Bannā's honor. The poem, which begins his poetry collection *The Muslims Are Coming*, reads:

> They thought you dead, yet you live forever,
> only the criminal tyrant dies.
> They thought you gone, yet you are present,
> with your teachings we shall illuminate any dark path.
> You built for Islam a castle
> whose bricks are Muslim youths;
> you wrote for the world a constitution of revival
> and made sure to sign it in blood.
> . . . .
> The love for you shall remain carved in [our] hearts,
> your light shall remain in [our] minds and your name on [our] tongues.[96]

Al-Qaraḍāwī and Hamas as a Muslim Brotherhood Movement

Al-Qaraḍāwī identifies with Hamas as a resistance movement affiliated with the MB.[97] He supplies Hamas with religious justification for its actions, even when these actions are questionable from a religious standpoint and even starkly contravene the *sharīʿa*. For example, he did so in the ruling he issued in February 2007, during the conflict between Fath and Hamas in the Gaza Strip, which included violent clashes between the two movements and culminated in the Hamas takeover of the Gaza Strip in June (what Fath calls the "Gaza coup"). During the clashes, Hamas militants took over Fath's institutions in Gaza and shot Fath activists to death. Al-Qaraḍāwī stated unequivocally that in the war between the two sides, the aggressor and oppressor was Fath. Fath, he explained, was fighting Hamas on behalf of the Zionists or their "Crusader" allies, such as the Americans, whereas Hamas was acting in legitimate self-defense and killing Fath members out of necessity, not out of choice. Hence, he concluded, a Fath member killed in the clashes would go to hell, whereas a Hamas member killed in them would go to heaven as a martyr (*shahīd*).[98]

In his ruling, al-Qaraḍāwī quoted a prophetic *ḥadīth* that on the face of it contradicts his position: "[The Prophet once proclaimed]: 'If two Muslims confront each other with swords, then both the killer and the killed will be in hellfire.' It was said [to him], 'O Messenger of Allah, [we understand that is the fate] of the killer, but what about the one killed?' The Prophet said, 'Verily, he intended to kill his companion.'" This *ḥadīth* states that in the case of a war among Muslims, both the killers and the killed are doomed to hell. However, in interpreting this *ḥadīth*, al-Qaraḍāwī argued that the punishment of hell applies only under certain conditions: if a Muslim fights his fellow Muslim out of pre-Islamic tribal bigotry (*'aṣabiyya*), out of love of this world (as opposed to love of the world to come), out of capitulation to impulse, or in submission and obedience to the enemies of the Muslim *umma*. All of these conditions apply to Fath, he said. The shaykh claimed further that the *ḥadīth* does not apply to a Muslim who fights his fellow Muslim out of *ijtihād* (i.e., in a sincere attempt to comply with the teachings of Islam), even if the *ijtihād* is misguided, and therefore the *ḥadīth* does not apply to Hamas. In other words, according to the shaykh, it is one's inner intention that determines whether the *ḥadīth* applies or not. Because Hamas members killed Fath members out of a pure and worthy intention, but Fath members killed Hamas members out of a condemnable intention, the latter are doomed to hell, but the former are not.[99]

This ruling, in which al-Qaraḍāwī gave a slanted interpretation of the *ḥadīth* in order to justify Hamas's acts of murder, contradicts what he wrote in his comprehensive book on jihad. In this book, he presents the same *ḥadīth* as evidence that a Muslim may not fight his fellow Muslim and that such warfare does not count as jihad in Islam. He also stresses that the Prophet in his farewell sermon (*khuṭbat al-wadā'*) warned the

Muslims against fighting one another: "After my departure, do not go back to being unbelievers, smiting each other's necks."[100] The shaykh's ruling in February 2007 shows that he favors the MB (in this case the MB's Palestinian branch, Hamas) even when this favoritism requires permitting what is forbidden by both the Qur'ān and the *ḥadīth*. It is owing to such rulings that the Salafis accuse al-Qaraḍāwī of being a partisan *muftī* who represents the MB rather than the Muslim *umma* as a whole.[101]

Hamas acknowledged al-Qaraḍāwī's contribution to the struggle in a conference it held in Gaza in 2010, titled "Dr. Yūsuf al-Qaraḍāwī's Efforts in the Service of Islam and in Promoting the Palestinian Cause." At the conference, held by Hamas's Ministry of Endowment and Islamic Affairs, Gaza Strip prime minister Ismā'īl Haniyya (b. 1963) said that the shaykh had "strengthened the Islamic character" of the Palestinian problem. This was necessary, he explained, in light of the conspiracy to withdraw this problem from the Islamic sphere and confine it to the Arab sphere—and ultimately to the Palestinian sphere alone. Haniyya added that, on top of these efforts as well as the shaykh's intensive activity in favor of Jerusalem,[102] al-Qaraḍāwī engages in extensive activity to liberate al-Aqṣā Mosque from the Zionists. This activity includes propaganda, fund-raising, and urging the Islamic countries to rally to the cause. Al-Qaraḍāwī considers jihad for the liberation of al-Aqṣā to be the most important kind of jihad today.

According to Hanniya, al-Qaraḍāwī is thus worthy of the title "Shaykh al-Aqṣā," alongside Shaykh Rā'id Ṣalāḥ (b. 1958), head of the Northern Branch of the Islamic Movement in Israel. Haniyya noted further that al-Qaraḍāwī supported the resistance (*muqāwama*) and the jihad in Palestine and that Hamas's resistance needed his voice and the voice of other *'ulamā'* who draw a distinction between legitimate resistance and terror (*irhāb*). He stressed that al-Qaraḍāwī also exhorted the Islamic *umma* to extend financial, political, moral, and material assistance to the jihad in Palestine. He specifically commended him for uttering "the word of truth [*kalimat al-ḥaqq*]" regarding martyrdom (*istishhād*) operations when other *'ulamā'* questioned their legitimacy. Finally, he praised al-Qaraḍāwī's position on the Gaza siege and his call for Muslims outside Gaza to organize convoys to break the siege.[103]

Al-Qaraḍāwī as an *ʿĀlim*

Al-Qaraḍāwī's role as a scholar (*ʿālim*) must be understood in light of the central place he attributes to religious scholars in Islam.[104] A well-known *ḥadīth* states that "the Islamic scholars are inheritors of the prophets [*al-ʿulamāʾ warathat al-anbiyāʾ*]."[105] Interpreting this *ḥadīth*, al-Qaraḍāwī explains that scholars, like prophets, serve as ambassadors of God to His creatures; their role is to guide people in His way, transmit His *daʿwa*, act as an honest judge in disagreements and disputes, and warn His people of dangers. The corruption of rulers, he says, often stems from the corruption of scholars, for the latter are responsible for the rulers' moral health, just as physicians are responsible for their patients' physical health. And if the physician is corrupt or incompetent, who then will heal the patient?[106] According to al-Qaraḍāwī, true scholars are *rabbāniyyūn*:[107] they revere God, and He alone is their guiding light. Hence, they serve truth and guide the nation, and they are the nation's salvation in times of crisis. True scholars do not distinguish between theory and practice or between learning and *daʿwa*: what they think and believe is also what they practice and preach. Al-Qaraḍāwī believes that scholars are "the victorious group [*al-ṭāʾifa al-manṣūra*]" mentioned in the eponymous *ḥadīth*—the group that will remain triumphant on the right path, can never be harmed by those who desert it, and will retain this status until the Day of Judgment.[108]

Al-Qaraḍāwī's Debate with al-Azhar's Establishment Shaykhs: "The *Fiqh* of the Revolution"

Al-Qaraḍāwī: The Muslim Brotherhood's Source of Authority

The debate between al-Qaraḍāwī and the establishment shaykhs hinges on two legal issues: (1) the boundaries of obedience to Muslim leaders against the backdrop of the Arab Spring; (2) the religious legitimacy of the Oslo Accords (1993, 1995) and al-Qaraḍāwī's confrontation with ʿAbd al-ʿAzīz b. ʿAbdallah Ibn Bāz (d. 1999), who served as the *muftī* of Saudi Arabia from 1992 to 1999.

Al-Qaraḍāwī expressed his criticism of "the ruler's clerics [*'ulamā' al-salāṭīn*]"—that is, the clerics subservient to the regime—and of al-Azhar as an arm of the regime in the context of the revolution in Egypt in 2011. This criticism can also shed light on the important role he played in shaping "the jurisprudence of the revolution" (*fiqh al-thawra*) especially in Egypt—namely, the body of rulings issued during this revolution that brought about the ouster of President Husni Mubarak in 2011 and the subsequent rise to power of Muhammad Mursi in June 2012 after the presidential elections in Egypt. According to the shaykh, his main role in the revolution was to counter the rulings of the regime's clerics—including Egypt's chief *muftī* at the time, 'Alī Gum'a (b. 1952, served as chief *muftī* from 2003 to 2013)[109]—which, he says, misled the youth. These misleading clerics, he says, ruled that the youth had reignited internal strife (*fitna*) among Muslims,[110] preached anarchy, championed the ideology of the Khawārij, and deviated from the correct path. His own rulings refuted these dubious accusations, al-Qaraḍāwī says.[111]

Al-Qaraḍāwī's rulings during the Arab Spring uprisings,[112] especially the revolution and counterrevolution in Egypt, are perhaps the best proof of the shaykh's strong affiliation with the MB despite his nonmembership in it.[113] His unreserved support for the Mursi regime and his complete identification with the MB are also evident in a ruling he gave in January 2014 in which he proclaimed it a religious duty to boycott the Egyptian referendum on 'Abd al-Fattah al-Sisi's proposed constitution. He ruled: "I regard participation in the constitutional referendum and in any activity that may strengthen this coup regime, lend it legitimacy, prolong its existence, or increase its might as cooperation in sin and aggression [Q5:2] and as an act that is forbidden [*muḥarram*] according to the *sharī'a* of Allah the Almighty." Al-Qaraḍāwī based his opposition to the referendum on Q5:2 and several other Qur'ānic verses as well as on *ḥadīth*s, by means of which he characterized the al-Sisi regime as "straying" from the path of religious truth (Q10:32) and al-Sisi and his officials as ones who "do wrong" (Q11:113) and as "criminals" (Q28:17). Quoting an Arabic proverb—"Allah delays but does not neglect [punishing transgressors] [*Allāh yumhilu wa-lā yuhmilu*]"—he warned those who carried out the coup to beware Allah's wrath and advised them not to think that they would escape punishment, even if the punishment were delayed.[114]

Al-Qaraḍāwī sees considerable resemblance between Mursi's fate and the treatment he himself received at the hands of the Egyptian regime as well as more broadly between the MB's bitter trials in the 1950s and 1960s and the movement's situation in Egypt today. He expressed this resemblance in his harsh criticism of the ruling an Egyptian court issued regarding Mursi in April 2015. The court sentenced Mursi to twenty years in prison for his role in the December 5–6, 2012, events at the Ittiḥādiyya, the presidential palace, in which Mursi's supporters clashed with demonstrators who were protesting against him and his proposed constitution. In his response to the court's ruling, al-Qaraḍāwī praised Mursi's steadfastness and the sacrifices he had made for his faith, homeland, and *umma*. In this statement, the shaykh also included several lines from his *qaṣīda nūniyya*: "O Lord, deliver Egypt from its enemies and help [us resist] its cursed idol [*ṭāghūt*], for the situation has become unbearable, and your decree requires only the letters *kāf* and *nūn* [i.e., your decree will be realized instantly]."[115] With this quote, al-Qaraḍāwī drew a direct link between his own imprisonment in the 1950s and Mursi's imprisonment today and implied that today, just like then, Egypt is ruled by cruel and idolatrous tyrants.[116]

In light of these statements, it is not surprising that ʿAbd al-Fattah al-Sisi's regime regards al-Qaraḍāwī as an MB propagandist and that it included him in the long list of MB leaders and activists sentenced to death in May 2015. The figures on the list, headed by Muhammad Mursi, were convicted (many of them, including al-Qaraḍāwī, in absentia) of involvement in the mass escape from the Wādī al-Natrūn prison during the uprising against Mubarak in 2011 and of leaking state secrets to Hamas. Following this death sentence, al-Qaraḍāwī issued an important statement, in which he said, inter alia:

> Is this the punishment you hand me for saying the truth out loud and because I supported the right of the [Egyptian] people to attain its liberty? Do you [think that] you scare me with this death sentence? My motto in life, since I began to seek knowledge [i.e., to study Islam] and to engage in *daʿwa*, has been "[Allah praises] those who convey the

> messages of Allah and fear Him and do not fear anyone but Allah. And sufficient is Allah as Accountant" [Q33:39]. Since my early youth, I have cried, like all my brethren: "Death for the sake of Allah is our highest hope [*al-mawt fī sabīl Allāh asmā amānīnā*]."[117]

Al-Qaraḍāwī versus 'Alī Gum'a: A Confrontation with the Religious Establishment

It is important to note that in his debate with 'Alī Gum'a, al-Qaraḍāwī describes himself as a true scholar (*'ālim ḥaqīqī*), in contrast to Gum'a and his ilk, whom he describes as "false" scholars (*'ulamā' mufta'alūn*) because, according to him, they are the Egyptian regime's mouthpieces. The controversy between al-Qaraḍāwī and Gum'a deepened in the wake of the Arab Spring events. The theological argument between al-Qaraḍāwī and Gum'a over these events, especially in Egypt, revolves around two main interrelated questions: (1) Do these popular uprisings constitute *fitna*, civil war and anarchy, which are forbidden by the *sharī'a*? (b) According to the *sharī'a*, what circumstances justify coming out (*khurūj*) against a Muslim ruler, and in the context of Egypt do the rebels who rose up against Mubarak and against Mursi constitute Khawārij and *bughāh* (in Muslim jurisprudence, *bughāh* is the term for rebels against a legitimate ruler, whom the ruler is entitled to fight), or was their rebellion legitimate?

In fact, al-Qaraḍāwī proclaimed all the Arab Spring revolutions—in Tunisia, Egypt, Libya, and later Syria—to be the greatest blessing bestowed by Allah upon the Muslim *umma*. When Egyptian *muftī* 'Alī Gum'a described the anti-Mubarak demonstrations as a form of forbidden civil strife, citing the *ḥadīth* that says, "*Fitna* is asleep; Allah curse the one who awakens it," al-Qaraḍāwī declared this utterance, which is not even a *ḥadīth*, to be immaterial from a juristic and religious point of view and reiterated that the Egyptian revolution was a divine blessing.[118] He accused Gum'a and other establishment clerics of misusing the term *fitna* by applying it to anything that displeased the regime. These clerics, he said, characterized any protest or uprising against the authorities as a call for anarchy, while welcoming any measure that protected the tyrants and their corruption as promoting stability and security.[119]

With respect to al-Qaraḍāwī's position on the scholars who serve the regimes, as he describes them, it should be noted, however, that he changed his religious opinion about loyalty to Muslim rulers and the circumstances that justify rebellion against them. His position before the Arab Spring differed considerably from his position after this historic development. Prior to 2011, al-Qaraḍāwī took issue with the *fiqh* of Islamic groups that waged violent jihad against the authorities in Islamic countries, such as the Egyptian Islamic Jihad, which was responsible for the assassination of Anwar Sadat in 1981. He argued that these groups' *fiqh* was false (*maz'ūm*) in that it justified the use of violence. He agreed with these groups that *sharī'a* law should be implemented in all domains of life and that the regimes in most Muslim countries were guilty of violating the *sharī'a*. He therefore shared their belief that these regimes required reform but not their belief that using force was a legitimate means to achieve this reform. He argued that reform should be achieved through wise and gentle *da'wa*—that is, by advising the rulers and guiding them, commanding right and forbidding wrong. Before the Arab Spring and in particular before the Egyptian revolution of January 25, 2011, al-Qaraḍāwī pointed to *ḥadīth*s that enjoin Muslims to patiently endure oppression by a ruler as long as he does not commit acts of blatant heresy (*kufr bawāḥ*) that are explicitly forbidden by the Qur'ān. He placed emphasis on *ḥadīth*s such as the following: "One who found in his emir something that he disliked should hold his patience, for one who separated from the main body of the Muslims, even to the extent of a handspan, and then he died, would die the death of one belonging to the days of Jāhiliyya."[120]

Elaborating on his position, al-Qaraḍāwī clarified that when fulfilling the commandment of "putting right what is wrong [*taghyīr al-munkar*]"—for instance, by deposing a government that is violating the *sharī'a*—a Muslim must observe the juristic principle of choosing the lesser evil (*akhaff al-ḍararayni*); that is, he must make sure that his action will not yield more evil than it prevents. Armed rebellion against sinful rulers (*fasaqa*) or oppressive ones, he said, can lead to a civil war in which innocents die, property is stolen, security is lost, and anarchy spreads; in that case, "the harm caused by deposing [he ruler] surpasses [the harm caused] by his remaining [in power]."[121]

Furthermore, in addressing the issue of rulers who fail to enforce certain *sharīʿa* laws—such as the Qur'ānic punishments (e.g., cutting off a thief's hand) and the prohibitions on usury and the drinking of wine—al-Qaraḍāwī distinguished two categories of contemporary Muslim rulers. In the first category are rulers who recognize Islam as the state religion and the *sharīʿa* as the source of legislation yet do not enforce *sharīʿa* law in all aspects of life. These rulers, argued the shaykh, are comparable to Muslims who recite the two testimonies and follow some of the religious commandments but also commit major sins; they are sinners but are not *murtaddūn*, apostates, who should be excluded from the fold of Islam. In the second category are radical secularist rulers who treat the *sharīʿa* with hostility and contempt, presenting it as the opposite of civilization and progress. These rulers permit what Allah forbids and forbid what Allah permits, and they work to divest the public of religion. Before the Arab Spring, al-Qaraḍāwī placed most of the Muslim rulers in the former category and ruled that violent rebellion against them was forbidden. Regarding rulers of the second kind, he ruled that they must be rebelled against as long as the Muslims have the ability to stage a successful uprising. But he asserted that even in their case it was preferable "to agree on peaceful means of bringing change and utilize [various methods] developed in the world, such as democratic means of bringing change or other methods that will not result in civil war upon the land and in great corruption." He also proclaimed that "the error of exonerating one hundred infidels is lighter than the error of shedding the blood of one innocent Muslim."[122]

However, after the outbreak of the Arab Spring, al-Qaraḍāwī changed his position, adopting a much more radical line on rebellion against authority. In the matter of the uprising against Mubarak, for example, he ruled that, according to Q4:59, Muslims are commanded to obey a ruler only if he is "a believer." The shaykh then quoted many additional verses to establish who counts as a "believer," including Q5:44–47, according to which "whosoever does not rule by what Allah has revealed" is counted among the infidels (*kāfirūn*), oppressors (*ẓālimūn*), and sinners (*fāsiqūn*).[123] Before 2011, the shaykh had claimed that Q5:44–47 refers to a class of rulers who are guilty only of lesser heresy, which does not exclude them from the fold of Islam, for they recognize Islam as the state religion and build mosques, and they pray and follow other Islamic commandments.[124] Among these rulers he presumably counted Mubarak. Conversely, after 2011, he ruled that Mubarak was not a believer who must be obeyed, for he did not recognize Islam as a source of authority, did not turn to Islam for judgment, and often rejected the word of Allah and His Messenger. Al-Qaraḍāwī added that "no ruler merits automatic obedience, especially if he is one of the *murtaddūn* or the hypocrites [*munāfiqūn*]."[125]

However, al-Qaraḍāwī's juridical objection to armed opposition to Muslim regimes and to accusing them of unbelief stands in stark contradiction to a number of his rulings in the framework of his "jurisprudence of the revolution" with respect to the Arab Spring. For example, in a Friday sermon in February 2011 he called for killing Muʿammar Gaddafi (d. 2011) because, he argued, the entire Libyan nation must not be sacrificed for the sake of its ruler; therefore, al-Qaraḍāwī proclaimed, "whoever can come close to Allah [that is, become a martyr] by killing him [Gaddafi], let him do so, and his blood shall be on me [literally, on my neck]."[126] He commanded the Libyan soldiers and commanders to disobey Gaddafi because the Prophet said in a *ḥadīth*: "It is obligatory upon a Muslim to listen [to the ruler] and obey whether he likes it or not, except when he is ordered to do a sinful thing; in such case, there is no obligation to listen or to obey."[127]

Contradictions in al-Qaraḍāwī's position can be found with respect to other issues as well. For example, he does not always follow the principles he sets out in his *fiqh al-ikhtilāf*. For example, as part of this *fiqh*, he advocates avoiding bitter rivalry and expressions of disrespect for *ʿulamāʾ*.[128] However, he has been known to violate this principle—for instance, in his clash with ʿAlī Gumʿa. During the 2011 revolution, Gumʿa supported the Mubarak regime and issued *fatwā*s against the protests demanding his ouster, a position that drew fire from al-Qaraḍāwī. Some of the shaykh's arguments against Gumʿa were academic and objective, but much of his criticism was extremely blunt and reflected a deep personal animus toward the *muftī*. He stated that upon attaining the role of *muftī*, Gumʿa had apparently lost his mind, causing him to issue misguided (*shādhdha*) *fatwā*s unanchored in accurate knowledge. He also said that the school of thought Gumʿa adhered to was known to all: the school of following the ruler, defending him, justifying his sins, and seeking justifications for his atrocities. Al-Qaraḍāwī also accused Gum'a of regarding the Egyptian people as rabble without rights.[129]

Rulings on the Peace Accords with Israel

The dispute between al-Qaraḍāwī and the establishment shaykhs is thrown into sharp focus by their debate on the peace agreements with Israel (in this case the Oslo Accords). An examination of their rulings can shed light on the difference between the approach of the *wasaṭī* al-Qaraḍāwī; the approach of 'Abd al-'Azīz Ibn Bāz, who served as Saudi Arabia's grand *muftī*; and the approach of the jihadi Salafīs.[130] Ibn Bāz ruled that a truce (*hudna*) with enemies is permissible if the Muslim ruler deems it beneficial, whether it is a permanent *hudna* (which he called *hudna muṭlaqa*) or a temporary one (which he called *hudna mu'aqqata*). He added that peace (*ṣulḥ*) with Jews or other infidels does not require the Muslims to love them or to be loyal to them (*muwālāh*). It entails only the avoidance of mutual harm. Moreover, there is nothing wrong with maintaining commercial and diplomatic relations with them, he explained.[131] Al-Qaraḍāwī rejects this ruling with respect to agreements with Israel, in this case the Oslo Accords. He says that Ibn Bāz's error stems from a deficient understanding—not of *sharī'a* law or of the textual evidence, but of the reality in Palestine, which has demonstrated that the "false" peace agreements, as al-Qaraḍāwī calls them, benefit only Israel, not the Palestinians.[132]

Like other rulings sanctioning peace with Israel (such as a *fatwā* by Egyptian *muftī* Jāda al-Ḥaqq 'Alī Jāda al-Ḥaqq [d. 1996] sanctioning the Camp David Accords of 1979), Ibn Bāz's *fatwā* permitting the Oslo Accords relies on Q8:61, which states that if the enemies "incline to peace [*janaḥū li-l-salm*]," the Muslims must incline to it as well.[133] Al-Qaraḍāwī rejects the application of this verse to the Jews on the grounds that the Jews, who stole the land of Palestine, are aggressive by nature and have never been inclined to peace. He proposes that the legitimacy of the peace accords with Israel be assessed on the basis of a different verse, Q47:35: "So do not weaken and call for peace while you are superior; and Allah is with you and will never deprive you of [the reward of] your deeds."[134] The two scholars' distinct interpretations of this verse reveal their different positions on the relations with non-Muslims in the context of war. Ibn Bāz holds that the verse refers to a situation where the oppressed have become stronger than their oppressors but not to a situation where the oppressed are weaker than their oppressors, as is the case in Palestine.[135] Al-Qaraḍāwī, in contrast, contends that this verse exhorts the Muslims to call for peace only from a position of strength. According to him, the intention of the verse is to remind them that they are always superior because Islam is a religion "that ascends and cannot be exceeded," as stated in a *ḥadīth*, and because the Muslims' truth supersedes the polytheists' falsehood and their monotheism supersedes the polytheists' idolatry (*shirk*). To his mind, Ibn Bāz's interpretation disrespects the Muslims and turns them into defeatists who consider only benefit rather than moral values when calling for peace.[136]

Al-Qaraḍāwī's interpretation implies that the Muslims always have the upper hand, for theirs is the true and victorious religion, and that this consideration should be the Muslims' point of departure in pursuing peace. He understands the verse to refer not only to military superiority, as most exegetes (including Ibn Bāz) have understood it, but also to religious and creedal superiority.[137] A view similar to al-Qaraḍāwī's is taken by the jihadi Salafī shaykh ʿAbd al-Raḥmān ʿAbd al-Khāliq (b. 1939), who has ruled that Muslims must not call for peace with the infidels, except in two cases. First, they can do so when the infidels are weak and inclined to peace. In that case, peace is in the Muslims' interest, for their religion is in a position of strength, and peace may create conditions favorable to the conversion of infidels. Second, they can do so when peace is the lesser evil from the Muslims' perspective.[138]

Ibn Bāz ruled similarly that peace with non-Muslims is permitted when the Muslims are unable to wage jihad against them and force them either to convert to Islam (if they are polytheists) or to pay the *jizya* (if they are People of the Book). In other words, he sanctions the making of peace if there is need (*ḥāja*) for it or if it is an unavoidable necessity (*ḍarūra*).[139] Al-Qaraḍāwī, in contrast, claims that this permission to make peace applies only to *jihād al-ṭalab*, where the Muslims seek out the enemy in the latter's territory and which is a collective (rather than an individual) duty. This type of war can be avoided if necessary, he says. However, the jihad in

Palestine is not *jihād al-ṭalab* but rather *jihād al-dafʿ*, a jihad to repel the enemy, which is an individual duty and must be undertaken at any cost. In other words, al-Qaraḍāwī's position is that in the case of Palestine peace is not an option; the enemy (Israel) must be driven out.[140]

Interestingly, al-Qaraḍāwī's criticism of Ibn Bāz's *fatwā* echoes statements made about this *fatwā* by Osama bin Laden. Like al-Qaraḍāwī, bin Laden accused Ibn Bāz of being ignorant of the reality in Palestine and claimed that the Jews are the aggressors, which mandates waging jihad against them. As another argument, he stated that the "apostate" Muslim rulers are fundamentally unqualified to assess the Muslim interest and therefore also unqualified to decide on making peace with the enemies. In fact, bin Laden accused Ibn Bāz of granting legitimacy to these "secular" regimes.[141] Ibn Bāz, in contrast, ruled that every Muslim leader must assess the interest of his people and take whatever course of action he deems beneficial as long as it does not contravene the *sharīʿa*. Moreover, once the leader has engaged in *ijtihād* and determined the good of the people, the latter must accept his decision.[142] Here again, al-Qaraḍāwī agreed with bin Laden and not with Ibn Bāz. He ruled that in the case of peace with Israel, there is no obligation to obey the ruler, for the duty of obedience to the ruler is not absolute but conditional: a Muslim ruler must be obeyed if his directives are religiously sound (*maʿrūf*), but not if they contravene the *sharīʿa*. The shaykh also asserted that the duty of obedience implied in Q4:59 does not apply to a leader who rules within boundaries prescribed by his enemies (as is the case in Palestine). Furthermore, it is his firm position that capitulating to the Jews and conceding Muslim land to them is never in the Muslims' interests.[143]

Al-Qaraḍāwī's position on peace with Israel also corresponds to the position of jihadi ideologue ʿAbdallah ʿAzzām (d. 1989), who ruled that Muslims must not sign a peace agreement with unbelievers that grants the latter sovereignty over any Muslim territory. "Muslim land," he wrote, "does not belong to any [specific Muslims], and nobody has the right to negotiate over it."[144] He also determined that when jihad is an individual duty (as in the case of Palestine, where the enemy has invaded Muslim land), no peace (*ṣulḥ*) with the occupier is possible. Al-Qaraḍāwī, too, pronounced the Oslo Accords null and void because they recognize Israel's right to and sovereignty over Muslim land.[145] Ibn Bāz, in contrast, stated in his *fatwā* that the Oslo Accords do not involve recognition that Palestine belongs to the Jews. Their ownership, he said, is temporary, until the Muslims are strong enough to drive them out of the country.[146]

Al-Qaraḍāwī rejects the main argument made in favor of peace agreements with Israel—namely, the precedent of the Treaty of al-Ḥudaybiyya between Muḥammad and the Quraysh tribe (628 CE). The shaykh makes two points on this argument: first, the Quraysh tribe was not an "alien corn" in Mecca, unlike Israel, which is a "foreign entity" (*kiyān dakhīl*) in Palestine; second, the Treaty of al-Ḥudaybiyya was a temporary peace, whereas the peace agreements with Israel, including the Oslo Accords, recognize the Jews' right to the land they stole and are therefore meant to be permanent.[147] Ibn Bāz's response to this argument is worth noting. He claims that the Quraysh stole the money and homes of the immigrants (*muhājirūn*) (Q59:8), yet Muḥammad nevertheless made a *hudna* with them because he judged it to be in the Muslims' best interest. However, two years later, after the Quraysh violated the agreement and when the Prophet was strong enough to fight them, he invaded their homes during the conquest (*fatḥ*) of Mecca and shattered the idols at the Ka'ba.[148]

Al-Qaraḍāwī's ruling on the peace agreements with Israel and in particular on the Oslo Accords is colored by his perception of the so-called "Zionist challenge." The Muslim *umma*, he believes, will never be able to realize its aspirations of progress and growth as long as it is faced with the Zionist enterprise, for this enterprise opposes the very existence of the Muslim *umma* and seeks to divide it, so fighting it is both a religious duty and an objective necessity. Thus, it is not surprising that, for al-Qaraḍāwī, the greatest danger of the peace agreements with Israel lies in the possibility of normalization (*taṭbī'*) between Israel and the Arab countries. Israel, he says, seeks integration in the region by affecting a psychological and cerebral change in the local peoples, causing them to accept its aggressive presence in their midst. Normalization—that is, the acceptance of the Zionist entity as a natural part of the landscape—is intended to realize the Jewish dream in the region: to eliminate the terms *Arab homeland* and *Muslim homeland* in favor of a neutral geographical designation, *the Middle East*. In other words, normalization is part of Israel's attempt to subjugate the Arabs and Muslims.[149] In stark contrast to this position, Shākir al-Nābulsī's neoliberal platform (a full translation of which is presented in appendix B) advocates political and cultural normalization with the enemies, stating that "normalization and cross-pollination [*talāquḥ*] among nations and cultures are the way to a lasting peace in the Middle East." It also stresses the importance of transforming the agreements with Israel (the Camp David Accords with Egypt, the Oslo Accords with the Palestinians, and the Wadi Araba Agreement with Jordan) into peace agreements not only between countries but between the peoples.[150]

Is the International Union of Muslim Scholars an Independent Body?

Upon its establishment in 2004, the IUMS declared itself to be different from other religious institutions, such as al-Azhar, which are subordinate to and financed by the state, so that the state largely controls their attitudes and their rulings. It also declared that it includes only true scholars (*'ulamā' ḥaqīqiyyūn*), whose role is to serve the truth and guide the Islamic nation to the correct path.[151] According to al-Qaraḍāwī, such scholars are devoted to God (*rabbāniyyūn*) and are deeply knowledgeable, and they are the ones of whom the Qur'ān says (33:39) that they "deliver God's messages and fear only Him and no other." As a matter of fact, this verse adorns the IUMS emblem (see p. 138).[152]

In his dispute with the *'ulamā'* of al-Azhar on the Egyptian revolution in 2011, al-Qaraḍāwī claimed that their rulings were biased in favor of the regime, whereas the rulings of the IUMS, which he heads, were objective and independent, resting solely upon the Qur'ān and the Sunna and uninfected by political agendas. This claim is belied, however, by the ruling the IUMS issued on January 30, 2011, which referred to the uprising as "the blessed intifada in Egypt" and proclaimed that the protesters killed by the security forces in late January 2011 had the status of martyrs (*shuhadā'*). The ruling stated: "The lord of all martyrs was Ḥamza b. 'Abd al-Muṭṭalib [the Prophet's uncle, who died in the battle of Uḥud in 625 CE], and whosoever rises up against an oppressing and tyrannical ruler and that ruler attacks him, captures him, and kills him [is a martyr of the

3. The emblem of the International Union of Muslim Scholars, founded by al-Qaraḍāwī in 2004. The emblem contains a quotation of Q33:39: “Those who convey the messages of Allah and fear Him and do not fear anyone but Allah. And sufficient is Allah as Accountant.” (From “International Union of Muslim Scholars Emblem,” *Wikipedia*, n.d., at https://en.wikipedia.org/wiki/File:International_Union_of_Muslim_Scholars_emblem.png.)

same caliber].” It added that the protestors had died in defense of their religion, their lives, their families, and their property.[153] The IUMS document not only refrained from reiterating the warning against civil strife, cited so often in al-Qaraḍāwī’s pre-revolution writings on the issue of rebellion, but also proclaimed that the uprising against Mubarak was a form of jihad.

It should be mentioned that Saudi Arabia’s Council of Senior Scholars (Hay’at Kibār al-‘Ulamā’) stated in October 2017 that the IUMS, headed by al-Qaraḍāwī, operates from a narrow partisan perspective that prioritizes the interests of his movement, the MB, over the interests of the Muslim *umma*. The council also accused the IUMS of sparking civil strife in Muslim countries.[154] In November, the anti-Qatar quartet (i.e., Saudi Arabia, the UAE, Bahrain, and Egypt, who imposed a boycott on Qatar in June 2017) added the IUMS to their list of terror organizations on the grounds that it spreads terrorism by manipulating religious discourse.[155] The IUMS responded with an official statement on its website, declaring that it preaches and promotes *wasaṭiyya* and opposes exaggeration in religion and therefore that the allegations against it are preposterous.[156] Al-Qaraḍāwī tweeted in response to the designation of the IUMS as a terrorist organization: “For decades, we have taken it upon ourselves to oppose the tendency toward excessive strictness [*tashaddud*] and extremism [*taṭarruf*], which [actually] originates there [in the four countries boycotting Qatar] and causes chaos in the Muslim arena. And today they place us on the terror list?!”[157] Especially noteworthy is the response from the IUMS secretary-general ‘Alī al-Qarra Dāghī, who is responsible, along with al-Qaraḍāwī, for shaping the organization’s messages. He tweeted: “Accusations of terrorism directed at the IUMS by regimes that are hostile to the freedom of the peoples and that fund terrorist coups against the will of the peoples are nothing but proof that the IUMS is taking the right path in addressing the problems of the nation.” He then quoted Q13:17, which states that truth and falsehood are like water and foam in a rushing torrent: the foam vanishes, while the life-giving water remains.[158] The implication, clearly, is that the accusations against the IUMS are false and will vanish but that its way and its message, which are beneficial and true, will endure.

An examination of the IUMS’s publications reveals that it is a mouthpiece for al-Qaraḍāwī and a platform for spreading the *wasaṭī* school ideology. A comprehensive analysis of this organization and its views is beyond the scope of this book, but its views undoubtedly correspond to al-Qaraḍāwī's. This means sweeping support for the MB and for Qatar and condemnation of the IS and its terrorist attacks, especially its attacks in Europe, but at the same time unequivocal support for terror by the resistance movements in Palestine, especially Hamas. In fact, the organization's views on Hamas constitute an interesting example of its approach, which mirrors that of al-Qaraḍāwī. After Egypt designated Hamas as a terrorist organization in November 2015, the IUMS issued a statement condemning this decision. The statement described Palestine as "the number one cause of the Muslim and Arab nation" and resistance (*muqāwama*) as "the crowning glory" of this nation, adding that "any attempt to harm the resistance is an attempt to benefit the brutal Zionist regime." The IUMS proclaimed that all the resistance movements in Palestine are movements of national liberation and that all their actions are sanctioned by the *sharīʿa* because the *sharīʿa* permits—in fact commands—Muslims to wage resistance and jihad in defense of the homeland and because international law sanctions resistance as well.[159]

In its founding charter, the IUMS describes itself as a popular Islamic organization with members from all over the Muslim world and from Muslim communities in non-Muslim countries, and it proclaims itself independent and unaffiliated with any state.[160] After the anti-Qatar quartet imposed the boycott on Qatar in June 2017 and placed the IUMS on its terror list, Secretary-General al-Qarra Dāghī declared that the organization is not subordinate to any ruler and does not follow any country but seeks the good of all humankind. "In a world full of problems and crises, we act to spread principles of freedom, justice, and peace across the globe," he said.[161] However, the IUMS's response to the boycott reflects absolute support for Qatar and its regime. The quartet presented Qatar with a list of thirteen demands, including that it reduce the level of Iran's diplomatic representation in Qatar; end contact with all terrorist and sectarian organizations in the region, first and foremost the MB, the IS, al-Qaʿida, the Levantine Conquest Front (Jabhat Fatḥ al-Shām, formerly the Victory Front [Jabhat al-Nuṣra]), and Hizbullah; stop funding figures, bodies, and organizations that are included on the terror lists of the quartet, the

United States, and the international community; and close down the al-Jazeera network.[162] These demands are directly linked to al-Qaraḍāwī and his relations with Qatar because he has established a support base for the MB in that country since he settled there in the early 1960s[163] and has been using al-Jazeera to spread the message of *wasaṭiyya*. The IUMS's ruling on the boycott of Qatar reflects these close ties: it ruled that Islam forbids a Muslim country to boycott a Muslim neighbor, for a boycott causes deliberate harm, which the *sharī'a* defines as an act of oppression. It also cited the Qur'ānic proclamation (49:10) that all believers are brothers and must reconcile their differences as well as the injunction against "severing ties of kinship" (47:22).[164] The latter in particular is regarded as a grave sin in the Qur'ān, for it is stated that Allah will curse those who commit it, blind their eyes, and shut their ears to the truth (47:23).

Also interesting is the ruling al-Qarra Dāghī issued about the MB and especially about its members in Qatar in response to the boycott. He denied that the MB is a terror organization, stressing that the United States and the West cannot make a case that it is. He also noted that the Egyptian people had elected the MB in the elections of 2012 and so wondered whether the majority of Egyptians should also be regarded as terrorists because of this support. As for the MB members in Qatar, al-Qarra Dāghī said—hinting at al-Qaraḍāwī and Hamas members sheltering there—that their status is that of asylum seekers (*mustajīrūn*) and that Qatar is therefore obliged to shelter them, especially al-Qaraḍāwī. He added that the boycott of Qatar was a response to its support for the Arab Spring.[165]

Al-Qaraḍāwī as a Scholar Who Politicizes Islam

Liberal writers accuse al-Qaraḍāwī of using religion to achieve political goals and call him a political (*siyāsī*) cleric. In contrast to al-Qaraḍāwī's perception of the MB, the liberals contend that the founding of the MB reflects mainly the politization of religion (*tasyīs al-dīn*).[166] Al-Nābulsī regards the MB as a fundamentalist (*uṣūlī*) religious-political movement whose ultimate goal is to establish a caliphate state. This, he argues, is why the fundamentalists came out against the Arab regimes, as exemplified by the struggle between the MB and al-Nasir's regime in the 1950s and by the struggle between the MB and the regime of Hafiz al-Asad (d. 2000) in Syria in the 1980s.[167] Prominent Kuwaiti liberal Aḥmad al-Baghdādī defines the politization of religion as exploitation of religion for political ends and states that societies in which clerics play political roles tend to be characterized by backwardness and cultural decline.[168]

Characterizing the difference between secular politicians and politicized clerics such as al-Qaraḍāwī, al-Nābulsī states that the former begins and ends his career as a politician, whereas the latter begins as a cleric and then develops an appetite for power. The clerics of the MB are a case in point, he says, in that they transformed from moral guides (*hudāh*) into judges (*quḍāh*) seeking to take over the Muslims' minds.[169] According to the liberals, the opinions voiced by al-Qaraḍāwī on certain issues are political positions rather than religious rulings. An example is his statement in September 2009 on Egypt's decision to erect a barrier on its border with Gaza, in which he proclaimed this move to be a violation of the *sharīʿa*. As evidence, he quoted Q49:10, which proclaims that the believers are brothers, as well as *ḥadīth*s that make a similar point, such as "A Muslim is a brother to his fellow Muslim and neither oppresses him nor abandons him nor deserts him." Noting that the Muslim public tends to construe al-Qaraḍāwī's opinions as religious rulings, liberals claim that each of his sermons has become a sort of weekly political communiqué.[170]

The blurring of the distinction between al-Qaraḍāwī's political views and his religious rulings is also condemned by his son, ʿAbd al-Raḥmān (b. 1940), a media figure and poet known for his harsh criticism of the Mubarak regime and support for the revolution in 2011. In an open letter to his father, he mentioned al-Qaraḍāwī's ruling in support of Mursi's presidency, stating:

> I respect every word you wrote, my lord and mentor, and I know that your intentions were good. But my objection is that your words were not presented as a political opinion, which can be regarded as correct or mistaken, and were not an opinion by "citizen" Yūsuf al-Qaraḍāwī, son of the village and the *kuttāb* [an allusion to the title of al-Qaraḍāwī's autobiography], but rather a *fatwā* by the *imām* of *wasaṭiyya* "Shaykh" al-Qaraḍāwī. That is what amazed, confounded, and pained me.[171]

ʻAbd al-Ḥamīd al-Anṣārī has voiced similar criticism of the shaykh's politization of religion. He accuses clerics, including al-Qaraḍāwī, of exploiting the pulpit to incite young Muslims to wage jihad and become human bombs that kill innocent people. With this exploitation, he says, these clerics assume a political role that harms both politics and religion.[172]

The Secret of al-Qaraḍāwī's Influence and Popularity in the Muslim World

Many researchers who study al-Qaraḍāwī attempt to explain how he became such a prominent scholar and an international figure of such far-reaching influence that some in the Western literature call him "the global *muftī*."[173] Ana Bélen Soage finds the answer in his leadership skills, which allowed him to identify *wasaṭiyya* as an inspiring idea, and in his charisma, which allowed him to transform this idea into a movement.[174] Muʻtazz al-Khaṭīb writes that al-Qaraḍāwī's authority stems from three factors: the central role of *fatwā*s in his activity; his use of the *sharīʻa* as a source of authority in his debate with secularists; and his use of *wasaṭiyya*, which he presents as the true spirit of Islam, in his debate with Islamic extremists.[175] Bettina Gräf contends that his popularity stems from his prominent presence in the written and electronic media,[176] and Gudrun Krämer states, in a similar vein, that al-Qaraḍāwī is a modern figure who could not have emerged or wielded religious authority before the age of mass communication.[177] In the 1990s, following the media and information revolution, al-Qaraḍāwī began to utilize the various types of electronic media to spread his ideology and reach wider audiences. The year 1996 saw the launch of his immensely popular television show *Sharīʻa and Life* (*Al-Sharīʻa wal-ḥayāh*) on al-Jazeera, in which he discusses various Islamic issues and answers viewers' questions.[178]

Although I agree that the media played an important role in making al-Qaraḍāwī a "global *muftī*," I do not believe that it is the key to his popularity. The media allow him to convey his message, but the message itself is just as important as the media. I argue that the secret of his appeal lies in his successful formulation of a juridical methodology that meets the needs of the modern age and that he applies in many of his legal opinions.

One of the principles of this methodology is that in issuing legal opinions, one must be lenient rather than strict, and one must address the people in contemporary language so that they understand the ruling.[179] The latter principle is also evident in the shaykh's mosque sermons, where he makes frequent use of colloquial Arabic even though Muslim jurists forbade the use of colloquial Arabic except in cases where the worshippers are unlikely to understand the classical Arabic. By adopting this colloquial style—and also by peppering his sermons with quotes from poetry, which is another characteristic of his rhetoric—al-Qaraḍāwī makes the sermons both easier to comprehend and more enjoyable for the audience.

This study argues that al-Qaraḍāwī's appeal, then, lies in his adoption of *wasaṭiyya* and his application of its principles in his legal opinions and *da'wa*. *Wasaṭiyya* is al-Qaraḍāwī's answer to contemporary Salafism, which he accuses of taking a rigid and overliteral approach to the religious texts and therefore calls it the "new Ẓāhiriyya."[180] *Wasaṭiyya* is also his answer to jihadi Salafism, which he claims is mistaken in its religious understanding of jihad. *Wasaṭiyya*, according to al-Qaraḍāwī, is a contemporary Muslim attempt to meet the challenges posed by modernity and by the West. It advocates maintaining a dialogue with the West and borrowing from it, but without being blinded by it and discarding Islam. Moreover, *wasaṭiyya* expects this dialogue to be mutual rather than one-sided and therefore makes demands of the West and presents conditions for Muslim openness toward the West. According to al-Qaraḍāwī, one of the conditions of such a dialogue is that the West must not regard Muslims as enemies to be feared, for they are not wild beasts; on the contrary, they are frequently the victims of centuries-long oppression by the West.[181] The secret of al-Qaraḍāwī's powerful influence is that he applies *wasaṭiyya* in all domains, including in his attitude toward other cultures, which is encapsulated in the principle "internal [Muslim] unity [*tamāsuk*] without self-seclusion; openness without assimilation."[182]

As the spokesman of *wasaṭī* Islam, al-Qaraḍāwī wishes to present a solution in the spirit of *wasaṭiyya* and its principles to every issue facing the Muslim *umma*. An example is his response to the incident of the Danish cartoons. The affair began on September 30, 2005, when the popular Danish newspaper *Jyllands Posten* published in its culture and satire section a series of twelve cartoons, most of which depicted the Prophet Muḥammad. In January and February 2006, Muslims reacted to the cartoons with violent demonstrations and riots in Europe and the Muslim world. The cartoonists were threatened with death, and Danish embassies in various capitals were torched. Al-Qaraḍāwī's response to this affair in a sermon in his Qatar mosque on February 3, 2006, sheds further light on the reasons for his popularity among the Muslim masses in both the Muslim world and the West. On the one hand, al-Qaraḍāwī stated that the Muslim *umma* was entitled—and indeed obliged—to be outraged by the offense to the Prophet Muḥammad, for a true Muslim is one who zealously defends the sanctities (*ḥurumāt*) of his faith. If the Muslim *umma* failed to be enraged and to rally to the defense of the Prophet, he said, it would lose its vitality, its significance, and its manliness. As he often does, he adorned his statements with quotations from Arab poets. He told the worshippers:

> We are unwilling to accept humiliation, to be wounded and harmed and disparaged, and yet remain silent, like passive observers. That is not [the behavior of] a living nation. We do not want to say, like [the poet] Abū al-Ṭayyib al-Mutanabbī [d. 965]: "Debased is he who envies those who live in debasement. Sometimes [a proud] death is better than life [in humiliation]. Those who are weak can more easily endure humiliation, [like] a corpse that does not feel the pain of a wound."[183]

With this quote from al-Mutanabbī, whose famous poems have yielded many proverbs and moral pronouncements familiar to every speaker of Arabic, al-Qaraḍāwī sharply conveyed the message that the Muslim *umma* must defend its pride and that even death is preferable to humiliation. However, in the same breath he warned the Muslims not to take revenge for the Danish cartoons by targeting the Christians in Muslim countries and burning their churches. This, he said, would be a grave error because the Danes who drew the cartoons were not Christians, but rather atheists whose only religion is hedonism.

Moving on to attack the Americans and Europeans, al-Qaraḍāwī accused them of hypocrisy: they purported to fight terror and oppose violence throughout the world, but in keeping silent about these cartoons they were instigating terror and violence. Addressing the Westerners, he warned them: "You have no choice, O people, but to take a position of justice [*inṣāf*] and courage and tell the truth about these insults, otherwise [the consequences] will be your own choice. You are creating a new *qā'ida* [literally "basis," but also an allusion to the terror organization al-Qa'ida] for violence. In fact, you create new bases for violence when you disparage the Islamic nation and its sanctities and the Muslims' taboos."[184]

Responding to al-Qaraḍāwī's role in the attacks on Denmark following the affair of the Danish cartoons and his call for a global day of Muslim rage on January 2, 2006, and later for an ongoing boycott of Denmark, liberal writer Shākir al-Nābulsī wondered if it was the cartoons that had hurt the Muslim world or rather the actions of certain Muslims who perpetrated terror in the name of Islam. Addressing al-Qaraḍāwī, he asked: "What about the victims in the two towers [of the World Trade Center], more than three thousand of them?" The cartoons, he implied, simply reflected the West's understandable apprehension in light of realities such as Iran's nuclear program and Hamas's victory in the Palestinian elections of 2006.[185]

Al-Qaraḍāwī's immense impact on his audience stems from, inter alia, his charisma and his rhetorical methods, which are vividly reflected in the Friday sermons he delivers in Qatar. For example, in his Friday sermon on March 14, 2003, the shaykh reminded his audience that the previous week he had given a scathing sermon against the United States. He had analyzed the reasons for the projected US invasion of Iraq and then said that America was destined to perish, just like tyrants of the past, such as Pharaoh. After this sermon, he said, some worshippers had come up to him and said: "Your sermon clarified things for us. You healed our hearts [i.e., gladdened us], moved us, made us cry. However, after your sermon we began to feel afraid." The worshippers were afraid for his safety, al-Qaraḍāwī explained. They were afraid that America would harm him. But now he reassured the audience that there was no need to worry. He was not afraid of America because America was not Allah and because he believed in fate and was not afraid to die as a martyr. "By Allah," he proclaimed, "[the thought of] being assassinated does not worry me! It does not frighten me or cause me to bat an eyelash. If it happens, they [the Americans] will [merely] be realizing a wish that, in my prayers, I have long been beseeching Allah to grant me. In my personal prayers in the third watch [of the night], I have beseeched him to let me die as a martyr for his sake and in order to please him, so that *istishhād* will end my life, purge me of sin, and be weighed in my favor."[186]

Conclusion

Al-Qaraḍāwī's autobiography reflects that his al-Azhar background and his association with the MB were the main factors that determined his course in life.[187] He was an official MB member only until the mid-1960s, but even after relinquishing his official membership, he continued to identify himself with the movement's *da'wa* and remained loyal to the MB as the wellspring of his ideology. The shaykh explains that he withdrew from the movement out of a desire to devote himself to "general Islamic activity" for the sake of all Muslims from all currents, countries, and Islamic schools.[188] In other words, he indeed regards himself as a "global *muftī*," as some in the Western research literature have called him. Nevertheless, he can also be described as an MB cleric who espouses the movement's ideology and aspires to spread it to all currents of Islam. The influence has been mutual, of course: al-Qaraḍāwī's *wasaṭī* ideals have had considerable influence on the MB, especially on its middle generation, whose members can now be identified as disciples of al-Qaraḍāwī who espouse his principles of *wasaṭiyya* and renewal.

Part Two

Wasaṭiyya versus Its Ideological Rivals

Jihadi Salafism and Islamic Liberalism

4

Wasaṭiyya

Between the Muslim Brotherhood and Jihadi Salafism

This chapter focuses on *wasaṭiyya*'s approach to the fundamental tenets of jihadi Salafism: the belief in God's oneness (*tawḥīd*), the perception of God's sovereignty (*ḥākimiyya*), the tenet of *al-walā' wa-l-barā'*, and the issue of accusing other Muslims of unbelief (*takfīr*). In discussing two of these concepts—*ḥākimiyya* and *takfīr*, along with the related issue of the attitude toward democracy—I also compare the *wasaṭī* and liberal views. Comparing *wasaṭiyya* to both jihadi Salafism and liberalism enables a more accurate and considered assessment of *wasaṭiyya*'s basic claim: that it reforms Muslim thought and constitutes an alternative to both contemporary Islamic extremism and radical secularism. As part of the ideological comparison between *wasaṭiyya* and Salafism, the chapter also examines the jihadi Salafīs' criticism of *wasaṭiyya* and their grounds for accusing al-Qaraḍāwī of heresy. At the same time, it also explores the points of agreement between *wasaṭiyya*—which is pragmatic by nature owing to its roots in the MB, whose worldview is characterized by pragmatism and realism within the boundaries of the *sharī'a*—and certain jihadi Salafī thinkers who likewise take a somewhat pragmatic view within the confines of the *sharī'a*. It must be stressed, however, that pragmatism is not the same as moderateness. Pragmatism, as *wasaṭiyya* construes it, involves rigidity in defining the long-term goals but flexibility in choosing the means to attain them. On the spectrum that has secular liberalism on one end and jihadi Salafism on the other, *wasaṭiyya* occupies a position much closer to the latter than to the former. This is evident from its views on core issues discussed in the context of the comparison to liberalism: the perception of *ḥākimiyya* and democracy and the issue of *takfīr*.

Wasaṭiyya versus Salafism in the Academic Literature

Ron Shaham notes in his interesting paper on the rhetoric of the debate between al-Qaraḍāwī and the Salafīs that on the Salafī side the anti-Qaraḍāwī rhetoric is quite extreme and consists of very serious charges as well as curses and insults. According to Shaham, most of al-Qaraḍāwī's Salafī critics who have written to refute his approach belong to the traditional purist trend, and about half of them are disciples of Shaykh Nāṣir al-Dīn al-Albānī (d. 1999), leader of a school called the "neo–*ahl al-ḥadīth*," or "partisans or followers of the *ḥadīth*," who tend to rely on the textual sources.[1]

Shaham focuses mainly on rhetoric and style in his discussion of the dispute between al-Qaraḍāwī and the traditional or purist Salafīs. But an analysis of the material arguments raised in the debate between al-Qaraḍāwī and the jihadi Salafīs, which Shaham does not address but which constitute a major topic in the present volume, shows that although the jihadi Salafīs occasionally use insults when referring to al-Qaraḍāwī, both sides also present serious arguments that reveal ideological similarities as well as differences between them. An examination of the arguments presented by the Salafīs and the *wasaṭīs* and not just of the style and rhetoric of the debate reveals the nature of the two basic approaches that today struggle over dominion of the Muslim world.

Shiraz Maher makes the interesting observation in his book on jihadi Salafism that individuals identify with this ideological or philosophical current but that it does not belong to any specific movement or group, although some players, such as Abū Muḥammad al-Maqdisī and Shaykh Abū Baṣīr al-Ṭarṭūsī, do have considerable influence on shaping some of this current's ideas.[2] Maher identifies five characteristic ideologies that define jihadi Salafism: *tawḥīd*, *ḥākimiyya*, *al-walā' wal-barā'*, *takfīr*, and jihad. In this chapter, I discuss four of the five, leaving the discussion of jihad for chapter 5. The section on the perception of *ḥākimiyya* also includes a broad discussion of democracy and the perception of it by the three streams: *wasaṭī*, Salafist, and liberal.

Tawḥīd

The Jihadi Salafī Perception of Tawḥīd

The unique feature of how jihadi Salafism perceives the concept of *tawḥīd*, God's oneness, is the way in which it links *tawḥīd* with jihad. Al-Maqdisī's website is named "Minbar al-Tawḥīd wal-Jihad"; he explains that *tawḥīd* is the primary objective and the basis of everything and that jihad is the way to achieve it. The link between Islamic creed—that is, *tawḥīd*—and jihad is expressed in the following statement by Ibn Taymiyya that al-Maqdisī chose as the heading for his website: "The basis of religion is in the Book, which guides to the right path, and a victorious sword. 'Your Lord is sufficient guide and helper' [Q25:31]."[3] This close connection between *tawḥīd* and jihad can explain why both al-Qa'ida and the IS adopted the black flag with the "two testimonies": "There is no God but Allah" and "Muḥammad is Allah's messenger." The second testimony is drawn in the shape of the Prophet's seal (and the words are to be read from the bottom up) (see p. 154).

Al-Maqdisī,[4] like other jihadi Salafī thinkers, insists that every Muslim who truly believes in *tawḥīd* must at all times and in all places implement the true meaning of the credo "there is no God but Allah," both in the negative sense of denying the existence of idols (*al-kufr bil-ṭāghūt*) and in the positive sense of faith in Allah (see Q2:256). Al-Maqdisī explains that adherence to the doctrine of *tawḥīd* is required of Muslims in the various acts of worship (*'ibāda*), including in government (*ḥukm*), legislation (*tashrī'*), and the determination of what is permitted (*taḥlīl*) and forbidden (*taḥrīm*). As a result, Muslims are required to refuse ("disavow," *barā'a*) to worship or obey anyone or anything except Allah. This, al-Maqdisī states, is the core of "the religion of Abraham" (*millat Ibrāhīm*), as reflected in Q60:4. Al-Maqdisī accepts the ruling of the founder of the Wahhābī movement, Muḥammad Ibn 'Abd al-Wahhāb (d. 1791), that the testimony "there is no God but Allah" is not sufficient to make one's person and property inviolable unless one adds a declaration that one rejects any other object of worship except Allah.[5]

4. The "flag of monotheism" adopted by jihadi Salafist organizations, in particular al-Qaʿida and IS: a black flag with the "two testimonies." The sentence "Muḥammad is Allah's Messenger" is written upside down from the bottom up. It is placed inside a circle that represents the Prophet's seal. (From "Flag of the Islamic State of Iraq and the Levant," Wikimedia Commons, n.d., https://commons.wikimedia.org/wiki/File:Flag_of_the_Islamic_State_of_Iraq_and_the_Levant2.svg.)

Al-Qaraḍāwī's Wasaṭī *Perception of* Tawḥīd

In *The Essence of Professing God's Oneness* (first published in the 1980s),[6] al-Qaraḍāwī, like the Salafīs, recognizes the three types of *tawḥīd* but, unlike them, does not mention the *tawḥīd* of God's sovereignty (*ḥākimiyya*). The three types of *tawḥīd* accepted by both al-Qaraḍāwī and the Salafīs are:

1. "Professing the *tawḥīd* of lordship" (*rubūbiyya*): Allah is the only creator (*khāliq*), the only sovereign (*rabb*) and provider, the only king, and the only manager (*mudabbir*) of the universe.

2. "Professing the *tawḥīd* of Godship" (*ulūhiyya*): Allah alone is to be the object of all the forms of worship, as commanded in Q6:162–63.

3. "Professing the *tawḥīd* of the names and attributes" (*al-asmā' wal-ṣifāt*): God's attributes are to be accepted literally, not as metaphors; they must be neither distorted nor abolished (*ta'ṭīl*) nor interpreted (*ta'wīl*), nor may God with His attributes be compared (*tashbīh*) with men.[7]

Like the Salafīs, al-Qaraḍāwī insists that *tawḥīd* is to be realized through the following: worshipping only Allah; rejecting all idols and disavowing those who worship them instead of Allah; refraining from all manner of idolatry (*shirk*). He accepts Ibn Qayyim's comprehensive definition of the term *ṭāghūt*: "Anything by means of which the servant transgresses his bound—that is, whatever he worships, follows, or obeys. The *ṭāghūt* of a group of people is anyone or anything to which they turn for judgment who is not Allah and His messenger, or worship instead of Allah, or follow without evidence from Allah, or obey in anything which they do not know that it constitutes obedience to Allah."[8] For al-Qaraḍāwī, as for the jihadi Salafīs, the adoption of a law giver and ruler who is not Allah constitutes "grave polytheism" (*al-shirk al-akbar*) because the entire world is Allah's kingdom and the people in it are His servants; only He has the authority to rule and legislate, to determine what is permitted and what is forbidden, and His subjects must listen and obey. The difference between al-Qaraḍāwī and the jihadi Salafīs on this point is that some things that the latter would consider idolatrous—such as loyalty to one's homeland, nationalism, a multiparty system, and an elected legislature—al-Qaraḍāwī, as a *wasaṭī*, considers licit.[9] Another difference is that al-Qaraḍāwī would reduce the number of cases in which he would agree to excommunicate other Muslims, in particular rulers who do not govern according to *sharī'a*.[10]

Ḥākimiyya

Jihadi Salafīs' Perception of Ḥākimiyya

Maher argues that at the most basic level there is no difference between the way jihadi Salafīs perceive the notion of *tawḥīd* and the way other Salafīs perceive it. They all rely heavily on Ibn ʿAbd al-Wahhāb's *Book of the Profession of God's Oneness* and the doctrine expounded therein.[11] However, as Maher mentions, a perusal of jihadi Salafi writings reveals that they add the concept of "the unity of [God's] sovereignty" (*tawḥīd al-ḥākimiyya*).[12] In his book on the faith's doctrines (*ʿaqīda*), al-Ṭarṭūsī maintains that *tawḥīd al-ḥākimiyya* is not a fourth type of *tawḥīd*, in addition to the three types listed earlier, but that it constitutes an element in each of them. He writes: "We stress the importance [of *tawḥīd al-ḥākimiyya*] and mention it in particular because we believe that the seduction [*fitna*] of the nation in this age is owing to opposition to God's unity in His sovereignty and deviation from His rule and His *sharīʿa* in favor of the rule and the laws of the idolatrous tyrant [*ṭāghūt*]."[13] Al-Maqdisī considers *tawḥīd al-ḥākimiyya* as part of *tawḥīd al-ulūhiyya*. The former term he defines as proclaiming *tawḥīd* by obedience to God and to God's laws only. If one associates idols with God in His rule, it is equivalent to associating idols in the worship of God. Al-Maqdisī derives his conclusion that *tawḥīd al-ḥākimiyya* is an inseparable part of *tawḥīd al-ulūhiyya* from Q7:54 and 12:40.[14]

Al-Qaraḍāwī's Perception of Ḥākimiyya

Although al-Qaraḍāwī does not mention *tawḥīd al-ḥākimiyya* in *The Essence of Professing God's Oneness*, he does mention it in his book on the principles of *wasaṭiyya* published in 2010, in which he writes: "The faith must be based on belief in Allah and the Day of Judgment and on pure profession of God's oneness: Allah as the unique Lord of the universe [*tawḥīd al-rubūbiyya*], as God [*al-ulūhiyya*], and *the unity of the sovereignty of God* [*tawḥid al-hākimiyya*]. In this way, man will be liberated from subservience to man and to anything that is not Allah."[15]

At this last stage in the evolution of al-Qaraḍāwī's thinking on *ḥākimiyya*, he, like the jihadi Salafis, considers *tawḥīd al-ḥākimiyya* as an aspect of *tawḥīd* as a whole. Before this stage (i.e., before 2010), he discussed the concept of *ḥākimiyya* and its meaning in two other contexts. In the first, he insisted that *ḥākimiyya* does not mean support for the establishment of a theocracy because it has a purely legislative force; it means that Allah is the law giver for His creatures and tells them what is permitted and what is forbidden. However, this still leaves Muslims with numerous domains in which they can legislate for themselves in social, economic, and political affairs.[16] In the second context, he noted that the call for democracy was not inconsistent with the principle of Allah's *ḥākimiyya*—that is, with the sovereignty of Allah's *sharīʿa* (on *ḥākimiyya* and democracy, see the discussion later in this chapter).

The Liberal Perception of Ḥākimiyya

The liberal perception of *ḥākimiyya* is clearly expounded in the writings of Muḥammad Saʿīd al-ʿAshmāwī. The liberal's fundamental claim is that the rule of Allah existed only in the time of the Prophet, whereas all later regimes were guided by human aspirations and ambitions. According to al-ʿAshmāwī, the slogan "Rule (or judgment) is Allah's alone," which was used by the Khawārij to justify their opposition to the fourth caliph, ʿAlī b. abī Ṭālib (reigned 656–61 CE), was not a true call for divine law but rather a political and partisan slogan aimed solely at deposing the caliph and seizing power. In using it against the caliph, the Khawārij were actually defying the consensus of the *umma* and the spirit of Islam and sowing fear among Muslims. Al-ʿAshmāwī adds that the idea embodied by this slogan has no basis in the Qur'ān and the Sunna; it originated in ancient Egypt and later gained currency in medieval Christian societies. The clerics who politicize religion today, among them al-Qaraḍāwī, are using the same slogan, which means that they, too, merit the title of "Khawārij," he argues.[17]

It is interesting to note that al-ʿAshmāwī offers a unique definition of the name "Khawārij": anyone who defies the spirit of the faith and makes manipulative use of the *sharīʿa* and of concepts such as Allah's *ḥākimiyya* to realize political and partisan ambitions. Al-ʿAshmāwī states that the Qur'ān and the Sunna provide no specific definition of the ruler's prerogatives, out of the awareness that endowing the ruler with religious authority may lead to tyranny in the name of Islam and the *sharīʿa*. For the same reason, he says, the Qur'ān and the Sunna refrain from explicitly defining the authority of the clerics and from establishing a formal priesthood but decree instead that every Muslim is the master of his own faith. He adds that "Islam has no [concept of] religious science [*'ilm li-dīn*] but only of studies about religion [*'ulūm ḥawla al-dīn*]."[18]

Al-Qaraḍāwī calls al-'Ashmāwī's ideas "extreme secularism [*ghulū 'ilmānī*]" and criticizes them in brutal terms: "The truth is that I never saw greater ignorance, folly, and hideousness than what the so-called Muḥammad Sa'īd al-Ashmāwī writes about Islam. Whenever I tried to read anything by him, I could not go on reading because [I was filled with] nausea and disgust. He causes the cool blood to boil."[19] In this context, the shaykh quotes two Qur'ānic verses (22:8–9), implying that without knowledge or evidence al-'Ashmāwī casts doubt on Allah's power and His oneness and causes people to stray from Allah's path, sins that the Qur'ān defines as deserving of hell.

Naṣr Ḥāmid Abū Zayd provides another interesting analysis and critique of the Islamist perception of *ḥākimiyya*, including al-Qaraḍāwī's view. He argues that this perception is rooted in an attack on rational thought and on the legitimacy of disagreement and pluralism. In addition, he says, it draws a contrast between the divine and the human, between Allah's way and man's way. According to Abū Zayd, the notion of *ḥākimiyya* is also completely incompatible with democracy because it mirrors Sayyid Quṭb's claim that in Islam there are only two parties, the party of Allah and the party of Satan and idols,[20] and its theoretical expression is the false assumption that the clerics have a monopoly over religious knowledge and over the right to define the true Islam and hence also false Islam. This assumption, adds Abū Zayd, can be found in al-Qaraḍāwī's writings—for example, in his claim that Islamic extremism stems, in part, from the fact that some Muslim governments allow Marxists and secularists to freely disseminate their ideas while restricting the freedom of those who preach "true Islam." According to al-Qaraḍāwī, this "true Islam" is the Islam of the Qur'ān and the Sunna, of the Prophet's Companions and the generation that followed them, of truth, power, might, honor, and jihad, and governments fear it because it carries a whiff of revolution against the ruler. Therefore, they encourage the spreading of a different, "friendly" Islam, which is an Islam of saints' birthdays (*mawālid*), forbidden innovations in ritual, and stagnant thinking, and they focus on religious trivialities instead of on core issues (here the reference is presumably to Ṣūfī Islam).[21]

Abū Zayd calls this approach al-Qaraḍāwī's "*ḥākimiyya* of the *fuqahā*'" and an attempt to establish a kind of Christian-style priesthood in Islam, which wields authority in matters of faith and religion and is entitled to determine what counts as the "true Islam."[22]

The *Wasaṭī*, Jihadi Salafī, and Liberal Views of Democracy

Ḥākimiyya *and Democracy: Are They Compatible?*

Al-Qaraḍāwī presents two arguments to prove that there is no contradiction between the sovereignty of Allah (*ḥākimiyyat Allāh*) and democracy. First, the essence of democracy involves not the rejection of Allah's sovereignty but rather the rejection of the despot's tyranny. Second, there are two types of *ḥākimiyya*, and neither contradicts democratic rule. One type is Allah's sovereignty over the universe and over destiny (*ḥākimiyya kawniyya qadriyya*)—that is, God's way of ruling over the cosmos; the other is legislative sovereignty (*ḥākimiyya tashrīʿiyya*). Al-Qaraḍāwī proposes to resolve the apparent conflict between democracy as the rule of the people and *ḥākimiyyat Allāh* by certain formulations in the constitution of the Islamic state that he envisions. He proposes that the constitution will contain an article that states that in addition to the state being a democracy, Islam will be its religion, and *sharīʿa* will be the source of legislation. This, in his view, will constitute a realization of the *ḥākimiyya* of the *sharīʿa*. Another article he proposes for the constitution would state that any law that contradicts explicit statements in the *sharīʿa* is null and void.[23]

Al-Qaraḍāwī argues that when Abū al-Aʿlā al-Mawdūdī and subsequently Sayyid Quṭb called for the implementation of *ḥākimiyya*, they had in mind only Allah's legislative authority but did not mean to imply that God appointed clerics and rulers. Legislative *ḥākimiyya*, al-Qaraḍāwī points out, was not invented by al-Mawdūdī and Quṭb but is something that all Muslims accept. He rejects the claim that in Sunnī Islam God appoints the ruler; rather, he says, this approach is characteristic of Shīʿīsm, which believes that Allah appointed the twelve *imām*s. This claim, he adds, is based on a faulty understanding of *ḥākimiyya*, as expressed in the following saying of the Khawārij: "Rule is only God's [*lā ḥukma illā li-Allāh*]."

With this statement, they expressed their opposition to ʿAlī after he agreed to the idea of arbitration (*taḥkīm*) with Muʿāwiya b. Abī Sufyān (d. 680), the founder and first caliph of the Umayyad caliphate (ruled 661–80). ʿAlī replied to them, "[This statement] is a word of truth whose intention is a falsehood," an assertion that reflects the Muslim approach to *ḥākimiyya*, according to al-Qaraḍāwī: the Khawārij maintained that only God rules, whereas ʿAlī only agreed that God is the legislator, but not the ruler.[24]

Al-Qaraḍāwī restricts al-Mawdūdī's and Quṭb's concept of *ḥākimiyya* to the legislative arena, although al-Mawdūdī's and Quṭb's writings make it very clear that for them it had a much broader application. Thus, for example, al-Mawdūdī states that "the Qur'ān explains the belief in *tawḥīd* in a way that makes it clear that Allah is alone, without any associate, not only in the religious but also in the political and legal sense."[25] He explains the term *ḥākimiyya* as meaning "supreme authority [*al-sulṭa al-ʿulyā*] and absolute authority [*al-sulṭa al-muṭlaqa*]"; in other words, Allah's dominion according to this view is unlimited, and humankind must obey Him.[26] Although al-Mawdūdī states that Allah does have "legal sovereignty" (*ḥākimiyya qānūniyya*), he agrees with al-Qaraḍāwī that Islam does not forbid humans to legislate, although, again like al-Qaraḍāwī, he maintains that human legislation is restricted to the domains on which *sharīʿa* remains silent.[27] Quṭb declares quite explicitly that "the meaning of *ḥākimiyya* in Islam is not restricted to receiving laws only from God." The reason for this is, according to Quṭb, that the term *sharīʿa* denotes not only the law and the foundations of government but also the foundations of faith, ethics, behavior, and knowledge.[28]

The Wasaṭī *Approach to Democracy: Essentially Apologetic*

Although the *wasaṭī* view on democracy claims to occupy a middle position between the secularists and the Salafīs, an analysis reveals that in fact it rejects both approaches and adopts instead a third position that is not a synthesis of the other two. *Wasaṭiyya* argues that democracy is essentially consistent with the commandments of Islam. Al-Qaraḍāwī notes that democracy shares the following principles with Islam: giving advice to the ruler (*naṣīḥa*), commanding right and forbidding wrong, commanding the truth and patience (*al-tawāṣī bil-ḥaqq wal-ṣabr*, based on Q103:3), establishing justice, removing iniquity, realizing benefits, rejecting harmful things, and more.[29]

It is worth emphasizing that although the shaykh presents himself as an advocate of democracy, he contends that the Muslims need a particular brand of it, which he calls "true democracy," suited to Muslim society—namely, a democracy within the confines of *sharīʿa*: "We do not want a licentious [*sā'iba*] democracy that permits whatever it pleases," he writes.[30] In fact, he rejects the Western term *democracy*. In a sermon in his Doha mosque on April 1, 2005, he declared: "Nothing suits us better than what is called democracy, but we do not wish to call it that, but rather to call it *shūrā*."[31] In the same sermon, he asserted that democracy involves not only *shūrā* (the ruler's consultation with his counselors) but also additional components—namely, dispensing advice to the ruler, commanding good and forbidding evil, and opposing tyranny and oppression. "Islamic democracy," as characterized by al-Qaraḍāwī, leaves certain elements beyond the scope of majority vote, such as the tenets of the faith and the basic prohibitions and explicit laws of Islam. Voting, in other words, applies only to issues that are subject to *ijtihād*, such as declaring war, making a truce, and raising taxes.[32]

Regarding al-Qaraḍāwī's conception of *shūrā*, Sayyid al-Qimnī (b. 1947), an Egyptian secular writer and thinker, points out that in the shaykh's view the people whom the ruler must consult—*ahl al-ḥall wa-l-ʿaqd*, literally "those who loosen and bind"—are clerics like himself, and that is why, al-Qimnī says, the shaykh decrees that the ruler must consult with them or else be deposed.[33] Aḥmad al-Baghdādī holds that *shūra* is an Islamic term that has nothing to do with democracy; it does not connote a form of government but rather a way of life, one that suits a primitive tribal society but not a modern state with complex social, political, and economic characteristics.[34] He notes further that this concept is mentioned only twice in the Qur'ān (3:159 and 42:38) and that the early Islamic jurists (*fuqahā'*) did not discuss it in their writings, and modern ones refer to it only in seeking to argue that democracy is the practical expression of an indigenous Islamic concept and is therefore compatible with the *sharīʿa*. Highlighting what he regards as the essential differences between *shūrā* and democracy, al-Baghdādī points out that *shūrā* is a vague concept, whereas democracy is sharply defined; that *shūrā* is not associated with an implementation mechanism, whereas democracy is; and that in *shūrā* the role of the people is absent, whereas in democracy it is central and clear.[35]

The *wasaṭī* conception of Muslim democracy in a Muslim state is that it takes democracy's best principles but is not a copy of Western democracy. It is similar to the latter in that it is the nation that chooses its ruler and may remove him from power if he strays from the right path, acts unjustly, or does not listen to his advisers. However, the Muslim state, according to *wasaṭiyya*, is superior to democracy because it gives every individual in the nation the right to advise the ruler and to "command right and forbid wrong" to him as one believer to another (based on Q9:71). *Wasaṭī*s stress that Western democracy, in contrast to its Muslim counterpart, is not limited by guiding principles, and therefore the people's representatives can allow what religion forbids and forbid what it allows. For example, American democracy allows alcohol. But in Islam the *sharī'a* enjoys absolute sovereignty over all branches of government, including the legislature, which is not allowed to change or abolish religious law.

Al-Qaraḍāwī's approach to the Islamic view of the state is an apologetic one: he seeks to anchor modern political concepts in the texts of the Qur'ān and the Sunna by finding evidence in them for democratic principles such as elections and voting. He contends, for example, that voting is equivalent to giving testimony because the voter testifies as to the candidate he considers worthy. According to Q65:2, a witness must be honest; al-Qaraḍāwī rules that this requirement can be relaxed in the context of modern elections to allow more members of the public to vote.[36] This claim sparked criticism from Mu'tazz al-Khaṭīb, who complained that al-Qaraḍāwī was creating a hybrid of the Islamic tradition and the modern concept of the state.[37] Al-Qaraḍāwī, it should be noted, does not set out a clear definition of the Islamic state in his writings, but his vision is clearly informed by the original Islamic state founded by the Prophet Muḥammad in Medina and on the model of the Righteous Caliphate (632–61 CE).

The Jihadi Salafī View of Democracy: Heresy

The *wasaṭī* view on democracy was formulated as a rebuttal to both the secularists' view and the Salafīs' view, especially the jihadi kind.[38] In the Salafī view, democracy is considered an innovation (*bid'a*), which is explicitly forbidden in the famous *ḥadīth* "He who innovates something in this matter of ours [i.e., Islam] that is not of it [that is, expresses an independent view that has no basis in the Qur'ān or the Sunna] will have it rejected."[39] In other words, the Salafīs view democracy as an import from the secular Christian West and therefore reject it out of hand and accuse those in the Muslim world who support it of unbelief.

As a *wasaṭī*, al-Qaraḍāwī does not accept the argument that democracy must be rejected because it is a Western import; Islam, he says, permits the importation of whatever is not harmful or already exists in Islam. In this context, he writes:

> We import from democracy its mechanisms and its guarantees, but not its philosophy, which exaggerates the value of the individual at the group's expense, exaggerates freedom at the expense of values and morals, and gives the majority the right to change anything, even democracy itself. We want a democracy of Muslim society and the Muslim *umma*, one that will preserve this society's beliefs, values, and religious, cultural, and ethical foundations. These are unchanging things that are not subject to evolution or the vote.[40]

Al-Qaraḍāwī preaches "careful openness" (*al-infitāḥ al-maḥdhūr*) to Western civilization. For him, the greatest danger lies in blind admiration and excessive empowerment of that civilization as well as a sense of Muslim inferiority to it. He proposes the following formula for Muslim interaction with other cultures: "Cohesiveness without self-isolation [*tamāsuk bilā inghilāq*] and openness without absorption [*infitāḥ bilā dhawabān*]."[41]

Jihadi Salafīs such as al-Maqdisī and al-Ṭarṭūsī accuse democracy of constituting "manifest unbelief and deviation from the faith."[42] Ayman al-Ẓawāhirī criticizes the MB sharply because of its acceptance of democracy, which, in his view, is a new religion based on the deification of man, who is granted an unlimited right to determine the law. He concludes that democracy is an infidel man-made faith (*dīn waḍʿī kāfir*), in which the lawmakers are "lords" (*arbāb*) equal to God. This is clearly contrary to the Qur'ān (for example, Q3:64), which explicitly forbids the believers to choose a substitute for God.[43]

Al-Ẓawāhirī enumerates a number of democratic principles that he considers to constitute heresy, in particular the fact that democracy involves granting a great deal of authority to the nation. According to the Qur'ān (Q4:59), disputes may be settled only by reference to the Qur'ān and the Sunna. In Islam, ultimate authority lies with the *sharīʿa* rather than with the civil nation or the people. Al-Ẓawāhirī argues that in a democracy the nation's authority is greater than God's, and in any conflict between the two the former prevails; he mentions as an example the fact that "apostate" Muslim regimes hold referenda on whether *sharīʿa* should be applied or not, in keeping with the principle of national sovereignty. Al-Ẓawāhirī declares that a Muslim who calls for democracy is like a Muslim who says of himself that he is a "Jewish Muslim" or a "Christian Muslim."[44] The jihadi Salafīs believe that Muslims must decide whether they follow Allah's faith and His *sharīʿa* or the religion of democracy, which the jihadi Salafīs consider polytheistic.[45]

The Moroccan jihadi Salafī shaykh Muḥammad b. Muḥammad al-Fazzāzī (b. 1949) accuses al-Qaraḍāwī of having ignored all the fundamental properties of democracy in his ruling on this system of government and of seeing no distinction and no contradiction between democracy and Islam. Al-Fazzāzī argues that it is strange if not ridiculous to use Islamic tools of jurisprudence to rule on the legitimacy of democratic principles from the perspective of *sharīʿa*, considering that such tools cannot properly be employed in non-Muslim environments. These tools must not be used to justify what is unjustifiable—democracy in this case—as al-Qaraḍāwī does. For al-Fazzāzī, doing so can be compared to using the rules of Arabic to analyze another language. He views al-Qaraḍāwī's ruling on democracy as assimilation to and imitation of the unbelievers and, worse, as the defeat of Islam by the unbelievers.[46]

The Liberal Approach to Democracy: An Antithesis of the Wasaṭī *Approach*

In contrast to al-Qaraḍāwī's claim that democracy is inherent in Islam, liberal writers such as Shākir al-Nābulsī argue that no trace of this concept exists in the Qur'ān or the Sunna or the writings of the early Muslims and that the political history of Islam presents no examples of democracy being implemented. Unlike al-Qaraḍāwī, al-Nābulsī regards democracy as Western in origin and as a secular-civil notion rather than as a religious one.[47] The liberal writer Aḥmad al-Baghdādī contends that the Muslim *fuqahā'*, including al-Qaraḍāwī, are ignorant of the philosophical underpinnings of Western democracy. They mistakenly believe that democracy means constitution, parliament, elections, and the rule of the majority, but these things, he says, are only the mechanisms for realizing the philosophy of democracy. The true essence of democracy is freedom and equal rights for all, regardless of ethnicity, skin color, gender, religion, or opinion.[48] This essence entails granting political rights to women and full equality to non-Muslims, for example, and respecting people's right to choose their religion. For al-Qaraḍāwī, however, the essence of democracy is the people's right to elect their leaders, and he believes that this right is also championed by Islam, as reflected in the *ḥadīth* stating that the best rulers are the ones the Muslims love and the worst are the ones the Muslims hate.[49]

Al-Qaraḍāwī criticizes Westernized secularists who believe that Western-style democracy with its liberal social attitudes, capitalism, and political freedom can provide the solution to the problems of the Muslim world. He dislikes the fact that they want to apply democracy in the Muslim world in the same manner as it is practiced in the West—a democracy that is not based on faith, that does not promote the worship of God or the implementation of *sharī'a*. He accuses these secularists of wanting to imitate both the good and the bad of the West.

Assessing why democracy failed to take hold in Arab and Muslim countries, Aḥmad al-Baghdādī and other liberals point out that it is alien to the heritage of the Muslim *umma*. "This nation," writes al-Baghdādī, "was characterized by a backward mentality that advocates a return to the past; moreover, this mentality has been revived and the number of its followers has increased. Sadly, the Muslim *umma* has a past more than it has a present and future."[50] Al-Nābulsī adds that political parties in the Arab world do not believe in democracy; they use it only as a slogan and as a means to gain power, but after they do, they fail to implement it, which causes the public to lose faith in them. He identifies this failure as one of the political factors that contributed to the emergence of the bin Laden phenomenon.[51] Al-Qimnī, too, alleges that al-Qaraḍāwī and the MB treat democracy as a means rather than an end, and so he calls them "opportunist[s]."[52]

An examination of al-Qaraḍāwī's view of democracy in comparison to the liberals' view confirms Khaled Abou El Fadl's conclusion that al-Qaraḍāwī's perception is mostly dogmatic. It does not reflect a deep understanding of the theoretical problems that democracy poses to Islam, which is why the shaykh discusses it only in vague and general terms. El Fadl assesses that al-Qaraḍāwī has a superficial understanding of democratic institutions and theories and regards democracy mainly as a mechanism for implementing the will of the majority. Because he expects the majority of citizens in a Muslim country to be observant Muslims, he sees no difficulty in implementing democracy in such a country.[53]

Muhammad Mursi provided an example of such a narrow perception of democracy during his short period as president of Egypt. One of the problems of the MB even before the election of Mursi, its representative, as president in 2012 was that it never clearly defined what kind of democracy is compatible with an Islamic state, and its perception of democracy thus remained vague. Alison Pargeter writes that "the Brotherhood has hardly been a bastion of democracy itself."[54] During his presidency, Mursi took measures that undermined democracy and human rights, but al-Qaraḍāwī nevertheless condoned these measures. This example sheds light on al-Qaraḍāwī's and the MB's utilitarian view that democracy serves as a tool for bringing an Islamic party (in this case the MB) to power, but once that party is in power, it is not required to respect democratic values.

Among Mursi's undemocratic measures were his constitutional declaration on November 22, 2012, that granted him sweeping powers; the new constitution that was formulated during his rule and ratified in a referendum in December 2012; and his handling of the opposition to and demonstrations against him. The constitutional declaration stated that no judicial body can dissolve the Shūrā Council (the upper house of Parliament) or the Constituent Assembly (the body charged with drafting Egypt's new constitution). It also stipulated that no decision made by Mursi after his election in June 2012 could be appealed by any judicial element until a new constitution was in place and a new People's Assembly elected.[55] Human rights organizations in Egypt described the declaration as an attack on Egypt's judiciary and the rule of law and as the beginning of a tyrannical regime that banned all opposition and criticism and undermined human rights and personal freedoms on the pretext of defending the revolution and its goals. Al-Qaraḍāwī, however, defended Mursi, saying that he was entitled to take these measures by virtue of "the responsibility placed on his shoulders by Allah" when he became Egypt's president. Citing the *ḥadīth* that says, "You [Muslims] are all shepherds, and each of you is responsible for his flock," he added that Mursi was acting in Egypt's best interest and that Mursi was responsible for governing it before Allah, before the people, and before history.[56]

The new constitution drafted during Mursi's presidency exemplifies the MB's and al-Qaraḍāwī's limited perception of democracy.[57] Human rights organizations complained that this constitution—which had been drafted by Islamic elements alone after the liberal, secular, and Christian members resigned from the Constitutional Assembly—cemented political and religious tyranny and paved the way for the establishment of a Sunnī theocracy similar to the Shī'ī theocracy in Iran. They claimed that the new constitution made no mention of gender equality and accorded religious freedom only to members of the monotheistic faiths.[58]

An examination of the Mursi constitution is beyond the scope of this study, but a few examples from it can illuminate the MB's and al-Qaraḍāwī's perception of democracy. Article 6, for instance, states that "the political regime is based on the principles of democracy and *shūrā*." This language was meant to appease both the liberals, who wished to define the Egyptian regime as democratic, and the Salafīs, who wanted to avoid the term *democracy* and replace it with the Islamic term *shūrā*. The Salafīs agreed to this phrasing because in their view it distinguished Egyptian democracy from Western democracy and defined Egypt as a parliamentary regime subject to Islamic tradition, which meant that practices such as same-sex marriage, for example, would not be permitted. Liberal circles accepted this phrasing on the grounds that *shūrā* is a component of democracy and does not detract from the regime's democratic character.[59] As we have seen, al-Qaraḍāwī, too, refers to Islamic democracy as *shūrā* to distinguish it from Western democracy.

Article 10 of the Mursi constitution states, inter alia, that the Egyptian state "shall enable the reconciliation between the duties of a woman toward her family and toward her work." The Mursi constitution omitted the article of the Constitution of 1971 that stipulated that the state would guarantee equality between men and women in the political, social, cultural, and economic spheres when doing so would not violate the directives of the Islamic *sharīʿa*.[60] The latter clause was rejected by women's organizations, which feared that subjecting women's equality to the directives of the *sharīʿa* would lead to lowering the legal age of marriage, segregating schools, mandating the *ḥijāb*, permitting female circumcision, and banning women from serving as president. The Salafīs, for their part, refused to let the equality clause stand without the inclusion of the reference to the *sharīʿa*, so the clause was eventually dropped altogether. As shown in chapter 6, Article 10 of the Mursi constitution conforms to al-Qaraḍāwī's perception of gender equality.

Article 43 of the Mursi constitution stipulates that "the state shall guarantee the freedom to practice religious rites and to establish places of worship for the divine religions." Human rights organizations protested that the article does not guarantee "absolute" freedom of belief, including the freedom to convert to another religion or to practice a nonmonotheistic faith.[61] Al-Qaraḍāwī takes a similar view to the one reflected in this article. He recognizes freedom of worship but not a Muslim's right to convert to another religion, which he regards as *ridda*, apostasy, a sin punishable by death.

Not surprisingly, al-Qaraḍāwī defended Mursi's constitution, calling it "a superb Egyptian constitution that defends the individual, the family, the group, the nation, and the religious and human moral and national values."[62] He did, however, have some reservations about it. He complained that it did not stipulate that faith in Allah is the foundation of Egyptian society and stressed that faith takes precedence over freedom, justice, and equality. He also took issue with Article 44, which prohibits insulting the messengers and prophets, on the grounds that it does not explicitly mention the Prophet Muḥammad alongside Jesus and Moses.[63] These reservations about Mursi's constitution—the most Islamic constitution in Egypt's history—indicate that al-Qaraḍāwī does not really advocate a civil state, as he claims, but a theocracy.

A press release published by human rights organizations one year after Mursi's election claimed that the state of human rights in Egypt had severely declined during that period and that Mursi's violations of human rights were worse even than Mubarak's during the latter's thirty years in power. This decline, they said, was manifest in the brutal suppression of political and social protest movements and the violence used against protestors not only by the security apparatuses but also by Mursi's supporters, who were given a free hand by the authorities.[64] One of the most intense conflicts between the regime's opponents and supporters took place in December 2012, when demonstrations against Mursi's constitutional declaration developed into clashes between anti-Mursi and pro-Mursi protesters in front of the presidential palace, in which seven people were killed and hundreds were injured.[65]

A characteristic of the Mursi regime was its effort to control the media and transform it into an MB mouthpiece. For example, the Shūrā Council, which was dominated by the MB, replaced more than fifty editors and editorial board managers of Egypt's state newspapers, and copies of the independent daily *Al-Dustūr* were seized after it criticized Mursi and the MB. In addition, the president's office and the office of the MB's supreme guide brought lawsuits against journalists for publishing "false reports" about the MB.[66] As stated in a Bedford Row International report on Mursi's presidency, "Morsi's pledge of forming a government for all Egyptians based on the principles of democracy and equality enabled him to win the election, but once in power his strategy changed markedly. Democracy and equality were relegated and replaced by a strategy of Islamification, publicly endorsed by Morsi and his government and controlled, from behind the scenes, by the MB."[67]

It is notable that al-Qaraḍāwī referred to Mursi's opponents as "Khawārij," whom he characterized as rebels against a legitimate leader to whom the *umma* had sworn a pledge of loyalty (*bay'a*), whether verbally or electorally.[68] Conversely, in discussing the protestors against Mubarak in the revolution of 2011, al-Qaraḍāwī ruled that they were not Khawārij because rebels count as Khawārij only if they come out against a legitimate ruler, as defined in the *sharī'a*, and if the uprising involves bloodshed and civil war among Muslims.[69] According to al-Qaraḍāwī, Mubarak was an illegitimate ruler, whereas Mursi, a member of the MB, was legitimate—hence, his differing rulings on the two revolutions. The shaykh's application of the damning name "Khawārij" thus essentially hinged on his political opinion about the two rulers.

Al-Qaraḍāwī's views on the anti-Mursi protests were also reflected in his sermon on June 21, 2013, in which he tried to dissuade Muslims from participating in demonstrations against Mursi and his government that were planned for the end of that month. In this sermon, he presented several arguments, only some of them religious, against calling for Mursi's ouster. He cited Q4:59, which exhorts the believers to obey Allah, Muḥammad, and the Muslim ruler, and added that, according to the *sharī'a*, opposing a Muslim ruler is permitted only if he orders the believers to commit sinful acts. Mursi, he elaborated, had commanded only good and had sought Egypt's welfare in all domains: religion, worldly affairs, matters of property and state, and the rights of its citizens.[70] This argument clearly places emphasis on the *shar'ī* criterion (i.e., whether Mursi commanded Egypt's citizens to sin) and disregards Mursi's violations of human rights, separation of powers, press freedom, and other fundamental democratic values.

Al-Qaraḍāwī argued further that Mursi's opponents were not sincere advocates of freedom but were simply hostile to the MB. During the entire monarchy period and the republic period up to Mubarak's ouster, he said, the Egyptians tolerated the regime's tyranny: the absence of free elections and the violation of human rights and freedoms. Yet when the MB came to power, they could not tolerate this absence and violation even for one year. The shaykh's unreserved support for Mursi and his movement as well as his failure to criticize their infringement on freedoms and human rights became even more blatant after 'Abd al-Fattah al-Sisi seized power.

It should be noted that al-Qaraḍāwī's conflict with Aḥmad al-Ṭayyib and 'Alī Gum'a (discussed in chapter 3) involves differing interpretations of Qur'ān and Sunna texts and their application to reality, in this case to the anti-Mursi revolution of 2013 and its aftermath. Following the attack by Egyptian security forces on pro-Mursi protesters in al-Naṣr Road, near Rābi'a al-'Adawiyya Square, on July 27, 2013, al-Ṭayyib, the shaykh of al-Azhar, issued a statement reminding both sides of the Prophet's warning: "If two Muslims clash swords, both the killer and the killed will be in hellfire."[71] (Al-Qaraḍāwī's use of this *ḥadīth* to justify Hamas's killing of Muslims is discussed in chapter 3.) Al-Qaraḍāwī argued, in response, that this *ḥadīth*—which condemns both sides in a violent conflict among Muslims—refers to a conflict between two groups of Muslims that are on an equal footing. Hence, he said, it does not apply to the al-Naṣr Road events because the two sides in that conflict were not equal: those who did the killing ('Abd al-Fattah al-Sisi's security forces) were oppressors and sinners, whereas those who were killed (Mursi's supporters) were righteous martyrs.[72] Al-Qaraḍāwī even made implicit threats against his rivals. In his response to al-Ṭayyib, he wrote: "O Shaykh of al-Azhar, I remind you how sinful it is to help kill a Muslim, even by uttering half a word"—in this statement hinting at a *ḥadīth* that proclaims that such a person will see no mercy from Allah on Judgment Day.[73]

Wasaṭīs' *and Liberals' Views of Human Rights*

Also pertinent to the *wasaṭīs*' and liberals' views of democracy are their divergent perceptions of human rights. Secular liberal writers regard democracy as a comprehensive philosophy anchored in a core system of human rights—chief among them the right to life, the right to freedom, and the right to define the welfare of the individual.[74] Al-Qaraḍāwī claims that Islam recognized human rights long before the West published its human rights conventions and that it was in fact an Islamic innovation: "Before the coming of Islam, people did not know they had rights. They only knew they had duties." He discerns several fundamental differences between the Islamic and Western perception of human rights. First, the West grants people rights but disregards their duties, whereas in Islam rights and duties are mutually linked: rights are granted when duties are fulfilled. Furthermore, in Islam, upholding rights is defined as a duty. For example, granting a child's right to material and spiritual care and to education is a duty that his parents must fulfill. Second, the human rights set out in the Qur'ān were not the result of a revolution that demanded them but rather a natural corollary of the high status accorded to man in the *sharīʿa*, for Allah honored man (Q17:70), appointed him as His *khalīfa*, viceroy, upon the earth (Q2:30), and created him in His image (Q95:4). Third, because what the West regards as rights Islam regards as duties, these duties are universally mandatory. For example, in the West gaining knowledge and education is a right, whereas in Islam "seeking knowledge" (*ṭalab al-ʿilm*) is the duty of every Muslim man and woman. According to the shaykh, human rights in Islam are anchored in two principles. First, the creed of monotheism liberated mankind from all forms of bondage except submission to Allah Himself. Al-Qaraḍāwī stresses that this creed also means that all men are brothers, for they are sons of a single Father and servants of a single Master. He states that the first human rights convention, held long before the UN Universal Declaration of Human Rights (1948), was Muḥammad's words in his farewell sermon (*khuṭbat al-wadāʿ*, delivered in 632 CE): "Verily your blood, your property are as sacred and inviolable as the sacredness of this day of yours, in this month of yours, in this town of yours." The second principle that underpins human rights in Islam, says al-Qaraḍāwī, is the dignity conferred by Allah upon Man, manifested by the soul Allah gave him (Q15:29), which distinguishes him from the beasts.[75]

Secular philosopher Fu'ād Zakariyyā rejects this claim that human rights are ancient and divine in origin rather than a modern man-made concept born of real-world human experience. He argues that al-Qaraḍāwī's approach, according to which God's decree is the only guarantee of human rights, is dangerous, for if the ruler is insufficiently pious, human rights may be in jeopardy. In other words, the Islamic view of human rights, including al-Qaraḍāwī's, assumes an ideal, God-fearing world, where the dignity conferred upon Man by Allah is sufficient to guarantee that his rights be respected. However, in the real world, which is governed by human beings with human flaws, interests, and ambitions, these rights must be safeguarded by man-made, nonreligious mechanisms. In the absence of such mechanisms, says Zakariyyā, violations of human rights are all too probable, as is in fact evident in Muslim history.[76]

Zakariyyā also points out that because the perception of human rights espoused by al-Qaraḍāwī and his fellow Islamists is not based on actual human experience, it is rigid and immutable. He notes that Western human rights developed gradually, over years of struggle, whereas the Islamic perception is of divinely decreed rights whose implementation was initially perfect but declined as time passed after the descent of the Qur'ān. Moreover, because the scriptures define these rights in very general terms, in real life their vagueness is exploited to justify every kind of tyranny and violation. According to Zakariyyā, this is why the gap between the theory and implementation of human rights is not a major topic of debate in the Muslim world. For example, the religious sources enshrine the right to life and prohibit murder (Q5:32), yet Islamic history is replete with violations of this right by the rulers because Muslim rulers who purported to govern according to the *sharī'a* ignored the prohibition on killing. In Zakariyyā's view, this discrepancy between ideal and reality stems from the fact that these laws are not associated with any practical means of enforcing them.[77]

Al-Qaraḍāwī counters that since the adoption of the Universal Declaration of Human Rights in 1948, much blood has been shed, much property has been stolen, and many people have been driven from their lands, especially Muslims—for instance, the Palestinians, who were expelled from Palestine. He asks: "Where are [your] human rights, O people . . . , in a jungle where the strong devour the weak or in a sea where the big fish eats the small one?" Conceding that Muslim countries fail to honor human rights, he argues that the remedy is to return to Islam and observe the rights and duties as decreed by Allah and Muḥammad.[78] Zakariyyā, too, observes a decline in human rights in Muslim countries, in particular those countries under military rule. He states that military regimes are especially intolerant of freedom of expression and thought and are inherently incapable of dealing with a rational opposition that raises logical arguments against them.[79] Zakariyyā would presumably reject al-Qaraḍāwī's remedy of implementing human rights as decreed in the Qur'ān, for although he does not contest the virtuous character of the Qur'ān and Sunna, he contends that "as long as the divine source of human rights is not surrounded by a protective fence, in the form of practical guarantees whose implementation is overseen by institutions, laws, and established traditions, nothing prevents the violation of human dignity and the usurpation of human rights at any given moment."[80]

Liberal writers such as Sayyid al-Qimnī[81] accuse al-Qaraḍāwī of presenting himself to the enlightened world as an advocate of democracy when in fact he denies basic human rights, such as freedom of belief, including the freedom to disagree with the *'ulamā'*. As evidence of this contradiction, al-Qimnī points to the shaykh's statement that "there is a consensus among the *'ulamā'* that whoever denies what is known by necessity in religion [*ma'lūm min al-dīn bi-l-ḍarūra*, i.e., essential religious truths] is an infidel who has strayed from the faith, and the ruler must demand that he repent and recant his views or else face the penalty for *ridda*." This statement, says al-Qimnī, shows that *'ulamā'* of al-Qaraḍāwī's ilk appoint themselves priests and purport to have a monopoly over the correct understanding of the religious texts.[82] Al-Qaraḍāwī indeed claims that secularists such as Fu'ād Zakariyyā deny the tenets of the faith when they reject the universal and eternal validity of the *sharī'a*.[83] According to al-Qimnī, al-Qaraḍāwī's position here includes all the components of Islamic fascism. Al-Qimnī identifies two camps in contemporary Islamic discourse: on the one hand the secularists, whose common denominator is a belief in individual freedoms, human rights, political democracy, and social justice, and on the other hand the purveyors of "terrorist" discourse, including al-Qaraḍāwī, whose beliefs al-Qimnī calls fascist, racist, sectarian, violent, and incompatible with individual freedoms and human rights.[84]

Al-Walā' wal-Barā'

Various Interpretations

The concept of "loyalty and disavowal," *al-walā' wal-barā'*, as Shiraz Maher has noted, is rather ill defined and has been given numerous and quite varied practical interpretations.[85] Traditional Muslim theology has applied this principle mainly to Muslims' personal behavior, taking it to mean that Muslims should be recognizable in their dress, their outward demeanor in general, their holidays, and so on.[86] Today, however, the principle of *al-walā' wal-barā'*, in Maher's words, "forms a distinct delineation between the Salafī-Jihadi constructions of Islam and everything else."[87] Salafīs and jihadi Salafīs consider Q5:51 as textual confirmation of this principle. This verse forbids the believers to "take the Jews and Christians as allies [*awliyā'*]" because "they are allies only to each other. Anyone who takes them as an ally becomes one of them [*wa-man yatawallahum minkum fa-innahu minhum*]."

One conclusion that the jihadi Salafīs derive from their interpretation of the concept of *al-walā' wal-barā'* is that one is commanded to hate unbelievers and forbidden to love them. According to Q58:22, the believers in Allah and the Day of Judgment should not give "their loyalty to those who oppose God and His Messenger, even though they may be their fathers, sons, brothers, or other relations." Al-Ẓawāhirī claims that the unbelievers, whether from among the People of the Book or from among the pagans, hate the Muslims and wish that the latter would not receive God's Revelation (2:105). According to the Qur'ān (3:100), he argues, Jews and Christians hope that Muslims will revert to unbelief after having believed. Al-Ẓawāhirī stresses the close link that love of Allah and the principle of loyalty only toward one's fellow believers have with jihad, for it is the latter that proves that the believer loves Allah.[88]

The dispute between al-Qaraḍāwī as *wasaṭī* and the jihadi Salafīs on the matter of *al-walā' wal-barā'* concerns first and foremost the way Q5:51 should be interpreted. Al-Qaraḍāwī insists that the Salafīs who quote this and other Qur'ānic verses as proof that Muslims are commanded to hate the unbelievers have misunderstood the text. His approach to Qur'ānic exegesis is based on understanding the context of the verse and the circumstances under which it was revealed.[89] Taking these into account, he maintains that Q5:51 and the subsequent verses do not speak about Jews and Christians generally, but only about those who were hostile toward the Muslims and fought against their *da'wa*. Verses 5:57–58 prove this interpretation, to his mind, because they command the faithful not to "take as allies those who ridicule your religion." But, adds al-Qaraḍāwī, in contrast to the Jews mentioned in these verses, those Jews and Christians who live in peace (*musālimūn*) with the Muslims are "People of the Book," whom the Qur'ān allows Muslims to eat with and even to marry (Q5:5).[90] However, we should note that in a decision within the framework of his "jurisprudence for Muslim minorities," al-Qaraḍāwī ruled that although it is permissible to marry the daughters of the People of the Book, one should refrain from doing so today because the principle of "prevention of harm takes precedence over benefit [*dar' al-mafsada muqaddam 'alā jalb al-maṣlaḥa*]." In the same decision, he also states that a Muslim may not marry a Jewess as long as there is war between Muslims and Jews because, so he claims, every Jewish woman is a soldier in Israel's army, in spirit if not in body.[91]

Al-Qaraḍāwī, therefore, takes an interpretative and apologetic approach to the tenet of *al-walā' wa-l-barā'* and to the texts in the Qur'ān and *ḥadīth* on which it is based. In contrast, liberals, such as the Tunisian liberal writer al-'Afīf al-Akhḍar, regard this tenet as the core of the *fiqh* of modern terrorism. Al-Akhḍar describes it as a "narcissistic" effort to maintain "a purity of identity" and claims that its practical implication is that all political, diplomatic, economic, and cultural ties with non-Muslims should be severed and that all non-Muslim lands must be regarded as *dār al-ḥarb*; moreover, millions of Muslims living in non-Muslim lands are to be regarded as fighting against Islam because they pay taxes to the states in which they live. This principle, he writes, is part of the *fiqh* of the Middle Ages and is a certain recipe for a collective Muslim suicide. He notes that this belief supplanted the approach expressed by Q2:62, which states that Muslims, Jews, Christians, and the Sabians who believe in Allah and in the Day of Judgment will be rewarded by Him and need not fear the Day of Judgment. According to al-Akhḍar, the latter verse sets out the common denominator among all nations, and it should be revived as a basis for interfaith dialogue in order to combat terrorism.[92]

Liberal writer Shākir al-Nābulsī identifies *al-walā' wa-l-barā'* as well as *dār al-Islām* and *dār al-ḥarb* as slogans of religious-political fundamentalism (*uṣūliyya*)—that is, of the MB—and as inventions by the *ikhwānī* and Salafī *fuqahā'* but not part of the Qur'ān and Sunna. These terms, he says, gained currency in Salafī and *uṣūlī* writings during the 1960s, when al-Nasir began persecuting the MB, prompting many of its members to leave Egypt for the Persian Gulf countries. It is these members who incorporated these terms in their curricula, thus making them part of Islam, he contends. He notes that these terms are also prominent in the rhetoric of al-Qaʿida and other "pseudo-Islamic" extremist groups.[93]

Seeking the Help of the Unbelievers as an Expression of al-Walāʾ wal-Barāʾ

One expression of the principle of loyalty and disavowal is the prohibition that forbids Muslims from helping non-Muslims against fellow Muslims (*al-istiʿāna bil-kuffār*).[94] According to al-Ẓawāhirī this rule is based on the Qurʾānic prohibition (Q5:51) against taking Jews and Christians as allies.[95] Al-Ẓawāhirī quotes Ibn Taymiyya's ruling that if even those who had fasted, prayed, and did not fight against Muslims were to be considered *murtaddūn*, apostates, because they had refused to pay the *zakāh* to Abū Bakr, then obviously Muslims who fought on the side of the Mongols against the Muslims should be considered *murtaddūn*. Al-Ẓawāhirī asks: "What would Ibn Taymiyya have said today had he seen the aircraft and troops of America and its allies using the Gulf States as bases from which to attack the Muslims in Iraq?"[96]

Jihadi Salafī jurists such as al-Maqdisī[97] maintain that such Muslims deserve to be fought even more than the Mongols because a *murtadd* deserves greater punishment than one who was originally an infidel (*al-kāfir al-aṣlī*). He also draws support from Muḥammad Ibn ʿAbd al-Wahhāb's list of ten "nullifiers of Islam" (*nawāqiḍ al-Islām*), the eighth of which is providing aid (*muẓāhara*) to polytheists against Muslims. Therefore, al-Maqdisī rules that anyone who helps the American "Crusaders" and the North Atlantic Treaty Organization forces against the Muslims in Afghanistan is an infidel.[98] Al-Ṭarṭūsī, too, considers loyalty to the "unbelieving polytheists," in the sense of helping them against Muslims with sword or word, as "major unbelief," whose perpetrator removes himself from the community of believers (*kufr akbar yukhriju ṣāḥibahu mina al-milla*).[99]

Al-Qaraḍāwī surveys the classical legal views on the issue of Muslims using non-Muslims in time of war.[100] He concludes that the basic rule (*aṣl*) is that Muslims should do their own fighting with no help from unbelievers, but that such help is permitted in case of necessity, under certain conditions as defined by jurists.[101] He recognizes the importance of taking reality into consideration (what he calls *fiqh al-wāqi*ʿ, "understanding reality") and thus rules that at present Muslims need to seek the help of others more than in the past because today there are individual Muslim states with no unifying caliph and lacking the needed strength. However, he sets the following conditions for seeking the help of non-Muslims, even those who are not protected people (*dhimmī*s): there is a clear need for such help; it must be ascertained that those whose help is sought are loyal to the Muslims and hostile to the Muslims' enemies; they must not be permitted to engage in proselytizing activities among the Muslims; and they will not be in positions of command but be subordinate to Muslim commanders.[102]

Following the Iraqi invasion of Kuwait in 1990, King Fahd (d. 2005) of Saudi Arabia allowed half a million American troops to enter Saudi territory to protect the kingdom against a possible attack by the Iraqi army. Al-Qaraḍāwī ruled that a necessity existed to use the troops of the infidels, American and British in this case, in order to expel Saddam Hussein's army from Kuwait; however, he opposed an American invasion of Iraq and the participation of Muslim countries in the coalition against Saddam Hussein (d. 2006) because Muslims are forbidden to side with unbelievers against their brethren, even when the latter do wrong. This is what he wrote concerning American assistance in expelling Iraq from Kuwait: "Seeking the assistance of a foreign (unbelieving) force is something that has been imposed by necessity, and necessity has its own laws; what is permitted because of necessity must be measured by the extent of the necessity [*wa-mā yubāḥ lil-ḍarūra yuqaddar bi-qadrihā*]." He added that the permission he gave for American troops to assist the Muslims to remove Saddam's forces from Kuwait was restricted to that specific mission, following which they should return whence they came.[103] He rejected the idea that Muslims were allowed to help the Americans against Saddam's regime because the latter was a *murtadd* and his Baath Party was secular. Indeed, he maintained that even if Saddam's regime was not Islamic, the Iraqi people as a whole were Muslims and Iraq was part of *dār al-Islām*, and therefore it was the duty of every Muslim to perform jihad in order to liberate Iraq from the American occupiers.[104]

It is important to point out that al-Qaraḍāwī's ruling on using American troops to expel the Iraqis from Kuwait is also in agreement with 'Abd al-'Azīz b. 'Abdallah Ibn Bāz's ruling that it was permissible (*jā'iz*) to use foreign troops to remove Saddam from Kuwait because of "necessity" and that therefore Saudi Arabia was duty bound to do so. Ibn Bāz also noted in his ruling that there is a duty to protect Islam, Muslims, and the "inviolability" (*ḥurma*) of the state, in this case Saudi Arabia, and its inhabitants.[105]

Al-Qaraḍāwī's and Ibn Bāz's rulings contradict the position of the *'ulamā'* of the Awakening (Ṣaḥwa) in Saudi Arabia, headed by Shaykh Safar al-Ḥawālī (b. 1955), and that of jihadi Salafī jurists such as al-Maqdisī. Al-Maqdisī declared that when Muslims aid the unbelievers in fighting other Muslims, as in the case of the Saudi regime's cooperation with the Americans, it constitutes giving aid to Allah's enemies. He therefore accused the Saudi government of unbelief and ruled that Muslims were duty bound to fight against the government and so declare *tawḥīd*, which, for him, means detaching oneself from any religion, idol, way, or law, or any object of worship except for Allah and Islam; it also means hostility (*'adāwa*) toward polytheists and loyalty (*muwālāh*) to the believers.[106]

In the *fatwā*s issued following 9/11, the attacks were condoned from the standpoint of Islamic law, specifically using the principle of *al-walā' wal-barā'* as justification. Hostility toward the polytheists, Americans in this case, was explained as constituting an element of *tawḥīd*, and disavowing unbelievers and polytheists, whether Jews or Christians, was stated to be a religious duty, derived from the negative part of the *shahāda*—the declaration "there is no God but Allah."[107] Al-Qaraḍāwī, in contrast, owing to his attempt to correct the image of Islam as a religion of violence and to assuage fears of Islam in the West, argued following the 9/11 attacks that Islam embraces humanity as a whole, despite differences in language, color, homeland, and religion, viewing it as "one family" that belongs to a single sovereign and that traces its roots back to Adam and Eve.[108]

It should be noted that al-Qaraḍāwī suggested after 9/11 that as part of the attempt to improve the reputation of Islam in the West, the unbelievers should be called "non-Muslims" (*ghayr al-Muslimīn*) rather than "infidels," although he emphasized that this change in terminology must not be perceived as a change in the position that Islam is the one true religion and that anyone who does not believe in Muḥammad's mission is an infidel.[109] In the same context, al-Qaraḍāwī urged Muslims in this age of globalization, especially after the 9/11 attacks, to adopt the term *brotherhood of mankind* to express the connection among all human beings. However, it is important to understand the way he meant this term to be used and his purpose in the representation of humankind as one family—namely, to bring non-Muslims closer to Islam and to close the gap between Muslims and non-Muslims in order to thwart the plots of Islam's enemies against it. These enemies, he wrote, seek to ignite internal war among Muslims as an excuse to conquer and rule them. Hence, "we should repel their plot by means of positions such as this [using different terminology], thus transforming the nation's forces into a unified front against their plotting and aggression."[110] Al-Qaraḍāwī's argument shows that rather than championing a fundamental change of attitude toward non-Muslims—that is, promoting reconciliation and brotherhood instead of hostility—he is concerned mainly with thwarting what he sees as the infidel conspiracies against Islam. This understanding of his view fits the rule that al-Qaraḍāwī formulated for the use of certain terminology: "The importance lies in what the names denote, not in the names themselves [*al-'ibra bil-musammayāt lā bil-asmā'*] because names can change."[111]

The Islamic legal status of Muslim soldiers who serve in the US armed forces is an issue that came to prominence following the 9/11 attacks and the US war in Afghanistan and highlighted the differences in approach between *wasaṭiyya* and jihadi Salafism with respect to the principle of *al-walā' wal-barā'*. Following 9/11, al-Qaraḍāwī issued a ruling that sparked an uproar and intense controversy in the Muslim world: that Muslims soldiers serving in the US military may take part in the war in Afghanistan against terrorists and those who shelter them. The religious justification he gave is that refusing to fight in Afghanistan would cast doubt on the Muslim soldiers' loyalty to their homeland, the United States, and this, in turn, would harm the American Muslim community as a whole. This harm to the community would be graver than the harm caused to the conscience of a Muslim soldier if he killed a fellow Muslim in his capacity as a US soldier. The *sharī'a* principle he cited in support of this view was that of choosing the lesser evil; he also cited the principle that it is more important to prevent harm to the collective than to prevent harm to an individual.[112]

Criticizing al-Qaraḍāwī's *fatwā*, al-Ṭarṭūsī wrote that al-Qaraḍāwī made loyalty to one's homeland (*al-walā' al-waṭanī*) more important than loyalty to God, the faith, and the Muslims.[113] Also contrary to al-Qaraḍāwī, al-Maqdisī ruled that Muslim soldiers in the US armed forces were fighting "on behalf of the idol [*fī sabīl al-ṭāghūt*]," an understanding based on Q4:76, and were therefore to be considered unbelievers. He added that the Muslim soldiers in the US armed forces must deny the existence of the idol (*al-kufr bil-ṭāghūt*, based on Q2:256) and "disavow" it (the principle of *barā'a*, based on Q16:36) by either fleeing from the American "Crusader" camp or performing jihad against the Americans in order to help the Muslims.[114] It should be noted that al-Qaraḍāwī later declared that his *fatwā* on this issue was an "anomalous ruling" (*fatwā shādhdha*) on his part, a mistake owing to his ignorance of the fact that soldiers in the US armed forces have a right to request not to participate in combat.[115]

In the year 2003, following the US invasion of Iraq, al-Qaraḍāwī did declare that Muslims have a duty to resist the American forces in every way but added that the old agreements between the United States and the Persian Gulf states allowing the Americans to build military bases in the Gulf must be respected.[116] The jihadi Salafīs fiercely attacked this ruling. One of them, Shaykh ʿAbd al-Ākhir Ḥammād al-Ghunaymī, argued that Arab rulers who open their air and sea ports to US forces and permit them to use their territories for invading Iraq become unbelievers. He added, contra al-Qaraḍāwī, that the Muslim rulers' agreements with the Americans are illegitimate according to *sharīʿa* because they do not govern by its laws, and they permit the military presence of unbelievers on Muslim soil, including the Arabian Peninsula, which violates the Prophet's commandment in *ḥadīth*: "Remove the polytheists from the Arabian Peninsula."[117]

Takfīr

The theological debate on the definition of faith and unbelief in Islam had already begun by the eighth century CE. The mainstream in Islam, the *ahl al-sunna wal-jamāʿa*, adhered to what Ibn Taymiyya called a "median position"[118] and adopted the view that faith involves utterance (*qawl*) in the heart and by the mouth; deeds (*ʻamal*) done by the heart, the tongue, and the limbs; and inner conviction (*niyya*). This position led to the idea that faith increases (*al-īmān yazīdu*) by observance of the commandments and decreases through sin (*yanquṣu bil-maʻṣiya*).[119] This definition of faith in turn directly affected Ibn Taymiyya's view on *takfīr*: he argued that no Muslim should be accused of unbelief based on sins he has committed, that such a Muslim remains within the faith despite his sins.[120] The *ahl al-sunna wal-jamāʻa* are considered to be located in the middle between two extreme approaches. One of these extremes is the *murji'a*,[121] which recognizes only inner conviction as the essence of faith and therefore maintains that faith neither increases nor decreases because deeds are external to faith.[122] At the other extreme are the Khawārij and the Muʻtazilites, both of whom consider deeds to be included in faith and therefore that whoever commits a major sin (*kabīra*) should be considered a nonbeliever. These two groups differ, however, in that the Khawārij consider such a person to be an unbeliever, whereas the Muʻtazilites see him as neither a believer nor an unbeliever but rather in a "position between the two positions [*manzila bayna manzilatayni*]."[123]

The fundamental concept of the jihadi Salafī approach is *ʻaqīda*, the basic articles of the faith, together with *minhaj*, the path toward the implementation of the *ʻaqīda*. ʻAbdallah ʻAzzām explained that the establishment of Islam must proceed by construction from the foundations, by sowing the seeds of faith deep inside the heart, as one sows seeds in the soil.[124] As a result, global jihad thinkers such as al-Maqdisī and al-Ṭarṭūsī wrote books on *ʻaqīda*.[125] IS, too, published a fundamental document of this kind that presents the *ʻaqīda* and IS's *minhaj*.[126] At the center of all these publications, one finds the terms *īmān* (faith) and *kufr* (unbelief) as well as the criteria for declaring someone an unbeliever. In these documents, faith is defined in line with the views of the *ahl al-sunna wal-jamāʻa*.[127]

Al-Qaraḍāwī's Engagement in Takfīr

It should be noted that although al-Qaraḍāwī did set out the conditions required for accusing someone of unbelief, *takfīr*, and endorsed Abū

Ḥamid al-Ghazālī's principle that "it is better to let a thousand unbelievers live than to shed even a cup's worth of Muslim blood,"[128] he has leveled accusations of *ridda*, for example, against the secularists, as we have seen. According to al-Qaraḍāwī, *takfīr* is justified in the following cases:

1. Muslims who openly and unabashedly declare their unbelief. However, anyone who is a Muslim on the outside (*ẓāhir*) but does not believe on the inside (*bāṭin*) is to be classified as a hypocrite (*munāfiq*). In this world, hypocrite Muslims are to be treated as Muslims, but in the next world they will occupy the "lowest depths [*al-darak al-asfal*] of hell" (Q4:145).

2. Adherents of communism as a philosophy and a way of life, which are inconsistent with the Muslim faith and *sharīʿa*.

3. Secular rulers and members of secular political parties who explicitly reject *sharīʿa* and promote the separation of state and religion. Such rulers wage war against those who call on the implementation of *sharīʿa*.

4. Sects that have manifestly deviated from Islam, such as the Druze, the Nuṣayrīs or Alawites, the Ismāʿīlīs, and today also the Bahāʾīs and the Ahmedis (al-Qādyāniyya).[129]

Al-Qaraḍāwī also directed accusations of *ridda* at the author Salmān Rushdī for his novel *The Satanic Verses* (1988). In a sermon delivered in April 1989, he called the novelist a *murtadd* and an atheist (*mulḥid*) and wondered how Muslim countries could defend him in the name of liberty and freedom of artistic creation. He stated that Rushdī had cursed the Prophet Muḥammad and that, in the opinion of most Muslim jurisprudents, whoever curses the Prophet can never absolve himself even if he repents his sin.[130] The shaykh thus effectively adopted Rūḥ Allah b. Muṣṭafā Khomeini's ruling on February 14, 1989, proclaiming Rushdī a *murtadd* deserving of death.

Another incident in which the religious establishment in Egypt acted to stifle creative freedom occurred in 2000, when the Egyptian Culture Ministry decided to republish the book *A Feast for the Seaweeds* (*Walīma li-aʿshāb al-baḥr*) by Syrian author Ḥaydar Ḥaydar (b. 1936). In response, Muḥammad Sayyid Ṭanṭāwī (d. 2010), the shaykh of al-Azhar, proclaimed that the book disrespected Allah, the Prophet, and the Qurʾān and moreover was replete with eroticism, which he said contravened the moral values of Islam. He ruled that the book contained heresy because it denied "what is known by necessity in religion [*maʿlūm min al-dīn bi-l-ḍarūra*]."[131] Al-Qaraḍāwī endorsed the al-Azhar position, which he proclaimed was authoritative, and praised the shaykh of al-Azhar for his clear and firm position.[132] He castigated the Culture Ministry for its position that reprinting the book would promote a culture of enlightenment; it would not promote *tanwīr*, enlightenment, he said, but rather *tabwīr*, the turning of Egyptian culture into uncultivated soil.[133]

Such rulings led the liberal writer Shākir al-Nābulsī to conclude that the *takfīr* practiced by scholars such as al-Qaraḍāwī reflects the moral bankruptcy of *uṣūliyya* as well as the intellectual deficiency of this stream, which stems from its ignorance of modern thought. He wrote: "The religious *uṣūliyya* does not confront thought with thought because it has no thought. Instead it confronts thought by means of fire, explosive belts, silencers, whips, knives, car bombs, invective, *takfīr*, and accusations of atheism—and those are the bare minimum of their faith [*aḍʿaf al-īmān*]."[134]

Muḥammad Saʿīd al-ʿAshmāwī, also a fierce critic of *takfīr*, claims that it contravenes the spirit of the Qur'ān. The holy book of Islam, he says, contends that anyone who utters the two testimonies (*shahādatāni*) cannot be described as a *murtadd* under any circumstances, and nobody is entitled to proclaim him as such. He adds that by employing *takfīr*, the tyrants—specifically clerics and those who politicize Islam—transform the compassionate and tolerant Islam into a religion of terror and create a situation in which both the Muslims and their rivals regard Islam as an inherently violent faith.[135]

Al-Qaraḍāwī regards *ridda* as the gravest danger to Muslim society; in fact, he believes that the most dangerous plot of Islam's enemies is to cause Muslims, by force or by cunning, to leave their faith. According to him, in the modern era the Muslim world has faced several violent attacks aimed at severing it from its roots—namely, the Islamic tenet of *tawḥid*, God's oneness—and at driving it to commit *ridda*. The worst of these attacks has been the "secularist invasion" that seeks to destroy the true Islam, and the Muslims' duty is to repel these attacks and refuse *ridda*, as Abū Bakr did in the Ridda Wars (632–33 CE).[136]

Al-Qaraḍāwī's definition of a society based on *tawḥīd* sheds light on his conception of *ridda*. An Islamic society, he says, cannot be materialistic, secular, polytheist, Jewish or Christian, liberal, capitalist, socialist, or Marxist. Paraphrasing a famous *ḥadīth*, he asserts that an Islamic society must not only accept *tawḥid* but recognize that *tawḥid* "is superior and that nothing is superior to it." Islam cannot occupy a marginal place in the life of this society, nor can this society permit any other creed (*ʻaqīda*)—the creed of communism, for example—to oppose Islam or to compete with it. For al-Qaraḍāwī, "revolutionary" ideologies such as communism and secularism are religions because they are comprehensive philosophies pertaining to many of life's domains.[137]

The Wasaṭī*-Liberal Debate on the Appropriate Punishment for* Ridda

Liberal writers such as al-Baghdādī note that the Qur'ānic verses on *ridda* do not specify that a *murtadd* must be put to death. In other words, according to al-Baghdādī, *ridda* is not one of the sins for which a Qur'ānic punishment (*ḥadd*) is specified. One of the verses on *ridda* (2:217) states that the actions of a *murtadd* will be "worthless in this world and the Hereafter" and that he will abide in hellfire forever. But even this verse, stresses al-Baghdādī, does not state that the *murtadd* must be killed.[138] Scholars who argue that a *murtadd* must be executed often cite the *ḥadīth* that says, "Whoever changes his religion—kill him [*man baddala dīnahu—fa-uqtulūhu*]." However, this is a *ḥadīth āḥād*, a *ḥadīth* transmitted by only a single source,[139] and the liberals accept the principle, which is accepted also by many *ʻulamā'*, that a *ḥadīth* of this kind does not constitute sufficient evidence for the validity of a punishment.

Al-Qaraḍāwī rejects these claims, stating that there is a consensus among jurists that *murtaddūn* are deserving of death. He does stress, however, that a Muslim can be convicted of *ridda* only by expert scholars with extensive knowledge and that the punishment must be carried out by the ruler after a *sharīʻa* court convicts the accused. In response to al-Baghdādī's claim that this punishment is not mentioned in the Qur'ān, the shaykh replies that Q5:33 (known as the *ḥadd al-ḥirāba* verse, specifying the punishment of those who commit highway robbery, rape, and terrorism) applies to *murtaddūn* and thus proclaims that they must be executed. The shaykh also justifies the severity of the punishment by asserting that Muslim society is based on faith, for faith is the foundation of its identity and the main pillar of its existence. Hence, declared *ridda* is the gravest crime in Islam, he says.[140]

Al-Baghdādī counters that "by calling on *murtaddūn* to be killed, we declare before all non-Muslims that Islam does not allow freedom of religion, when Qur'ānic verses clearly state otherwise." He quotes Q2:256, "there is no coercion in religion," and asserts: "We ignore this great verse and insist, in a bewildering fashion, on [accepting] the *ḥadīth al-āḥād* 'whoever changes his religion kill him'?!" Those who call on the execution of *murtaddūn*, he adds, open schools whose graduates are criminals with a license to kill. "Is this what we want for our Muslim societies on the brink of the twenty-first century?" he wonders.[141]

In an attempt to settle the contradiction between Q2:256 ("there is no coercion in religion") and his ruling that *murtaddūn* are deserving of death, the shaykh distinguishes between two types of *murtaddūn*: those who openly advocate *ridda*, whose sin is therefore "severe" (*ghalīẓa*), and those who keep their *ridda* to themselves, whose *ridda* is therefore "light" (*khafīfa*). *Murtaddūn* of the former type, says the shaykh, are guilty not only of renouncing Islam but of fighting Allah and His Messenger and spreading corruption in the land; hence, they are deserving of death according to Q5:33. Such *murtaddūn*, he elaborates, must be killed because they threaten the very identity of the society in which they live. He compares their status in Islam to the status of traitors and collaborators in non-Muslim societies, who are likewise regarded as the worst of criminals.[142]

Rejecting al-Qaraḍāwī's apologetic stance, al-Baghdādī notes that freedom of religion must be absolute and cannot apply to those who wish to embrace Islam but not to those who wish to leave it.[143] Another critic of al-Qaraḍāwī, al-Nābulsī, asserts that al-Qaraḍāwī knows in his heart of hearts that democracy is anchored in secularism and liberalism, which guarantee political, ideological, and personal freedom. These freedoms, he says, are the foundations of the Universal Declaration of Human Rights. But for the Islamists, the Declaration of Human Rights is heresy because it assumes that all human beings are equal, regardless of their gender and religion.[144]

The shaykh's interpretation of *takfīr* evoked harsh criticism from 'Abd al-Razzāq 'Īd, who wrote: "If we count all those the shaykh [al-Qaraḍāwī] wishes to slaughter [for heresy], then Genghis Khan and Hulagu [Khan] will seem like amateurs next to this 'tolerant' shaykh who wants to kill the nation out of love, following in the footsteps of his *imām*, Ḥasan al-Bannā, who wanted to invade [people's hearts] with love."[145]

Wasaṭiyya *and Jihadi Salafism on* Takfīr*: Similarities*

Comparing al-Qaraḍāwī's and Ḥasan al-Bannā's views on *takfīr*, we find that the *wasaṭī* al-Qaraḍāwī has gone much further than his mentor, drawing close to the position of the jihadi Salafīs. Al-Bannā's approach to *takfir* was formulated as one of his twenty principles (*uṣūl*) enunciated in "Message of Teachings":

> Never label any Muslim as an unbeliever [*kāfir*] because of an opinion [*ra'y*] or a sin [*ma'ṣiya*] if he has confessed the two testimonies [*shahādatāni*] of faith, acts accordingly, and performs the obligatory [*farḍ*] duties of Islam, unless he clearly professes the word of unbelief, refuses to acknowledge a fundamental principle of Islam [*ma'lūm min al-dīn bi-l-ḍatūra*: literally, "things in religion that are known of necessity"],[146] denies the purity of the Qur'an, or commits an evident act of unbelief.[147]

Al-Qaraḍāwī formulated a number of rules based on the Qur'ān and the Sunna for determining when one may accuse a Muslim of unbelief. It should, however, be pointed out that some jihadi Salafī thinkers, such as al-Maqdisī and al-Ṭarṭūsī, also expressed their concern, as did al-Qaraḍāwī, about exaggerated accusations of unbelief and so attempted to formulate rules for the application of *takfīr*.[148] An examination of their writings shows that their rules encompass al-Qaraḍāwī's rules. It also makes it clear that both al-Qaraḍāwī the *wasaṭī* and al-Maqdisī and al-Ṭarṭūsī the jihadi Salafīs share their objection to *takfīriyyūn*, those who "exaggerate" in their accusations of unbelief.[149] Al-Qaraḍāwī can certainly accept al-Maqdisī's major contentions on the subject of *takfīr* as they appear in *This Is Our Faith*, such as the need to double-check the facts before accusing anyone of unbelief because "permission to shed the blood of those who pray to the one God is a great danger; the mistake of letting a thousand unbelievers be is lesser than the mistake of shedding a cup of blood of a single Muslim."[150]

The rules that al-Qaraḍāwī shares with al-Maqdisī and al-Ṭarṭūsī include:

1. One must distinguish between attributing "absolute unbelief" (*al-kufr al-muṭlaq*), also called "generic unbelief" (*kufr an-naw'*)—that is, attribution of unbelief to the cause and not the person—and accusing a specific person of unbelief (*takfīr al-mu'ayyan*). In the former case, it is the deed that is accused of unbelief, whereas in the latter case the accusation is against a person who said or did something that constitutes unbelief. In the latter case, it is necessary to determine whether the conditions (*shurūṭ*) for an accusation of unbelief have been met and whether there are no *shar'ī* bases for preventing such an accusation.[151] Al-Qaraḍāwī, al-Maqdisī, and al-Ṭarṭūsī base their distinction between the two cases on Ibn Taymiyya, among others.[152]

2. One judges whether a person is a believer or an unbeliever by what can be perceived from the outside (*ẓāhir*) rather than on what people think within themselves (*bāṭin*), for only God knows a person's innermost secrets (*sarā'ir*).[153]

3. Whoever utters the two testimonies becomes a Muslim definitively (*yaqīn*) and cannot be expelled from the faith without a similarly definitive testimony, in accordance with the principle "Certainty is not removed by doubt [*al-yaqīn lā yuzāl bil-shakk*]." Therefore, no Muslim may be removed from Islam unless he commits an explicit act of unbelief (*kufr bawāḥ*) that is not open to any other interpretation (*ta'wīl*).[154]

4. Unbelief can be either "major" (*al-kufr al-akbar*) or "minor" (*al-kufr al-aṣghar*); the former causes one to be removed from Islam, but the latter does not. One who commits a minor act of unbelief remains a Muslim in this world, and in the next world his fate is determined by God, who may punish or forgive him. But even if such a sinner is punished, he will not remain in hell forever, unlike those who are guilty of major unbelief and die as unbelievers or polytheists.[155]

The Difference between the Wasaṭī *and Jihadi Salafī Perceptions of* Takfīr

The difference between the *wasaṭī* and jihadi Salafī perceptions of *takfīr* is subtle and sometimes seems to be a difference in phrasing rather than in content: *wasaṭiyya* uses deliberately vague language in discussing this issue, whereas jihadi Salafism uses clear and decisive language. A good example is provided by their rulings regarding the Shī'a. Al-Ṭarṭūsī ruled that the Twelver Shī'a is "a sect of *shirk* and *ridda*."[156] Al-Qaraḍāwī, in contrast, ruled that although the Shī'a sect introduced forbidden innovations in Islam (i.e., is guilty of *ibtidā'*), this act is not blatant heresy that excludes its adherents from the fold of Islam.[157] The shaykh rejects the claim made by some Sunnīs that the Shī'īs are infidels because they believe that the Qur'ān has been distorted and that chapters have been omitted from it. He notes that only some Shī'īs believe this, but most of them accept the Qur'ān as it is known to the Sunnīs.[158] Despite this clarification, however, as noted earlier, he accuses the Shī'a of attempting to infiltrate Sunnī countries and calls the Shī'ī party Hizbullah "Ḥizb al-Shayṭān" (Party of Satan) and "Ḥizb al-Ṭāghūt" (Party of Idols), which is essentially an act of *takfīr* against Hizbullah.[159]

A fundamental difference between the *wasaṭī* and jihadi Salafī perceptions of *takfīr* is evident in their rulings about parliamentary elections, the legitimacy of secular parties, and the legitimacy of nationalism. An important difference between the three streams—*wasaṭī*, jihadi Salafī, and liberal—involves the issue of *takfir* against Muslim rulers who do not govern according to the *sharī'a*. The disagreement between them on this point is reflected in their respective interpretations of verses 44, 45, and 47 in the fifth *sūra* of the Qur'ān, which the jihadi Salafīs regard as the basis for accusing such rulers of heresy.

The jihadi Salafīs, such as al-Maqdisī, rule that parliamentary elections are a form of *shirk* because the parliament, as a legislative body, infringes upon Allah's exclusive authority to pass laws. "Whoever follows and obeys [an authority] other than Allah in legislation," writes al-Maqdisī, "even with respect to a single issue, attributes a partner to Allah the Almighty, for he accepts that authority as a sovereign, even if he does not worship it, pray to it, or fast in order to draw close to it." If this is the case, he adds, what can be said about someone who "assumes or grants someone else the absolute and comprehensive authority to pass laws??" Al-Maqdisī thus determines that anyone who runs in parliamentary elections is a *murtadd* and a *mushrik*, even if he does not manage to gain a seat and take part in legislation, for merely by submitting his candidacy he has accepted the heretical notion of human legislation and failed to renounce the constitution and the *shirk* of democracy. For the same reason, al-Maqdisī rules that whoever votes in parliamentary elections is a *mushrik* as well.[160]

Al-Qaraḍāwī, in contrast, does not accuse parliamentarians and voters of *ridda*; in fact, he regards elections as a means by which Islamic parties can rise to power, as the MB did in Egypt in 2012. As noted earlier, he advocates "Islamic democracy," in which the tenets of the faith and explicit *sharīʿa* laws are not subject to amendment or approval by majority vote. He holds that Allah is the supreme legislator but also that there is nevertheless some room for human legislation in those areas that are not regulated by clear-cut religious permissions and prohibitions but are subject to *ijtihād* and to human considerations of cost and benefit.[161] Unlike the jihadi Salafīs, then, al-Qaraḍāwī does not regard all parliamentary legislation as a form of heresy. However, he stresses that in order for man-made laws to be legitimate, they must exist within the general framework of the *sharīʿa* and conform to the philosophy of Islam; furthermore, the force of these laws does not emanate from the authority of the parliament but from the authority of Allah, who is their ultimate source.[162]

A significant difference between al-Qaraḍāwī and the jihadi Salafīs concerns their view of secular parties. Al-Ṭarṭūsī rules that, based on the texts of the *sharīʿa*, "secular parties" and "heretical parties" cannot be considered legitimate and must not be allowed to exist and certainly not to govern, even if elected by majority vote. In fact, he states that "the espousal of secularism and of heretical schools of thought by Muslims is tantamount to heresy and to leaving the fold of Islam."[163] This *fatwā* is part of the Islamic debate on the wider issue of party pluralism. In ruling on this issue, al-Ṭarṭūsī distinguishes between two cases: an Islamic state governed by a caliph and a state that is not governed by *sharīʿa* law. In the former kind of state, he says, no parties are allowed at all, and the Muslims are required to preserve their unity and obey the Qur'ān and the Sunna. In the second kind of state, observant Muslims are allowed—and in fact required—to form an organized movement in order to gain power and oppose the ruling tyrant.[164]

Al-Qaraḍāwī allows party pluralism but prohibits the founding of secular parties. However, although he generally denounces secularism as a form of heresy and atheism, unlike al-Ṭarṭūsī he refrains from explicitly stating that secular parties constitute "great heresy." Using more cautious language, he states that a party is legitimate as long as it respects the tenets of the Muslim faith—in other words, the directives of the *sharīʿa* and of the religion at large.[165] This ruling drew criticism from al-Ṭarṭūsī, who objected that this condition is insufficient and allows even heretical and apostate parties to participate in elections.[166]

Also interesting is the two streams' distinct approach to the issue of nationalism, or "national loyalty" (*al-walāʾ al-waṭanī*). For al-Ṭarṭūsī, national loyalty means that rights and duties are based on copresence within the geographical boundaries of the homeland—namely, on citizenship. According to him and to other jihadi Salafis, this means the rejection of the only valid basis for mutual loyalty among individuals, which is shared religious faith. Jihadi Salafism in fact rejects the division of the world into nation-states. Al-Ṭarṭūsī writes:

> In the name of the homeland, of nationalism, and of national loyalty, they tore up the world into homelands and gave each of them borders and a slogan. They composed a national anthem for each homeland, and the sons of this homeland, young and old, know this anthem by heart and are proud of it, rather than of some other [anthem]. In this way, they scattered the Muslims, who are brothers, in separate, misshapen countries that are dispersed throughout [the globe].

He adds that nationalism sets up the homeland as "an idol that is worshipped instead of Allah."[167] The jihadi Salafis thus regard loyalty to the homeland as *jāhilī*, idolatrous.

Al-Qaraḍāwī takes a different approach. He accepts the division of the world into nation-states and even advocates national jihad to liberate the homeland from an occupier, such as Hamas's jihad. He argues that there are many possible bases for loyalty and brotherhood, including nationalism, and that the latter is legitimate as long as it does not come at the expense of loyalty to the faith. Nationalism, he elaborates, has no ideological content, either religious or secular, and it becomes a problem only when it is excessive and takes the place of religion. Al-Qaraḍāwī in fact proposes citizenship (*muwāṭana*) as a basis for granting rights to religious minorities in Muslim-majority states, such as the Copts in Egypt.[168] At the same time, he stresses that nationalism must not become "excessive" and take the place of religion. In the case of a conflict between religion and homeland, he says, religion must always take precedence, for there are alternatives to the homeland but no valid alternatives to Islam. He adds: "Brotherhood based on Islam takes precedence to tribal or national loyalties [*ʿaṣabiyyāt*]. The bond of faith supersedes all bonds, and *dār al-Islām* supersedes all homelands." Very like the jihadi Salafīs, al-Qaraḍāwī proclaims that a society cannot be regarded Islamic if it reveres the homeland as an idol that is worshipped in place of Allah.[169]

The Differences in Exegetic Approaches: Interpretations of Q5:44–47 as a Basis for Takfīr *against Rulers*

An important source of justification for the violence that jihadi Salafī groups use against what they call the "near enemy," the Muslim regimes whom they accuse of *ridda*, is a group of Qur'ānic verses, 5:44, 45, and 47.[170] According to traditions concerning the "occasions or circumstances of revelation" (*asbāb al-nuzūl*), these verses are aimed at the Jews, who had replaced the biblical punishment for adultery, stoning to death, with blackening of the face and flogging of the perpetrator. Al-Qaraḍāwī does not accept the jihadi Salafī view that these verses are aimed at rulers who do not govern in accordance with *sharīʿa* and are therefore to be treated as iniquitous infidels who have strayed from the straight path (*fāsiqūn*). Abū Muḥammad al-Maqdisī argues that the word *al-ḥukm* (government, judgment) mentioned in verse 44 has two meanings: (1) acts of iniquity (*jawr*), which constitute "minor unbelief" or, according to a tradition ascribed to the Prophet's cousin Ibn ʿAbbās (d. 619 CE), "an unbelief that is less than unbelief [*kufr dūna kufr*]"; (2) legislation (*tashrī'*), which is "manifest unbelief" (*kufr bawāḥ*) and causes the perpetrator to no longer be considered a Muslim. Al-Maqdisī explains that Ibn 'Abbās interpreted the unbelief in the verse in question as belonging to the minor kind (*kufr dūna kufr*, "an unbelief that is less than unbelief") because he referred to the criticism that the Khawārij expressed toward the caliph at the time, 'Alī b. Abī Ṭālib. Al-Maqdisī notes that at that time no Muslim rule claimed to possess the authority to legislate together with God. Rather, the issues on which the Khawārij disagreed with the caliph, 'Alī, were those that needed *ijtihād* for their resolution, such as the arbitration (*taḥkīm*) between 'Alī and Mu'āwiya. Al-Maqdisī declares that the application of these verses in Q5 to contemporary Muslim rulers, whom he considers to be polytheists, involves the literal reading of a revelation that criticizes the Jews for having agreed to implement laws that are not of divine origin, just as today's Muslim rulers do. In other words, the unbelief mentioned in this verse as applied to the rulers is major unbelief.[171]

Al-Ṭarṭūsī, in contrast, states that ruling not in accordance with divine law is a violation that can cause the sinner to be expelled from Islam, but not in every case. He divides rulers who do not govern according to *sharī'a* into different groups. Some rulers are not infidels because they do obey *sharī'a* in general but stray from it only on certain matters. Such a ruler realizes that he sins and will not be considered an infidel as long as he does not think that his actions are legitimate (that is, does not perform *istiḥlāl*—literally, making or considering something that is prohibited [*ḥarām*] lawful [*ḥalāl*] instead) and does not deny *sharī'a* law. A ruler of this kind, according to al-Ṭarṭūsī, can be compared to a Muslim who steals or commits adultery (*zinā*), and in this case Ibn 'Abbās's interpretation of Q5:44 may be applied: the ruler is considered to have committed *kufr dūna kufr* and is not guilty of major unbelief. Another type of ruler does not apply *sharī'a* at all and therefore commits major unbelief and is no longer a Muslim. One condition that must be fulfilled in order for a ruler to belong to this category is that he must reject the revealed principle of God's unity; he is to be considered a polytheist who denies God's revelation. A third type of ruler uses erroneous *ijtihād* but, like any Muslim who does so, still deserves reward, recompense.[172]

Al-Qaraḍāwī ruled that forms of the verb *yaḥkum* in these verses denote not only judgment but also legislation, administration, and policy—in other words, government. However, like Shaykh Nāṣir al-Dīn al-Albānī, he rejects the jihadi Salafī interpretation that the verses constitute a legal basis for declaring Muslim rulers who do not govern according to the *sharīʿa* to be *murtaddūn*.[173] He believes that today only a very small number of Muslim rulers are "extreme secularists"[174] who are explicitly hostile to *sharīʿa*, which they consider an obstacle to culture and progress. For al-Qaraḍāwī, such rulers are like the devil (Iblīs), who refused to obey Allah's command to bow down to Adam (Q2:34, 7:11–12). Muslims should refuse to obey such rulers, says al-Qaraḍāwī, because they are the intended subjects of the Prophet's command to Muslims to obey their rulers unless the rulers behave in a way that constitutes evident unbelief, for which God Himself will provide the proof.[175]

In this context, it is pertinent to examine the liberals' interpretation of Q5:44–47, as set out by al-ʿAshmāwī, for example. Al-ʿAshmāwī firmly rejects the contention that these verses refer to any Muslim regime that does not implement the laws of *sharīʿa*. He makes two major exegetic arguments regarding these verses. First, they must be interpreted in light of the context in which they descended—namely, as part of a reference to the People of the Book, not to Muslims. Although al-Qaraḍāwī and the Salafīs do not ignore this context, states al-ʿAshmāwī, they nevertheless apply the verses to Muslims rulers based on the principle that interpretations should be general rather than specific ("interpretation [must be based] on general meaning, not specific circumstances [*al-ʿibra bi-ʿumūm al-lafẓ, lā bikhuṣūṣ al-sabab*]").[176] Al-ʿAshmāwī notes that this is not a *sharīʿa* principle that appears in the Qur'ān or the Sunna, but rather an invention of the *fuqahā'*, which, he claims, contravenes the spirit of Islam and the true meaning of the Qur'ān. Second, in the Qur'ān the word *ḥukm* does not designate political government, as it does in modern Arabic, but rather judgment and the settlement of disputes as well as wisdom and insight. Political government is referred to in the Qur'ān as *amr*, hence the word *amīr* (emir), designating one who holds the reins of power. Al-ʿAshmāwī claims further that the word *kufr* in Q5:44 does not denote disbelief in Allah but rather the renouncement (*inkār*) of Allah's law, meaning that the

People of the Book, to whom the verse refers, renounced Allah's laws and judgment.[177] According to this interpretation, the verses do not refer to government and heresy at all. This view is in stark contrast to the position taken by al-Qaraḍāwī and the jihadi Salafīs.

Based on his interpretation of Q5:44–47, al-ʿAshmāwī distinguishes two approaches in Egypt and in the Muslim world at large: the approach of extremism (*taṭarruf*)—which he presumably ascribes to al-Qaraḍāwī as well—and the approach of "rationalism" (*taʿaqqul*). The first approach is that of the Khawārij: its proponents seek to gain power by means of the religion; the second approach is that of the Prophet's Companions and their successors, whose aim is to discover religious truth. Al-ʿAshmāwī holds that those who politicize Islam, first and foremost the MB, are motivated by political and partisan goals, not by a desire to preserve the *sharīʿa*.[178]

Wasaṭiyya: Between the Muslim Brotherhood and Jihadi Salafism

The Jihadi Salafīs' Perception of the Muslim Brotherhood

Gilles Kepel shows that the jihadi Salafīs criticize members of the MB in countries in which *sharīʿa* is not the law of the land and who are politically active, form political parties, and participate in elections. They accuse MB members of being "deceivers of the faithful" for giving religious legitimacy to regimes that should be toppled.[179] Shaykh Nāṣir al-Dīn al-Albānī, the founder of purist Salafism, accused the MB of paying more attention to politics than to religious knowledge. This accusation, according to Roel Meijer, presaged the current split between the Salafīs and the MB.[180] Ayman al-Ẓawāhirī defined the ideological foundations for al-Qaʿida's criticism of the MB in *Bitter Harvest: The Muslim Brotherhood in Sixty Years*, first published in the late 1980s or early 1990s.[181]

In this book, Ayman al-Ẓawāhirī presents himself vis-à-vis the MB as a physician who is treating a terminally ill patient who suffers from stomach cancer. He feels himself duty bound to apprise his patient of his serious condition and to warn him that the disease may spread throughout his body.[182] His criticism of the MB focuses on three main issues:

1. According to al-Ẓawāhirī, a Muslim ruler who does not govern in accordance with *sharīʿa* but replaces *sharīʿa* with man-made laws is an infidel; a regime of this kind rules through "the Mongol system of laws [*yāsa*] laws" and can no longer be considered Muslim. Al-Ẓawāhirī attacks the MB for its refusal to declare rulers who do not govern according to *sharīʿa* to be infidels and for, in fact, its condemnation of such declarations.[183] We have seen, however, that al-Qaraḍāwī's *wasaṭiyya* does level accusations of heresy at rulers who do not implement the *sharīʿa* and whom he defines as "secular."

2. Al-Ẓawāhirī considers democracy to be a "new religion" based on the deification of man, for it gives human beings unlimited legislative authority. Democracy is thus a man-made, heretical religion. He condemns the MB because it has called for democracy, has announced that democracy is the legitimate way to bring change to the country, and has taken part in parliamentary elections in a number of Muslim countries that are governed by unbelieving apostate regimes, including Egypt.[184] The *wasaṭī* al-Qaraḍāwī, as we have seen, does not regard democracy as heresy, but he rejects democratic values such as freedom of belief, sexual freedom, and equality between men and women.

3. Al-Ẓawāhirī accuses the MB of having violated the following laws of loyalty and disavowal: (*a*) the prohibition on alliances and friendships with the infidel, as stated, for example, in Q3:28,[185] and (*b*) the demand to dislike/hate the infidel.[186]

A good example of a jihadi Salafī attack on the MB can be found in issue number 14 of *Dabiq*, IS's English-language magazine,[187] where in a long article entitled "The Murtadd Brotherhood" we read that "over the past few decades, a devastating cancer has emerged, mutated, and spread, attempting to drown the entire *umma* in *ridda*." Abū Muḥammad al-ʿAdnānī (d. 2016), former spokesman of the IS, described the Brotherhood as "a secular party in Islamic garb; they are the worst and most corrupt of secularists. A party that worships seats and parliaments. They will perform jihad and die for democracy but cannot perform jihad and die for Allah. I heard their preacher [viz., al-Qaraḍāwī] at a gathering of hundreds of thousands saying quite explicitly: Beware of going backward; die for democracy."[188]

Among the ideological criticisms leveled at the MB by both al-Qaʿida and the IS is that it advocates interfaith dialogue. I examine this issue in the next section to show that although al-Qaraḍāwī's *wasaṭiyya* is a development of MB ideas, it is closer in spirit to jihadi Salafism.

Wasaṭiyya, *Jihadi Salafism, and Liberalism on the Issue of Interfaith Dialogue*

The IS accuses the Muslim Brotherhood of pioneering the "deviant call" for interreligious dialogue with Jews and Christians. The MB's insistence that Egypt's Copts are brother citizens of Egypt is, according to IS, a violation of the duty of disavowal mentioned in Q5:51. Indeed, al-Qaraḍāwī said in his historical sermon at Tahrir Square in Cairo on February 18, 2011, after the fall of Mubarak: "It is the custom of preachers to say 'Oh Muslims!' But I say here on this square: 'Oh Muslims and Copts! Oh sons of Egypt!' This day is the day of all Egyptians and not the day of only the Muslims."[189]

In anti-Qaraḍāwī Salafī and jihadi Salafī polemical writings, he is accused of preaching love for the People of the Book, similar to the accusations leveled at the MB.[190] Here is not the place to expand on al-Qaraḍāwī's attitude toward Jews and Christians; I merely note that jihadi Salafīs accuse him of liking the Jews and the Christians, although in fact al-Qaraḍāwī considers both groups infidels who refuse to believe in Muḥammad, whom God, according to the Qur'ān, sent to all mankind (Q21:107) and in particular to the Jews and the Christians (Q5:19).[191]

Regarding the Jews, al-Qaraḍāwī states that their religion is closer to Islam than to Christianity because they, unlike the Christians, do not believe in the Trinity or claim that Moses was the son of God. On this basis, he denies the claim that the war in Palestine is a religious one, having to do with the Jews' rejection of Muḥammad's mission or their distortion of the Torah. However, in describing the enemy that the Muslims are fighting in Palestine, the shaykh uses a term that is applied to the Jews in the Qur'ān (2:74), "hard-hearted," and based on this Qur'ānic description he concludes that the Jews are violent and aggressive.[192]

More than that, in the context of the war in Palestine, he writes that although it is a war over land, it is religious in character and has religious goals, stating: "Any fight that a Muslim joins with the aim of defending truth and opposing falsehood or to enact justice and rise up against oppression is a religious fight because it is a fight for the sake of Allah." As evidence, he quotes Q4:76, which draws a dichotomy between the believers, who fight for Allah, and the unbelievers, who fight for the idol (*ṭāghūt*).[193] In this statement, al-Qaraḍāwī essentially claims, in contrast to what he writes elsewhere, that the war in Palestine is a war between the true faith of Islam and the heresy of Judaism. It is rulings like these that have prompted Egyptian liberal thinker Ashraf 'Abd al-Qādir (b. 1965) to accuse al-Qaraḍāwī of taking a terrorist stance that ignites religious war and permits the killing of innocents.[194]

Al-Qaraḍāwī permits dialogue between Islam and the revealed religions, Christianity and Judaism, but only providing that this dialogue does not aim to blur what he sees as the essential differences between them. For example, this dialogue must not question or deny that the Qur'ān is free of error because Allah ensured it to be so (Q15:9), whereas the Torah and the New Testament were changed and distorted by the Jews and the Christians (as stated in Q5:13, for instance).[195]

In practice, however, the shaykh takes part in interfaith dialogue with Christians but not with Jews. He refused to attend the dialogue conference in Doha in 2013, for example, on the grounds that he would not sit on the same panel with Jews as long as they continued to usurp Palestine and al-Aqṣā Mosque and to destroy mosques and as long as the matter of Palestine remained unresolved.[196] He found justification for this refusal in Q29:46, which instructs the believers to argue with the People of the Book "in a way that is best, except for those who commit injustice among them"—an exception that al-Qaraḍāwī believes applies to the Jews. In a sermon given in December 2014, he forbade his listeners to participate in dialogue even with those Jews who do not recognize the State of Israel because, he said, they constitute a tiny minority of Jews, "a drop in the ocean," and Islam instructs the believers to judge groups by the behavior of the majority of their members.[197] The liberal Kuwaiti thinker Aḥmad al-Baghdādī observes that *'ulamā'* who accept dialogue with Christianity tend to reject dialogue with other faiths, especially Judaism,[198] a practice that is indeed exemplified by al-Qaraḍāwī.

It should be noted that al-Qaraḍāwī also disagrees with the liberals on the goals of interfaith dialogue. According to al-Baghdādī, the goal of such dialogue is to foster global understanding among the followers of all faiths through mutual familiarity and respect for the values and perceptions of each religion. He adds that "today's world completely rejects the notion of the victory of one faith over the others" but rather advocates rapprochement for the sake of peace.[199] Al-Qaraḍāwī, in contrast, identifies three legitimate domains for cooperation between Muslims and Christians: the joint fight against atheism, which denies that man was created by God; the joint fight against what al-Qaraḍāwī terms promiscuity, including the legalization of same-sex marriage and abortion; and the joint campaign in support of downtrodden or occupied peoples, first and foremost the Palestinians.[200] In other words, al-Qaraḍāwī mainly wants to enlist the help of Christians in the campaign for Palestine and in the Islamist fight against the secularists and liberals.

To accurately assess al-Qaraḍāwī's position on interfaith dialogue, one must also compare it to the *fatwā* issued on this matter by the Saudi jihadi Salafī Shaykh Ḥamūd b. 'Uqalā' al-Shu'aybī (d. 2002). Al-Shu'aybī ruled that all faiths other than Islam are false and that any Muslim who does not reject the Jews and the Christians as unbelievers or who regards their religions as valid is himself an unbeliever.[201] Although al-Qaraḍāwī, too, regards the Jews and the Christians as infidels in some of his writings, he stresses that there are different degrees of unbelief and that a distinction must be made between the People of the Book—to whom Q9:29 applies (the verse that exhorts Muslims to fight them until they pay the *jizya* according to their financial ability and while in a state of humiliation)—and the polytheists, to whom the Verse of the Sword (Q9:5) applies (stating that they must be killed).[202] Yet in other writings he stresses that the unbelievers are a single nation (*al-kufr milla wāḥida*) and the "allies of one another" (Q8:73).

Jihadi Salafism Accuses al-Qaraḍāwī of Unbelief (*Takfīr*)

In the polemic between al-Qaraḍāwī's *wasaṭiyya* and the jihadi Salafī stream, the latter levels *takfīr* against the former. For example, a prominent jihadi Salafī thinker, al-Ṭarṭūsī, has accused al-Qaraḍāwī of heresy.[203] However, this does not necessarily indicate a deep ideological rift between the two streams. In fact, the jihadi Salafīs apparently recognize that *wasaṭiyya* is a creed quite similar to their own but tempered with a measure of flexibility and pragmatism that makes it attractive to many Muslims. For this reason, they fiercely attack *wasaṭiyya*, focusing precisely on these realistic and pragmatic aspects.

Al-Ṭarṭūsī is particularly incensed at several legal decisions made by al-Qaraḍāwī that, he argues, constitute a breach of the principle of God's oneness. Al-Ṭarṭūsī accuses al-Qaraḍāwī of assistance to Buddhism because al-Qaraḍāwī ruled that the Buddha statues in Afghanistan should not be destroyed. According to al-Ṭarṭūsī, al-Qaraḍāwī's ruling on this issue was motivated by a desire to placate "idolatrous" Muslim rulers (*ṭawāghīt*), and so it constitutes "evident heresy" (*kufr bawāḥ*) because it contradicts the principle of God's oneness, which rejects all idols and idol worshippers.[204]

In March 2001, two statues of Buddha in Bamiyan, Afghanistan, were destroyed by the Taliban regime, following an edict the regime had promulgated at the beginning of the year that ordered all such statues in the country to be destroyed because of their idolization by the infidel. In 2003, the remnants of these statues as well as a number of other sites in the Bamiyan Valley were declared World Heritage sites by the UN Education, Scientific, and Cultural Organization. Al-Qaraḍāwī was a member in a delegation of clerics representing the Organization of the Islamic Conference (Munaẓẓamat al-Mu'tamar al-Islāmī) headed by Egypt's *muftī*, Shaykh Naṣr Farīd Wāṣil (b. 1937, in this position from 1996 to 2002) that was sent to Afghanistan to plead with the Taliban not to destroy the sixth-century CE statues.[205] In his ruling on this issue, al-Qaraḍāwī attacked the jihadi Salafī rulings in support of the statues' destruction.[206]

In his ruling on the Buddhas, al-Qaraḍāwī relied on principles of *shar'īa* governance.[207] For example, he used the principle that consequences of actions must be taken into account to ask the Taliban's clerics to consider the results of destroying the statues. He noted that it would not be wise for the Taliban to anger countries such as China and Japan, whose political and economic support was needed, especially against the West, in particular the United States, which was hostile toward the Taliban. He also feared that the destruction of the statues would endanger the Muslims who lived in Buddhist countries. Al-Qaraḍāwī also used the principle of prioritization (*fiqh al-awlawiyyāt*); in this case, he was of the view that Afghanistan had more pressing problems than the statues, problems that should be given priority—for example, feeding the hungry; providing clothing to those who had none, medicine to the ill, and work to the unemployed; and preventing bloodshed. He therefore urged the Taliban to turn its attention elsewhere for the moment or at least to postpone its decision to destroy the statues and convene an international Islamic conference that would decide the issue.

Al-Qaraḍāwī's fundamental argument in his ruling on this case was that the statues deserved to be destroyed if they constituted a temptation that threatened Muslims' faith. But in Afghanistan today, he pointed out, Muslims view those statues as works of art, as proof that their ancestors excelled in the art of sculpture, in the same way that Egyptians view the statue of Ramses in the center of Cairo as an archaeological remnant of ancient pharaonic civilization.

Conclusion

In sum, a comparison of the *wasaṭī* approach to the jihadi Salafī and liberal approaches shows that with respect to core issues of Islamic discourse, such as Allah's sovereignty and democracy, *wasaṭiyya* is quite close in spirit to jihadi Salafism and diametrically opposed to liberalism. This chapter has shown that, despite the jihadi Salafīs' criticism of al-Qaraḍāwī's *wasaṭiyya*, the two streams actually have much in common. Al-Qaraḍāwī developed the doctrine of the MB into a school of thought that occupies a point midway between this doctrine and jihadi Salafism.

The distance between *wasaṭiyya* and liberalism, however, is vast. At the heart of the ideological dispute between them is the concept of freedom: the liberals claim that the Islamic *fuqahā'*, including al-Qaraḍāwī, assume a monopoly over religious exegesis and consider their interpretation to be synonymous with the religion itself. Accordingly, the *fuqahā'* reject all alternative interpretations, including those of the liberals, and accuse the latter of heresy and atheism. Al-Qaraḍāwī counters this accusation by directing allegations at the secularist liberals. In his sermon titled "The Battle between Islam and *'Ilmāniyya*" in July 1997, he said: "They [the secularists] demand freedom of heresy rather than freedom of thought; freedom of straying from the straight path rather than the freedom [to enjoy] rights; freedom of atheism and tyranny rather than human freedom." Challenging the secularists, the shaykh said that if they truly believe in democracy, they should hold a referendum among Muslims, asking them whether they prefer *sharīʿa* or secularism. The results of such a referendum are known in advance, he says: the Muslim *umma* will side with the *sharīʿa*, with Muḥammad, and with the Qur'ān, never with foreign rules and perceptions.[208] This statement obviously misrepresents the secularists' outlook in that it describes them as being antireligious. They stress, however, that they do not oppose religion but only the clerics' takeover of politics and all other domains of life. Al-Qaraḍāwī's oversimplified presentation of his rivals' positions is meant to cast them in a negative light so that Muslims are left with no choice but to reject them and sympathize with the shaykh and his fellow *fuqahā'*.

5

The Conception of Jihad

Wasaṭī *Apologetics, Jihadi Salafī Selective Reading, and Liberal Claims of Distorted Interpretation*

This chapter deals with the conception of jihad in Islam, focusing on a comparison between the *wasaṭī* view; the position of the jihadi Salafīs, whose approach is espoused by the global jihad organizations; and the view of liberal writers, in particular Muḥammad Saʿīd al-ʿAshmāwī and Gamāl al-Bannā. Both *wasaṭiyya* and jihadi Salafism claim that their conception of jihad reflects the way it was originally understood in early Islam, the period of the pious forefathers. The *wasaṭīs*, however, contend that the jihadi Salafīs' conception is excessively radical owing to a misapplication of Islamic jurisprudence. *Wasaṭiyya* seeks to correct this juristic flaw and proposes that what it presents is a more moderate view of jihad. The liberals, for their part, accuse both of these streams of distorting the true meaning of jihad in Islam. The chapter examines the three streams' views on several issues pertaining to jihad, especially the core issues: the goals of jihad; the identity of the enemy and the division of the world into *dār al-Islām* and *dār al-ḥarb*; and the legal status of martyrdom (*istishhād*) operations and the killing of civilians.

In the statement in which IS took responsibility for the Paris attacks of November 13, 2015, in which 129 people were killed, the attacks were called "a blessed raid [*ghazwa mubāraka*]."[1] The term *ghazwa* was used to denote the battles that the Prophet waged after his immigration to Medina in 622 CE. The declaration of responsibility characteristically opened with a Qur'ānic verse (59:2) and ended with one (63:8).[2] In the text of the announcement, we find what for IS constitutes the reason for the attacks.

There Paris was called the capital of "fornication and depravity" and was accused of being the flag bearer of the cross in Europe. The French were called "Crusaders," and France was accused of leading the crusade. The Bataclan Theater, in which four of the terrorists killed eighty-nine people during a rock concert, was depicted as a place where multitudes of polytheists gathered for a "celebration of fornication and debauchery." The French were also accused of having had the temerity to curse the Prophet, of taking pride in fighting against Islam in France, and of bombing the Muslims in the lands of the caliphate with their airplanes.

The attacks' success was ascribed first and foremost to Allah, who, according to the announcement, "put terror in the Crusaders' hearts within their own home [*fī ʿuqr dārihim*]." The expression "Allah put terror in the Crusaders' hearts" echoes Q8:12 ("put terror into the hearts of the disbelievers"), which speaks of the polytheists of Mecca who were to be defeated and commands the Muslims in the Battle of Badr (624 CE) to behead the enemy ("strike above their necks"). The IS statement described the terrorists as having abandoned the vanities of this world in favor of the fight against the enemy out of a desire to die for Allah, His religion (Islam), and His Prophet.

In a public condemnation of the attack published by IUMS and signed by the union's head, al-Qaraḍāwī, and its secretary-general, ʿAlī al-Qarra Dāghī, the events in Paris were called "criminal acts of terrorism [*aḥdāth irhābiyya ijrāmiyya*]." The announcement went on to declare that no divine religion, no decent conscience, and no ethics can condone such terrorism. The acts were called inhumane. The document quotes Q5:32 to stress the fact that, for Allah, killing a person is considered a grievous sin. This verse is said to have been revealed after the first murder in human history, the murder of Abel by Cain (Genesis 4; Q5:27–31). It states that "if anyone kills a person—unless in retribution for murder or spreading corruption in the land—it is as if he kills all mankind, while if any saves a life, it is as if he saves the lives of all mankind."[3]

These two documents, IS's declaration of responsibility for the attacks and the IUMS's condemnation, reflect the dispute within the Muslim world on the key issues of the goals of jihad, the legal status of operations in which civilians are killed, and the difference between legitimate jihad and terrorism. To borrow a term taken from the Western laws of war as they evolved from the sixteenth century into the orderly doctrine of *bellum iustum*, "just war" or "war according to the law," in contemporary Islam the question arises of what constitutes a "just war" in terms of the *sharīʿa*.[4]

This question has been hotly debated since the 9/11 attacks. Three main positions are taken: the jihadi Salafī approach, adopted by global jihadi organizations, especially al-Qaʿida and IS (formerly ISIS, which changed its name from the Islamic State of Iraq and al-Sham to Islamic State after the declaration of the caliphate in June 2014);[5] the *wasaṭī* approach led by al-Qaraḍāwī, who in this case is joined by innumerable Sunnī clerics and official Sunnī legal institutions, all of whom condemn the kind of jihad waged by IS; and the approach taken by the liberals, such as Shākir al-Nābulsī and al-ʿAfīf al-Akhḍar, which regards *wasaṭiyya* and the MB as breeding grounds for terror in the name of Islam.

Al-Qaraḍāwī: A Terrorist or a Champion of Peace and Moderation?

The entry on Yūsuf al-Qaraḍāwī in the *Militant Ideology Atlas* describes him as an important voice in today's Muslim world, where he is generally considered to be a moderate conservative, making him a target for attacks from both the left and the right.[6] More liberal voices in the Muslim world as well as most of his Western critics disagree with his support for what he calls martyrdom (*istishhād)* operations in Israel and with his legal opinion that such actions are a legitimate means of Palestinian resistance (*muqāwama*).[7] They also oppose his uncompromising views on certain social issues, such as homosexuality[8] and the status of women[9] (both discussed in chapter 6), and his rejection of secularism (*ʿilmāniyya*).[10] These critics regard al-Qaraḍāwī as an extremist Islamic scholar—a proponent of jihadi Salafism, which is the ideological wellspring of global jihad. Conversely, contemporary jihadis oppose al-Qaraḍāwī for his rejection of violence outside Palestine and for what they consider his liberal approach to Islamic jurisprudence. In fact, some jihadi Salafī thinkers, such as Abū Baṣīr al-Ṭarṭūsī, even accuse him of heresy, as noted in earlier chapters.

Al-Qaraḍāwī Accused of Being Two-Faced

Some liberals—for instance, al-Nābulsī—claim that there are "two al-Qaraḍāwīs" with two different opinions on every key issue: one for the Muslims in the East and one for the Muslims in the West. When addressing the West, al-Qaraḍāwī says that the grounds for the war on the Jews in Palestine is their occupation of Muslim land, not their Jewish identity. But when addressing Muslims in the East, he curses the "treacherous" Jews and asks Allah to torment them.[11] In a Friday sermon in October 1994, he praised the martyrs of Palestine:

> As long as there are young people who sell their souls to Allah, take their lives and their souls in their hands, and say, "O winds of Paradise, blow; O steeds of Allah, speed forth"; as long as there is a believing youth who cares not whether he finds death or death befalls him; as long as the youths from whom Allah has purchased their lives and their wealth, giving them Paradise in their stead [based on Q9:111], continue on their path, we will do well, Allah willing.[12]

Al-Qaraḍāwī also has many critics in both the Muslim world and the West. The criticism surfaced, for example, in the summer of 2004, when the then mayor of London, Ken Livingstone, invited the shaykh for a one-week visit. This invitation sparked a heated debate in the press: many British newspapers described al-Qaraḍāwī as "the *muftī* of terror" and a propagandist for extremism and called on the British authorities to ban him from the country, as the United States had done.[13] The protests were to no avail, however, and the visit took place, culminating in a joint press conference with Livingstone in London's town hall. As part of the public debate surrounding this affair, prominent Saudi journalist ʻAbd al-Raḥmān al-Rāshid (b. 1956), the former editor of the London-based Arabic daily *Al-Sharq al-Awsaṭ*, accused al-Qaraḍāwī of being both tolerant (*mutasāmiḥ*) and extremist (*mutaʻaṣṣib*) at the same time. Al-Qaraḍāwī, he clarified, was tolerant when it came to social issues but not when it came to political ones. Moreover, owing to his ties with the MB, al-Qaraḍāwī addressed issues from a narrow, partisan view, not from the perspective of the Islamic nation as a whole. As an example of the shaykh's inconsistencies, al-Rāshid noted that in countering the attacks of the British papers against him, the shaykh stressed that he advocated peace and opposed violence, but in his Qatar sermons he spoke in very different terms. Likewise, in order to obtain permission to enter Britain, he had advocated dialogue with the Christians, but at the same time he spoke against dialogue with the Jews.[14]

ʿAbd al-Razzāq ʿĪd, a fearless critic of al-Qaraḍāwī, likewise describes him as two-faced, noting that, on the one hand, he emulates Osama bin Laden, proclaiming that anyone who disagrees with him is a *murtadd* deserving of death, but, on the other hand, clothes himself in "Western" garb, claiming that democracy is the spirit of Islam.[15] Whereas the liberals regard al-Qaraḍāwī as a terrorist and the spiritual father of Osama bin Laden and Abu Muṣʿab al-Zarqāwī, the IS regards him as an agent of the Qatari regime—one of the *ʿumalāʾ*, agents, rather than one of the *ʿulamāʾ*, scholars—and has placed him on its hit list.[16]

Al-Qaraḍāwī Accused of Encouraging Terror

In late 2004, a group of 2,500 Muslim intellectuals presented a petition of protest, "International Communiqué against Terrorism," to the UN in which they called on the UN to establish a court to prosecute the "theologians of terror" and the "shaykhs of death" who tarnished the image of Islam and fostered intercultural hatred—among them al-Qaraḍāwī.[17]

It should be noted that in December 2014 Interpol put al-Qaraḍāwī on its wanted list at Egypt's behest.[18] This decision prompted an unprecedented campaign by his students and supporters in the Muslim world to remove him from the list, a campaign that eventually achieved its aim in September 2017.[19] One of the announcements published in his defense was by a group of *ʿulamāʾ* and thinkers who described him as the *imām* of *wasaṭiyya* and one of the most prominent *mujaddidūn* of Islam of our age, a scholar guided by Allah (*ʿālim rabbānī*), a man of ideas and opinions who answers argument with argument and thought with thought.

To target him, they wrote, is to target the moderate and honest *wasaṭī* way ("al-manhaj al-wasaṭī al-muʿtadil al-rashīd"). They added that his inclusion on Interpol's wanted list was an attempt to harm all *ʿulamāʾ* and would only cause Muslim youths to embrace violence and extremism by leaving them vulnerable to the influence of "the enemies and deceivers inside and outside [the Muslim world], in the absence of genuine *ʿulamāʾ*."[20] In December 2015, the Saudi Ministry of Education decided to remove from school libraries eighty books by MB ideologues, including Ḥasan al-Bannā, Sayyid Quṭb, and al-Qaraḍāwī. A Saudi official explained that these books incited violence, sectarianism, and terror and should be not only banned but also burned.[21]

The four countries boycotting Qatar—Saudi Arabia, Bahrain, UAE, and Egypt, which likewise regard al-Qaraḍāwī as a Qatari agent—not only included his organization the IUMS on its terror list (as mentioned earlier) but also as part of their conflict with Qatar added the shaykh to a list of fifty-nine individuals linked to terrorism in July 2017.[22] Al-Qaraḍāwī responded with the following tweet: "All my ideological writings have been a call for moderation [*iʿtidāl*], tolerance, and dialogue, and they belie these baseless accusations." The tweet included a link to a segment from an al-Jazeera program (apparently from 2004) on which al-Qaraḍāwī says,

> Throughout my life I have been preaching moderation, dialogue, openness, and lenience, and that is a well-known fact. I therefore regard it as an injustice to accuse me [of preaching extremism]. All my writings belie this accusation. Are people entitled to make accusations without evidence? I have written over 130 books, some of which have been published in several world languages and some of which have been printed in dozens of editions. I have [delivered] lectures and sermons. So how can they say such things?[23]

Several days later he wrote on his Facebook page: "I want what is good for people, all people. I bear no ill will or hostility toward anyone because all people are my brothers: either coreligionists or compatriots or fellow human beings. I bear hostility only for those who are hostile to my nation, and I fight only those who fight my faith."[24]

Al-Qaraḍāwī a Revered Figure in the Eyes of His Students

Al-Qaraḍāwī is a fascinating figure who has always sparked controversy both in the Muslim world and in the West. His popularity and eminence in the Muslim world are evident from the many awards he has received. For example, in 2000 Dubai gave him the International Holy Qur'ān Award and named him Islamic Personality of the Year. In stating its reasons for selecting him, the award committee noted his contribution to fighting violence and extremist ideas, preaching love and dialogue, and seeking the liberation of Muslim society through a fundamental moral revolution to bring it back to the Qur'ān and the Sunna.[25] The admiration al-Qaraḍāwī commands is also reflected in a two-volume anthology of studies compiled in his honor on the occasion of his seventieth birthday (published in 2004). In a short essay contributed to this anthology, Muṣṭafa al-Zarqā (d. 1994), who is considered to be one of the great reformists of Islam in the modern age, wrote that al-Qaraḍāwī is one of the great boons bestowed by Allah upon the Muslims in contemporary times and called him the authoritative source for his generation (*ḥujjat al-ʿaṣr*). According to al-Zarqā, al-Qaraḍāwī's uniqueness lies in his deep understanding of the social, economic, and political reality, what al-Qaraḍāwī himself calls "the understanding of priorities [*fiqh al-awlawiyyāt*]."[26] Some writers have even dubbed al-Qaraḍāwī "the Muslim pope"[27] because during the 1980s he represented Islam in debates with secularists (the secularist side was represented by, among others, the Egyptian philosopher Fu'ād Zakariyyā). Also, after Pope Benedict XVI criticized Islam in a lecture in 2006, it was al-Qaraḍāwī who answered him in the name of Islam.[28] Following each of these debates, al-Qaraḍāwī published a book presenting Islam's answers to its critics.[29]

In contrast to the image of al-Qaraḍāwī as "the Muslim pope," liberals such as Shākir al-Nābulsī regard him as one of the "jurisprudents of terrorism" (*fuqahā' al-irhāb*), and some of them even call him "the jurisprudent of blood[shed]." Al-Nābulsī said of him in an interview in 2005: "We respect al-Qaraḍāwī as a Muslim jurisprudent, as a supreme juristic authority [*marjiʿiyya*], and as a great scholar of jurisprudence, but we are critical of his position on terror."[30]

Given these two diametrically opposed views of al-Qaraḍāwī, this chapter attempts an in-depth examination of his views on issues of jihad. Because his rulings on jihad figure prominently in the reasoning of those who accuse him of encouraging terrorism, this chapter focuses on these rulings and compares them to the views of the jihadi Salafīs, on the one hand, and of the liberals, on the other.

Al-Qaraḍāwī's Mapping of Approaches to Jihad

As is the case with other issues, al-Qaraḍāwī maps the approaches of various *'ulamā'* to jihad and locates the *wasaṭī* approach between two extremes, between "deficiency" (*tafrīṭ*) and "excess" (*ifrāṭ*), between those who want to "kill jihad" and those who want to "wage war against the whole world." Among the former are the Ṣūfīs[31] and westernized secularists in the Muslim world,[32] who, he claims, want to take jihad out of the life of the Muslim *umma* and educate it on the basis of spiritual values alone.[33]

However, a close examination of the positions expressed by those whom al-Qaraḍāwī calls "westernized secularists" reveals that their views on jihad are much more nuanced than he implies. In fact, he seems to be exaggerating and simplifying both their views and those of the jihadi Salafīs in order to present his own opinion as the moderate middle. Contra al-Qaraḍāwī's claim, the liberal thinker al-'Ashmāwī, whose views of jihad are discussed in detail later in this chapter, does not seek to eliminate the concept of jihad. He argues that jihad has two different meanings in Muslim tradition: its original religious meaning and a political-historical one. In its true, religious sense, he says, jihad is first and foremost a spiritual, moral, and self-oriented concept: it connotes an individual's ongoing spiritual effort to overcome his flaws and instincts and to attain a strong and pure faith. It means striving to embrace compassion and justice as a genuine product of one's living conscience and to instill these values in Muslim society and humankind at large. This religious concept of jihad includes war (*ḥarb*) and fighting (*qitāl*) as well, but only in self-defense, never in permanent aggression and hostility or endless conflict. Conversely, the political-historic sense of jihad, says al-'Ashmāwī, is that of unjustified war against both Muslims and non-Muslims, coups against governments and societies, and threats directed at philosophers, free thinkers, and proponents of human reasoning (*ijtihād*). Sadly, says al-ʿAshmāwī, this interpretation and implementation of jihad—which he considers an act of "drawing a sword" against the genuine Islam—has become dominant, but the original, religious sense must nevertheless prevail. When that happens, "jihad will be compassion rather than a sword, justice rather than war, transcendence rather than killing, and self-elevation rather than destruction."[34]

Al-Qaraḍāwī also opposes the approach taken by the "exaggerators," who declare war on the entire world. He calls them "extremist warmongers" and "proponents of offensive jihad." These people are the members of global jihad organizations, or "groups of violence," as al-Qaraḍāwī refers to them, who adopt the jihadi Salafī approach.[35] Al-Qaraḍāwī explains that for these groups unbelief is reason enough to wage war against non-Muslims, even if the latter have neither attacked Muslims nor invaded their lands. They believe that Islam must be disseminated by the sword rather than by *daʿwa* and argument and that war rather than peace is the fundamental relation between Muslims and non-Muslims. Jihadi Salafīs reject the UN Charter and international conventions and agreements on the treatment of prisoners of war because they believe these things aim to prevent the Muslim *umma* from engaging in jihad.[36] But al-Qaraḍāwī, according to his own testimony, adopts the position of the Syrian cleric Wahba al-Zuḥaylī (d. 2015) and the Egyptian Muḥammad Abū Zahra (d. 1974), according to whom the laws of war in Islam are compatible with international law.[37] In the twenty-first century, al-Qaraḍāwī wants to present *wasaṭī* Islam as an alternative to jihadi Salafism and to the Islamist groups that have adopted that approach, especially al-Qaʿida and the IS.

Between these two extremes—westernizing secularists on one hand and jihadi Salafīs on the other—al-Qaraḍāwī locates his own *wasaṭiyya* as a "balanced middle approach,"[38] an approach he explains thoroughly in his very extensive book on jihad published in 2009 under the title *The Jurisprudence of Jihad: A Comparative Study of Its Laws and Philosophy in Light of the Qur'ān and the Sunna*.[39] The *wasaṭī* view of jihad, as clarified in this book, is based on the tools of *wasaṭī* jurisprudence and on the interpretation of Qur'ān and Sunna texts, which are presented as proof that the laws of Islam in no way promote violence or terrorism. *Wasaṭiyya* also addresses the activists of the Islamist movements and asks them to accept its guidance.[40]

The Clash within Islam: The Debate on Issues Pertaining to Jihad

The Meaning of the Term Jihad

One point of departure for the discussion of what the term *jihād* means and what the various types of jihad are lies in the meaning of the Arabic root *j h d*, which means "make an effort." A secondary meaning is "overcoming difficulties" and so also "struggle." In classical Arabic, the word *jihād* has no association with war. In the Qur'ān, words derived from the root *j h d* occur about forty times, but only in a few cases is the context clearly that of fighting; almost every occurrence of the root concerns some laudable deed performed by the believers, but not necessarily a deed involving fighting.[41] It should be noted that in contrast to the Arabic word *jihād*, which can denote efforts of different kinds, including war, the Qur'ān contains dozens of verses calling for war using words derived from the root *q t l*, which in Form I means "kill" and in Form III means "fight."[42] Ella Landau-Tasseron notes that the original meaning of *jihād* is "effort" and not "war," a distinction that plays an important role in debates concerning the nature of jihad in particular and of Islam in general: Is Islam a warlike or peaceful religion? Such debates have been taking place unabated since the eighth and ninth centuries.[43]

Controversy over the Concept of Jihad and the Flaws in Interpretation of It

All of the streams in this debate—al-Qaraḍāwī the *wasaṭī*, jihadi Salafī thinkers such as al-Ṭarṭūsī and 'Abdallah 'Azzām, liberal thinkers such as al-'Ashmāwī and Gamāl al-Bannā—claim that the concept of jihad has been distorted and that it is their aim to set it aright. Al-Qaraḍāwī identifies a distortion in understanding the concept both inside and outside the Muslim world. In the Muslim world, he maintains, there are those who restrict the concept of jihad to fighting (*qitāl*). For them, jihad means taking up arms to fight against the enemies of Islam, including in some cases Muslim rulers who do not govern in accordance with the *sharīʿa*. He calls these individuals the "violent groups," who accuse their fellow Muslims of heresy (that is, they commit the act of *takfīr*) and believe that they have the right to kill them. Outside the Muslim world, jihad is perceived, wrongly according to al-Qaraḍāwī, as fighting against all non-Muslims in order to force them to convert to Islam or to subordinate them to Muslim rule.[44]

Wasaṭiyya wishes to correct this distortion by stressing the basic facts that in the Qur'ān there is an essential difference between the terms *jihād* and *qitāl* and that fighting is only one form of jihad. Al-Qaraḍāwī stresses the fundamental difference between jihad and fighting. Jihad is a duty that every Muslim man and woman must carry out with their souls or property, tongue and heart, as in the following famous *ḥadīth*: "Whoever sees a wrong [*munkar*] and is able to put it right with his hand, let him do so; if he can't, then with his tongue; if he can't, then with or in his heart, which is the bare minimum of faith [*aḍʿaf al-īmān*]."[45] However, al-Qaraḍāwī insists that it is not necessary for every Muslim to be a "fighter" (*muqātil*) because fighting is a duty only in certain circumstances, and even then there are cases in which only some members of the Muslim *umma* are required to fight—namely, when jihad is a "collective duty" (*farḍ kifāya*) rather than an "individual duty" (*farḍ ʿayn*).[46]

Jihadi Salafīs, in contrast, claim that Muslims are commanded to fight, not just to "strive," as they say is explicitly stated in Q2:216: "fight is ordained for you [*kutiba ʿalaykum al-qitāl*]" (the same formulation in Arabic is used in the command to fast, Q2:183: "fasting is prescribed for you [*kutiba ʿalaykum al-ṣiyām*]"). ʿAbd al-Salām Faraj (d. 1982) notes that there are those who maintain that a Muslim can fulfill his duty to perform jihad by preaching rather than by fighting, but in this case he has not fulfilled a Muslim's real duty, which is to fight.[47] ʿAzzām accuses clerics who try to abolish jihad by the sword of doing so to appease the West; he replies to them: "Jihad is a divine command imposed on the Muslim *umma* in order to save the earth in its entirety from the tyranny of the idols [*jawr al-ṭawāghīt*] and in order to subordinate the despots to Islam's justice and mercy."[48] He further notes that all four heads of the orthodox schools of jurisprudence agreed that jihad means combat and combat support.[49]

To obtain a clear picture concerning the differences between *wasaṭiyya*'s and jihadi Salafism's views on jihad, it may be useful to examine the "distortion" that the concept of jihad has undergone according to al-Ṭarṭūsī, a prominent jihadi Salafī shaykh. To his mind, the main "distortion" in how jihad is understood today is that it has become restricted to fighting the external enemy—that is, to fighting non-Muslims (or, more specifically, the Christian "Crusaders" and the Jews) who have attacked Muslim countries, to the exclusion of jihad aimed at the local, internal enemy—namely, Muslim rulers who have abandoned Islam (*murtaddūn*, or apostates). This is the case despite the fact that the internal enemy's heresy and evil, according to al-Ṭarṭūsī, are greater even than those of the external enemy. The "distorters" of jihad consider fighting against heretic or apostate Muslim regimes as "civil war" (*fitna*), a claim that al-Ṭarṭūsī rejects out of hand.[50]

Liberal writers likewise contend that the understanding of the term *jihād* in Islam has been distorted. Al-ʿAshmāwī claims that it is politicians who have distorted it, with the support of jurisprudents, and that the essence of the mistake is the failure to understand that the laws of "the lesser jihad"—that is, jihad in the sense of war—are temporary and valid only in certain circumstances, whereas the laws of "the greater jihad"—the spiritual jihad—are permanent. Over time, politics and *fiqh* marginalized the greater jihad while glorifying the lesser, he says, and as a result Muslims "began living under the illusion that jihad means declaring war on everyone and raising a sword over every neck. Islam thus came to be perceived as war against everyone and fighting all of mankind, although its genuine and original [message] is peace and compassion for the worlds."[51]

Gamāl al-Bannā also contends, like al-Qaraḍāwī, that the misrepresentation of the term *jihād* stemmed from understanding it as synonymous with fighting. But, unlike al-Qaraḍāwī, he believes that this interpretation results in backwardness. He argues that *jihād* (in its original sense) is a spiritual term that encapsulates the moral values of Islam and Muslim society. Moreover, the jihadi nature of Islam means that Muslims are always ready to fight their baser instincts, for they are aware that Satan flows in their very blood, and so they are ever ready to resist him. Jihad, according to Gamāl al-Bannā, is a way of life based on a constant striving to do good. For example, it is a tool for confronting and correcting the ills of society, as expressed by the commandment to preach virtue and prohibit vice.[52]

The difference between Gamāl al-Bannā's conception of jihad and al-Qaraḍāwī's is highlighted by the former's explanation of "jihad by means of money" (*jihād bi-l-māl*). In Gamāl al-Bannā's opinion, this type of jihad includes not only arming fighters but also helping the needy, building charitable institutions, and even pursuing entrepreneurship that creates jobs and helps to improve people's quality of life. He adds that the Qur'ān often gives precedence to this type of jihad over the "jihad of the soul" (i.e., self-sacrifice in battle) because jihad by means of money is a duty incumbent upon every individual every day, whereas self-sacrifice in battle is required only in times of war, which are not the norm.[53] According to al-Qaraḍāwī, however, "jihad by means of money" refers exclusively to financing military gear and activity and is the duty of Muslims who are unable to participate in the fighting for some physical, mental, or social reason. They are required to equip a Muslim fighter in lieu of actual participation in the war.[54]

Spiritual Jihād

The *wasaṭī*, jihadi Salafī, and liberal streams have disparate views on a famous *ḥadīth* of the Prophet according to which the "greater jihad" is spiritual, striving against desire, rather than military. After one of the Muslim raids (*ghazwa*), probably the raid on Tabūk (629 CE), the Prophet said: "We returned from the lesser jihad [*jihād aṣghar*] to the greater jihad [*jihād akbar*]. When asked what he meant by the greater jihad, he answered: the jihad against oneself." It is worth noting that in premodern times the "greater jihad," the fight against desire, was rarely discussed in the Muslim legal literature.[55] Ibn Taymiyya, for example, claimed that this *ḥadīth* is untrustworthy and was not transmitted by any of those who were acquainted with the Prophet's sayings and deeds. He ruled that jihad against the infidel is "a huge deed [*aʿẓam al-aʿmāl*]."[56] Indeed, this *ḥadīth* does not appear in the canonical *ḥadīth* collections.

Al-Qaraḍāwī shares the opinion that this *ḥadīth* is not reliable (*ṣaḥīḥ*). It should be noted that the traditional, purist shaykhs, such as the Saudi shaykh Muḥammad b. Ṣāliḥ al-ʿUthaymīn (d. 2001), have ruled, like al-Qaraḍāwī, that the *ḥadīth* about fighting one's soul is not *ṣaḥīḥ*. In fact, he said that this *ḥadīth* has no roots whatsoever in the literature of authentic *ḥadīth*s, although it has gained currency among Muslims. He, too, believes that jihad against one's desires is the basis for jihad by warfare and for jihad against the hypocrites (*munāfiqūn*) and infidels.[57] Jihadi Salafīs such as ʿAbdallah ʿAzzām have done more than just question the reliability of the *ḥadīth* in which the spiritual jihad is considered as the "greater jihad." ʿAzzām has written that this *ḥadīth* is forged (*mawḍūʿ*), contradicts texts in the Qur'ān and Sunna, and is inconsistent with reality.[58] Faraj explains that this *ḥadīth* was fabricated to diminish the value of fighting with the sword and to lead Muslims away from fighting against the infidel.[59]

Al-Qaraḍāwī, like the Salafīs and jihadi Salafīs, draws a connection between "jihad against the soul's desires" and jihad by warfare, stating that the former is a prerequisite for the latter: in order to fight on the battlefield, a warrior must first struggle with his soul, which desires life rather than death. This is especially the case if the nation around him suffers from the weakness of love for this world and hatred of death.[60] The association between the two types of jihad, the inner mental struggle and the external physical struggle against an enemy, exists among Muslims in general and has been used to explain the fact that Islam has achieved victories during the month of Ramaḍān throughout its history. This is a month in which Muslims view themselves as fighting against their own desires and as existing in a state of purity that prepares them for fighting victoriously against the enemy.[61]

IS, too, calls on its fighters to redouble their jihadi efforts during Ramaḍān. Thus, for example, in a video to mark the beginning of Ramaḍān in June 2015, the IS spokesman, Abū Muḥammad al-ʿAdnānī (d. 2016), called on Muslims to use the month of fasting for the performance of good deeds, adding that jihad is the commandment that more than any other brings the believer close to God. He therefore urged Muslims: "Hasten and persevere in the attack [*ghazw*] in this distinguished month and in martyrdom [*shahāda*] in it."[62] Al-ʿAdnānī called on IS soldiers to repent and ask for absolution during the month of fasting and at the same time to engage in jihad.

The lesson al-Qaraḍāwī draws from the *ḥadīth* in question is that the Muslims must always start with the lesser jihad, with fighting. He writes in this context: "If we accept, for the sake of the argument, that this *ḥadīth* is authentic, its reasoning compels us to start with the lesser jihad and gradually move on to the greater jihad—for this is Allah's way in all things: to begin with the lesser and proceed to the greater. If, according to the reasoning of this *ḥadīth*, fighting for Allah is the lesser jihad, let us start with it and not postpone it."[63] He also juxtaposes this *ḥadīth* with others that describe self-sacrifice in battle as the highest form of jihad. According to one of them, the Prophet was asked which kind of *hijra* (migration) is most noble, and he replied: forsaking what Allah has forbidden. Asked what kind of jihad is most noble, he answered: jihad against the polytheists with one's life and one's property. Asked what kind of death is most commendable, he said: when one's blood is spilt and one's horse is killed.[64]

Interestingly, Ḥasan al-Bannā's position on this matter is closer to that of the jihadi Salafis. He, too, rejects the tradition's authenticity and adds that even if it were authentic, it would still not make it legitimate to abandon jihad by warfare, whose objective is to protect the lands of Islam and to repel the attacks against them by the infidel. Inner jihad, al-Bannā stresses, involves the duty to fight the soul's desires so that it becomes purified and acts purely in God's name, but it is only if a Muslim kills and is killed for God's sake in war that he will receive the recompense of a jihad fighter.[65] It should be remembered, however, that Ḥasan al-Bannā wrote in the context of the struggle against British control in Egypt (1882–1922),[66] Egypt's fight for independence, and the jihad against the newly established State of Israel (1948).

Taking an apologetic approach and seeking to exonerate Islam of terrorist actions carried out in its name, al-Qaraḍāwī argues that the spiritual jihad should be given its rightful place in Islam and its value should be neither understated nor overstated.[67] He gives the name "greater jihad" to the dissemination (*tablīgh*) of Islam using all available means, in an allusion to the phrase *jihādan kabīran* in Q25:52: "strive hard [*jihādan kabīran*] against them with this Qur'ān."

In a letter condemning the leader of IS, Abū Bakr al-Baghdādī (b. 1971), the authors, among them al-Qaraḍāwī, raise an interesting point about the *ḥadīth* on "greater jihad." They argue that even if this tradition is "weak" or fabricated, the Prophet stressed the importance of the spiritual jihad in yet another *ḥadīth*, where he is reported as having said that mentioning God's name is more worthy than fighting the enemy and cutting off his head. The letter's authors refer to Q8:45, in which both types of jihad are mentioned: "standing firm" in the face of the enemy, the "lesser jihad," which in this verse is associated with the "greater jihad," "keeping God firmly in mind" and asking Him to help achieve victory.[68]

A comparison between al-Qaraḍāwī's position on "jihad in one's soul" and the liberals' position reveals how far al-Qaraḍāwī is from their view and how close to the jihadi Salafīs' view. Al-ʿAshmāwī writes that the Prophet called this type of jihad "greater" after he realized that the physical aspect of jihad had gained more importance than the spiritual aspect and so wanted to clarify to the believers that jihad on the battlefield, even if it ends in *istishhād*, is less noble than the effort to abstain from evil, purify the soul, and attain high moral standards of forgiveness, compassion, and generosity. Al-ʿAshmāwī describes this "greater jihad" as "the common human struggle against greed, meanness, fear, ignorance, [spiritual] illness, corruption, and tyranny."[69] Interesting, too, is ʿAbd al-Ḥamīd al-Anṣārī's definition of "greater jihad." He also contends that to address the roots of terrorism, the understanding of jihad needs to be corrected because it has been distorted by "the preachers of hatred." The greater jihad, he says, is "living, building, creating, advancing, spreading virtue, defending truth, and helping the oppressed for the sake of Allah, not just dying for the sake of Allah." It means combatting backwardness, fanaticism, and the culture of hate. Conversely, the lesser jihad means fighting enemies even when the Muslims are in a state of weakness.[70]

The Meaning of Irhāb

Following the 9/11 terror attacks, al-Qaraḍāwī sharpened the distinction he made between jihad and *irhāb* (terrorism).[71] He maintains that he condemns the latter but preaches jihad, which is legitimate according to the *sharīʿa*.[72] He notes that the term *irhāb* in its common denotation does not exist in the Muslim lexicon and is therefore not mentioned as one of the sins for which *sharīʿa* requires punishment. The Arabic word for terror or terrorism, *irhāb*, is a translation from other languages and has never received an unambiguous definition because, he claims, America intentionally wants the concept to remain fuzzy so that it can be used as a derogatory term for anyone who opposes America or its policies. As an example, he mentions the fact that America defines all those who resist the Israeli occupation (say, Hamas) as terrorists and accuses those who contribute to Islamic charities of assisting terrorism. Islam, he insists, forbids terrorism in the sense of terrorizing people because people have the right to live in security, as proven by the Prophet's words in a *ḥadīth*: "The believer is the one from whom the people's lives and wealth are safe."[73]

However, al-Qaraḍāwī, like the jihadi Salafīs, makes a sharp distinction between two types of *irhāb* (which literally means "to terrify"). The difference between *wasaṭiyya* and jihadi Salafism on this matter lies in determining what should be considered terror and therefore should be condemned and what comes under the divine command to terrify the enemy, which is a Muslim's duty. The two types of *irhāb* are:

1. *The terrorization that Muslims are commanded to carry out.* For example, Q8:60 (also 8:12 and 3:151, where the word *ruʿb*, "terror," is used) says: "Prepare whatever forces you [believers] can muster, including warhorses, to frighten off God's enemies and yours and warn others unknown to you [according to commentators, the hypocrites (*munāfiqūn*) and the Jews] but known to God." Al-Qaraḍāwī explains that this verse commands the Muslims to "frighten off" their enemies in order to deter them from attacking. He adds that such deterrence of the enemy is "legitimate terrorization" (*irhāb mashrūʿ*); if each of the belligerents is of equal strength and deters the other, then what he calls "armed peace" (*al-silm al-musallaḥ*) will ensue.[74]

ʿAbdallah ʿAzzām provides an important expression of the notion that Muslims are commanded to terrorize the enemy. He writes that "every Muslim must be an *irhābī* [i.e., a terrorizer of the enemy, as commanded in Q8:60], for *irhāb* is a duty specified in the Qurʾān and Sunna." He adds that the Prophet was the first to fulfill this commandment and thus was the first *irhābī* and that any Muslim who fails to do the same is not following the true path of Islam.[75]

Al-Qaraḍāwī ruled that the Palestinian resistance (*muqāwama*) groups, such as Hamas, are not terrorists, either with respect to their objectives or with respect to the means they use; indeed, he believes that their actions constitute the most sublime form of terrorizing (*irhāb*) and jihad in God's name for the purpose of protecting Islam's holy places and the Muslim homeland.[76] As part of this resistance, he permits the Palestinians to attack Israeli settlements and settlers, to capture Zionist officers and soldiers, and to kidnap them and hold them in order to negotiate the release of Palestinian prisoners or withdrawal of the forces of occupation from the homeland. For al-Qaraḍāwī, the terrorism that should be the first to be condemned is that of the Zionist state, a state, he argues, that is based on terrorism and adopted the use of terrorism after its establishment. In contrast, one who defends his homeland and fights against the occupier using whatever force he may have—for example, by turning himself into a human bomb (*qunbula bashariyya*) and exploding himself among the enemy—is a martyr of the highest order.[77] *Istishhād* attacks in Israel in which civilians are killed should not be considered terrorism because, to his mind, there are no innocent Jews. (For further discussion of this issue, see the section on *istishhād* in this chapter.)

2. *Illegitimate terrorism carried out for illegitimate purposes using illegitimate means*, such as Zionist terrorism. Acts of terrorism committed for legitimate purposes but using illegitimate means—for example, skyjacking[78]—are also considered illegitimate, as are taking hostages with a view toward imprisoning them and threatening to execute them if the hostage takers' demands are not met or killing tourists, as in the Luxor massacre in 1997. In all these cases, al-Qaraḍāwī considers the means illegitimate because they involve punishing the innocent for the sins of others.[79] Al-Qaraḍāwī defines a terrorist as someone who kills innocent people unjustly, fails to distinguish between the innocent and the guilty, and uses civilians to achieve his aims. Thus, in his view, the passengers in the aircraft used in the 9/11 attacks were innocent and had no connection to the crimes committed by America.[80]

The distinction between the two types of "terrorization" led Abū Muḥammad al-Maqdisī to rule that the 9/11 attacks came under the Qur'ānic command to "arouse fear" in the enemy, in contrast to al-Qaraḍāwī, who considers the 9/11 attacks as acts of terror to be condemned, although he views acts of *istishhād* against Israel as legitimate from a *shar'ī* perspective. Al-Maqdisī rejects descriptions of jihad as terrorism and jihad fighters as terrorists and calls such descriptions "whispers and wiles of the devil"; he accuses those who make such comparisons of imitating the Jews and Christians, which is forbidden in Islam.[81] Owing to the distinction between these two types of terrorization, IS can claim that its own terrorist attacks in Europe against civilians are not terror at all but rather expressions of the Qur'ānic command to frighten or terrify the enemy.

Liberal writers such as al-Nābulsī accuse al-Qaraḍāwī of employing a double standard with respect to terror because although he condemned the car bombing in Qatar on March 19, 2005, perpetrated by an Egyptian national, 'Umar Aḥmad 'Abdallah, against a British school in Doha, he does not condemn terror attacks in Iraq and Palestine. Al-Qaraḍāwī seems to think that there is permissible terror and forbidden terror, al-Nābulsī says and so asks: "Did 'Umar Aḥmad 'Abdallah perhaps pray behind you [al-Qaraḍāwī] at the 'Umar b. al-Khaṭṭāb mosque in Doha and listen to the Friday sermons you give, in which you extol the jihad and jihad fighters in the Muslim world?"[82] It should be noted that in the March 25, 2005, sermon in which al-Qaraḍāwī condemned the Qatar bombing, he remarked that the perpetrator couldn't possibly have been one of the people who attended his mosque, for "the minds [of these worshippers] are illuminated with the true Islam."[83] But al-Nābulsī is presumably thinking of sermons such as the one al-Qaraḍāwī delivered on June 13, 2003, in which he said, "The believer is not afraid of death but seeks *istishhād*," and then quoted Q9:52 and explained that the phrase "one of the two best things" in this verse means either victory or *istishhād*.[84] Al-Qaraḍāwī's firm condemnation of the Doha bombing and his participation in the protests against it also stand out in comparison to his feeble condemnation of the 9/11 attacks. About the Doha bombing, he stated unequivocally that it was "an act denounced by the religion, by custom [*'urf*], and by the law,"[85] and he ascribed it to the perpetrators' mental defect and twisted understanding of the religion and of life.[86] But in the case of 9/11, as we saw, al-Qaraḍāwī ascribed the attacks to the Americans' unjust behavior, foreign policy, and support for Israel.

Jus ad Bellum: The Causes and Aims of War

Al-Qaraḍāwī the *wasaṭī* claims to be among those in the Muslim world who preach peace and who believe that relations between Muslims and non-Muslims should basically be peaceful unless the non-Muslims attack Muslims—their souls, property, land, or faith, the latter through attempts to convert Muslims to another faith. Preachers of peace, he claims, view jihad as a defensive measure because, according to *sharīʿa*, jihad is intended only for defense, and Muslims should therefore never go on the offensive without due cause. He adds that jihad is not an aim in itself but rather a religious instrument for achieving the Muslim *umma*'s aims. Islam, according to al-Qaraḍāwī, does not want war and wages it only when it is forced to, as stated in Q2:216: "Fighting is ordained for you, though you dislike it." He rejects accusations such as those leveled at Islam by Pope Benedict XVI, for example, that Islam is a religion of the sword and of war.[87]

Al-Qaraḍāwī contrasts his own conception of defensive jihad with the conceptions of those whom he calls the "preachers of war," by which he means global jihad organizations, whom he accuses of preaching offensive jihad and of viewing Muslim–infidel relations as being based primarily on war. For them, others' nonbelief in Islam is cause enough to go to war, even with no prior aggression against Muslims. Al-Qaraḍāwī claims that these organizations promote offensive jihad and attributes to them the view that Islam and the Qur'ān are truths that must be supported by the sword; they view Islam as a mission that presents non-Muslims with three choices, as enumerated in classical Muslim law: conversion to Islam or payment of the poll tax (*jizya*) or fighting (*qitāl*).[88] It is important to note here that the views on the causes of war and its aims that al-Qaraḍāwī ascribes to global jihad organizations are in fact identical to those found in classical Muslim jurisprudence. For example, Ibn Rushd (d. 1198) wrote that it is a duty to fight all polytheists and that the People of the Book should either convert to Islam or pay the *jizya*.[89]

Jihadi Salafīs such as ʿAzzām criticize clerics such as al-Qaraḍāwī for presenting jihad as only defensive. ʿAzzām writes:

> Our religion is offensive [*dīn hujūmī*] toward the idols [*ṭawāghīt*] that enslave men to them rather than to Allah. This religion has come to destroy the political, economic, and social obstacles to Muslim *daʿwa*, which must encompass all of humanity. The idols will never enable you to transmit [*tablīgh*] Allah's religion, and therefore the objective of jihad is to remove the political obstacles that prevent Allah's religion [according to Q3:19, Islam is God's religion] from reaching mankind. Subsequently this religion will be presented to the people and "let those who wish to believe in it do so, and let those who wish to reject it do so" [Q18:29].[90]

These words were inspired by Sayyid Quṭb.[91] The jihadi Salafī thinker Abū Baṣīr al-Ṭarṭūsī has also sharply criticized the proponents of defensive jihad, whom he disparagingly calls "the secularist hypocrites," because, to his mind, they adopt an overly reticent and apologetic approach to jihad. He accuses them of discrediting the principle of jihad in Islam by calling it "terrorism" and an uncivilized option that is not fit for our times.[92]

The Controversy within Islam over the Goals of Jihad

Wasaṭiyya and jihadi Salafism agree that one of the legitimate objectives of jihad according to *sharīʿa* is to ward off aggression, whether against Islam or against the homeland and the soil. One difference between the two schools in this respect, however, is that al-Qaraḍāwī accepts the nationalist (*waṭanī*) jihad waged by Hamas for the purpose of liberating the soil of Palestine because for Hamas nationalism is part of the faith.[93] Jihadi Salafism, in contrast, views nationalism and loyalty to the homeland as idolatry (*ṭāghūt*) or unbelieving (*jāhilī*) allegiance. In contrast to al-Qaraḍāwī, Quṭb and his jihadi Salafī followers are of the opinion that land in itself has no value; its value derives from the rule of *sharīʿa* over it. The preservation of the *dār al-Islām* is thus not the ultimate objective of jihad, according to Quṭb, but only a means toward the establishment of Allah's kingdom in the *dār al-Islām*, which will subsequently serve as a base from which Islam will be imposed on the entire world.[94]

Another bone of contention between *wasaṭiyya* and jihadi Salafism is the latter's claim that jihad has the aim of combating unbelief everywhere, in accordance with Q2:193 and 8:39, where Muslims are urged to fight until there is no *fitna* in the world, a term that jihadi Salafīs, like classical exegetes, understand as denoting unbelief and polytheism.[95] Al-Qaraḍāwī rejects the interpretation of the word *fitna* in these verses as *shirk*, or heresy, which is the most common meaning it is given in classical Muslim Qur'ānic exegesis.[96]

Al-Qaraḍāwī, in contrast to the traditional Muslim interpretation adopted by jihadi Salafism, insists that the word *fitna* in these verses must be understood in its original meaning of "temptation." For him, *fitna* means that Muslims should be free of religious persecution, free of pressure and of material and psychological coercion with respect to their faith, and free to preach Islam so that whoever believes will do so of his own free will and whoever rejects the faith will also do so of his own free will because, as the beginning of Q2:256 states, "there is no coercion in religion [*lā ikrāha fī al-dīn*]."[97] However, most classical Muslim exegetes consider this verse (2:256) to have been abrogated (*mansūkh*) by the Verse of the Sword, as discussed later.

Al-Qaraḍāwī provides further evidence for his claim that it is not true that the objective of fighting the infidel is to force him to convert. He argues that the idea of fighting the infidel merely because he is an infidel contradicts the Qur'ān, which states that the differences in people's beliefs and religions and the division of humankind into believers and nonbelievers is God's will (e.g., Q10:99, 11:118). He uses arguments contained in Ibn Taymiyya's epistle "Brief Statement on Fighting the Infidel, Armistice with Them, and the Prohibition to Kill Them Only for Their Unbelief" in order to bolster his position that war against the infidel is to be waged not because of their unbelief but only because of their war against the Muslims.[98] Muhammad Qasim Zaman remarks that because al-Qaraḍāwī could not find strong evidence for his position, he was forced to rely on the latter composition ascribed to Ibn Taymiyya even though he (al-Qaraḍāwī) admits that Saudi clerics refuse to list the epistle among Ibn Taymiyya's rulings because his authorship of it is in doubt.[99]

A different and interesting interpretation of the *fitna* verses on the objective of jihad (Q8:39, 2:193) is proposed by Gamāl al-Bannā, who can be taken as a representative of the liberal approach. According to him, the word *fitna* refers to forced conversion, which Islam forbids. The expression "wa-yakūn al-dīn kulluhu li-llāh" in Q8:39—"the religion, all of it, is for God"—does not refer just to Islam but to all religions, he argues; interpreting it as referring to Islam only contravenes other Qur'ānic verses stating that Judaism and Christianity will endure and that Allah will judge between the religions on Judgment Day. If understood as referring specifically to Islam, the verse would imply that non-Muslims are required to convert whether they like it or not, but that amounts to "compulsion in religion," which Islam explicitly rejects (Q2:256), Gamāl al-Bannā says. He also notes that whereas war occupies a central place in *fiqh* and in the Prophet's biographies, the Qur'ān devotes most of its verses to moral guidance and only a handful of verses to the issue of warfare. Unlike *fiqh* and history, the Qur'ān sanctifies life and the individual's right to life, claims Gamāl al-Bannā. It should be noted that this argument is apologetic because the Qur'ān does contain numerous verses that set out the framework for war between Muslims and non-Muslims, modeled upon the Prophet's raids on his enemies. According to al-Bannā, many Islamist writers who evoke the verses of fighting as evidence for their rulings are ignorant of the true nature of these verses—that is, of the fact that they are anchored in the fundamental principle of freedom of religion. This is why fighting is permitted only in cases of *fitna*: when Muslims are being forced to embrace beliefs other than Islam.[100]

Here it is pertinent to mention Gamāl al-Bannā's view on the goals of jihad for the sake of Allah. To his mind, war has two legitimate objectives. The first objective is to replace tyranny with a regime that is politically and economically fairer. Muslim soldiers, he said, should not fight their enemies because the latter are unbelievers but because their enemies defend the corrupt order and prevent the instatement of the justice brought by Islam. The second objective is to remove any obstacle that prevents Muslims from delivering the message of Islam. Al-Bannā stresses, however, that Islam must not be imposed by force and that anyone is free to reject it and enjoy freedom of religion under Muslim rule, provided he pay the *jizya*.[101]

Also noteworthy is the harsh criticism leveled by the Tunisian liberal al-ʿAfīf al-Akhḍar at the jihadi movement for waging a religious war against the entire world, including Muslim countries it regards as apostate. According to al-Akhḍar, the term *jihad* is synonymous with the term *terror*, and the threat jihad poses to global stability today is comparable to the threat posed by fascism in the 1930s, a claim that al-Qaraḍāwī obviously rejects. Al-Akhḍar warns that a religious war is bound to end in a Muslim defeat, and so he offers Muslims a way out: to recognize other religions, especially Judaism, Christianity, and Sabianism, which the Qur'ān recognizes (2:62, 5:69, 22:17). He states that the medieval Muslim *fuqahā'*, acting out of "religious narcissism," ruled that the Qur'ānic verses recognizing other religions had been abrogated by other verses, such as 3:19 ("The religion in the sight of Allah is Islam") and 3:85 ("If anyone desires a religion other than Islam, never will it be accepted of him"). Taking the opposite approach, al-Akhḍar explains that the latter two verses descended during a period of intense conflict between Islam and the other Abrahamic religions—Judaism and Christianity—and were suitable for that period. But in the current era, which is one of dialogue between faiths and civilizations, the moderate verses are more appropriate.[102]

Taking a starkly different approach, al-Qaraḍāwī contends that the Prophet Muḥammad was sent as a messenger to the entire world when Allah deemed mankind ready to receive the final, eternal, and universal message of Islam. It is Allah, in His infinite wisdom, who designated the *sharīʿa* as the seal of all revelations, superseding every revelation that preceded it, al-Qaraḍāwī claims. It is Allah who made religion complete through the revelation of Islam (5:3) and who guarantees the eternal nature of the Qur'ān (15:9) by ensuring that it cannot be distorted, as the Torah and the New Testament were.[103] In other words, al-Qaraḍāwī takes a view similar to that of the Islamic sources, the Qur'ān and the Sunna, which the jihadi Salafīs have also adopted: that Allah's religion is one—namely, Islam, as stated in Q3:19—and that all the divine messengers conveyed the message of Islam, but the Jews and Christians distorted this message. Quoting Q5:48, al-Qaraḍāwī states that Islam confirms the revealed religions that preceded it and corrects their scriptures, which have been corrupted.[104]

Disseminating Islam by the Sword

Since the attacks of 9/11 and even more so since the IS began to execute people by beheading, the *wasaṭīyya* school has sharpened the distinction between jihad and violence: jihad is acceptable in *sharīʿa*, whereas violence is to be condemned. Al-Qaraḍāwī points out that although both use physical force to attain their goals, jihad is unique in the clarity of its aim, the clarity of the means it uses, and its commitment to the laws of *sharīʿa*, to Islam's ethical values, and to the laws of war, both in the course of fighting and in its aftermath.[105]

As part of its effort to present Islam as a peaceful religion that eschews violence, *wasaṭiyya* must deal with a large repository of texts in the Qur'ān and the Sunna that, at least on the face of it, refute this claim. The *wasaṭiyya*'s effort to present Islam as a peaceful religion has given rise to a debate between the *wasaṭī*s and jihadi Salafīs regarding the manner in which Islam was first spread. Whereas the jihadi Salafīs quote Qur'ānic verses and prophetic *ḥadīth*s that mention war and the use of force against the infidels as the means to attain the victory of Islam, the *wasaṭīs* employ creative interpretations and apologetics to claim that Islam was not spread by the force of the sword but rather through persuasion and *daʿwa*. Among the important texts that are the topic of a heated debate between the *wasaṭī*s, the jihadi Salafīs, and the liberals is the so-called Verse of the Sword (Āyat al-Sayf).

The Debate on the Verse of the Sword

Resolving Contradictions between Qur'ānic Verses on Relations with non-Muslims

In the Qur'ān, the message concerning the issue of war is unsystematic and uneven, with contradictions among different verses. On the one hand, there are passages that imply recognition of nonbelievers' right to retain their faith—for example, Q109:6 ("you have your religion and I have mine")[106] and the opening sentence of Q2:256 ("there is no coercion in religion"). On the other hand, other verses command war against the infidel (Q9:14) and demand that they be killed (Q9:5). Many Qur'ānic verses are about war. Some command the believers to engage in unlimited warfare against the infidel, kill idolaters, and refuse offers of peace until Islam reigns supreme.

Reuven Firestone first presents the traditional approach, which he calls "evolutionary theory," used in Islam to resolve the contradictions between the warlike verses in the Qur'ān and those urging recognition of the infidel. This approach relies on the "occasions of revelation" (*asbāb al-nuzūl*) and assumes that the war verses were revealed in direct connection with Muḥammad's actual needs during his lifetime. In other words, the verses reflect an evolving situation. During his stay in Mecca, the Prophet was still weak, with few followers, and so the Qur'ān urged him to avoid a physical confrontation with the idolaters of Mecca. After his immigration to Medina (622 CE), Muḥammad and his believers were commanded to take up arms to defend themselves against the infidel. During the next phase, when the Muslim *umma* was already larger and stronger, it was commanded to fight almost irrespective of time and place. The main weakness of this evolutionary theory is that early exegetes did not agree on the "occasion of revelation" of the various warlike verses, their times, or which verses were abrogated by other verses.[107]

Firestone proposes an alternative approach to classifying the warlike verses in the Qur'ān, in which he takes into account neither the chronology of their revelation nor their context within the Qur'ān. He divides these verses into four types: verses expressing nonmilitant means of propagating or defending the faith; verses that place restrictions on fighting; verses expressing conflict between God's command and the reaction of Muḥammad's followers; and verses strongly advocating war for God's religion.[108] Michael Bonner points out a difficulty in this analysis: that the Qur'ān, in his opinion, contains "war verses" that do not fall into any of Firestone's categories.[109]

The Wasaṭī, *Jihadi Salafī, and Liberal Positions on the Verse of the Sword*

A major bone of contention that highlights the difference between the *wasaṭī* and the jihadi Salafī positions concerns the status of the Verse of the Sword (Āyat al-Sayf).[110] Classical commentators on the Qur'ān disagree on which verse in Q9 is the Verse of the Sword, but the most common view is that it is Q9:5: "When the [four] forbidden months [i.e., months in which it is forbidden to fight the polytheists: Dhū al-Qa'da, Dhū al-Ḥijja, Muḥarram, and Rajab] are over, wherever you encounter the idolaters, kill them, seize them, besiege them, wait for them at every lookout post; but if they turn [to God], maintain the prayer, and pay the prescribed alms [*zakāh*], let them go on their way, for God is most forgiving and merciful." This verse explains the cause of the fighting: to make men testify to God's oneness (this is the classical interpretation of the verb *tābū*, "they turn to God"), "maintain the prayer, and pay the prescribed *zakāh*."

In classical Qur'ānic exegesis, Q9:5 is said to have abrogated more than 120 verses that were perceived as inconsistent with it. In other words, according to the classical exegetical tradition, the command to fight the infidel and make him convert to Islam is the one that is valid. The purpose of fighting as reflected in this verse is clarified in classical exegesis by means of a *ḥadīth* in which the Prophet is quoted as saying, "I was commanded to fight the people until they gave the witnessing: 'There is no god but God, and that Muḥammad is the Messenger of God,' and that they establish prayer and give *zakāh*."[111]

It is pertinent to examine al-Qaraḍāwī's position on two issues that come up regarding the Verse of the Sword: (*a*) how to handle the explicit message of the verse and the *ḥadīth* used to clarify it, which implies that infidels must be forced to convert; (*b*) the question of whether the Verse of the Sword abrogates other Qur'ānic verses that imply otherwise. As for the first issue, al-Qaraḍāwī rejects the classical interpretation of Q9:5 that the purpose of fighting is to force the infidel to convert to Islam. He believes that the purpose of fighting, rather than to force people to convert to Islam, is to ensure the safety of those who proselytize for Islam—to safeguard the liberty to disseminate the message of Islam through the use of sound logic and convincing arguments.[112]

Regarding the *ḥadīth*, Yohanan Friedmann notes that *ḥadīth* commentators have held various views on the identity of the people against whom the Prophet commanded the believers to fight until they convert to Islam. Some commentators say that the phrase "the people" in this *ḥadīth* refers to all of mankind, including the People of the Book who agreed to pay the *jizya*. However, it should be pointed out that in some versions of this *ḥadīth* the word *polytheists* appears instead of *people*; according to these versions, the Muslims are commanded to fight the idolaters, but not the People of the Book, against whom one should not fight after they agree to pay the *jizya*, according to Q29:9.

In an apologetic attempt to show that the purpose of fighting according to the Qur'ān is to defend Islam and the Muslims, not to forcefully convert the infidel, al-Qaraḍāwī interprets the word *people* in this tradition as denoting only those who fight (*al-muḥāribūn*) against the Muslims and are mentioned at the beginning of Q9—that is, idolaters who violated their agreement with the Muslims. Al-Qaraḍāwī accepts the view of his spiritual mentor, Shaykh Muḥammad al-Ghazālī, that the tradition in question has been "wronged" (*maẓlūm*). According to al-Ghazālī, Muslim religious scholars agree that the tradition does not speak about the People of the Book (Jews and Christians).[113]

The liberal thinker Muḥammad Sa'īd al-'Ashmāwī also proposes an apologetic interpretation of this *ḥadīth* similar to al-Qaraḍāwī's. He argues that the word *people* in the *ḥadīth* refers only to the people of Mecca or to the Quraysh tribe, which means that the Prophet was commanded to fight only the polytheists of Mecca. Interpreted this way, he notes, the *ḥadīth* is in line with Q9:36, which commands the Muslims to fight all the polytheists, referring to those in Mecca.[114]

As for the claim that the Verse of the Sword abrogates (*nāsikh*) the verses that express recognition of the infidel, al-Qaraḍāwī rejects it, whereas the jihadi Salafis accept it. He rejects the very idea of abrogation in the Qur'ān and thus naturally cannot accept the claim made in classical Qur'ānic exegesis or the jihadi Salafis' interpretation that the Verse of the Sword abrogates other verses in which non-Muslims are shown indulgence. Al-Qaraḍāwī insists that any claim concerning the abrogation of a Qur'ānic verse requires unequivocal proof and that there is no proof of this kind concerning any verse.[115]

Contrary to al-Qaraḍāwī, 'Azzām in his will (*waṣiyya*) wrote that the Verse of the Sword is either Q9:5 or Q9:36, "fight the pagans all together as they fight you all together," and accepted the classical interpretation, concluding that the Verse of the Sword abrogates 120 or 140 Qur'ānic verses that contradict it. 'Azzām added that the Verse of the Sword is a conclusive answer to all who have tried to evade the warlike verses of the Qur'ān by giving them a nonliteral interpretation.[116] Note that bin Laden quoted the "verses of the sword" (Q9:5 and 9:36) in "Declaration of Jihad on the Americans Occupying the Country of the Two Sacred Places [*bilād al-ḥaramayni*—i.e., Saudi Arabia]," issued on August 23, 1996, as well as in "Declaration Announcing the Establishment of the World Islamic Front for Jihad against Jews and Crusaders," issued on February 23, 1998.[117] Based on the Verse of the Sword and on several other verses quoted in his announcement about the new front, bin Laden declared that every able-bodied Muslim, wherever he be, had an individual duty to kill Americans and their allies, civilians and soldiers, until the al-Aqṣā Mosque and the Holy Mosque in Mecca were liberated from American control and until the US Army was defeated and expelled from the Land of Islam and became incapable of threatening any Muslim.[118] He interpreted Q9:5 as saying that every tribe in the Arabian Peninsula was duty bound to wage jihad for God and to purify Saudi Arabia of the American occupier.[119]

Al-Qaraḍāwī's understanding of the Verse of the Sword was influenced by the approach taken by his teacher Muḥammad al-Ghazālī, who showed *wasaṭī* tendencies in his writings.[120] Al-Ghazālī denies the very existence of a Verse of the Sword in the Qur'ān; he argues instead that Q9 contains a number of verses that address the issue of Islam's relationship to its foes and the fight against them, for reasons that legists in the past and at present agree justify fighting and yet do not infringe on the religious liberty of non-Muslims. For example, in Q9:1 God declares a release (*barā'a*) from His and the Prophet's commitment to the agreements between the Muslims and the polytheists. According to al-Ghazālī, this step does not constitute a violation of an agreement by the Muslims, but only a response to the polytheists' violation of their commitments. This interpretation is proven by the chapter's fourth verse (9:4), which states that Muslims must fulfill treaties that have been honored by the infidel.[121]

It should be noted that, just like al-Qaraḍāwī, Gamāl al-Bannā, who can be taken to represent the liberal approach, also rejects the principle of *naskh* in the Qur'ān. According to his view, the Qur'ānic verses on fighting do not abrogate the verses that instruct the Muslims to tolerate the harm caused to them by the infidels. Each set of verses, he argues, descended in certain circumstances and is applicable today in the same circumstances. As an alternative to *naskh*, he adopts the view that the Qur'ān allows the Muslims to choose between different options, according to the prevailing conditions.[122] Explaining the aggressive stance of the verses in Sūrat al-Tawba, including the Verse of the Sword, he takes an apologetic line, stating that the aggressive stance of the verses in Sūrat al-Tawba was required by the circumstances: after a series of battles with the non-Muslims, Islam was triumphant and established its state, but there were still pockets of resistance that had to be eliminated. In other words, fighting the infidels was a precautionary measure, necessary to ensure the future of the Islamic state. Al-Bannā adds that although Sūrat al-Tawba commands Muslims to fight the infidels, it also states that the infidels should be given a chance to repent.[123]

Al-ʿAshmāwī also takes an apologetic approach regarding certain Qur'ānic verses that command the believers to kill (such as 2:191). He argues that some of these verses do not command Muslims to kill the polytheists but rather to fight them and to do this only until they stop fighting the Muslims. Moreover, the fighting is required to be proportional to the threat.[124]

The "Ḥadīth *of the Sword*"

The dispute between the *wasaṭī* movement and jihadi Salafism on whether Islam should be disseminated by the sword is also reflected in the way each group views the statement ascribed to the Prophet and known as the "*ḥadīth* of the sword": "I have been sent [by God] to bear the sword at the approach of the Hour [*bayna yaday al-sāʿa*—that is, when the Day of

Judgment draws near]. My sustenance has been placed in the shadow of my spear; humiliation and debasement are the lot of those who oppose me." This tradition is a source of difficulty for al-Qaraḍāwī's claim that Islam was spread benevolently, by *da'wa* and convincing arguments. To cope with this text, he adopts an apologetic approach in interpreting it.

First, he argues that this *ḥadīth* is doubtful because its chain of transmission is flawed; *ḥadīth* scholars cast doubt on the reliability of one of the tradition's transmitters.[125] He adds that its content, too, contradicts numerous verses in the Qur'ān, which never once states that the Prophet was sent with a sword but, to the contrary, says that he was sent with the task to instruct people in the right path (*hudā*), the true religion, mercy, and so on.[126] Al-Qaraḍāwī insists that it is impossible for there to exist a valid tradition that contradicts the clear evidence and explicit statements (*muḥkamāt*) of the Qur'ān; if a contradiction is found, it means that the Sunna in question is false, that we understand it incorrectly, or that the contradiction is only apparent but not real. In any case, the Qur'ān has priority over the Sunna.[127] Al-Qaraḍāwī declares that Islam raised the sword only against those who resisted it by force or first raised the sword against it.[128] Indeed, most Muslim experts on Islamic jurisprudence agree that the Sunna cannot invalidate Qur'ānic texts; however, some scholars have ruled to the contrary, among them several jurists of the Ḥanafī school.[129]

IS states in its videos, after mentioning the Prophet's name, that he was sent with a sword as a mercy to all creatures.[130] The authors of the critical epistle addressed to the head of IS, Abū Bakr al-Baghdādī, wrote that the claim that the Prophet was "sent to bear the sword" is incorrect. They pointed out that, according to Q21:107, it was only as a mercy that Allah sent Muḥammad "to all people, for all creatures." They added that the expression "sent to bear the sword" appears in a *ḥadīth* that refers to a specific time, a specific place, and specific circumstances. They argue that it is important to distinguish the overall absolute attribute of mercy ascribed to God in the Qur'ān and the use of the sword, which is limited to the specific circumstances in which the *ḥadīth* was uttered.[131]

'Abd al-Salām Faraj and 'Abdallah 'Azzām, who represent the jihadi Salafī approach to this *ḥadīth*, explain that Allah helped Islam with the sword after Muḥammad provided proof of Islam's truth. In this context, they quote the "*ḥadīth* of the sword." Faraj explains that the Prophet made this statement because the idolaters were so powerful that they would have prevailed unless defeated by the sword. Faraj writes that the Prophet Muḥammad addressed Mecca's idolaters as follows: "Listen, people of Quraysh, by the life of Him who holds Muḥammad's soul in His hand, I was sent to you with the authority to slaughter [*laqad ji'tukum bil-dhabḥ*] [God's opponents]." With these words, according to Faraj, the Prophet, when specifically in the heart of the city of Mecca, defined unambiguously the way the infidel should be treated.[132] 'Abdallah 'Azzām, in contrast to al-Qaraḍāwī, claims that Islam brought the sword, arose through the sword, will continue to exist thanks to the sword, and will disappear if it loses the sword. Islam, he declares, is a religion of terrorization, force, and bravery; weakness is a crime whose deserved punishment is hellfire (Q4:97).[133] To those who accuse Islam of having been established with the sword, 'Azzām replies: "Our religion is one of love, peace, and eternal mercy, but it arose through the sword, our Prophet was sent with a sword, and our religion and our faith in the oneness of God [*tawḥīd*] have been preserved only thanks to the sword."[134]

This *ḥadīth* of the sword is often quoted in jihadi Salafī texts in order to give *shar'ia* legitimacy to the use of the sword. Thus, bin Laden quoted it in the preamble to his declaration announcing the establishment of the World Islamic Front for Jihad against Jews and Crusaders, and al-Maqdisī quoted it at the beginning of the *fatwā* in which he provided legal justification for the 9/11 attacks.[135]

Defining the Enemy and the Battlefield

Most *fuqahā'* divide the world into two parts, *dār al-Islām* and *dār al-ḥarb*. This division affects the way Muslim thinkers perceive the global order because it could imply that Islam does not recognize the division of the world into numerous sovereign nations, each with its own law and religion. Another kind of "house" discussed in Muslim legal literature is the "house of covenant" (*dār al-'ahd*) or the "house of treaty" (*dār al-ṣulḥ*)—that is, territory not occupied by the Muslims but whose inhabitants have a *ṣulḥ*, treaty, with the Muslims, its conditions agreed to by both sides. The Shāfiʿī school created the concept of this third category, *dār al-ʿahd*.[136] It is important to note that some contemporary Muslim jurists, such as Muḥammad Abū Zahra, have argued that the concept of *dār al-ʿahd* emerged in response to evolving relations between the Muslim state and its neighbors. Thus, when a state of war existed between the parties, Muslims perceived the world as divided into *dār al-Islām* and *dār al-ḥarb*, but when the war was over, relations between the states came to be codified in agreements (*muʿāhadāt*). These jurists maintain that in our day all nations of the world, including the Muslim states, belong to the UN and share a commitment to its laws and that therefore non-Muslim states can no longer be considered *dār al-ḥarb* but are *dār al-ʿahd*. Abū Zahra adds that Muslim states must respect international agreements, including the UN Charter, because the Qur'ān commands the believers to honor their commitments (e.g., Q5:1: "fulfill your obligations").[137]

Al-Qaraḍāwī's Realistic Interpretation of the Division of the World

Although al-Qaraḍāwī accepts the division of the world, he makes two very significant caveats:

1. He rules that all "Muslim states" where the majority of the population is Muslim are part of *dār al-Islām*, even though some implement the *sharīʿa* only partially, and others, such as Turkey under Muṣṭafā Kamāl Atatürk (d. 1938), are self-declared secular states. For al-Qaraḍāwī, it is enough that such states are fundamentally and historically Muslim, most of their populace is Muslim, and their rulers are at least nominally Muslim. In these countries, Islam's rites are given public religious and social expression—for example, in the call to prayer (*adhān*), Qur'ān readings, mosques, Friday prayers, and so on. Most of these countries also state in their constitutions that Islam is the state religion, and some even declare that *sharīʿa* is a chief or *the* chief source of legislation. Al-Qaraḍāwī thus supports those jurists, especially those in the Ḥanafī and Shāfiʿī schools of jurisprudence, who place very strict conditions on the possibility of removing a state from *dār al-Islām* and considering it *dār al-ḥarb*.[138]

2. The entire world, with the exception of Israel, is to be considered *dār al-ʿahd* with respect to the Muslims: "We are connected to the world

around us by means of the UN Charter, being, all of us Muslims, members of this body."[139] Al-Qaraḍāwī adds that Muslim states must obey the UN Charter but are forbidden to sign agreements that contradict the laws of *sharīʿa*—for example, the convention that abolishes discrimination against women because the convention both forbids polygamy, which *sharīʿa* allows (for a discussion of polygamy, see chapter 6), and allows marriage between a Muslim woman and a non-Muslim man, which *sharīʿa* forbids. As for Israel, he declares that it is the Muslims' duty in solidarity to engage in jihad in order to liberate Palestine, but he adds that in the case of countries that have signed peace treaties with Israel, such as Egypt and Jordan, Israel is *dār al-hudna*, "the abode of (temporary) armistice or truce." Al-Qaraḍāwī opposes separate peace agreements between Muslim states and Israel because they bring about a division that is harmful to the Muslim *umma*'s general interests.[140]

The shaykh considers the political reality in addressing the *dār al-ḥarb*/*dār al-Islām* distinction. In referring to the status of Muslims living in the West, he replaces these terms with *dār al-daʿwa*, "the abode of preaching," and *dār al-ijāba*, "the abode of heedfulness." He explains that the entire world is "the nation of Muḥammad" because the Prophet was sent by Allah as a mercy to all creatures (Q21:107). Some parts of the world heeded the Prophet's message and can therefore be referred to as *dār al-ijāba*, whereas other parts have not yet heeded it and should therefore be designated *dār al-daʿwa*.[141] He stresses that although America and Europe would be considered *dār al-ḥarb* according to the classical division, and although war with them is a possibility, in practice they are not *dār al-ḥarb*. He suggests they be referred to instead as *dār al-ʿahd*, "the house of covenant." This ruling relies on the fundamental assumption that the Muslims, as a nation with a global mission, must establish an influential presence in the West, which currently leads the world.

Al-Qaraḍāwī prefers to consider Muslims in the West as people who entered *dār al-ḥarb* under protection (*amān*) or what may be called a treaty, consisting of the visa they receive and their naturalized status. He insists that Muslims must respect this treaty and should neither steal from those who give them protection nor betray them. He finds a precedent for this state of affairs in the Prophet's own actions when he was in Mecca, which was then still *dār al-ḥarb*. The idolaters of the city gave him *wadīʿa*, property and possessions entrusted to him as collateral, which he returned, as he was obliged to do. From this, we may deduce that al-Qaraḍāwī views Western countries to which Muslims have immigrated as *dār al-ʿahd* or *dār al-amān* and the Muslims who live there as "seekers of protection" (*mustaʾminūn*).[142]

Al-Qaraḍāwī's approach is part of the *fiqh* for minorities, a field of jurisprudence that he largely shaped. His jurisprudence for minorities seeks to allow the Muslim communities a measure of flexibility and openness so that they do not remain isolated. The ultimate goal is for these communities to interact with their surroundings and become integrated—but without losing their unique identity and completely assimilating into the non-Muslim society.[143] As part of this flexibility, al-Qaraḍāwī permits Muslims in the West to become citizens of their host countries as long as these countries are not at war with the Muslims. He states that "citizenship is neither good nor bad in itself; the ruling regarding it depends on whether it is useful to the Muslims or harmful to them." Citizenship is beneficial, for example, in that it gives the immigrants power by allowing them to vote in municipal and national elections and protects them against expulsion.[144]

Al-Qaraḍāwī also rules that a Muslim, "based on his commitment to the laws of the Islamic *sharīʿa*, must honor the laws and regulations of any country he visits or resides in, for these are the terms of his entry permit, and he must not violate them." He notes that the Prophet said in a *ḥadīth*: "The Muslims [honor] their commitments [*al-Muslimūn ʿinda shurūṭihim*]," which means their commitments to both fellow Muslims and non-Muslims.[145] As in his other rulings, here, too, al-Qaraḍāwī takes reality into account (in this case the reality in Western societies) and rules pragmatically, recognizing certain constraints that apply to Muslims, both individuals and communities. The shaykh stresses, however, that the *fiqh* for minorities should focus less on the interests of the individual and more on the interests of the Muslim *umma*, with its particular identity and goals: "Jurisprudents should consider this collective entity [the Muslim *umma*], its requirements and needs. [They should ask] how this collective can live by the light of Islam in a non-Muslim society, as a group that is strong and united yet believes in diversity within the framework of its unity."[146]

A very significant difference between the IS and both *wasaṭiyya* and some jihadi Salafī thinkers concerns the issue of whether Muslims living in the West are permitted to perform acts of jihad and *istishhād* against and inside their host countries. Unlike the jihadi Salafī al-Ṭarṭūsī, who considers the Muslims of Europe as seekers of protection who may not attack their host country—for example, Great Britain, which has given them citizenship—the IS calls on its Muslim supporters in Europe and the United States to carry out attacks inside these countries. On the eve of Ramaḍān in 2016, in a video dated May 22, the IS spokesman, Abū Muḥammad al-ʿAdnānī, called on IS supporters in Europe and America to perform jihad in their respective countries and explained that "the smallest operation that you carry out in their [the Europeans' and Americans'] home is preferable and more desirable to us than the greatest operation here [on the battlefields of the IS in Syria and Iraq]. Such an operation [in Europe and America] benefits us more and harms them more." In the video, the IS spokesman noted that the purpose of jihad in Europe is to instill fear in the "Crusaders." He added that the citizenry of the Crusaders who fight Islam should not have immunity from having their blood spilled in their homes, quoting the principle of reciprocity, which al-Qaʿida also used to justify the 9/11 attacks.[147] Al-ʿAdnānī claimed that the European and American aircraft attacking the IS did not distinguish between armed and unarmed people, between men and women, and therefore the IS is justified in killing civilians in Europe and America. The IS thus instructed its supporters in the West: "Know that your attacks on civilians is more desirable and beneficial to us, for it hurts them more, gives them more pain, and deters more."[148]

However, al-Ṭarṭūsī, an immigrant in Britain and a resident of London after he left Syria in the 1980s, condemned the attacks on the London Underground in July 2005. In his statement of condemnation, he wrote:

> The British Muslim dispersion [*jāliya*] living on British soil, like every Muslim exile community residing in any Western country, is in a state of "covenant and contract" with the country and the society in which

> it lives, and therefore it is forbidden for any individual member of such an exile community to betray and violate these covenants and contracts that were entered into freely on both sides, nor is he allowed to live and behave toward the other side as a party to the contract and as a fighter at one and the same time.[149]

Al-Qaraḍāwī's approach to the division of the world into *dār al-Islām* and *dār al-ḥarb* is diametrically opposed to the approach taken by the jihadi Salafīs, for whom existing Muslim states are to be considered the "house of unbelief." From the perspective of some Salafī elements, especially the IS, the war against these "infidel" Muslim states takes precedence even over the war against Israel. The head of the IS, Abū Bakr al-Baghdādī, expressed this view very clearly in an address to the Palestinians in February 2008, when he was a member of al-Qa'ida in Iraq, also known as the Islamic State of Iraq. He said: "Let our people in Palestine know that the first solution is jihad. Under the pure flag of *tawḥīd*, they will not distinguish or discriminate between fighting against the white and fighting against the black, between the Jewish nonbeliever and the Palestinian *murtadd*. There is no difference between Olmert and his criminals and 'Abbās [Abū Māzen] and his gang. In fact, they ['Abbās and his gang] come first [i.e., jihad against them precedes the jihad against the Jews]."[150]

For jihadi Salafīs such as al-Ṭarṭūsī, the Muslim *umma* at present is under occupation by two kinds of infidels. In this case, Muslims have an individual duty to carry out jihad against (1) original infidels—that is, non-Muslims; and (2) apostates from Islam—that is, the nonbelieving Muslim regimes.[151] Al-Ṭarṭūsī considers the current borders that separate the Muslim countries today as artificial, the result of a conspiracy between the external imperialists and the internal enemy, the idolatrous Muslim rulers. Islam, he declares, does not recognize these borders and rejects the idea of basing the principle of loyalty and disavowal (*al-walā' wal-barā'*) on nationalist foundations.[152] He concludes that it is the entire Muslim nation's duty to repel both types of infidel.[153]

In a ruling that declares the 9/11 attacks legitimate, "This Is What I Believe in and Worship Allah with,"[154] al-Maqdisī defines *dār al-ḥarb* as any *dār kufr* that does not have a covenant (*'ahd*) or a protection agreement (*dhimma*) with the Muslim state. He adds that an infidel state does not have to be engaged in fighting against the Muslims or in helping the enemies of Islam in their fight in order for it to be considered *dār al-ḥarb*, but, of course, it goes without saying that it is to be defined as such if it does engage in such actions. Al-Maqdisī classifies the Unites States as a country that is de facto fighting against the Muslims because of its support of Israel in helping the Jews fight the Muslims and because of its help to Muslim rulers who fight against jihadi Salafī fighters.[155]

Al-Maqdisī declares that the battlefield of the war against the enemy who fights Islam is not limited to the territory that the enemy has invaded or occupied but wherever the enemy and his property may be.[156] He bases this ruling on the Qur'ān—for example, Q2:191 ("kill them wherever you encounter them") and Q9:5 ("wherever you encounter the idolaters kill them"). He insists that the ally (*ḥalīf*) of those who fight against Islam should be treated like those who fight it and is a legitimate target of jihad everywhere. He therefore dismisses al-Qaraḍāwī's ruling that Palestine alone is the arena where the confrontation with the Zionist enemy is to take place. Such a ruling, al-Maqdisī says, does not befit a scholar who is proficient in the laws of jihad in Islam. Indeed, he says, it is permissible and even obligatory to fight against the Jews and their allies everywhere, as defensive jihad, because they fight, attack, and occupy the lands of the Muslims.[157]

In contrast to the jihadi Salafīs and the *wasaṭī*s, the liberals, such as al-'Ashmāwī, contend that the distinction between *dār al-Islām* and *dār al-ḥarb* is not part of Islam and the *sharī'a*, which are peaceful, but is part of religious thinking. Moreover, this distinction was born of the unique circumstances that prevailed during the period of early Islam but no longer prevail today.[158] Al-'Ashmāwī's most intriguing claim, which completely undermines the notions of *dār al-Islām* and *dār al-ḥarb*, has to do with the meaning of the words *Islām* and *Muslim*. He contends that *Islām* refers to all the revealed religions and that all righteous human beings are Muslims. What differs from nation to nation and from prophet to prophet is the method (*sharī'a* or *manhaj*) of proselytizing, he asserts. Allah never intended for hostility to prevail between Muslims and non-Muslims, nor did He mean to brand non-Muslims as infidels. The sole purpose of Muḥammad's *sharī'a*, whose essence is compassion and forgiveness, is to open the gates of mercy and the path of righteousness to all and to establish tolerance as the bond connecting all of mankind. The essence of Islam, according to al-'Ashmāwī, is encapsulated in Q2:62, which implies that Allah condones diversity while explicitly recognizing the Jews, Christians, and Sabeans. The verse spells out the principle that whoever believes in Allah and is righteous has nothing to fear in the world to come and no cause for regret in this world.[159]

Al-'Ashmāwī states further that religion is concerned with individuals and society, not with states and empires. Establishing states and empires is not part of religion but is required by human nature and by international and social circumstances. The Qur'ān and the Sunna, he notes, contain no verses or *ḥadīths* on the establishment of states or regimes, for religion addresses the individual with the aim of elevating mankind and has nothing to do with territory and statehood.[160] 'Abd al-Ḥamīd al-Anṣārī expresses a similar thought when he states that the essence of the crisis afflicting contemporary Muslim discourse is the absence of a universalist perspective: "This discourse does not address human beings as human beings. We lack what I call the 'culture of humanity.' We want to make our youth love human beings as human beings, before they love them for being Muslim or non-Muslim, Shī'ī or Sunnī."[161]

Jus in Bello: The Killing of Civilians

In *Jihad and Just War*, Alia Brahimi claims that "the Muslims had inherited a vast source of custom from the city-states of pre-Islamic Arabia," including diplomatic codes of behavior and laws of war that dealt with the treatment of prisoners of war, arbitration, alliances, spies, cessation of hostilities, and the like. She notes that the Qur'ān had a great effect on the ethics of warfare owing to the verses on mercy and "commanding the good and forbidding evil." As an example, she gives Q5:8, in which the Muslims are urged to "adhere to justice" even toward those whom they hate.[162] An important issue in the laws of war is the way noncombatants are to be treated. In this context, writers quote traditions ascribing to the Prophet statements on the prohibition to kill women and children. In some of the traditions, the Prophet is said to have forbidden the Muslims to kill an old man (shaykh) who is no longer of use to the infidel and cannot harm the Muslims (such an old man is called *fānin* in *ḥadīth*).[163]

Ella Landau-Tasseron states in her study of the attitude in classical Muslim law toward the treatment of people not involved in the fighting that the term *noncombatant* in use in Western "just-war" doctrines is not appropriate in the context of Islamic law. She notes that in early Muslim sources the list of people who may not be hurt include women, children, the elderly, and monks. However, in the course of fighting, the prohibition on attacking those who do not participate in the battle has practically no validity. Such casualties in battle are almost always defined as "unpremeditated" (*ghayr ʿamd*) and in fact are permitted; the attackers thus bear no responsibility and are not punished. There is in fact a broad consensus among the *fuqahāʾ* that noncombatants who take part in fighting may be killed just like the fighters themselves. Such participation does not have to take the form of bearing arms but can also consist of spying, turning Muslims over to the enemy, inciting others to fight or agitate, giving advice to fighters, or even being capable of fighting. Based on her careful perusal of the Muslim legal literature, Landau-Tasseron concludes that the Islamic law on noncombatants does not make the same distinction between fighters and civilians as international law does today, even if at first glance the rules seem similar.[164]

The Legal Status of *Istishhād* Operations

Suicide or martyrdom (*istishhād*) attacks in modern times, including attacks of the kind carried out by Hamas in the 1990s and the attacks in 2011, raise two legal difficulties with respect to *sharīʿa*. First, because the Muslim who carries out such an attack kills himself—for example, by detonating explosives on his body—there is the question of whether this is an act of suicide (*intiḥār*), which is forbidden in Islam, or one of martyrdom (*istishhād*). Second, in such attacks, innocent bystanders, which include even fellow Muslims, may be killed. Both Hamas and al-Qaʿida have found legal justifications for making careful distinctions between forbidden *intiḥār* and laudable *istishhād* and also for killing civilians, whom one is not permitted to kill with premeditation.[165]

Al-Qaraḍāwī ruled that acts of *istishhād* in Palestine, performed by Palestinian resistance groups against the Zionist occupation, are not to be considered criminal acts of terrorism, even if they result in civilian casualties. To the contrary, he argues, they are the most sublime form of jihad for Allah, acts that come under the definition of "licit terrorization" (*al-irhāb al-mashrūʿ*), which the Qur'ān commands in Q8:60: "to frighten off God's enemies and yours."[166]

In rebutting the claim that *istishhād* operations are suicide, al-Qaraḍāwī evokes their objective: to deliver a deadly blow to the enemy. He cites classical Qur'ānic commentators and jurists who ruled that a lone Muslim soldier may carry out an operation of infiltrating enemy lines (*inghimās*), even if he has no chance of surviving, on the condition that his intention is to harm the enemy (*nikāya bi-l-ʿadū*). Al-Qaraḍāwī quotes al-Qurṭubī (d. 1273), who wrote in a commentary on Q2:195, "There is no prohibition against a lone Muslim carrying out an attack even against an enormous army if he has the power to do so and if his motives are pure and for the sake of Allah. If he does not have the power, it is regarded as an act of suicide."[167] In a ruling in 2005 that proclaimed *istishhād* operations a form of suicide, the jihadi Salafī al-Ṭarṭūsī argued that the ruling regarding *inghimās* operations does not apply to *istishhād* attacks because the two cases differ substantially. In an *inghimās* operation, if the attacker is eventually killed, it is by the hand of the enemy, whereas a suicide attacker dies by his own hand. Moreover, in an *inghimās* operation, the attacker has a chance, however slim, of surviving the attack, whereas a suicide attacker has no chance at all.[168]

The most comprehensive and detailed *fatwā* against *istishhād* operations and the targeting of innocent civilians was issued in 2010 by "Shaykh al-Islam" Muḥammad Ṭāhir al-Qadrī (b. 1951), a Pakistani cleric and politician and the founder of the Way of the Quran (Minhāj al-Qur'ān) institute, whose stated objective is to lay foundations for understanding and dialogue among peoples and countries.[169] The *fatwā*, written in Urdu, states that Allah alone is the master of life and death and that because murdering a single soul is likened to murdering all of mankind (Q5:32), suicide is an equally despicable act. As evidence, it cites Q2:195: "Do not throw [yourselves] with your [own] hands into destruction."[170] ʿAbd al-Ḥamīd al-Anṣārī commends al-Qadrī for this *fatwā* and accuses other *'ulamā'* of failing in their duty to save the Muslim youth from committing acts of terrorism by failing to agree that *istishhād* operations, in which both Muslim and non-Muslim innocents are killed, are forbidden according to the *sharī'a*. "When will the *'ulamā'* discharge their responsibility of [stopping] the rivers of blood flowing in the Arab and Muslim world?" al-Anṣārī asks. "True, we hear many condemnations of terror in all its forms, and they [the *'ulamā'*] reiterate that 'terror has no religion' while stressing that Islam is innocent of it. However, they do not tell us unequivocally whether the bombings, killings, and massacres that take place in Iraq, Afghanistan, or Somalia are terrorism or rather resistance and jihad!"[171]

As we saw, al-Anṣārī's criticism is directed at, among others, al-Qaraḍāwī, especially after al-Qaraḍāwī stated in his *fatwā* sanctioning *istishhād* operations that Q2:195 does not refer to *istishhād* operations at all. Contrary to al-Qadrī's position and based on Islamic commentary on this verse, al-Qaraḍāwī contends that *istishhād* operations are permissible if they benefit the Muslims, sow death and fear in the enemy ranks, and raise the Muslims' morale. According to him, such operations are forbidden only when it is certain and clear in advance that the perpetrator will die and that the Muslims will derive no benefit from his action.[172]

The Evolution of al-Qaraḍāwī's Ruling on Istishhād *Operations*

After ruling in the 1990s that *istishhād* operations in Palestine were permitted, during the 2000s al-Qaraḍāwī revisited this *fatwā* several times. His reassessment was apparently prompted by several factors, including the changing times, the development of new means of warfare more effective than *istishhād* attacks, and the criticism directed at him by various figures, Muslim and Western, who presented this *fatwā* as proof that he merited the epithet "*muftī* of terror."

In *Fiqh al-jihād*, Al-Qaraḍāwī makes two significant comments with respect to the permission he gives to carry out *istishhād* operations in Israel.

First, this permission has been given to the Palestinians owing to their special circumstances, which force them to protect themselves, their families and children, and other inviolable things (*ḥurumāt*). Because of their situation, he adds, the Palestinians have been forced to carry out acts of *istishhād* when no alternative has been available. He further states:

> We did not permit such acts [of *istishhād*] outside of Palestine because there was no necessity [*ḍarūra*] that made it obligatory or that would make it permissible. The analogy [*qiyās*] between Palestine and other countries where such acts are committed against Muslims—for example in Algeria, Egypt, Yemen, Saudi Arabia, Iraq, Pakistan, and the like—is one that is inappropriate; it is an analogy between things that are not the same, and therefore it is invalid from the perspective of *sharī'a*.[173]

As an example of such a false analogy, he gives the case of the 9/11 attacks, if one were to conclude that they were legitimate based on the analogy of Palestine.[174]

Al-Qaraḍāwī's ruling permitting *istishhād* operations in Palestine would seem to contradict his ruling in the case of the 9/11 attacks, which he called acts of terrorism and not a case of legitimate jihad, as well as his views on the Muslim ethics of warfare, which, he maintains, forbids the use of means that do not distinguish between fighters and noncombatants. He ruled that hijacking of aircraft is a crime, and one of the reasons he gave was the Islamic principle that "does not permit attacking [*i'tidā'*] the innocent under any circumstances, no matter who they are, whether the attack is on the person's life, family honor ['*irḍ*], or property."[175]

Brahimi has stated that not a single "maverick" cleric who supported *istishhād* operations in Palestine supported the 9/11 attacks, including al-Qaraḍāwī.[176] Indeed, the latter made a sharp distinction between *istishhād* attacks in Israel and acts such as 9/11 or the terror attacks in London in July 2005:

> The [suicide] operations in Palestine have a clear objective—namely, self-defense and defending the homeland; the means are clear—namely, [a martyr] who risks his life. But the other acts [such as the 9/11 attacks, on which he was asked] are not like that. Those who carry them out invade another country not in order to defend his own homeland, and he did not use his own spirit, soul, and self but airplanes with their

> passengers and used them to attack noncombatants. The people in the Twin Towers were clerks in corporations, some of them were Arabs and Muslims, and others had no connection at all with the issue.[177]

Of possible relevance to this issue is al-Qaraḍāwī's ruling concerning a Muslim's right to carry out *istishhād* bombings in Syria against the Bashar al-Asad regime and its supporters. On his al-Jazeera program *Sharīʿa and Life* on March 17, 2013, he was asked if a Muslim in Syria were allowed to carry out such an attack even if it was likely to result in civilian casualties as well. Are "regime supporters" not civilians? In his response, he did not mention the issue of civilian casualties at all but ruled that a private person is forbidden to carry out such an operation; permission to do so depends on the collective need for such an act. If the collective decides that there is such a need, it would know how to operate so that the number of casualties is minimized, and if the person sent to carry it out is able to perform his task and also save his own life, he is obliged to do so.[178] In this ruling, the consideration that makes an act of *istishhād* permissible is the need of the group fighting against the al-Asad regime; the fact that civilian casualties would result from such an operation seems not to have given al-Qaraḍāwī any pause.[179]

Second, al-Qaraḍāwī noted in 2009 that the Palestinians possess missiles that can hit Israel and may therefore constitute an alternative to *istishhād*. Although, as he points out, these missiles do not have the same range as the missiles that Israel possesses, they do enable Hamas to worry and harass Israel.[180] Needless to say, in either case, *istishhād* attacks or missiles fired into Israel, it is impossible to make a distinction between fighters and innocent civilian noncombatants.

Al-Qaraḍāwī made an interesting comment about *istishhād* in an interview by Shaykh Salmān al-ʿAwda in November 2016. Asked about the legitimacy of *istishhād* operations, he replied: "I do not consider them permitted today. I permitted them owing to a certain necessity. [The principle] is that 'necessity renders the forbidden permissible.'"[181] The shaykh, it should be noted, no longer considers *istishhād* operations necessary because the Palestinians now possess more effective weapons, such as rockets, the employment of which he already ruled permissible in

Fiqh al-jihād.[182] It should be stressed that al-Qaraḍāwī did not reverse his *fatwā* permitting the killing of Israeli civilians. Moreover, some of his recent remarks contradict his claim that *istishhād* operations are no longer permitted. Following the incident on July 21, 2017, in which a Palestinian entered a home in a Jewish settlement and stabbed to death several family members, al-Qaraḍāwī tweeted: "Israel no longer fears anything, except for the young people, who take their lives in their hands and sell their souls to Allah and care not whether they meet death or death finds them."[183] He posted a similar tweet in December 2017 following US president Donald Trump's declaration recognizing Jerusalem as Israel's capital. In this tweet, he also repeated his wish to die as a martyr, writing: "How I wish I could answer the call of the first *qibla* [Jerusalem] and take some part in the jihad for Jerusalem and the beloved al-Aqṣā and gain the honor of martyrdom [*shahāda*] on that sacred soil." The tweet was accompanied by a video in which al-Qaraḍāwī said, in a similar vein, that he wished he could walk or even be carried in a wheelchair to participate in the jihad for Jerusalem and then be struck by a bullet that would sever his head from his body and thus be killed for the sake of Allah.[184]

Al-Qaraḍāwī's Justification for Killing Civilians in Israel

Brahimi analyzes the arguments that bin Laden used to justify his call for jihadis to kill noncombatants and identifies three that appear to be similar to those that al-Qaraḍāwī uses to justify killing the innocent in Israel. First, bin Laden argued that there is no such thing as an innocent American: they all pay taxes to the government and participate in the political process in their country. Second, the principle of reciprocity applies—that is, although it is true that al-Qa'ida kills innocents, many innocent Muslims were also killed by the Americans. Third, some innocent people were unintentionally killed by al-Qa'ida.[185]

An examination of al-Qaraḍāwī's *fatwā* justifying the killing of civilians in Israel reveals arguments very similar to those of jihadi Salafī jurists:

1. Israeli society is imperialistic and militaristic; its ostensible civilians are in reality also soldiers. Israel is a society of invaders who came

to occupy the land and to expel the people living in it. Al-Qaraḍāwī declares that it is the right of anyone whose land has been invaded to fight against the criminals using every available means. He adds that anyone in Israel who passes the age of childhood, man or woman, is conscripted into the army.

Al-Maqdisī declared in the ruling in which he pronounced the 9/11 attacks legitimate under *sharīʿa* that, according to Muslim law, a child becomes an adult (*bāligh*) the moment he shows signs of sexual maturity in the form of nocturnal emission (*iḥtilām*) or the growth of pubic hair (*inbāt*). A person can be an adult at age twelve or even younger and from that moment must observe the religious commandments. Al-Maqdisī concluded that the same criteria of adulthood should be applied to non-Muslims and that an adult according to this definition would no longer fall under the prohibition of killing children. He therefore declared that many of the "children" under current international laws and conventions are not considered children in Muslim law and therefore are not protected from being killed.[186]

2. Innocent Israelis or Jews killed in jihadi actions, including children, were not intentionally targeted but were casualties of the "necessity of war" (*ḍarūrat al-ḥarb*). Indeed, most classical jurists of all schools rule that the prohibition on killing civilians applies only to intentional attacks.[187] Al-Qaraḍāwī claims that the "necessity of war" justification should not be overused, that it should remain an exception rather than the rule, in accordance with the principle "What has been permitted out of necessity is to be measured by the extent of the necessity [and no more] [*mā ubīḥa li-l ḍarūra yuqaddar bi-qadrihā*]."[188] However, Landau-Tasseron has shown that this argument by Muslim apologists is not quite accurate because Muslim law, unlike the situation in contemporary international law, does not punish those who violate the rules, which over time have become mere empty words.[189]

Al-Maqdisī used the same argument to justify the killing of women and children in the 9/11 attacks, adding that it is permissible to kill women and children in a "night attack [*tabyīt*]" and when the chaos of the battlefield makes it impossible to avoid such killing. He stated that the prohibition on killing women and children is in effect only when it is possible to refrain from doing so or in case of intentional attacks on targets where such people are found, such as schools, buses, and so on. In this context, he wrote: "That is why we always advised our brothers the jihad fighters not to kill them deliberately and not to attack concentrations [of women and children], even among the Jews occupying Palestine, but to focus always on prominent military and political targets so as to deliver a severe blow to the enemies of Allah."[190]

In classical Muslim law, non-Muslims are divided into two categories. A "peaceable" (*musālim*) is a non-Muslim who does not fight against Muslims; the Qur'ān (Q60:8) urges Muslims to treat such non-Muslims with "kindness" (*birr*) and "justice" (*qisṭ*). The other kind of non-Muslim is a "belligerent" (*muḥārib*), who fights against Islam and must in turn be attacked (Q2:190, 193).[191] In his justification of the 9/11 attacks, al-Maqdisī, following classical Muslim law, ruled that women, children, and the elderly are to be treated like combatants if they participate in the fighting or if they assist the fighters with counsel, opinion, propaganda, and so on.[192]

3. Al-Qaraḍāwī notes that *fuqahā'* have ruled that it is permissible to kill Muslims forced by an attacking army to serve as live shields (*tatarrus*). He argues that if one is permitted to kill Muslims who were forced to act as shields for the infidel in order to protect the larger group of Muslims, it is certainly permissible to kill non-Muslims in order to liberate Muslim land from its occupiers.[193]

4. In our times, civilian society is also mobilized and participates in the war, either directly or indirectly. Al-Maqdisī, like al-Qaraḍāwī, declares that in war civilian casualties are unavoidable, a fact recognized by the infidel, too, as demonstrated by an American commander who used this explanation for the death of Afghan civilians during the US offensive in Afghanistan.[194]

Al-Qadrī, however, ruled that permitting the killing of civilians is tantamount to heresy. As evidence, he cited Abū Manṣūr al-Māturīdī (d. 944), among other sources. Al-Māturīdī wrote in commentary on Q5:32 ("whoever kills a soul unless for a soul or for corruption [done] in the land, it is as if he had slain mankind entirely") that "one who seeks the unjustified killing of a soul that Allah forbade to kill, it is as though he has sought to kill all of mankind, for one who renounces one verse of Allah's Book, it is as though he has renounced it all."[195] Al-Qaraḍāwī also refers to Q5:32, but he adopts the ruling of Ibn Taymiyya, from which he derives that although murder is among the gravest of sins, killing is permitted when there is an overriding benefit (*maṣlaḥa rājiḥa*)—that is, when refraining from killing might bring about an even greater evil than the killing itself. Ibn Taymiyya ruled that killing is permitted only as part of retaliation in kind (*qiṣāṣ*) or in case of corruption (*fasād*), which, according to him, refers to the act of tempting a Muslim to abandon his faith and to highway robbery.[196] Al-Qaraḍāwī adds that killing is also justified in cases of repelling an attacker who has invaded Muslim land (*daf' al-ṣā'il*) or quelling a rebellion.[197] This argument allows him to provide religious sanction for the killing of Jews in Palestine, whom he regards as aggressors; the killing of rebels against Hamas's rule in Gaza (such as the members of Soldiers of the Supporters of Allah [Jund Anṣār Allāh] who were killed in the Rafah mosque in August 2009); and, as discussed later, the killing of Americans in Iraq.

According to al-Qadrī, the killing of noncombatants is forbidden even in times of war. He bases this argument on Q5:8, which exhorts the Muslims to be just, including with those they hate. Al-Qadrī takes this verse to mean that the Muslims must not oppress other nations, even if extreme hostility prevails between them. Accordingly, he rejects the terrorists' claim that their actions are justified because they are directed at foreign aggressors occupying Muslim land. Such acts, he says, contravene the Islamic rules of war even when they are directed at the Muslims' enemies.[198]

It should be noted that al-Qaraḍāwī, too, regards Q5:8 as one of the foundations of religious tolerance in Islam and understands it as a directive to behave justly with all human beings.[199] However, he finds ways to limit the prohibition against killing noncombatants. For example, he rules that killing Jewish Israeli women is permitted because they serve in the army and must therefore be treated no differently than armed soldiers. He also states that in the modern era it is not only the military but society as a whole that participates in war because civilians, such as factory workers, assist the army even if they do not bear arms. The only exception, he says, are people who actively oppose and condemn war, but in Israel's case such people generally reside outside the country.[200] This statement essentially eliminates any distinction between combatants and civilians in Israel, thus permitting the indiscriminate killing of both. Anyone who can be argued to assist or support the armed forces in any way is fair game.[201]

Al-Qaraḍāwī's Ruling on the Killing of Americans in Iraq

According to Muhammad Qasim Zaman, al-Qaraḍāwī's ruling that permits the indiscriminate killing of Jews in Palestine reflects his anti-Israel and anti-Zionist position. For al-Qaraḍāwī, Israel today is the only extant *dār al-ḥarb* and constitutes an example of state terrorism.[202] We may well ask if there are any other cases beside Israel in which al-Qaraḍāwī permits the killing of civilians. Another relevant ruling by him in this context is the ruling he made in the wake of the American invasion of Iraq in 2003 that every single American in Iraq is to be considered a fighter and that no difference should be made between military and civilian personnel. American civilians must be fought and killed, he stated, because they came to Iraq to serve the occupation. He supposedly said this at a conference of the Egyptian Association of Journalists in August 2004 but has explained that this was not his ruling and that he did not use the word *qatl*, "killing," but rather *muqāwama*, "resistance," which has a much broader range of meanings and does not necessarily imply killing.[203]

Of interest here is liberal writer Shākir al-Nābulsī's response to al-Qaraḍāwī's *fatwā* permitting the killing of all Americans in Iraq, both combatants and civilians. Wondering what enables "jurists of bloodshed" such as al-Qaraḍāwī to take to their "political pulpits" and issue such rulings, al-Nābulsī stated that the Arab world is governed by instinct rather than by thought and that this enables the clerics to steer Arab political activity, which has become nothing but a call for bloodshed in the name of a new religion created by al-Qaraḍāwī and the fundamentalist terror organizations. *Fatwā*s of this sort, he added, are the hallmark of a nation that is politically bankrupt. The solution, he suggested, is for liberal Arab thinkers to petition the UN to found a special tribunal for terrorists that will try every jurist who issues a ruling encouraging terror.[204] Al-Nābulsī also claimed that al-Qaraḍāwī did not base his *fatwā* on any Qur'ānic verse or *ḥadīth*. Liberal writer 'Abd al-Khāliq Ḥusayn wrote that this *fatwā* had stripped the mask from al-Qaraḍāwī's face, exposing him as a terrorist and as the jurist and advocate of terrorists. He also called al-Qaraḍāwī and his ilk "jurists of bloodshed" and said that they had turned Muslim thought into a terrorist ideology, thereby harming the Muslims, Islam, and this religion's reputation around the world.[205]

Samuel Helfont claims in his book on al-Qaraḍāwī that al-Qaraḍāwī's definition of innocents in Iraq is similar to the definition he uses with respect to Israel.[206] Although al-Qaraḍāwī denied that he ruled that it is permissible to kill any American in Iraq, whether military or civilian, Helfont's claim is confirmed by a sermon al-Qaraḍāwī gave at his mosque in Qatar on March 7, 2003, in which he stated that if the Americans were to invade Iraq that month, it would be a war of aggression.[207] Therefore, just as in the case of the liberation of Palestine, he believed that in Iraq the entire Muslim *umma* should mobilize to liberate it from America. He perceived the root of the problem to lie with America's despotism; he told his audience in the mosque that this despotism would cease to exist, just as the despotic nations mentioned in the Qur'ān disappeared. But in the same sermon in which he defined America as an aggressor, he also made a distinction between the American nation, against which the Muslim should have no rancor, and the American regime, which he describes as bullying, aggressive, and opposed to Islam and the Muslims.[208]

Al-Qaraḍāwī's Ruling on *Istishhād* versus Other Jurists' Rulings

To assess al-Qaraḍāwī's claim that *wasaṭiyya* is a moderate voice in the Islamic discourse and an alternative to the extremism of the jihadi Salafīs, it is pertinent to examine other jurists' rulings on *istishhād* operations and compare them to al-Qaraḍāwī's.[209]

Traditional Salafī Jurists

Shaykh Nāṣir al-Dīn al-Albānī ruled that *istishhād* operations are illicit today and that anyone who perpetrates them risks being doomed to hell for eternity. He explained that the fighting going on in the Muslim world today is not jihad but war motivated by nationalism. Jihad, he elaborated, can take place only under an Islamic banner, in a Muslim caliphate governed by *sharīʿa* law. In such a caliphate, a soldier does not act on his own judgment but follows the orders of his commander, who in turn is appointed by the caliph. But today, in the absence of such a caliphate, so-called *istishhād* operations are nothing but acts of suicide that are based on fanatical youths' misguided *ijtihād* and that do not benefit Muslim *daʿwa* in any way. He urged young Muslims: "Protect your lives by studying your religion and your Islam, by truly knowing it, and by acting within the boundaries of your abilities."[210]

Also in contrast to al-Qaraḍāwī, Ibn al-ʿUthaymīn contends that operations in which the perpetrator knows he will die are suicide and are forbidden according to the *sharīʿa*. In fact, he regards such operations as a grave sin, based on the *ḥadīth* "If somebody commits suicide with anything in this world, he will be tortured with that very thing on the Day of Resurrection." He adds that such operations bring more harm than good to the Muslims because they provoke severe retaliation by the enemy and arouse sympathy for the enemy while blackening the reputation of the Muslims. He also states that the perpetrators of these operations are doomed to hell.[211]

Al-Azharī Establishment Shaykhs

Al-Qaraḍāwī's *fatwā* permitting *istishhād* operations in Palestine also contravenes the rulings of establishment clerics such as the al-Azhar shaykh Muḥammad Sayyid Ṭanṭāwī (who served from 1996 until his death in 2010). In December 2001, Ṭanṭāwī denounced any attack on innocent civilians, regardless of their political, ethnic, or national affiliation, stating that the *sharīʿa* protects human life and regards the killing of a single soul as the killing of mankind in its entirety (Q5:32). In response to the *istishhād* bombings in Israel that year, he rejected the claim that Jewish children in Palestine are legitimate targets because they will grow up to be soldiers. Such claims are hideous and depraved, he said, and contravene the Prophet Muḥammad's directives.[212] This comment provoked a fierce response from al-Qaraḍāwī, who wondered how Ṭanṭāwī could regard the Israelis as innocent when they came to Palestine, stole it by force, and killed and expelled its inhabitants. Ṭanṭāwī's *fatwā*, he opined, disregarded reality and was an act of abandoning the jihad fighters who were fighting against Israel. He added that many Muslim scholars are ignorant of reality and do not realize that Israeli society is militarized and therefore that none of its citizens can be regarded as civilians.[213] Ṭanṭāwī, it should be noted, changed his opinion in March 2002, when he proclaimed that a person who blows himself up among the aggressors that demolish homes and kill *āminūn*—namely men, women, and children entitled to security and protection—is a martyr. He also sanctioned the killing of Israeli civilians as long as they are not deliberately targeted.[214] Ṭanṭāwī reiterated this ruling in April 2004, stating that any action that is aimed at defending land, life, property, and honor against the aggressor and does not deliberately target those entitled to security is legitimate and that whoever dies while carrying it out is a martyr.[215] It should be noted that in his ruling from 2001 al-Qaraḍāwī permitted the killing of Israeli children and elders on the grounds that if a child (*ṭifl*) or elderly person (shaykh) is killed in a martyrdom operation, the killing is not deliberate but accidental, and this is permitted by the *sharīʿa* because it is a necessity (*ḍarūra*) in war.[216] In his book *Fiqh al-jihād*, al-Qaraḍāwī ruled that every Israeli past the age of childhood (*sinn al-ṭufūla*), man or woman, is drafted to the Israeli army and therefore no longer counts as a civilian (*madanī*).[217]

Jihadi Salafīs

Al-Qaraḍāwī's rulings on *istishhād* operations in Palestine are quite similar to rulings by jihadi Salafī clerics, such as Abū Qatāda al-Filasṭīnī (b. 1960, also known as ʿUmar b. Maḥmūd Abū ʿUmar) and Shaykh Ḥamūd b. ʿUqalāʾ al-Shuʿaybī. When al-Shuʿaybī was asked in 2002 about the legitimacy of *istishhād* operations in Palestine, Chechnya, and elsewhere, he ruled, like al-Qaraḍāwī, that they are permitted by the *sharīʿa* and constitute a form of jihad for the sake of Allah. In fact, he stated that such operations are among the most effective forms of jihad. He also stressed, again like al-Qaraḍāwī, that they are not a form of suicide, which is forbidden in Islam, for the suicide takes his own life out of impatience or bitterness over his lot or to end his pain and suffering, whereas an *istishhād* seeker is motivated by his longing for paradise and by the desire to hurt the enemy and bring about the victory of Islam.[218] Al-Filasṭīnī ruled, in a similar vein, that the modern operations in which the fighter blows himself up are not acts of suicide but of *sharī'a*-sanctioned *istishhād* because the objectives of the martyrdom seeker are to hurt the enemy and to raise the morale of the Muslims.[219] Unsurprisingly, al-Qaraḍāwī's and al-Shu'aybī's *fatwās* on *istishhād* are quoted in a ruling issued by the Palestinian Scholars Union (Rābiṭat 'Ulamā' Filasṭīn), which described the martyrs as paragons of heroism and jihad, saying: "You fulfilled your duty toward your Lord, your religion, your Jerusalem, your al-Aqṣā, and your homeland."[220]

Pragmatic Jihadi Salafī Shaykhs

Interestingly, the London-based jihadi Salafī shaykh Abū Baṣīr al-Ṭarṭūsī expressed a different opinion on *istishhād* operations following the London bombing on July 7, 2005 (although al-Ṭarṭūsī denied that there was any connection between his ruling and the bombing, describing his *fatwā* as a combination of past rulings on the matter of *istishhād*). Unlike al-Qaraḍāwī, Abū Qatāda al-Filasṭīnī, and al-Shu'aybī, he ruled that the perpetrators of such operations have committed suicide because they take their lives with their own hands. He also stated that these operations are forbidden because they generally result in the death of innocents, both Muslim and non-Muslim, the killing of whom is forbidden by Islam. The evidence demonstrating the unlawfulness of this act is clear, he said, whereas the evidence suggesting otherwise is ambiguous.[221]

To prove that *istishhād* operations are permissible even against civilians, however, al-Qaraḍāwī cites the consensus among jurists regarding the issue of Muslims used by the enemy as human shields (*tatarrus*).[222] Jurists ruled it permissible to kill Muslim captives that the enemy has placed in front of his forces to serve as human shields if the alternative is letting the enemy breach the Muslims' ranks, resulting in the deaths of even more Muslims. The criterion here is one of preferring the lesser evil. Al-Qaraḍāwī argues that "if it is permissible to kill innocent Muslims that have been forced to serve as a shield, it is certainly permissible to kill non-Muslims [in an *istishhād* operation] in order to liberate Muslim land from the oppressive occupier."[223] Al-Ṭarṭūsī rejected this argument as well, though, again on the grounds that the two cases are not analogous: the Muslims used as human shields, he noted, are killed by others, whereas the perpetrator of an *istishhād* operation kills himself—that is, he commits the forbidden act of suicide. Moreover, according to al-Ṭarṭūsī, the killing of human shields is licit only in case of absolute necessity, when there is no other way to fight the infidels and the benefit to the Muslim *umma* is clear. These conditions, he stated, are not met by the contemporary *istishhād* operations in question.[224]

Another text presented to justify *istishhād* operations is the story known as "The Boy and the King" or "The People of the Trench" ("Aṣḥāb al-ukhdūd"), which is mentioned in both the Qur'ān (85:4) and the Sunna. The story tells of a boy who by virtue of his deep faith in Allah attains the ability to perform miracles such as healing the blind. When the king hears about this, he summons the boy to the palace and asks him how he performs these acts of healing, and the boy replies that it is not he but only his Lord, Allah, who heals. Enraged by the suggestion that there is a lord more powerful than himself, the king tries to force the boy to renounce his faith by threatening to kill him, but every time he tries to kill the boy, the boy prays to Allah, and Allah saves him. Finally, in a bid to open the king's eyes to the truth of Islam, the boy tells him how he may be killed: the king must shoot him with an arrow while saying, "In the name of Allah, the Lord of the boy." The king does this and succeeds in killing the boy. But the people who witness the boy's execution are moved to embrace Islam, declaring, "We believe in the Lord of the boy."[225]

Because the boy in the story effectively brings about his own death to convince others of the truth of Islam, many jurists present the story as proof that *istishhād* is permissible if it benefits the religion. Al-Qaraḍāwī is among those who make this argument, citing Ibn Taymiyya's commentary about the story.[226] Another jurist who refers to it is Abū Qatāda al-Filasṭīnī, a prominent authority for jihadi Salafism, who writes in a *fatwā* permitting *istishhād* operations: "Behold this boy, who showed the polytheist [the king] how to kill him, showed him the only way he could be killed. He did it to attain the beneficial goal of demonstrating [the truth of] Islam and spreading Islam."[227] Al-Ṭarṭūsī's ruling, however, rejects this story as justification for *istishhād* operations on the grounds that the boy's action was meant to achieve a supreme goal—converting an entire nation of polytheists to Islam—whereas suicide bombers do not have such lofty objectives.[228] It is interesting to note that in this case the *wasaṭī* al-Qaraḍāwī seems to be more extremist than the jihadi Salafī al-Ṭarṭūsī.

Al-Ṭarṭūsī's ruling also mentions a practical consideration that al-Qaraḍāwī does not address: that a jihad fighter eager to sacrifice himself for the sake of Allah is a rare and precious asset, so "dooming him to blow himself up upon taking his first step in jihad" is a waste and serves only to "gladden the hearts of the enemies." Such individuals should instead be allowed to fight as long as possible so as to inflict maximum harm upon the enemy. Al-Ṭarṭūsī argues further that sending fighters to kill themselves in their very first operation may discourage young men from joining the jihad in the first place.[229] This consideration is part of governance in accordance with the *sharīʿa* (*al-siyāsa al-sharʿiyya*; see chapter 6). Curiously, al-Qaraḍāwī, who generally devotes much attention to considerations of cost versus benefit, does not address this angle at all in his ruling about *istishhād* operations.

Finally, al-Ṭarṭūsī also evokes the argument of the damage caused to the image of Islam. *Istishhād* operations, he says, give the erroneous impression that Islam permits the killing of innocent people and so cause people to abhor jihad and refrain from helping the jihad warriors (*mujāhidūn*). "Some of the misguided actions that are occasionally associated with jihad and the *mujāhidūn* and are perpetrated in the name of jihad and the *mujāhidūn* distort the image of jihad in the minds of many people," he writes.[230] The Pakistani shaykh Muḥammad Tāhir al-Qadrī writes that the same consideration motivated him to issue his own *fatwā* against *istishhād* operations. In the introduction to this *fatwā*, he states that these operations—namely, the acts of terrorism perpetrated in the name of Islam—not only threaten the West but also harm Islam, the Muslim world, and mankind as a whole. He argues that these operations breed atheism on one hand and further extremism on the other: atheism because some young Muslims who lack in-depth knowledge of their religion are influenced by the media to think that terror and extremism originate in the directives of Islam, which drives them away from Islam and toward atheism; extremism because the West, too, comes to associate Islam with terror and therefore adopts anti-Muslim policies, which in turn fills some young Muslims with hatred toward the West and drives them to seek revenge and to embrace extremist ideologies. "The Muslim *umma* and mankind thus both head towards disaster," al-Qadrī concludes.[231]

In his important book on "the fruits of jihad" (2004), al-Maqdisī writes that *istishhād* operations, unlike traditional forms of warfare that are sanctioned without any doubt, are subject to special juristic constraints: they are religiously sanctioned only "if the jihad fighter cannot wage jihad by any other means, if jihad will otherwise be paralyzed and the infidels and their religion will reign supreme."[232] As mentioned, in his *fatwā* on *istishhād* operations in Palestine, al-Qaraḍāwī ruled that all Israelis are combatants, and in this way he rendered irrelevant many of the arguments presented by pragmatic scholars of global jihad.

The Liberal Approach

The views of the liberal thinker ʿAbd al-Ḥamīd al-Anṣārī on *istishhād* are also worthy of notice. According to him, the Muslim sources are clear: they indicate that a Muslim must not blow himself up among enemy soldiers, let alone among civilians. Al-Anṣārī stressed that the principle of retaliation in kind (*al-muʿāmala bi-l-mithl*) does not legitimize sinful actions such as the killing of children and that Muslims must not lose their moral bearings in search of revenge against the enemy because revenge is not one of the objectives of jihad. Rather, it is one of the excuses used by the jurists of political Islam, who sympathize with the ideology of political groups that chant hollow slogans of resistance and jihad. These jurists, especially al-Qaraḍāwī, says al-Anṣārī, encourage *istishhād* operations by describing them in their rulings as the noblest form of jihad. By doing so, they skew the Muslims' moral compass and introduce forbidden innovation (*bidʿa*) into the literature of jihad, for not a single text about the battles of the Prophet and his Companions indicates that *istishhād* operations are legitimate. Such operations not only harm Islam but also yield no political benefit and involve the needless loss of the most precious thing in creation: human life. Al-Anṣārī also embraces the view that *istishhād* operations, including those in Palestine, are the most blatant manifestation of Islam's ideological and moral crisis and that Islam must be purged of this "moral and ideological evil."[233] He notes that in permitting indiscriminate *istishhād* operations against both combatants and civilians in Iraq, al-Qaraḍāwī relies on the same ideological and juristic principles as jihadi Salafī jurists such as Abū Muṣʿab al-Zarqāwī and Abū Muḥammad al-Maqdisī.[234]

Al-Anṣārī points to Salafī rulings against *istishhād* operations as support for his claim that the Islamic scriptures regard it a grave sin for a Muslim to blow himself up amid the enemy's ranks.[235] A salient example is a *fatwā* by the al-Albānī Center, which stated that the perpetrators of such actions rely not on any esteemed religious authority but rather on the "illusions" of "a partisan agent who wastes his time on useless activities, destroys countries and harms people." Addressing the "*rabbānī*" scholars, whose only guiding light is Allah and whose rulings are not influenced by political interests, the *fatwā* calls on these scholars to condemn these operations and to warn Muslims against this grave sin.[236]

A comparison of al-Qaraḍāwī's rulings on *istishhād* operations and other jurists' rulings reveals that his perspective is very similar to that of the jihadi Salafīs. Traditional Salafī jurists such as al-Albānī, establishment shaykhs such as Ṭanṭāwī, and pragmatic jihadi Salafī jurists such as al-Ṭarṭūsī express reservations about *istishhād* operations and even see them as forbidden acts of *intiḥār*, suicide. They also oppose them on the grounds that the damage they cause to Islam and to the jihad organizations exceeds the benefit they bring. Although al-Qaraḍāwī makes extensive use of the juristic principle of balancing costs and benefits (as shown in chapter 6), in the case of Palestine he rules that *ishtishhād* operations are the noblest form of jihad.

Conclusion

Wasaṭiyya and jihadi Salafism share the view of Islam as a global mission that, in the words of the *ḥadīth*, "will enter every house, whether made of clay or of camel hair." Both consider Islam as the only true religion from which all other religions deviate. But although they agree on the vision as expressed in the texts of the Qur'ān and the Sunna, they disagree on issues that concern the way in which the vision is to be achieved. The liberals, in contrast, believe that Islam, in the sense of submission and devotion to God, was not only Muḥammad's religion but also the religion of all the messengers who preceded him and therefore that all the revealed religions were and still are valid faiths. Accordingly, they hold that many Qur'ānic verses that call on people to embrace "Islam" do not refer to Islam in the narrow sense but rather to the faith in God shared by all the messengers. Iraqi liberal writer ʻAbd al-Khāliq Ḥusayn puts it especially well. He notes that the Qur'ānic verses calling for tolerance and pluralism, which descended during the Meccan period, are numerous. The problem, he says, is that the preachers of violence and intolerance give precedence to other verses calling for intolerance that descended during the Medina period and that they argue that these latter verses abrogate the former.[237]

Wasaṭiyya adopts an apologetic approach and argues that Islam is a religion of peace; *wasaṭiyya* thus distances itself from the traditional heritage of classical Qur'ān and *ḥadīth* exegesis. The way it copes with the "obstacles" that the fundamental texts put on the path of attempts to represent Islam as a tolerant religion is by reinterpreting those texts that appear to contradict its desire to present Islam as preferring peace to the sword, especially after 9/11. We saw an example of this in the way *wasaṭiyya* deals with the Verse of the Sword and the *ḥadīth* of the sword. Jihadi Salafism thus reflects the classical exegetical tradition more accurately when it adheres to the interpretation that the Verse of the Sword abrogates the Qur'ānic passages that are in conflict with it and that imply recognition of the infidels and their religion. The liberals, in contrast, accuse both the *wasaṭī*s and the jihadi Salafīs of encouraging terrorism by treating the Qur'ānic verses that call for violence as universally valid while disregarding the historical context in which these verses were revealed.[238]

The liberals' diagnosis is that Islam's current enemies are neither the liberals nor the non-Muslims, as the Islamists claim, but rather the preachers of political Islam. The latter, claim liberals such as ʻAbd al-Khāliq Ḥusayn, destroy the religion of Islam by trying to transform it into an inhuman ideology locked in a violent conflict with the civilized world, a conflict that breeds terror. "Political Islam" is from 'political' to 'its sake' more dangerous than the racist fascist movements, for it distinguishes between people based on their faith and sanctifies this distinction. [Furthermore,] it promises its followers Paradise if they fight for its sake."[239]

The liberals note that political Islam applies this discrimination (*tamyīz*) not only to non-Muslims but also to other schools of Islam. They blame political Islam and its preachers—first and foremost al-Qaraḍāwī—for the spread of terrorism and the consequent damage to the image of Islam. These political preachers, the liberals explain, threaten those whom they call the "enemies of Allah" and the "enemies of Islam" based on verses such as the "verse of preparation" (8:60).[240] Al-Qaraḍāwī's commentary on this verse sheds light on the convoluted path of *wasaṭīyya*. According to him, the "warhorses" mentioned in the verse refer in the present-day context to modern military weapons and gear, such as tanks. The Muslims are ordered to prepare military might—including even nuclear weapons—in order to establish an "armed peace" and to strike fear in the hearts of the infidels so as to deter them from fighting the Muslims, he says.[241] Such pronouncements support the liberals' claim that the political Islam represented by al-Qaraḍāwī is "the warm breast that nurtures the ideologies of the jihadi Salafī militias."[242] This claim seems doubly valid in view of the similarity between the *wasaṭī* conception of jihad and the jihadi Salafī conception.

In a sermon al-Qaraḍāwī gave in Qatar on June 8, 2001, he praised the young people who carried out *istishhād* attacks against innocents in Israel: "This heroic youth, that sacrifices itself [*fidā'ī*], that detonates itself in the midst of God's enemies, is proof of this nation's vitality [*ḥayawiyya*]. It behooves us to pray for those who have martyred themselves for God, to pray that they be granted mercy in Paradise to the highest degree by Allah. Let us pray for the Palestinian people and may it produce more students like this, students of Muḥammad's school of jihad [*madrasat al-jihād al-Muḥammadī*], the prophetic jihad."[243] Although al-Qaraḍāwī here speaks about martyrs in Palestine, his audience could very well have interpreted his words as encouragement to join what he calls the "school of jihad" and to carry out such acts outside Palestine as well.

6

Principles of *Wasaṭī* Judicial Decisions

Salafī and Wasaṭī *Dogmatism versus Liberal Openness to Reform*

This chapter addresses one of the most important domains of *wasaṭī* activity and influence: legal decisions under Muslim law. This issue also merits a comparison between the *wasaṭī*, Salafī, and liberal views, but here I focus mainly on a comparison between al-Qaraḍāwī's *wasaṭī* jurisprudence and the liberal approach to Islamic law, especially on matters related to the status of women and other social issues, such as homosexuality and female circumcision (*khitān*).

The chapter opens with a presentation of the historical context of *wasaṭī* legal decisions, which shares certain features with the legal reform proposed by the Islamic reformists headed by Muḥammad Rashīd Riḍā. It then discusses three main topics: (1) *ijtihād* and its use in *wasaṭiyya* to create more flexible maneuvering room for legal decisions; (2) the two main tools that enable *wasaṭīs* to be creative in their decisions, which are the consideration of *maṣlaḥa* as an independent juridical principle (permitting or not permitting something based on public interest), perhaps *wasaṭīyya*'s most significant innovation, and the field of governance in accordance with *sharīʿa* (*al-siyāsa al-sharʿiyya*)—that is, running the country and making policy in accordance with *sharīʿa*; and (3) the principles of *wasaṭī* jurisprudence as realized in rulings on and exegetic approaches to social matters such as women's issues and homosexuality.

Al-Qaraḍāwī has been defined as "the knight of Islamic legal rulings" in our times because this is probably the sphere of activity in which he has been most influential and by means of which he believes the *wasaṭiyya* approach can best be implemented on the ground. One important characteristic of the *wasaṭī* school's policy in the domain of legal decisions is its adoption of the principle of *maṣlaḥa* as an independent legal source—permitting or not permitting something based on public interest or benefit—not only in the field of political law but in general. Al-Qaraḍāwī may be said to have enhanced the position of this principle in contemporary Islamic law beyond the status that it had gained with Abū Isḥāq al-Shāṭibī (d. 1388). Al-Qaraḍāwī's writings may therefore quite justly be classified as belonging to what Wael Hallaq calls "religious utilitarianism."[1] *Wasaṭī fatwās* purport to reflect an approach that takes the law's goal into account, in contrast to Salafī rulings, which al-Qaraḍāwī characterizes as being based on a literal understanding of the religious texts. For this reason, he calls the Salafists "the new Ẓāhiriyya."[2] He accuses the Ẓāhiriyya of coming to strange conclusions, which are condemned by both the *sharī'a* and common sense. *Wasaṭī* claims that its legal decisions are based on the premise that *sharī'a* law intends to protect the interests of Muslims.[3]

These *wasaṭī* claims should be put to scrutiny because, according to liberal writers such as Shākir al-Nābulsī, both the Salafiyya (jihadi and nonjihadi) and the *uṣūliyya* (e.g., the MB) flatly reject the historical interpretation of the Qur'ān and the Sunna and adhere to an absolutely literal interpretation of these sacred texts.[4] Saudi journalist 'Abd al-Raḥmān al-Rāshid (b. 1956), the former editor-in-chief of the daily *Al-Sharq al-Awsaṭ*, writes about al-Qaraḍāwī that, despite his image as one of the most tolerant Muslim scholars on social issues, when addressing political issues he becomes a completely different kind of *muftī*: an extremist one.[5] This chapter examines the truth of this claim by exploring al-Qaraḍāwī's judicial decisions on issues of women's status and other social matters and by comparing them to Muslim liberals' views and obviously to Salafī jurisprudents' views as well.

The Emergence of the *Wasaṭī* School in Islamic Jurisprudence

Since the end of the nineteenth century, Islamic law has undergone dramatic changes, owing in no small part to Western influences. These changes are so profound that Wael Hallaq has concluded that "traditional *sharī'a* can surely be said to have gone without return." Hallaq does not believe that *sharīʿa* can be renewed as a code of law in the modern sense.[6] Aharon Layish claims that today Muslim clerics' ability to "Islamize" foreign laws is quite limited when compared to what their eighth- and ninth-century counterparts were able to do at a time when Muslim law was taking shape. However, he does believe that modern clerics can demonstrate judicial creativity.[7] As shown in this chapter, al-Qaraḍāwī demonstrates precisely the kind of creativity Layish mentions. His main contribution to Muslim law is the cohesive and comprehensive legal methodology that he created in an attempt to adapt *sharīʿa* to the changing times.

The reform that took place in Muslim law toward the end of the nineteenth century was characterized by a number of tendencies that can also be seen in al-Qaraḍāwī's rulings: the principle that the texts of the Qur'ān and the Sunna cannot possibly be inconsistent with reason; the principle of returning to Islam in its pristine form and its scriptural sources, the Qur'ān and the Sunna; the need to abandon the practice of blind imitation (*taqlīd*) of any single school of Islamic jurisprudence, which must be replaced with the practice of direct perusal of the textual sources to find legal indications of how to rule. In this reform, *ijtihād*, independent reasoning, was considered the main instrument for reviving Muslim law, making it more flexible, and adapting it to the changing needs of Muslim societies. *Maṣlaḥa* was a legal instrument subordinate to *ijtihād* and served to modify the law, legitimize new rulings, and deal with situations that are not mentioned in the textual sources.[8] Like the earlier reformists, al-Qaraḍāwī highlights the elements of flexibility in *sharīʿa*, the most important of which is *istiṣlāḥ*, or the use of "unattested [i.e., not mentioned in Qur'ān or Sunna] benefit or interest [*al-maṣlaḥa al-mursala*]" as a legitimate legal consideration.[9]

Unique Aspects of the Wasaṭī *System of Juridical Decision Making:* Wasaṭiyya *as a School*

The *wasaṭī* method of Islamic legal rulings possesses a number of distinctive features that can explain its great popularity. These features make it a distinct school of jurisprudence with its own legal methodology.

1. The link between legal practice and preaching. Al-Qaraḍāwī is occasionally called "the preachers' legist and the legists' preacher" because of this link.[10]

2. *Wasaṭiyya* and the evil/benefit balance (*i'tidāl*) in jurisprudence.

3. Facilitation (*taysīr*) in legal rulings.

4. Realism (*wāqi'iyya*). In his legal decisions, al-Qaraḍāwī often uses the term *understanding reality* (*fiqh al-wāqi'*), as influenced by Ibn Qayyim al-Jawziyya.[11] In a practical sense, this means that his rulings show a tendency to strike a balance between benefits and evils and to take changing reality into consideration.

5. Refraining from partisanship toward any single specific school of Islamic jurisprudence (*al-'aṣabiyya al-madhhabiyya*).[12]

6. Understanding texts in light of the goals of the *sharī'a*.

7. The interpretation of Qur'ānic verses or statements of *ḥadīth* used to determine the appropriate ruling in a given case in light of "universals" (*kulliyyāt*) of *sharī'a*. These "universals" are of two kinds: one consists of general principles found in the Qur'ān and the Sunna, such as Q5:1: "fulfill your obligations [*awfū bil-'uqūd*]," or the principle enunciated in the *ḥadīth* that "neither harm nor harmful requital shall be inflicted [*lā ḍarar wa-lā ḍirār*]";[13] the other encompasses the "general goals" of *sharī'a*, including legal maxims (*al-qawā'id al-fiqhiyya*), which al-Qaraḍāwī frequently invokes in his rulings (discussed later in this chapter).

8. The distinction between definitive (*qaṭ'ī*) and presumptive (*ẓannī*) matters in religion.

9. An amalgamation of Salafism and *tajdīd*, renewal.[14]

In this book, I define *wasaṭiyya* as a "school." This is especially true with respect to the domain of Islamic legal rulings, where *wasaṭiyya* pursues, according to its own view of itself, a middle road and *tajdīd*. An inquiry into the juridical methodology al-Qaraḍāwī uses and into his actual legal decisions leads us to justify viewing *wasaṭiyya* not just as a legal school but also as an intellectual school because it sees a direct link between the domain of ideas and *da'wa* and the domain of legal rulings, and it uses the latter to express its ideas of balance or *wasaṭiyya* and renewal (*tajdīd*). It is therefore not to be wondered that the IUMS, founded in 2004, declared its adoption of "the jurisprudence of the *wasaṭī* school [*fiqh al-madrasa al-wasaṭiyya*].” It is also no wonder that on his Facebook page al-Qaraḍāwī designates himself as *imām*, the title given to each of the heads of the orthodox schools of jurisprudence.

Al-Qaraḍāwī expresses the notion of *tajdīd* in his writings in the field of legal rulings in three ways: *ijtihād*; *tajdīd* of “legal methodology” (*uṣūl al-fiqh*); and consideration of the goals of *sharīʿa* when a ruling is made.[15] These innovative aspects of al-Qaraḍāwī’s legal method are the focus of this chapter.

Ijtihād

Al-Qaraḍāwī sees *ijtihād* as the key to what he calls “the *tajdīd* of the *fiqh*.”[16] According to al-Qaraḍāwī, *ijtihād* is necessary as long as life goes on and society evolves and if *sharīʿa* is to remain relevant to all times and all places, as he believes it should.[17] He rejects the claim that the “gates” of *ijtihād* “closed” as something that both tradition and logic cannot accept. Indeed, he asks, “Who can close a door that Allah and His Messenger opened?”[18] He notes that in the past Muslim clerics called for “closing the gates” of *ijtihād* to prevent its improper use or its use by those not fit to use it.[19] However, the very fact that he has called for the *tajdīd* of *ijtihād* shows that even he admits the “gates” had indeed been closed.[20]

Al-Qaraḍāwī distinguishes three approaches to *ijtihād*, among which he positions his own *wasaṭī* view. One approach restricts the use of *ijtihād* quite severely. This approach, he argues, is taken by two groups. One group consists of strict adherents of a single school of Islamic jurisprudence, who agree to use *ijtihād* in new cases only in accordance with the rulings of that school, which are usually based on previous rulings of later clerics of the same school. When such jurists are asked questions concerning pecuniary transactions and other interpersonal issues, they search for an answer in the writings of their own school; if they find nothing, they rule that the subject of the query is forbidden, as if in matters of *muʿāmalāt*, social and pecuniary issues, the basic rule (*aṣl*) is to forbid and to permit only what their predecessors declared to be permissible. Al-Qaraḍāwī, in contrast, makes the reverse basic assumption—namely, that in the domain of *muʿāmalāt* the rule is that everything that God has not forbidden is permitted: "the basic rule in [matters of] *mu'āmalāt* and contracts is permission [*al-aṣl fī al-mu'āmalāt wal-'uqūd al-idhn wal-ibāḥa*]."[21]

The other group that, according to al-Qaraḍāwī, restricts the use of *ijtihād* is the Salafīs, whom he calls "the new Ẓāhirīs" (after a medieval school of Islamic thought that advocated a literal interpretation of the Islamic sources) and who base their rulings on a literal understanding of the texts. They take *ḥadīth* into consideration but do not deal with *fiqh* and its methodology; as a result, they ignore the variety of views among jurists, almost totally ignore the goals of *sharī'a* and the *ratio legis*, and pay no attention to the principles of "maintaining benefits" and the need to adapt rulings to time, place, and circumstances.

One of the issues in contention between the *wasaṭī* jurists, on the one hand, and the Salafī and jihadi Salafī jurists, on the other, is the status of the arts, in particular music and singing. The controversy between al-Qaraḍāwī and the Salafīs on this issue hinges on the interpretation of Qur'ān and Sunna texts that the Salafīs present as proof that music is forbidden, such as Q31:6: "but there is the sort of person who pays for distracting tales [purchases idle tales][,] anything that amuses people [referring also to music, according to some exegetes], intending without any knowledge [that it is a sin] to lead others from God's way and to hold it [the Qur'ān] up to ridicule. There will be humiliating torment for him." The clerics who forbid music also quote exegetical traditions associated with this verse, in which the Prophet's Companions are said to have placed a total ban on music, no matter of what kind. Al-Qaraḍāwī expresses a number of reservations concerning the use of this verse as evidence for the prohibition of music. In particular, he notes that the interpretation of the phrase *lahw al-ḥadīth*, "distracting tales," as song is not the only possible interpretation. According to some exegetical traditions, the phrase refers to tales of Persian and Byzantine kings. Al-Qaraḍāwī also points out that a Companion's interpretation of a Qur'ānic verse reflects that Companion's understanding of it and that it is often the case that the interpretations of different Companions are mutually contradictory. But, he continues, even if the phrase in question is interpreted as referring to song, it still cannot be taken as evidence for prohibiting singing, for the verse condemns and threatens to punish not those who listen to music, but those who use song to lead the people astray and to make them deviate from God's path, which they "hold up to ridicule."[22]

In his ruling on music, al-Qaraḍāwī takes a position between those who say that music is lawful and those who prohibit it. He states that music is permissible, but under certain restrictions and reservations: the content of the songs should be consistent with the Muslim faith, the *sharīʿa*, and morality; the song's execution should be free of enticement; the music should not be accompanied by forbidden things, such as wine drinking; and music and song should not be listened to excessively. Al-Qaraḍāwī's *wasaṭī* ruling on music may explain his great popularity among Muslims. He declares that Islam is realistic and takes into account a person's inborn characteristics (*fiṭrat al-bashar*) and aspects: physical, spiritual, mental, and moral. Islam requires one to nourish these characteristics, but in a balanced manner. Just as sport nourishes the body, so the worship of God nourishes the spirit, knowledge nourishes the mind, and art nourishes the soul.[23]

Salafī jurists, such as the Moroccan jihadi shaykh Muḥammad b. Muḥammad al-Fazzāzī, sharply criticize al-Qaraḍāwī's ruling in favor of music and song. Al-Fazzāzī writes that in this ruling al-Qaraḍāwī once again treaded grossly on Muslims' faith and spread corruption (*fasād*) in the form of forbidden song. He accuses al-Qaraḍāwī of permitting what is unlawful and therefore levels the charge of heresy against him. Al-Fazzāzī insists that he does not dispute al-Qaraḍāwī's view with respect to "Islamic hymns" (*al-anāshīd al-Islāmiyya*), with no instrumental accompaniment.[24] (It is worth noting, too, that such hymns figure regularly in jihadi Salafī videos, including IS videos.)

An exception to the Salafī prohibition on music is *anāshīd* (sing. *unshūda*), vocal hymns with religious lyrics that are usually sung a cappella or are accompanied by percussion instruments. Some Salafī jurists have ruled that listening to such hymns is permitted under certain conditions. Ibn al-ʿUthaymīn, for instance, states that they are allowed as long as they do not feature drums, are not performed in a lewd manner, and do not use the melodies of other, forbidden songs.[25] Ibn Bāz ruled that the permissibility of the song depends on its lyrics. Songs that preach virtuous conduct such as obeying Allah and His Messenger or encourage defending the homeland against the plots of the enemies and preparing for war against the enemy are permissible.[26] The global jihad organizations, including al-Qa'ida and the IS, make extensive use of *anāshīd* to spread their message and goad their activists to wage jihad.[27] Other Salafī jurists, however, have banned even these hymns. Saudi shaykh Ṣāliḥ al-Fawzān states that the term *Islamic nashīd* is misleading, for they, too, are nothing but forbidden songs (*aghānī*), and, like Ṣūfī songs, they constitute a forbidden innovation (*bid'a*). Moreover, he stresses that listening to them constitutes emulation of the Christians, who sing as part of their worship, and he cites the Prophetic prohibition on emulating the Christians and the Jews.[28]

The second approach to *ijtihād* uses it excessively, even in the face of clear-cut, unambiguous texts (*al-nuṣūṣ al-muḥkama*). Here, too, al-Qaraḍāwī identifies two groups. One is the school founded by Najm al-Dīn al-Ṭūfī (d. 1316), a Ḥanbalī jurist, which allows considerations of benefit to overrule the text in cases of contradictions between the two.[29] According to al-Qaraḍāwī, this school uses doubtful cases (*shubuhāt*), which it presents as valid arguments. Among such instances, he mentions several cases of *ijtihād* by 'Umar b. al-Khaṭṭāb—for example, his decision not to distribute alms (*zakāh*) to "those whose hearts need winning over [*al-mu'allafa qulūbuhum*]," despite the fact that this category is mentioned explicitly in Q9:60 as having the right to receive *zakāh*.[30] But al-Qaraḍāwī argues that a more careful analysis will show that 'Umar's uses of *ijtihād* do not in fact contradict the texts.[31]

Another group that al-Qaraḍāwī places under this approach consists of clerics appointed by rulers, who strive to please their employers and therefore find excuses for a state of affairs created under the influence of the various types of material and spiritual foreign invasions. These clerics' mission is to grant legitimacy to the rulers by seeking out esoteric *shar'ī* interpretations (*ta'wīlāt*) that will enable them to remain in power.

Al-Qaraḍāwī maintains that the *wasaṭiyya* approach to legal rulings occupies the middle ground between the two aforementioned approaches because it combines respect for the texts with maintenance of the goals (*maqāṣid*) of the *sharī'a*. The *wasaṭī* school takes cognizance of the need to benefit mankind, as long as this does not contradict a text whose correctness has been conclusively proven in transmission (*ṣaḥīḥ al-thubūt*), whose meaning is clear (*ṣaḥīḥ al-dalāla*), and which does not contradict any fundamental principle of *sharīʿa* for which there is a consensus (*ijmāʿ*). This approach combines the fundamentals of *sharīʿa* with the needs of the times.[32]

Al-Qaraḍāwī's approach to *ijtihād* draws fire from both the Salafīs and the liberals. The former accuse him of seeking to create a new religion through false *ijtihād* and a rejection of the principle of *taqlīd* (imitation). An interesting Salafī critique of his writings, titled *Al-Qaraḍāwī Exposed*, systematically documents and challenges what it calls al-Qaraḍāwī's violation of both the correct tradition and common sense.[33] The author, Usāma al-Sayyid, wonders how al-Qaraḍāwī allows himself to perform *ijtihād* when most of the Companions of the Prophet did not consider themselves qualified to do this and therefore relied on the rulings of scholars who were recognized as capable *mujtahidūn*. The book also takes issue with al-Qaraḍāwī's claim that some imitators (*muqallidūn*)—that is, Muslim scholars who, according to al-Qaraḍāwī, are overstrict in following various schools of jurisprudence—are similar to the Jews and Christians, who take their rabbis and priests as their masters (*arbāb*) alongside Allah (an accusation that is directed at the Jews and Christians in Q9:31).[34] The book claims that this comparison is unfair because the Jews and Christians believe their rabbis and priests have the right to distort the Word of Allah, whereas the imitators are innocent of this sin and merely believe that the school of jurisprudence they follow faithfully interprets what is said in the Qur'ān and the Sunna. The book gravely warns the Muslims against following al-Qaraḍāwī's writings: "[Fulfilling the duty of] commanding good and forbidding evil, we warn against perusing these books, for they contain deadly poison and diseased thinking." It also cautions the Muslims not to heed the rulings al-Qaraḍāwī dispenses on satellite TV and elsewhere, for he "insolently challenges Allah, His Messengers, and his *sharīʿa*."[35] The Salafīs, then, regard al-Qaraḍāwī's jurisprudence to be overlax, a claim that is examined in this chapter.

Conversely, liberal writers such as Aḥmad al-Baghdādī argue that the *tajdīd* of contemporary Islamic thought, whose most prominent representative is al-Qaraḍāwī, focuses on *ijtihād* while ignoring the principle of freedom of thought. But *ijtihād*, says al-Baghdādī, is the exclusive province of individuals possessing specialized religious knowledge: a mastery of Qur'ānic law (including the circumstances in which the verses were revealed, abrogating and abrogated verses, etc.), a vast knowledge of *ḥadīth* and of Arabic grammar, and more. This means that clerics, such as al-Qaraḍāwī, have an absolute monopoly over the interpretation of the *sharī'a* and can present their interpretation as synonymous with the religion itself while presenting all other interpretations as heresy. Al-Baghdādī therefore proposes to replace the concept of *ijtihād* with the Western concept of freedom of thought and opinion, which accords individuals the universal right to express their opinion and be heard with respect. Western civilization, he says, liberated thought from the shackles of the medieval religious mentality, and this is the way forward for the Muslim world as well.[36]

Maṣlaḥa as an Independent Legal Principle in *Wasaṭī* Legal Practice

Background: Maṣlaḥa *and* Istiṣlāḥ *in Muslim Law*

As part of its *ijtihād*, *wasaṭiyya* employs two juridical tools that make *sharī'a* more flexible and capable of adapting to changing times and places: *maṣlaḥa* and *al-siyāsa al-shar'iyya*. This section is devoted to examining these two tools.

Use of considerations of *maṣlaḥa* appear in Muslim legal rulings beginning in the eighth and ninth centuries CE, although then a different term was used to denote it: *istiḥsān*, which literally means "consider something to be good" and in the legal context means "discretion (in the application of the law)." The term *maṣlaḥa* first received a legal definition in the eleventh century CE by Abū Ḥāmid al-Ghazālī, an adherent of the Shāfi'ī school of jurisprudence, who also determined the parameters for the future interpretation of this concept in Islamic law. After al-Ghazālī, the elements that constitute *maṣlaḥa* did not change, although its standing in legal practice did. For al-Ghazālī, *maṣlaḥa* was a secondary principle and not an independent source of the law; in fact, he classified *istiṣlāḥ* as belonging to the class of "illusory fundamentals" (*al-uṣūl al-mawhūma*).[37] In contrast, Abū Isḥāq al-Shāṭibī, a jurist of the Mālikī school by whom al-Qaraḍāwī was greatly influenced, considered *maṣlaḥa* as the principle on which the entire theory of the law is based.[38] Felicitas Opwis is of the opinion that in his focus on the aims and goals of *sharīʿa* al-Shāṭibī took the concept of *maṣlaḥa* to new heights and recast its existing interpretations into a comprehensive and coherent theory.[39]

Opwis states that most modern *fuqahāʾ* have used some aspects of various models of *maṣlaḥa*, which they combine or interpret eclectically. She comes to the conclusion that Muslim legists choose their interpretations of *maṣlaḥa* depending on their education, personal views, and historical environment.[40] This is also true of al-Qaraḍāwī, who has adopted the *maṣlaḥa* principle in the juridical model of Abū Ḥāmid al-Ghazālī and al-Shāṭibī but has expanded and introduced some innovations into their theory.

Al-Qaraḍāwī's Innovations in the Domain of Maṣlaḥa

In principle, al-Qaraḍāwī accepts al-Ghazālī's definition of *maṣlaḥa* but modifies it somewhat. According to al-Ghazālī, *maṣlaḥa* involves the preservation of the goals (*maqāṣid*) of the Islamic law—namely, to preserve religion, life, reason, property, and offspring. For him, whatever can be subsumed under the preservation of these five "necessities" (*ḍarūriyyāt*) is a *maṣlaḥa* and whatever cannot is harm (*mafsada*), whose prevention in turn is also a *maṣlaḥa*.[41]

Al-Qaraḍāwī has two reservations about this definition. First, he believes that al-Ghazālī's restriction of *maṣlaḥa* to the preservation of just the five "necessities" is too restrictive and that it should also encompass human "needs" (*ḥājiyyāt*) and moral "improvements" (*taḥsīnāt*), such as good manners and proper behavior (as discussed later). Second, al-Qaraḍāwī points out that in addition to the five "necessities" listed by al-Ghazālī, one should also include the following: preservation of the family honor (*ʿirḍ*), security, justice, solidarity, preservation of public rights and liberties, and the establishment of an *umma wasaṭ*, literally "a middle nation," a Qurʾānic phrase that appears in Q2:143, as already noted, and that has provided the inspiration for the name of the *wasaṭiyya* school.[42]

Al-Qaraḍāwī accepts the division of "goals" as formulated by al-Ghazālī and the jurists who followed him. As al-Shāṭibī notes in *The Correspondences*, the goals of the *sharīʿa* commandments were meant for the welfare of mankind and are of three kinds:

1. Things that are absolutely necessary for the maintenance of benefits (*maṣāliḥ*) in religion and in the world. Five such things are usually mentioned: preservation of religion, life, reason, property, and offspring.

2. Needs (*ḥājiyyāt*), things that are needed to prevent hardship (*raf' al-ḥaraj*) and whose absence causes difficulties. This category includes religious observances (*'ibādāt*), customs (*'ādāt*), pecuniary transactions (*mu'āmalāt*), and the penal code (*jinā'iyyāt*).

3. Improvements (*taḥsīnāt*), by which is meant the adoption of good habits and moral behavior. According to Muḥammad al-Ṭāhir Ibn 'Āshūr (d. 1973), it is the *taḥsīnāt* that make it possible for the Muslim *umma* to live peacefully and safely and that attract others and make them wish to join the *umma*. He enumerates several "good customs" (*maḥāsin al-'ādāt*), both of a general nature, such as covering one's private parts, and some that apply specifically to some nations, such as letting one's beard grow (*i'fā' al-liḥya*).[43]

*Al-Qaraḍāwī as a "Purposive Jurist" (*Faqīh al-Maqāṣid*)*

Understanding of the law's goals is an important principle in al-Qaraḍāwī's legal method; in fact, he has been called a "purposive jurist," *faqīh al-maqāṣid*.[44] David Johnston, in his interesting and thorough study of al-Qaraḍāwī's theory of the law's goals, comes to the conclusion that despite the frequent use that al-Qaraḍāwī makes of this concept in his rulings, he was and remains a mainstream, conservative, traditionalist jurist. Johnston describes al-Qaraḍāwī as "the eternal opportunist, simply jumping on a useful bandwagon the better to push his consistent agenda, to unite the Islamic umma under the banner of the benevolent *'ulamā'*." Johnston writes that if the focus of the formulation and issuance of *fatwā*s is transferred from the text to human reason, the authority of preachers who are not *'ulamā'* and of Muslim intellectuals will be strengthened at the expense of the long-term standing of the *'ulamā'*. He concludes that by stressing the law's goals, al-Qaraḍāwī would lose his standing as an *'ālim*.[45]

However, an analysis of al-Qaraḍāwī's rulings and of his use of the law's goals as a legal source, as performed in this chapter, can lead one to conclude that his use of this principle enables him to maneuver more easily in his rulings, to take Muslims' changing needs into account, and to adapt the law to the spirit of the times, of course without going beyond the bounds of the *sharīʿā*. This method for deriving legal decisions may explain al-Qaraḍāwī's great attraction as a jurist. Johnston is right when he states that al-Qaraḍāwī's distinction between "definite" and "ambiguous" legal texts and his use of the law's goals only for the latter result in his accepting *sharīʿā* laws in full where the prohibition on usury (Q3:130) and the punishments set out in the Qur'ān and the like are concerned. However, his use of *ijtihād* and his reliance on the principle of the laws' goals enables him to be more flexible in his rulings and to take changes in time and place into consideration. Furthermore, al-Qaraḍāwī adopts criteria for the interpretation of the Qur'ān and the *ḥadīth* that enable him to rule that on many issues *sharīʿā* neither absolutely prohibits nor absolutely commands; for example, music is not prohibited, a woman's voice is not immodest per se, and the full face veil (*niqāb*) is not absolutely obligatory.

Female Circumcision: Applying the Principle of Maṣlaḥa

In his rulings on women's issues, al-Qaraḍāwī claims to adopt the *wasaṭī* line, taking care to maintain "benefits" (*maṣālīḥ*) and the law's goals.[46] One of the issues that enables us to assess this claim and that highlights the differences among the *wasaṭī*, Salafī, and liberal approaches is female circumcision (*khafḍ* or *khitān al-unthā*). Muslim legists consider this act as having one of the following four statuses:

1. "An act of nobility by women [*makruma lil-nisā'*]," although abstaining from it is not a sin. This is the Mālikī approach, which is anchored in the *ḥadīth*.
2. "A good practice" (*sunna*)—that is, less than obligatory but very strongly encouraged. This is the Ḥanbalī legal approach.
3. "Permissible or neutral" (*jā'iz*), a category that is neutral with respect to the *sharīʿa* and of course does not imply any obligation to perform it.
4. "Obligatory" (*wājib*) for women just as it is for men. This is the Shāfiʿī view.

The two first views are the most common; they are also the least well defined and the most flexible. Shaykh Maḥmūd Shaltūt (d. 1963), former al-Azhar shaykh, ruled that because no texts in the Qur'ān or the Sunna support female circumcision, the ruling must be based on the *sharī'a* law that forbids causing pain to a living creature, unless there are benefits significant enough to make the pain worthwhile. He rejects the claim that circumcision keeps women chaste, saying that some circumcised women nevertheless engage in forbidden sexual behaviors. Virtue depends on proper education and supervision and on a proper environment, he says, not on circumcision.[47] Al-Qaraḍāwī's ruling on female circumcision is largely similar to that of Maḥmūd Shaltūt, whom al-Qaraḍāwī, not surprisingly, regards as a *wasaṭī* jurist.[48]

The Salafī Ruling on Female Circumcision. Salafī shaykh Muḥammad b. Ṣāliḥ al-'Uthaymīn ruled that male circumcision is obligatory, whereas female circumcision is *sunna*—that is, optional. He explained that for men, circumcision confers *maṣlaḥa* of purity and is also a condition for the acceptability (*ṣiḥḥa*) of their prayers, whereas in the case of women the only benefit of circumcision is that it curbs their libido. Unlike male circumcision, he added, female circumcision does not remove a flaw, and therefore it is not compulsory.[49] Ibn Bāz ruled that both male circumcision and female circumcision are permitted by the *sharī'a* (*mashrū'*), adding that female circumcision is desirable (*mustaḥabb*) as long as there is a competent professional to perform it and that male circumcision is confirmed *sunna* (*sunna mu'akkada*)—that is, compulsory.[50]

In order to fully assess al-Qaraḍāwī's ruling, it should also be compared to that of traditional *'ulamā'*, such as former al-Azhar shaykh Jāda al-Ḥaqq 'Alī Jāda al-Ḥaqq. Al-Ḥaqq ruled that both male and female circumcision are acts of cleansing (*naẓāfa*) and that female circumcision creates parity between the man and the woman and is therefore beneficial for both. "By taking care not to cut too severely [following the *ḥadīth* that recommends to reduce the clitoris but not eliminate it entirely], Muslims can avoid the effects that have prompted the calls to abolish female circumcision," he wrote. He dismissed the claim that female circumcision, in any form, causes medical and social problems on the grounds that Muslims have been performing it for centuries without complaint. Al-Ḥaqq also argued that because female circumcision is part of the *fiṭra* (based on the *ḥadīth* that proclaims this), there is no need to consult with medical or other professionals about it, especially since medical professionals are divided on the issue. He contended that the practice of circumcision helps to subdue the female libido, especially during adolescence, which is the most dangerous stage in a girl's sexual development. This, he said, is why the Prophet called it "an act of nobility" (*makruma*): it helps to preserve the woman's honor by keeping her from forbidden sexual acts. According to al-Ḥaqq, female circumcision also has health benefits, helping to prevent urinary and uterine infections, which can lead to severe illness.[51]

The Wasaṭī *al-Qaraḍāwī's Ruling on Female Circumcision.* Al-Qaraḍāwī, in dealing with this issue, first examines the existing evidence and concludes that from the Qur'ān, the Sunna, the consensus of legal opinion, and the principle of "analogy" (*qiyās*), no evidence can be adduced that female circumcision is obligatory (*wājib*) or even recommended (*mustaḥabb*); nor is there evidence that it is prohibited (*ḥarām*) or abominable (*makrūh*). He adds that there were *fuqahā'*, both within the schools of jurisprudence as well as others, who maintained that the act was obligatory, desirable, or noble. This state of affairs, according to al-Qaraḍāwī, proves that Muslim *fuqahā'* implicitly agreed that female circumcision is "permissible" (*jā'iz*).[52]

For this reason, al-Qaraḍāwī uses the principles of "legal maxims" and the "law's goals" to rule on this issue. He states that something that is "permitted" (*jā'iz* or *mubāḥ*) may be forbidden partially or wholly if it can be proven to be harmful because Allah has permitted things to His servants in order to alleviate (*taysīr*) their situation (Q4:28). Thus, if something that is permitted is harmful to all or most people, it must be declared forbidden owing to the principle of "neither harm nor harmful requital shall be inflicted [*lā ḍarar wa-lā ḍirār*]." In other words, if it proves to be the case that female circumcision causes certain or almost certain harm, it must be forbidden under the rule of "blocking misuse" (*sadd al-dharī'a*). However, if expert medical opinion shows that some girls are in need (*ḥāja*) of circumcision, these cases should be treated as an exception to the prohibition in order to bring about a *maṣlaḥa* and prevent harm (*dar' al-mafsada*).[53]

Al-Qaraḍāwī mentions a number of principles based on which he rules that female circumcision should be avoided:

1. The fundamental principle in the Qur'ān and the Sunna is that God's creation should not be changed because any such change is the

devil's work (Q4:119). This in turn means that removing part of a woman's body with no overriding justification is forbidden (*maḥẓūr*) according to the *sharīʿa*. Male circumcision is an exception because revealed texts bear conclusive evidence in transmission and meaning (*ṣaḥīḥat al-thubūt* and *ṣaḥīḥat al-dalāla*), according to which male circumcision is a "natural innate characteristic" (*sunan al-fiṭra*) and part of the Abrahamic tradition and so is also part of the rites of Islam (*shaʿāʾir al-Islām*). Furthermore, physicians agree that male circumcision is medically and hygienically desirable and that it prevents disease.

2. If removing part of a woman's body does her body or mind any harm or prevents her from enjoying a natural right, such as the right to sexual pleasure with her husband and her right to sexual gratification, it is forbidden because in Islam it is forbidden for anyone to cause harm to himself or to others (according to the *ḥadīth* that has become a legal principle: "neither harm nor harmful requital shall be inflicted [*lā ḍarar wa-lā ḍirār*]."[54]

Muḥammad Salīm al-ʿAwwā issued a *wasaṭī* ruling on female circumcision that gives greater weight to the woman's rights and feelings. In his legal opinion on this practice, he calls it an assault on the woman's body and therefore a violation of the penal code, and he adds that anyone involved in it, including doctors who perform it, bears legal and civil responsibility and should be punished. The woman's sex organ, as God created it, is neither a disease nor the cause of any disease or discomfort, he says, so there is no need to surgically alter it. Circumcision is a brutal violation of the woman's right to enjoy a warm relationship with her husband and the mental ease that results from such a relationship. He concludes: "Those pious men who permit what is not permitted and ascribe to the *sharīʿa* what is not part of it, must remember the Prophet's last directive regarding women: 'Be good to the women.' They should put themselves in the place of those poor girls who, owing to this [practice of] circumcision, which is not mentioned in the *sharīʿa*, have been deprived of pleasure. Had men been deprived of the same pleasure, nothing could ever compensate them [for the loss]."[55]

The Liberal View of Female Circumcision. Liberal writers such as Gamāl al-Bannā go much further than al-Qaraḍāwī, describing female circumcision as a heinous crime. Gamāl al-Bannā believes that it must be fought first of all by refuting the false notion that it is a noble act and part of the religion. Female circumcision, he says, is merely an entrenched social custom in religious guise, which has no basis in the Qur'ān and the Sunna, and the public must be made aware of this. An important difference between Gamāl al-Bannā and al-Qaraḍāwī is that the former gives much thought to the woman's perspective, her suffering, and the effects of circumcision on her. He explains that this custom originates in ancient times, when ignorance and patriarchality prevailed, and was part of the overall oppression of women, which lasted for centuries, and was also manifested in forcing them to wear the *ḥijāb* and denying their rights. Circumcision was a means of controlling the woman's body and her sexuality, with the aim of suppressing her natural urges. It was a kind of castration, similar to what is done to animals and to slaves, Gamāl al-Bannā says. Religion subsequently associated circumcision with various myths, such as the biblical story of Abraham's circumcision (Genesis 17). Circumcision is the first commandment given to Abraham as a sign of God's covenant with him and his descendants. After the advent of Islam, Muslim exegetes copied this idea wholesale from the Torah and from other Jewish and Christian texts, thus turning circumcision into a Muslim custom as well.[56]

Gamāl al-Bannā claims that, unlike Europe, the Muslim world has yet to free itself from ancient customs such as female circumcision. In Europe, where quality of life gradually improved, freedom and culture blossomed, and women joined the work force as part of the industrial revolution, such customs were unable to gain traction. He concludes that Muslim women must be rescued from the crime of circumcision, which violates their honor and causes them many illnesses, both physical and mental.[57]

Principles of *al-Siyāsa al-Shar'iyya*

Having addressed the principle of *maṣlaḥa*, let us now turn to the other legal tool extensively used by *wasaṭiyya* to issue creative rulings: governance in accordance with *sharī'a*, or *al-siyāsa al-shar'iyya*. The term *al-siyāsa al-shar'iyya* refers to leadership and administration (*siyāsa*) based on the principles, laws, and instructions of *sharī'a*. A *siyāsa* may be inconsistent with *sharī'a* or even hostile to it—for example, if it is based on secular philosophical principles, whether liberal or communist. *Shar'ī* governance, in contrast, is founded on the *sharī'a*, which it strives to implement on the ground and to inculcate among Muslims. The juridical branch of "political jurisprudence" (*al-fiqh al-siyāsī*) or *shar'ī* governance consists of rulings on issues having to do with the relations between the individual and the state or between ruler and subject.[58] It is similar in nature to what is known as constitutional monetary, administrative, and international law.[59]

Aharon Layish notes that the classical doctrine of *shar'ī* governance recognizes a Muslim ruler's right to complement the *sharī'a* with legislation of his own for the public welfare in case of a legal gap in the Qur'ān, the Sunna, or legal doctrine. In fact, the tool of *shar'ī* governance provides Muslim legal legitimacy to statutory legislation. In our day, this doctrine can be used to adapt the *sharī'a* to changing circumstances and to "Islamize" the body of law that has accumulated in the Muslim world since the second half of the nineteenth century, in particular in the domains of criminal and economic law.[60] Both *wasaṭī*s and jihadi Salafīs use the tools of *shar'ī* governance in their legal rulings.

Al-Qaraḍāwī formulated several fundamental principles for *shar'ī* governance: understanding the religious texts in light of the general goals of *sharī'a*; understanding reality and changes in *fatwā*s in accordance with changes in the reality; understanding the balances between benefits and evils (*fiqh al-muwāzanāt*); understanding priorities (*fiqh al-awlawiyyāt*); and understanding change (*fiqh al-taghyīr*). To examine how these principles are put into practice, let us peruse the *wasaṭī* ruling on peaceful demonstrations against the ruler in comparison to the rulings made by the Salafīs and establishment scholars.

Jurisprudence of the Revolution: Rulings on Peaceful Protest Demonstrations

Salafī Rulings on Nonviolent Demonstrations. Shaykh Nāṣīr al-Dīn al-Albānī has ruled that protests are forbidden because they violate the Prophet's principle that Muslims should strive to distinguish and differentiate themselves from the infidel (*mukhālafat al-kuffār*). He states that the demonstrations are an imitation of the infidel way of protest against their rulers. He adds yet another reason for rejecting the use of demonstrations: that they are not a method sanctioned by *sharīʿa* for bringing about social and political reform, which, he claims, is to be achieved in Islam by the dissemination of knowledge and education and not by demonstrating. Al-Albānī thus concludes that the participants in demonstrations stray from the right path shown by the Prophet and will therefore suffer the punishment threatened by Q4:115: hellfire.[61]

The Saudi Salafī cleric Ibn al-ʿUthaymīn ruled that demonstrations are an innovation (*amr ḥādith*) that was unknown in the days of the Prophet, the right-guided caliphs, and the Prophet's Companions. He added that they should also be prohibited because they foment anarchy, bring men and women together, and give rise to other abominations (*munkarāt*). Furthermore, in his opinion they cannot succeed as a means for putting pressure on a government: if the government is Muslim, the Qur'ān should be enough to guide it, and if it is infidel, it will in any case not heed the demonstrators. He therefore concludes that demonstrations are an abomination.[62]

Ibn Bāz ruled that demonstrations, far from being a solution, are in fact a cause for civil war (*fitna*), iniquity, and unjust trespass. The way to bring about reform, he believes, is not through violent protests but through friendly advice (*naṣīḥa*) to rulers. He mentions the fact that during the thirteen years the Prophet spent in Mecca, he never demonstrated or marched and never threatened anyone's property. Ibn Bāz thinks that demonstrations have a negative effect on preaching efforts and harm the dissemination of the faith.[63]

Establishment Scholars' Ruling on Demonstrations. Al-Qaraḍāwī's ruling in the matter of demonstrations is at odds with that of the establishment scholars in both Egypt and Yemen. The Yemeni Scholars' Association (Jamʿiyyat ʿUlamāʾ al-Yaman) ruled on September 27, 2011, that coming out against the rulers, either in deed or in word, contravenes the *sharīʿa*, for it contravenes both the Qur'ān and the Sunna. The Qur'ān (4:59) states that the believers must obey Allah, the Messenger, and "those in authority" among them—namely, the rulers. As for the Sunna, a *ḥadīth* says: "One who found in his emir [*amīr*] something that he disliked should hold his patience, for one who separated from the main body of the Muslims, even to the extent of a handspan, and then he died would die the death of one belonging to the days of *jāhiliyya* [pre-Islamic paganism]." The association stated further that the demonstrations against President ʿAlī ʿAbdallah Ṣāliḥ (d. 2017) violated both the *sharīʿa* and the civil law because they involved bloodshed, a threat to security, the disruption of public order, and the uttering of slogans that contravened the *sharīʿa*.[64]

Al-Qaraḍāwī responded to this *fatwā* by stating that the reactionary *fiqh* that panders to the rulers even when they oppress their peoples must vanish in favor of the revolutionary *fiqh* (*al-fiqh al-thawrī*) that acts to strengthen the peoples and to cure the regimes of their ills. Obeying the ruler, he said, is obligatory as long as the latter obeys Allah and His Messenger, enacts the *sharīʿa*, and honors his contract with his people. Moreover, although taking up arms against the ruler is prohibited, peaceful protests are permissible.[65]

Furthermore, Al-Qaraḍāwī argued, the *fatwā*s that forbid demonstrating against oppressive rulers cast Islam in a negative light, for they present it as a religion that prevents people from opposing tyranny. Worse, it presents Islam as a religion that shields tyrants and sanctions their crimes, when in fact it is a religion that forbids its adherents to remain silent in the face of oppression and treats this behavior itself as a form of oppression. This is evident from the *ḥadīth* that says, "Whoever witnesses oppression and does not act to prevent it, Allah shall soon punish him with the oppressor's punishment." According to al-Qaraḍāwī, protests against an oppressive regime constitute uttering "a word of truth before a despotic ruler [*kalimat ḥaqq ʿinda sulṭān jāʾir*]," which is described in another famous *ḥadīth* as "the best form of jihad." Such protests are a kind of peaceful jihad, he states, comparable to "jihad by means of the tongue," and engaging in them is a fulfillment of the duty to "forbid wrong and change it [*taghyīr al-munkar*]."[66]

Al-Qaraḍāwī's Ruling on Demonstrations. Al-Qaraḍāwī ruled that Muslims have the right to organize protest demonstrations for expressing legitimate demands from their rulers and decision makers. This they may do because the collective will is greater than that of the individual, as God indicated in the Qurʾān (Q5:2), "Help one another to do what is right and good, in righteousness and piety," and as the Prophet is said to have declared in the following *ḥadīth*: "The relationship of the believer with another believer is like (the bricks of) a building, each strengthens the other. He illustrated this by interlacing the fingers of both his hands." The demonstrations of the Arab Spring, according to al-Qaraḍāwī, were within the realm of custom (*'ādāt*) and civil life, where the fundamental rule is permission.[67] This is why, according to al-Qaraḍāwī, the domain of forbidden things in Islam is small, whereas the domain of permissible things is large.

Based on the principles that al-Qaraḍāwī formulated for ruling on matters of *shar'ī* governance, he refuted the arguments raised against the legitimacy of the demonstrations. The argument that demonstrations are an innovation in Islam has no substance, he declared, because the concept of innovation refers only to purely religious obligations that men have toward their God. This can be seen in the deeds of the Prophet's Companions and their disciples, who made numerous innovations—such as 'Umar b. al-Khaṭṭāb, who introduced the *hijrī* calendar, military cities, and prisons. Later generations introduced further innovations, such as Muslim coins to replace the Persian *dirham* and the Byzantine *denarius* and the postal service, and developed new fields of knowledge, such as the science of the "fundamentals of Islamic jurisprudence."[68]

It should be noted that to expand the spectrum of issues that can be dealt with using *ijtihād* and *tajdīd*, *wasaṭī*s make a distinction between religious observances and social and pecuniary issues. *Wasaṭiyya* adopts the view of al-Shāṭibī, Rashīd Riḍā, and Ḥasan al-Bannā: the basic rule is that religious observances (*'ibādāt*) must be performed irrespective of their goals, whereas in the domain of pecuniary transactions (*mu'āmalāt*) the goals must be taken into account.[69] In this connection, al-Qaraḍāwī adds that in the field of worship—that is, in purely religious matters—the basic principle is to obey (*ittibā'*) the text, whereas in the field of customs—that is, of worldly matters—it is necessary to innovate (*ibtidā'*) and develop. For this reason, the *ḥadīth* that says, "If anyone innovates something in this matter of ours [i.e., Islam] that is not of it, he will have it rejected," applies only to matters of worship, but in the domains of customs and interpersonal relations the people rather than God have decided what the law should be, and Allah has only refined and corrected it.

To the claim that demonstrations are a Western import, al-Qaraḍāwī replies that this fact alone does not make them forbidden according to *sharīʿa*, as long as they are permissible in and of themselves and the Muslims think they are beneficial. After all, according to one tradition, "wisdom is the believer's most avid desire; wherever he finds it is the place most worthy of it." He mentions the fact that the Prophet's Companions borrowed the land tax (*kharāj*) from the Persians, adding that in our day Muslims have made numerous borrowings from the West in many different fields, including the concept of a constitution, elections, separation of powers, and use of the Internet. He states that there is nothing intrinsically wrong in borrowing from the West, especially in light of the fact that in the past the West borrowed from the Muslim world, with great benefit for its science at the beginning of the Renaissance. The important point, according to al-Qaraḍāwī, is to ensure that what one borrows is consistent with the Muslims' faith, values, and *sharīʿa* and that it is beneficial to the borrower. He adds that Muslims borrow mainly things associated with the changing aspects of life, which are flexible by their very nature, and not with fixed objectives and principles.[70]

In order to confirm the licit status of demonstrations, al-Qaraḍāwī uses two tools of *sharīʿa*:

The first tool is an unattested benefit or interest (*al-maṣlaḥa al-mursala*) (i.e., a benefit or interest not mentioned in Qur'ān or Sunna), which in his view encompasses anything that did not exist in the times of the Prophet and the right-guided caliphs, as long as they fulfill the following conditions: that the borrowed items not belong to the domain of man's duty toward God; that they bring about a benefit allowed by *sharīʿa*; and that they be reasonable and not contradict any *sharīʿa* text or principle.

The second tool is the principle that the permissibility of a means depends on whether its use is consistent with the *sharīʿa*; according to this principle, a means is never prohibited on its own merits but is to be judged on whether it is acceptable in *sharīʿa*. Al-Qaraḍāwī adds that this tool can be applied to demonstrations. If their purpose is acceptable according to the *sharīʿa*—for example, if they call for application of the *sharīʿa*, for the release of unjustly imprisoned people, for putting an end to trials of civilians by the military courts, or for an end to the state of emergency or if they sound demands for bread, sugar, and medications—then they are legitimate. Other issues that al-Qaraḍāwī accepts as legitimate are protests against what is being done to the Palestinians, the excavations at the al-Aqṣā Mosque, the war in Iraq, and offensive cartoons of the Prophet Muḥammad.[71]

Jurisprudence on Women's Issues (*Fiqh al-Mar'a*)

This part of the chapter focuses on the *wasaṭī* ruling on women's issues, comparing it to the approach of the Salafīs and the liberals. As in other domains surveyed in this book, al-Qaraḍāwī presents his *wasaṭī* approach in this matter as taking the middle road between two extremes: the "extremists" (apparently the Salafī clerics) and the "exaggerators" (the liberals). The former, he says, are trapped in ancient Oriental traditions and are excessively strict in their rulings regarding women. They regard women with contempt and see them as tools of Satan's cunning and therefore rule that women should be confined to the house and forbidden from seeking religious knowledge and even from attending the mosque. They base this approach, says al-Qaraḍāwī, on unreliable *ḥadīth*s or on texts that are ambiguous (*mutashābihāt*) instead of on texts that are decisive and clear (*muḥkamāt*). At other times, says al-Qaraḍāwī, the extremists cite *ḥadīth*s that are reliable (*ṣaḥīḥ*) but present them in a different context than intended, such as the *ḥadīth* (discussed later in this chapter) that calls women "deficient in intelligence and religion [*nāqiṣāt 'aql wa-dīn*]."[72]

Regarding the "exaggerators," the liberals, al-Qaraḍāwī says they are trapped in exported Western traditions and take the notion of women's liberation too far, overstepping the boundaries set out by Allah and disregarding the distinct inborn traits Allah instilled in women and men (*ḥudūd al-fiṭra*). He accuses them of wanting to erase the differences between the sexes, when the fact is that Allah made them different, as evident even from the physical differences between them. Allah, in His wisdom, gave men and women different traits and abilities, which suit their different roles in life, says the shaykh. A central part of the woman's role is motherhood, and this should be taken into account, for example, in issuing rulings about women's education and employment.[73]

Some westernized jurists, adds al-Qaraḍāwī, forbid what Allah allowed, such as polygamy (to be discussed later), in stark contradiction to what is said in the Qur'ān (4:2–3) and to the example provided by the Prophet and by the caliphs who succeeded him. Al-Qaraḍāwī also condemns these jurists for advocating equality between men and women in inheritance, when the unequal division of inheritance is mandated by Q4:11, by the Sunna, and by the consensus of legal opinion, making it an essential of the faith (*mā ʿulima bi-l-ḍarūra min dīn al-Islām*).[74]

One of the principles that al-Qaraḍāwī as a follower of *wasaṭiyya* added to Ḥasan al-Bannā's original twenty principles (see chapter 2) concerns the respect owed to women in Islam. He formulated this principle as follows: "Just treatment of women, respect for them, preservation of their natural disposition, stress on what Islam has introduced: rights, status, and respect for women, [their] liberation from the traces of periods of backwardness and withdrawal in Islam and from the evils of the Western cultural invasion that has taken women out of their innate nature and does not preserve their femininity."[75] This formulation, especially at the end, shows clear signs of Muḥammad al-Ghazālī's influence on al-Qaraḍāwī.[76] Al-Ghazālī wrote in his own additions to al-Bannā's principles, "Women are like men; seeking knowledge is obligatory on both sexes, as well as commanding the good and forbidding evil or wrong. Women, within the bounds of Islamic morality, have the right to participate in the construction and preservation of society."[77]

To assess the scope and essence of the change represented by the *wasaṭī* perspective on women, it is instructive to compare it to al-Nābulsī's neoliberal platform. In addressing the issue of women's status, this platform makes "a demand to grant women full equality in rights, duties, employment, education, inheritance, testimony, and [the right to] hold office," and it advocates "adopting the Tunisian Personal Status Law of 1957, which is considered an ideal example of an Arab [law] liberating women and making them equal to men."[78] Al-Qaraḍāwī, in contrast, cites the Tunisian Personal Status Law of 1957 as evidence that Tunisia is afflicted with "extreme secularism," even more extreme than that of Muṣṭafā Kamāl Atatürk's republic. One of the clauses of this law criminalizes polygamy, a criminalization that, al-Qaraḍāwī points out, contradicts the

Qur'ān's (4:3) permission to take multiple wives. He also accuses the Tunisian law of encouraging debauchery because, denied the right to take a second wife, a man might take a woman as a girlfriend instead.[79]

Al-Qaraḍāwī's and the liberals' different views on this law and on other reforms introduced by Tunisian president Habib Bourguiba (d. 2000, held office 1957–87) sheds light on their different perspectives in general. Al-Nābulsī and his fellow liberals regard Bourguiba as a paragon of religious reform and women's equality. As examples they cite not only the Personal Status Law but also Bourguiba's introduction of a law revoking the *qiwāma* (a concept mentioned in Q4:34, establishing men's responsibility for and authority over women), which he deemed insulting to women. He also introduced a law permitting a non-Muslim man to marry a Muslim woman.[80] These very same reforms, however, motivated al-Qaraḍāwī to accuse Bourguiba of resenting and despising Islam, the Qur'ān, and the Prophet. According to the shaykh, the only difference between Atatürk and Bourguiba is that the former openly declared his secularism, whereas the latter was a hypocrite who pretended to be a Muslim. This hypocrisy (*nifāq*) is much more dangerous than Atatürk's open heresy, he says.[81]

It is important to stress that al-Qaraḍāwī accepts and justifies the principle of *qiwāma*, explaining that it is granted to the man for two reasons. The first reason has to do with men's and women's different roles: it is the man, more than the woman, who invests in building the family. The second reason has to do with men's and women's different *fiṭra*, inborn characteristics. According to al-Qaraḍāwī, Allah granted men an innate ability to examine things rationally and foresee consequences, whereas women were blessed with keen emotions, as mandated by their role of motherhood.[82]

The Muslim Woman's Dress Code

The Wasaṭīs *View of the Dress Code.* The issue of the Muslim woman's dress code is a major point of contention between *wasaṭiyya*, Salafism, and liberalism. According to al-Qaraḍāwī, the *sharīʿa* necessarily has an opinion on this issue, as entailed by the all-encompassing nature of Islam (*shumūl al-Islām*). He contends that women must cover their head, neck, and chest, but he shares Shaykh al-Albānī's opinion that a woman's face and hands are not to be considered "private parts" (*'awra*) and therefore do not have to be covered.[83] The *niqāb*, he says, is not obligatory or even desirable (*mustaḥabb*), but it is permissible (*mubāḥ*); wearing one is the Muslim woman's right, which nobody may deny her.[84]

The shaykh bases his ruling on Q24:31, especially on exegesis of the part of the verse that exhorts women not to "expose their adornment except that which appears thereof." He holds that the phrase "that which appears thereof" refers to the face and hands, and he presents numerous arguments in favor of this particular interpretation. For example, he notes that the Qur'ān instructs men to lower their gaze (24:30) and that this would not have been necessary had women been required to cover their faces. He also presents the practical argument that various everyday activities, such as buying and selling, as well as other activities, such as testifying in court, require women to be identifiable to those they come into contact with.[85]

He enumerates the following considerations that led him to this conclusion, which provided the basis for his *wasaṭī* ruling on the matter:[86]

1. Whatever is not forbidden in a reliable (*ṣaḥīḥ*) and explicit text is permitted (*mubāḥ*).

2. The ruling on any issue may change with the changing times, circumstances, customs, and situation. In our times, says al-Qaraḍāwī, women's status has changed, and it is necessary to adopt positions that are supportive of women and help strengthen them. He notes that the "enemies of Islam," such as the secularists, blame Islam for the sad state of Muslim women in many Muslim countries and have tried to distort the laws of *sharī'a* concerning women. This is yet another reason, he adds, for ruling in favor of women and enabling them to realize their natural and legal rights.

3. The very fact that something is widespread (*'umūm al-balwā*) is reason enough to rule leniently on it. Today women commonly attend schools and universities and go out to work; they are no longer restricted to their homes, as they were in the past. This makes it necessary for them to expose their faces and hands in order to move and maintain contact with their surroundings. Today's battle, according to al-Qaraḍāwī, is not about exposing a woman's face and hands but rather about standing up to those

who wish that Muslim women become copies of Western women and become totally exposed like them.

4. There is a legal principle that says, "Difficulty begets facility [*al-mashaqqa taghlibu al-taysīr*]."[87] The requirement that women cover their faces and hands presents a difficulty for women, especially in this day and age, and Allah, al-Qaraḍāwī reminds us, wants Islam to be a religion of "facility" (Q2:185).

The Salafī Ruling on the Ḥijāb. Ibn Bāz has ruled that a woman's face is a "private part" and that the *niqāb* is obligatory. A woman, he states, must hide her face and her entire body from all men who are strangers to her. Ibn Bāz relies on Q33:53, "When you ask his [the Prophet's] wives for something, do so from behind a screen: this is purer both for your hearts and for theirs, that makes for greater purity for your hearts and for theirs," and Q33:59, "Prophet, tell your wives, your daughters, and women believers to make their outer garments hang low over them so as to be recognized and not insulted (molested): God is most forgiving, most merciful."[88] Al-Qaraḍāwī, however, argues that these verses do not constitute evidence for the obligatory nature of the *niqāb*. He argues that because verse 53 speaks about the Prophet's wives and Companions, the "greater purity for your hearts" does not refer to sexual thoughts that may enter their hearts but rather to thoughts of licit marriage. Nor does al-Qaraḍāwī agree that the phrase "do so behind a screen [*ḥijāb*]" can be deemed evidence for the *niqāb* because it specifically refers to the Prophet's wives, who cannot be said to represent women in general, as the Qur'ān states in Q33:32: "Wives of the Prophet, you are not like any other woman." In other words, the Qur'ān requires that the Prophet's wives be treated with greater strictness than women in general.[89]

As for verse 59, which commands women to wrap themselves in a *jilbāb*, al-Qaraḍāwī notes that exegetes do not agree on what this garment is or on the action required with respect to it. Some have argued that the verse requires women to hide the entire face so nothing but one eye can be seen. Other commentaries say that the *jilbāb* is a shorter and wider garment than the woman's headdress (*khimār*). At any rate, al-Qaraḍāwī concludes, verse 59 does not require the face to be hidden, and neither is there evidence for such a requirement elsewhere in the Qur'ān, the Sunna, or the consensus of legal opinion.[90]

In addressing the *jilbāb* verse, al-Qaraḍāwī applies the principle that even where the *sharīʿa* does provide an instrument for the implementation of its goal, this instrument is not binding but may evolve with changing circumstances. Al-Qaraḍāwī criticizes clerics who confuse the instrument with the goal. Thus, Q33:59 mentions the outer garments (*jalābīb*), which women should wrap around themselves. However, al-Qaraḍāwī says that *jalābīb* are merely one possible kind of garment with which a woman can fulfill the demand for a chaste and modest appearance. Other garments are possible as well, according to *sharīʿa*, because clothing differs in different countries and environments and may change with changing times, places, and needs.

The Muslim Liberals' Approach to the Issue of the Woman's Dress Code. The liberal Muḥammad Saʿīd al-ʿAshmāwī takes a completely different approach to the issue of the *ḥijāb*.[91] He contends that the *ḥijāb* in the sense of a head veil is not a religious commandment at all, but rather a social custom. In fact, he argues that issues of dress code are among the aspects of life that depend on social customs (*aʿrāf*) and traditions (*taqālīd*) and have nothing to do with religion and the *sharīʿa*. Islam, he says, merely commands women to be modest and chaste (*iḥtishām, ʿiffa*). The real sense of the *ḥijāb* is therefore spiritual: restraining lust and sinful desires.

According to al-ʿAshmāwī, the *ḥijāb* is essentially a political slogan of Islamic movements that emerged as part of the Islamic awakening of the 1970s and 1980s in Egypt, which falsely present it as a sign of piety. It is an example of the use of religion for political and partisan purposes. He also points out that many women wear the *ḥijāb* but at the same time decorate their faces with makeup in complete contradiction to the purpose of the veil. Those who regard a woman's hair as *ʿawra*, he adds, will also regard her face, her voice, and her entire body as *ʿawra*. This notion, he argues, belongs to past eras; today it is espoused only by extremists and fanatics, and the result is a return to the *jāhiliyya*, a pre-Islamic situation.[92]

Like many other liberals, al-ʿAshmāwī contends that nobody has a right to impose a certain dress code on women, either by physical coercion or by spiritual coercion—for example, by accusing them of heresy. "It is not the way of the Qur'ān and of Islam to coerce [*ikrāh*] compliance with a commandment [*ḥukm*] or even with the laws of Allah's punishments [*ḥudūd*]. [Islam's] way is always to set a good example and dispense good advice." He mentions the Qur'ān proclamation that "there is no coercion in religion [*lā ikrāha fī al-dīn*" (2:256), arguing that if this is true for the religion as a whole, it must surely be true for individual laws and commandments. Even if failing to wear the *ḥijāb* is a sin, he says, that is between the individual and Allah and is not a matter for intervention by anyone else.[93]

Another argument al-'Ashmāwī raises, also typical of the liberal thinking on this issue, is that the particular definitions of the term *'awra* were not provided by Allah in the Qur'ān, but rather by Muslim jurists. Because the definition of the term is human rather than divine in origin, adapting it to the norms of the time and place does not contravene Islam or the *sharī'a*. In fact, al-'Ashmāwī contends that neither the Qur'ān nor the *ḥadīth* contain an explicit directive to wear a headdress. As for Q24:31, which forms the basis for al-Qaraḍāwī's ruling that women are required to wear the *khimār*, head scarves, al-'Ashmāwī asserts that it was required by specific circumstances that prevailed during the Prophet's day. According to him, women in the Prophet's time used to cover their head but not the upper part of their chest. The verse therefore instructed the Muslim women to cover their chests in order to clearly differentiate them from the nonbelieving women around them. But today, when Islam is an established religion, there is no longer any need for this differentiation.[94] The important aspect of this explanation is the principle it illustrates: in understanding Qur'ānic verses and laws, al-'Ashmāwī relates them to the particular circumstances that prevailed in the Prophet's day and consequently regards them as temporary and as subject to change.

Al-'Ashmāwī also differs from al-Qaraḍāwī in his interpretation of the "*jilbāb* verse" (Q33:59). As stated earlier, al-Qaraḍāwī rejects the Salafī claim that this verse requires women to wear a face veil (today called a *niqāb*) on the grounds that exegetes do not agree on the nature of the garment mentioned in the verse or on how it is meant to be worn.[95] Al-'Ashmāwī does not agree with this approach, but instead, as in the case of the previous verse, he examines the circumstances in which the verse descended. He notes that, according to exegetes, women in those days used to relieve themselves in the open desert because homes were not equipped with toilets. Sinful men used this opportunity to harass the women, especially slave girls, who dressed immodestly and did not cover their faces. Muslim women who dressed immodestly would be mistaken for slave girls and be molested as well. The verse therefore instructed the Muslim women to wear a *jilbāb*—a garment that, according to al-ʿAshmāwī, covered the whole body, including the face—so as to differentiate themselves from the slave girls and avoid molestation. According to al-ʿAshmāwī, this law, too, was valid as long as the circumstances that warranted it prevailed, but today circumstances are different, so the law no longer holds.[96]

Another writer who expresses the liberal approach to the Muslim woman's dress code is Gamāl al-Bannā, whose views on the matter are similar to al-ʿAshmāwī's but more radical. He asserts that Muslim clerics have falsely presented various issues related to women, in particular the issue of the *ḥijāb*, as sacred Islamic tenets when in fact they are nothing but *jāhilī* (pre-Islamic) customs. These customs have been "anointed with the oil of Islam" and dressed up as essentials of the faith ("*al-maʿlūm min al-dīn bi-l-ḍarūra*") in order to depict women as the enemies of virtue and piety. But, according to Gamāl al-Bannā, this presentation is far from the true spirit of the Qur'ān and the Sunna, which treat women objectively and justly.[97]

Perusing the context in which the word *ḥijāb* appears in the Qur'ān, al-Bannā comes to the conclusion that it does not refer to a garment at all. Regarding Q24:31, which forbids a woman to expose her beauty "except for that which appears thereof," and on which al-Qaraḍāwī based his ruling about the obligatory nature of the *khimār*, al-Bannā contends that its wording is deliberately vague in order to allow a range of different interpretations. Had the Qur'ān wished to be more definite, he says, the verse would have been worded more explicitly. It is vague because the Qur'ān intended Muslims to adapt its interpretation to the specific time, place, and values.[98]

According to Gamāl al-Bannā, Islam advocates equity and equality between the sexes in both rights and duties, but it also stresses the importance of women's modesty and places constraints on sexual relations. This was a revolution in women's status in comparison to their inferior status during the *jāhiliyya*. He argues that women during the Prophet's era did not wear a *niqāb*, for they took an active part in public life, attended the mosque, performed pilgrimage, and even took part in war, activities with which wearing a face veil is not suitable. It was only later, he says, after the period of the Righteous Caliphs, that the custom of wearing a face veil emerged, as women's status declined and they were gradually isolated from society. This decline was due in part to the infiltration of foreign influences, such as the Persian in the Abbasid period and the Turkish and Greek in subsequent periods, he speculates.[99]

Like al-Qaraḍāwī, Gamāl al-Bannā rejects the Salafī *fatwā*s that mandate the *niqāb* for women on the grounds that it is what is meant by *ḥijāb* in the Qur'ān. Addressing Ibn Bāz's ruling on this matter, he condemns it in even harsher terms than al-Qaraḍāwī's: "The weakness and arrogance of this ruling are very clear. This is what convinces us that the enthusiasm for the *niqāb* does not originate in Qur'ānic texts but rather in the [jurists'] temperament, in an entrenched prejudice that regards women as temptresses, and in a tendency to judge [both] men and women harshly."[100]

Gamāl Al-Bannā asserts that it is the veil that led to the exclusion of Muslim women from society, to the elimination of their personhood, and to the disregard of their abilities, which, in turn, led to the paralysis and backwardness of Muslim society at large. He emphasizes that no matter how the *ḥijāb* is defined, it is not part of the faith, and women who choose not to wear it must not be accused of violating the laws of Islam. "We must not allow ourselves to interfere in an issue that is a woman's private business and on which she alone, as a human being, has the right to decide."[101]

Liberal intellectual Fu'ād Zakariyyā, who, as mentioned, clashed horns with al-Qaraḍāwī in the debates between the Islamists and secularists in Egypt, accuses the contemporary Muslim movements of focusing on the outward aspects of the faith, such as the *ḥijāb* and the woman's dress code in general, instead of on crucial aspects of public and social life. Dress codes, he argues, have particular social functions that differ from society to society and from period to period. Hence, religious texts referring to dress codes are not absolute and must be interpreted according to the prevailing social norms. He also wonders why modern Muslims should adopt ancient dress codes when they would not even dream of adopting other obsolete practices from the past, such as traveling on pack animals or living in tents.[102]

Interpreting the Texts Concerning Women

Wael Hallaq distinguishes between two approaches. There are those whom he calls "reformists of Muslim law," headed by Muḥammad 'Abduh, Rashīd Riḍā, and Ḥasan al-Turābī (d. 2016), who proposed the principle of "religious utilitarianism," with its cornerstone *maṣlaḥa*. According to Hallaq, they proposed a concept without developing a comprehensive legal methodology, so their initiative remained relative. The liberal approach to Islamic law as represented by Muḥammad Sa'īd al-'Ashmāwī, in contrast, understands revelation as both text and context; it does not perceive the link between the text and modern society to be based on a literal understanding of the former, but rather on an interpretation of the text's spirit and its broad goals.[103] The analysis of al-Qaraḍāwī's rulings in this chapter leads to the conclusion that in comparison to the liberal interpretation, the *wasaṭī* interpretation considers the literal meaning of the texts more than their general spirit and goals. The two approaches are also examined and compared here in the context of social issues.

The debate between the *wasaṭī* and liberal streams pivots on the interpretation of texts from the Qur'ān and *ḥadīth*. The difference in their approaches is clearly illustrated by their responses to Salafī rulings that limit women's freedom and exclude them from public life on the basis of various scriptural texts. The liberals and al-Qaraḍāwī agree that Islam liberated women from their pre-Islamic state of bondage and that the current state of women in the Islamic world does not reflect the spirit of the Qur'ān and the Sunna. But the difference between them is evident, for example, in their interpretation of the Qur'ānic passage that addresses the Prophet's wives and instructs them to "abide in your houses [*wa-qarna fī buyūtikunna*]" (Q33:33). The Salafī Ibn Bāz cited this verse in a *fatwā* that banned women from driving, stating that it instructs the Prophet's wives in particular but also Muslim women in general to abide (*istiqrār*) indoors.[104]

Al-Qaraḍāwī and Gamāl al-Bannā, in contrast, hold that the passage is addressed exclusively to the Prophet's wives, not to all Muslim women. Al-Qaraḍāwī points out that Muslim women certainly leave their homes, to study and to work in various professions, such as teaching and even practicing medicine. He argues further that the verse did not prescribe confinement even for the Prophet's wives, for they definitely left their homes: 'Ā'isha joined the Battle of the Camel (656 CE) to take revenge upon 'Alī for killing 'Uthmān. The Qur'ān, he says, prescribes confinement only as punishment for women who commit a lewd act (*fāḥisha*), as stated in 4:15.[105]

Gamāl al-Bannā, in explaining Q33:33, adopts a different interpretation of the verb that is usually read as *qarna*, "abide." Following classical exegete Ibn Jarīr al-Ṭabarī (d. 923), he reads it as *qirna*, "possess prestige and honor." He adds that had Allah wanted women to cover their hair and face, remain indoors, and avoid contact with men, the Qur'ān would have stated this explicitly. The Qur'ān instead deliberately states its directives, including those pertaining to women, in very general terms, open to a range of interpretations. "There is no need to put words in the mouth of the Qur'ān when the Qur'ān does not actually say them, and there is no need to invent interpretations and ascribe them to the Qur'ān when they actually originate in the minds of the interpreters," he states.[106]

The essential difference between the *wasaṭī* al-Qaraḍāwī and the liberals, including Gamāl al-Bannā, is that, according to the latter, the interpretation of the Qur'ān must be adapted to the prevailing circumstances and norms, even to the extent of discarding certain laws if they are at odds with modern values and the circumstances that warranted them no longer prevail. For example, Gamāl al-Bannā argues that the value of justice mandates complete equality and lack of discrimination between men and women—for example, in laws of inheritance and testimony, even if this contradicts specific verses in the Qur'ān. He attempts to justify this view by citing Q25:73, from which he infers that men must not be "deaf and blind" in reading the Word of God but must approach it with open eyes and ears.[107] Al-'Ashmāwī calls this principle "the temporality of Qur'ānic laws [*waqtiyyat al-aḥkām*]." As stated earlier, he denounces the streams that "politicize Islam," reject this temporality—that is, deny man the right to legislate and to adapt the divine law to the changing times and values—and, moreover, attempt to enforce their views using violence and terror. Like other liberals, he points out that the Qur'ān includes only a small number of laws pertaining to interpersonal relations (*mu'āmalāt*) and that the few laws it does contain are phrased very generally and therefore require *ijtihād* by the Muslim *umma* in order to interpret and implement them. This was deliberate, he argues; Allah meant

> to leave legislation, with the exception of very general principles, to the nation, which is required to perform *ijtihād* using its faculties of reasoning [*ra'y*], inventiveness [*ibtidā'*], and innovation and with sensitivity to the changing circumstances. This is necessary because whereas Islam itself is a universal and comprehensive religion with a humane and eternal *sharī'a*, the laws themselves are, by their very nature, local rather than global and temporary rather than permanent.[108]

Hence, the eternal values of the *sharī'a* need to be translated into temporary worldly laws.

Whereas the liberals recommend adapting the *sharī'a* to reality, al-Qaraḍāwī points out that many aspects of the reality in Muslim countries are at odds with the *sharī'a*. "We must elevate reality to the level of the *sharī'a*, not drag the *sharī'a* down to the abysmal level of reality," he says. "People's reality as well as their deeds and behavior must be subordinated to the *sharī'a*, for the *sharī'a* is Allah's Word, and Allah's Word is supreme." The shaykh complains that many domains of life are governed by foreign man-made laws (*qawānīn waḍ'iyya*), as opposed to divine laws, owing to the influence of Western imperialism. The Muslims do need to catch up with the developed world in many areas, he concedes, but this does not mean that Islam should be divested of its mission of guiding human life.[109]

Moreover, al-Qaraḍāwī states that any attempt to permit what Allah forbade on the pretext of adapting to modernity or to Western ways constitutes abandoning the "Muslim identity," defying Allah, and distorting His Word. This is a form of weakness in religion, asserts the shaykh. In fact, he encourages the Muslims "to shake off their inferiority complex vis-à-vis Western civilization and thought." In stark contrast to the liberals, he forbids any attempt to learn from the West or to borrow from it in matters of religion, morality, or ideology, for "the West has its religion, and we have ours, and we shall never abandon our religion in favor of Western [norms]. The West has its civilization, its heritage, its thought, and its values, and we have our own civilization, heritage, thought, and values, which emanate from our faith. We are not obliged to follow the West inch by inch, step by step, and enter the lizard's hole if [the West] enters it" (the last sentence is based on a *ḥadīth*).[110]

According to the liberals, the main reason for what they call the backwardness of Muslim thought and Muslim society is that Islam in its current form is not the Islam of Allah and His Messenger but rather the Islam of the *fuqahā'* and the schools of jurisprudence, formulated more than a thousand years ago. They propose that modern Islam be based on a new way of thinking anchored primarily in the Qur'ān itself, unsullied by medieval human interpretation. As Gamāl al-Bannā puts it, "The goal is Man, and the means is the Qur'ān." The Qur'ān, says al-Bannā, sets out principles of freedom, justice, tolerance, and forgiveness, whereas the *fuqahā'* and the schools of jurisprudence came up with the notion of *takfīr*. The Qur'ān recognizes that human beings err and therefore provides ways to repent, whereas the *fuqahā'* found errors unforgivable and originated the principle of *sadd al-dharī'a* (literally "blocking the means or eliminating pretexts")—that is, preventing misuse of legal means to illegal ends. Women were the first victims of this principle, he states, because it formed the basis for banning them even from the mosque to preclude any possibility of temptation.[111]

The liberals' harsh criticism of "the Islam of the *fuqahā'*" is also reflected in the epithets they apply to clerics such as al-Qaraḍāwī. Shākir al-Nābulsī, for example, calls them the "jurists of darkness and ignorance [*fuqahā' al-ẓalām wa-l-jahāla*]," writing, "None of the infidels of the West and the East, for all their atheism, did as much harm to Islam as the gang of jurists of darkness and ignorance."[112] Khālid Muḥammad Khālid wrote in his book *From Here We Begin* that the clerics, whom he called "members of the ranks of reactionaries [*rijāl al-ṭābūr al-raj'ī*]" reject women's rights in the name of religion or in the name of age-old Muslim customs or both and claim that women were created for one purpose only: to care for their homes, their husbands, and their children.[113] It should be mentioned that the liberals apply these epithets to al-Qaraḍāwī, among others, not only because of his rulings on women but also because of his rulings and statements about jihad, discussed in the previous chapter. As shown in the next subsection, the dispute between the three streams—*wasaṭī*, liberal, and Salafī—lies in their different interpretations of the texts of the Qur'ān and the Sunna.

Dealing with Textual Traditions That Discriminate against Women

Despite their different outlook on the relationship between the *sharī'a* and modernity, both al-Qaraḍāwī and the liberals have to contend with the same "textual heritage," which creates difficulties for both of them. One especially problematic text pertaining to women is the *ḥadīth* in which the Prophet describes women as "deficient in intelligence and religion [*nāqiṣāt 'aql wa-dīn*]." According to the *ḥadīth*, the Prophet said: "I have not seen anyone more deficient in intelligence and religion than you. An opinionated and sensible [*ḥāzim*] man could be led astray by some of you." The women then asked, "O Allah's Messenger! What is deficient in our intelligence and religion?" He said, "Is not the evidence of two women equal to the witness of one man?" They replied in the affirmative. He said, "This is the deficiency in her intelligence. Isn't it true that a woman can neither pray nor fast during her menses?" The women replied in the affirmative. He said, "This is the deficiency in her religion."[114]

Al-Qaraḍāwī, in addressing this *ḥadīth*, cites the analysis by 'Abd al-Ḥalīm Muḥammad Abū Shaqqa (d. 1995), which he describes as a *wasaṭī* analysis. In his book about women in Islam, Abū Shaqqa refers to the circumstances in which the *ḥadīth* was uttered, as part of a holiday sermon, and asks: "Do we [really] believe that the honorable Prophet, with his towering morality, would demean the status of women, their honor or their personality, in such festive circumstances?!" Not unlike Gamāl al-Bannā, he claims that the Prophet's intention was to express his amazement that "women, who have weaknesses, can overcome men of intelligence, namely his amazement at Allah's wisdom!" He adds that the Prophet uttered the phrase "deficient in intelligence and religion" only once, to grab people's attention before conveying an important message for women: that Allah gave them the power to befuddle even men of wisdom and that they must not abuse this power but use it only for virtuous purposes.[115]

It should be stressed that although Abū Shaqqa's argument is in some ways similar to Gamāl al-Bannā's, his basic assumption is that women have weaknesses and are indeed inferior to men in their intelligence. In fact, Abū Shaqqa (whose position is endorsed by al-Qaraḍāwī) argues that women are intellectually deficient for various biological, social, and psychological reasons, including their excessively emotional natures. He remarks, however, that the *ḥadīth* does not necessarily imply that women are intellectually inferior from birth; that, he says, is a matter for science to determine. Regarding the Prophet's utterance that women are also deficient in religion because they cannot pray or fast during their menses, Abū Shaqqa states that this can cause deficient piety in some women, although not necessarily in all of them.[116]

Gamāl al-Bannā argues that the *ḥadīth* has been misunderstood and that it instead means to praise women for their ability to influence the thinking of even sensible and opinionated men (an apologetic argument that al-Qaraḍāwī makes as well). He adds that the law regarding women's testimony and the law forbidding them to pray or fast during their menses are religious rulings that have nothing to do with their intelligence or piety.[117]

The liberal Qatari academic ʿAbd al-Ḥamīd al-Anṣārī also believes that the *ḥadīth* does not mean to describe women as less intelligent than men or inferior to them in any way. Explaining the inequality of men and women in matters of testimony, he says that it is limited to financial and criminal affairs and is motivated by the concern that women, owing to their lack of interest in finance or their "emotionality and forgetfulness," may be less reliable than men. "However, this was only a precaution, to remove any doubt in such cases." He concludes that men and women are equal in their mental faculties and that this *ḥadīth* cannot be used, for example, as grounds for denying women political rights.[118]

The Issue of Polygamy

An issue that is a topic of heated debate between the three streams and sheds light on their approaches is polygamy (*ta'addud al-zawjāt*). Ibn Bāz notes that Allah permitted a man to take up to four wives as long as he is confident of his ability to treat them fairly, as stated in Q4:3. In fact, Ibn Bāz contends that polygamy is preferable to monogamy as long as the conditions are met, for it has many advantages: it prevents promiscuity and adultery, raises the birth rate, and provides a solution for older unmarried women (*'awānis*), who are better off becoming third or fourth wives than remaining single. "Had polygamy not been necessary and lawful according to the *sharī'a*, and very beneficial, the Prophet would not have practiced it," he writes. In his ruling, he therefore urges governments to encourage polygamy and denounce those who oppose it.[119]

Taking an apologetic approach, al-Qaraḍāwī argues that polygamy is more moral and humane than the situation that prevails in the West, where men have "multiple girlfriends" rather than multiple wives. The West effectively allows multiple partners, he says, but the man's extramarital partners have no official status and therefore no financial rights; their number is not limited; and any children born to them are regarded as bastards. Moreover, he adds, polygamy provides a solution in cases of necessity—for instance, when the woman is barren or when she cannot satisfy her husband's sexual appetite because her libido is weak or because she is ill or has a prolonged menstrual period. In such cases, the wife "does not satisfy the man's desire and does not keep his eye from wandering toward this or that woman, for men are unable to control [their desire] for women. Should [the man] then not be allowed to take another legal wife, instead of looking for a girlfriend or divorcing his first wife?" he asks.[120]

Al-Qaraḍāwī acknowledges that Muslims often abuse the practice of polygamy in ways that harm the family—for instance, by favoring a new wife over the old one, so that the old wife feels that "she is neither married nor divorced," or by favoring the children of one wife over the children of the other, thus causing jealousy between the children. However, the flaw is not in the law itself but in the way it is implemented, he stresses, and, in any case, polygamy is still preferable to the adultery that prevails in the West.[121]

The shaykh points out that "the propagandists of westernization [*du'āt al-taghrīb*]" who wish to ban polygamy often base their position on the Qur'ān, verse 4:129, which says "you will never be able to treat wives equally, even if you should strive [to do so]." They argue that the Qur'ān essentially bans polygamy because it requires the man to treat his wives equally and then proclaims that no man is able to meet this condition. This argument is false, says the shaykh, because it misconstrues Q4:129. This verse refers not to the man's actions but to his feelings, proclaiming that men will inevitably love one wife or want one wife more than the others, for such is human nature. The Qur'ān does not forbid this, says the shaykh; it only forbids the husband from acting on this preference, exhorting him to provide for his wives equally in food, drink, housing, finances, and the time he spends with each of them.[122]

It should be noted that although al-Qaraḍāwī presumes to follow in the footsteps of the Islamic reformers (*muṣliḥūn*) of the late nineteenth and early twentieth centuries, such as Muḥammad 'Abduh, his ruling on the central issue of polygamy is completely different from 'Abduh's. The latter observed that polygamy tends to characterize societies where women's status is low and to disappear in societies where their status is high. Showing understanding and empathy for women, he described polygamy as degrading and painful for them because "no woman enjoys sharing her husband with another, just as no man would tolerate sharing his love for his wife with another." Like Gamāl al-Bannā, he rejected the view (espoused by al-Qaraḍāwī, among others) that the Qur'ān does not expect a man to love his wives in equal measure. To his mind, polygamy is unjustified even if the woman is ill and unable to fulfill some of her marital duties. If this happens, the husband must tolerate it, just as the wife is required to tolerate it if her husband falls ill, he says. Polygamy, concluded 'Abduh, is just an excuse (*ḥīla*) to satisfy bestial desires with a religious stamp of approval and is "a sign of moral corruption, confusion, and hedonism." Based on Q4:3 and Q4:129, he asserted, like others, that the Qur'ān essentially banned polygamy by associating it with an impossible condition.[123]

Al-Qaraḍāwī's position on polygamy again contrasts with that of Gamāl al-Bannā. The latter points out that Q4:3 permits polygamy, but only in the context of justice for orphans: "And if you fear that you will not deal justly with the orphans, then marry those that please you of [other] women, two or three or four."[124] It should be mentioned that exegetes provided different explanations for the first half of the verse. Some suggested that it forbids a man to marry orphan girls under his protection if he fears he may not treat them justly—for example, in terms of their dowries. Others suggested that it refers to men who are providing for orphans and is intended to ban them from marrying more than four wives if they fear that this will leave them with insufficient funds to properly care for the orphans. It is curious that al-Qaraḍāwī, who generally considers the context of Qur'ānic verses, fails to address this point at all.

Gamāl Al-Bannā also stresses that in its second half Q4:3 reiterates that polygamy depends on the ability to be just, saying, "If you fear that you will not be just, then [marry only] one." In other words, this verse, which is presented as main prooftext for the lawfulness of polygamy, implicitly criticizes this practice as unjust and undesirable. Gamāl al-Bannā argues further that the main motivation for polygamy is men's desire to vary their love life and that the jurists who condone it view it from this masculine perspective while completely ignoring the woman and her feelings. When a man takes a second wife, he says, the first wife is usually devastated, even if her husband treats her fairly in material terms, because women value their husband's love and devotion above anything else. As for the claim that polygamy saves some women from the fate of remaining "old maids," unmarried and childless, Gamāl al-Bannā notes that if a woman remains childless, that is God's will. Moreover, some men accuse their wives of being barren when it is they themselves who are the source of the problem, as modern medical tests can show. Even if it is the wife who is barren, it is not her fault, and the husband should accept this rather than act selfishly by taking another wife, says al-Bannā.[125]

Gamāl al-Bannā rejects al-Qaraḍāwī's claim about Q4:129, that the Qur'ān regards the man's unequal feelings toward his wives as an inescapable fact and therefore excuses it. The Qur'ān, insists al-Bannā, describes marriage as based on affection and mercy (Q30:21) and therefore surely acknowledges that emotional discrimination can destabilize a marriage. He also rejects al-Qaraḍāwī's denouncement of the Western practice of "multiple girlfriends," stating that the Islamic practice of polygamy grants the wife only "half a husband" or less, whereas the Western practice of a husband having girlfriends and a wife having boyfriends does not discriminate between men and women. He concludes that in modern times there is no justification for polygamy and that it should be allowed only in special cases and only with the first wife's consent.[126]

Al-Qaraḍāwī's *Wasaṭī* Dogmatism: The Case of Homosexuality

Al-Qaraḍāwī's rulings on homosexuality shed further light on his approach to issues involving a clash between the *sharīʿa*, on the one hand, and social realities and human rights, on the other. In his book *The Lawful and the Prohibited in Islam* (1960), directed at Muslims living in non-Muslim countries, especially in the West, he refers to male homosexuality as "a depraved act [*ʿamal khabīth*] that contravenes innate human nature (*fiṭra*), plunges [the perpetrator] into the depths of contamination and filth, corrupts masculinity, and is a crime against rightful femininity." When this sin spreads in a community, he adds, it corrupts and enslaves the community, causing it to forget every moral standard. This is evident from the story of the people of Lot (Q26:165–66, the Qur'ānic version of the story of Sodom and Gomorrah), who performed homosexual acts and forsook their women. According to al-Qaraḍāwī, they perverted their inborn nature and lost their reason and their morals, and the same happens to anyone who engages in homosexual sex.[127]

The shaykh elaborated on the issue of (male and female) homosexuality in an episode of his television program *Sharīʿa and Life* in June 2006. Here he again relied mainly on the key concept of *fiṭra*, saying that it is in man's inborn nature—instilled in him by God—to be attracted to the opposite sex. Same-sex attraction is therefore at odds with God's wisdom and intention, a perversion (*shudhūdh*) that cannot be proper or beneficial. Moreover, it cannot be innate but must be an individual choice. He finds support for this view in Q15:72, which states that the people of Lot were drunk when they engaged in homosexual behavior—that is, were in a state of altered consciousness. In the television program, he characterized homosexuality as a mental disorder, dismissing scientific theories that claim otherwise and the fact that homosexuality has been removed from the list of mental illnesses. The cure, he said, is to abstain from such acts, and the treatment, to be developed and administered by physicians, sociologists, and clerics, should involve education and the promotion of marriage.[128]

Interestingly, in order to achieve this "cure," he advocates easing some of the constraints of conservative Muslim society so as to allow more opportunities for men and women to meet. The largest threat, in his opinion, is allowing public displays of homosexuality, which can cause society to view it as normal. He warns the Muslims not to emulate the West in this regard, but to preserve its norms of behavior, virtue, and masculinity, for instance by forbidding men to wear women's clothing and vice versa. The religious duty of commanding right and forbidding wrong, he adds, obligates Muslims to fight the phenomenon of homosexuality, including by shunning homosexuals and refraining from giving them any encouragement.[129]

This ruling, which proclaims homosexuality an illness that needs to be cured, in contrast to the scientific consensus on this issue, also contradicts one of the fundamental juristic principles set out by al-Qaraḍāwī himself: the principle that rulings must change to suit the time, place, norms, and circumstances—for instance, when new information becomes available. An example of al-Qaraḍāwī's application of this principle is his ruling on smoking. Modern science, he notes, has found that smoking is harmful because it causes lung cancer and other diseases; consequently, jurists must ban it. "Since [the state of medical] knowledge has changed, the *fatwā* must also change," he explains. "The jurists' ruling must be based on a doctor's opinion. If a doctor says something is harmful, the jurist must proclaim it forbidden [*ḥarām*]."[130] However, when it comes to homosexuality, al-Qaraḍāwī does not apply the same principle. On the contrary, he denounces clerics and physicians who accept this aspect of humanity, accusing them of succumbing to Western culture and using science as an excuse, all with the aim of spreading homosexuality and presenting it as natural.[131]

Regarding the punishment for homosexuality, the shaykh states that it should be identical to the punishment for *zinā*, adultery. However, of the various punishments that jurists have suggested for *zinā*, he advocates choosing the lighter ones owing to the prevalence of homosexuality in our times. He believes that the prevalence of a negative practice (*'umūm al-balwā*, to use the Islamic term) indicates that it fulfills a need and therefore should not be punished too severely.[132] As another example, he mentions the practice of watching television. Some of the content on television contravenes the *sharī'a*, he says, but because watching television has become a ubiquitous pastime, it apparently fulfills a need and should not be proclaimed forbidden in itself.[133]

This does not mean that al-Qaraḍāwī advocates letting homosexuals go unpunished. In justifying the need to punish them, he argues (as already mentioned) that homosexuality is a conscious choice because it cannot be innate: Allah would never forbid a behavior that cannot be helped because it is part of human nature. Al-Qaraḍāwī likens homosexuality to Adam's eating from the Tree of Knowledge (Q2:35–36): it is essentially a sin of failing to withstand temptation, and as such it merits a penalty. The shaykh does, however, make a distinction between *liwāṭ* (intercourse between two men) and *siḥāq* (intercourse between two women), saying that the latter does not involve penetration and therefore merits a lighter punishment.[134]

Classical jurists are divided on the proper penalty for intercourse between two men, but most of them agree that it merits the death penalty, based on the following *ḥadith*: "If you find anyone doing as Lot's people did, kill the one who does it and the one to whom it is done." Some contend that homosexuals must be thrown to their death from a high place (such as a roof or a cliff) and then stoned, based on the punishment meted out to the people of Lot in the Qur'ān (15:74): "We made the highest part [of the city] its lowest and rained upon them stones of hard clay." As mentioned, al-Qaraḍāwī wishes to choose the punishment most suitable to our period, in which homosexuality is fairly common, and so opts for the punishment specified for *zinā*. This means stoning to death if the perpetrator is married and flogging if he is not.[135]

Regarding intercourse between two women, al-Qaraḍāwī rules, following the classical jurists, that it does not constitute *zinā* because no penetration takes place, and therefore the penalty (*ta'zīr*) is at the discretion of the *qāḍī*, the judge, and its goal is education and prevention.[136]

The liberal response to al-Qaraḍāwī's ruling on homosexuality is harsh. Āmal Qarāmī (b. 1962), a Tunisian professor of gender studies, writes: "It is clear and obvious that al-Qaraḍāwī and other religious preachers of his ilk lack scientific knowledge or any accurate understanding of the modern methodologies of gender analysis. Consequently, they are unable to understand the behavior of homosexuals or to present political, economic, social, and psychological analyses of the basic problems that trouble the young people and the challenges they face."[137]

According to Qarāmī, the solutions proposed by al-Qaraḍāwī and other preachers are unrealistic and irrelevant to the present age. The rationale of adhering to the rulings of the past is a sterile one, she says, for their validity is not eternal, despite the sanctity that has been attributed to them. "Can homosexuals be burned today, as the Companions of the Prophet used to do?" she asks. "Can Muslims be expected to follow the principle of excluding, expelling, marginalizing, and condemning them and using every kind of violence against them?" She describes al-Qaraḍāwī's view as reflecting a culture of intimidation, exclusion, criminalization, and violence.[138]

Saudi shaykh Salmān al-ʿAwda (b. 1956), one of the leaders of the Saudi Awakening (Ṣaḥwa) movement in the 1980s and 1990s, sparked an uproar in the Muslim world when he said in an interview with a Swedish newspaper in 2016 that homosexuality is a sin (*ithm*), but one that can be punished only in the world to come, not in this world. He explained that Islam grants individuals freedom of choice, and they must bear the consequences of their choices in the afterlife; but this does not mean that homosexuals are excluded from the fold of Islam. He stressed, however, that homosexuals must not flaunt their inclinations in public.[139]

Al-Qaraḍāwī's ruling on homosexuality exemplifies his dogmatism and conservatism. He essentially adopts the opinion of Salafis such as Ibn Bāz, who regard it as one of the gravest sins (*kabā'ir*).[140] As Scott Kugle and Stephen Hunt state, al-Qaraḍāwī's view is "actually an aggressive retrenchment of patriarchal masculinity, refusing dialogue with Muslim homosexuals, denying homosexuality as a cultural construct, and subsequently eliding homosexuals and their experience as members of the Islamic community."[141] Al-Qaraḍāwī's view contrasts with that of the liberals, who regard secularism and democracy as "the two wings of the bird of liberty"[142] and whose basic premise is respect for human rights and human freedom, including sexual freedom. As in the case of the women's issues discussed earlier, in addressing the issue of homosexuality the liberals believe in the temporality of Qur'ānic laws and in the need to adapt them (and even discard them) to the changing times and circumstances.

Conclusion

An examination of the *wasaṭī*, Salafī, and liberal approaches to social issues in general and to women's issues in particular reveals that *wasaṭiyya* and Salafism are basically similar in their approaches, whereas liberalism takes a very different line. The Salafīs and *wasaṭī*s share the belief that the laws set out in the Qur'ān and *ḥadīth* about these issues are binding—not only the general principles but also the specific laws, such as those pertaining to the *ḥijāb*. The liberals, in contrast, point out that specific laws of this kind form a very small portion of the Qur'ān, whereas the majority of verses set out general moral guidelines, leaving room for *ijtihād* to adapt the particulars to the circumstances and the spirit of the age. This difference in perspective yields very different rulings, with the liberals giving much weight to the principles of human and women's rights and to individual freedoms, the *wasaṭī*s and Salafīs taking a patriarchal approach, with little consideration for women's feelings and needs. The *wasaṭī*s and Salafīs assume, as their point of departure, that men and women are different in their inborn nature and roles and that women are innately suitable for domestic functions. The liberals, however, regard women first of all as human beings, entitled to the same rights and freedoms as men, such as the freedom to dress as they please, to partake in political life, and to assume public roles, up to and including that of president. Aḥmad al-Baghdādī writes that "the essence of the issue is that, as human beings, women, just like men, are entitled to achieve everything men have achieved in society. The issue basically comes down to human rights." He states further that the twenty-first century will be "the century of the woman," in which women will act within parliament to change the laws that discriminate against them.[143]

Far from dismissing the core texts of Islam, the liberals hold that the Qur'ān and Sunna lay down the foundations for women's equality and rights and thus provide the key for liberating women from the shackles of conservative social customs. They argue that the scriptural laws that differentiate between men and women, such as the testimony law, were born of specific circumstances that no longer prevail, rendering these laws obsolete. Regarding directives that are stated more generally or vaguely, such as the *ḥijāb* law, the liberals contend that these laws, in their fundamental spirit, uphold rather than contravene the modern values of human equality and dignity. Accordingly, the liberals advocate a flexible interpretation of these laws that reflects this spirit and is compatible with contemporary norms.

According to the liberals, it is not the Islam of the Qur'ān and the Sunna but rather "the Islam of the *fuqahā*'" that rejects such flexibility and that is responsible for the oppression of women in the Muslim world. Indeed, the *wasaṭī*s take a dogmatic approach that rejects any possibility of abolishing scriptural laws. They contend with "problematic texts" by allowing a limited degree of flexibility, or pragmatism, in their implementation and by offering apologetic interpretations that seek either to disguise or to justify the texts' discriminatory nature in order to defend the image of Islam, especially in the eyes of the West.

Conclusion

Islam at a Crossroads

The Clash within Islam: *Wasaṭī* and Jihadi Salafism versus Liberalism

The clash within Islam pitches the Salafīs—comprising a wide spectrum of ideologies, from *wasaṭī* to jihadi—against the liberals. The Egyptian leftist Muḥammad Rif'at al-Sa'īd (d. 2017), the head of the Tajammu' Party and a fierce opponent of the MB, characterized this clash very aptly:

> The battle with the "purported Muslims" [*muta'aslimūn*] is neither easy nor close to a conclusion. The danger stems from the fact that it is not a democratic struggle between two ways of thinking, but rather [a struggle between] progressive thinking armed with understanding, knowledge, and subtlety and thinking that is armed with guns, knives, and inquisition courts. Moreover, the enlightened secularists enter the fray openly and by the light of day, whereas the purported Muslim groups operate under the cover of darkness, sometimes employing *taqiyya* [concealment] and sometimes granting religious legitimacy to their false claims.[1]

Rif'at al-Sa'īd calls the Islamists "purported Muslims" because, according to him, they claim to represent the genuine Islam when the opposite is true. This name also suits the political groups that hide behind the religion—chiefly the MB, he says.[2]

Rif'at al-Sa'īd states further that despite the impotence of these streams' ideology, which in his opinion is rife with contradictions and rejects the modern age along with its science and its achievements, this ideology is capable of attracting and misleading large sectors of Muslim societies, both Arab and non-Arab. This stems from the ignorance of these societies, many of whose members are illiterate and suffer from a lack of true enlightenment and education, even among the so-called educated circles. Their backwardness constitutes fertile ground for the growth of the "false Islam," he explains.[3]

The liberal writers identify a crisis in the contemporary religious discourse. In an interview in 2016, al-Anṣārī described this discourse as being out of touch with society, for while society changes, this discourse remains married to the past. It seeks to preoccupy the Muslims with obsolete issues such as the woman's veil, the mingling of men and women, accusations of heresy, invective toward the Jews and the Christians, and the like, while the Muslim youth is preoccupied with completely different matters.[4] In an earlier interview, he had commented that the religious discourse had failed to achieve what should be its main goals: strengthening the common denominator between all religions and between all schools and sects of Islam, in particular between the Sunnīs and Shīʿīs; fostering diligence and productiveness in the Muslim youth; promoting openness toward non-Muslims; improving the image of Islam; and protecting Muslim societies from the ills of religious extremism and excess while inoculating the youth against the virus of terrorist thinking.[5]

Although al-Qaraḍāwī claims to support openness toward other cultures, he places many constraints on this openness. For example, he warns against becoming mesmerized with the West and developing feelings of inferiority toward it as well as against the "dangerous infiltration" of Western culture: "The loyal guardians of this *umma* and its conscience must guard against invasion and infiltration. They must be alert and confront this dangerous infiltration, especially today, in the age of so-called globalization, which America is spreading in the world, . . . economic, social, political, and cultural globalization."[6]

Addressing the *tajdīd*, renewal, of religious discourse, ʿAbd al-Ḥamīd al-Anṣārī identifies several obstacles that hinder it. The main obstacle, in his eyes, is the Muslim clerics' commitment to the past and its heritage. He clarifies that he does not advocate discarding the Islamic heritage as a whole, only its negative extremist and inhumane aspects. Another obstacle he discerns is excessive reverence for various scholars, contemporary ones but especially ancient ones, whose rulings were relevant to the problems of the past but are not relevant to those of the present.[7] An interesting example of such reverence is in fact provided by al-Qaraḍāwī's disciples and their admiration for the shaykh. Mas'ūd Ṣabrī, for instance, calls al-Qaraḍāwī "a unique and rare [scholar]," "the Ibn Taymiyya of our age," and "a gift from Allah," blessed with exceptional abilities.[8]

Al-Qaraḍāwī's *wasaṭiyya* displays many of the characteristics that the liberals identify as the faults of contemporary Islamic discourse. Al-Anṣārī and other liberals, chiefly Naṣr Ḥāmid Abū Zayd, describe this discourse as "excluding" or "exclusionary" (*iqṣā'ī*), meaning that it excludes and rejects anyone who disagrees with it. The Islamists, says al-Anṣārī, including al-Qaraḍāwī and the ideologues of global jihad, brand all their opponents as infidels, just as the Egyptian nationalists of the 1970s branded all their opponents as traitors. They claim a monopoly over Islam and its interpretation, although neither they nor anyone else is entitled to claim such a monopoly. According to al-Anṣārī, the root of all evil is the politicization of the religion, whose most blatant representative today is al-Qaraḍāwī. This politicization is expressed first of all in using the mosque pulpits to promote political and partisan agendas. The mosque, al-Anṣārī argues, should dispense religious guidance to worshippers, regardless of their political affiliation; Friday sermons must not be transformed into political manifestos; and preachers must not become political analysts. Hinting at al-Qaraḍāwī, he adds: "One of the prominent stars of political Islam, whose many disciples[9] describe him as 'the jurist of the Awakening' [*faqīh al-ṣaḥwa*], has turned his Friday pulpit into a private political platform from which he dispenses his personal political views and opinions on a weekly basis."[10]

The remedy for this politicization, according to the liberals, is what al-Anṣārī calls "the humanization of the religious discourse [*ansanat al-khiṭāb al-dīnī*]." Two aspects of this humanization are fostering in the Muslim youth a love of life, labor, growth, and development and encouraging them to devote their abilities to the advancement of culture instead of destruction and killing. Describing the religious discourse he would like to see, al-Anṣārī says: "We want a humane, tolerant discourse that is compatible with the spirit of the age and is open to human cultures. [A discourse] that allays the world's fear of us and our own fears of the world. We have lost much in rejecting the world, more than the world lost in rejecting us."[11]

As stated, the liberals condemn al-Qaraḍāwī as a "political scholar" and contend that the politicization of Islam leads to terror in the name of the faith. Al-Qaraḍāwī, in contrast, believes that the true Islam, as established by Allah, is necessarily political. "If you divest Islam of politics, you turn it into a different religion, which might be Buddhism, Christianity, or what have you but is not Islam," he writes.[12] According to the shaykh, Islam is political because it has clear positions on many issues that are blatantly political in nature. Moreover, Muslims must necessarily be political in their character, for each and every one of them is commanded by his faith to promote good and forbid evil—for instance, by fighting corruption. As for the function of the mosque, the shaykh states that since the dawn of Islam, the mosque has always played an important part in goading Muslims to wage jihad for Allah and oppose their enemies.[13] In fact, he claims that during the glory days of Islam, the mosque was not only a place of worship but also a place of politics. It was only during periods of Islam's decline that it served solely as a place of prayer and ritual. When this happens, Friday sermons become "dead sermons" that deal only with otherworldly topics, such as the tortures of the grave, and not with current affairs, he says. Accordingly, al-Qaraḍāwī believes that jurists are qualified to rule on any topic, including political ones, after studying the issue at hand.[14]

The liberals contend that the solution to the crisis of Islam lies in secularism, which is eventually bound to defeat what they call *uṣūliyya*—the fundamentalist Islam of the MB and jihadi Salafism. "These forces of darkness," says the liberal Shākir al-Nābulsī, "move backward every day, while the forces of light and enlightenment move forward every day, albeit slowly, because darkness always spreads more quickly than light." Al-Nābulsī believes that *uṣūliyya* is bankrupt and that not a single one of its clerics or jurists can hold his ground against a secular liberal philosopher or writer.[15]

Muslim clerics, headed by al-Qaraḍāwī, claim that secularism is "against religion," by which claim they mean to discredit it in the eyes of

Muslim societies. The liberals, for their part, argue that secularism is not antireligion; on the contrary, it aims to protect religion by distancing it from politics—that is, by "distancing the sacred from the profane [*ib'ād al-muqaddas 'an al-mudannas*]" and the eternal from the turbulent and ever changing, as al-Nābulsī puts it. Moreover, al-Nābulsī contends that secularism in the Muslim world must not involve a departure from religion but must coexist with—and in fact grow out of—the religion. The failure of past attempts to promote secularism in the Muslim world has demonstrated that Arab liberalism must be Islamic, he explains, if only in order to prevent clerics such as al-Qaraḍāwī from attacking liberals as "un-Islamic," "atheists," or Khawārij. He adds that this kind of Islamic secularism requires knowledge of the religion and its sources.[16]

According to the liberals, the notion of "Islamic secularism" is not an oxymoron because the seeds of *'ilmāniyya* exist within Islam itself. The Islam of the Qur'ān (like liberalism and unlike the Islam of the *fuqahā'*) allows freedom of belief, preaches equality, and holds that human beings are responsible for changing their own state of being (Q13:11). Regarding Qur'ānic texts that make a distinction between men and women and are thus at odds with liberal values (such as the texts on testimony that were addressed in this book), the liberals contend that they were appropriate for their time and place but are no longer relevant in our day and age.[17]

In his book *The Arabs between Liberalism and Religious Fundamentalism*, al-Nābulsī predicts that the twenty-first century will be the century of liberalism, especially in the Arab world. He writes: "Political Islam and the religious *uṣūliyya* are on their last legs and are drawing their last gasps. The wave of political Islam and religious *uṣūliyya* that we witnessed beginning in the 1970s and whose river-foam we saw floating upon the water,[18] has been in decline and retreat since 2005, like every other historical trend that has been dashed upon the shores of modernity and liberalism. That is the way of the universe and the thrust of history."[19] However, the events of the past few years have made this prediction seem more like wishful thinking. Political Islam indeed appears to be in temporary decline, but its place has been taken by the jihadi Salafīs and their ultraextremist brand of Islam. Al-Nābulsī speculates that the appeal of these "forces of darkness" (both the streams of political Islam and the jihadi Salafīs) stems from the very fact that they employ violence and terrorism and boast of this in the media—in contrast to the liberals, who are armed only with words and have no sword but "the blade that opens up people's minds."[20]

Another reason why liberalism does not possess the mass appeal of the MB's ideology, suggests al-Nābulsī, is the liberals' superior attitude and their disdain for the common folk, whom they regard as ignorant. This attitude may stem from the fact that they never formed a unified party or sought to seize power and therefore never made the effort to learn the language of the masses and garner broad popular support. In contrast, the parties of political Islam, chief among them the MB, have managed to appeal to the masses by providing social services that the state has failed to provide. They have also peddled a populist brand of religion that emphasizes jihad on the one hand and charity on the other—jihad to attain power and charity to finance their social and religious services. Moreover, they present Islam using simple language that the masses can readily understand, whereas the elitist liberals use sophisticated language and direct their messages mainly at other educated elites.[21]

The academic literature often presents *wasaṭiyya* as occupying a point midway between two poles: that of the militant Islamists, who wish to model contemporary Muslim society on the Muslim society of the seventh century, and that of the secularists, who wish to emulate the West.[22] However, this study has concluded that the development of *wasaṭī* ideology from the 1980s until the 2000s proceeded along two lines. On the one hand, al-Qaraḍāwī developed Ḥasan al-Bannā's theory into a comprehensive juridical method that affords room for maneuver within the boundaries of *sharī'a*, as shown in chapter 2; on the other hand, *wasaṭiyya* moved away from the doctrine of the MB and al-Bannā, drawing closer to the jihadi Salafī ideology. This process was especially apparent after 9/11. At that historical juncture, *wasaṭiyya* presented itself to the world as the face of moderate Islam and the alternative to global jihad. Yet at the same time, within the Muslim arena *wasaṭiyya* was challenged by the jihadi Salafī ideology and consequently moved toward it, taking an intermediate position between jihadi Salafī and *ikhwānī* Islam. This movement is exemplified by its position on *takfīr*, as shown in chapter 4, as well as in its position on jihad and terrorism, as shown in chapter 5. Thus, *wasaṭiyya* can be regarded as a brand of Salafism and called "*wasaṭī* Salafism." It is Salafī in that it purports to return to the Qur'ān and the Sunna; in fact, it can even be regarded as a type of jihadist Salafism in that it shares the vision of the ultimate victory of Islam over all other religions. It is *wasaṭī* in that it advocates pragmatism, realism, and gradualness in choosing a path toward attaining its goals.

Interpretation of the Qur'ān and Sunna Texts

This study has shown that the controversy between *wasaṭiyya* and jihadi Salafism on the one hand and liberalism on the other, whether on jihad or on social issues such as the status of women, pivots on their differing interpretation of texts in the Qur'ān and the Sunna. The liberals' fundamental premise is that the Qur'ān is multifaceted (*ḥammāl awjuh*), an expression attributed to 'Umar b. al-Khaṭṭāb. The liberals take this to mean that there are multiple ways to understand Qur'ānic texts and so condemn clerics such as al-Qaraḍāwī for claiming the exclusive authority to interpret the Qur'ān and for rejecting any opinion different from their own.[23] Mapping the different approaches to Qur'ānic exegesis, Shākir al-Nābulsī came to the conclusion, shared by other liberal writers, that it is the literal reading (*qirā'a ḥarfiyya*) of the Qur'ān that lays the foundations for terrorism. The liberals contend that both *wasaṭiyya* and jihadi Salafism endorse this type of interpretation,[24] whereas they themselves employ a historical reading that considers the political, social, and economic circumstances in the time of the Qur'ān, especially in the context of social and economic legislation.[25]

Egyptian intellectual Ḥasan Ḥanafī (b. 1935), considered the father of the Islamic Left, incurred the ire of the Egyptian religious establishment when in a lecture at the newly opened library of Alexandria in 2006 he likened the Qur'ān to a "supermarket" in which anyone can find evidence for his views by cherry-picking the right texts, especially if he chooses to ignore either their literal meaning or their overall Qur'ānic context. This, he said, is because the Qur'ānic verses contradict one another, especially when it comes to relations with non-Muslims (some verses calling for tolerance and others calling for battle against them).[26] Although disliking his comparison of the Qur'ān to a supermarket, which they consider crude, many liberals basically agree with Ḥanafī's point and say that this metaphor is merely meant to convey in laymen's terms that the Qur'ān is multifaceted.[27] Ḥanafī's statement, blunt even by liberal standards, nevertheless accords with the liberals' claim that they are not against the religion itself but against the tendentious interpretations of the Qur'ān that are motivated by political and ideological agendas. An example is the Verse of the Sword, calling on Muslims to fight and kill the infidels, which serves as the ideological platform of the global jihad movements but which, according to the liberals, is not relevant to today's political and social reality.[28]

As discussed elsewhere in this book, al-Qaraḍāwī contends that it is the Salafīs who employ an overliteral interpretation of the Qur'ān and *ḥadīth* (he even calls them "new Ẓāhirīs"), but that his own exegetic method is the remedy. However, from the liberal point of view, both al-Qaraḍāwī and the Salafīs can be classified as literalists, for they share the basic premise that the Qur'ān and Sunna are relevant to all times and places. The liberals' own premise, as set out in al-Nābulsī's liberal platform, is that the laws of the *sharī'a* should be understood "as laws legislated for their specific time and place, not as laws that cut through [i.e., are valid throughout] history, as some clerics claim."[29]

Accordingly, the liberals claim—and this is the crux of the controversy between their perspective and that of the *wasaṭī*s and Salafīs—that the principle of *naskh* (abrogation) must be applied to Qur'ānic texts and *ḥadīth*s that do not accord with the interests of the Muslims or humanity today, as al-'Afīf al-Akhḍar has suggested. For example, texts calling for jihad, which threaten the peace among Muslims or among the nations of the world, must be abrogated.[30] Based on this outlook, the liberals also advocate abrogating the Qur'ānic testimony and inheritance laws that create inequality between men and women, whereas al-Qaraḍāwī presents apologetic arguments to explain the need for the differences between the treatment and behavior of men and women. Another example is provided by the issue of homosexuality. The liberals contend that the Qur'ānic story about the people of Lot and the punishment they incurred belongs to a former era, in which norms and circumstances were different. It cannot be applied to homosexuals today, for this would violate the fundamental and broad values of freedom and human rights, which the Qur'ān essentially accepts and enshrines. For this reason, the liberals distinguish between "the Islām of the Qur'ān" and "the Islām of the *fuqahā'*," such as al-Qaraḍāwī. Addressing women's issues such as polygamy and the *ḥijāb*, Gamāl al-Bannā states that the Qur'ān upholds a woman's dignity and freedom and that the rulings that disregard the woman and her personhood are the product of Islamic jurists. The Qur'ān, he says, liberated women, whereas the *fuqahā'* chained them. He makes similar arguments about freedom of belief: the Qur'ān gives people the freedom to choose their beliefs, and the punishment for *ridda* (*ḥadd al-ridda*) is an invention by jurists. Gamāl al-Bannā and other liberals therefore regard the authority granted to the jurists as a great danger that threatens freedom of thought.[31] Al-Qaraḍāwī, in contrast, holds that the Qur'ānic law is still valid and applicable, although he argues, based on juristic principles, that the current prevalence of the phenomenon justifies a degree of lenience in the punishment meted out to homosexuals.

As we saw throughout this book, especially in the discussions of jihad and of women's issues, al-Qaraḍāwī's juristic methodology does consider the circumstances in which verses were revealed and *ḥadīth*s were uttered.[32] But al-Qaraḍāwī accuses the liberals, such as Muḥammad Sa'īd al-'Ashmāwī, of going too far in considering the particular circumstances in which texts emerged, to the point of interpreting certain general Qur'ānic directives as narrow and specific directives relevant only to the particular circumstances that prevailed in the time of the Prophet. This approach, he says, cannot be accepted by any reasonable Muslim, for it flies in the face of the premise that God's Word is eternally and universally valid. Therefore, in interpreting certain verses conveying general pronouncements—such as Q5:44, 45, 47, on the duty of implementing divine law—al-Qaraḍāwī follows the juristic principle of relying on the general meaning and goal of the texts, not on the specific historical circumstances in which they emerged (*al-'ibrā bi-'umūm al-lafẓ, lā bi-khuṣūṣ al-sabab*).[33] Liberals such as al-'Ashmāwī counter that with this principle the shaykh essentially "severs Qur'ānic verses from their Qur'ānic context, from the reasons for their revelation, and from all historic circumstances. Then he applies the verse universally based exclusively on its phrasing and literal meaning, without considering any other factor."[34]

An interesting example of this principle in action involves the verses in Sūrat al-Mā'ida (Q5:44–47), which are often presented as grounds for leveling accusations of heresy at Muslim leaders who do not govern according to the laws of the *sharī'a*. Because in their Qur'ānic context these verses refer to the Jews, liberals consider them inapplicable to Muslim rulers, whereas al-Qaraḍāwī and the Salafis regard them as applicable to all rulers who fail to enforce the *sharī'a*. *Wasaṭiyya*, which I have argued can justifiably be termed "*wasaṭī* Salafism," regards its interpretation of the Qur'ān and *ḥadīth* as the only valid interpretation, synonymous with Islam itself. Al-Qaraḍāwī claims an exegetical monopoly when he says that *wasaṭiyya* "corrects" the juristic flaws of the global jihad movements while also providing an Islamic alternative to secularism. The liberals, however, make a sharp distinction between the "Islam of the Qur'ān" and the "Islam of the *fuqahā'*," of which al-Qaraḍāwī is a typical representative. Clearly, the liberals are guilty of the fault they ascribe to al-Qaraḍāwī—branding their own interpretation as the "true" Islam, rejecting other interpretations, and choosing readings of the texts that suit their agendas. As we saw, the liberal Gamāl al-Bannā claims that the Qur'ān does not preach military jihad, but that the "*fuqahā'* of terror" create the impression that it does by cherry-picking the militant verses as the basis for their rulings. According to al-Bannā, Islam *is* "*jihādī*," not in the military sense but rather in the sense of requiring its adherents to invest effort in every domain. The term *jihād*, he says, has been misunderstood by both Orientalists and the Islamic groups (*al-jamā'āt al-Islāmiyya*).[35]

The liberals, who believe that the role of the clerics is to promote justice and virtue, ask: "Who is and was more dangerous for Islam: bin Laden and al-Qa'ida or Faraj Fūda? How is it that *fatwās* have been issued calling to kill liberal intellectuals like Fūda but not to kill bin Laden and the leaders of al-Qa'ida?" Al-Nābulsī describes this as a double standard employed by Muslim jurists.[36]

Is *Wasaṭiyya* Truly an Alternative to Radicalism, Both Religious and Secularist, as It Claims?

As stated, al-Qaraḍāwī presents *wasaṭiyya* as an alternative to radical secularism on the one hand and religious extremism on the other. However, this study has shown that the *wasaṭī* ideology is actually an incubator for extremism and violence in the name of Islam. Al-Qaraḍāwī's *wasaṭiyya* and jihadi Salafism share a single vision and differ mainly in the means they advocate for realizing this vision. *Wasaṭiyya*'s point of departure, like that of the jihadi Salafīs, is that Islam is the one true religion, whose ultimate victory over all has been promised by Allah. Both streams evoke Q9:32–33, which states that the infidels are bent on extinguishing the light of Allah, but Allah shall "perfect His light, although the disbelievers dislike it."[37] Accordingly, al-Qaraḍāwī sees the relations between Islam and the West through the prism of the basic premise he shares with the global jihad movements: that Islam is a global mission and that therefore the West, just like the East, is part of Allah's great kingdom (2:115) and part of the world to which the Prophet Muḥammad was sent.[38]

In enumerating the challenges facing Muslims in the twenty-first century, al-Qaraḍāwī indeed points to Western imperialism, which he says has taken a new form: the form of globalism that threatens to Westernize or Americanize the entire world. "Globalization," he writes, "is a refined name for a new [kind of] imperialism that has shed its old garb and discarded its old methods in order to launch a new era of takeover under this attractive new label." He adds that this new imperialism is "arrogant without right" (Q28:39) and is similar to Pharaoh, who "exalted himself in the land and made its people into factions" (28:4). However, imperialism is even worse than Pharaoh because the latter oppressed only one faction (the Children of Israel, as stated in Q38:4), whereas the Americans and the new imperialism wish to "spread arrogance and corruption throughout the world and oppress not only one faction but all the world's nations in order to benefit a tiny minority."[39]

The shaykh ascribes the tension between Islam and the West to the West's "distorted perception" of Islam, which he believes is the legacy of the Crusader period. Like the global jihad movements, he regards the West primarily as an imperialist power, which in the past used to impose its dominance by military force and today spreads its influence through cultural and ideological infiltration. The shaykh seeks to change the West's image of Islam by convincing it that Islam is a benevolent and peace-loving religion. He admits that certain Islamic groups employ unjustified violence but contends that they are small and marginal and do not represent Muslims at large. Moreover, he argues that the extremism and violence of these groups are a response to the West's injustice and aggression, its consistent hostility toward the Muslims, and its unreserved support for Israel, which has usurped Muslim land.[40] With these arguments, the shaykh effectively justifies terror in the name of Islam, including the September 11 attacks.

It is precisely this perception, which presents terror as a natural and legitimate reaction to Western injustice toward Muslims, that draws fire from liberals such as 'Abd al-Ḥamīd al-Anṣārī. The liberals argue that such explanations are nothing but false and misleading excuses and that the real reason for terror is the terrorists' aspiration to restore "the absent commandment [*al-farīḍa al-ghā'iba*]" (i.e., jihad, as stated in 'Abd al-Salām Faraj's book by that name), to establish the Islamic state, and to enact the *sharī'a* according to their aggressive interpretation of it. Al-Anṣārī ascribes terrorism to the culture of hate that is cultivated and spread by shaykhs such as al-Qaraḍāwī and to the religious discourse that prevails in the Muslim world. This discourse, he says, fills the hearts and minds of young Muslims with loathing toward the West by presenting it as materialistic and promiscuous and as bent upon the ideological, religious, and military subordination of the Muslims—all in order to divide and subjugate the Muslims and plunder their resources. Al-Anṣārī acknowledges that not every Muslim exposed to such messages will necessarily internalize them and heed the call to violent jihad, but even if only one Muslim in a hundred responds, this is still a very great number, he notes.[41]

In light of al-Qaraḍāwī's views on jihad—his sweeping approval of *istishhād* operations in Palestine and Syria and of the killing of American soldiers and civilians in Iraq as well as the distinction he draws between "Western terrorism," which he calls despicable, and the terrorizing of the infidels, which he describes as the religious duty of every Muslim (based on Q8:60)—liberal writers have called him one of the "jurists of terrorism." A petition submitted by a group of Arab liberals to the UN in November 2004, titled "International Communique against Terrorism?", stated that these "jurists of terrorism" foster violence by means of their *fatwās*, which describe terror not as a crime but as the implementation of divine justice or as a duty incumbent upon Muslims. Among the *fatwās* it mentioned were three by al-Qaraḍāwī: the *fatwā* permitting the killing of Israeli babies in their mothers' wombs because if they are allowed to be born they will grow up to be soldiers in the Israeli army; the *fatwā* he issued at the September 2004 conference of the Egyptian Journalists Union in Cairo permitting the killing of any American national in Iraq; and his *fatwā* in July 2004 permitting the killing of "apostate" Muslim intellectuals (*murtaddūn*), for, he claimed, there is a consensus among most schools of Islamic jurisprudence that a *murtadd* is deserving of death.[42]

As we have seen, al-Qaraḍāwī's inclusion among the "jurists of terrorism" is not without basis; however, the question arises: What distinguishes al-Qaraḍāwī from the jihadi Salafīs? Rafīq Ṣamū'īl puts forward an interesting answer to this question. He states that the terms *wasaṭī* (centrist), *mu'tadil* (balancing), and *mustanīr* (enlightened) appeared in the Muslim discourse only with the emergence of terror in the name of the faith, and therefore moderation in the Muslim world has come to be measured in terms of its distance from terrorism. However, says Ṣamū'īl, in assessing al-Qaraḍāwī's positions, we must not be misled by his use of progressive Western terms such as *citizenship*, *democracy*, *freedom*, *liberalism*, and *secularism*, for even as he uses these terms, he espouses the same notions as the global jihad groups that use violence to achieve the goal of establishing a global Islamic state. Therefore, according to Ṣamū'īl, "the difference between al-Qaraḍāwī's *wasaṭiyya* and bin Laden's terrorism is tactical, not strategic." The only real difference Ṣamū'īl identifies between the two is that in calling for violence, al-Qaraḍāwī also advocates considering the consequences for the Islamic nation, whereas bin Laden encouraged his followers to kill in order to attain paradise, with complete disregard of the consequences.[43]

As evidence of his position, Ṣamū'īl presents several examples from al-Qaraḍāwī's writings, including his ruling on opposing Muslim rulers who do not govern according to the *sharī'a*. As mentioned, al-Qaraḍāwī ruled that "radical secularists" who are openly hostile to the *sharī'a* and reject it out of hand must be opposed, but only within the limits of what is possible, for Allah "does not charge a soul except [with that within] its capacity" (Q2:286). He stresses that the uncalculated use of force can often bring about great calamity and may even delay the ultimate reinstatement of the *sharīʿa* by a long or short length of time.[44] Ṣamūʾīl concludes from this ruling that, just like bin Laden, al-Qaraḍāwī preaches killing anyone who opposes him, such as the secularists, as long as it does not jeopardize the mission of Islamic outreach.[45]

Another example Ṣamūʾīl presents as evidence of the similarity between al-Qaraḍāwī and the jihadi Salafīs is the shaykh's perception of *al-walāʾ wal-barāʾ*, the principle of loyalty and disavowal. Describing his vision of the ideal Islamic society, al-Qaraḍāwī states that it is characterized by "loyalty to Islam and the Muslims and hatred for the enemies of Islam who conspire against the Muslims and are an obstacle on the path of Islam." To support this view, he cites the *ḥadīth* stating that the strongest bonds of the faith are "love for the sake of Allah and hatred for the sake of Allah, loyalty for the sake of Allah and enmity for the sake of Allah."[46] A society that embraces the values of homeland and nationality as "idols" (*awthān*) that are worshipped in place of Allah is not a Muslim society. By saying this, he essentially espouses the jihadi Salafī view that regards as heretical any society in which citizenship is the basis of loyalty and affiliation. Ṣamūʾīl writes that, "in this sense, al-Qaraḍāwī is a replica of bin Laden; there is no difference. The insistence on *al-walāʾ wal-barāʾ*, on Islam as the homeland, and on the Muslim as its citizen [is shared by both]."[47]

Although the *wasaṭī* vision is indeed largely similar to that of jihadi Salafism, there is an essential difference between them: *wasaṭiyya* advocates the gradual implementation of this vision. The principle of gradualness (set out by Ḥasan al-Bannā based on precedents derived from the *ḥadīth*), realism, and a clear-headed reading of reality are the foundations of *wasaṭiyya*'s pragmatism within the limits of the *sharīʿa*. This pragmatism is by no means synonymous with moderateness, however. Its essence is rigidity in defining long-term goals but flexibility in selecting the means and mechanisms for achieving them. *Wasaṭiyya* adopted this pragmatism as a principle of jurisprudence but implements it in all domains of its activity, first and foremost in politics, which, as mentioned, it regards as an integral part of the religion. This pragmatism affords *wasaṭiyya* a measure of maneuverability that might be mistaken for moderateness.

As part of this pragmatism, *wasaṭiyya* believes that Islamic *da'wa* should address every culture in its own language, a notion espoused by the Qur'ān (14:4): "And We did not send any messenger except [speaking] in the language of his people to state clearly for them." Interpreting the verse very broadly in the context of globalization, al-Qaraḍāwī writes: "The verse means not just that the Chinese must be addressed in Chinese and the Russians in Russian. It means that the privileged must be addressed in the language of the privileged, the simple folk in the language of the simple folk, the people of the East in the language of the East, and the people of the West in the language of the West. [Furthermore,] people of the twentieth century must be addressed in the language of the twentieth century, not in the language of past centuries."[48]

Two interesting examples illustrate al-Qaraḍāwī's sophisticated pragmatism. First, his commentary on Q8:60—"Prepare against them whatever you are able of power and of steeds of war by which you may terrify the enemy of Allah and your enemy"—the first word of which is incorporated in the MB's logo. Commenting on this verse, al-Qaraḍāwī states: "When the enemy sees what you have prepared for him—weapons and well-trained men—he will think a thousand times before drawing near you or harming you, for he will be terrified of you and wary of your power. It is this [fear] that will maintain the peace between you. This is called 'armed peace.'"[49] Based on the same verse, al-Qaraḍāwī also rules that the Muslims are obligated to develop every kind of weapon, including chemical and nuclear weapons, as long as others possess them and can use them to threaten Islam.[50] The oxymoronic term *armed peace*, used by al-Qaraḍāwī to characterize the readiness for jihad, is a quintessential example of the sophistication and complexity of *wasaṭiyya* and the built-in contradictions that form its very essence.

The second example involves al-Qaraḍāwī's vision of "the conquest of Rome." Based on eschatological *ḥadīth*s, the shaykh is confident that Islam will eventually return to Europe and conquer this city. However, using another oxymoronic term, he calls the future conquest of Rome a "peaceful conquest [*fatḥ silmī*]." He notes that Islamic history provides a precedent for this kind of conquest—namely, the treaty of al-Ḥudaybiyya (628 CE), which paved the way for the Muslim conquest (*fatḥ*) of Mecca and which the Qur'ān (48:1) calls a "clear victory" (*fatḥ mubīn*).[51] This peaceful conquest of Rome is part of the advent of the global Islamic state, which, al-Qaraḍāwī believes, will be actualized through a combination of *da'wa* and jihad, in accordance with the fundamental vision shared by him, the MB, and the jihadi Salafīs.

Al-Qaraḍāwī derives the philosophy of gradualness and realism from the principles of *sharī'a* politics. These principles are also adopted by jihadi Salafī ideologues such as Abū Muḥammad al-Maqdīsī and Abū Basīr al-Ṭarṭūsī, which explains the similarity between their rulings and al-Qaraḍāwī's. For example, based on the principles of *sharī'a* politics, both al-Qaraḍāwī and al-Ṭarṭūsī contend that Muslims living in the West must not be called upon to wage jihad there, for this would be a breach of their contract with their host countries.[52] This is further evidence for this study's conclusion that the MB's ideology serves as a legacy for both *wasaṭiyya* and jihadi Salafism. It is not surprising, therefore, that the global jihad movements and the political Islam movements have a great deal in common.[53]

Wasaṭiyya's Weakness: Its Use of Doublespeak

Because of its tendency to support both sides of an argument, *wasaṭiyya* has been criticized both by Salafīs, who find its rulings too liberal and permissive, and by liberals and secularists, who accuse it of excessive conservatism. Al-Qaraḍāwī admits that he has been accused of showing both too much leniency (*tasāhul*) and too much strictness (*tashaddud*), adding that "this is always the problem of anyone who takes an intermediate position; he is liked neither by the people on the right nor by the people on the left."[54] The *wasaṭī* insistence on taking a middle course but also on pleasing both extremes occasionally results in doublespeak. This can very clearly be seen, for example, in the way al-Qaraḍāwī expressed himself on the 9/11 attacks when speaking to the West and to Muslims. In his addresses to both, he condemned the attacks as well as hijacking and hostage taking in general. However, when speaking to a Muslim audience in his mosque in Qatar, he noted that America's crimes, especially its cooperation with Israel, make the appearance of "bin Ladens" understandable.[55]

In this same sermon, he explained that the way to defeat terrorism is by establishing justice on earth, resisting lies, and supporting the weak against the strong, the oppressed against the oppressor. He added that if the strong (i.e., America) will continue to attack the weak, terrorism will continue, and even if America were to kill bin Laden, a thousand others like him will arise: "The world will continue to give birth to people like bin Laden if America continues on its present course. It is the despotic power that will rule as it wishes rather than [with] truth and reason." Here al-Qaraḍāwī provides what amounts to a rationalization of the motives for the 9/11 attacks, putting the blame on America and its behavior.[56]

Who Will Be al-Qaraḍāwī's Successor?

For his disciples, al-Qaraḍāwī is a revered authority (*marji'iyya*) of the type familiar from Shī'ī Islam. The circle of his students and associates is organized as an institution, alongside many other institutions the shaykh has established. It holds regular conventions, which, according to al-Qaraḍāwī, are intended "to produce leaders . . . for the future of the nation [because] this nation will prosper only if led by *'ulamā'*." These leaders, he adds, must possess knowledge of both religion and the world around them; moreover, they must be "men of hand and eye"—that is, possess both capability and vision. He notes that he does not expect his students to agree with and follow all his opinions but hopes that they will adopt his innovative *wasaṭiyya* and embrace the spirit of knowledge.[57]

The shaykh has also said that he regards his students as his sons and that a man feels prouder of his sons than of his forefathers. Asked in a televised interview with Saudi shaykh Salmān al-'Awda who his greatest student is, he declined to provide a name.[58] It seems that al-Qaraḍāwī is less interested in naming a successor than he is in leaving a well-ordered *wasaṭī* legacy. His numerous books, encompassing most domains of Islamic study, especially jurisprudence, certainly constitute such a legacy. Moreover, he claims to be working on an encyclopedia summarizing all his works.

Also noteworthy is the manner in which al-Qaraḍāwī wishes to end his life, as he expressed at a conference held by his students in 2007. On that occasion, he asked his students to join his prayer that Allah allow him to die as a martyr: "I pray to Allah to end my life with *istishhād* for His sake at the hands of the enemies of Islam. I do not want to die at the hands of a Muslim, be he an extremist or a radical. I ask Allah for *istishhād*, which is the best way to end one's life."[59] The message these words conveyed to his students and associates is that they, too, should aspire to die as martyrs at the hands of the enemies of Islam.

Appendixes

Glossary

Notes

Bibliography

Index

Appendix A

Fundamental Principles of the *Wasaṭiyya* and Renewal Movement

The text given here is from Shaykh Yūsuf al-Qaraḍāwī, *Fiqh al-wasaṭiyya al-Islāmiyya wal-tajdīd: Maʿālim wa-manārāt* (The *Fiqh* of Islamic *Wasaṭiyya*: Characteristics and Beacons) (Cairo: Dār al-Shurūq, 2010), 242–46.

1. Profound knowledge and a comprehensive and balanced understanding of Islam, revealing its two unique properties: Islam is all-encompassing and perfect—faith and law, knowledge and action, worship and interpersonal relations, culture and ethics, truth and power, *daʿwa* and state, religion and this world, civilization and nation.[1] The second property: a balanced blend between parallel elements—for example, a blend of spirituality and materialism, divinity and humanity, thought and conscience, idealism and realism, individualism and collectivism.
2. Faith in the authority [*marjiʿiyya*] of the Holy Qur'ān and the true prophetic Sunna as a source of legislation for directing the lives of Muslims,[2] with the necessity to understand partial texts in light of general goals.
3. The creed [*ʿaqīda*] is based on a belief in God, the Day of Judgment, and God's unity: unity of lordship [*tawḥīd al-rubūbiyya*], oneness of divinity [*tawḥīd al-ulūhiyya*], and oneness of God's sovereignty [*ḥākimiyya*], so that man can be liberated from slavery to his fellow man and from anything that is not God. Belief in Muḥammad as God's messenger, sent with an eternal and universal message, the "seal of the prophets."
4. Approach to God alone, by means of the rites that He has determined and focusing on God's worship, as the goal for which man was created.[3] Worship consists of the four "major commandments" [prayer, almsgiving, fasting, and pilgrimage] and also mention of God (*dhikr*), supplication, and asking for forgiveness. This is in addition to "worship in the heart": pure intentions and loyalty [*ikhlāṣ*] to God, fear of God, and the

like. These observances are the foundation of true *ṣūfism*, based on [the saying] "Be true to God and ethical toward mankind."

5. The soul must be purified and fought so that it comes to possess the virtues in which Islam is interested, whether this morality concerns the individual or society. Rejection of the view that ceremonial duties are everything and also the view that ethics is everything.
6. Stress on the obligation to preach [call, *daʿwa*] for God, enjoin the good and forbid evil, give counsel [*naṣīḥa*] in matters of religion, "urge one another to the truth, and urge one another to steadfastness [*ṣabr*]."[4]
7. Instilling humanitarian and social values such as justice, *shūrā*, liberty, and human dignity and rights.
8. Respect for reason in addition to revelation. Call for study, thought, and the shaping of a scientific way of thinking; opposition to paralysis and blind imitation of forefathers or lords, the great or the masses. Abolishing the contradiction between true tradition [*al-naql al-ṣaḥīḥ*] and common sense [*al-ʿaql al-ṣarīḥ*].
9. *Tajdīd* of the religion from within by means of a renewed understanding of it; *tajdīd* of the faith, of deeds according to religion; and *tajdīd* of the call (*daʿwa*) to adhere to it. Revival of the principle of *ijtihād*, the only principle that makes *sharīʿa* alive, but only on condition that such *ijtihād* be practiced by an appropriate person at an appropriate place.
10. A call for a new *fiqh* in the world and in religion. A number of different kinds of *fiqh* are desired: *fiqh* of the ways [*sunan*] of the universe; goals of the *sharīʿa*; results of actions [*al-maʾālāt*]; balances, priorities, and conflict; cultural *fiqh*; *fiqh* of change; and *fiqh* of reality.
11. Justice and respect for women, guarding their inborn characteristics, and emphasis on what Islam has given to women: their rights, status, and honor. Women are to be liberated from the effects of the period of backwardness and recession in Islam and freed from the evil results of the cultural invasion by the West, which removed women from their innate nature and did not preserve their femaleness.
12. Focus on (and preservation of) the family as the core and basic foundation of every decent society. Each spouse must guard the other's rights. Divorce should be considered only if no agreement proves possible. Polygamy is condoned in *sharīʿa* with certain restrictions and conditions; it should neither be forbidden nor made use of excessively. The term *family* should be expanded to include *ʿaṣaba* and *arḥām*.[5]

13. Formation of a decent society with mutual assistance, a society based on mutual care and mercy among its members, with the rich supporting the poor, the strong holding the hands of the weak, and all fortifying each other.
14. Faith in the Muslim *umma*, its mission, its everlastingness and loyalty to it. Faith in the duty of unity and of religious brotherhood among its members, of all schools of jurisprudence. All the sects are to be considered part of the one nation as long as they pray in the direction of prayer [i.e., toward Mecca] and believe in the noble Qur'ān and the Prophet's noble Sunna.
15. Establishment of a just state that promotes *da'wa*, a state that leads the believers toward the truth and the good, establishes Allah's justice on earth, and adopts as judge what God has revealed—that is, the Qur'ān and the scales [Q57:25]. Such a state respects nations' right to choose their rulers without distortion of the people's will and without imposing a ruler by force. It is the right of nations, in fact their duty, to demand an accounting from their ruler and to dismiss him peacefully if he continues to err.
16. One should as far as possible refrain from accusing [one's fellow Muslims] of deviating from the straight path [; declaring someone to be a *fāsiq* is act of *tafsīq*] or of unbelief [*takfīr*], especially if the cause of such an accusation depends on textual interpretation. One should be forbearing toward anyone who says the Two Testimonies, prays in the direction of prayer, and does not utter anything that is clearly in contradiction to [Islam]. The basic rule whenever possible is to consider any Muslim to be righteous.
17. The Muslim economy should be strengthened based on knowledge and experience, faith and morality, which should complement each other. The economy should be based on an understanding of *sharī'a* and its goals. Practical steps should be taken toward the establishment of a unique Muslim economy, distinct from both capitalist and communist economies.
18. Belief in the necessity for pluralism, mutual recognition, and tolerance among nations. Belief that humanity is one family and that cultures should coexist, enrich each other, interact with and borrow from each other, neither withdrawing within themselves nor being condescending toward others.

19. Establishment of a civilization of science and faith, a civilization based on the divine [*ḥaḍāra rabbāniyya*], humane, ethical, and global that combines science and faith, spirit and matter, that creates an equilibrium between mind and heart and links heaven and earth, that creates balance and justice between the individual and society and makes truth more powerful than force.
20. Advancement and promotion of the arts, which are to be used in the service of the nation's mission. The essence of art is the aesthetic sense and its expression in beauty; Islam revitalizes this sense in the Muslim soul and teaches one to see beauty in the world and in man, himself a creation of the divine, for God is good at all He does. Islam welcomes the high arts, both auditory and visual, the fruit of production. It uses art in the service of truth and good and prevents it from being used as an instrument for arousing the passions and appetites of this world.
21. Building the land, developing and protecting the environment. Cooperation in making life easier for people and in whatever promotes beauty in life. This is to be deemed worship of God and jihad for His sake.
22. Peace with whoever wants peace and jihad against the aggressors. The nation must be made aware that jihad is a duty of the individual [*farḍ ʿayn*], whose purpose is to liberate its [the nation's] territory of any foreign rule imposed on it. All forces, groups, and movements operating to help Islam and revive its nation must be directed in one direction.
23. The Muslim minorities throughout the world must be paid attention to, for they are part of the Muslim *umma*. The nation must help them live in accordance with Islam in their societies as active members, and they should have their own *fiqh*. The slogan of Muslim minorities will be: to proceed on the straight path in religion without seclusion and to become integrated into society without being absorbed in it.
24. The religious minorities within our Muslim societies must be treated in a way that accords with the requirements of Islam in this respect: to allow them to retain their faith and to emphasize that they "are residents of *dār al-Islām*." In contemporary terms, this means that they are citizens with the same rights as ours and the same duties as well, with the exception of the things that are dictated by the difference in religion.
25. Adoption of the principle of facilitation [*taysīr*] in religious rulings and jurisprudence. Even in cases where strictness [*tashdīd*] is required, this

should be applied only in "roots" and not in "branches." The facilitation that is urged here does not mean justification of a state of affairs, Westernization, or the placation of the rulers.

Furthermore, in *da'wa* the path of bringing joy and good tidings [*tabshīr*] should be chosen. *Da'wa* to Muslims should be performed with wisdom and good teaching, while *da'wa* to non-Muslims should consist of dialogue, which is the better way [a formulation based on Q16:125] and in keeping with the spirit and style of the times.

26. Adherence to gradualism and Allah's other ways, wise gradualism in *da'wa*, teaching, legal decisions, and making changes. One must not hurry to do something whose time has not come or pick the fruit before it has ripened. At the same time, God's ways in the universe and in society should be retained. Those who protect God's ways are protected by them, and those who cause them to be lost will themselves be lost through them.
27. A balance must be struck between the constant elements of *sharī'a* and the variables of the times. Constancy must be preserved in aims and objectives, fundamental principles and generalities [*kulliyyāt*], while flexibility should be shown in means and mechanisms, branches and secondary principles. Constant things should not be changed, nor should variable things be fixed.
28. Religious commandments must be given their *shar'ī* status through a balanced understanding, so that each commandment may receive its standing in accordance with what is said in unambiguous texts [*muḥkamāt al-nuṣūṣ*] and their goals. What should be postponed must not be hastened, nor is what should be hastened be postponed. This is what we have called "understanding priorities" [*fiqh al-awlawiyyāt*].
29. Comprehensive reform [*iṣlāḥ*] and radical change are necessary. A reform that will not be limited to the superficial and will not refrain from diving into the depths. Reform will not be real unless it is done of our own will and by our own hands, without being imposed from the outside. The key to every reform is reforming despotic political regimes. The basis of every change is changing man from within [a statement based on Q13:11].
30. We must benefit from our rich heritage in the sciences, the arts, and ethics. Yet we must also remember that this heritage is not infallible. It can be criticized, reevaluated, and debated; some things in it may be

declared fitting and appropriate, whereas others may be deemed weak. But as the Prophet is quoted as saying, "My nation will not unite on misguidance." It is also necessary to revive this heritage using the methods and tools of the modern age. We must choose whatever is appropriate from it and disseminate it to the masses of the nation, while leaving the other things to be studied by experts.

Appendix B

The Neoliberal Platform by Shākir al-Nābulsī

The text given here is from Shākir al-Nābulsī, *Al-Lībirālīyyūn al-judud: Jadal fikrī* (The New Liberals: An Intellectual Discussion) (Cologne, Germany: Manshūrāt al-Jamal, 2005), 21–25.[1]

The platform sets out twenty-five principles:

1. A persistent demand to reform the religious education, which is in darkness [*ẓalāmī*] owing to the domination of religious terror after Islam has been hijacked and distorted into a militant and bloodthirsty ideology.
2. A call for fighting the militant and bloodthirsty religious, nationalist, and political terror in all its forms.
3. Enabling the subjection of prevailing sacred values, traditions, legislations, and moral values to in-depth scrutiny. Employing rational scientific scrutiny based on the interpretational principle of "genealogy," whose essence is the interpretational question of "who" and the analytical question of "why" [i.e., interpreting and assessing texts and ideas by asking who formulated them and why], so that the criticism will constitute interpretation and assessment, not just contempt and invective. Because [the principle of] genealogy is a tool for understanding modernity, true criticism will serve as a path to true wisdom.
4. Considering religious hostility toward others as a position that emanated from specific political and social circumstances that existed 1,500 years ago. These circumstances no longer exist but have fundamentally changed. Therefore, the religious positions that were expressed in the Qur'ān fifteen centuries ago should not be used at all today to attack others and shed their blood. Interests change, and positions change. Change is part of life.

5. Considering the laws of the *sharīʿa* as laws legislated for their specific time and place and not as laws that cut through [i.e., are valid throughout] history, as some clerics claim. Examples are [the laws pertaining to] women *ḥijāb*,[2] women's inheritance,[3] women's testimony,[4] the appointment of women to political and senior judicial positions,[5] and so on.
6. The religious ideologies were formulated by religious scholars and jurists, not by the religion of the Prophet himself. They are an obstacle to free thinking and its development and to the emergence of scientific reasoning.
7. There can be no absolute loyalty to the past as such and no dwelling on the past. An understanding of the present obligates us to reexamine the values of the past and [impresses upon us] the necessity of creating a future, which is the essence of modernity.
8. The present cannot be built upon the record of the past but only upon the records of the present, and the same is true for the future. The key to transcending the past lies in the present, not in the past, especially not in our history and cultural heritage, which massacred their own knowledge by their own hand. The past [Muslim scholarship], headed by [the medieval scholars] Ibn Taymiyya, Jalāl al-Dīn al-Suyūṭī [d. 1505], Ibn Qayyim al-Jawziyya, and others, rejected philosophy, banished reason, persecuted the *muʿtazila*, shut the gates of *ijtihād*, forbade [the study of] theology [*ʿilm al-kalām*], exiled rational thinkers [*aṣḥāb al-manṭiq*; i.e., philosophers], and allowed distorted religious texts to battle philosophy, wisdom, and logic. Whoever adopted the way of the philosophers [was thought to] court heresy.[6] Rational thinkers were [branded] heretics. The natural and medical sciences were rejected, branded as "foreign sciences" [*ʿulūm dakhīla*], and replaced with religious sciences and prophetic medicine, to the point where the Prophet was [considered] a more famous and knowledgeable [physician] than the father of medicine, Hippocrates. Music, painting, poetry, and all the high human arts were banned. How can this past serve as a bridge from the present to the future?
9. It is our weakness, inferiority, ignorance, and lack of scientific and rational knowledge that drive us to rely on the past in building the future, which is the worst possible option, for the past can support the past alone and is not valid in the present. Turning to the outside world to build the present is the lesser evil.

10. The Arabs must discard the ideal that they purport to represent out of their arrogance and conceit (that they [must] either take leadership of the worlds or [choose] the grave).[7]
11. Recognizing that history is governed by laws and not by people's passions, delusions, or dwelling on their past. No nation can forge its history at will by going backward, embracing [past] glories, and restoring bygone culture and civilization. Human perfection, as [Egyptian Islamic modernist] Qāsim Amīn [d. 1908] said, is not necessarily to be found in the past.[8]
12. Understanding that renouncing reason will achieve nothing but the dominance of barbarism, demagogy, and bloodthirsty societies.
13. Raising all the questions that were not asked by the enlightened [Muslim liberals] of the nineteenth century and the first half of the twentieth century, from [Sayyid Jamāl al-Dīn] al-Afghānī to Ṭaha Ḥusayn, addressing the issues they glossed over and subjecting them to analysis.
14. Embracing Arab modernity [*ḥadātha*] without reserve, for it is the key to liberty, [while] distinguishing between Arab and Western modernity. Each nation has its own unique [brand of] modernity.
15. Liberating the Arab soul from its illusions and from the witchcraft, amulets, and deception in which it is immersed.
16. Emancipating the Arab soul from its past and from the forefathers [*aslāf*] who still dominate it from the grave.
17. Discarding false claims to absolute knowledge or immutable laws. There is no absolute knowledge, and one should [always] be open to the truth.
18. Creating a new Arab personality that moves away from violence, subservience, irrationality, asceticism, tribalism, and racism to become rational, realistic, scientific, nationalist, but not racist.
19. Reembracing the self and self-criticism as well as self-knowledge not as individuals but as a nation. Myths must not only be defeated but pursued to the very caverns [from which they emanate].
20. There is no harm in using the assistance of outside forces to defeat the terrifying tyranny, to completely eradicate the virus of despotism, and to implement Arab democracy, in light of the inability of the domestic elite and the fragile political parties to defeat this dictatorship and implement such democracy. This is not unprecedented in history: Europe was helped by the United States in defeating Nazism and the

Japanese military fascism in World War II, and the United States freed Europe just as it freed Kuwait and Iraq.

21. There is nothing wrong with reform coming from without as long as it is done through diplomacy [rather than by force]. The most important thing is that it does arrive, be it on the back of an Arabian camel, a British tank, an American warship, or a French submarine. The early Arab philosopher [Abū Yūsuf b. Yaʿqūb Ibn Isḥāq al-Ṣabbāḥ] al-Kindī (d. 873 CE) said, "We should take the truth from anyone, whether he shares our religion or not."
22. There is no solution to Arab conflicts with others, be it in Palestine or anywhere else, except through dialogue, negotiations, and peaceful solutions in view of the imbalance in military, scientific, economic, and rational capabilities between the Arabs and their enemies.
23. A belief in political and cultural normalization [*taṭbīʿ*] with the enemies and acceptance of the Arab political reality without burying [our] heads in the destructive, scorching, Arab desert sand. Normalization and cross-pollination [*talāquḥ*] among nations and cultures are the way to a lasting peace in the Middle East. Peace agreements, such as the Camp David Accords of 1979, the Oslo Accords of 1993, and the (Wadi) Araba Treaty [between Israel and Jordan] of 1994 should turn into agreements among peoples instead of being mere agreements between states without any links to the peoples themselves. This is a waste of time and a distortion of the political facts on the ground, whether we like it or not. The aversion of the divided Arab intelligentsia, on the one hand, and of the common folks, on the other, to normalization does not detract from the real possibilities of peace, which is crucial for the region and is the path toward comprehensive change.
24. Support for globalization because it is one of the ways that lead to Arab economic modernization, which may bring about political and cultural modernization.
25. A demand for total equality between men and women in rights, duties, employment, education, inheritance, testimony, and appointment [to public office]. Adopting the Tunisian Personal Status Laws of 1957, which are considered the best Arab example of the emancipation of Arab women without having to embrace Western values of women's liberation and equality to men.

Glossary of Key Terms

***ʿālim* (pl. *ʿulamāʾ*):** an Islamic scholar
***ʿaqīda*:** the creed, the faith's main doctrines
***bidʿa* (pl. *bidaʿ*):** an innovation, contrary to Sunna
***dār al-ʿahd*:** the abode of covenant
***dār al-daʿwa*:** the abode of preaching
***dār al-ḥarb*:** the abode of war
***dār al-ijāba*:** the abode of heedfulness
***dār al-Islām*:** the abode of Islam
***dār al-kufr*:** the abode of unbelief
***daʿwa*:** preaching, proselytizing
***faqīh* (pl. *fuqahāʾ*):** Muslim jurists
***fatwā*:** religious ruling
***fiqh*:** Islamic jurisprudence
***fiqh al-aqalliyyāt*:** jurisprudence for Muslim minorities
***fiqh al-awlawiyyāt*:** understanding of priorities
***fiqh al-ikhtilāf*:** jurisprudence of controversy
***fiqh al-muwāzanāt*:** understanding of balances
***fiqh al-thawra*:** jurisprudence of revolution, rulings concerning the revolutions of the Arab Spring
***fitna*:** temptation; civil war, internal strife, unbelief
***fiṭra*:** inborn characteristics, innate human nature
***ghulū*:** exaggeration
***ghulū ʿilmānī*:** extreme secularism
***ḥākimiyya*:** God's sovereignty
***ḥijāb*:** veil, scarf that covers the head and neck but not the face
***ʿibāda* (*ʿibādāt*):** worship, religious observances
***iftāʾ*:** the issuing of legal rulings

ijtihād: independent human reasoning in juristic effort based on the primary sources of Islam, the Qur'ān and the Sunna

'ilmāniyya: secularism

'ilmāniyyūn: secularists

intiḥār: suicide (forbidden in Islam), in contrast to *istishhād*, self-sacrifice for the sake of Allah (*fī sabīl Allāh*)

al-irhāb al-mashrū': licit or legitimate terrorization of the enemy

iṣlāḥ: reform

istishhād: martyrdom

jāhiliyya: originally referring to the pre-Islamic period; Sayyid Quṭb used the term *jāhiliyya* to describe a non-Islamic state of affairs in which men are ruled and enslaved by their fellow men

jihād al-daf': jihad of repelling the enemy from Muslim territory

jihād al-ṭalab: literally, "jihad of request"—that is, jihad in which Muslims "seek" the infidel in the latter's territory

jizya: the poll tax. The *jizya* verse (Q9:29) commands the Muslims to "fight those of the People of the Book who do not [truly] believe in God and the Last Day, who do not forbid what God and His Messenger have forbidden, [and] who do not obey the rule of justice until they pay the *jizya* according to their financial ability and while in a state of humiliation."

khimār: woman's veil

mafsada: harm, damage

maṣlaḥa: literally, a cause or source of something good and beneficial; public interest, well-being, welfare, and social weal

al-maṣlaḥa al-mursala: benefit or interest that is unattested (i.e., not mentioned in the Qur'ān or Sunna); *maṣlaḥa* that is neither supported nor rejected by any clear-cut text in the Qur'ān and the Sunna

mansūkh: abrogated

maqāṣid al-sharī'a: the goals or intentions of the Islamic law

mu'āmalāt: interpersonal relationships and social behavior

mujaddid: renewer

murtadd: apostate

mushrikūn: polytheists

naskh: abrogation

niqāb: full-face veil

rabbāniyyūn: scholars who are devoted to God, whose only guiding light is Allah, and whose rulings are not influenced by political interests

***ridda*:** apostasy
***al-salaf al-ṣāliḥ*:** the pious forefathers
***shahīd*:** martyr
***shirk*:** polytheism, attributing partners to Allah
***shūrā*:** consultation, the ruler's consultation with his counselors
***al-siyāsa al-shar'iyya*:** making policy in accordance with *sharī'a*; leadership and administration (*siyāsa*) based on the principles, laws, and instructions of *sharī'a*
***ṭāghūt* (pl. *ṭawāghīt*):** idol, "idolatrous" Muslim ruler
***tajdīd*:** renewal
***takfīr*:** the act of accusing fellow Muslims of unbelief
***tawḥīd*:** God's oneness
***tawḥīd al-asmā' wal-ṣifāt*:** unity of the names and attributes, with God's attributes being accepted literally
***tawḥīd al-ḥākimiyya*:** the unity of [God's] sovereignty
***tawḥīd al-rubūbiyya*:** unity of lordship
***tawḥīd al-ulūhiyya*:** unity of divinity, Godship, with Allah alone as the object of all forms of worship
***al-walā' wal-barā'*:** loyalty and disavowal

Notes

Note on Transliteration and Translations

1. *The Qur'an: A New Translation*, trans. M. A. S. Abdel Haleem (Oxford: Oxford Univ. Press, 2005).

The Clash within Islam

1. This statement was made by al-Qaraḍāwī in a sermon after he quoted the following statement ascribed to the Prophet, who was asked: "O messenger of God, which of the two cities will be conquered first, Constantinople [i.e., Istanbul, captured by the sultan Mehmet I in 1453 CE] or Rome?" To which the Prophet replied: "The city of Heraclius [the Byzantine emperor, ruled from Constantinople in the years 610–641 CE] will be conquered first."

2. Shaykh Yūsuf al-Qaraḍāwī, "Al-Mustaqbal lil-Islām," c. 2000–2003, in *Khuṭab al-Shaykh al-Qaraḍāwī*, ed. Shaykh Khālid al-Sa'd, 6 vols. (Cairo: Maktabat Wahba, 2003), 5:285–86.

3. Shaykh Yūsuf al-Qaraḍāwī, *Al-Mubashshirāt bi-intiṣār al-Islām*, 2nd ed. (Cairo: Maktabat Wahba, 1999), 30, parentheses around "ideologies" in the original.

4. 'Abdallah 'Azzām, *Dhikrayāt Filasṭīn* (Peshawar, Pakistan: Markaz 'Azzām al-I'lāmī, n.d.), 17, electronic copy at http://www.ilmway.com/site/maqdis/MS_9006.html; the first two sets of ellipses are in the original, but some material has also been omitted after the second set.

5. Ayman al-Ẓawāhirī, head of al-Qa'ida, *Tawjīhāt 'āmma lil-'amal al-jihādī*, (N.p.: Mu'assasat al-Saḥāb, 1434 [2013]), electronic copy at http://www.ilmway.com/site/maqdis/MS_10765.html.

6. Abū Bakr al-Baghdādī (b. 1971), head of the Islamic State, in a video titled *Infirū khifāfan wa-thiqālan* [So Go Out, No Matter Whether You Are Lightly or Heavily Armed (the first words of Q9:41)], Mu'assasat al-Furqān, Apr. 15, 2015, at https://tawhid.website/?video=3059.

7. Shākir al-Nābulsī, *Tahāfut al-uṣūliyya: Naqd fikrī li-l-uṣūliyya al-Islāmiyya min khilāl wāqi'ihā al-mu'āsh* (Beirut: al-Mu'assasa al-'Arabiyya lil-Dirāsāt wal-Nashr, 2009), 15.

8. Muḥammad Sa'īd al-'Ashmāwī, *Al-Islām al-siyāsī*, 4th ed. (Cairo: Maktabat Madbūlī al-Ṣaghīr, 1996), 138.

9. Naṣr Ḥāmid Abū Zayd, *Al-Tajdīd wa-l-taḥrīm wa-l-ta'wīl bayna al-ma'rifa al-'ilmiyya wa-l-khawf min al-takfīr* (Al-Dār al-Bayḍā', Morocco: Al-Markaz al-Thaqāfī al-'Arabī, 2010), 27.

Introduction

1. CNN Arabic, "Muftī al-Su'ūdiyya: 'DĀ'SH' wal-Qā'ida mina al-Khawārij yastaḥillāni al-dimā' wa-lā naḥsabuhumā 'alā al-Muslimīna," Aug. 19, 2014, at https://arabic.cnn.com/middleeast/2014/08/19/saudi-mufti-isis.

2. On the negative characteristics of the Khawārij as reflected in *ḥadīth* literature and evoked to this day, see Abū Baṣīr 'Abd al-Mun'im Muṣṭafā Ḥalīma al-Ṭarṭūsī, *Hādhihi hiya khiṣāl al-Khawārij fa-iḥdharūhā* (N.p.: n.p., 2013), electronic copy at www.abubaseer.bizland.com/books/read/b%2047.doc. In the case of some publications, especially jihadi Salafī ones, the publication details are often unavailable, and the only option is to refer to the online copies of these texts.

3. *Shorouk News*, "Muntadā al-Samāḥa wal-Wasaṭiyya bil-awqāf yuṭālibu bi-ta'āwun mukhtalif al-mu'assasāt li-intāj khiṭāb dīnī muttazin," May 26, 2015, at http://www.shorouknews.com/news/view.aspx?cdate=26052015&id=5e0f8692-b6ca-4fc7-bdc1-e1e72e445d1a.

4. Shākir al-Nābulsī, *Sujūn bi-lā quḍbān: Yaḥduthu fī al-'ālam al-'Arabī al-'ān* (Beirut: Al-Mu'assasa al-'Arabiyya lil-Dirāsāt wal-Nashr, 2007), 106.

5. Shākir al-Nābulsī, *Bin Lādin wal-'aql al-'Arabī: Kayfa fakkara al-'Arab ba'da 11 Sibtambir 2001* (Cologne, Germany: Manshūrāt al-Jamal, 2007), 198–99.

6. See, for example, al-Majlis al-Islāmī al-A'lā fī Ustrāliyā, Dār al-Fatwā, "Al-Azhar al-sharīf ramz al-i'tidāl wal-wasaṭiyya wa-bihimā naḥmī al-mujtama' min khaṭar al-taṭarruf al-baghīḍ," Dec. 22, 2015, at https://tinyurl.com/y8q5xly6.

7. Muḥammad Mukhtār Gum'a, "Al-Khiṭāb al-dīnī al-muftarā 'alayhi," Nov. 7, 2014, at https://tinyurl.com/y6v5mq98.

8. Mawqi' Samāḥat al-Shaykh Yūsuf al-Qaraḍāwī, "Inṭilāq a'māl multaqā 'al-imām al-Qaraḍāwī' bil-Dawḥa," July 11, 2007, at https://www.al-qaradawi.net/node/1708 (Mawqi' Samāḥat al-Shaykh Yūsuf al-Qaraḍāwī is al-Qaraḍāwī's website); Muḥammad 'Abd al-Quddūs, "Al-Shaykh Yūsuf al-Qaraḍāwī: Imām al-wasaṭiyya," Mawqi' Samāḥat al-Shaykh Yūsuf al-Qaraḍāwī, Oct. 13, 2015, at https://www.al-qaradawi.net/node/2371.

9. On the meaning of the village's name, see Shaykh Yūsuf al-Qaraḍāwī, *Ibn al-qarya wal-kuttāb: Malāmiḥ sīra wa-masīra*, 4 vols. (Cairo: Dār al-Shurūq, 2002), 1:15–20.

10. Al-Qaraḍāwī, *Ibn al-qarya wal-kuttāb*, 1:101; Shaykh Yūsuf al-Qaraḍāwī, "Kalimat al-'allāma al-Qaraḍāwī bi-munāsabat al-jā'iza," Dec. 16, 2000, in *Al-Shaykh al-Qaraḍāwī: Shakhṣiyyat al-'ām al-Islāmiyya 1421 A.H./2000* (Cairo: Maktabat Wahba, 2001), 136.

11. Al-Qaraḍāwī, "Kalimat al-'allāma al-Qaraḍāwī bi-munāsabat al-jā'iza," 136.

12. Al-Qaraḍāwī, *Ibn al-qarya wal-kuttāb,* 1:151; Mu'tazz al-Khaṭīb, *Al-Qaraḍāwī faqīh al-ṣaḥwa al-Islāmiyya: Sīra fikriyya taḥlīliyya* (Beirut: Markaz al-Ḥaḍāra li-Tanmiyat al-Fikr al-Islāmī, 2009), 29.

13. Shaykh Yūsuf al-Qaraḍāwī, *Al-Ḥayāh al-rabbāniyya wal-'ilm: Fī-l-ṭarīq ilā Allāh,* Taysīr fiqh al-sulūk fī ḍaw' al-Qur'ān wal-Sunna no. 1 (Cairo: Maktabat Wahba, 1995), 7–9.

14. Mawqi' Samāḥat al-Shaykh Yūsuf al-Qaraḍāwī, "Multaqā talāmīth al-Qaraḍāwī: Ṣinā'at qāda li-mustaqbal al-umma," June 2, 2010, at https://www.al-qaradawi.net/node/5017.

15. Naṣr Ḥāmid Abū Zayd, *Naqd al-khiṭab al-dīnī,* 2nd ed. (Cairo: Sīnā lil-Nashr, 1994), 67–71, quotation marks around *mu'tadil* and *mutaṭarrif* in the original.

16. 'Abd al-Razzāq 'Īd, *Yūsuf al-Qaraḍāwī bayna al-tasāmuḥ wal-irhāb (sadanat hayākil al-wahm/naqd al-'aql al-fiqhī)* (Beirut: Dār al-Ṭalī'a, 2005), 210, quotation marks around *wasaṭiyya* and *ifranjiyya* in the original.

17. 'Īd, *Yūsuf al-Qaraḍāwī,* 228–29, quotation marks around *ifranjiyya* in the original.

18. Bettina Gräf, "The Concept of Wasaṭiyya in the Work of Yūsuf al-Qaraḍāwī," in *Global Mufti: The Phenomenon of Yusuf al-Qaradawi,* ed. Bettina Gräf and Jakob Skovgaard-Petersen (New York: Columbia Univ. Press, 2009), 214–15.

19. Mohammad Hashim Kamali, *The Middle Path of Moderation in Islam: The Qur'ānic Principle of Wasaṭiyyah* (Oxford: Oxford Univ. Press, 2015).

20. Among the many works on *wasaṭiyya,* the following should be mentioned: 'Alī Muḥammad al-Ṣalābī, *Al-Wasaṭiyya fī al-Qur'ān al-karīm* (Cairo: Dār Ibn al-Jawzī, 2007), and Ṣalāḥ al-Ṣāwī, *Al-Wasaṭiyya: Al-'Aqīda, al-'ilm, al-'ibādāt, al-mu'āsharāt, al-mu'āmalāt, al-akhlāq* (Cairo: Dār al-Kitāb al-Ḥadīth, 2010).

21. Sagi Polka, "The Centrist Stream in Egypt and Its Role in the Public Discourse Surrounding the Shaping of the Country's Cultural Identity," *Middle Eastern Studies* 39, no. 3 (July 2003): 39–64, and "Between Liberalism and Fundamentalism" (in Hebrew), PhD diss., Bar Ilan Univ., 2000.

22. Shaykh Yūsuf al-Qaraḍāwī, *Al-Khaṣā'iṣ al-'āmma lil-Islām,* 6th ed. (Cairo: Maktabat Wahba, 2003), 115, and *Fiqh al-wasaṭiyya al-Islāmiyya wal-tajdīd: Ma'ālim wa-manārāt* (Cairo: Dār al-Shurūq, 2010), 37–38.

23. Muḥammad 'Imāra, *Ma'ālim al-minhāj al-Islāmī,* 3rd ed. (Cairo: Dār al-Rashād, 1997), 79–80.

24. Uriya Shavit, *Sharī'a and Muslim Minorities: The Wasaṭī and Salafī Approaches to Fiqh al-Aqalliyyāt al-Muslima* (Oxford: Oxford Univ. Press, 2015), 24–25.

25. Shaykh Yūsuf al-Qaraḍāwī, *Min ajli ṣaḥwa rāshida: Tujaddidu al-dīn wa-tanhaḍu bi-l-dunyā,* 2nd ed. (Cairo: Dār al-Shurūq, 2005), 51–52.

26. Shaykh Yūsuf al-Qaraḍāwī, *Kalimāt fī al-wasaṭiyya al-Islāmiyya wa-ma'ālimihā* (Cairo: Dār al-Shurūq, 2008), 16–19.

27. Mu'tazz al-Khaṭīb, "Fī naqd al-qawl bi-l-wasaṭiyya wa-l-i'tidāl," *Majallat al-Kalima: Muntadā al-Kalima li-l-Dirāsāt wa-l-Abḥāth,* Winter 2007, 113–18, at https://archive.islamonline.net/?p=50.

28. Gräf, "The Concept of Wasaṭiyya in the Work of Yūsuf al-Qaraḍāwī," 214.

29. Muḥammad ʿImāra, *Al-Salafiyya wāḥida? Am salafiyyāt?* (Giza, Egypt: Nahḍat Miṣr, 2008), 7. On the definition of the term *Salafiyya*, see Muḥammad Saʿīd Ramaḍān al-Būṭī, *Al-Salafiyya marḥala zamaniyya mubāraka lā madhhab Islāmī* (Beirut: Dār al-Fikr al-Muʿāṣir, 2009), 9–23.

30. On this *ḥadīth*, see Muḥammad Rātib al-Nābulsī, "Mazāyā al-Ṣaḥāba al-kirām," June 29, 1997, at http://www.nabulsi.com/green/ar/print.php?art=2973.

31. Muḥammad ʿImāra, *Izālat al-shubuhāt ʿan maʿānī al-muṣṭalaḥāt* (Cairo: Dār al-Salām, 2010), 490–92.

32. Bernard Haykel, "On the Nature of Salafi Thought and Action," in *Global Salafism: Islam's New Religious Movement*, ed. Roel Meijer (New York: Columbia Univ. Press, 2009), 33.

33. Henri Lauzière, *The Making of Salafism: Islamic Reform in the Twentieth Century* (New York: Columbia Univ. Press, 2016), 20–22.

34. Lauzière, *The Making of Salafism*, 33–44.

35. Lauzière, *The Making of Salafism*, 201.

36. Haykel, "On the Nature of Salafi Thought," 47.

37. Haykel, "On the Nature of Salafi Thought," 38–39.

38. Muḥammad ʿImāra, *Al-Salaf wal-Salafiyya* (Cairo: Maktabat Wahba, 2011), 8; Henri Lauzière, "The Construction of Salafiyya: Reconsidering Salafism from the Perspective of Conceptual History," *International Journal of Middle East Studies* 42 (2010): 369–89; Quintan Wiktorowicz, "Anatomy of the Salafi Movement," *Studies in Conflict and Terrorism* 29 (2006): 207–8.

39. Wiktorowicz, "Anatomy of the Salafi Movement," 208.

40. Wiktorowicz, "Anatomy of the Salafi Movement," 217–21.

41. Daniel Lav, *Radical Islam and the Revival of Medieval Theology* (Cambridge: Cambridge Univ. Press, 2012), 86–119; Joas Wagemakers, *A Quietist Jihadi: The Ideology and Influence of Abu Muhammad al-Maqdisi* (Cambridge: Cambridge Univ. Press, 2012), 102–3.

42. Wagemakers, *A Quietist Jihadi*, 99–101.

43. Wagemakers, *A Quietist Jihadi*, 34.

44. Thomas Hegghammer, "Jihadi-Salafis or Revolutionaries? On Religion and Politics in the Study of Militant Islamism," in *Global Salafism*, ed. Meijer, 251.

45. Abū Muḥammad al-Maqdisī, "Suʾāl ʿan ṣiḥḥat muṣṭalaḥ (al-Salafiyya al-jihādiyya)?" *Muntadā Minbar al-Tawḥīd wal-Jihād*, question no. 120 (2009), at http://www.ilmway.com/site/maqdis/FAQ/MS_3034.html.

46. For a discussion of the term *Salafiyya jihādiyya*, see al-Bāshā Abū Dajjāna, *Taʾammulāt fī muṣṭalaḥ al-Salafiyya al-jihādiyya* (N.p.: Shabakat al-Fidāʾ al-Islāmiyya, Feb. 23, 2012), electronic copy at https://tinyurl.com/y9me7v3l.

47. Abū Muḥammad al-Maqdisī, "Ḥiwār maʿa al-shaykh Abī Muḥammad al-Maqdisī sanat 1423," 1423 [2002–3], at http://www.ilmway.com/site/maqdis/MS_121.html.

48. Wiktorowicz, "Anatomy of the Salafi Movement," 225–28.

49. Shiraz Maher, *Salafi-Jihadism: The History of an Idea* (Oxford: Oxford Univ. Press, 2016), 16–18.

50. Lav, *Radical Islam*, 126–35.

51. For more on Abū Muṣʿab al-Sūrī, see Philip Holtmann, *Abu Musab al-Surī's Jihad Concept* (Tel Aviv: Moshe Dayan Center, Tel Aviv Univ., 2009), 53–69. See also Abū Muṣʿab al-Sūrī, *Daʿwat al-muqāwama al-Islāmiyya al-ʿālamiyya* (N.p.: n.p., Dec. 2004), electronic copy at http://www.ilmway.com/site/maqdis/MS_808.html.

52. Al-Sūrī, *Daʿwat al-muqāwama al-Islāmiyya al-ʿālamiyya*, 693–94.

53. Ḥasan al-Bannā, *Majmūʿat rasāʾil al-imām al-shahīd Ḥasan al-Bannā* (Cairo: Dār al-Tawzīʿ wal-Nashr al-Islāmiyya, 1992), 356.

54. Ḥ. al-Bannā, *Majmūʿat rasāʾil*, 191. The latter part of the last sentence is based on Q8:39 and 2:193; see the importance of these verses for global jihad in chapter 5.

55. Ḥ. al-Bannā, *Majmūʿat rasāʾil*, 361.

56. Ḥ. al-Bannā, *Majmūʿat rasāʾil*, 144–45.

57. Ḥ. al-Bannā, *Majmūʿat rasāʾil*, 361.

58. Shaykh Yūsuf al-Qaraḍāwī, *Al-Ikhwān al-Muslimūn: Sabʿūn ʿāman fī al-daʿwa wal-tarbiya wal-jihād, bi-munāsabat murūr sabʿīn ʿāman ʿalā taʾsīs Jamāʿat al-Ikhwān al-Muslimīn wa-khamsīn ʿāman ʿalā istishhād muʾassis al-jamāʿa Ḥasan al-Bannā* (Cairo: Maktabat Wahba, 1999), 215–16.

59. On Quṭb's time in the MB, see John Calvert, *Sayyid Qutb and the Origins of Radical Islamism* (New York: Columbia Univ. Press, 2013), 157–95.

60. Ayman al-Ẓawāhirī, *Fursān taḥta rāyat al-nabī*, 2nd ed. (N.p.: Muʾassasat al-Saḥāb lil-Intāj al-Iʿlāmī, 1431 [2010]), part I, 10, electronic copy at http://www.ilmway.com/site/maqdis/MS_874.html.

61. ʿAbdallah ʿAzzām, "Sayyid Quṭb ʿishrūna ʿāman ʿalā al-shahāda," Oct. 23, 1986, 2, at http://www.ilmway.com/site/maqdis/MS_9077.html.

62. ʿAzzām, "Sayyid Quṭb," 6–7.

63. On Quṭb and the MB and on his radicalization, see Calvert, *Sayyid Qutb*, 157–227.

64. Al-Mawdūdī was the founder of the Islamic Group in India, which he led for thirty years. On him and his teachings, see Seyyed Vali Reza Nasr, "Mawdudi and the Jamaʿat-I Islami: The Origins, Theory, and Practice of Islamic Revivalism," in *Pioneers of Islamic Revival*, ed. Ali Rahnema (London: Zed Books, 2008), 98–124.

65. Sayyid Quṭb, *Fī ẓilāl al-Qurʾān*, 6 vols., 25th ed. (Cairo: Dār al-Shurūq, 1996), 2:904 (commentary on Q5:50), and *Maʿālim fī al-ṭarīq* (Cairo: Dār al-Shurūq, n.d.), 133, 148, electronic copy at http://www.ilmway.com/site/maqdis/MS_705.html. See also Emmanuel Sivan, *Radical Islam, Medieval Theology, and Modern Politics* (New Haven, CT: Yale Univ. Press, 1985), 21–22; Calvert, *Sayyid Qutb*, 217–20; and Abū al-Ḥasan al-Nadwī, *Mādhā khasira al-ʿālam bi-inḥiṭāṭ al-Muslimīn* (Al-Manṣūra, Egypt: Maktabat al-Īmān, n.d.).

66. Quṭb, *Maʿālim fī al-ṭarīq*, 79–82.

67. Calvert, *Sayyid Qutb*, 217.

68. Quṭb, *Maʿālim fī al-ṭarīq*, 97.

69. Quṭb, *Maʿālim fī al-ṭarīq*, 9–17.

70. ʿUmar ʿAbd al-Raḥmān, *Kalimat ḥaqq: Murāfaʿat al-Shaykh ʿUmar ʿAbd al-Raḥmān fī qaḍiyyat al-jihād* (Cairo: Dār al-Iʿtiṣām, 1987), 78, electronic copy at http://www.ilmway.com/site/maqdis/MS_8860.html.

71. Fawaz A. Gerges, *The Far Enemy: Why Jihad Went Global*, 2nd ed. (Cambridge: Cambridge Univ. Press, 2010), 7.

72. Al-Nābulsī, *Tahāfut al-uṣūliyya*, 47, 78–79. See also François Gugart, *Islamism in the Shadow of al-Qaʿida*, trans. Patrick Hutchinson (Austin: Univ. of Texas Press, 2008), 100–120.

73. Quṭb, *Maʿālim fī al-ṭarīq*, 30–31.

74. Quṭb, *Maʿālim fī al-ṭarīq*, 57.

75. Quṭb, *Maʿālim fī al-ṭarīq*, 122–23, 129–30.

76. Al-Qaraḍāwī, *Ibn al-qarya wal-kuttāb*, 3:51. On the MB's ambivalence toward Quṭbism, see Alison Pargeter, *The Muslim Brotherhood: The Burden of Tradition* (London: Saqi, 2010), 185.

77. Shaykh Yūsuf al-Qaraḍāwī, "Waqfa maʿa al-shahīd Sayyid Quṭb," in *Sayyid Quṭb wal-ʿunf wa-takfīr: Azmat afkār am mushkilat qurrāʾ?* ed. Muʿtazz al-Khaṭīb (Cairo: Maktabat Madbūlī, 2009), 60–62.

78. On Quṭb's views on jihad, see Calvert, *Sayyid Qutb*, 221–27, and Richard Bonney, *Jihad from Qurʾān to Bin Laden* (New York: Palgrave Macmillan, 2007), 215–23.

79. Shaykh Yūsuf al-Qaraḍāwī, *Fiqh al-jihād: Dirāsa muqārana li-aḥkāmihi wa-falsafatihi fī ḍawʾ al-Qurʾān wal-Sunna*, 2 vols. (Cairo: Maktabat Wahba, 2009), 1:394–404. All references to *Fiqh al-jihād* are to this first edition, with the exception of note 175 in chapter 5.

80. Quṭb, *Maʿālim fī al-ṭarīq*, 60–69.

81. On al-Mawdūdī's conception of jihad as a global revolution, see Bonney, *Jihad*, 200–211, and al-Qaraḍāwī, *Fiqh al-jihād*, 1:394–95.

82. Calvert, *Sayyid Qutb*, 221–27. For al-Qaraḍāwī's own interpretation of the Verse of the Sword, see al-Qaraḍāwī, *Fiqh al-jihād*, 1:267–314.

83. This tendency in the shaykh's efforts is particularly evident in the following writings: Shaykh Yūsuf al-Qaraḍāwī, *Al-Islām wal-ʿunf: Naẓarāt taʾṣīliyya*, 2nd ed. (Cairo: Dār al-Shurūq, 2007); *Khiṭābunā al-Islāmī fī ʿaṣr al-ʿawlama* (Cairo: Dār al-Shurūq, 2004), 158–72; and *Naḥnu wal-gharb: Asʾila shāʾika wa-ajwiba ḥāsima* (Cairo: Dār al-Tawzīʿ wal-Nashr al-Islāmiyya, 2006), especially his condemnation of terrorism, 47–56.

84. Quṭb, *Maʿālim fī al-ṭarīq*, 3.

85. Shaykh Yūsuf al-Qaraḍāwī, *Al-Islām: Ḥaḍārat al-ghad* (Cairo: Maktabat Wahba, 1995), 149.

86. Quoted in Shaykh Yūsuf al-Qaraḍāwī, "Al-Iṣlāḥ alladhī nanshuduhu: Ahdāfuhu wa-shurūṭuhu wa-majālātuhu," Jan. 16, 2004, in *Khuṭab al-Shaykh al-Qaraḍāwī*, ed. al-Sa'd, 6:267–68.

87. Azzam Tamimi, "The Origins of Arab Secularism," in *Islam and Secularism in the Middle East*, ed. John L. Esposito and Azzam Tamimi (New York: New York Univ. Press, 2000), 17.

88. Shaykh Yūsuf al-Qaraḍāwī, *Al-Taṭarruf al-'ilmānī fī muwājahat al-Islām* (Al-Manṣūra, Egypt: Andalūsiyā li-l-Nashr wa-l-Tawzī', 2000), 13–18.

89. Nadav Safran, *Egypt in Search of Political Community: An Analysis of the Intellectual and Political Evolution of Egypt, 1804–1952*, 2nd ed. (Cambridge, MA: Harvard Univ. Press, 1981), 275; Meir Hatina, *Identity Politics in the Middle East: Liberal Thought and Islamic Challenge in Egypt* (London: I. B. Tauris, 2007), 6.

90. On the generations of liberals, see Shākir al-Nābulsī, *Al-Lībirāliyyūn al-judud: Jadal fikrī* (Cologne, Germany: Manshūrāt al-Jamal, 2005), 19–28.

91. S. al-Nābulsī, *Al-Lībirāliyyūn al-judud*, 15–16. See also David Govrin, *The Journey to the Arab Spring: The Ideological Roots of the Middle East Upheaval in Arab Liberal Thought* (London: Vallentine Mitchell, 2014), 89–117, and Meir Hatina, "Arab Liberal Thought in Historical Perspective," in *Arab Liberal Thought after 1967: Old Dilemmas, New Perceptions*, ed. Meir Hatina (New York: Palgrave Macmillan, 2015), 26–40.

92. Govrin, *Journey to the Arab Spring*, 89–117.

93. S. al-Nābulsī, *Al-Lībirāliyyūn al-judud*, 15–16.

94. S. al-Nābulsī, *Al-Lībirāliyyūn al-judud*, 21–25.

95. Al-Qaraḍāwī, *Fiqh al-wasaṭiyya al-Islāmiyya wal-tajdīd*, 208–41.

96. Shākir al-Nābulsī, *Al-'Arab bayna al-lībirāliyya wal-uṣūliyya al-dīniyya* (Beirut: Al-Mu'assasa al-'Arabiyya lil-Dirāsāt wal-Nashr, 2010), 17.

97. Abū Zayd, *Naqd al-khiṭab al-dīnī*, 62.

98. Shaykh Yūsuf al-Qaraḍāwī, *Al-Islām wal-'ilmāniyya wajhan li-wajhin: Radd 'ilmī 'alā Dr. Fu'ād Zakariyyā wa-jamā'at al-'ilmāniyyīn*, 2nd ed. (Cairo: Dār al-Ṣaḥwa, 1994), 42–54.

99. Shaykh Yūsuf al-Qaraḍāwī, "Ma'rakat al-Islām wal-'ilmāniyya," June 13, 1997, in *Khuṭab al-Shaykh al-Qaraḍāwī*, vol. 7, ed. Muḥammad Ḥūṭar and Akram 'Abd al-Sattār Kassāb (Cairo: Maktabat Wahba, 2006), 173.

100. Al-Qaraḍāwī, *Al-Taṭarruf al-'ilmānī*, 16.

101. S. al-Nābulsī, *Al-'Arab bayna al-lībirāliyya*, 109–18; S. al-Nābulsī, *Sujūn bi-lā quḍbān*, 52–53.

102. Abū Zayd, *Naqd al-khiṭāb al-dīnī*, 63–64.

103. Naṣr Ḥāmid Abū Zayd, *Al-Tafkīr fī zaman al-takfīr: Ḍidda al-jahl wal-zayf wal-khurāfa*, 2nd ed. (Cairo: Maktabat Madbūlī, 1995), 21–24, 37–40.

104. S. al-Nābulsī, *Al-Lībirāliyyūn al-judud*, 15–16.

105. Shaykh Yūsuf al-Qaraḍāwī, *Al-Islām alladhī nad'ū ilayhi* (Cairo: Maktabat Wahba, 2004), 8.

106. Al-Qaraḍāwī, *Al-Islām wal-'ilmāniyya*, 73–74.

107. Al-Qaraḍāwī, *Al-Islām wal-'ilmāniyya*, 73–74.

108. Al-Qaraḍāwī, *Al-Islām wal-'ilmāniyya*, 83; the quotation marks around *aydiyūlūjiyya* (ideology) are in the original.

109. Shaykh Yūsuf al-Qaraḍāwī, *Al-Ṣaḥwa al-Islāmiyya bayna al-jumūd wal-taṭarruf* (Cairo: Dār al-Shurūq, 2001), 43.

110. Al-Qaraḍāwī, *Al-Ṣaḥwa al-Islāmiyya bayna al-jumūd wal-taṭarruf*, 48.

111. Al-Qaraḍāwī, *Al-Taṭarruf al-'ilmānī*, 93.

112. On the distinction between a theocracy and an Islamic state, see al-Qaraḍāwī, *Al-Taṭarruf al-'ilmānī*, 96–110.

113. Abū Zayd, *Al-Tafkīr fī zaman al-takfīr*, 24–25.

114. Abū Zayd, *Al-Tajdīd wa-l-taḥrīm*, 45.

115. S. al-Nābulsī, *Al-'Arab bayna al-lībirāliyya*, 104–5.

116. Al-'Ashmāwī, *Al-Islām al-siyāsī*, 122–23.

117. 'Alī 'Abd al-Rāziq, *Al-Islām wa-uṣūl al-ḥukm: Baḥth fī al-khilāfa wal-ḥukūma fī al-Islām* (Cairo: Dār al-Hilāl, 1925).

118. Khālid Muḥammad Khālid, *Min hunā nabda'u*, 11th ed. (Cairo: Maktabat al-Anjilū al-Miṣriyya, 1969), 150–64.

119. Shaykh Yūsuf al-Qaraḍāwī, *Al-Ḥulūl al-mustawrada wa-kayfa janat 'alā ummatinā* (Cairo: Maktabat Wahba, 1993), 52.

120. S. al-Nābulsī, *Sujūn bi-lā quḍbān*, 49.

121. S. al-Nābulsī, *Sujūn bi-lā quḍbān*, 51.

122. For the full text of the National Charter, see Gamal 'Abd al-Nasir, "Kalimat al-ra'īs Gamāl 'Abd al-Nāṣir fī taqdīm al-mīthāq al-waṭanī fī Jāmi'at al-Qāhira," May 21, 1962, at http://nasser.bibalex.org/Speeches/browser.aspx?SID=1015&lang=ar.

123. On the publication of this series, see al-Qaraḍāwī, *Ibn al-qarya wal-kuttāb*, 3:194, and al-Qaraḍāwī, *Al-Ḥulūl al-mustawrada*, 3–6.

124. Al-Qaraḍāwī, *Al-Ḥulūl al-mustawrada*, 3–6.

125. Shaykh Yūsuf al-Qaraḍāwī, *Al-Ḥall al-Islāmī: Farīḍa wa-ḍarūra*, 5th ed. (Cairo: Maktabat Wahba, 1993), 38–39.

126. Al-Qaraḍāwī, *Al-Ḥall al-Islāmī*, 70–71.

127. See Shimon Shamir, "Liberalism: From Monarchy to Postrevolution," in *Egypt from Monarchy to Republic: A Reassessment of Revolution and Change*, ed. Shimon Shamir (Boulder, CO: Westview Press, 1995), 202–3.

128. On these writers, see Shamir, "Liberalism," 202–3.

129. About Zakariyyā, see Hatina, *Identity Politics in the Middle East*, 134–37.

130. Al-Qaraḍāwī, *Al-Islām wal-'ilmāniyya*, 13.

131. Al-Qaraḍāwī, *Al-Islām wal-'ilmāniyya*, 24–26.

132. Shaykh Yūsuf al-Qaraḍāwī, "Bayān al-Duktūr Yūsuf al-Qaraḍāwī bi-sha'n tafjīrāt Amrīkā," *Shabakat Mishkāh al-Islāmiyya*, Sept. 12, 2001, http://www.almeshkat.net/vb/showthread.php?t=6554#gsc.tab=0.

133. Shaykh Yūsuf al-Qaraḍāwī, "Man al-mas'ūl 'an aḥdāth al-ḥādī 'ashar min Sibtimbir?" Sept. 21, 2001, in *Khuṭab al-Shaykh al-Qaraḍāwī*, ed. al-Sa'd, 6:82–95.

134. "Al-Irhāb wa-ḥamalāt al-karāhiya ḍidda al-'Arab wal-Muslimīn," episode of *Al-Sharī'a wal-ḥayāh*, al-Jazeera, Sept. 16, 2001, at https://tinyurl.com/yb2vfl5a.

135. Al-Qaraḍāwī, "Bayān al-duktūr al-Qaraḍāwī bi-sha'n tafjīrāt Amrīkā," 6:83; "Al-Irhāb wa-ḥamalāt al-karāhiya ḍidda al-'Arab wal-Muslimīna."

136. Al-Qaraḍāwī, "Man al-mas'ūl," 6:82–83; Shaykh Yūsuf al-Qaraḍāwī, "Al-Qimma al-Islāmiyya al-Masīḥiyya al-'ūlā fī Rūmā ḥawla al-irhāb wa-asbābihi," Oct. 12, 2001, in *Khuṭab al-Shaykh al-Qaraḍāwī*, ed. al-Sa'd, 6:96–109; al-Qaraḍāwī, "Bayān al-duktūr al-Qaraḍāwī bi-sha'n tafjīrāt Amrīkā."

137. "Al-Irhāb wa-ḥamalāt al-karāhiya ḍidda al-'Arab wal-Muslimīna."

138. Al-Qaraḍāwī, "Man al-mas'ūl," 6:92.

139. Alia Brahimi, *Jihad and Just War in the War on Terror* (Oxford: Oxford Univ. Press, 2010), 116–17.

140. Al-Qaraḍāwī, "Al-Qimma al-Islāmiyya al-Masīḥiyya," 6:101–4.

141. Abū Muḥammad al-Maqdisī, *Hādhā mā adīnu Allāh bihi: Wujūb nuṣrat al-Muslimīn fī Afghānistān wa-kufr man ẓāhara 'alayhim 'abadat al-ṣulbān wa-kashf talbīs al-aḥbār wal-ruhbān* (N.p.: n.p., 2001), 33–34, electronic copy at http://www.ilmway.com/site/maqdis/MS_65.html; Samuel Helfont, *Yusuf al-Qaradawi: Islam and Modernity* (Tel Aviv: Moshe Dayan Center, Tel Aviv Univ., 2009), 82–83.

142. Al-Maqdisī, *Hādhā mā adīnu Allāh bihi*, 2–3. On al-Qaraḍāwī's *fatwā* to boycott Israeli and American products, see Shaykh Yūsuf al-Qaraḍāwī, *Fatāwā mu'āṣira: Min hady al-Islām*, vols. 1, 3, 4 (Cairo: Dār al-Qalam, 2001), 3:498–502. On *ahl al-zaygh*, see 'Abd al-'Azīz b. Fawzān al-Fawzān, "Minhaj ahl al-zaygh fī al-istidlāl," *al-Bayān* 281 (Dec. 2010), at http://albayan.co.uk/MGZarticle2.aspx?id=509.

143. Al-Maqdisī, *Hādhā mā adīnu Allāh bihi*, 12.

144. 'Abd al-Ḥamīd al-Anṣārī, "Judhūr al-irhāb," *Al-'Arabiyya*, video, May 11, 2007, at https://www.youtube.com/watch?v=urvxEFTszjs&t=10s.

145. S. al-Nābulsī, *Bin Lādin*, 8–9.

146. S. al-Nābulsī, *Al-Lībirāliyyūn al-judud*, 21, 24.

147. S. al-Nābulsī, *Al-Lībirāliyyūn al-judud*, 24.

148. Al-'Afīf al-Akhḍar, "Kayfa nujaffifu yanābī' al-irhāb?" *Al-Ḥiwār al-Mutamaddin* 504 (May 31, 2003), at http://www.ahewar.org/debat/show.art.asp?aid=7812.

149. 'Abd al-Ḥamīd al-Anṣārī, *Thaqāfat al-karāhiya wa-mustaqbal al-tasāmuḥ al-insānī ilā ayna?* (Beirut: Dār Madārik lil-Nashr, 2012), electronic copy at https://aafaqcenter.com/post/826.8.

150. Al-Anṣārī, *Thaqāfat al-karāhiya wa-mustaqbal al-tasāmuḥ al-insānī ilā ayna?*

151. Shaykh Yūsuf al-Qaraḍāwī, "Wā Islāmāh," n.d., in *Khuṭab al-Shaykh al-Qaraḍāwī*, ed. al-Sa'd, 5:249–51. The date of the sermon is not specified; however, its content indicates that it was delivered in the mid-1990s, during the Bosnia War.

152. Shaykh Yūsuf al-Qaraḍāwī, "Al-Ḥarb al-thaqāfiyya 'alā al-Muslimīn," Jan. 11, 2002, and "Al-Umma al-Islāmiyya taḥta wiṣayat al-gharb," Jan. 18, 2002, both in *Khuṭab al-Shaykh al-Qaraḍāwī*, ed. al-Sa'd, 6:133–36, 6:152–59.

153. Al-'Afīf al-Akhḍar, "Min madrasat al-jihād ilā madrasat al-ijtihād," *Īlāf*, Feb. 3, 2002, at http://elaphjournal.com/Web/Archive/1012748707481471100.html.

154. Shaykh Yūsuf al-Qaraḍāwī, *Al-Ṣaḥwa al-Islāmiyya min al-murāhaqa ilā al-rushd*, 3rd ed. (Cairo: Dār al-Shurūq, 2008), 84–115, 277–338.

155. Al-Qaraḍāwī, *Khiṭābuna al-Islāmī fī 'aṣr al-'awlama*, 44–47; Shaykh Yūsuf al-Qaraḍāwī, *Thaqāfatunā bayna al-infitāḥ wal-inghilāq* (Cairo: Dār al-Shurūq, 2000), 71–79.

156. Al-Qaraḍāwī, *Naḥnu wal-gharb*, 10.

157. George Bush, "9/11 George Bush: This Crusade Is Gonna Take a While," Sept. 17, 2001, at https://www.youtube.com/watch?v=7TRVcnX8Vsw.

158. Shaykh Yūsuf al-Qaraḍāwī, *Fatāwā mu'āṣira: Min hady al-Islām*, vol. 2, 2nd ed. (Al-Manṣūra, Egypt: Dār al-Wafā', 1993), 623–35; Shaykh Yūsuf al-Qaraḍāwī, *Min fiqh al-dawla fī al-Islām: Makānatihā, ma'ālimihā, ṭabī'atihā, mawqifihā mina al-dīmuqrāṭiyya wal-ta'addudiyya wal-mar'a wa-ghayr al-Muslimīn* (Cairo: Dār al-Shurūq, 1997), 88–100; Shaykh Yūsuf al-Qaraḍāwī, *Al-Islām kamā nu'minu bihi: Ḍawābiṭ wa-malāmiḥ* (Cairo: Nahḍat Miṣr, 1999), 37–49.

159. Olivier Roy, *Globalized Islam: The Search for a New Ummah* (New York: Columbia Univ. Press, 2004), 58.

160. Martin Kramer, "Coming to Terms: Fundamentalists or Islamists," *Middle East Quarterly*, Spring 2003, 65–77; Gilles Kepel, "Islamism Reconsidered: A Running Dialogue with Modernity," *Harvard International Review*, Summer 2000, 2–5.

161. S. al-Nābulsī, *Al-'Arab bayna al-lībirāliyya*, 17.

162. S. al-Nābulsī, *Tahāfut al-uṣūliyya*, 11.

163. S. al-Nābulsī, *Tahāfut al-uṣūliyya*, 9, 15.

164. S. al-Nābulsī, *Tahāfut al-uṣūliyya*, 17–18, 47.

165. S. al-Nābulsī, *Tahāfut al-uṣūliyya*, 150.

166. Al-Qaraḍāwī, *Al-Ṣaḥwa al-Islāmiyya bayna al-jumūd wal-taṭarruf*, 23–24.

167. Al-Qaraḍāwī, *Al-Ṣaḥwa al-Islāmiyya bayna al-jumūd wal-taṭarruf*, 72.

168. S. al-Nābulsī, *Tahāfut al-uṣūliyya*, 39–40.

169. Shaykh Yūsuf al-Qaraḍāwī, *Kayfa nata'āmalu ma'a al-Qur'ān al-'aẓīm?* 2nd ed. (Cairo: Dār al-Shurūq, 2000), 252.

170. Al-'Ashmāwī, *Al-Islām al-siyāsī*, 67; Muḥammad Sa'īd al-'Ashmāwī, *Uṣūl al-sharī'a*, 4th ed. (Cairo: Maktabat Madbūlī al- Ṣaghīr, 1996), 65–75.

171. S. al-Nābulsī, *Al-Lībirāliyyūn al-judud*, 22 (Art. 5).

172. Olivier Roy, *The Failure of Political Islam*, trans. Carol Volk (London: I. B. Tauris, 1994), 48–55; John L. Esposito, *The Islamic Threat: Myth or Reality?* (New York: Oxford Univ. Press, 1992), 136–39.

173. Al-Qaraḍāwī, *Al-Ṣaḥwa al-Islāmiyya bayna al-jumūd wal-taṭarruf*, 72.

174. Abū Zayd, *Al-Tajdīd wa-l-taḥrīm*, 27.

175. Al-ʿAshmāwī, *Al-Islām al-siyāsī*, 82.

176. Al-Qaraḍāwī, *Min fiqh al-dawla fī al-Islām*, 30.

177. Abū Zayd, *Naqd al-khiṭāb al-dīnī*, 78–79 (quoting Abū Ṭālib), 121–22; see also S. al-Nābulsī, *Sujūn bi-lā quḍbān*, 44–45.

178. Gräf and Skovgaard-Petersen, eds., *Global Mufti*.

179. Gudrun Krämer, preface to *Global Mufti*, ed. Gräf and Skovgaard-Petersen, xi.

180. Helfont, *Yusuf al-Qaradawi*.

181. Muhammad Qasim Zaman, *Modern Islamic Thought in a Radical Age: Religious Authority and Internal Criticism* (Cambridge: Cambridge Univ. Press, 2012).

182. Raymond William Baker, *Islam without Fear: Egypt and the New Islamists* (Cambridge, MA: Harvard Univ. Press, 2003).

183. Shavit, *Sharīʿa and Muslim Minorities*, 17.

184. R. Hrair Dekmejian, *Islam in Revolution: Fundamentalism in the Arab World*, 2nd ed. (Syracuse, NY: Syracuse Univ. Press, 1995), 213.

185. Al-Qaraḍāwī, *Kalimāt fī al-wasaṭiyya al-Islāmiyya*, 39.

186. Al-Qaraḍāwī, *Fiqh al-wasaṭiyya al-Islāmiyya wal-tajdīd*.

187. Mawqiʿ Samāḥat al-Shaykh Yūsuf al-Qaraḍāwī, "Multaqā talāmīdh al-Qaraḍāwī."

188. Al-Qaraḍāwī, *Khiṭābunā al-Islāmī fī ʿaṣr al-ʿawlama*, 9–13.

189. Ḥasan al-Bannā, "Risālat al-taʿālīm" (1940), electronic copy at https://tinyurl.com/ydxe5gtu, and reprinted in al-Bannā, *Majmūʿat rasāʾil*, 355–70.

190. Al-Qaraḍāwī, *Al-Islām ḥaḍārat al-ghad*, 124–26, 149.

191. Shaykh Yūsuf al-Qaraḍāwī, *Al-Muslimūn wal-ʿawlama* (Port Said, Egypt: Dār al-Tawzīʿ wal-Nashr al-Islāmiyya, 2000), 138–39.

1. *Wasaṭiyya*, an Innovating Salafism

1. John L. Esposito and John O. Voll, eds., *Makers of Contemporary Islam* (Oxford: Oxford Univ. Press, 2001).

2. John L. Esposito and John O. Voll, "Introduction: Muslim Activist Intellectuals and Their Place in History," in *Makers of Contemporary Islam*, ed. Esposito and Voll, 3, 17.

3. Esposito and Voll, "Introduction," 12–21.

4. On al-Afghānī, see Nikki R. Keddie, "Sayyid Jamal al-Din al-Afghani," in *Pioneers of Islamic Revival*, ed. Ali Rahnema (London: Zed Books, 1994), 11–29.

5. On Muḥammad ʿAbduh, see Yvonne Haddad, "Muhammad Abduh: Pioneer of Islamic Reform," in *Pioneers of Islamic Revival*, ed. Rahnema, 30–63.

6. On religious reform (*iṣlāḥ*) in the thought of Muḥammad ʿAbduh, see Muḥammad ʿImāra, *Al-Imām Muḥammad ʿAbduh: Mujaddid al-dunyā bi-tajdīd al-dīn*, 3rd ed. (Cairo: Dār al-Shurūq, 2009), 45–80.

7. On the difference between today's Salafism and the Salafism of al-Afghānī, ʿAbduh, and Riḍā, see Wagemakers, *A Quietist Jihadi*, 6–7; Lauzière, "The Construction of Salafiyya," 369–89; and Lauzière, *The Making of Salafism*, 33–49.

8. Ana Belén Soage, "Rashīd Riḍā's Legacy," *The Muslim World* 98, no. 1 (Jan. 2008): 2–3.

9. For al-Bannā's concept of *tajdīd*, which was influenced by the modernists, see Muḥammad ʿImāra, "Al-Tajdīd fī al-mashrūʿ al-ḥaḍārī lil-Imām Ḥasan al-Bannā," in *Al-Mashrūʿ al-iṣlāḥī lil-Imām Ḥasan al-Bannā: Tasāʾulāt li-qarn jadīd: Buḥūth muʾtamar miʾawiyyat al-Imām al-Bannā*, 2nd ed., ed. Ṭāriq al-Bishrī (Cairo: Markaz al-Iʿlām al-ʿArabī, 2007), 21–37.

10. Malcolm H. Kerr, *Islamic Reform: The Political and Legal Theories of Muḥammad ʿAbduh and Rashīd Riḍā* (Berkeley: Univ. of California Press, 1966), 187–208. On *ijtihād* in the thought of the modernists and al-Qaraḍāwī, see Zaman, *Modern Islamic Thought in a Radical Age*, 75–107.

11. ʿImāra, *Al-Imām Muḥammad ʿAbduh*, 47–80.

12. Shaykh Yūsuf al-Qaraḍāwī, "Al-Mīthāq al-Islāmī li-l-Ittiḥād al-ʿĀlamī li-ʿUlamāʾ al-Muslimīn," 2006, 58, at http://www.iumsonline.org/uploads/books/IslamicCharter-Arabic.pdf.

13. Muhammad Qasim Zaman, *The Ulama in Contemporary Islam: Custodians of Change* (Princeton, NJ: Princeton Univ. Press, 2002), 178–80. See also David H. Warren, "The ʿUlamāʾ and the Arab Uprisings 2011–13: Considering Yusuf al-Qaradawi, the 'Global Mufti,' between the Muslim Brotherhood, the Islamic Legal Tradition, and Qatari Foreign Policy," *New Middle Eastern Studies* 4 (2014): 2–4.

14. Al-Qaraḍāwī, "Al-Iṣlāḥ alladhī nanshuduhu," 6:266.

15. Al-Qaraḍāwī quotes the text by Muḥammad Iqbāl in "Al-*Wasaṭiyya* fī al-Islām," episode of *Al-Sharīʿa wal-ḥayāh*, al-Jazeera, Oct. 26, 1997, at https://tinyurl.com/y7agxjsr.

16. Muṣṭafā Ṣādiq al-Rāfiʿī, *Taḥta Rāyat al-Qurʾān—Al-Maʿraka bayna al-Qadīm wal-ḥadīth* (Beirut, 7th ed.: Dār al-Kitāb al-ʿArabī, 1974), at https://ia600603.us.archive.org/29/items/FP11523/11523.pdf.

17. Al-ʿAfīf al-Akhḍar, "Iṣlāḥ al-Islām ḍarūrī wa-mumkin," *Al-Ḥiwār al-Mutamaddin* 5380 (Dec. 23, 2016), at http://www.ahewar.org/debat/show.art.asp?aid=336211.

18. Shaykh Yūsuf al-Qaraḍāwī, *Al-Umma al-Islāmiyya: Ḥaqīqa lā wahm* (Cairo: Maktabat Wahba, 1995), 16.

19. ʿAbd al-Ḥamīd al-Anṣārī, "Thaqāfat al-karāhiya wa-intishār al-taṭarruf wa-l-tajdīd al-dīnī," interview on *Ḥadīth al-ʿArab*, program on *Sky News*, Aug. 5, 2016, at https://www.youtube.com/watch?v=fA0edaPSCvU&t=792s.

20. Al-Qaraḍāwī, *Fiqh al-jihād*, 2:1156–57.

21. Shākir al-Nābulsī, "Al-'Arab bayna taḥadiyyāt al-'aṣr wa-'awā'iq al-taghayyur," *Al-Ḥiwār al-Mutamaddin*, Apr. 13, 2005, at http://www.m.ahewar.org/s.asp?aid=35398&r=0.

22. Al-Akhḍar, "Iṣlāḥ al-Islām ḍarūrī wa-mumkin."

23. Tamimi, "The Origins of Arab Secularism," 18; Bernard Lewis, *What Went Wrong? Western Impact and Middle Eastern Response* (Oxford: Oxford Univ. Press, 2002), 18–34.

24. Tamimi, "The Origins of Arab Secularism," 17; Lewis, *What Went Wrong?* 104–5.

25. Ṭaha Ḥusayn, *Mustaqbal al-thaqāfa fī Miṣr* (Cairo: Mu'assasat al-Hindāwī, 2014), 43.

26. Muḥammad 'Abduh, "Ta'addud al-zawjāt," in *Al-A'māl al-kāmila lil-imām al-Shaykh Muḥammad 'Abduh*, 5 vols., ed. Muḥammad 'Imāra (Cairo: Dār al-Shurūq, 1993), 2:85. On the apologetics of Islamic modernism, see William E. Shepard, "Islam and Ideology: Towards a Typology," *International Journal of Middle East Studies* 19 (1987): 313.

27. Shaykh Yūsuf al-Qaraḍāwī, *Markaz al-mar'a fī al-ḥayāh al-Islāmiyya*, 2nd ed. (Cairo: Maktabat Wahba, 2005), 119–20.

28. Shaykh Yūsuf al-Qaraḍāwī, *Ummatunā bayna qarnayni* (Cairo: Dār al-Shurūq, 2000), 92–95.

29. Al-Qaraḍāwī, *Ummatunā bayna qarnayni*, 93–95.

30. Al-Qaraḍāwī, *Fatāwā mu'āṣira*, 2:636–51.

31. Al-Qaraḍāwī, *Min fiqh al-dawla fī al-Islām*, 138–46. On al-Qaraḍāwī's principles on borrowing from others, see al-Qaraḍāwī, *Al-Ḥall al-Islāmī*, 81–85.

32. 'Umar Baṭīsha, *Al-'Allāma al-Duktūr al-Qaraḍāwī: Shāhid 'alā al-'aṣr* (Giza, Egypt: Dār al-Fārūq li-l-Istithmārāt al-Thaqāfiyya, 2009), 50–59; al-Qaraḍāwī, *Al-Ḥall al-Islāmī*, 7–38.

33. Mirna Hammoud, "Causes for Fundamentalist Popularity in Egypt," in *Islamic Fundamentalism: Myths and Realities*, ed. Ahmad S. Moussalli (London: Ithaca Press, 1998), 303; al-Qaraḍāwī, *Al-Ḥall al-Islāmī*, 7–38.

34. Al-Qaraḍāwī, *Ummatunā bayna qarnayni*, 112–13.

35. Shaykh Yūsuf al-Qaraḍāwī, *Mustaqbal al-uṣūliyya al-Islāmiyya* (Cairo: Maktabat Wahba, 1997), 32–44.

36. Al-Qaraḍāwī, *Mustaqbal al-uṣūliyya al-Islāmiyya*, 17–19.

37. Al-Qaraḍāwī, *Mustaqbal al-uṣūliyya al-Islāmiyya*, 19–27.

38. Al-Qaraḍāwī, *Mustaqbal al-uṣūliyya al-Islāmiyya*, 27–32.

39. Shaykh Yūsuf al-Qaraḍāwī, *Al-Saḥwa al-Islāmiyya wa-humūm al-waṭan al-'Arabī wal-Islāmī*, 2nd ed. (Cairo: Maktabat Wahba, 1997), 247–48.

40. Al-Qaraḍāwī, *Ummatunā bayna qarnayni*, 114.

41. Al-Qaraḍāwī, *Fiqh al-jihād*, 1:18–19.

42. Shaykh Yūsuf al-Qaraḍāwī, *Liqā' maftūḥ ma'a al-'allāma al-Qaraḍāwī fī l-Baḥrayn* (Cairo: Maktabat Wahba, 2011), 22. On the definition of the term *tajdīd* (renewal), see al-Qaraḍāwī, *Fiqh al-wasaṭiyya al-Islāmiyya wal-tajdīd*, 184–206; *Tajdīd al-dīn alladhī nans-huduhu* (Cairo: Maktabat Wahba, 2011), 25–29; and *Al-Islām alladhī nad'ū ilayhi*, 9.

43. Al-Qaraḍāwī, *Liqā' maftūḥ ma'a al-'allāma al-Qaraḍāwī*, 20–24. On al-Qaraḍāwī and modernity, see Helfont, *Yusuf al-Qaradawi*, 41–57.

44. On Ibn Taymiyya's renewing Salafism, see 'Imāra, *Al-Salafiyya wāḥida?* 31–54.

45. Shaykh Yūsuf al-Qaraḍāwī, *Awlawiyyāt al-ḥaraka al-Islāmiyya fī al-marḥala al-qādima*, 4th ed. (Cairo: Maktabat Wahba, 1992), 101–4. On the "*tajdīd ḥadīth*," see Ella Landau-Tasseron, "The 'Cyclical Reform': A Study of the Mujaddid Tradition," *Studia Islamica* 70 (1989): 79–117, and al-Qaraḍāwī, *Min ajli ṣaḥwa rāshida*, 11–56.

46. Uriya Shavit, "Can Muslims Befriend Non-Muslims? Debating *al-Walā' wa-al-Barā'* (Loyalty and Disavowal) in Theory and Practice," *Islam and Christian Relations* 25, no. 1 (2014): 67–68.

47. Hegghammer, "Jihadi-Salafis or Revolutionaries?" 249.

48. Al-Qaraḍāwī, *Awlawiyyāt al-ḥaraka al-Islāmiyya*, 96–97.

49. Al-Qaraḍāwī, *Awlawiyyāt al-ḥaraka al-Islāmiyya*, 96–100.

50. Abū Baṣīr 'Abd al-Mun'im Muṣṭafā Ḥalīma al-Ṭarṭūsī, *Muṣṭalaḥāt wa-mafāhīm shar'iyya 'alāhā ghubār ta'wīlāt al-mubṭilīn yajibu taṣḥīḥuhā* (N.p.: n.p., 2007), 4–13, 229–33, electronic copy at http://www.ilmway.com/site/maqdis/MS_145.html.

51. For more on the "victorious community," see Abū Baṣīr 'Abd al-Mun'im Muṣṭafā Ḥalīma al-Ṭarṭūsī, *Ṣifat al-ṭā'ifa al-manṣūra allatī yajibu an tukaththira sawādahā* (N.p.: n.p., 1993), electronic copy at http://www.abubaseer.bizland.com/books/read/b12.doc, and Abū Qatāda al-Filasṭīnī (a.k.a. 'Umar b. Maḥmūd Abū 'Umar), *Ma'ālim al-ṭā'ifa al-manṣūra fī 'uqr dār al-Mu'minīn (Bilād al-Shām)* ([Copenhagen]: Dār al-Nūr al-Islāmī, n.d.), at http://www.ilmway.com/site/maqdis/MS_35525.html.

52. Al-Ṭarṭūsī, *Ṣifat al-ṭā'ifa al-manṣūra*, 154.

53. Al-Ṭarṭūsī, *Ṣifat al-ṭā'ifa al-manṣūra*, 154–56. For al-Ṭarṭūsī's "correction" of the term *wasaṭiyya*, see al-Ṭarṭūsī, *Muṣṭalaḥāt wa-mafāhīm shar'iyya*, 233–37, and Shaykh 'Abd al-Ākhir Ḥammād al-Ghunaymī, *Muṣṭalaḥāt wa-mafāhīm* (Beirut: Dār al-Bayāriq, 1999), term no. 7: *al-wasaṭiyya*, electronic copy at http://www.ilmway.com/site/maqdis/MS_21389.html.

54. Al-Qaraḍāwī, *Min ajli ṣaḥwa rāshida*, 30.

55. Al-Qaraḍāwī, *Awlawiyyāt al-ḥaraka al-Islāmiyya*, 101–4.

56. Landau-Tasseron, "The 'Cyclical Reform,'" 84.

57. On the idea of *tajdīd* in the Qur'ān, see al-Qaraḍāwī, *Fiqh al-wasaṭiyya al-Islāmiyya wal-tajdīd*, 187–88.

58. Landau-Tasseron, "The 'Cyclical Reform,'" 82–83.

59. On the identity of the "renewers" (*mujaddidūn*) in Muslim literature, see Landau-Tasseron, "The 'Cyclical Reform,'" 84–96.

60. Al-Qaraḍāwī, *Fiqh al-wasaṭiyya al-Islāmiyya wal-tajdīd*, 188–99, and *Min ajli ṣaḥwa rāshida*, 54–56.

61. Landau-Tasseron, "The 'Cyclical Reform,'" 85n26.

62. The word *fiqh* as al-Qaraḍāwī uses it here does not have its more familiar meaning of "Islamic jurisprudence" but rather the more basic meaning of "understanding" that it has

in the Qur'ān and the Sunna—for example, Q6:98. It appears also in *ḥadīth*: "Whomsoever God wishes to grant a favor, he gives him understanding in religion."

63. Al-Qaraḍāwī, *Tajdīd al-dīn alladhī nanshuduhu*, 25.

64. Abū Zayd, *Al-Tajdīd wa-l-taḥrīm*, 21–36.

65. Aḥmad al-Baghdādī, *Tajdīd al-fikr al-dīnī: Da'wa li-istikhdām al-'aql* (Beirut: Mu'assasat al-Intishār al-'Arabī, 2008), 253, electronic copy at https://www.books4arab.com/2016/03/pdf_764.html.

66. The term *ḥisba* refers to the state's authority to enforce compliance with principles and commandments of Islam. Unlike in civil lawsuits, in *ḥisba* lawsuits the plaintiff is not required to prove that the defendant's action caused him any direct personal harm, but only that the defendant behaved in an "un-Islamic" manner. In Egypt, *ḥisba* lawsuits have been filed against thinkers and artists who were accused of expressing anti-Islamic opinions, such as the liberal Abū Zayd.

67. Aḥmad al-Baghdādī, *Tajdīd al-fikr al-dīnī*, 267.

68. On al-Qaraḍāwī's *fatwā* forbidding Muslims to greet non-Muslims on the non-Muslims' holidays, see Shaykh Yūsuf al-Qaraḍāwī, *Fī fiqh al-aqalliyyāt al-Muslima: Ḥayāt al-Muslimīn wasṭa al-mujtama'āt al-ukhrā* (Cairo: Dār al-Shurūq, 2001), 145–50, and Uriya Shavit, "The *Wasaṭī* and *Salafī* Approaches to the Religious Law of Muslim Minorities," *Islamic Law and Society* 19, no. 4 (2012): 433–44.

69. Aḥmad al-Baghdādī, *Tajdīd al-fikr al-dīnī*, 260–65.

70. Aḥmad al-Baghdādī, *Tajdīd al-fikr al-dīnī*, 53–252.

2. The *Wasaṭiyya* School as Shaped by Yūsuf al-Qaraḍāwī

1. For the complete proceedings of the conference, which took place on December 3–4, 2014, see *Bawwābat al-Ahrām*, "Tawṣiyāt Mu'tamar al-Azhar al-'Ālamī fī Muwājahat al-Taṭarruf wal-Irhāb," Dec. 4, 2014, at http://gate.ahram.org.eg/News/568856.aspx.

2. See, for example, the closing statement of the conference "Islam and the War on Terror," held in Saudi Arabia in February 2015: *Al-Rā'id Ittiḥād al-Munaẓẓamāt al-Ijtimā'iyya fī Ūkrāniyā*, "Al-Bayān al-khitāmī al-ṣādir 'an al-Mu'tamar al-Islāmī al-'ālamī "al-Islām wa-Muḥārabat al-Irhāb," Feb. 26, 2015, at http://www.arraid.org/ar/node/4352.

3. *Shorouk News*, "Muntadā al-Samāḥa wal-Wasaṭiyya."

4. See, for instance, a video of 'Abd al-Fattah al-Sisi's speech on the Prophet Muḥammad's birthday (*Mawlid al-Nabī*): *Al-Sīsī fī iḥtifāl al-Mawlid al-Nabawī*, video, Jan. 2015, at https://www.youtube.com/watch?v=OPoIJEDcPEo. For an important treatise on the need to exterminate IS and its terrorism, see Muḥammad Mukhtār Gum'a, "Ḥatmiyyat al-qaḍā' 'alā al-irhāb," Aug. 24, 2004, at http://www.awkafonline.com/portal/wp-content/uploads/2015/03/arabic.pdf.

5. 'Īsā 'Abd al-Wahhāb, "Majlis Jāmi'at al-Azhar yuwāfiqu 'alā tadrīs thaqāfat al-wasaṭiyya fī al-Islām," *al-Waṭan*, June 7, 2015, at http://www.elwatannews.com/news/details/746030.

6. ʿAbd al-Quddūs, "Al-Shaykh Yūsuf al-Qaraḍāwī."

7. On al-Qaraḍāwī's role in the Islamic Awakening, see Armando Salvatore, *Islam and the Political Discourse of Modernity* (London: Ithaca Press, 1997), 197–217.

8. On Fūda and his liberal approach, see Hatina, *Identity Politics in the Middle East*, 47–116.

9. Gräf, "The Concept of *Wasaṭiyya* in the Work of Yūsuf al-Qaraḍāwī," 214–23.

10. Gräf, "The Concept of *Wasaṭiyya* in the Work of Yūsuf al-Qaraḍāwī," 214. For more on the role of the media in the dissemination of *wasaṭī* ideas, see Shaykh Yūsuf al-Qaraḍāwī, "Al-*Wasaṭiyya* wa-dawr al-iʿlām fī ibrāziha," Mawqiʿ Samāḥat al-Shaykh Yūsuf al-Qaraḍāwī, Oct. 15, 2006, at https://www.al-qaradawi.net/new/304-2014-01-26-18 . . . /4783, and Bettina Gräf, "Sheikh Yūsuf al-Qaraḍāwī in Cyberspace," *Die Welt des Islams* 47, nos. 3–4 (2007): 403–21.

11. Shaykh Yūsuf al-Qaraḍāwī, "Al-Wasaṭiyya 1," episode of the program *Fiqh al-ḥayāh*, Anā TV, Sept. 15, 2009, at https://www.youtube.com/watch?v=oHSzIM6SqlQ; al-Qaraḍāwī, *Fiqh al-wasaṭiyya al-Islāmiyya wal-tajdīd*, 26–32.

12. Shaykh Yūsuf al-Qaraḍāwī, *Liqāʾāt wa-muḥāwarāt ḥawla qaḍāyā al-Islām wal-ʿaṣr*, 2 vols. (Cairo: Maktabat Wahba, 2001), 2:49.

13. Al-Qaraḍāwī, *Liqāʾāt wa-muḥāwarāt ḥawla qaḍāyā al-Islām wal-ʿaṣr*, 2:49–50.

14. Al-Qaraḍāwī, *Fiqh al-wasaṭiyya al-Islāmiyya wal-tajdīd*, 91–95.

15. Al-Qaraḍāwī, *Fiqh al-wasaṭiyya al-Islāmiyya wal-tajdīd*, 101–2. Here al-Qaraḍāwī quotes a passage from Taqī al-Dīn Ibn Taymiyya, *Al-Jawāb al-ṣaḥīḥ li-man baddala dīn al-Masīḥ* (Riyadh: Dār al-ʿĀṣima, 1999), electronic copy at https://tinyurl.com/ycdhpjky), in which the Muslim nation is defined as "centrist" (*umma wasaṭ*).

16. Al-Qaraḍāwī, *Fiqh al-wasaṭiyya al-Islāmiyya wal-tajdīd*, 102–5. Al-Qaraḍāwī quotes Ibn Qayyim's book *Al-Rūḥ* on the concept of "the middle road" (*al-iqtiṣād*): Ibn Qayyim al-Jawziyya, *Al-Rūḥ fī al-kalām ʿalā arwāḥ al-amwāt wal-aḥyāʾ bil-dalāʾil min al-Kitāb wal-Sunna wal-āthār wa-aqwāl al-ʿulamāʾ* (Beirut: Dār al-Kutub al-ʿIlmiyya, 1999), 288–89.

17. Al-Qaraḍāwī, *Fiqh al-wasaṭiyya al-Islāmiyya wal-tajdīd*, 105. He quotes Abū Isḥāq Ibrāhīm b. Mūsā al-Shāṭibī, *Al-Muwāfaqāt*, 2 vols. (Cairo: Dār al-Faḍīla, 2010), 2:159–65 (where al-Shāṭibī discusses the "mean road," *wasaṭ*, in the enforcement of religious commands on Muslim believers).

18. Shaykh Yūsuf al-Qaraḍāwī, *Al-Ḥalāl wal-ḥarām fī al-Islām*, 29th ed. (Cairo: Maktabat Wahba, 2007). Al-Qaraḍāwī describes the composition of this book in *Ibn al-qarya wal-kuttāb*, 2:291–305 (esp. 293, where he explains the *wasaṭī* approach he takes in that book).

19. Al-Qaraḍāwī, *Al-Ḥalāl wal-ḥarām fī al-Islām*, 10–12.

20. The *ḥadīth* says, "If a judge judges, performs *ijtihād*, and is right, he has double recompense from Allah; but if he judges, performs *ijtihād*, and errs, he has a single recompense." See Abū Zakariyyā al-Nawawī, *Sharḥ al-Nawawī ʿalā Muslim* (Al-Dammām, Saudi Arabia: Dār al-Khayr, 1996), electronic copy at https://tinyurl.com/ya4uow25.

21. Al-Qaraḍāwī, *Al-Ḥalāl wal-ḥarām fī al-Islām*, 11–12.

22. Shaykh Yūsuf al-Qaraḍāwī, *Fiqh al-zakāh: Dirāsa muqārana li-aḥkāmihā wa-Falsafatihā fī ḍaw' al-Qur'ān wal-Sunna*, 2 vols., 21st ed. (Cairo: Maktabat Wahba, 1994), 1:38.

23. Al-Qaraḍāwī, *Al-Ṣaḥwa al-Islāmiyya bayna al-jumūd wal-taṭarruf*. In another edition of this book, the Arabic word *al-juḥūd* (unbelief) appears instead of *al-jumūd* (apathy). See Shaykh Yūsuf al-Qaraḍāwī, *Al-Ṣaḥwa al-Islāmiyya bayna al-juḥūd wal-taṭarruf*, 12th ed. (al-Manṣūra, Egypt: Dār al-Wafā', 1992).

24. Al-Qaraḍāwī, *Al-Ṣaḥwa al-Islāmiyya bayna al-jumūd wal-taṭarruf*, 97.

25. Al-Qaraḍāwī, *Al-Ṣaḥwa al-Islāmiyya bayna al-jumūd wal-taṭarruf*, 163.

26. Al-Qaraḍāwī, *Al-Islām wal-'ilmāniyya*, 35.

27. Al-Qaraḍāwī, *Al-Islām wal-'ilmāniyya*, 36–47; Ḥ. al-Bannā, "Risālat al-ta'ālīm."

28. Al-Qaraḍāwī, *Al-Islām wal-'ilmāniyya*, 37–38.

29. Al-Qaraḍāwī, *Kalimāt fī al-wasaṭiyya al-Islāmiyya*, 39–56; al-Qaraḍāwī, *Fiqh al-wasaṭiyya al-Islāmiyya wal-tajdīd*, 207–46.

30. Al-Qaraḍāwī, *Al-Ṣaḥwa al-Islāmiyya wa-humūm al-waṭan*, 49.

31. Al-Qaraḍāwī, *Al-Ṣaḥwa al-Islāmiyya wa-humūm al-waṭan*, 51–124.

32. Al-Qaraḍāwī, *Al-Islām wal-'ilmāniyya*, 36–47.

33. The session was held from December 31, 2003, to January 1, 2004. The twenty principles were set out in its closing statement.

34. Al-Qaraḍāwī, *Kalimāt fī al-wasaṭiyya al-Islāmiyya*, 57–61.

35. Al-Qaraḍāwī, *Fiqh al-wasaṭiyya al-Islāmiyya wal-tajdīd*, 242–46.

36. Al-Qaraḍāwī, *Al-Islām wal-'ilmāniyya*, 38.

37. Al-Majlis al-Ūrūbī lil-Iftā' wal-Buḥūth, "Al-Bayān al-khitāmī lil-dawra al-'ādiyya al-thāniya 'ashra lil-majlis al-ūrūbī lil-iftā' wal-buḥūth," Jan. 31, 2014, at https://tinyurl.com/yddfpdft. The language is based on Q8:60–61.

38. Civil jihad, according to al-Qaraḍāwī, is intended to address the various needs and problems of society in various domains: cultural, social, educational, economic, and so on. On this type of jihad as well as on jihad through *da'wa*, see al-Qaraḍāwī, *Fiqh al-jihād*, 1:213–21.

39. Al-Qaraḍāwī, *Kalimāt fī al-wasaṭiyya al-Islāmiyya*, 59.

40. Al-Qaraḍāwī, *Fiqh al-jihād*, 1:41, 2:1029–67.

41. Al-Qaraḍāwī, *Fiqh al-wasaṭiyya al-Islāmiyya wal-tajdīd*, 244.

42. Al-Qaraḍāwī, *Kalimāt fī al-wasaṭiyya al-Islāmiyya*, 58.

43. Al-Qaraḍāwī, *Fiqh al-wasaṭiyya al-Islāmiyya wal-tajdīd*, 243. Principle 17 of the version written in 2008 is very similar; see al-Qaraḍāwī, *Kalimāt fī al-wasaṭiyya al-Islāmiyya*, 59.

44. Muḥammad al-Ghazālī, *Dustūr al-waḥda al-thaqāfiyya bayna al-Muslimīn*, 3rd ed. (Al-Manṣūra, Egypt: Dār al-Wafā', 1992), 220–21.

45. Al-Qaraḍāwī, *Fiqh al-wasaṭiyya al-Islāmiyya wal-tajdīd*, 244. The equivalent in the version of 2008 is Principle 25; see al-Qaraḍāwī, *Kalimāt fī al-wasaṭiyya al-Islāmiyya*, 60.

46. M. al-Ghazālī, *Dustūr al-waḥda*, 221 (Art. 10–19).

47. Abū Baṣīr 'Abd al-Mun'im Muṣṭafā Ḥalīma al-Ṭarṭūsī, *Al-Ṭāghūt* (N.p.: n.p., Jan. 1996), 107–8, electronic copy at http://www.abubaseer.bizland.com/books.htm.

48. According to this *ḥadīth*, the Prophet was asked which city would be "opened" (i.e., conquered) first, Constantinople or Rome, and he replied: "The city of Heraclius [Constantinople] will be opened first!"

49. Al-Qaraḍāwī, *Al-Mubashshirāt bi-intiṣār al-Islām*, 30–31.

50. Al-Qaraḍāwī, *Ummatunā bayna qarnayni*, 245.

51. Shaykh Yūsuf al-Qaraḍāwī, *Jīl al-naṣr al-manshūd*, 6th ed. (Cairo: Maktabat Wahba, 2013), 36–37.

52. Al-Qaraḍāwī, *Fiqh al-jihād*, 2:1192–93.

53. Uriya Shavit, *Islamism and the West: From "Cultural Attack" to "Missionary Migrant"* (London: Routledge, 2014), 13–14.

54. For more on the idea that the twenty fundamentals form the basis for Muslim unity, see M. al-Ghazālī, *Dustūr al-waḥda*, 3–15.

55. Al-Qaraḍāwī, *Al-Ikhwān al-Muslimūn*, 11–23, 154–206.

56. On al-Qaraḍāwī's links to the MB, see Husam Tammam, "Yūsuf al-Qaraḍāwī and the Muslim Brothers: The Nature of a Special Relationship," in *Global Mufti*, ed. Gräf and Skovgaard-Petersen, 55–83.

57. See H. al-Bannā, *Majmūʿat rasāʾil*, 356–59.

58. Soage, "Rashīd Riḍā's Legacy," 15.

59. Binyamin Abrahamov, "Ibn Taymiyya on the Agreement of Reason with Tradition," *The Muslim World* 82, nos. 3–4 (July–Oct. 1992): 256–72.

60. Al-Bannā, *Majmūʿat rasāʾil*, 359–60.

61. On how Muslim society should be shaped in al-Qaraḍāwī's view, see Shaykh Yūsuf al-Qaraḍāwī, *Madkhal li-maʿrifat al-Islām: Muqawwimātihi, khaṣāʾiṣihi, ahdāfihi, maṣādirihi*, 3rd ed. (Cairo: Maktabat Wahba, 2001), 234–45, and *Malāmiḥ al-mujtamaʿ al-Muslim alladhī nanshuduhu* (Cairo: Maktabat Wahba, 1993).

62. Al-Qaraḍāwī, *Fiqh al-wasaṭiyya al-Islāmiyya wal-tajdīd*, 220–24; al-Qaraḍāwī, *Madkhal li-maʿrifat al-Islām*, 193–288, 258–69.

63. Shaykh Yūsuf al-Qaraḍāwī, *Shumūl al-Islām fī ḍawʾ sharḥ mufaṣṣal li-l-usūl al-ʿishrīn li-l-Imām Ḥasan al-Bannā*, 3rd ed. (Cairo: Maktabat Wahba, 2003), 19.

64. Al-Qaraḍāwī, *Shumūl al-Islām*, 12.

65. Shaykh Yūsuf al-Qaraḍāwī, *Kayfa nataʿāmalu maʿa al-turāth wal-tamadhhub wal-ikhtilāf?* (Cairo: Maktabat Wahba, 2001), 6.

66. Al-Qaraḍāwī, *Shumūl al-Islām*, 33–34.

67. Al-Bannā, *Majmūʿat rasāʾil*, 356.

68. For the *wasaṭī* principles of Qurʾānic exegesis, see al-Qaraḍāwī, *Kayfa nataʿāmalu maʿa al-Qurʾān al-ʿaẓīm?* 215–63. For the *wasaṭī* principles for interpreting the Sunna, see Shaykh Yūsuf al-Qaraḍāwī, *Kayfa nataʿāmalu maʿa al-Sunna al-nabawiyya?* (Cairo: Dār al-Shurūq, 2000), 111–200.

69. Al-Qaraḍāwī, *Kayfa nataʿāmalu maʿa al-Qurʾān al-ʿaẓīm?* 238–55.

70. Al-Qaraḍāwī, *Fiqh al-jihād*, 1:295–98.

71. Gamāl al-Bannā, *Al-Jihād* (Cairo: Dār al-Fikr al-Islāmī, 2002), 74.

72. Al-Qaraḍāwī, *Fiqh al-jihād*, 1:299; see also al-'Ashmāwī, *Al-Islām al-siyāsī*, 134.

73. G. al-Bannā, *Al-Jihād*, 102.

74. Shaykh Yūsuf al-Qaraḍāwī, *Ghayr al-Muslimīn fī al-mujtama' al-Islāmī*, 6th ed. (Beirut: Mu'assasat al-Risāla, 1994), 32–34; [Muḥammad] Rashīd Riḍā, *Tafsīr al-manār*, 12 vols., 2nd ed. (Cairo: Dār al-Manār, 1948), 10:290 (Q9:29), electronic copy at http://waqfeya.com/book.php?bid=786.

75. For more on the principle that a *ḥadīth* must be understood within the context in which it was said and the intention behind it, see al-Qaraḍāwī, *Kayfa nata'āmalu ma'a al-Sunna al-nabawiyya?* 145–57.

76. Al-Maqdisī, *Hādhā mā adinu Allāh bihi*, 30; Shaykh Yūsuf al-Qaraḍāwī, *Al-Waṭan wal-muwāṭana fī ḍaw' al-uṣūl al-'aqdiyya wal-maqāṣid al-sharī'iyya* (Cairo: Dār al-Shurūq, 2010), 70–73.

77. Al-Qaraḍāwī, *Fī fiqh al-aqalliyyāt al-Muslima*, 33–34. See also Alexandre Caeiro and Mahmoud al-Saify, "Qaraḍāwī in Europe, Europe in Qaraḍāwī? The Global Mufti's European Politics," in *Global Mufti*, ed. Gräf and Skovgaard-Petersen, 109–48.

78. Al-Qaraḍāwī, *Fiqh al-jihād*, 1:325–26. On the principle of understanding the Sunna in light of the Qur'ān, see al-Qaraḍāwī, *Kayfa nata'āmalu ma'a al-Sunna al-nabawiyya?* 113–22.

79. Al-Qaraḍāwī, *Kayfa nata'āmalu ma'a al-Sunna al-nabawiyya?* 166.

80. Al-Bannā, *Majmū'at rasā'il*, 358. For al-Qaraḍāwī's explanation of this principle, see *Kayfa nata'āmalu ma'a al-turāth wal-tamadhhub wal-ikhtilāf?* 127–256.

81. Al-Qaraḍāwī, *Kayfa nata'āmalu ma'a al-turāth wal-tamadhhub wal-ikhtilāf?* 127–256. Al-Qaraḍāwī's book *Fiqh al-ikhtilāf* is worth comparing to al-Ṭarṭūsī's writings on the same issue. See Abū Baṣīr 'Abd al-Mun'im Muṣṭafā Ḥalīma al-Ṭarṭūsī, *Fiqh al-ikhtilāf 'ind ahl al-Sunna wa-ahl al-bida'* (N.p.: n.p., Dec. 2006), electronic copy at http://www.ilmway.com/site/maqdis/MS_145.html.

82. Al-Qaraḍāwī, *Kayfa nata'āmalu ma'a al-turāth?* 176–201.

83. Shaykh Yūsuf al-Qaraḍāwī, *Mabādi' fī al-ḥiwār wa-l-taqrīb bayna al-madhāhib al-Islāmiyya* (Cairo: Maktabat Wahba, 2005), 28–31.

84. Al-Qaraḍāwī, *Mabādi' fī al-ḥiwār wa-l-taqrīb*, 28–36.

85. Abū Baṣīr 'Abd al-Mun'im Muṣṭafā Ḥalīma al-Ṭarṭūsī, *Al-Shī'a al-Rawāfiḍ ṭā'ifat shirk wa-ridda* (N.p.: n.p., Aug. 2002), electronic copy at http://www.abubaseer.bizland.com/books/read/b%2044.pdf.

86. Abū Muṣ'ab al-Zarqāwī, *Hal atāka ḥadīth al-Rāfiḍa?!* ([Baghdad]: Warshat 'Amal al-Burāq, no. 2, June 2006), 62, electronic copy at http://www.ilmway.com/site/maqdis/MS_26057.html.

87. Quoted in Rāniyā Badawī, "Al-Duktūr Yūsuf al-Qaraḍāwī ra'īs al-Ittiḥād al-'Ālamī li-'Ulamā' al-Muslimīn (2:2): Naṣīḥatī lil-ra'īs Mubārak lā tumaddid walā tūrith walā taẓlim ibnaka bil-ḥukm," *Al-Maṣrī al-Yawm*, Sept. 9, 2008, at https://tinyurl.com/y83dv8zq.

88. Shaykh Yūsuf al-Qaraḍāwī, "Naṣṣ bayān al-Qaraḍāwī ḥawla mawqifihi min al-Shī'a," Sept. 2008, at https://archive.islamonline.net/?p=9502.

89. For an analysis of Jabrīn's *fatwā* and al-Qaraḍāwī's opposing *fatwā*, see Sagi Polka, "Taqrib al-madhahib: Qaradawi's Declaration of Principles Regarding Sunni-Shi'i Ecumenism," *Middle Eastern Studies* 49, no. 3 (2013): 422–24.

90. Al-Qaraḍāwī, *Fatāwā mu'āṣira*, 4:880–81, 884–85.

91. For al-Qaraḍāwī's sermon, see Shaykh Yūsuf al-Qaraḍāwī, *Al-Qaraḍāwī yaṣifu Ḥizb Allāh bi-Ḥizb al-Shayṭān wa-yad'ū duwal al-Nātū li-mazīd al-tadakhkhul fī Sūriyā*, video, May 2013, at https://www.youtube.com/watch?v=-2d0LBXsYFg.

92. Abū Zayd, *Al-Tajdīd wa-l-taḥrīm*, 27; Al-'Ashmāwī, *Al-Islām al-siyāsī*, 44.

93. Al-'Ashmāwī, *Al-Islām al-siyāsī*, 44–46.

94. Taqī al-Dīn Ibn Taymiyya, *Iqtiḍā' al-ṣirāṭ al-mustaqīm li-mukhālafat ahl al-jaḥīm*, 2 vols. (Riyadh: Maktabat al-Rushd, n.d), 1:210–15, electronic copy at http://waqfeya.com/book.php?bid=11466, vol. 1 also at https://ia800409.us.archive.org/4/items/FP158171/01_158171.pdf.

95. Al-Qaraḍāwī, *Kayfa nata'āmalu ma'a al-turāth?* 210–15.

96. Ibn Taymiyya, *Iqtiḍā' al-ṣirāṭ*, 132.

97. Al-Ṭartūsī, *Fiqh al-ikhtilāf*, 19–20.

98. Al-Qaraḍāwī, *Kayfa nata'āmalu ma'a al-turāth?* 213–15.

3. Al-Qaraḍāwī, al-Azhar, and the Muslim Brotherhood

1. In the eighth decade of his life, al-Qaraḍāwī decided—after much hesitation, he says—to write his autobiography, titled *Ibn al-qarya wal-kuttāb: Malāmiḥ sīra wa-masīra* (Son of the Village and the *Kuttāb*: My Biography and Path). So far four volumes of the work have been published, covering his life up to the 1990s. On the shaykh's biography, see Ana B. Soage, "Shaykh Yusuf al-Qaradawi: Portrait of a Leading Islamic Cleric," *Middle East Review of International Affairs* 12, no. 1 (Mar. 2008), at http://www.globalpolitician.com/print.asp?id=4328; Gudrun Krämer, "Drawing Boundaries: Yūsuf al-Qaraḍāwī on Apostasy," in *Speaking for Islam: Religious Authorities in Muslim Societies*, ed. Gudrun Krämer and Sabine Schmidtke (Leiden: Brill, 2006), 185–194; and al-Khaṭīb, *Al-Qaraḍāwī faqīh al-ṣaḥwa al-Islāmiyya*, 27–61.

2. Soage, "Shaykh Yusuf al-Qaradawi," 5; Krämer, "Drawing Boundaries," 186; Jakob Skovgaard-Petersen, "Yūsuf al-Qaraḍāwī and al-Azhar," in *Global Mufti*, ed. Gräf and Skovgaard-Petersen, 33, 36, 48.

3. On Shaykh Muḥammad al-Ghazālī, see Nūr al-Dīn b. Rābiḥ A'zīz, *Al-Wasaṭiyya wal-i'tidāl fī al-manhaj al-da'wī 'ind al-Shaykh Muḥammad al-Ghazālī* (Damascus: Dār al-Fikr, 2010), 21–29, and Mohammed Moussa, *Politics of the Islamic Tradition: The Thought of Mohammad al-Ghazali* (New York: Routledge, 2016), 13–21.

4. For al-Qaraḍāwī's comments on this affair, see Shaykh Yūsuf al-Qaraḍāwī, *Al-Shaykh al-Ghazālī kamā 'araftuhu: Riḥlat niṣf qarn* (Cairo: Dār al-Shurūq, 2000), 50.

5. Ḥusām Tammām, "Qaraḍāwī wal-Ikhwān: Qirā'a fī jadaliyyat al-shaykh wal-ḥaraka," *Islamism Scope*, July 2008, at https://tinyurl.com/y9he4ul4.

6. This *ḥadīth* says, "The Islamic scholars are the heirs of the prophets, and they shall inherit the knowledge" (Islam.web, "Sharḥ ḥadīth Inna al-'ulamā' warathat al-anbiyā,'" Oct. 5, 2005, at http://fatwa.islamweb.net/fatwa/index.php?page=showfatwa&Option=FatwaId&Id=67822).

7. Shaykh Yūsuf al-Qaraḍāwī, *Risālat al-Azhar bayna al-ams wal-yawm wal-ghad*, 3rd ed. (Cairo: Maktabat Wahba, 2009), 49. On this book, see Skovgaard-Petersen, "Yūsuf al-Qaraḍāwī and al-Azhar," 40–43.

8. Malika Zeghal, "Religion and Politics in Egypt: The Ulema of al-Azhar, Radical Islam, and the State (1952–94)," *International Journal of Middle East Studies* 31 (1999): 371–99; Tamir Moustafa, "Conflict and Cooperation between the State and Religious Institutions in Contemporary Egypt," *International Journal of Middle East Studies* 32 (2000): 3–22.

9. See IUMS's self-characterization on its website: al-Ittiḥād al-'Ālamī li-'Ulamā' al-Muslimīn, "Al-Ta'rīf," Mawqi' al-Ittiḥād, n.d., at http://www.iumsonline.org/ar/ContentDetails.aspx?ID=8150. See also Skovgaard-Petersen, "Yūsuf al-Qaraḍāwī and al-Azhar," 45–47.

10. On this *ḥadīth* and its interpretation, see Khālid b. Sa'ūd al-Bulayhid, "Sharḥ ḥadīth 'al-Dīn al-naṣīḥa,'" *Ṣayd al-Fawā'id*, n.d., at https://tinyurl.com/ycbpqtem.

11. For al-Qaraḍāwī's letter of resignation from al-Azhar's Council of Senior Scholars, see Mawqi' Samāḥat al-Shaykh Yūsuf al-Qaraḍāwī, "Istiqālat al-Qaraḍāwī min Hay'at Kibār al-'Ulamā' bil-Azhar," Dec. 2, 2013, at https://www.al-qaradawi.net/node/4760. For a legal opinion by al-Qaraḍāwī mandating a boycott of the constitution of the *inqilābiyyūn* (performers of the coup), meaning 'Abd al-Fattah al-Sisi and his supporters, see Mawqi' Samāḥat al-Shaykh Yūsuf al-Qaraḍāwī, "Al-Qaraḍāwī yuftī bi-wujūb muqāṭa'at dustūr al-inqilābiyyīna," Aug. 1, 2014, at https://www.al-qaradawi.net/node/861.

12. Shaykh Yūsuf al-Qaraḍāwī, *Khuṭbat Yūsuf al-Qaraḍāwī bi-Jāmi' al-Azhar,*" video, Nov. 16, 2012, https://www.youtube.com/watch?v=M8lVhA2nzGY.

13. Al-Qaraḍāwī, *Risālat al-Azhar*, 81–82.

14. Al-Qaraḍāwī, *Risālat al-Azhar*, 74–95.

15. Al-Qaraḍāwī, *Ibn al-qarya wal-kuttāb*, 1:183–87, 221–35 (criticism of his elementary school studies).

16. Al-Qaraḍāwī, *Ibn al-qarya wal-kuttāb*, 1:234.

17. Al-Qaraḍāwī, *Risālat al-Azhar*, 99–104.

18. Al-Qaraḍāwī, *Risālat al-Azhar*, 104–8, and *Ibn al-qarya wal-kuttāb*, 1:221–22.

19. Shavit, *Islamism and the West*, 2.

20. Al-Qaraḍāwī, *Ibn al-qarya wal-kuttāb*, 1:348–49; Shaykh Yūsuf al-Qaraḍāwī, "Al-Ihdā'," in *Al-Muslimūn qādimūn* (Port Said, Egypt: Dār al-Tawzī' wal-Nashr al-Islāmiyya, 2000), 3–4.

21. Al-Qaraḍāwī, *Ibn al-qarya wal-kuttāb*, 1:149–50.

22. Al-Qaraḍāwī, *Ibn al-qarya wal-kuttāb*, 1:242.

23. Al-Qaraḍāwī, *Ibn al-qarya wal-kuttāb*, 1:176–78.

24. Al-Qaraḍāwī, *Ibn al-qarya wal-kuttāb*, 1:313–14. The concept of an all-inclusive Islam is one of the twenty fundamental principles (*usūl*) Ḥasan al-Bannā set out in his treatise "Message of the Teachings" ("Risālat al-ta'ālīm") (as given in *Majmū'at rasā'il*, 356). Al-Qaraḍāwī's book *Shumūl al-Islām* is devoted to this principle.

25. Richard P. Mitchell, *The Society of the Muslim Brothers* (New York: Oxford Univ. Press, 1993), 2–4.

26. Ḥ. al-Bannā, *Majmū'at rasā'il*, 122–23 (from the epistle "Risālat al-mu'tamar al-khāmis"); al-Qaraḍāwī, *Al-Ḥayāh al-rabbāniyya wal-'ilm*, 9.

27. Al-Qaraḍāwī devoted a book to al-Ghazālī: *Al-Shaykh al-Ghazālī kamā 'araftuhu*.

28. Al-Qaraḍāwī, *Ibn al-qarya wal-kuttāb*, 1:313–19.

29. On al-Qaraḍāwī's time in prison, see al-Qaraḍāwī, *Ibn al-qarya wal-kuttāb*, 1:360–96. On the dissolution of the MB in 1948, see Mitchell, *Society of the Muslim Brothers*, 58–79.

30. Al-Qaraḍāwī, *Ibn al-qarya wal-kuttāb*, 1:344–52.

31. Mitchell, *Society of the Muslim Brothers*, 67–71.

32. Al-Qaraḍāwī, *Ibn al-qarya wal-kuttāb*, 1:394–96; Shaykh Yūsuf al-Qaraḍāwī, *'Ālim wa-ṭāghiya: Sa'īd b. Jubayr wal-Ḥajjāj b. Yūsuf, Masraḥiyya tārīkhiyya*, 7th ed. (Cairo: Maktabat Wahba, 1998). Al-Qaraḍāwī wrote another version of this play in 1967.

33. Al-Qaraḍāwī, *Ibn al-qarya wal-kuttāb*, 1:394–96.

34. Skovgaard-Petersen, "Yūsuf al-Qaraḍāwī and al-Azhar," 32. About these shaykhs' impact on al-Qaraḍāwī, see Akram Kassāb, *Al-Manhaj al-da'wī 'ind al-Qaraḍāwī* (Cairo: Maktabat Wahba, 2008), 42–53; al-Sayyid Sābiq, *Fiqh al-Sunna*, 3 vols. (Cairo: Dār al-Fatḥ lil-I'lām al-'Arabī, 2000).

35. Mitchell, *Society of the Muslim Brothers*, 125–33. On the term *miḥna*, see Shaykh Yūsuf al-Qaraḍāwī, *Al-Miḥna fī wāqi' al-ḥaraka al-Islāmīyya al-mu'āṣira* (Cairo: Maktabat Wahba, 2009). On this agreement and the circumstances that led to it, see Mitchell, *Society of the Muslim Brothers*, 130–33.

36. Mitchell, *Society of the Muslim Brothers*, 151–62; Gilles Kepel, *The Prophet and Pharaoh: Muslim Extremism in Egypt*, trans. Jon Rothschild (London: Alsaqi Books, 1985), 26–27; al-Qaraḍāwī, *Ibn al-qarya wal-kuttāb*, 2:80–92.

37. Al-Qaraḍāwī, *Ibn al-qarya wal-kuttāb*, 2:170–72.

38. Al-Qaraḍāwī wrote monographs on several of these fundamentals as part of the series Naḥwa waḥda fikriyya lil-'āmilīn lil-Islām (Toward Intellectual Unity of Those Working on Behalf of Islam), in which six volumes have appeared so far.

39. Al-Qaraḍāwī, *Fiqh al-zakāh*.

40. According to al-Qaraḍāwī, Aḥmad Ḥasan al-Bāqūrī chose to ignore the directives of the security forces regarding his employment (*Ibn al-qarya wal-kuttāb*, 2:248).

41. The name of the feature, "Yastaftūnaka," which means "they request from you [a religious ruling]," is taken from Q4:127, 176.

42. Al-Qaraḍāwī, *Ibn al-qarya wal-kuttāb*, 2:256.

43. Al-Qaraḍāwī, *Al-Ḥalāl wal-ḥarām fī al-Islām*.

44. On *Al-Ḥalāl wal-ḥarām fī al-Islām*, see al-Qaraḍāwī, *Ibn al-qarya wal-kuttāb*, 2:256; for al-Qaraḍāwī's responses to the criticism of the book, see 2:304–5.

45. Ṣāliḥ al-Fawzān, *Al-I'lām bi-naqd kitāb "Al-Ḥalāl wal-ḥarām fī al-Islām"* (Riyadh: Maktabat al-Ma'ārif lil-Nashr wal-Tawzī', 2003), electronic copy at https://islamhouse.com/ar/books/314806/. For the story behind the writing of *Al-Ḥalāl wal-ḥarām fī al-Islām*, see al-Qaraḍāwī, *Ibn al-qarya wal-kuttāb*, 2:291–302.

46. Al-Qaraḍāwī, *Fī fiqh al-aqalliyyāt al-Muslima*, 30–39. On the objectives of the ECFR, see its website at http://www.e-cfr.org/ar/index.php?cat_id=005. On al-Qaraḍāwī's activity in the European arena, see Caeiro and al-Saify, "Qaraḍāwī in Europe, Europe in Qaraḍāwī?"; Said Fares Hassan, *Fiqh al-Aqalliyyāt: History, Development, and Progress* (New York: Palgrave Macmillan, 2013), 57–85; and Shavit, *Sharī'a and Muslim Minorities*, 77–137.

47. Al-Qaraḍāwī, *Ibn al-qarya wal-kuttāb*, 3:380 (this sentence appeared in al-Qaraḍāwī's letter to the MB members who offered him the role of supreme guide in 1976).

48. Al-Qaraḍāwī, *Ibn al-qarya wal-kuttāb*, 4:160.

49. Al-Qaraḍāwī, *Ibn al-qarya wal-kuttāb*, 35–40; Pargeter, *The Muslim Brotherhood*, 99–100.

50. Allen J. Fromherz, *Qatar: A Modern History* (London: I. B. Tauris, 2012), 150–51.

51. Quoted in Martin Kramer, "Hour of Power with an Islamist Superstar," Nov. 13, 2002, at http://www.martinkramer.org/sandbox/2002/11/hour-of-power-with-an-islamist-superstar/.

52. Mawqi' Samāḥat al-Shaykh Yūsuf al-Qaraḍāwī, "Maktab faḍīlat al-'allāma yanfī mā turaddiduhu al-mawāqi' al-mashbūha," June 29, 2013, at https://www.al-qaradawi.net/node/928.

53. Al-Qaraḍāwī, *Ibn al-qarya wal-kuttāb*, 4:635–36. On al-Qaraḍāwī's preaching at various Qatar mosques, see al-Qaraḍāwī, *Ibn al-Qarya wal-kuttāb*, 3:333–34.

54. Al-Qaraḍāwī, *Liqā'āt wa-muḥāwarāt ḥawla qaḍāyā al-Islām wal-'aṣr*, 2:138.

55. Mubarak appointed Aḥmad Shafīq, considered to be close to Mubarak, as prime minister on January 29, 2011, but Shafīq resigned after a month. He then ran in Egypt's presidential elections in 2012, but after losing to Mursi and being implicated in election fraud and financial irregularities, he fled to Abu Dhabi.

56. Shaykh Yūsuf al-Qaraḍāwī, *Khuṭbat al-Jum'a lil-Shaykh al-Qaraḍāwī 'an dhikrā thawrat 25 Yanāyir*, video, Jan. 24, 2014, at https://www.youtube.com/watch?v=7KtfIQyT6cw

(praise for Qatar at time segment 27:07; condemnation of the UAE at 41:11, condemnation of Gulf Arabs at 45:12).

57. Mawqiʿ Samāḥat al-Shaykh Yūsuf al-Qaraḍāwī, "Al-Qaraḍāwī: Lā uʿādī aḥadan wa-kull mā yahummunī al-Islām wal-Muslimīn," Feb. 8, 2015, at https://www.al-qaradawi.net/node/421.

58. Bassām Ramaḍān, "Wazīr khārijiyyat Qaṭar: Isā'at 'al-Qaraḍāwī' lil-Imārāt lā tuʿabbiru ʿan siyāsatina al-khārijiyya," *Al-Maṣrī al-Yawm*, Feb. 1, 2014, at http://www.almasryalyoum.com/news/details/386434.

59. Quoted in ʿIṣām Talīma, *Al-Qaraḍāwī: Faqīh al-duʿāh wa-dāʿiyat al-fuqahā'* (Damascus: Dār al-Qalam, 2001), 24.

60. Al-Qaraḍāwī, *Ibn al-qarya wal-kuttāb*, 4:43.

61. Al-Qaraḍāwī, *Ibn al-qarya wal-kuttāb*, 42–43.

62. On Ḥasan al-Huḍaybī's time as supreme guide, see al-Qaraḍāwī, *Ibn al-qarya wal-kuttāb*, 3:293–302, and Barbara H. E. Zollner, *The Muslim Brotherhood: Hasan al-Hudaybi and Ideology* (London: Routledge, 2009), 19–49.

63. Pargeter, *The Muslim Brotherhood*, 101.

64. Al-Qaraḍāwī, *Ibn al-qarya wal-kuttāb*, 4:343–44.

65. Al-Qaraḍāwī, *Ibn al-qarya wal-kuttāb*, 4:43–44.

66. Al-Qaraḍāwī, *Ibn al-qarya wal-kuttāb*, 4:42–44. On al-Qaraḍāwī's relations with the MB, see Tammam, "Yūsuf al-Qaraḍāwī and the Muslim Brothers."

67. Al-Tilmisānī held this post from the early 1970s until the journal was shuttered again in 1981.

68. Al-Qaraḍāwī, *Ibn al-qarya wal-kuttāb*, 4:342; Shaykh Yūsuf al-Qaraḍāwī, *Thaqāfat al-dāʿiya*, 10th ed. (Cairo: Maktabat Wahba, 1996). On the renewed publication of *Al-Daʿwa* during the Anwar Sadat period, see Carrie Rosefsky Wickham, *The Muslim Brotherhood: Evolution of an Islamist Movement* (Princeton, NJ: Princeton Univ. Press, 2013), 30.

69. For the full text of the letter, see al-Qaraḍāwī, *Ibn al-qarya wal-kuttāb*, 3:380–84.

70. On the relationship between jurisprudence and politics (*siyāsa*) in al-Qaraḍāwī's thought, see "Al-Fatwā wal-siyāsa," episode of *Al-Sharīʿa wal-ḥayāh*, al-Jazeera, Jan. 13, 2010, at https://www.youtube.com/watch?v=VKLOsxSLDAU.

71. Al-Qaraḍāwī, *Ibn al-qarya wal-kuttāb*, 3:382–83.

72. Al-Qaraḍāwī, *Al-Umma al-Islāmiyya*, 10–18.

73. Shaykh Yūsuf al-Qaraḍāwī, "Risāla ilā al-mu'tamar al-Islāmī al-tāsiʿ," Nov. 10, 2000, in *Khuṭab al-Shaykh al-Qaraḍāwī*, ed. al-Saʿd, 5:191–96.

74. Tammam, "Yūsuf al-Qaraḍāwī and the Muslim Brothers."

75. See, for example, the poem "Naḥnu al-Ikhwān," in *Al-Muslimūn qādimūn*, 53–54.

76. On al-Qaraḍāwī's diatribe against Sayyid Quṭb, see al-Qaraḍāwī, "Waqfa maʿa al-shahīd Sayyid Quṭb." See also Ḥasan al-Huḍaybī, *Duʿāh lā quḍāh* (Cairo: Dār al-Tawzīʿ wal-Nashr al-Islāmiyya, 1987), and on al-Huḍaybī's book, see Zollner, *The Muslim Brotherhood*, 64–145.

77. Reem Ahmed El Mahdy, "The Compatibility of Yusuf al-Qaradawi's Wasateyya School of Thought with the Second Generation of the Muslim Brotherhood," MA thesis, American Univ. in Cairo, 2014, at http://dar.aucegypt.edu/handle/10526/4298.

78. On "the Islamic cultural program" (*al-mashrūʿ al-ḥaḍārī al-Islāmī*), see Muḥammad ʿImāra, *Al-Qaraḍāwī: Al-Madrasa al-fikriyya wal-mashrūʿ al-fikrī* (Cairo: Nahḍat Miṣr, 1997), 63–74. "Cultural Islam" seeks to revive and renew the faith in order to offer an Islamic solution for the problems of the modern Muslim *umma* and as an alternative to Western culture.

79. Joshua A. Stacher, "Post-Islamist Rumblings in Egypt: The Emergence of the Wasat Party," *Middle East Journal* 56, no. 3 (Summer 2002): 417–18, 425; Wickham, *The Muslim Brotherhood*, 76–95; Pargeter, *The Muslim Brotherhood*, 46–53.

80. On the Wasaṭ Party's program, see Mawqiʿ Ḥizb al-Wasaṭ, "Barnāmaj al-ḥizb," n.d., at https://tinyurl.com/yb9amq5o. On the establishment of this party in Egypt, see Stacher, "Post-Islamist Rumblings in Egypt"; Wickham, *The Muslim Brotherhood*, 76–95; and Hatina, *Identity Politics in the Middle East*, 158–81.

81. Tammam, "Yūsuf al-Qaraḍāwī and the Muslim Brothers," 68–69, 73; ʿIṣām Talīma, "Al-Mufakkir wal-tanẓīm fī al-ḥaraka al-Islāmiyya . . . ʿalāqa mutawattira," Mar. 17, 2017, at https://www.facebook.com/ikhwanturk/posts/1918540955045808:0.

82. Wickham, *The Muslim Brotherhood*, 59; Pargeter, *The Muslim Brotherhood*, 36–46.

83. The Secret Apparatus—or the Special Section, as it was known within the MB—was conceived in the 1930s and formed in the early 1940s. Its first head was Ṣāliḥ ʿAshmāwī. See Mitchell, *Society of the Muslim Brothers*, 30–32, and Pargeter, *The Muslim Brotherhood*, 27–29.

84. Wickham, *The Muslim Brotherhood*, 67–68.

85. Wickham, *The Muslim Brotherhood*, 68.

86. Wickham, *The Muslim Brotherhood*, 68. See also Pargeter, *The Muslim Brotherhood*, 38.

87. Kepel, *The Prophet and Pharaoh*, 107. It should be mentioned that in the literature the name "New MB" is sometimes applied not just to the MB's middle generation but to the global *wasaṭī* stream founded by al-Qaraḍāwī. See Lorenzo Vidino, *The New Muslim Brotherhood in the West* (New York: Columbia Univ. Press, 2010), 48–50.

88. Chris Harnisch and Quinn Mecham, "Democratic Ideology in Islamist Opposition? The Muslim Brotherhood's Civil State," *Middle Eastern Studies* 45, no. 2 (Mar, 2009): 190.

89. Amānī Mājid, "Al-Qaraḍāwī: Lā ʿalāqa lī bi-tanẓīm al-Ikhwān," *Al-Ahrām*, Feb. 21, 2011, at http://www.ahram.org.eg/Archive/450/2011/2/21/12/63784.aspx; Shaykh Yūsuf al-Qaraḍāwī, *25 Yanāyir sanat 2011m: Thawrat shaʿb: Al-Shaykh al-Qaraḍāwī wal-thawra al-Miṣriyya: Bayānāt wa-khuṭab wa-fatāwā wa-maqālāt wa-ṣuwar* (Cairo: Maktabat Wahba, 2012), 195–96.

90. Al-Qaraḍāwī, *Al-Waṭan wal-muwāṭana*, 42–59; David H. Warren and Christine Gilmore, "One Nation under God? Yusuf al-Qaradawi's Changing Fiqh of Citizenship in the Light of the Islamic Legal Tradition," *Contemporary Islam* 8, no. 3 (2014): 217–37.

91. Israel Elad Altman, *Strategies of the Muslim Brotherhood Movement 1928–2007* (Washington, DC: Hudson Institute, 2009), 11–13; al-Qaraḍāwī, *Fatāwā muʿāṣira*, 4:831–33.

92. ʿAbd al-Munʿim Abū al-Futūḥ, "Al-Qaraḍāwī nāẓir al-madrasa al-Ikhwāniyya," Mawqiʿ Samāḥat al-Shaykh Yūsuf al-Qaraḍāwī, Sept. 12, 2007, at https://www.al-qaradawi.net/node/3404.

93. Abū al-Futūḥ, "Al-Qaraḍāwī nāẓir al-madrasa al-Ikhwāniyya," ellipses in the original.

94. Al-Qaraḍāwī, *Al-Ikhwān al-Muslimūn*, 154–206.

95. Al-Qaraḍāwī, *Al-Ikhwān al-Muslimūn*, 207–21.

96. Al-Qaraḍāwī, "Al-Ihdā'," 3–4.

97. The latest research to concentrate on the subject explored in this section is Shaul Bartal and Nesya Rubinstein-Shemer, *Hamas and Ideology: Sheikh Yūsuf al-Qaraḍāwī on the Jews, Zionism, and Israel* (London: Routledge, 2018), 99–102, 139–51.

98. Mawqiʿ Samāḥat al-Shaykh Yūsuf al-Qaraḍāwī, "Al-Qaraḍāwī: Qatlā al-ṣirāʿ al-dākhilī al-Filasṭīnī laysū sawā'," Feb. 18, 2007, at https://www.al-qaradawi.net/node/4297.

99. Mawqiʿ Samāḥat al-Shaykh Yūsuf al-Qaraḍāwī, "Al-Qaraḍāwī: Qatlā al-ṣirāʿ al-dākhilī al-Filasṭīnī laysū sawā'."

100. Al-Qaraḍāwī, *Fiqh al-jihād*, 1:42, 179.

101. Usāma al-Sayyid, *Al-Qaraḍāwī fī al-ʿarā': Dirāsa naqdiyya manhajiyya muwaththaqa tubayyinu mukhālafāt al-Qaraḍāwī li-ṣaḥīḥ al-naql wa-ṣarīḥ al-ʿaql* (Beirut: Sharikat Dār al-Mashārīʿ, 2002), electronic copy at https://tinyurl.com/y9ldahv6.

102. For example, in 2001 al-Qaraḍāwī founded and became the head of the International Jerusalem Institute (Mu'assasat al-Quds al-Duwaliyya). The purpose of this institute is to actively oppose Zionist programs for the Judaization (*tahwīd*) of Jerusalem and to help Palestinian residents of Jerusalem maintain their struggle steadfastly (Bartal and Rubinstein-Shemer, *Hamas and Ideology*, 54–55).

103. Ismāʿīl Haniyya, "Kalimat al-ustādh Ismāʿīl Haniyya, ra'īs wuzarā' Filasṭīn," in *Juhūd al-Duktūr al-Qaraḍāwī fī khidmat al-Islām wa-nuṣrat al-qaḍiyyā al-Filasṭīniyya*, Mu'tamar Wizārat al-Awqāf wa-l-Shu'ūn al-Dīniyya, Ghazza, Filasṭīn, ed. Ismāʿīl Haniyya, Ṭālib Abū Shiʿr, ʿAbdallah Abū Jarbūʿ, Wā'il Muḥyī al-Dīn al-Zirr, Yūsuf Farḥāt, Ibrāhīm Aḥmad al-Kurd, ʿIṣām al-ʿAbd Zuhd, et al. (Giza, Egypt: Markaz al-Iʿlām al-ʿArabī, 2012), 7–13.

104. On the "phenomenon" of al-Qaraḍāwī as a scholar, see Jakob Skovgaard-Petersen, "In Defense of Muhammad: ʿUlama', Daʿiya, and the New Islamic Internationalism," in *Guardians of Faith in Modern Times: ʿUlama' in the Middle East*, ed. Meir Hatina (Leiden: Brill, 2009), 291–309.

105. On this *ḥadīth*, see *Shabakat Saḥāb al-Salafiyya*, "Kalām al-ʿulamā' wa-sharḥuhum ʿalā ḥadīth inna al-ʿulamā' warathat al-anbiyā'," Aug. 26, 2010, at https://www.sahab.net/forums/index.php?app=forums&module=forums&controller=topic&id=113380.

106. This view is anchored in a *ḥadīth* that states, "There are two kinds of people who if [they] are good, people are good, and if [they] are corrupted, people become corrupted:

[they are the] scholars and rulers" (Muḥammad b. Ismā'īl Al-Amīr al-Ṣan'ānī, *Al-Tanwīr sharḥ al-jāmi' al-ṣaghīr* [Riyadh: Maktabat Dār al-Salām, 2011], electronic copy at http://shamela.ws/browse.php/book-122096/page-3630).

107. On the term *rabbānī*, see Shaykh Yūsuf al-Qaraḍāwī, *Al-Rabbāniyya abraz khaṣā'iṣ al-tarbiya al-Islāmiyya* (Cairo: Maktabat Wahba, 2009). On the relationship between the *'ulamā'* and the state and rulers, see Zaman, *The Ulama in Contemporary Islam*, 144–80; Meir Hatina, "The Clerics' Betrayal? Islamists, 'Ulama', and the Polity," in *Guardians of Faith in Modern Times*, ed. Hatina, 247–64.

108. On this *ḥadīth*, see Ibrāhīm 'Abdallah Salqīnī, *Sharḥ ḥadīth lā tazālu ṭā'ifa min ummatī* (Beirut: Dār al-Muqtabis, 2014).

109. 'Alī Gum'a, "Al-Ḥiwār al-kāmil lil-Shaykh 'Alī Gum'a ma'a Khayrī Ramaḍān," episode of the television program *Mumkin*, CBC, Aug. 23, 2013, at https://www.youtube.com/watch?v=DcAoD8FttnU. 'Alī Gum'a claimed that the shaykh had Alzheimer's disease and accused him of asking the "jihad fighters" (meaning the MB) to kill the Egyptian people. Al-Qaraḍāwī responded to these claims in a lengthy article: Shaykh Yūsuf al-Qaraḍāwī, "Rudūd 'ilmiyya 'alā al-shaykh aw al-jinirāl 'Alī Gum'a," Mawqi' Samāḥat al-Shaykh Yūsuf al-Qaraḍāwī, Sept. 17, 2013, https://www.al-qaradawi.net/node/2849.

110. This statement evokes a *ḥadīth* (which is considered unreliable): "Fitna exists; cursed are those who awaken it."

111. Al-Qaraḍāwī, *25 Yanāyir sanat 2011m*, 7–8; Waṣfī 'Āshūr Abū Zayd, *Al-Imām al-thā'ir: Dirāsa taḥlīliyya uṣūliyya . . . fī ma'ālim ijtihādihi li-l-thawra al-Miṣriyya* (Britton, MI: Sulṭān li-l-Nashr, 2011).

112. Warren, "The 'Ulamā' and the Arab Uprisings," 20–30.

113. On al-Qaraḍāwī's role in the Egyptian revolution, see W. Abū Zayd, *Al-Imām al-thā'ir*, 169–76, and Warren, "The 'Ulamā' and the Arab Uprisings," 20–30.

114. The *fatwā* is given in Mawqi' Samāḥat al-Shaykh Yūsuf al-Qaraḍāwī, "Al-Qaraḍāwī yuftī bi-wujūb muqāṭa'at dustūr al-inqilābiyyīn."

115. This is an allusion to Q2:117, which states that when Allah wants to decree something, He must only say to it, "Kun!" (Be!).

116. Mawqi' Samāḥat al-Shaykh Yūsuf al-Qaraḍāwī, "Ta'līq al-Shaykh al-Qaraḍāwī 'alā al-ḥukm 'alā al-duktūr Muḥammad Mursī wa-Ikhwānihi," Apr. 21, 2015, at https://www.al-qaradawi.net/node/550.

117. This is part of the MB slogan coined by al-Bannā. The slogan consists of several elements that al-Bannā explained in "Message of Teachings": "Allah is our objective. The Prophet is our model, the Qur'an is our constitution, jihad is our way, dying for the sake of Allah is our highest hope" (in H. al-Bannā, *Majmū'at rasā'il*, 359–62).

118. "Al-Thawra: Fitna am raḥma," episode of *Al-Sharī'a wal-ḥayāh*, al-Jazeera, Sept. 15, 2011, at https://tinyurl.com/ybjo8w54.

119. Al-Qaraḍāwī, *25 Yanāyir sanat 2011m*, 139–40.

120. Quoted i n al-Qaraḍāwī, *Fiqh al-jihād*, 2:1055–63.

121. Al-Qaraḍāwī, *Fiqh al-jihād*, 2:1051–52, 1061.

122. Al-Qaraḍāwī, *Fiqh al-jihād*, 2:1064–67.

123. Al-Qaraḍāwī, *25 Yanāyir sanat 2011m*, 147–49.

124. Al-Qaraḍāwī, *Fiqh al-jihād*, 2:1064–66.

125. Al-Qaraḍāwī, *25 Yanāyir sanat 2011m*, 149.

126. Shaykh Yūsuf al-Qaraḍāwī, *Al-Qaraḍāwī yuftī bi-qatl Muʿammar al-Qadhdhāfī*, video, Feb. 21, 2011, at https://www.youtube.com/watch?v=QrXN1FVIhio.

127. Shaykh Yūsuf al-Qaraḍāwī, *Al-Shaykh al-Qaraḍāwī yuftī bi-jawāz qatl al-Qadhdhāfī*, video, Feb. 21, 2011, at https://www.youtube.com/watch?v=X8fpg8_hR2Q. See also Warren, "The 'Ulamā' and the Arab Uprisings," 14–17, and Yahya M. Michot, "The Fatwa of Shaykh Yusuf al-Qaradawi against Gaddafi," Scribd.com, Mar. 15, 2011, at https://www.scribd.com/doc/51219918/The-fatwa-of-Shaykh-Yusuf-al-Qaradawi-against-Gaddafi.

128. Al-Qaraḍāwī, *Kayfa nataʿāmalu maʿa al-turāth?* 223–32.

129. Al-Qaraḍāwī, "Rudūd ʿilmiyya ʿalā al-shaykh aw al-jinirāl ʿAlī Gumʿa."

130. On the juristic debate between al-Qaraḍāwī and Ibn Bāz on the Oslo Accords, see Yitzhak Reiter, *War, Peace, and International Relations in Islam: Muslim Scholars on Peace Accords with Israel* (Brighton, UK: Sussex Academic Press, 2011), 120–34.

131. ʿAbd al-ʿAzīz b. ʿAbdallah Ibn Bāz, *Ḥukm al-ṣulḥ maʿa al-Yahūd fī ḍawʾ al-sharīʿa al-Islāmiyya* (Riyadh: Riʾāsat Idārat al-Buḥūth al-ʿIlmiyya wa-l-Iftāʾ, 1996), 4–14, electronic copy at http://waqfeya.com/book.php?bid=2287.

132. Shaykh Yūsuf al-Qaraḍāwī, *Fatāwā min ajli Filasṭīn* (Cairo: Maktabat Wahba, 2010), 8, 19–20.

133. Ibn Bāz, *Ḥukm al-ṣulḥ maʿa al-Yahūd*, 4–5; al-Qaraḍāwī, *Fatāwā min ajli Filasṭīn*, 8–9, 21–22.

134. Al-Qaraḍāwī, *Fatāwā min ajli Filasṭīn*, 9–26.

135. Ibn Bāz, *Ḥukm al-ṣulḥ maʿa al-Yahūd*, 25.

136. Al-Qaraḍāwī, *Fatāwā min ajli Filasṭīn*, 25.

137. See, for example, ʿImād al-Dīn Abī al-Fidāʾ Ibn Kathīr, *Tafsīr al-Qurʾān al-ʿaẓīm*, 6 vols. (Beirut: Dār al-Kitāb al-ʿArabī, 2004), 5:607.

138. ʿAbd al-Raḥmān b. ʿAbd al-Khāliq, "Ḥukm muʿāhadāt al-ṣulḥ wa-l-salām maʿa al-Yahūd wa-mawqif al-Muslim minhā" (2008), 3–4, at http://www.ilmway.com/site/maqdis/MS_8332.html.

139. Ibn Bāz, *Ḥukm al-ṣulḥ maʿa al-Yahūd*, 20–21.

140. Al-Qaraḍāwī, *Fatāwā min ajli Filasṭīn*, 26–27.

141.Osama bin Laden, "Risāla ilā Ibn Bāz bi-buṭlān fatwāhu bi-l-ṣulḥ maʿa al-Yahūd," Rajab 27, AH 1415 [Dec. 30, 1994], at http://www.ilmway.com/site/maqdis/MS_852.html.

142. Ibn Bāz, *Ḥukm al-ṣulḥ maʿa al-Yahūd*, 19–20.

143. Al-Qaraḍāwī, *Fatāwā min ajli Filasṭīn*, 27–28.

144. ʿAbdallah ʿAzzām, *Al-Difāʿ ʿan arāḍī al-Muslimīn ahamm furūḍ al-aʿyān* (ʿAmmān, Jordan: Maktabat al-Risāla al-Ḥadītha, 1987), 40, electronic copy at http://www.ilmway.com/site/maqdis/MS_10202.html.

145. Al-Qaraḍāwī, *Fatāwā min ajli Filasṭīn*, 10–11.

146. Ibn Bāz, *Ḥukm al-ṣulḥ maʿa al-Yahūd*, 17.

147. Al-Qaraḍāwī, *Fatāwā min ajli Filasṭīn*, 22–23.

148. Ibn Bāz, *Ḥukm al-ṣulḥ maʿa al-Yahūd*, 25.

149. Al-Qaraḍāwī, *Ummatunā bayna qarnayni*, 182–83.

150. S. al-Nābulsī, *Al-Lībirālīyyūn al-judud*, 23 (Art. 5).

151. These statements appear on the "Taʿrīf" (Who We Are) page of the IUMS website: http://iumsonline.org/portal/ar.

152. On the IUMS, see Bettina Gräf, "The International Association of Muslim Scholars: Yusuf al-Qaradawi and the Foundation of a 'Global Muslim Authority,'" *Qantara* 1 (2005), at http://en.qantara.de/wcsite.php?wc_c=6081&printmode=1.

153. The ruling is titled "Bayān al-Ittiḥād al-ʿĀlamī li-ʿUlamāʾ al-Muslimīn bi-shaʾn al-intifāḍa al-mubāraka fī Miṣr" and is given in al-Qaraḍāwī, *25 Yanāyir sanat 2011m*, 52.

154. CNN Arabic, "Kibār al-ʿUlamāʾ" tuḥadhdhiru min "Ulamāʾ al-Muslimīn": Tuqaddimu maṣlaḥat ḥaraka ʿalā al-Islām," Oct. 27, 2017, at https://arabic.cnn.com/middle-east/2017/10/27/saudi-muslim-scholars-union-warning.

155. Al-Jazeera.net, "Duwal al-ḥiṣār tudriju Ittiḥād ʿUlamāʾ al-Muslimīn bi-qawāʾim al-irhāb," Nov. 23, 2017, at https://tinyurl.com/yba8dp62.

156. Mawqiʿ Samāḥat al-Shaykh Yūsuf al-Qaraḍāwī, "Al-Ittiḥād al-ʿĀlamī li-ʿUlamāʾ al-Muslimīn: Ittihāmunā bi-l-irhāb bāṭil lā asāsa lahu," Dec. 2, 2017, at https://www.al-qaradawi.net/node/4592.

157. Quoted in *Al-Quds al-ʿArabī*, "Ramatni bi-dāʾihā wa-insallat: Al-Qaraḍāwī yaruddu ʿalā duwal al-ḥiṣār wa-ittihāmihi bi-l-irhāb," Nov. 25, 2017, at http://www.alquds.co.uk/?p=833102. In the last sentence of the quotation, al-Qaraḍāwī uses the Arabic expression *ramatni bi-dāʾihā wa-insallat*, meaning "to impute one's own fault to someone else and then sneak away," implying that his accusers are the ones fostering terrorism.

158. Quoted in *Al-ʿArab*, "Al-Qarra Dāghī: '95 alf dāʿiya wa-ʿālim bi-l-ittiḥād aṣbaḥū irhābiyyīn!'" Nov. 24, 2017, at https://tinyurl.com/y9obwe58.

159. *Dunyā al-Waṭan*, "Al-Ittiḥād al-ʿĀlamī lil-ʿUlamāʾ yastankiru waṣf Ḥamās bil-irhābiyya wa-yaʿtabiru al-qarār al-Miṣrī musayyasan," Mar. 2, 2015, at https://www.alwatanvoice.com/arabic/news/2015/03/02/671012.html.

160. *Al-Mīzān al-Bawwāba al-Qānūniyya al-Qaṭariyya*, "Wathīqa taʾsīsiyya li-l-Ittiḥād al-ʿĀlamī li-ʿUlamāʾ al-Muslimīn," Mar. 3, 2011, at http://www.almeezan.qa/LawPage.aspx?id=4361&language=ar.

161. Quoted in Mawqiʿ Samāḥat al-Shaykh Yūsuf al-Qaraḍāwī, "Al-Qarra Dāghī: Ittiḥād al-ʿUlamāʾ qāma bi-aʿmāl jalīla ḍidda al-taṭarruf wa-l-irhāb," Feb. 12, 2017, at https://www.al-qaradawi.net/node/44.

162. *RTonline*, "Qaṭar tatasallamu maṭālib al-duwal al-muqāṭi'a," June 23, 2017, at https://tinyurl.com/yd5xu35f.

163. David H. Warren, "Qatari Support for the Muslim Brotherhood Is More Than Just Realpolitik; It Has a Long, Personal History," *Maydan Politics & Society*, July 12, 2017, 1–7, at https://tinyurl.com/yd7aou65.

164. *Al-'Arabī al-Jadīd*, "Al-Ittiḥād al-'Ālamī li-'Ulamā' al-Muslimīn yad'ū ilā taghlīb al-ḥikma wa-raf' al-ḥiṣār 'an Qaṭar," June 12, 2017, at https://tinyurl.com/ybf8m6ve.

165. *Al-Sharq*, "Al-Qarra Dāghī li-al-Sharq: 'Muḥāṣarat sha'b Muslim lā tajūzu shar'an fī kull al-ẓurūf,'" Sept. 22, 2017, at https://tinyurl.com/yak65y3q.

166. On the main arguments of the proponents of *tasyīs al-dīn*, see al-'Ashmāwī, *Al-Islām al-siyāsī*, 45–46.

167. S. al-Nābulsī, *Tahāfut al-uṣūliyya*, 29–30.

168. Aḥmad al-Baghdādī, *Tajdīd al-fikr al-dīnī*, 241–48.

169. Shākir al-Nābulsī, "Qaraḍāwiyyāni, lā Qaraḍāwī wāḥid," *Al-Ḥiwār al-Mutamaddin* 894 (July 2004), at http://www.ahewar.org/debat/show.art.asp?aid=20677.

170. Mishārī al-Dhāyadī, "Al-Qaraḍāwī wa-ḥālat al-qarḍana," *Al-Sharq al-Awsaṭ*, Jan. 15, 2018, at https://tinyurl.com/y8j5lylx; *Al-Yawm al-Sābi'*, "'Abd al-Raḥmān Yūsuf al-Qaraḍāwī Yaktubu: 'Afwan Abī al-ḥabīb . . . Mursī lā shar'iyya lahu," July 7, 2013, at https://tinyurl.com/ya8gpkuq.

171. Quoted in *Al-Yawm al-Sābi'*, "'Abd al-Raḥmān Yūsuf al-Qaraḍāwī Yaktubu."

172. 'Abd al-Ḥamīd al-Anṣārī, "Mā ḥaqīqat faza' al-Qaraḍāwī min al-tashayyu'?" Oct. 15, 2008, at http://www.siironline.org/alabwab/maqalat&mohaderat(12)/1311.htm.

173. See, for example, Gräf and Skovgaard-Petersen, eds., *Global Mufti*, and Jakob Skovgaard-Petersen, "The Global Mufti," in *Globalization and the Muslim World: Culture, Religion, and Modernity*, ed. Birgit Schaebler and Leif Stenberg (Syracuse, NY: Syracuse Univ. Press, 2004), 153–65.

174. Soage, "Shaykh Yusuf al-Qaradawi," 8.

175. Al-Khaṭīb, *Al-Qaraḍāwī faqīh al-ṣaḥwa al-Islāmiyya*, 122–27.

176. Gräf, "Sheikh Yūsuf al-Qaraḍāwī in Cyberspace," 404–5, and "The Concept of Wasaṭiyya in the Work of Yūsuf al-Qaraḍāwī," 224–27; Skovgaard-Petersen, "The Global Mufti."

177. Krämer, "Drawing Boundaries," 193. See also Helfont, *Yusuf al-Qaradawi*, 41–57.

178. For episodes of *Al-Sharī'a wal-ḥayāh* and transcripts of episodes, see http://www.aljazeera.net/program/religionandlife.

179. Shaykh Yūsuf al-Qaraḍāwī, *Al-Fatwā bayna al-inḍibāṭ wal-tasayyub*, 2nd ed. (Cairo: Dār al-Ṣaḥwa, 1994), 107.

180. The Ẓāhirī school of Islamic jurisprudence, founded by Dāwud b. Khalaf (d. 884), advocated a literal reading of the Qur'ān and *hadīth* and rejected the use of reason and analogy. Ibn Ḥazm (d. 1064) is considered one of this school's most characteristic and

prominent representatives. On this school, see Ignaz Goldziher, *The Ẓāhirīs: Their Doctrine and Their History*, trans. Behn Wolfgang (1883; reprint, Leiden: Brill, 2008).

181. Al-Qaraḍāwī, *Thaqāfatunā bayna al-infitāḥ wal-inghilāq*, 69–79, and *Ummatuna bayna qarnayni*, 244–45.

182. Al-Qaraḍāwī, *Thaqāfatunā bayna al-infitāḥ wal-inghilāq*, 79.

183. Shaykh Yūsuf al-Qaraḍāwī, "Nuṣrat al-nabī," Feb. 3, 2006, in *Khuṭab al-Shaykh al-Qaraḍāwī*, vol. 8, ed. al-Maktab al-I'lmī li-l-Shaykh bil-Dawḥa (Cairo: Maktabat Wahba, 2009), 366. For the quotation from al-Mutanabbī, see Abū al-Ḥasan 'Alī b. Aḥmad al-Wāḥidī, *Sharḥ Dīwān al-Mutanabbī* (N.p.: n.p., n.d.), electronic copy at http://islamport.com/w/adb/Web/754/124.htm.

184. Al-Qaraḍāwī, "Nuṣrat al-nabī," 8:364.

185. Shākir al-Nābulsī, *Al-Islām wa-jirāb al-ḥāwī: Limādhā ḥawwalnā al-Islām ilā ḥijāb wa-irhāb?* (Beirut: al-Mu'assasa al-'Arabiyya lil-Dirāsāt wal-Nashr, 2011), 158–59.

186. Shaykh Yūsuf al-Qaraḍāwī, "Lā akhāfu al-ightiyāl, bal atamannā al-shahāda," Mar. 14, 2013, in *Khuṭab al-Shaykh al-Qaraḍāwī*, ed. al-Sa'd, 6:205–9. For the sermon against the American invasion of Iraq, "Qaḍiyyat al-'Irāq," Mar. 7, 2003, see pages 188–204 in this same volume.

187. On al-Qaraḍāwī and al-Azhar, including his criticism of this organization, see Skovgaard-Petersen, "Yūsuf al-Qaraḍāwī and al-Azhar." On al-Qaraḍāwī and the MB, see Tammām, "Qaraḍāwī wal-Ikhwān," and Ana Belén Soage, "Yusuf al-Qaradawi: The Muslim Brothers' Favorite Ideological Guide," in *The Muslim Brotherhood: The Organization and Policies of a Global Islamist Movement*, ed. Barry Rubin (New York: Palgrave Macmillan, 2010), 19–37.

188. Al-Qaraḍāwī, *Ibn al-qarya wal-kuttāb*, 4:40–41.

4. *Wasaṭiyya*

1. Ron Shaham, "The Rhetoric of Legal Disputation: Neo-Ahl al-Ḥadīth vs. Yūsuf al-Qaraḍāwī," *Islamic Law and Society* 22 (2015): 114–41. On Shaykh al-Albānī and his influence on the neo-*ahl al-ḥadīth* school, see Stéphane Lacroix, "Between Revolution and Apoliticism: Nasir al-Din al-Albani and His Impact on the Shaping of Contemporary Salafism," in *Global Salafism*, ed. Meijer, 58–80.

2. Maher, *Salafi-Jihadism*, 16.

3. Abū Muḥammad al-Maqdisī, "Al-Tawḥīd wal-jihād 'unwān al-tamayyuz," Aug. 3, 2009, at http://www.ilmway.com/site/maqdis/MS_36546.html. The sentence from Ibn Taymiyya is quoted from Taqī al-Dīn Ibn Taymiyya, *Majmū'at al-fatāwā*, multiple vols. (Cairo: Al-Maktaba al-Tawfīqiyya, n.d.), 10:11.

4. For al-Maqdisī's view of jihad against contemporary Muslim rulers, see Wagemakers, *A Quietist Jihadi*, 58, 66–70.

5. Abū Muḥammad al-Maqdisī, *Kashf al-niqāb ʿan sharīʿat al-ghāb* (N.p.: n.p., 1988), 12, electronic copy at http://www.ilmway.com/site/maqdis/MS_38438.html. For al-Maqdisī's view on "the religion of Abraham," see Abū Muḥammad al-Maqdisī, *Millat Ibrāhīm wa-daʿwat al-anbiyāʾ wal-mursalīn wa-asālīb al-ṭughāh fī tamyīʿihā wa-ṣarf al-duʿāh ʿanhā* (N.p.: n.p., 1984), 13–36, electronic copy at http://www.ilmway.com/site/maqdis/MS_20383.html.

6. Shaykh Yūsuf al-Qaraḍāwī, *Ḥaqīqat al-tawḥīd*, 8th ed. (Cairo: Maktabat Wahba, 2006), 40–41.

7. Abū Muḥammad al-Maqdisī, *Hādhihi ʿaqīdatunā* (N.p.: n.p., 1997), 4–7, electronic copy at http://www.ilmway.com/site/maqdis/MS_35422.html; Abū Baṣīr ʿAbd al-Munʿim Muṣṭafā Ḥalīma al-Ṭarṭūsī, *Hādhihi ʿaqīdatunā wa-hādhā alladhī nadʿū ilayhi* (N.p.: n.p., 2002), 2–5, electronic copy at http://www.ilmway.com/site/maqdis/MS_35310.html; al-Ṭarṭūsī, *Muṣṭalaḥāt wa-mafāhīm sharʿiyya*, 4–13; Roel Meijer, introduction to *Global Salafism*, ed. Meijer, 1–32.

8. Al-Qaraḍāwī, *Ḥaqīqat al-tawḥīd*, 40–41.

9. On the view that rulers who do not follow *sharīʿa* should be considered *ṭawāghīt*, see al-Ṭarṭūsī, *Al-Ṭāghūt*, 94–102; Ibn Qayyim al-Jawziyya, *Aʿlām al-muwaqqiʿīn ʿan Rabb al-ʿālamīn*, 2 vols. (Al-Manṣūra, Egypt: Maktabat al-Īmān, 1999), 1:53–54.

10. For more on actions that, according to jihadi Salafis, make one no longer a Muslim, see Abū Baṣīr ʿAbd al-Munʿim Muṣṭafā Ḥalīma al-Ṭarṭūsī, *Aʿmāl tukhriju ṣāḥibahā mina al-milla* (N.p.: n.p., 2001), electronic copy at http://www.abubaseer.bizland.com/books/read/b10.doc. On al-Qaraḍāwī's criteria in this matter, see Shaykh Yūsuf al-Qaraḍāwī, *Ẓāhirat al-ghulū fī al-takfīr*, 5th ed. (Cairo: Maktabat Wahba, 2010), and *Jarīmat al-ridda wa-ʿuqūabat al-murtadd fī ḍawʾ al-Qurʾān wal-Sunna* (Beirut: Muʾassasat al-Risāla, 2001).

11. Muḥammad Ibn ʿAbd al-Wahhāb, *Kitāb al-tawḥīd* (Al-Manṣūra, Egypt: Maktabat ʿIbād al-Raḥmān, Maktabat al-ʿUlūm wal-Ḥikam, 2008), electronic copy at http://waqfeya.com/book.php?bid=7781.

12. Maher, *Salafi-Jihadism*, 187.

13. Al-Ṭarṭūsī, *Hādhihi ʿaqīdatunā wa-hādhā alladhī nadʿū ilayhi*, 4–5.

14. Abū Muḥammad al-Maqdisī, "Mā al-farq bayna tawḥīd al-ḥākimiyya wa-tawḥīd al-ulūhiyya?" n.d., at http://www.ilmway.com/site/maqdis/MS_38161.html.

15. Al-Qaraḍāwī, *Fiqh al-wasaṭiyya al-Islāmiyya wal-tajdīd*, 212–13, 242.

16. Al-Qaraḍāwī, *Fatāwā muʿāṣira*, 4:858–64, and *Min fiqh al-dawla fī al-Islām*, 61–65.

17. Al-ʿAshmāwī, *Al-Islām al-siyāsī*, 49–50.

18. Al-ʿAshmāwī, *Al-Islām al-siyāsī*, 49–50, 52–53, 78–79.

19. Shaykh Yūsuf al-Qaraḍāwī, *Al-Duktūr Muḥammad ʿImāra al-ḥāris al-yaqiẓ al-murābiṭ ʿalā thughūr al-Islām* (Cairo: Dār al-Muqāṣid, 2015), 31–32.

20. Quṭb, *Maʿālim fī al-ṭarīq*, 121.

21. Al-Qaraḍāwī, *Al-Ṣaḥwa al-Islāmiyya bayna al-jumūd wal-taṭarruf*, 96–97.

22. Abū Zayd, *Naqd al-khiṭāb al-dīnī*, 114–17.

23. Al-Qaraḍāwī, *Min fiqh al-dawla fī al-Islām*, 61.

24. Al-Qaraḍāwī, *Min fiqh al-dawla fī al-Islām*, 61.

25. Abū al-Aʿlā al-Mawdūdī, *Al-Ḥukūma al-Islāmiyya* (Cairo: Al-Mukhtār al-Islāmī, 1980), 130.

26. Abū al-Aʿlā al-Mawdūdī, *Naẓariyyat al-Islām wa-hadyihi fī al-siyāsa wal-qānūn wal-dustūr*, trans. Jalīl Ḥasan al-Iṣlāḥī (Damascus: Dār al-Fikr, 1964), 250–57, electronic copy at http://elibrary.mediu.edu.my/books/2014/MEDIU16880.pdf.

27. Al-Mawdūdī, *Al-Ḥukūma al-Islāmiyya*, 131.

28. Quṭb, *Maʿālim fī al-ṭarīq*, 109–10.

29. For more on al-Qaraḍāwī's views on democracy, see al-Qaraḍāwī, *Min fiqh al-dawla fī al-Islām*, 130–46; *Al-Ṣaḥwa al-Islāmiyya wa-humūm al-waṭan*, 100–103; and *Fatāwā muʿāṣira*, 2:636–65.

30. Al-Qaraḍāwī, "Al-Dīmuqrāṭiyya," Apr. 1, 2005, in *Khuṭab al-Shaykh al-Qaraḍāwī*, ed. Ḥūṭar and ʿAbd al-Sattār Kassāb, 7:283.

31. Al-Qaraḍāwī, "Al-Dīmuqrāṭiyya," 7:282.

32. "Al-Islām wa-ʿalāqatuhu bi-l-dīmuqrāṭiyya," episode of *Al-Sharīʿa wal-ḥayāh*, al-Jazeera, June 6, 2004, at https://tinyurl.com/y9qwbecv.

33. Sayyid al-Qimnī, *Ahl al-dīn wa-l-dīmuqrāṭiyya* (Cairo: Dār Miṣr al-Maḥrūsa, 2005), 222–23.

34. Aḥmad al-Baghdādī, *Tajdīd al-fikr al-dīnī*, 47–48.

35. Aḥmad al-Baghdādī, *Tajdīd al-fikr al-dīnī*, 445–46.

36. Al-Qaraḍāwī, *Min fiqh al-dawla fī al-Islām*, 138–39.

37. Muʿtazz al-Khaṭīb, "Al-Wasaṭiyya al-Islāmiyya wa-fiqh al-dawla: Qirāʾa naqdiyya," *Tabayyun li-l-Dirāsāt al-Fikriyya wa-l-Thaqāfiyya*, 1, no. 3 (Winter 2013): 186–88, at https://tinyurl.com/y8ofwm9t.

38. Shaykh Yūsuf al-Qaraḍāwī, *Al-Dīn wal-siyāsa: Taʾṣīl wa-radd shubuhāt* (Cairo: Dār al-Shurūq, 2007), 174–81. See also Meir Litvak, "Islamic Democracy vs. Western Democracy: The Debate among Islamists," in *Middle Eastern Societies and the West*, ed. Meir Litvak (Tel Aviv: Moshe Dayan Center, Tel Aviv Univ., 2006), 199–219. For the *wasaṭī* view on democracy, see Mawqiʿ Samāḥat al-Shaykh Yūsuf al-Qaraḍāwī, "Al-Islām wa-l-dīmuqrāṭiyya," Apr. 19, 2017, at https://www.al-qaradawi.net/node/3775. For a refutation of the centrist view of democracy, see Muḥammad b. Muḥammad al-Fazzāzī, "Munāqashat al-Shaykh Yūsuf al-Qaraḍāwī fī mawḍūʿ al-dīmuqrāṭiyya," Dec. 24, 1996, at http://www.ilmway.com/site/maqdis/MS_23711.html.

39. For more on this *ḥadīth* and its interpretation by al-Qaraḍāwī, see Shaykh Yūsuf al-Qaraḍāwī, *Fī riḥāb al-Sunna: Sharḥ aḥādīth nabawiyya* (Cairo: Maktabat Wahba, 2010), 90–99.

40. Al-Qaraḍāwī, *Al-Dīn wal-siyāsa*, 174–77.

41. Al-Qaraḍāwī, *Thaqāfatunā bayna al-infitāḥ wal-inghilāq*, 79.

42. Al-Maqdisī, *Hādhihi ʿaqīdatunā*, 26–29; al-Ṭarṭūsī, *Hādhihi ʿaqīdatunā wa-hādhā alladhī nadʿū ilayhi*, 13. On this view, see Joas Wagemakers, "'The Kāfir Religion of the West':

Takfīr of Democracy and Democrats by Radical Islamists," in *Accusations of Unbelief in Islam: A Diachronic Perspective on Takfir*, ed. Camilla Adang, Hassan Ansari, Maribel Fierro, and Sabine Schmidke (Leiden: Brill, 2016), 327–53.

43. Ayman al-Ẓawāhirī, *Al-Ḥiṣād al-murr: Al-Ikhwān al-Muslimīn fī sittīn ʿāman*, 2nd ed. (N.p.: Markaz al-Fajr lil-Iʿlām, 2005), 32–37, electronic copy at http://www.ilmway.com/site/maqdis/MS_25064.html.

44. Al-Ẓawāhirī, *Al-Ḥiṣād al-murr*, 32–37.

45. Abū Muḥammad al-Maqdisī, *Al-Dīmuqrāṭīyya dīn* (N.p.: n.p., n.d.), 11–15, electronic copy at http://www.ilmway.com/site/maqdis/MS_26238.html; al-Ẓawāhirī, *Al-Ḥiṣād al-murr*, 37.

46. Al-Fazzāzī, "Munāqashat al-Shaykh Yūsuf al-Qaraḍāwī fī mawḍūʿ al-dīmuqrāṭiyya," 11–12, 22.

47. Shākir al-Nābulsī, "Dīmuqrāṭiyyat al-Qaraḍāwī al-Islāmawiyya al-zāʾifa," *Al-Ḥiwār al-Mutamaddin*, June 15, 2004, at http://www.m.ahewar.org/s.asp?aid=19430&r=0.

48. Aḥmad al-Baghdādī, *Tajdīd al-fikr al-dīnī*, 44.

49. Al-Qaraḍāwī, *Fatāwā muʿāṣira*, 2:637–38.

50. Aḥmad al-Baghdādī, *Tajdīd al-fikr al-dīnī*, 450.

51. S. al-Nābulsī, *Bin Lādin wal-ʿaql al-ʿArabī*, 220.

52. Al-Qimnī, *Ahl al-dīn wa-l-dīmuqrāṭiyya*, 233–35. For the MB's reform platform, see al-Jazeera.net, "Mubādarat Jamāʿat al-Ikhwān al-Muslimīn lil-iṣlāḥ al-dākhilī fī Miṣr," May 16, 2005, at https://tinyurl.com/y8yhkolg.

53. Khaled Abou El Fadl, "Reply," in *Islam and the Challenge of Democracy: Khaled Abou El Fadl*, ed. Joshua Cohen and Deborah Chasman (Princeton, NJ: Princeton Univ. Press, 2004), 120–21.

54. Alison Pargeter, *The Muslim Brotherhood from Opposition to Power* (London: Saqi Books, 2013), 248.

55. Al-Jazeera.net, "Al-Iʿlān al-dustūrī li-l-raʾīs Mursī," Dec. 7, 2012, at https://tinyurl.com/y9gsf66j; *Markaz al-Qāhira li-Dirāsāt Ḥuqūq al-Insān*, "Al-Iʿlān al-dustūrī al-jadīd yamnaḥu Mursī sulutāt ilāhiyya wa-yuwajjihu ḍarba qāḍiya li-istiqlāl al-qaḍā," Nov. 24, 2012, at https://tinyurl.com/ycp2ov23; Navit Shamni, *Egypt under Muslim Brotherhood Rule: The Constitutional Declaration, Dictatorship in the Name of the Revolution*, Inquiry & Analysis Report no. 907 (Washington, DC: Middle East Media Research Institute, Dec. 7, 2012), at https://tinyurl.com/ybx3rwr7.

56. "Ḥalqa khāṣṣa ḥawla al-shaʾn al-ʿāmm li-l-umma," episode of *Al-Sharīʿa wal-ḥayāh*, al-Jazeera, Nov. 25, 2012, at https://tinyurl.com/y9awubsb; Shaykh Yūsuf al-Qaraḍāwī, *Khuṭbat al-Jumʿa li-l-Duktūr Yūsuf al-Qaraḍāwī*, video, Nov. 23, 2012, at https://www.youtube.com/watch?v=nJrImaCkxo4&t=35s.

57. For the Constitution as drafted by the Constitutional Assembly, see al-Jamʿiyya al-Taʾsīsiyya li-Waḍʿ Mashrūʿ Dustūr Jadīd lil-Bilād, "Mashrūʿ dustūr Jumhūriyyat Miṣr

al-ʿArabiyya," Nov. 30, 2012, at https://egelections-2011.appspot.com/Referendum2012/dostor_masr_final.pdf.

58. International Federation for Human Rights (FIDH), "One Year into Mohamed Morsi's Term: Manifold Abuses and the Systematic Undermining of the Rule of Law," press release by twenty rights organizations, including FIDH member organizations in Egypt, July 3, 2013, at https://tinyurl.com/y9aqv29k.

59. Limor Lavi, *An Examination of Egypt's Draft Constitution Part I: Religion and State: The Most Islamic Constitution in Egypt's History*, Inquiry & Analysis Report no. 904 (Washington, DC: Middle East Media Research Institute, Dec. 3, 2012), at http://www.memri.org/report/en/print6846.htm, and *An Examination of Egypt's Draft Constitution Part II: The Egyptian Public Debate over Religion and State*, Inquiry & Analysis Report no. 906 (Washington, DC: Middle East Media Research Institute, Dec. 5, 2012), at http://www.memri.org/report/en/print6851.htm.

60. For the Constitution of 1971, see Al-Jazeera.net, "Dustūr Miṣr 1971," Dec. 7, 2015, at https://tinyurl.com/yagox2bc.

61. Lavi, "An Examination of Egypt's Draft Constitution Part II," 7.

62. "Ḥalqa khāṣṣa ḥawla al-sha'n al-ʿāmm li-l-umma."

63. Al-Qaraḍāwī, *Khuṭbat al-Jumʿa li-l-Duktūr Yūsuf al-Qaraḍāwī.*

64. FIDH, "One Year into Mohamed Morsi's Term."

65. Bedford Row International, *The Egyptian Experience of the Muslim Brotherhood in Power 2012–2013* (London: Bedford Row International, June 3, 2015), 83–85, at http://9bri.com/wp-content/uploads/2015/06/Report-II.9BRi.Muslim-Brotherhood-in-Power.pdf.

66. On the MB's takeover of the media during Mursi's presidency, see Limor Lavi, *Muslim Brotherhood Efforts to Take Over Egyptian Media*, Inquiry & Analysis Report no. 875 (Washington, DC: Middle East Media Research Institute, Aug. 22, 2012), https://www.memri.org/reports/muslim-brotherhood-efforts-take-over-egyptian-media.

67. Bedford Row International, *The Egyptian Experience of the Muslim Brotherhood in Power 2012–2013*, 54–55, 83–85.

68. "Al-Khawārij bayna al-dīn wa-l-tārīkh wa-l-siyāsa," episode of *Al-Sharīʿa wal-ḥayāh*, al-Jazeera, Aug. 25, 2011, at https://tinyurl.com/y955zsax.

69. Al-Qaraḍāwī, *25 Yanāyir sanat 2011m*, 142; al-Qaraḍāwī, "Rudūd ʿilmiyya ʿalā al-shaykh aw al-jinirāl ʿAlī Gumʿa."

70. Shaykh Yūsuf al-Qaraḍāwī, *Khuṭbat al-Jumʿa li-l-Duktūr al-Qaraḍāwī*, video, June 21, 2013, at https://www.youtube.com/watch?v=iKb8048QjLQ; "Al-Radd ʿalā istifsārāt al-mushāhidīn ḥawla al-sha'n al-ʿāmm," episode of *Al-Sharīʿa wal-ḥayāh*, al-Jazeera, Apr. 21, 2013, at https://tinyurl.com/yay59hlk; Mawqiʿ Samāḥat al-Shaykh Yūsuf al-Qaraḍāwī, "Al-Ittiḥād yuḥadhdhiru min zaʿzaʿat al-istiqrār fī Miṣr wa-yuṭālibu al-muʿāraḍa bi-ittibāʿ qawāʿid al-dīmuqrāṭiyya," June 26, 2013, at https://www.al-qaradawi.net/node/4788.

71. Basma ʿAbd al-ʿAzīz, *Saṭwat al-naṣṣ khiṭāb al-Azhar wa-azmat al-ḥukm* (Giza, Egypt: Dār Ṣafṣāfa, 2016), 259–60.

72. Shaykh Yūsuf al-Qaraḍāwī, "Waqafāt maʿa shaykh al-Azhar wa-qaḍiyyat al-inqilāb ʿalā al-sharʿiyya," Sept. 4, 2013, at https://tinyurl.com/y79sfua8.

73. Al-Qaraḍāwī, "Waqafāt maʿa shaykh al-Azhar."

74. Govrin, *Journey to the Arab Spring*, 174.

75. Shaykh Yūsuf al-Qaraḍāwī, "Ḥuqūq al-insān fī al-Islām," n.d., in *Khuṭab al-Shaykh al-Qaraḍāwī*, ed. al-Saʿd, 2:178–84.

76. Fuʾād Zakariyyā, *Al-Ṣaḥwa al-Islāmiyya fī mīzān al-ʿaql* (Alexandria, Egypt: Dār al-Wafāʾ, 2006), 100–102.

77. Zakariyyā, *Al-Ṣaḥwa al-Islāmiyya fī mīzān al-ʿaql*, 108–9.

78. Al-Qaraḍāwī, "Ḥuqūq al-insān fī al-Islām," 2:191–92, ellipses in the original.

79. Zakariyyā, *Al-Ṣaḥwa al-Islāmiyya fī mīzān al-ʿaql*, 113–14.

80. Zakariyyā, *Al-Ṣaḥwa al-Islāmiyya fī mīzān al-ʿaql*, 111.

81. On al-Qimnī, see Govrin, *Journey to the Arab Spring*, 98–99.

82. Al-Qimnī, *Ahl al-dīn wa-l-dīmuqrāṭiyya*, 249–51; for the statement from al-Qaraḍāwī, see al-Qaraḍāwī, *Al-Islām wal-ʿilmāniyya wajhan li-wajhin*, 148.

83. Al-Qaraḍāwī, *Al-Islām wal-ʿilmāniyya wajhan li-wajhin*, 145.

84. Al-Qimnī, *Ahl al-dīn wa-l-dīmuqrāṭiyya*, 239–40.

85. Maher, *Salafi-Jihadism*, 111. On the differences between *wasaṭiyya* and Salafism on the issue of "loyalty and disavowal," see Shavit, "Can Muslims Befriend Non-Muslims?" 5–16.

86. On the historical evolution of the principle of *al-walāʾ wal-barāʾ*, see Joas Wagemakers, "The Transformation of a Radical Concept: *Al-Walaʾ Wa-l-Baraʾ* in the Ideology of Abu Muhammad al-Maqdisi," in *Global Salafism*, ed. Meijer, 81–106.

87. Maher, *Salafi-Jihadism*, 111.

88. Ayman al-Ẓawāhirī, *Al-Walāʾ wal-barāʾ: ʿAqīda manqūla wa-wāqiʿ mafqūd* (N.p.: n.p., 2002), 8–11, electronic copy at http://www.ilmway.com/site/maqdis/MS_20361.html.

89. Al-Qaraḍāwī, *Kayfa nataʿāmalu maʿa al-Qurʾān al-ʿaẓīm?* 238–55.

90. Al-Qaraḍāwī, *Fiqh al-jihād*, 2:1145–47.

91. Al-Qaraḍāwī, *Fī fiqh al-aqalliyyāt al-Muslima*, 98–104.

92. Al-Akhḍar, "Kayfa nujaffifu yanābīʿ al-irhāb?"

93. S. al-Nābulsī, *Tahāfut al-uṣūliyya*, 164–65.

94. Wagemakers, *A Quietist Jihadi*, 147–88; Shaykh Ḥamūd b. ʿUqalāʾ al-Shuʿaybī, *Al-Qawl al-mukhtār fī ḥukm al-istiʿāna bil-kuffār* (N.p.: n.p., 1999), electronic copy at http://www.ilmway.com/site/maqdis/MS_15136.html; Maher, *Salafi-Jihadism*, 126–33.

95. Al-Ẓawāhirī, *Al-Ḥiṣād al-murr*, 27–44.

96. Al-Ẓawāhirī, *Al-Walāʾ wal-barāʾ*, 16–17; Ibn Taymiyya, *Majmūʿat al-fatāwā*, vol. 15, part 28:311.

97. For more on al-Maqdisī's views concerning *al-walāʾ wal-barāʾ*, see Wagemakers, "The Transformation of a Radical Concept," and Joas Wagemakers, "Framing the 'Threat

to Islam': *Al-Wala' Wa al-Bara'* in Salafi Discourse," *Arab Studies Quarterly* 30, no. 4 (Fall 2008): 1–22.

98. Al-Maqdisī, *Hādhā mā adīnu Allāh bihi*, 15–19; Ibn Taymiyya, *Majmū'at al-fatāwā*, vol. 15, part 28:313.

99. Al-Ṭarṭūsī, *A'māl tukhriju ṣāḥibahā min al-milla*, 102–11.

100. On the issue of seeking or taking help from non-Muslims (*al-isti'āna bil-kuffār*), see Wagemakers, *A Quietist Jihadi*, 147–64.

101. Al-Qaraḍāwī, *Fiqh al-jihād*, 1:703–7. The same legal views are also expressed by 'Abdallah 'Azzām in *Al-Difā' 'an arāḍī al-Muslimīn ahamm furūḍ al-a'yān*, 35–37.

102. Al-Qaraḍāwī, *Fiqh al-jihād*, 1:707–9. See also 'Azzām, *Al-Difā' 'an arāḍī al-Muslimīn ahamm furūḍ al-a'yān*, 35–39.

103. Al-Qaraḍāwī, *Fiqh al-jihād*, 1:713; the parentheses around the Arabic term for "unbelieving" are in the original.

104. Al-Qaraḍāwī, *Fiqh al-jihād*, 1:714–19.

105. 'Abd al-'Azīz b. 'Abdallah Ibn Bāz, "Mawqif al-sharī'a al-Islāmiyya min al-ghazw al-'Irāqī lil-Kuwayt," n.d., at www.binbaz.org.sa/article/177.

106. Abū Muḥammad al-Maqdisī, *Al-Kawāshif al-jaliyya fī kufr al-Dawla al-Su'ūdiyya*, 2nd ed. (N.p.: n.p., 2000–2001), 162–67, electronic copy at http://www.ilmway.com/site/maqdis/MS_65.html.

107. Al-Maqdisī, *Hādhā mā adīnu Allāh bihi*, 19–22; Ḥamūd b. 'Uqalā' al-Shu'aybī, *Ḥukm mā jarā fī Amrīkā min aḥdāth* (N.p.: n.p., 2001), 2–3, electronic copy at http://www.al-oglaa.com/?section=subject&SubjectID=176.

108. Shaykh Yūsuf al-Qaraḍāwī, "Thaqāfat al-tasāmuḥ 'inda al-Muslimīn," Mawqi' Samāḥat al-Shaykh Yūsuf al-Qaraḍāwī, Nov. 23, 2015, at https://www.al-qaradawi.net/node/2293.

109. Al-Qaraḍāwī, *Khiṭābunā al-Islāmī*, 45.

110. Al-Qaraḍāwī, *Khiṭābunā al-Islāmī*, 49.

111. Shaykh Yūsuf al-Qaraḍāwī, *Al-Taḥdhīr min al-'urf al-khāṭi' wal-khidā' al-lafẓī wal-tarkīz 'alā al-'aqīda wa-ta'thīrihā fī al-'amal* (Cairo: Maktabat Wahba, 2013), 39–40.

112. Imām Muḥammad Imām, "Fatwā min al-Qaraḍāwī wal-'Awwā wal-Bishrī wa-ākharīn tujīzu lil-'askariyyīn al-Amīrikiyyīn al-Muslimīn al-mushāraka fī al-ghārāt 'alā Afghanistān," *Al-Sharq al-Awsaṭ*, Oct. 14, 2001, at http://archive.aawsat.com/details.asp?issueno=8070&article=61545#.W_CCu-hvbIU; Basheer M. Nafi, "Fatwā and War: On the Allegiance of the American Muslim Soldiers in the Aftermath of September 11," *Islamic Law and Society* 2, no. 1 (2004): 78–116. On the *sharī'a* principle of choosing the lesser evil, see 'Abd al-'Azīz Muḥammad 'Azzām, *Al-Qawā'id al-fiqhiyya* (Cairo: Dār al-Ḥadīth, 2005), 160–64.

113. Abū Baṣīr 'Abd al-Mun'im Muṣṭafā Ḥalīma al-Ṭarṭūsī, "Limādhā kaffartu Yūsuf al-Qaraḍāwī . . . ?" Nov. 1, 2008, at http://www.abubaseer.bizland.com/articles/read/a%20118.doc.

114. Al-Maqdisī, *Hādhā mā adīnu Allāh bihi*, 18–19.

115. Shaykh Yūsuf al-Qaraḍāwī, *Al-Fatāwā al-shādhdha: Maʿāyīruhā wa-taṭbīqātuhā wa-asbābuhā wa-kayfa nuʿālijuhā wa-natawaqqāhā* (Cairo: Dār al-Shurūq, 2010), 124–26. On this issue, see also Shavit, "The *Wasaṭī* and *Salafī* Approaches to the Religious Law of Muslim Minorities," 450–56.

116. "Dalālāt wa-rasāʾil al-muẓāharāt fī al-gharb li-ṣāliḥ al-ʿIrāq," episode of *Al-Sharīʿa wal-ḥayāh*, al-Jazeera, Feb. 16, 2003, at https://tinyurl.com/ybf44ze9.

117. Shaykh ʿAbd al-Ākhir Ḥammād al-Ghunaymī, "Waqafāt maʿa fatwā al-Qaraḍāwī ḥawla al-qawāʿid al-Amrīkiyya," n.d., 4–5, at http://www.ilmway.com/site/maqdis/MS_21378.html.

118. Taqī al-Dīn Ibn Taymiyya, *Al-ʿAqīda al-wāsiṭiyya: Jāmiʿ al-durūs al-ʿaqdiyya fī sharḥ al-ʿaqīda al-wāsiṭiyya li-shayk al-Islām Ibn Taymiyya* (Cairo: Dār Ibn Ḥazm, 2009), 557–58. According to Ibn Taymiyya, "[*Ahl al-Sunna wal-Jamāʿa*, the branch of Islam that claims to follow the example of the Prophet (Sunna) and belong to the group (*jamāʿa*) and a name the Salafis apply to themselves,] is the middle [*wasaṭ*] among the nation's sects, just as the [Muslim] nation is the middle among the nations" (according to Q2:143).

119. Ibn Taymiyya, *Al-ʿAqīda wal-wāsiṭiyya*, 728–47.

120. Ibn Taymiyya, *Al-ʿAqīda wal-wāsiṭiyya*, 728.

121. On the classical *murjiʾa*, see Lav, *Radical Islam*, 13–29.

122. Ibn Taymiyya, *Al-ʿAqīda al-wāsiṭiyya*, 735; Lav, *Radical Islam*, 24–27.

123. Ibn Taymiyya, *Al-ʿAqīda al-wāsiṭiyya*, 735–38.

124. ʿAbdallah ʿAzzām, *Al-ʿAqīda wa-atharuhā fī bināʾ al-jīl* (Beirut: Dār Ibn Ḥazm, 1990), 6, electronic copy at http://www.ilmway.com/site/maqdis/MS_161.html.

125. Al-Maqdisī, *Hādhihi ʿaqīdatunā*; al-Ṭarṭūsī, *Hādhihi ʿaqīdatunā wa-hādhā alladhī nadʿū ilayhi*.

126. The IS document is titled *Hādhihi ʿaqīdatunā wa-hādhā minhajunā*. For an analysis of this document, see Ella Landau-Tasseron, *A Self Profile of the Islamic State: The Creedal Document*, Inquiry & Analysis Report no. 1253 (Washington, DC: Middle East Media Research Institute, June 1, 2016).

127. Al-Maqdisī, *Hādhihi ʿaqīdatunā*, 23; al-Ṭarṭūsī, *Hādhihi ʿaqīdatunā wa-hādhā alladhī nadʿū ilayhi*, 10.

128. Al-Qaraḍāwī, *Fiqh al-jihād*, 2:1065; Abū Ḥāmid al-Ghazālī, *Al-Iqtiṣād fī al-iʿtiqād* (Beirut: Qutayba li-l-Ṭibāʿa wa-l-Nashr wa-l-Tawzīʿ, 2003), 176, electronic copy at http://www.ghazali.org/books/iqtisad-ramadan.pdf.

129. Al-Qaraḍāwī, *Ẓāhirat al-ghulū fī al-takfīr*, 25–26.

130. Shaykh Yūsuf al-Qaraḍāwī, "Qaḍiyyat al-murtadd Salmān Rushdī," Mar. 1989, in *Khuṭab al-Shaykh al-Qaraḍāwī*, ed. al-Saʿd, 1:170.

131. On al-Azhar's ruling on the novel, see Jābir ʿAsfūr, *Ḍidda al-taʿaṣṣub* (Cairo: Maktabat al-Usra, 2000), 415–40.

132. Al-Qaraḍāwī, *Fatāwā muʿāṣira*, 3:715–16.

133. Al-Qaraḍāwī, *Thaqāfatunā bayna al-infitāḥ wal-inghilāq*, 63–64.

134. S. al-Nābulsī, *Al-'Arab bayna al-lībirāliyya*, 49.

135. Al-'Ashmāwī, *Al-Islām al-siyāsī*, 76–77.

136. Al-Qaraḍāwī, *Jarīmat al-ridda*, 30.

137. Al-Qaraḍāwī, *Jarīmat al-ridda*, 24–27.

138. Aḥmad al-Baghdādī, *Tajdīd al-fikr al-dīnī*, 156–57.

139. The term *ḥadīth āḥād*, a *ḥadīth* from an individual narrator, is the opposite of *ḥadīth mutawātir*, a *ḥadīth* transmitted by multiple sources—that is, multiply transmitted prophetic reports, which is therefore accepted as authentic (*ṣaḥīh*). See Islamqa, "Mā huwa khabar al-āḥād?" May 4, 2013, at https://islamqa.info/ar/197554.

140. Al-Qaraḍāwī, *Jarīmat al-ridda*, 37, 40–46.

141. Aḥmad al-Baghdādī, *Tajdīd al-fikr al-dīnī*, 156–57.

142. Al-Qaraḍāwī, *Jarīmat al-ridda*, 37–39.

143. Aḥmad al-Baghdādī, *Tajdīd al-fikr al-dīnī*, 156.

144. Al-Nābulsī, "Qaraḍāwiyyāni, lā Qaraḍāwī wāḥid."

145. 'Īd, *Yūsuf al-Qaraḍāwī bayna al-tasāmuḥ wal-irhāb*, 223. 'Īd is alluding to a saying attributed to al-Bannā: "We shall invade people's [hearts] with love rather than the sword" (quoted in al-Qaraḍāwī, *Khiṭābunā al-Islāmī*, 107).

146. Muṣṭafā Mahdī, "Al-Ma'lūm min al-dīn bil-ḍarūra," *Al-Alūka al-Shar'iyya*, Apr. 30, 2009, http://www.alukah.net/sharia/0/5654.

147. H. al-Bannā, *Majmū'at rasā'il*, 359.

148. Abū Muḥammad al-Maqdisī, *Al-Risāla al-thalāthīniyya fī al-taḥdhīr min al-ghulū fī al-takfīr* (N.p.: n.p., 1998–99), electronic copy at http://www.ilmway.com/site/maqdis/MS_14491.html; Abū Baṣīr 'Abd al-Mun'im Muṣṭafā Ḥalīma al-Ṭarṭūsī, *Qawā'id fī al-takfīr* (N.p.: n.p., 1994), electronic copy at http://www.abubaseer.bizland.com/books/read/b16.pdf.

149. Al-Maqdisī attacks "exaggeration in accusations of unbelief [*al-ghulū fī al-takfīr*]" in *Al-Risāla al-thalāthīniyya*, 11–29. On the term *takfīriyyūn*, see Hegghammer, "Jihadi-Salafis or Revolutionaries?" 246–48.

150. Al-Maqdisī, *Hādhihi 'aqīdatuna*, 28. See also al-Qāḍī 'Iyāḍ, *Kitāb al-shifā bi-ta'rīf ḥuqūq al-Muṣṭafā* (Beirut: Dār al-Fikr, 2002), electronic copy at https://tinyurl.com/ycc9u3gp.

151. On the conditions (*shurūṭ*) for leveling an accusation of unbelief and the "hindrances" (*mawāni'*) to such an accusation, see al-Maqdisī, *Al-Risāla al-thalāthīniyya*, 34–77.

152. Al-Qaraḍāwī, *Ẓāhirat al-ghulū fī al-takfīr*, 27–28; al-Maqdisī, *Al-Risāla al-thalāthīniyya*, 83–86; al-Ṭarṭūsī, *Qawā'id fī al-takfīr*, 48–53.

153. Al-Qaraḍāwī, *Ẓāhirat al-ghulū fī al-takfīr*, 28–29, 32–35; al-Ṭarṭūsī, *Qawā'id fī al-takfīr*, 115; al-Maqdisī, *Hādhihi 'aqīdatunā*, 83–86.

154. Al-Qaraḍāwī, *Fiqh al-jihād*, 2:1064; al-Maqdisī, *Hādhihi 'aqīdatunā*, 29; al-Ṭarṭūsī, *Qawā'id fī al-takfīr*, 176–77.

155. Al-Qaraḍāwī, *Ẓāhirat al-ghulū fī al-takfīr*, 51–57; al-Ṭarṭūsī, *Qawā'id fī al-takfīr*, 11–15; al-Maqdisī, *Hādhihi 'aqīdatunā*, 25.

156. Al-Ṭarṭūsī, *Al-Shīʿa al-Rawāfiḍ ṭāʾifat shirk wa-ridda*, 6.

157. Al-Qaraḍāwī, "Naṣṣ bayān al-Qaraḍāwī ḥawla mawqifihi mina al-Shīʿa."

158. Al-Qaraḍāwī, *Mabādiʾ fī al-ḥiwār wa-l-taqrīb*, 76–77; al-Ṭarṭūsī, *Al-Shīʿa al-Rawāfiḍ ṭāʾifat shirk wa-ridda*, 13–22.

159. Shaykh Yūsuf al-Qaraḍāwī, "Al-Qaraḍāwī: Ḥizb Allāh Ḥizb al-Ṭāghūt wal-Shayṭān . . . wal-jihād bi-Sūriyā maṭlūb," June 9, 2013, at https://mz-mz.net/158239.

160. Abū Muḥammad al-Maqdisī, *Al-Jawāb al-mufīd bi-anna al-mushāraka fī al-barlamān wa-intikhābātihi munāqiḍa li-l-tawḥīd* (N.p.: n.p., 2010), 7, 20, 25, electronic copy at http://www.ilmway.com/site/maqdis/MS_65.html; the double question marks are in the original.

161. Al-Qaraḍāwī, *Fatāwā muʿāṣira*, 2:647.

162. Al-Qaraḍāwī, *Malāmiḥ al-mujtamaʿ al-Muslim*, 173.

163. Abū Baṣīr ʿAbd al-Munʿim Muṣṭafā Ḥalīma al-Tarṭūsī, *Ḥukm al-Islām fī al-dīmuqrāṭiyya wa-l-taʿaddudiyya al-ḥizbiyya*. 2nd ed. (N.p.: n.p., 1999), 57–58, electronic copy at http://www.abubaseer.bizland.com/books/read/b11.pdf.

164. Al-Tarṭūsī, *Ḥukm al-Islām fī al-dīmuqrāṭiyya*, 57–58, 66–98.

165. "Ruʾyat al-Islām lil-taʿaddudiyya al-siyāsiyya," episode of *Al-Sharīʿa wal-ḥayāh*, al-Jazeera, Apr. 4, 1999, at https://tinyurl.com/kdemb4b; Shaykh Yūsuf al-Qaraḍāwī, *Al-Ḥurriyya al-dīniyya wal-taʿaddudiyya fī naẓar al-Islām* (Beirut: Al-Maktab al-Islāmī, 2007), 55–86.

166. Al-Tarṭūsī, *Ḥukm al-Islām fī al-dīmuqrāṭiyya*, 113.

167. Al-Ṭarṭūsī, *Aʿmāl tukhriju ṣāḥibahā min al-milla*, 156–58.

168. Al-Qaraḍāwī, *Al-Waṭan wal-muwāṭana*, 42–45, 47–49.

169. Al-Qaraḍāwī, *Malāmiḥ al-mujtamaʿ al-Muslim*, 86.

170. Al-Qaraḍāwī discusses these verses and their interpretation in *Min fiqh al-dawla fī al-Islām*, 104–15, and *Fatāwā muʿāṣira*, 2:697–714.

171. Abū Muḥammad al-Maqdisī, *Kashf shubuhāt al-mujādilīn ʿan ʿasākir al-shirk wa-anṣār al-qawānīn*, 2nd ed. (N.p.: n.p., 1999), 13–16, at http://www.ilmway.com/site/maqdis/MS_23039.html.

172. Al-Ṭarṭūsī, *Aʿmāl tukhriju ṣāḥibahā min al-milla*, 37–101; Abū Baṣīr ʿAbd al-Munʿim Muṣṭafā Ḥalīma al-Ṭarṭūsī, "Faṣl al-kalām fī masʾalat al-khurūj ʿalā al-ḥukkām," Apr. 11, 2001, at http://www.ilmway.com/site/maqdis/MS_8756.html.

173. For more on al-Qaraḍāwī's views on the meaning of these verses, see *Fatāwā muʿāṣira*, 2:697–714, and *Min fiqh al-dawla fī al-Islām*, 101–17. On al-Albānī's interpretation of these verses and the way Ibn ʿAbbās's exegesis is perceived by jihadi Salafis, see Lav, *Radical Islam*, 151–58.

174. For an explanation of "secularist extremism" (*al-taṭarruf al-ʿilmānī*) in the Muslim world, see al-Qaraḍāwī, *Al-Taṭarruf al-ʿilmānī*, 127 and 128–36 (the example of Turkey); al-Qaraḍāwī, *Al-Islām wal-ʿilmāniyya wajhan li-wajhin*; and Polka, "Between Liberalism and Fundamentalism," chap. 1, 54–145.

175. Al-Qaraḍāwī, *Fiqh al-jihād*, 2:1066–67. ʿAbd al-Salām Faraj used this *ḥadīth* as proof for the duty to rebel against apostate Muslim rulers. See ʿAbd al-Salām Faraj, *Al-Jihād: Al-Farīḍa al-ghāʾiba* (N.p.: n.p., 1981), 14–15, electronic copy at http://unfulfilledduty.weebly.com/uploads/1/8/5/3/18537222/__.pdf.

176. Al-ʿAshmāwī, *Al-Islām al-siyāsī*, 64. Al-Qaraḍāwī accepts this exegetic principle. See al-Qaraḍāwī, *Kayfa nataʿāmalu maʿa al-Qurʾān al-ʿaẓīm?* 252–53.

177. Al-ʿAshmāwī, *Al-Islām al-siyāsī*, 57–58, 76.

178. Al-ʿAshmāwī, *Al-Islām al-siyāsī*, 63–64.

179. Gilles Kepel, *Jihad: The Trail of Political Islam*, trans. Anthony F. Roberts (Cambridge, MA: Belknap Press of Harvard Univ. Press, 2002), 220–21.

180. Meijer, introduction to *Global Salafism*, 9.

181. Al-Ẓawāhirī, *Al-Ḥiṣād al-murr*. For more on al-Ẓawāhirī's book against the MB, see Meir Hatina, "Redeeming Sunni Islam: Al-Qaʿida's Polemic against the Muslim Brethren," *British Journal of Middle Eastern Studies* 39, no. 1 (2012): 101–13.

182. Al-Ẓawāhirī, *Al-Ḥiṣād al-murr*, 4.

183. Al-Ẓawāhirī, *Al-Ḥiṣād al-murr*, 27.

184. Al-Ẓawāhirī, *Al-Ḥiṣād al-murr*, 37.

185. Q3:28: "The believers should not make the disbelievers their allies rather than other believers—anyone who does such a thing will isolate himself completely from God."

186. Al-Ẓawāhirī, *Al-Ḥiṣād al-murr*, 27–44. Al-Ẓawāhirī quotes al-Ṭabarī's commentary on the verse's last sentence ("wa-man yatwallahum minkum fa-innahu minhum" [Q5:51]), which states that whoever helps the Jews or Christians becomes one himself.

187. *Dabiq* (in English), "The Murtadd Brotherhood," no. 14 (Rajab 1437 [Sept. 2016]): 28–43, at https://www.clarionproject.org/docs/Dabiq-Issue-14.pdf.

188. Abū Muḥammad al-ʿAdnānī, the IS spokesman, in a video recording entitled "Al-Silmiyya dīn man?" Aug. 2013, at https://justpaste.it/6151. The video to which the IS spokesman alludes, where al-Qaraḍāwī calls for fighting for democracy, is Shaykh Yūsuf al-Qaraḍāwī, *Yūsuf al-Qaraḍāwī yaqūlu innahu yuqātilu fī sabīl al-dīmuqrāṭiyya*, video, May 5, 2012, recording, at https://www.youtube.com/watch?v=6O1Abw6JG3k.

189. Al-Qaraḍāwī, *25 Yanāyir sanat 2011m*, 16.

190. Aḥmad b. Muḥammad b. Manṣūr al-ʿAdīnī, *Rafʿ al-lithām ʿan mukhālafāt al-Qaraḍāwī li-sharīʿat al-Islām*, 2nd ed. (Ṣanʿāʾ, Yemen: Dār al-Āthār, 2001), 28–62.

191. Shaykh Yūsuf al-Qaraḍāwī, *Mawqif al-Islām al-ʿaqdī min kufr al-Yahūd wal-Naṣārā* (Cairo: Maktabat Wahba, 1999), 37–40, 65–66.

192. Shaykh Yūsuf al-Qaraḍāwī, *Al-Quds: Qaḍiyyat kull Muslim* (Beirut: Al-Maktab al-Islāmī, 2002), 121–24.

193. Al-Qaraḍāwī, *Al-Quds*, 51.

194. Ashraf ʿAbd al-Qādir, "Al-Qaraḍāwī ʿAdū li-ḥiwār al-adyān," *Al-Ḥiwār al-Mutamaddin* 11507 (Apr. 1, 2006), at http://www.ahewar.org/debat/show.art.asp?aid=61121.

195. Al-Qaraḍāwī, *Fī fiqh al-aqalliyyāt al-Muslima*, 66.

196. *France 24*, "Al-Qaraḍāwī yuqāṭi'u Mu'tamar Ḥiwār al-Adyān fī al-Dawḥa i'tirāḍan 'alā al-ḥuḍūr al-Yahūdī," Apr. 23, 2013, at https://tinyurl.com/y85cagz2.

197. Shaykh Yūsuf al-Qaraḍāwī, *Ḥiwār al-adyān al-shaykh Yūsuf al-Qaraḍāwī*, video, Dec. 30, 2014, at https://www.youtube.com/watch?v=sCTN9qpQQPU.

198. Aḥmad al-Baghdādī, *Tajdīd al-fikr al-dīnī*, 174.

199. Aḥmad al-Baghdādī, *Tajdīd al-fikr al-dīnī*, 175.

200. "Ḥiwār al-adyān," episode of *Al-Sharī'a wal-ḥayāh*, al-Jazeera, Nov. 4, 2001, at https://tinyurl.com/y9lg3vpu.

201. Ḥamūd b. 'Uqalā' al-Shu'aybī, "Ḥukm al-da'wa ilā waḥdat al-adyān," Sept. 17, 2000, at http://www.ilmway.com/site/maqdis/MS_22437.html.

202. Al-Qaraḍāwī, *Mawqif al-Islām al-'aqdī min kufr al-Yahūd wal-Naṣārā*, 7.

203. 'Abd al-Mun'im Muṣṭafā Ḥalīma al-Ṭarṭūsī, *Al-Mawqif al-shar'ī min al-Qaraḍāwī* (N.p.: n.p., n.d.), electronic copy at http://www.ilmway.com/site/maqdis/MS_23692.html.

204. Al-Ṭarṭūsī, "Limādhā kaffartu Yūsuf al-Qaraḍāwī . . . ?" 4–5. Al-Qaraḍāwī's legal opinion on the statues in Afghanistan is given in al-Qaraḍāwī, *Fatāwā mu'āṣira*, 4:803–18.

205. Mawqi' Samāḥat al-Shaykh Yūsuf al-Qaraḍāwī, "Ṭālibān dammarat al-tamāthīl al-Būdhiyya wa-wasāṭat al-'ulamā' fashilat," May 8, 2001, at https://www.al-qaradawi.net/node/2035; *Al-Sharq al-Awsaṭ*, "Al-Yūnīskū tad'ū al-wafd al-Islāmī li-badhl dawr yunqidhu mā tabaqqā min tamāthīl Bāmiyān," Mar. 12, 2001, at https://tinyurl.com/yd8yq3ss.

206. As indicated in al-Ṭarṭūsī, "Limādhā kaffartu Yūsuf al-Qaraḍāwī . . . ?" See also Al-Qaraḍāwī, *Fatāwā mu'āṣira*, 4:803–18.

207. Al-Qaraḍāwī, *Fatāwā mu'āṣira*, 4:803–18. He stated his juridical principles on *shar'ī* governance in Shaykh Yūsuf al-Qaraḍāwī, *Al-Siyāsa al-shar'iyya fī ḍaw' nuṣūṣ al-sharī'a wa-maqāṣidihā* (Beirut: Mu'assasat al-Risāla, 2001), 207–307.

208. Al-Qaraḍāwī, "Ma'rakat al-Islām wal-'ilmāniyya," 7:186–88.

5. The Conception of Jihad

1. Islamic State, "Risāla bi-sha'n ghazwat Bārīs al-mubāraka," audio recording, Nov. 14, 2015, at https://archive.org/details/mksnd73iu4; Islamic State, "Bayān 'an ghazwat Bārīs al-mubāraka 'alā Faransā al-Ṣalībiyya" Nov. 14, 2015, at https://tinyurl.com/y8nvaxle.

2. Q59:2 is said to have been revealed in connection with the Jewish tribe al-Naḍīr, which the Prophet drove out of Medina. The verse—which states that although the Jews "thought their fortifications would protect them against God," God "put panic into their hearts"—was apparently thought fitting for an operation that surprised the "Crusaders" in France and "put panic into their hearts." The closing verse (63:8) of the announcement is aimed at the "hypocrites" (*munāfiqūn*), who are made to realize that "power belongs to God."

3. Mawqiʿ Samāḥat al-Shaykh Yūsuf al-Qaraḍāwī, "Ittiḥād ʿUlamāʾ al-Muslimīn yudīnu hajamāt Bārīs," Nov. 14, 2015, at https://www.al-qaradawi.net/node/4656.

4. Brahimi, *Jihad and Just War*, 17–26; John Kelsay, *Arguing the Just War in Islam* (Cambridge, MA: Harvard Univ. Press, 2007), 43–96; Ella Landau-Tasseron, *"Non-combatants" in Muslim Legal Thought* (Washington, DC: Hudson Institute, 2006).

5. For more on the formation of the IS, see William McCants, *The ISIS Apocalypse: The History, Strategy, and Doomsday Vision of the Islamic State* (New York: St. Martin's Press, 2015), 5–29, and Fawaz A. Gerges, *ISIS: A History* (Princeton, NJ: Princeton Univ. Press, 2016), 50–97.

6. William McCants, Jarret Brachman, and Lieutenant Colonel Joseph Felter, *Militant Ideology Atlas: Research Compendium* (West Point, NY: Combating Terrorism Center, 2006), 357–58.

7. For al-Qaraḍāwī's legal opinion permitting *istishhād* operations in Palestine, see al-Qaraḍāwī, *Fatāwā muʿāṣira*, 3:503–10, and *Fatāwā min ajli Filasṭīn*, 31–44.

8. For al-Qaraḍāwī's views on homosexuality, see "Fiṭrat Allāh fī khalqihi," episode of *Al-Sharīʿa wal-ḥayāh*, al-Jazeera, June 7, 2006, at https://tinyurl.com/yac86hus. For a discussion of these views, see Āmāl Qarāmī, "Manzilat al-mithliyyīn fī khiṭāb al-Islāmiyyīn: Al-Qaraḍāwī namūdhajan," *Al-Ḥiwār al-Mutamaddin*, June 29, 2006, at http://www.ahewar.org/debat/show.art.asp?aid=68755, and Scott Kugle and Stephen Hunt, "Masculinity, Homosexuality, and the Defence of Islam: A Case Study of Yusuf al-Qaradawi's Media Fatwa," *Religion and Gender* 2, no. 2 (2012): 254–79.

9. For al-Qaraḍāwī's juridical approach on issues pertaining to women, see ʿAmr ʿAbd al-Karīm, *Qaḍāyā al-marʾa fī fiqh al-Qaraḍāwī*, 2nd ed. (Giza, Egypt: Qaṭr al-Nadā li-l-Nashr wal-Tawzīʿ, 2009).

10. For al-Qaraḍāwī's rebuttal of *ʿilmāniyya*, see *Al-Islām wal-ʿilmāniyya wajhan li-wajhin* and *Al-Taṭarruf al-ʿilmānī*. For al-Qaraḍāwī's criticism of *ʿilmāniyya*, see Polka, "Between Liberalism and Fundamentalism," 54–145.

11. S. al-Nābulsī, "Qaraḍāwiyyāni, lā Qaraḍāwī wāḥid." For other writers who describe al-Qaraḍāwī as both tolerant and extremist, see ʿAbd al-Raḥmān al-Rāshid, "Al-Qaraḍāwī mutasāmiḥ wa-mutaʿaṣṣib," *Al-Sharq al-Awsaṭ*, July 10, 2004, at https://tinyurl.com/ya33mjc6, and ʿĪd, *Yūsuf al-Qaraḍāwī bayna al-tasāmuḥ wa-l-irhāb*, 6–7, 210–12.

12. Shaykh Yūsuf al-Qaraḍāwī, "Maʿrakat al-ḥijāb fī Faransā," Oct. 1994, in *Khuṭab al-Shaykh al-Qaraḍāwī*, ed. al-Saʿd, 2:209.

13. On al-Qaraḍāwī's visit to London in 2004 and the uproar it sparked, see Vidino, *The New Muslim Brotherhood in the West*, 144–46.

14. Al-Rāshid, "Al-Qaraḍāwī mutasāmiḥ wa-mutaʿaṣṣib."

15. ʿĪd, *Yūsuf al-Qaraḍāwī bayna al-tasāmuḥ wa-l-irhāb*, 231, 228, quotation marks around the Arabic term for "Western" in the original.

16. Islamic State, *ʿUmalāʾ, lā ʿulamāʾ*, video, May 26, 2017, at https://www.youtube.com/watch?v=HJeVOsSA9qI.

17. On this petition, "Al-Bayān al-umamī ḍidda al-irhāb," see *Arab News*, "Stop Terror Sheikhs, Muslim Academics Demand," Oct. 30, 2004, at http://www.arabnews.com/node/257332; *Multaqā Rābiṭat al-Wāḥa al-Thaqāfiyya*, "Naṣṣ al-Bayān al-umamī ḍidda al-irhāb," Nov. 2004, at https://tinyurl.com/yaxmjtcv.

18. *Orient Net*, "Al-Intirbūl yudriju al-Qaraḍāwī 'alā qā'imat al-maṭlūbīn," Dec. 6, 2014, at https://tinyurl.com/ydxu73b7.

19. *Al-Quds al-'Arabī*, "Al-Intirbūl yaḥdhifu ism al-Qaraḍāwī min al-maṭlūbīn wa-Miṣr tasta'limu 'an al-asbāb," Sept. 11, 2017, at http://www.alquds.co.uk/?p=787587.

20. Waṣfī 'Āshūr Abū Zayd, *Al-Imām al-Qaraḍāwī wa-malḥamat al-Intirbūl al-duwalī* (Cairo: Dār al-Bashīr li-l-Thaqāfa wa-l-'Ulūm, 2015), 28–30. The pamphlet is dated December 15, 2014.

21. *Nāẓūr 24*, "Al-Su'ūdiyya tuṣdiru qarāran bi-'ḥarq' kutub al-Qaraḍāwī wa-l-Bannā," Dec. 7, 2015, at https://tinyurl.com/yd7l8ejh.

22. 'Abdallah al-Barqāwī, "Rasmiyyan, 4 duwal tuṣannifu Yūsuf al-Qaraḍāwī irhābiyyan," *Saḥīfat Sabq al-Iliktrūniyya*, June 9, 2017, at https://tinyurl.com/yavcm3st.

23. Shaykh Yūsuf al-Qaraḍāwī, tweet, July 9, 2017, at https://twitter.com/alqaradawy.

24. Shaykh Yūsuf al-Qaraḍāwī, Facebook post, July 15, 2017, at https://facebook.com/alqaradawy.

25. Shaykh Yūsuf al-Qaraḍāwī, "Bayān Majlis Umanā' Mu'assasat Sulṭān B. 'Alī al-'Awīs al-Thaqāfiyya ḥawla manḥ al-Shaykh al-Duktūr Yūsuf 'Abd Allāh al-Qaraḍāwī jā'izat al-injāz al-thaqāfī wal-'ilmī 1998–1999," in *Al-Shaykh al-Qaraḍāwī: Shakhṣiyyat al-'ām al-Islāmiyya 1421/2000*, 149–51. For the awards al-Qaraḍāwī has received, see pages 38–39 in this volume.

26. Muṣṭafa Aḥmad al-Zarqā, "Yūsuf al-Qaraḍāwī: Ḥujjat al-'aṣr wa-huwa min ni'am Allāh 'alā al-Muslimīn," in *Al-Qaraḍāwī: Kalimāt fī takrīmihi wa-buḥūth fī fikrihi wa-fiqhihi muhdāh ilayhi bi-munāsabat bulūghihi al-sab'īn*, 2 vols., ed. 'Abd al-'Aẓīm al-Dīb (Cairo: Dār al-Salām, 2004), 1:43.

27. Al-Khaṭīb, *Al-Qaraḍāwī faqīh al-ṣaḥwa al-Islāmiyya*, 117.

28. In the lecture, delivered on September 12, 2006, at the University of Regensburg in Germany, Pope Benedict XVI quoted a passage by the fourteenth-century Byzantine emperor Manuel II Palaiologos, who said that Muḥammad had brought nothing but evil and inhuman things, such as the command to spread the faith by the sword. Al-Qaraḍāwī gave his response to the pope's claims in *Al-Bābā wal-Islām: Radd 'ilmī 'alā al-bābā Banadīkt al-sādis 'ashar fī kalimatihi fī-Almāniyā allatī asā'a bihā ilā al-Islām* (Cairo: Maktabat Wahba, 2007).

29. Al-Qaraḍāwī summarized his polemic with the secularists in his book *Al-Islām wal-'ilmāniyya wajhan li-wajhin*.

30. Shākir al-Nābulsī, "Al-Qaraḍāwī wa-l-Sibā'ī wa-Bakrī 'alā lā'iḥat fuqahā' al-irhāb," *Īlāf* interview on al-Ḥurra TV, Aug. 10, 2005, at https://tinyurl.com/yaespyja.

31. On al-Qaraḍāwī's rejection of this type of "passive" Ṣūfism, see Mawqi' Samāḥat al-Shaykh Yūsuf al-Qaraḍāwī, "Tajdīd al-īmān: Al-Taṣawwuf al-maqbūl wal-mardūd,"

Feb. 22, 2017, https://www.al-qaradawi.net/node/2148, and al-Qaraḍāwī, *Fatāwā muʿāṣira*, 1:734–43.

32. An example of the kind of jihad that al-Qaraḍāwī may well have had in mind is given in al-ʿAshmāwī, *Al-Islām al-siyāsī*, 127–45.

33. Al-Qaraḍāwī, *Fiqh al-jihād*, 1:13–14, 129.

34. Al-ʿAshmāwī, *Al-Islām al-siyāsī*, 138–45.

35. For more on jihadi Salafism, see Lav, *Radical Islam*, 120–47; Hegghammer, "Jihadi-Salafis Or Revolutionaries?"; and Jarret M. Brachman, *Global Jihadism: Theory and Practice* (London: Routledge, 2009), 22–51.

36. Al-Qaraḍāwī, *Fiqh al-jihād*, 1:251–52. On the principles of Muslim/non-Muslim relations, see Wahba al-Zuḥaylī, *Āthār al-ḥarb: Dirāsa fiqhiyya muqārana* (Damascus: Dār al-Fikr, 2009), 121–28; Muḥammad Abū Zahra, *Al-ʿAlāqāt al-duwaliyya fī al-Islām* (Cairo: Dār al-Fikr al-ʿArabī, 1995), 50–56; and Reiter, *War, Peace, and International Relations*, 36–60. Among the jihadis, the UN Security Council is considered an idol (*ṭāghūt*): see al-Ṭarṭūsī, *Al-Ṭāghūt*, 114–15. On the laws of prisoners of war in Islam, see al-Qaraḍāwī, *Fiqh al-jihād*, 2:839–63.

37. Al-Qaraḍāwī, *Fiqh al-jihād*, 1:252. For more on the laws of war in Islam, see al-Qaraḍāwī, *Fiqh al-jihād*, 2:839–63, and Reiter, *War, Peace, and International Relations*, 36–60.

38. Al-Qaraḍāwī, *Fiqh al-jihād*, 1:12–13, 15–17.

39. The full title in Arabic is *Fiqh al-jihād: Dirāsa muqārana li-aḥkāmihi wa-falsafatihi fī ḍaw' al-Qur'ān wal-Sunna*. For an analysis of al-Qaraḍāwī's view of jihad as laid out in *Fiqh al-jihād*, see Zaman, *Modern Islamic Thought in a Radical Age*, 261–308. An important critical review of *Fiqh al-jihād* is Rāshid al-Ghannūshī, "Mā al-jadīd fī *Fiqh al-jihād* lil-Qaraḍāwī?" Al-Jazeera, Sept. 20, 2009, at https://tinyurl.com/yahwk596.

40. Al-Qaraḍāwī, *Fiqh al-jihād*, 1:32–33. For al-Qaraḍāwī's method of ruling on jihad, see *Fiqh al-jihād*, 1:20–31, and Zaman, *Modern Islamic Thought in a Radical Age*, 304–8.

41. On the meanings of the root *j h d* in the Qur'ān, see Ella Landau-Tasseron, "Jihād," in *EQ (Encyclopaedia of the Qur'ān)*, vol. 3 (Leiden: Brill, 2003), 36, and Bonney, *Jihad*, 27–29.

42. Landau-Tasseron, "Jihād," 3:38–42. On occurrences of the root *q t l* in the Qur'ān, see Majmaʿ al-Lugha al-ʿArabiyya, *Muʿjam alfāẓ al-Qur'ān al-karīm*, 2 vols. (Cairo: Sharikat al-Iʿlānāt al-Sharqiyya, 1990), 2:876–80.

43. Ella Landau-Tasseron, "The Origins of the Idea of Jihad," in *War and Peace* (in Hebrew), ed. Shlomo Avineri (Jerusalem: Zalman Shazar Center, 2010), 100.

44. Al-Qaraḍāwī, *Khiṭābunā al-Islāmī*, 162–63. On the dispute concerning the nature of jihad, see Michael Bonner, *Jihad in Islamic History: Doctrines and Practice* (Princeton, NJ: Princeton Univ. Press, 2006), 1–4, and Ella Landau-Tasseron, "Is Jihād Comparable to Just War? A Review Article," *Jerusalem Studies in Arabic and Islam* 34 (2008): 535–50. On the identification of *jihād* with *qitāl* and a possible explanation for it, see Landau-Tasseron, "Jihād," 3:38.

45. Michael Cook, *Commanding Right and Forbidding Wrong in Islamic Thought* (Cambridge: Cambridge Univ. Press, 2000), 32–45.

46. Al-Qaraḍāwī, *Fiqh al-jihād*, 1:53, 130–31.

47. Faraj, *Al-Jihād*, 18.

48. Abdallah 'Azzām, "Jihād . . . lā irhāb," Jan. 1987, 6, at http://www.ilmway.com/site/maqdis/MS_9045.html.

49. 'Abdallah 'Azzām, *Fī al-jihād ādāb wa-aḥkām* (N.p.: n.p., n.d.), 2–4, electronic copy at http://www.ilmway.com/site/maqdis/MS_10190.html; 'Abdallah 'Azzām, *'Ibar wa-baṣā'ir lil-jihād fī al-'aṣr al-ḥāḍir* ('Ammān, Jordan: Maktabat al-Riṣāla al-Ḥadītha, 1987), 1, electronic copy at http://www.ilmway.com/site/maqdis/MS_10040.html. See also Landau-Tasseron, "Jihād," 3:38–39, and E. Tyan, "Djihād," EI^2 2 (1991): 538–40.

50. Al-Ṭarṭūsī, *Muṣṭalaḥāt wa-mafāhīm shar'iyya*, 124–27; al-Ṭarṭūsī, "Faṣl al-kalām fī mas'alat al-khurūj 'alā al-ḥukkām."

51. Al-'Ashmāwī, *Al-Islām al-siyāsī*, 138.

52. G. al-Bannā, *Al-Jihād*, 36–40.

53. G. al-Bannā, *Al-Jihād*, 33–35.

54. Al-Qaraḍāwī, *Fiqh al-jihād*, 1:573–78.

55. For Ibn Taymiyya's views, see Rudolph Peters, *Jihad in Classical and Modern Islam: A Reader* (Princeton, NJ: Markus Wiener, 1996), 116–18, and Bonney, *Jihad*, 40–41.

56. Ibn Taymiyya, *Majmū'at al-fatāwā*, 11:1196.

57. Yaḥyā b. Sharaf al-Nawawī, *Riyāḍ al-ṣāliḥīn min kalām sayyid al-mursilīn*, with interpretive commentary by al-Shaykh Muḥammad b. Ṣāliḥ al-'Uthaymīn, 3 vols. (Cairo: Dār Ibn al-Haytham, n.d,), 3:370.

58. 'Abdallah 'Azzām, *Ilḥaq bil-qāfila* (Ṣan'ā', Yemen: Maktabat al-Jīlal-Jaḍīd, 1990), 24–26, electronic copy at http://www.ilmway.com/site/maqdis/MS_10191.html); 'Abdallah 'Azzām, "Jihād . . . lā irhāb," 7–8.

59. Faraj, *Al-Jihād*, 19.

60. Al-Qaraḍāwī, *Fiqh al-jihād*, 1:515–20.

61. Sālim Mubārak al-Falaq, "Ramaḍān shahr al-jihād," *Ṣayd al-Fawa'id*, n.d., at http://www.saaid.net/mktarat/ramadan/216.htm.

62. Abū Muḥammad al-'Adnānī, "Tafrīgh al-kalima al-ṣawtiyya bi-'unwān (yā qawmanā ajībū dā'iya Allāh, Q46:31) lil-Shaykh Abī Muḥammad al-'Adnānī," June 24, 2015, at https://justpaste.it/lxzf.

63. Al-Qaraḍāwī, *Fiqh al-jihād*, 1:519.

64. Al-Qaraḍāwī, *Fiqh al-jihād*, 1:519–20.

65. H. al-Bannā, *Mujmū'at rasā'il*, 437.

66. P. J. Vatikiotis, *The History of Modern Egypt: From Muhammad Ali to Mubarak*, 4th ed. (Baltimore: Johns Hopkins Univ. Press, 1991), 169–78.

67. On al-Qaraḍāwī's view on "jihad against the soul" (*jihād al-nafs*), see al-Qaraḍāwī, *Fiqh al-jihād*, 1:143–53.

68. See "Risāla maftūḥa ilā Abī Bakr al-Baghdādī," letter to Abū Bakr al-Baghdādī by several persons, Sept. 19, 2014, at http://lettertobaghdadi.com/14/arabic-v14.pdf. The

ḥadīth quoted by the authors of the letter to al-Baghdādī is: "Shall I not inform you of the best of your actions which are the purest to your Lord, which exalt you to the high ranks, which are more efficacious than spending gold and silver (in charity), and better for you than you should encounter your enemies, whom you will smite their necks, and they will smite your necks?" They said, "Certainly." He said, "Remembrance of Allah the Exalted." For an analysis of the letter, see Ella Landau-Tasseron, *Delegitimizing ISIS on Islamic Grounds: Criticism of Abu Bakr al-Baghdadi by Muslim Scholars*, Inquiry & Analysis Report no. 1205 (Washington, DC: Middle East Media Research Institute, Nov. 19, 2015), 7, at https://tinyurl.com/y6wf3ads.

69. Al-'Ashmāwī, *Al-Islām al-siyāsī*, 130.

70. 'Abd al-Ḥamīd al-Anṣārī, "Thaqāfat al-karāhiya wa-intishār al-taṭarruf wa-l-tajdīd al-dīnī," interview on *Ḥadīth al-'Arab*, program on Sky News, Aug. 5, 2016, at https://www.youtube.com/watch?v=fA0edaPSCvU&t=792s.

71. On the term *terrorism* (*irhāb*), see Aaron Y. Zelin, "Jihadis and the Use of the Terms *Terror*, *Terrorist*, and *Terrorism*: A Contextual and Semantic Understanding from Islamic Tradition," 2011, at https://tinyurl.com/ydylay4p.

72. Al-Qaraḍāwī, "Man al-mas'ūl 'an aḥdāth al-ḥādī 'ashar min Sibtimbir," 6:100–101.

73. Al-Qaraḍāwī, *Fiqh al-jihād*, 2:1071–75. Al-Ṭarṭūsī discusses the reasons why the international community has failed to define the term *irhāb* (terrorism) in "Al-Irhāb ma'nāhu wa-wāqi'uhu min manẓūr Islāmī," n.d., 15–18, at http://www.ilmway.com/site/maqdis/MS_28456.html.

74. Al-Qaraḍāwī, *Fiqh al-jihād*, 2:1071–72; al-Qaraḍāwī, *Khiṭabunā al-Islāmī*, 169–70.

75. 'Abdallah 'Azzām, *Muqaddima fī-l-hijra wa-l-i'dād* (N.p.: n.p., n.d.), 58, electronic copy at http://www.ilmway.com/site/maqdis/MS_9006.html.

76. "Al-Irhāb wa-ḥamalāt al-karāhiya ḍidda al-'Arab wal-Muslimīn."

77. Al-Qaraḍāwī, *Khiṭābunā al-Islāmī*, 161.

78. Al-Qaraḍāwī's ruling on hijacking airplanes is given in al-Qaraḍāwī, *Fatāwā mu'āṣira*, 2:497–502.

79. Al-Qaraḍāwī, *Fiqh al-jihād*, 2:1084–85. Al-Ṭarṭūsī makes a similar distinction between "reprehensible terror" (*al-irhāb al-madhmūm*) and "praiseworthy terror" (*al-irhāb al-mamdūḥ*) to instill fear in the enemy. See Abū Baṣīr 'Abd al-Mun'im Muṣṭafā Ḥalīma al-Ṭarṭūsī, "Ta'rīf al-irhāb," Feb. 10, 2005, at http://www.ilmway.com/site/maqdis/MS_28487.html, and "Al-Irhāb ma'nāhu wa-wāqi'uhu min manẓūr Islāmī," 4–12. The same kind of distinction is also made in Shaykh Ḥamūd b. 'Uqalā' al-Shu'aybī, "Ma'nā al-irhāb wa-ḥaqīqatihi," Nov. 20, 2001, 3–4, at http://www.ilmway.com/site/maqdis/MS_516.html.

80. Al-Qaraḍāwī, "Al-Qimma al-Islāmiyya al-Masīḥiyya" 6:98; al-Qaraḍāwī, *Khiṭābunā al-Islāmī*, 160–61.

81. Al-Maqdisī, *Hādha mā adīnu Allāh bihi*, 35–36. For another *fatwā* that rejects the accusation of terrorism with respect to the 9/11 attacks, see al-Shu'aybī, *Ḥukm mā jarā fī Amrīkā min aḥdāth*, 5.

82. S. al-Nābulsī, *Sujūn bi-lā quḍbān*, 100–103.

83. Shaykh Yūsuf al-Qaraḍāwī, "Tafjīrāt masraḥ Qaṭar 'amal mustankar," Mar. 25, 2005, in *Khuṭab al-Shaykh al-Qaraḍāwī*, vol. 7, ed. Ḥūṭar and 'Abd al-Sattār Kassāb, 263.

84. Shaykh Yūsuf al-Qaraḍāwī, "Al-Durūs al-mustafāda min aḥdāth Filasṭīn wal-'Irāq," June 13, 2003, in *Khuṭab al-Shaykh al-Qaraḍāwī*, vol. 8, ed. al-Maktab al-'Ilmī li-l-Shaykh bil-Dawḥa, 114.

85. Al-Qaraḍāwī, *Fatāwā mu'āṣira*, 4:787.

86. Al-Qaraḍāwī, "Tafjīrāt masraḥ Qaṭar 'amal mustankar," 7:257.

87. For al-Qaraḍāwī's response to the pope's statement that Islam was spread by the sword, see al-Qaraḍāwī, *Al-Bābā wal-Islām*, 133–56.

88. Al-Qaraḍāwī, *Fiqh al-jihād*, 1:256; see also Yohanan Friedmann, *Tolerance and Coercion in Islam: Interfaith Relations in the Muslim Tradition* (Cambridge: Cambridge Univ. Press, 2003), 87–120. On the internal debate in Islam concerning defensive versus offensive jihad, see John L. Esposito, *Unholy War: Terror in the Name of Islam* (Oxford: Oxford Univ. Press, 2002), 64–68.

89. Abū al-Walīd Muḥammad b. Aḥmad Ibn Rushd, *Bidāyat al-mujtahid wa-nihāyat al-muqtaṣid* (Cairo: Maktabat Ibn Taymiyya, 1994–95), 426, 433–34, electronic copy at http://waqfeya.com/book.php?bid=9940.

90. 'Abdallah 'Azzām, *Dhikrayāt Filasṭīn*, 19.

91. Quṭb, *Ma'ālim fī al-ṭarīq*, 60–69.

92. Abū Baṣīr 'Abd al-Mun'im Muṣṭafā Ḥalīma al-Ṭarṭūsī, *Rasā'il fī al-i'dād wal-jihād* (N.p.: n.p., n.d.), electronic copy at https://tinyurl.com/y7kucd6j; Faraj, *Al-Jihād*, 8, 15–16.

93. Jihadi Salafīs define the attachment to a homeland and nationalism as "idolatry," for example, in al-Ṭarṭūsī, *Al-Ṭāghūt*, 99–102, and *Ṣifat al-ṭā'ifa al-manṣūra*, 98–104. See also al-Qaraḍāwī, *Al-Waṭan wal-muwāṭana*, 45–48 (al-Qaraḍāwī's concept of *waṭaniyya*), and the Hamas Charter given in al-Jazeera.net, "Mīthāq Ḥarakat al-Muqāwama al-Islāmiyya (Ḥamās)," Aug. 1988, sec. 12 on nationalism, at https://tinyurl.com/mzbsbew. On al-Qaraḍāwī's conception of nationalism, see Warren and Gilmore, "One Nation under God?"

94. Quṭb, *Ma'ālim fī al-ṭarīq*, 67–68; see also 'Abdallah 'Azzām, *'Ibar wa-baṣā'ir*, 25.

95. Al-Ṭarṭūsī, *Muṣṭalaḥāt wa-mafāhīm shar'iyya*, 129–30, and *Rasā'il fī al-i'dād wal-jihād*, 12–13; 'Abdallah 'Azzām, *Ilḥaq bil-qāfila*, 2–3.

96. Al-Qaraḍāwī, *Fiqh al-jihād*, 1:259–66, 402.

97. Al-Qaraḍāwī, *Fiqh al-jihād*, 1:259–66, 402. On this verse and its interpretation, see Friedmann, *Tolerance and Coercion in Islam*, 100–106, and H. al-Bannā, *Majmū'at rasā'il*, 434–35.

98. Al-Qaraḍāwī, *Fiqh al-jihād*, 1:376–83; see also Zaman, *Modern Islamic Thought in a Radical Age*, 264–66. The title of Ibn Taymiyya's epistle in Arabic is "Qā'ida mukhtaṣara fī qitāl al-kuffār wa-muhādanatihim wa-taḥrīm qatlihim li-majarrad kufrihim (qā'ida tubayyinu al-qiyam al-sāmiya lil-ḥaḍāra al-Islāmiyya fī al-ḥarb wal-qitāl)."

99. Zaman, *Modern Islamic Thought in a Radical Age*, 304, referring to al-Qaraḍāwī, *Fiqh al-jihād*, 1:376–83.

100. G. al-Bannā, *Al-Jihād*, 51–52, 70, 62–63, 83.

101. G. al-Bannā, *Al-Jihād*, 102.

102. Al-ʿAfīf al-Akhḍar, "Kayfa nuṣāliḥu al-Islām maʿa al-ʿālam?" *Al-Ḥiwār al-Mutamaddin* 1500 (Mar. 25, 2006), at http://www.ahewar.org/debat/show.art.asp?aid=60508.

103. Shaykh Yūsuf al-Qaraḍāwī, *Sharīʿat al-Islām ṣāliḥa lil-taṭbīq fī kull zamān wa-makān* (Cairo: Maktabat Wahba, 1997), 12–13.

104. Al-Qaraḍāwī, *Madkhal li-maʿrifat al-Islām*, 11.

105. Al-Qaraḍāwī, *Al-Islām wal-ʿunf*, 8–9, 30.

106. Friedmann, *Tolerance and Coercion in Islam*, 88, 95–96.

107. Reuven Firestone, *Jihad: The Origin of Holy War in Islam* (New York: Oxford Univ. Press, 1999), 47–65.

108. Firestone, *Jihad*, 67–97.

109. Bonner, *Jihad in Islamic History*, 22–27.

110. A number of verses in Q9 have been identified as the Verse of the Sword: 5, 29, 36, and 41. See al-Qaraḍāwī, *Fiqh al-jihād*, 1:268–69, 284–99.

111. Firestone, *Jihad*, 60–63.

112. Al-Qaraḍāwī, *Fiqh al-jihād*, 1:289.

113. Al-Qaraḍāwī, *Fiqh al-jihād*, 1:327–36; Muḥammad al-Ghazālī, *ʿIlal wa-adwiya: Dirāsāt fī amrāḍ ummatinā wa-wasāʾil al-istishfāʾ minhā maʿa taṣḥīḥ limā wujjiha ilā al-tārīkh al-Islāmī min akhṭāʾ* (Alexandria, Egypt: Dār al-Daʿwa, 1991), 247–49.

114. Al-ʿAshmāwī, *Al-Islām al-siyāsī*, 137–38.

115. For al-Qaraḍāwī's discussion of *naskh*, see al-Qaraḍāwī, *Fiqh al-jihād*, 1:271–81.

116. ʿAbdallah ʿAzzām, "Waṣiyyat al-shahīd ʿAbdallah ʿAzzām," *Muntadā al-Tawḥīd*, Apr. 20, 1986, at http://www.eltwhed.com/vb/showthread.php?4285; ʿAbdallah ʿAzzām, *Fī ẓilāl sūrat al-Tawba* (Peshawar, Pakistan: Markaz al-Shahīd ʿAzzām al-Iʿlāmī, n.d.), 77, electronic copy at http://www.ilmway.com/site/maqdis/MS_9006.html.

117. For an analysis of bin Laden's declarations, see Rosalind W. Gwynne, "Usama bin Laden, the Qur'an, and Jihad," *Religion* 36 (2006): 61–90.

118. Osama bin Laden, "Naṣṣ bayān al-Jabha al-Islāmiyya al-ʿĀlamiyya li-Jihād al-Yahūd wal-Ṣalībiyyīn," "Hal Yuʿtamadu "Bayān al-Jabha al-Islāmiyya al-ʿĀlamiyya?" Feb. 23, 1998, at https://tinyurl.com/yc66cpmo.

119. Osama bin Laden, "Iʿlān al-jihād ʿalā al-Amrīkān al-muḥtallīn li-Bilād al-Ḥaramayni (akhrijū al-mushrikīn min Jazīrat al-ʿArab)," Aug. 23, 1996, 20, at https://tinyurl.com/yb84rz43. For an analysis of al-Qaʿida's conception of jihad under bin Laden, see Brahimi, *Jihad and Just War*, 99–155.

120. For al-Ghazālī's centrist approach, see Aʿzīz, *Al-Wasaṭiyya wal-iʿtidāl fī al-manhaj al-daʿwī ʿind al-Shaykh Muḥammad al-Ghazālī*.

121. Muḥammad al-Ghazālī, *Jihād al-da'wa bayna 'ajz al-dākhil wa-kayd al-khārij*, 4th ed. (Giza, Egypt: Nahḍat Miṣr, 2009), 68–81. For al-Ghazālī's interpretation of Q9, "Sūrat al-Barā'a," see Muḥammad al-Ghazālī, *Naḥwa tafsīr mawḍū'ī li-suwar al-Qur'ān al-karīm*, 2nd ed. (Cairo: Dār al-Shurūq, 1996), 141–55.

122. Gamāl al-Bannā, *Tafnīd da'wat al-naskh fī al-Qur'ān al-karīm wa-maqālāt ukhrā* (Cairo: Dār al-Shurūq, 2004), 87–88, 103–4.

123. G. al-Bannā, *Al-Jihād*, 73.

124. Al-'Ashmāwī, *Al-Islām al-siyāsī*, 133.

125. The transmitter in question is 'Abd al-Raḥmān b. Thābit b. Thawbān. For the opinion that Muslim *ḥadīth* scholars have of him, see al-Qaraḍāwī, *Fiqh al-jihād*, 1:321–24.

126. Al-Qaraḍāwī, *Fiqh al-jihād*, 1:325–26.

127. On the relationship between the Sunna and the Qur'ān, see Ignaz Goldziher, *Muslim Studies*, trans. C. R. Barber and S. M. Stern (London: Allen & Unwin, 1890), 31–37.

128. Al-Qaraḍāwī, *Kayfa nata'āmalu ma'a al-Sunna al-nabawiyya?* 113.

129. For more on the issue of whether *ḥadīth* may or may not abrogate a Qur'ānic verse, see Nāṣir 'Abd al-Ghafūr, "Naskh al-Qur'ān bil-Sunna," *Al-Alūka al-Shar'iyya*, Dec. 22, 2014, at https://tinyurl.com/yblne3jg.

130. For example, see Abū Muḥammad al-'Adnānī, *Walayumakkinanna lahum dīnahum alladhī irtaḍā lahum: He Will Empower the Religion He Has Chosen for Them (Q24:55)*, video, Apr. 3, 2014, at https://archive.org/details/al_adnani2.

131. The letter is discussed in Landau-Tasseron, *Delegitimizing ISIS on Islamic Grounds*, 4–5.

132. Faraj, *Al-Jihād*, 2–3. See also 'Abdallah 'Azzām, *Al-Difā' 'an arāḍī al-Muslimīn ahamm furūḍ al-a'yān*, 7.

133. 'Abdallāh 'Azzām, "Jihād . . . lā irhāb," 6. On this view, see Friedmann, *Tolerance and Coercion in Islam*, 87–120.

134. 'Abdallāh 'Azzām, *Dhikrayāt Filasṭīn*, 17. On 'Azzām's view that Islam is not defensive but expands by using force, see Holtmann, *Abu Musab al Surī's Jihad Concept*, 48–49.

135. Bin Laden, "Naṣṣ bayān al-Jabha al-Islāmiyya al-'Ālamiyya li-Jihād al-Yahūd wal-Ṣalībiyyīn"; al-Maqdisī, *Hādhā mā adīnu Allāh bihi*, 1.

136. Reiter, *War, Peace, and International Relations in Islam*, 28.

137. Abū Zahra, *Al-'Alāqāt al-duwaliyya fī al-Islām*, 58–60. See also al-Zuḥaylī, *Āthār al-ḥarb*, 196–98.

138. Al-Qaraḍāwī, *Fiqh al-jihād*, 2:900–901.

139. Al-Qaraḍāwī, *Fiqh al-jihād*, 2:901.

140. Al-Qaraḍāwī, *Fiqh al-jihād*, 2:901–8.

141. "Al-Jāliyāt al-Islāmiyya fī bilād al-gharb," part 2, episode of *Al-Sharī'a wal-ḥayāh*, al-Jazeera, May 9, 1999, at https://tinyurl.com/y7w49ywz.

142. "Fiqh al-Jāliyāt al-Islāmiyya fī al-gharb," part 3, episode of *Al-Sharī'a wal-ḥayāh*, al-Jazeera, May 16, 1999, at https://tinyurl.com/lm6nem3.

143. Al-Qaraḍāwī, *Fī fiqh al-aqalliyyāt al-Muslima*, 33–35.

144. Al-Qaraḍāwī, *Al-Waṭan wal-muwāṭana*, 78.

145. Al-Qaraḍāwī, *Fatāwā mu'āṣira*, 3:642.

146. Al-Qaraḍāwī, *Fī fiqh al-aqalliyyāt al-Muslima*, 46.

147. Brahimi, *Jihad and Just War*, 113–15.

148. Abū Muḥammad al-'Adnānī, "Wa-yaḥyā man ḥayya 'an bayyina" ("Those who were to live might live after seeing a clear proof" [Q8:42]), May 23, 2016, at https://archive.org/details/ntheer14_mail.

149. Abū Baṣīr 'Abd al-Mun'im Muṣṭafā Ḥalīma al-Ṭarṭūsī, "Bayān ḥawla al-tafjīrāt allatī ḥaṣalat fī Madīnat Landan," July 10, 2005, at http://tartosi.blogspot.co.il/2005/07/blog-post_09.html. When jihadis criticized this statement, al-Ṭarṭūsī published a clarification in which he declared that he still adhered to jihad: "Ḥubb al-tashaffī am al-ḥukm al-shar'ī," July 11, 2005, at http://tartosi.blogspot.co.il/2005/07/blog-post_11.html.

150. Abū Bakr al-Baghdādī, "Al-Dīn al-naṣīḥa [Religion Is Counsel]," Feb. 24, 2007, at http://alaqsagate.org/vb/showthread.php?t=30133, with a heading taken from a well-known prophetic *ḥadīth*. Ehud Olmert was the prime minister of Israel from 2006 to 2009, and Muḥmūd 'Abbās has been the president of the Palestinian National Authority since 2005.

151. On the war against the "near enemy" in the 1980s and 1990s, see Gerges, *The Far Enemy*, 43–56.

152. For more on the principle of loyalty and disavowal, see Wagemakers, "Framing the Threat to Islam," and chapter 4 in this book.

153. Al-Ṭarṭūsī, *Muṣṭalaḥāt wa-mafāhīm shar'iyya*, 140–41.

154. Al-Maqdisī's ruling on the 9/11 attacks is titled *Hādhā mā adīnu Allāh bihi.*

155. Al-Maqdisī, *Hādhā mā adīnu Allah bihi*, 24.

156. For a discussion of al-Maqdisī's conception of the battlefield where jihad can be waged, see Wagemakers, *A Quietist Jihadi*, 54–59, 70–71.

157. Al-Maqdisī, *Hādhā mā adīnu Allāh bihi*, 27–29.

158. Al-'Ashmāwī, *Al-Islām al-siyāsī*, 97–102.

159. Muḥammad Sa'īd al-'Ashmāwī, *Jawhar al-Islām* (Cairo: Maktabat Madbūlī al-Ṣaghīr, 1996), 109–10.

160. Al-'Ashmāwī, *Uṣūl al-sharī'a*, 94–98.

161. Al-Anṣārī, "Judhūr al-irhāb."

162. Brahimi, *Jihad and Just War*, 158.

163. In the classical *ḥadīth* collections, there are chapters devoted to the ethics of warfare. See, for example, Muḥammad b. 'Alī b. Muḥammad al-Shawkānī, *Nayl al-awṭār: Sharḥ Muntaqā al-Akhbār min aḥādīth Sayyid al-akhyār*, 4 vols. (Cairo: Dār al-Ḥadīth, 2000), vol. 4, part 7:253–55.

164. Landau-Tasseron, *"Non-combatants" in Muslim Legal Thought*, 5, 10–12, 15–17, 19–22.

165. Nawāf Hāyil al-Takrūrī, *Al-'Amaliyyāt al-istishhādiyya fī al-mīzān al-fiqhī* (Cairo: Dār al-Fikr, 1997), electronic copy at https://www.goodreads.com/book/show/18306943. For more on Hamas's conception of jihad, see Meir Hatina, *Martyrdom in Modern Islam: Piety, Power, and Politics* (New York: Cambridge Univ. Press, 2014), 117–22. On al-Qa'ida's view on *istishhād*, see Hatina, *Martyrdom in Modern Islam*, 136–61.

166. Al-Qaraḍāwī, *Fatāwā min ajli Filasṭīn*, 31 (the *fatwā* permitting acts of suicide terror in Palestine is found on pages 31–34); al-Qaraḍāwī, *Fatāwā mu'āṣira*, 3:503–10. For more on this ruling, see Wagemakers, *A Quietist Jihadi*, 87, and Kelsay, *Arguing the Just War in Islam*, 141–50.

167. Shams al-Dīn al-Qurṭubī, *Al-Jāmi' li-aḥkām al-Qur'ān*, 24 vols. (Beirut: Mu'assasat al-Risāla, 2006), 3:256–63, commentary on Q2:195, electronic copy at https://ia801406.us.archive.org/13/items/waq73651/03_73653.pdf, quoted in al-Qaraḍāwī, *Fatāwā min ajli Filasṭīn*, 37–39.

168. Abū Baṣīr 'Abd al-Mun'im Muṣṭafā Ḥalīma al-Ṭarṭūsī, "Munāqashat adillat wa-i'tirāḍāt al-mukhālifīn ḥawla al-'amaliyyāt al-intiḥāriyya," Sept. 23, 2005, 8–9, at http://tartosi.blogspot.com/2005/09/blog-post_23.html.

169. The institute's website, Munaẓẓamat Minhāj al-Qur'ān al-'Ālamiyya, is at https://www.minhaj.org/arabic/index.html.

170. Muhammad Tahir ul-Qadri [Muḥammad Ṭāhir al-Qadrī], *Fatwa on Terrorism and Suicide Bombings*, foreword by John L. Esposito; introduction by Joel S. Hayward (Lahore, Pakistan: Minhaj ul-Quran International, 2010), 78.

171. 'Abd al-Ḥamīd al-Anṣārī, "Al-Intiḥāriyyūn abṭāl lākin fī al-jaḥīm," *Al-Waṭan*, May 21, 2016, at https://www.minhaj.org/english/oid/11082/Aljareeda.html.

172. Al-Qaraḍāwī, *Fatāwā min ajli Filasṭīn*, 33–43.

173. Al-Qaraḍāwī, *Fiqh al-jihād*, 2:1092. On this ruling, see also Zaman, *Modern Islamic Thought in a Radical Age*, 275.

174. This example is given in the fourth edition of al-Qaraḍāwī's comprehensive work on jihad: *Fiqh al-jihād: Dirāsa muqārana li-aḥkāmihi wa-falsafatihi fī ḍaw' al-Qur'ān wal-Sunna. Ḥaẓiyat hādhihi al-ṭab'a bi-taṣḥīḥāt wa-tanqīḥāt wa-iḍāfāt bālighat al-ahamiyya*, 2 vols., 4th ed., with additions and corrections (Cairo: Maktabat Wahba, 2014), 2:1199. His office also made a clarification concerning his position on acts of *istishhād* in Mawqi' Samāḥat al-Shaykh Yūsuf al-Qaraḍāwī, "Bayān tawḍīḥī ḥawla ra'y al-'allāma al-Qaraḍāwī fī al-'amaliyyāt al-istishhādiyya," July 27, 2015, at https://www.al-qaradawi.net/node/433.

175. Al-Qaraḍāwī, *Fatāwā mu'āṣira*, 2:498–99. For his views on the ethics of war, see al-Qaraḍāwī, *Fiqh al-jihād*, 1:723–49.

176. Brahimi, *Jihad and Just War*, 172.

177. Al-Qaraḍāwī, *Naḥnu wal-gharb*, 123 (interview for the *Guardian*).

178. "Ḥalqa khāṣṣa lil-ijāba 'alā istifsārāt al-mushāhidīn," episode of *Al-Sharī'a wal-ḥayāh*, al-Jazeera, Mar. 17, 2013, at https://tinyurl.com/y7shufdl.

179. Middle East Media Research Institute (MEMRI), "Sheikh al-Qaradhawi: Permission Previously Given to Palestinians to Carry Out Suicide Attacks—No Longer Valid; They Now Have Missiles That Can Strike Deep Inside Israel," Special Dispatch no. 6116, July 28, 2015, at www.memri.org/report/en/print8678.htm.

180. Al-Qaraḍāwī, *Fiqh al-jihād*, 2:1092.

181. Shaykh Yūsuf al-Qaraḍāwī, *Al-Shaykh Salmān al-'Awda yuḥāwiru al-'allāma Yūsuf al-Qaraḍāwī fī liqā' khāṣṣ 'alā Qanāt al-Ḥiwār*, video, Nov. 18, 2016, at https://www.youtube.com/watch?v=C825fzdDm6A&t=28s; MEMRI, "Sheikh al-Qaradhawi Retracts *Fatwā* Permitting Palestinian Suicide Bombings: No Need for Them Anymore," *MEMRI TV* Clip no. 5760, Nov. 18, 2016, at http://www.memritv.org/clip_transcript/en/5760.htm.

182. Al-Qaraḍāwī, *Fiqh al-jihād*, 2:1092.

183. Al-Qaraḍāwī, tweet, July 25, 2017, at https://twitter.com/alqaradawy/status/889893078428864512.

184. Al-Qaraḍāwī, tweet, Dec. 10, 2017, at https://twitter.com/alqaradawy/status/939918929882779648. See also Middle East Media Research Institute (MEMRI), "Sheikh Yousuf al-Qaradawi Calls for Resistance, Jihad, and Martyrdom Following Trump's Recognition of Jerusalem as Israel's Capital," Special Dispatch no. 7264, Jan. 4, 2018, at https://tinyurl.com/ybkzmn49.

185. Brahimi, *Jihad and Just War*, 179–85.

186. Al-Maqdisī, *Hādhā mā adīnu Allāh bihi*, 32. In this connection, al-Maqdisī quoted the Prophet's criterion with respect to the Banū Qurayẓa: he allowed the killing of anyone who had pubic hair.

187. Landau-Tasseron, *"Non-combatants" in Muslim Legal Thought*, 10–11.

188. Al-Qaraḍāwī, *Fiqh al-jihād*, 2:1090. For more on this principle, see Shaykh Aḥmad b. Shaykh Muḥammad al-Zarqā, *Sharḥ al-qawā'id al-fiqhiyya*, 6th ed. (Damascus: Dār al-Qalam, 2001), 187–88, and 'Azzām, *Al-Qawā'id al-fiqhiyya*, 151–53.

189. Landau-Tasseron, *"Non-combatants" in Muslim Legal Thought*, 2, 9.

190. Al-Maqdisī, *Hādhā mā adīnu Allāh bihi*, 30–31. See also al-Shu'aybī, *Ḥukm mā jarā fī Amrīkā min aḥdāth*, 4.

191. Al-Qaraḍāwī, *Fiqh al-jihād*, 2:1086–87; 'Abdallah 'Azzām, *Fī al-jihād ādāb wa-aḥkām*, 8–14; Landau-Tasseron, *"Non-combatants" in Muslim Legal Thought*, 14–15.

192. Al-Maqdisī, *Hādhā mā adīnu Allāh bihi*, 32–33.

193. Al-Qaraḍāwī, *Fiqh al-jihād*, 2:1087; see also al-Shu'aybī, *Ḥukm mā jarā fī Amrīkā min aḥdāth*, 5.

194. Al-Maqdisī, *Hādhā mā adīnu Allāh bihi*, 31–32.

195. Ul-Qadri, *Fatwa on Terrorism and Suicide Bombings*, 94–95, citing Abū Manṣūr al-Māturīdī, *Tafsīr al-Qur'ān al-'aẓīm al-musammā ta'wīlāt ahl al-Sunna*, 10 vols. (Beirut: Mu'assasat al-Risāla, 2004), 2:31–32, electronic copy at https://tinyurl.com/yavrdjhm.

196. Taqī al-Dīn Ibn Taymiyya, *Qā'ida mukhtaṣara fī qitāl al-kuffār wa-muhādanatihim wa-taḥrīm qatlihim li-mujarrad kufrihim* (Riyadh: n.p., 2004), 204; al-Qaraḍāwī, *Fiqh al-jihād*, 1:381–82.

197. Al-Qaraḍāwī, *Fiqh al-jihād*, 2:963.

198. Ul-Qadri, *Fatwa on Terrorism and Suicide Bombings*, 119–20.

199. Al-Qaraḍāwī, *Khiṭābunā al-Islāmī*, 103–4.

200. Al-Qaraḍāwī, *Fiqh al-jihād*, 1:736, 2:1087–88.

201. Al-Qaraḍāwī, *Fiqh al-jihād*, 2:1085–88; al-Qaraḍāwī, *Fatāwā min ajli Filasṭīn*, 33.

202. Zaman, *Modern Islamic Thought in a Radical Age*, 273–76.

203. Middle East Media Research Institute (MEMRI), "Reactions to Sheikh al-Qaradhaei's Fatwa Calling for the Abduction and Killing of American Civilians in Iraq," Special Dispatch no. 794, Oct. 6, 2004, at https://tinyurl.com/y9y4c4dx. Al-Qaraḍāwī's denial is given in Mawqi' Samāḥat al-Shaykh Yūsuf al-Qaraḍāwī, "Al-Qaraḍāwī yanfī al-iftā' bi-qatl al-madaniyyīn fī al-'Irāq," Nov. 9, 2004, at https://www.al-qaradawi.net/node/4441. For more on this *fatwā*, see Jean-Charles Brisard and Damien Martinez, *Zarqawi: The New Face of al-Qa'ida* (Cambridge: Polity Press, 2005), 147–50.

204. Shākir al-Nābulsī, "Fuqahā' safk al-dimā'," *Al-Ḥiwār al-Mutamaddin Mūbāyil*, Sept. 4, 2004, at http://www.m.ahewar.org/s.asp?aid=22960&r=0.

205. 'Abd al-Khāliq Ḥusayn, "Al-Qaraḍāwī dā'iya li-l-irhāb," *Al-Ḥiwār al-Mutamaddin*, Sept. 11, 2004, at http://www.ahewar.org/debat/show.art.asp?aid=23079.

206. Helfont, *Yusuf al-Qaradawi*, 78–79.

207. Al-Qaraḍāwī, "Qaḍiyyat al-'Irāq," 6:192–93.

208. Al-Qaraḍāwī, ""Qaḍiyyat al-'Irāq," 6:202–3.

209. On the juristic debate on these operations in Islam, see al-Takrūrī, *Al-'Amaliyyāt al-istishhādiyya fī al-mīzān al-fiqhī*, 71–111, and Hatina, *Martyrdom in Modern Islam*, 187–215.

210. Muḥammad Nāsir al-Dīn al-Albānī, "Mā ḥukm al-'amaliyyāt al-intiḥāriyya?" audio recording no. 533 of *Silsilat al-Hudā wal-l-nūr*, Aug. 16, 2004, at http://alathar.net/home/esound/index.php?op=tadevi&id=424&coid=4893.

211. Muḥammad b. Ṣāliḥ al-'Uthaymīn, *Majmū' fatāwā wa-rasā'il faḍīlat al-Shaykh Muḥammad b. Ṣāliḥ al-'Uthaymīn*, 26 vols., ed. Fahd b. Nāṣir b. Ibrāhīm al-Sulaimān (Riyadh: Dār al-Thurayyā, 2008), 25:357–64.

212. *Al-Sharq al-Awsaṭ*, "Al-Azhar yudīnu al-i'tidā' 'alā al-madaniyyīn min ayy jiha," Dec. 4, 2001, at https://tinyurl.com/y88mwulz. For al-Qaraḍāwī's claim, see *Fiqh al-jihād*, 2:1086.

213. *Al-Arab News*, "Al-Shaykh al-Qaraḍāwī yaruddu 'alā taṣrīḥāt shaykh al-Azhar," Dec. 7, 2001, at http://alarabnews.com/alshaab/GIF/07-12-2001/n23.htm; Imām Muḥammad Imām, "Al-Shaykh al-Qaraḍāwī: Istihdāf al-madaniyyīn al-Isrā'īliyyīn juz' min muqāwamat al-iḥtilāl wa-mujāhadatihi," *Al-Sharq al-Awsaṭ*, Dec. 12, 2001, at http://archive.aawsat.com/details.asp?article=77264&issueno=8415#.W_PApehvbIU.

214. Al-Jazeera.net, "Ṭanṭāwī: Qatl al-madaniyyīn al-Isrā'īliyyīn jā'iz," Mar. 21, 2002, at https://tinyurl.com/ybsancf8.

215. Muḥammad Khalīl, "Shaykh al-Azhar: Al-'Amaliyyāt al-istishhādiyya ḍidda al-mu'tadīn jā'iza," *Al-Sharq al-Awsaṭ*, Apr. 20, 2004, at https://tinyurl.com/yaeb9etk.

216. Al-Qaraḍāwī, *Al-Fatāwā al-mu'āṣira*, 3:504; "Al-Intifāḍa al-Filasṭīniyya wal-'amaliyyāt al-fidā'iyya," episode of *Al-Sharī'a wal-ḥayāh*, al-Jazeera, Dec. 9, 2001, at https://tinyurl.com/y7mfrvnu.

217. Al-Qaraḍāwī, *Fiqh al-jihād*, 2:1086.

218. Ḥamūd b. 'Uqalā' al-Shu'aybī, "Ḥukm al-'amaliyyāt al-istishhādiyya," Apr. 2001, 2, 7, at http://www.ilmway.com/site/maqdis/MS_5788.html.

219. Abū Qatāda al-Filasṭīnī (a.k.a. 'Umar b. Maḥmūd Abū 'Umar), "Jawāz al-'amaliyyāt al-istishhādiyya wa-innahā laysat bi-qatl li-l-nafs," Apr. 5, 1995, 4–6, at http://www.ilmway.com/site/maqdis/MS_5864.html.

220. Rābiṭat 'Ulamā' Filasṭīn, "Al-'Amaliyyāt al-istishhādiyya jihād fī sabīl Allāh . . . ḥalāl shar'an," n.d., at http://www.ilmway.com/site/maqdis/MS_5833.

221. Abū Baṣīr 'Abd al-Mun'im Muṣṭafā Ḥalīma al-Ṭarṭūsī, "Maḥādhīr al-'amaliyyāt al-istishhādiyya aw al-intiḥāriyya," Aug. 2005, at http://tartosi.blogspot.co.il/2005/08/blog-post_24.html.

222. On the issue of *tatarrus*, see Maher, *Salafi-Jihadism*, 59–67.

223. Al-Qaraḍāwī, *Fiqh al-jihād*, 2:1087.

224. Al-Ṭarṭūsī, "Munāqashat adillat wa-i'tirāḍāt," 6–7, and "Maḥādhīr al-'amaliyyāt," 4–5.

225. For an interesting analysis of this story, see Abū Baṣīr 'Abd al-Mun'im Muṣṭafā Ḥalīma al-Ṭarṭūsī, "Al-Ghulām wal-malik," Dec. 1, 2004, at http://www.ilmway.com/site/maqdis/MS_35815.html.

226. Al-Qaraḍāwī, *Fatāwā min ajli Filasṭīn*, 42; Ibn Taymiyya, *Majmū'at al-fatāwā*, 28:317.

227. Al-Filasṭīnī, "Jawāz al-'amaliyyāt al-istishhādiyya," 5–6.

228. Al-Ṭarṭūsī, "Munāqashat adillat wa-i'tirāḍāt," 5–6.

229. Al-Ṭarṭūsī, "Maḥādhīr al-'amaliyyāt," 5–6.

230. Abū Baṣīr 'Abd al-Mun'im Muṣṭafā Ḥalīma al-Ṭarṭūsī, *Al-Jihād wal-siyāsa al-shar'iyya: Munāṣaḥa wa-mukāshafa lil-jamā'āt al-jihādiyya al-mu'āṣira* (N.p.: n.p., n.d.), 42–43, electronic copy at www.abubaseer.bizland.com/books/read/b%2025.doc.

231. Muhammad Tahir ul-Qadri [Muḥammad Ṭāhir al-Qadrī], *Introduction to the Fatwa on Suicide Bombings and Terrorism: Table of Contents, Summary, & Bibliography*, trans. Shaykh Abdul Aziz Dabbagh (London: Minhaj ul Quran International, 2010), 26–27.

232. Abū Muḥammad al-Maqdisī, *Waqafāt ma'a thamarāt al-jihād: Bayna al-jahl fī al-shar' wa-l-jahl bi-l-wāqi'*, nuskha mazayyada, iḍāfat al-waqfa al-tāsi'a 'ashar (revised version with addition) (N.p.: n.p., 2008), 2, electronic copy at http://www.ilmway.com/site/maqdis/MS_155.html.

233. ʿAbd al-Ḥamīd al-Anṣārī, "ʿAlā al-majāmiʿ al-fiqhiyya taḥrīm al-aʿmāl al-intiḥāriyya," *Al-Bayān*, Apr. 16, 2007, at https://tinyurl.com/yawt2ufl. On suicide operations as an ideological and moral crisis, see also Jamāl Khāshuqjī, "Al-ʿAmaliyyāt al-intiḥāriyya akbar azma fikriyya wa-akhlāqiyya tuwājihu al-Islām," *Al-Ittiḥād*, July 19, 2005, at https://www.alittihad.ae/WejhatArticle/13358/.

234. ʿAbd al-Ḥamīd al-Anṣārī, "Limādhā yaqtulūna? Limādhā yufajjirūna? Limādhā yantaḥirūna?" *Al-Rāya al-Qaṭariyya*, July 25, 2005, at https://tinyurl.com/y7w69jv3; Middle East Media Research Institute (MEMRI), "Leading Progressive Qatari Cleric: By Permitting Suicide Operations, al-Qaradhawi and His Ilk Have Caused a Moral Crisis in Islam," Special Dispatch no. 968, Aug. 25, 2005, at http://www.memri.org/report/en/print1453.htm.

235. Al-Anṣārī, "Limādhā yaqtulūna?"

236. Al-Jazeera.net, "Naṣṣ fatwā Markaz al-Albānī bi-ḥurmat al-ʿamaliyyāt al-intiḥāriyya," Jan. 20, 2010, at https://tinyurl.com/yb8659t3.

237. ʿAbd al-Khāliq Ḥusayn, "Hal al-Islām dīn al-tasāmuḥ?" *Al-Ḥiwār al-Mutamaddin* 1587 (June 20, 2006), at http://www.ahewar.org/debat/show.art.asp?aid=67943.

238. See, for instance, S. al-Nābulsī, *Al-Lībirālīyyūn al-judud*, 21 (Art. 4), and Middle East Media Research Institute (MEMRI), "An Arab Nationalist Attack on the Arab Progressives," Special Dispatch no. 759, Aug. 6, 2004, at https://www.memri.org/reports/arab-nationalist-attack-arab-progressives.

239. ʿAbd al-Khāliq Ḥusayn, "Al-Islām bayna al-tafkhīkh wa-l-tafkhīdh . . . !" *Al-Ḥiwār al-Mutamaddin* 1829 (Feb. 17, 2007), at http://www.ahewar.org/debat/show.art.asp?aid=88920.

240. A. Ḥusayn, "Al-Islām bayna al-tafkhīkh."

241. Al-Qaraḍāwī, *Khiṭābunā al-Islāmī*, 169–70.

242. S. al-Nābulsī, *Tahāfut al-uṣūliyya*, 15.

243. Shaykh Yūsuf al-Qaraḍāwī, "Muḥammad al-rasūl al-mujāhid," June 8, 2001, in *Khuṭab al-Shaykh al-Qaraḍāwī*, vol. 8, ed. al-Maktab al-Iʿlmī li-l-Shaykh bil-Dawḥa, 30–31.

6. Principles of *Wasaṭī* Judicial Decisions

1. Wael B. Hallaq, *A History of Islamic Legal Theories: An Introduction to Sunnī Uṣūl al-Fiqh* (Cambridge: Cambridge Univ. Press, 1997), 214–31.

2. On the Ẓāhiriyya school, see Goldziher, *The Ẓāhirīs*.

3. Shaykh Yūsuf al-Qaraḍāwī, *Madkhal li-dirāsat al-sharīʿa al-Islāmiyya*, 4th ed. (Cairo: Maktabat Wahba, 2001), 57–58; Shaykh Yūsuf al-Qaraḍāwī, *Al-Marjiʿiyya al-ʿulyā fī al-Islām lil-Qurʾān wal-Sunna: Ḍawābiṭ wa-maḥādhīr fī al-fahm wal-tafsīr* (Cairo: Maktabat Wahba, 1992), 244–56; Shaykh Yūsuf al-Qaraḍāwī, *Al-ʿIbāda fī al-Islām*, 15th ed. (Cairo: Maktabat Wahba, 1985), 119–21; al-Shāṭibī, *Al-Muwāfaqāt*, 2:172–76.

4. S. al-Nābulsī, *Tahāfut al-uṣūliyya*, 39.

5. Al-Rāshid, "Al-Qaraḍāwī mutasāmiḥ wa-mutaʿaṣṣib."

6. Wael B. Hallaq, "Can the Sharī'a Be Restored?" in *Islamic Law and the Challenge of Modernity*, ed. Yvonne Y. Haddad and Barbara F. Stowasser (Walnut Creek, CA: Altamira Press, 2004), 42; Aharon Layish, "Islamic Law in the Modern World: Nationalization, Islamization, Reinstatement," *Islamic Law and Society* 21 (2014): 277.

7. Layish, "Islamic Law in the Modern World," 292; Ron Shaham, "Western Scholars on the Role of the 'Ulamā' in Adapting Sharī'a to Modernity: A Critical Review," in *Guardians of Faith in Modern Times*, ed. Hatina, 180–81, 184.

8. Felicitas Opwis, "Maṣlaḥa in Contemporary Legal Theory," *Islamic Law and Society* 12, no. 2 (2005): 187, 197; Hallaq, *A History of Islamic Legal Theories*, 207–54.

9. Al-Qaraḍāwī gives the term *maṣlaḥa mursala* the same definition as Shihāb al-Dīn Aḥmad b. Idrīs al-Qarāfī (d. 1285). On this definition, see Felicitas Opwis, *Maṣlaḥa and the Purpose of the Law: Islamic Discourse on Legal Change from the 4th/10th to the 8th/14th Century* (Leiden: Brill, 2010), 165–293, and Layish, "Islamic Law in the Modern World," 284.

10. Al-Qaraḍāwī, *Liqā'āt wa-muḥāwarāt ḥawla qaḍāyā al-Islām wal-'aṣr*, 2:3; Ṭaha Jābir al-'Alawānī, "Faqīh al-du'āh wa-dā'iyat al-fuqahā': Al-Shaykh Yūsuf al-Qaraḍāwī," in *Al-Qaraḍāwī*, ed. al-Dīb, 1:371–88; Talīma, *Al-Qaraḍāwī*.

11. Ibn Qayyim al-Jawziyya, *A'lām al-muwaqqi'īn*, 1:87–88.

12. Al-Qaraḍāwī, *Kayfa nata'āmalu ma'a al-turāth wal-tamadhhub wal-ikhtilāf?* 62–125.

13. Al-Zarqā, *Sharḥ al-qawā'id al- fiqhiyya*, 165–77; 'Azzām, *Al-Qawā'id al-fiqhiyya*, 126–37; Yaḥyā b. Sharaf al-Nawawī, Ibn Daqīq al-'Īd, and Shaykh Ṣāliḥ b. 'Uthaymīn, *Al-Riyāḍ al-Nadiyya: Sharḥ al-Arba'īn al-Nawawiyya* (Alexandria, Egypt: Dār al-Baṣīra, 2002), 181–83.

14. 'Iṣām Talīma, *Al-Qaraḍāwī faqīhan* (Cairo: Dār al-Tawzī' wal-Nashr al-Islāmiyya, 2000), 59–154.

15. Al-Qaraḍāwī, *Sharī'at al-Islām ṣāliḥa lil-taṭbīq*, 105–80.

16. For more on *ijtihād*, see Shaykh Yūsuf al-Qaraḍāwī, *Al-Ijtihād fī al-sharī'a al-Islāmiyya ma'a naẓarāt taḥlīliyya fī al-ijtihād al-mu'āṣir*, 3rd ed. (Kuwait: Dār al-Qalam, 1999), 11–13, and Hallaq, *A History of Islamic Legal Theories*, 117–21.

17. Al-Qaraḍāwī, *Min ajli ṣaḥwa rāshida*, 45.

18. Shaykh Yūsuf al-Qaraḍāwī, *Al-Ijtihād al-mu'āṣir bayna al-inḍibāṭ wal-infirāṭ* (Cairo: Dār al-Tawzī' wal-Nashr al-Islāmiyya, 1994), 3–18.

19. Al-Qaraḍāwī, *Min ajli ṣaḥwa rāshida*, 45.

20. For a discussion on whether the "gates of *ijtihād*" were closed, see Wael B. Hallaq, "Was the Gate of *Ijtihad* Closed?" in *Law and Legal Theory in Classical and Medieval Islam*, ed. Wael B. Hallaq (London: Variorum, 1994), 3–41.

21. Shaykh Yūsuf al-Qaraḍāwī, *Al-Qawā'id al-ḥākima li-fiqh al-mu'āmalāt* (Cairo: Dār al-Shurūq, 2010), 15; Al-Qaraḍāwī, *Al-Ḥalāl wal-ḥarām fī al-Islām*, 20–23.

22. Shaykh Yūsuf al-Qaraḍāwī, *Fiqh al-ghinā' wal-mūsīqā fī ḍaw' al-Qur'ān wal-Sunna* (Cairo: Maktabat Wahba, 2001), 29–34.

23. Al-Qaraḍāwī, *Fiqh al-ghinā'*, 185–94.

24. Muḥammad b. Muḥammad al-Fazzāzī, "Fatāwā mutasayyiba al-Qaraḍāwī yuḥillu al-ghinā'," 1998, at http://www.ilmway.com/site/maqdis/MS_23753.html. See also Nāṣir b. Ḥamad al-Fahd, "Risāla fī ḥukm al-ghinā' bil-Qur'ān," Aug. 2001, at http://www.ilmway.com/site/maqdis/MS_22514.html.

25. 'Alī b. Muḥammad al-Ḍab'ān, "Ḥukm al-anāshīd al-Islāmiyya," *Ṣayd al-Fawā'id*, n.d., at http://www.saaid.net/fatwa/f46.htm.

26. Al-Ḍab'ān, "Ḥukm al-anāshīd al-Islāmiyya."

27. On these hymns, see Menashe Shemesh, *The Songs of the Islamic State: A Major Tool for Reinforcing Its Narrative, Spreading Its Message, Recruiting Supporters*, Inquiry & Analysis Report no. 1179 (Washington, DC: Middle East Media Research Institute, Aug. 10, 2015), at https://tinyurl.com/y75e2bco.

28. Shabakat Saḥāb al-Salafiyya, "Fatāwā 'ulamā' al-Sunna fīmā yussamā bi-l-anāshīd al-Islāmiyya," Oct. 26, 2009, at https://tinyurl.com/y7s8rob2.

29. For al-Ṭūfī's theory of *maṣlaḥa*, see Opwis, *Maṣlaḥa and the Purpose of the Law*, 200–246, and Hallaq, *A History of Islamic Legal Theories*, 150–53.

30. On this case, see al-Qaraḍāwī, *Fiqh al-zakāh*, 2:643–48, and *Madkhal li-dirāsat al-sharī'a al-Islāmiyya*, 218.

31. For an analysis of 'Umar's ruling on "those whose hearts need winning over [*al-mu'allafa qulūbuhum*]," see al-Qaraḍāwī, *Al-Siyāsa al-shar'iyya*, 157–71.

32. Al-Qaraḍāwī, *Al-Ijtihād al-mu'āṣir bayna al-inḍibāṭ wal-infirāṭ*, 88–91, and *Al-ijtihād fī al-sharī'a al-Islāmiyya*, 229–34.

33. Al-Sayyid, *Al-Qaraḍāwī fī al-'ara'*.

34. Shaykh Yūsuf al-Qaraḍāwī, *Al-Ṣaḥwa al-Islāmiyya bayna al-ikhtilāf al-mashrū' wal-tafarruq al-madhmūm* (Cairo: Dār al-Shurūq, 2001), 132.

35. Al-Sayyid, *Al-Qaraḍāwī fī al-'arā'*, 260–62, 361.

36. Aḥmad al-Baghdādī, *Tajdīd al-fikr al-dīnī*, 259–60.

37. Opwis, "Maṣlaḥa in Contemporary Islamic Legal Theory," 187–88, and *Maṣlaḥa and the Purpose of the Law*, 77–78; al-Qaraḍāwī, *Al-Siyāsa al-shar'iyya*, 77–78, 89.

38. For al-Shāṭibī's conception of *maṣlaḥa*, see Opwis, "Maṣlaḥa in Contemporary Islamic Legal Theory," 187–88; Opwis, *Maṣlaḥa and the Purpose of the Law*, 247–333; and Hallaq, *A History of Islamic Legal Theories*, 162–206.

39. Opwis, *Maṣlaḥa and the Purpose of the Law*, 77–78; al-Qaraḍāwī, *Al-Siyāsa al-shar'iyya*, 247.

40. Opwis, "Maṣlaḥa in Contemporary Islamic Legal Theory," 197, 220–23.

41. Opwis, *Maṣlaḥa and the Purpose of the Law*, 67; Muhammad Qasim Zaman, "The 'Ulama' of Contemporary Islam and Their Conceptions of the Common Good," in *Public Islam and the Common Good*, ed. Armando Salvatore and Dale F. Eickelma (Leiden: Brill, 2004), 134; al-Qaraḍāwī, *Al-Siyāsa al-shar'iyya*, 80; Abū Ḥāmid al-Ghazālī, *Al-Mustaṣfā fī*

ʿilm uṣūl al-fiqh, 4 vols. (Al-Madīna, Saudi Arabia: Sharikat al-Madīna al-Munawwara lil-Ṭibāʿa, n.d.), 2:481–85, electronic copy at https://ia800509.us.archive.org/22/items/FPmustasfa/mustasfa2.pdf.

42. Al-Qaraḍāwī, *Al-Siyāsa al-sharʿiyya*, 84; Zaman, "The ʿUlamaʾ of Contemporary Islam," 134–35; Zaman, *Modern Islamic Thought in a Radical Age*, 109–39.

43. Al-Shāṭibī, *Al-Muwāfaqāt*, 2:9–12; Muḥammad al-Ṭāhir Ibn ʿĀshūr, *Maqāṣid al-sharīʿa al-Islāmiyya*, 5th ed. (Cairo: Dār al-Salām, 2012), 86–92.

44. Aḥmad al-Rīsūnī, "Al-Qaraḍāwī: Faqīh al-maqāṣid," in *Al-Qaraḍāwī*, ed. al-Dīb, 1:111.

45. David L. Johnston, "Yusuf al-Qaradawi's Purposive Fiqh: Promoting or Demoting the Future Role of the 'Ulamā'," in *Maqāṣid al-Sharīʿa and Contemporary Reformist Muslim Thought: An Examination*, ed. Adis Duderija (New York: Palgrave Macmillan, 2014), 39–71; David L. Johnston, "Shaykh Yusuf al-Qaradawi: Standard Bearer of the 'New Purposive Fiqh,'" paper presented at the *Journal of Law and Religion* conference "Emerging Voices in Islamic Jurisprudence," Sept. 28, 2012, St. Paul, MN, quotation on 8; and David L. Johnston, "Emerging Voices in Islamic Jurisprudence," *Humantrustees*, Oct. 8, 2012, at http://humantrustees.org/blogs/item/74-qemerging-voices.

46. On al-Qaraḍāwī's principles when ruling on women's issues, see ʿAbd al-Karīm, *Qaḍāyā al-marʾa fī fiqh al-Qaraḍāwī*, 29–64.

47. Maḥmūd Shaltūt, *Al-Fatāwā: Dirāsa li-mushkilāt al-Muslim al-muʿāṣir fī ḥayātihi al-yawmiyya al-ʿāmma*, 18th ed. (Cairo: Dār al-Shurūq, 2004), 285–86.

48. Al-Qaraḍāwī, *Fiqh al-wasaṭiyya al-Islāmiyya wal-tajdīd*, 108–12.

49. Muḥammad b. Ṣāliḥ al-ʿUthaymīn, "Mā ḥukm al-khitān fī ḥaqq al-rijāl wa-l-nisāʾ?" *Ṭarīq al-Islām*, Dec. 1, 2006, at https://tinyurl.com/y7u78y95; al-ʿUthaymīn, *Majmūʿ fatāwā wa-rasāʾil faḍīlat al-Shaykh Muḥammad b. Ṣāliḥ al-ʿUthaymīn*, 11:117–18.

50. ʿAbd al-ʿAzīz b. ʿAbdallah Ibn Bāz, "Ḥukm khitān al-ināth," n.d., at https://www.binbaz.org.sa/noor/7735.

51. Jāda al-Ḥaqq ʿAlī Jāda al-Ḥaqq, *Bayān li-l-nās* (Cairo: Dār al-Fārūq, 2014), 651–52.

52. Al-Qaraḍāwī, *Fatāwā muʿāṣira*, 4:516–17, and Shaykh Yūsuf al-Qaraḍāwī, *Al-Ḥukm al-sharʿī fī khitān al-ināth* (Cairo: Maktabat Wahba, 2007), 18.

53. Al-Qaraḍāwī, *Fatāwā muʿāṣira*, 4:507–23. See also al-Qaraḍāwī, *Al-Ḥukm al-sharʿī fī khitān al-ināth.*

54. Al-Qaraḍāwī, *Fatāwā muʿāṣira*, 4:519–23. See also al-Qaraḍāwī, *Al-Ḥukm al-sharʿī fī khitān al-ināth*, 19–24.

55. Salīm al-ʿAwwā's *fatwā* on female circumcision in 1994 is quoted in Gamāl al-Bannā, *Khitān al-banāt laysa Sunna wa-lā makruma wa-lākinna jarīma* (Cairo: Dār al-Fikr al-Islāmī, 2011), 139–44, electronic copy at https://tinyurl.com/yat6zryg.

56. G. al-Bannā, *Khitān al-banāt*, 178–80.

57. G. al-Bannā, *Khitān al-banāt*, 178–80.

58. This phrase is based on a *ḥadīth* according to which the Prophet said, "You are all shepherds, and each one of you is responsible for his sheep." The relationship between ruler and subject is just one of the examples in this *ḥadīth*.

59. Much has been written on the subject of *al-siyāsa al-shar'iyya*, including Abū al-Ḥasan 'Alī b. Muḥammad al-Māwardī, *Al-Aḥkām al-sulṭāniyya wal-wilāyāt al-dīniyya* (Kuwait City: Dār Ibn Qutayba, 1989), electronic copy at http://waqfeya.com/book.php?bid=356; Taqī al-Dīn Ibn Taymiyya, *Al-Siyāsa al-shar'iyya fī iṣlāḥ al-rā'ī wal-ra'iyya* (Alexandria, Egypt: Dār al-Baṣīra, 2003).

60. Layish, "Islamic Law in the Modern World," 292–93.

61. *Shabakat Saḥāb al-Salafiyya*, "Ilā al-'uqalā': Ḥukm al-muẓāharāt bayna al-Shaykh al-Albānī wal-Ḥawīnī," Aug. 30, 2010, at http://www.sahab.net/forums/index.php?showtopic=113495.

62. *Shabakat al-Da'wa al-Salafiyya mina al-Aqṣā al-Mubārak*, "Ḥukm al-muẓāharāt fī al-Islām," Jan. 26, 2011, at http://vb.alaqsasalafi.com/showthread.php?2500.

63. *Muntadayāt 'Ālam Ḥawwā'*, "Ḥukm al-muẓāharāt," Jan. 22, 2009, at https://www.hawaaworld.com/showthread.php?t=3038114.

64. Jam'iyyat 'Ulamā' al-Yaman, "Naṣṣ bayān Jam'iyyat 'Ulamā' al-Yaman alladhī yataḍammanu fatwā bi-taḥrīm al-muẓāharāt," Sept. 29, 2011, at https://yemen-press.com/news3298.html. On the *ḥadīth* quoted, see Ibn Ḥajar al-'Asqalānī, *Fatḥ al-bārī sharḥ Ṣaḥīḥ al-Bukhārī*, 13 vols. (Giza, Egypt: Dār al-Kutub al-Salafiyya, n.d.), 5:5–7, electronic copy at https://ia801303.us.archive.org/3/items/FP2021/13_2034.pdf.

65. Al-Jazeera.net, "Al-Qaraḍāwī yantaqidu fatwā 'Ulamā' bil-Yaman," Oct. 3, 2011, at https://tinyurl.com/y9xvus8t. Al-Qaraḍāwī's response to those forbidding demonstrations against the rulers is given in *25 Yanāyir sanat 2011m*, 138–62.

66. Al-Qaraḍāwī, *25 Yanāyir sanat 2011m*, 156–60, and Al-Jazeera.net, "Al-Qaraḍāwī yantaqidu fatwā 'Ulamā' al-Yaman."

67. Al-Qaraḍāwī, *Al-Ḥalāl wal-ḥarām fī al-Islām*, 20–21.

68. Shaykh Yūsuf al-Qaraḍāwī, *Al-Sunna maṣdaran lil-ma'rifa wal-ḥaḍāra*, 3rd ed. (Cairo: Dār al-Shurūq, 2002), 245–47.

69. Al-Shāṭibī, *Al-Muwāfaqāt*, 2:298–307; al-Qaraḍāwī, *Al-Siyāsa al-shar'īyya*, 298–307; Kerr, *Islamic Reform*, 187–90; Hallaq, *A History of Islamic Legal Theories*, 215–16.

70. Al-Qaraḍāwī, *Fatāwā mu'āṣira*, 4:825–27.

71. Al-Qaraḍāwī, *Fatāwā mu'āṣira*, 4:827–30.

72. Shaykh Yūsuf al-Qaraḍāwī, introduction (*taqdīm*) to 'Abd al-Ḥalīm Muḥammad Abū Shaqqa, *Taḥrīr al-mar'a fī 'aṣr al-risāla: Dirāsa 'an al-mar'a jāmi'a li-nuṣūṣ al-Qur'ān al-karīm wa-ṣaḥīḥay al-Bukhārī wa-Muslim*, 3 vols., 7th ed. (Cairo: Dār al-Qalam, 2011), 1:13–17. The introduction also appears in Shaykh Yūsuf al-Qaraḍāwī, *Al-Muqaddimāt* (Cairo: Dār al-Rawḍa, 2015), 159–87.

73. Al-Qaraḍāwī, introduction to Abū Shaqqa, *Taḥrīr al-mar'a fī 'aṣr al-risāla*, 1:18.

74. Al-Qaraḍāwī, introduction to Abū Shaqqa, *Taḥrīr al-mar'a fī 'aṣr al-risāla*, 1:19.

75. Al-Qaraḍāwī, *Fiqh al-wasaṭiyya al-Islāmiyya wal-tajdīd*, 243.

76. See especially Muḥammad al-Ghazālī, *Qaḍāyā al-mar'a bayna al-taqālīd al-rākida wal-wāfida*, 6th ed. (Cairo: Dār al-Shurūq, 1996).

77. M. al-Ghazālī, *Dustūr al-waḥda*, 220.

78. S. al-Nābulsī, *Al-Lībirāliyyūn al-judud*, 25 (Art. 25).

79. Al-Qaraḍāwī, *Al-Taṭarruf al-'ilmānī*, 137–42.

80. S. al-Nābulsī, *Al-'Arab bayna al-lībirāliyya*, 69–72.

81. Al-Qaraḍāwī, *Al-Taṭarruf al-'ilmānī*, 137–38.

82. Al-Qaraḍāwī, *Markaz al-mar'a*, 30–31.

83. Al-Albānī's ruling on this issue can be found in Muḥammad Nāsir al-Dīn al-Albānī, *Jilbāb al-mar'a al-Muslima fī al-Kitāb wal-Sunna* (Cairo: Dār al-Salām, n.d.).

84. Shaykh Yūsuf al-Qaraḍāwī, *Al-Niqāb lil-mar'a bayna al-qawl bi-bid'iyyatihi wal-qawl bi-wujūbihi*, 2nd ed. (Cairo: Maqtabat Wahba, 1999), 30–33, 47; "Libās al-mar'a al-Muslima," episode of *Al-Sharī'a wal-ḥayāh*, al-Jazeera, July 8, 2007, at https://tinyurl.com/ycegfzbp.

85. Al-Qaraḍāwī, *Al-Niqāb lil-mar'a bayna al-qawl*, 29–34.

86. Shaykh Yūsuf al-Qaraḍāwī, *Fiqh al-usra wa-qaḍāyā al-mar'a* (Istanbul: Al-Dār al-Shāmiyya, 2017), 561–65; al-Qaraḍāwī, *Al-Niqāb lil-mar'a bayna al-qawl*, 65–71.

87. For more on this principle, see 'Azzām, *Al-Qawā'id al-fiqhiyya*, 114–20, and al-Zarqā, *Sharḥ al-qawā'id al-fiqhiyya*, 157–62.

88. 'Abd al-'Azīz b. 'Abdallah Ibn Bāz, "Ḥukm al-niqāb lil-mar'a," n.d., at https://tinyurl.com/y7sln8jy.

89. Al-Qaraḍāwī, *Al-Niqāb lil-mar'a bayna al-qawl*, 52–53.

90. Al-Qaraḍāwī, *Al-Niqāb lil-mar'a bayna al-qawl*, 48–50. On the meanings of *jilbāb*, see al-Albānī, *Jilbāb al-mar'a al-Muslima*, 82–87. Al-Albānī, too, agrees that the verse does not constitute evidence that a woman's face is a "private part" that must be covered (87).

91. Muḥammad Sa'īd al-'Ashmāwī, *Ḥaqīqat al-ḥijāb wa-ḥujjiyyat al-ḥadīth*, 2nd ed. (Cairo: Maktabat Madbūlī al-Ṣaghīr, 1995), 16–68.

92. Al-'Ashmāwī, *Ḥaqīqat al-ḥijāb*, 20–21, 43.

93. Al-'Ashmāwī, *Ḥaqīqat al-ḥijāb*, 19.

94. Al-'Ashmāwī, *Ḥaqīqat al-ḥijāb*, 36–39.

95. Al-Qaraḍāwī, *Al-Niqāb lil-mar'a bayna al-qawl*, 48–50.

96. Al-'Ashmāwī, *Ḥaqīqat al-ḥijāb*, 16–17.

97. Gamāl al-Bannā, *Al-Ḥijāb* (Cairo: Dār al-Fikr al-Islāmī, 2002), 79–80.

98. G. al-Bannā, *Al-Ḥijāb*, 96–97.

99. G. al-Bannā, *Al-Ḥijāb*, 125–28.

100. G. al-Bannā, *Al-Ḥijāb*, 133.

101. G. al-Bannā, *Al-Ḥijāb*, 140.

102. Zakariyyā, *Al-Ṣaḥwa al-Islāmiyya fī mīzān al-'aql*, 17–22.

103. Hallaq, *A History of Islamic Legal Theories*, 214–62.

104. ʿAbd al-ʿAzīz b. ʿAbdallah Ibn Bāz, "Ḥukm qiyādat al-mar'a al-sayyāra," in *Al-Fatāwā al-sharʿiyya fī al-masā'il al-ʿaṣriyya: Min fatāwā ʿulamā' al-Balad al-Ḥarām*, ed. Khālid b. ʿAbd al-Raḥmān al-Jeraysī (Riyadh: Mu'ssasat al-Jeraysī, 1999), 1096, electronic copy at http://waqfeya.com/book.php?bid=338.

105. Al-Qaraḍāwī, *Fatāwā muʿāṣira*, 2:374–75, 3:285–86; Abū Shaqqa, *Taḥrīr al-mar'a*, 3:16.

106. G. al-Bannā, *Al-Ḥijāb*, 127.

107. G. al-Bannā, *Al-Ḥijāb*, 76. It should be mentioned that the Qur'ānic context does not lend itself to this interpretation. The straightforward interpretation of Q25:73 is an appeal to the believers not to close their eyes and ears to Allah's directives—that is, to hear and obey them.

108. Al-ʿAshmāwī, *Al-Islām al-siyāsī*, 66–67.

109. Al-Qaraḍāwī, *Sharīʿat al-Islām ṣāliḥa lil-taṭbīq*, 139.

110. Al-Qaraḍāwī, *Sharīʿat al-Islām ṣāliḥa lil-taṭbīq*, 143.

111. G. al-Bannā, *Al-Ḥijāb*, 77–78.

112. S. al-Nābulsī, *Al-Islām wa-jirāb al-ḥāwī*, 61.

113. Khālid, *Min hunā nabda'u*, 195.

114. On this ḥadīth and its meaning, see Abū Shaqqa, *Taḥrīr al-mar'a*, 1:281–94.

115. Abū Shaqqa, *Taḥrīr al-mar'a*, 1:281–82.

116. Abū Shaqqa, *Taḥrīr al-mar'a*, 1:292–93.

117. G. al-Bannā, *Al-Ḥijāb*, 129.

118. ʿAbd al-Ḥamīd al-Anṣārī, *Qaḍāyā al-mar'a bayna taʿālīm al-Islām wa-taqālīd al-mujtamaʿ* (Cairo: Dār al-Fikr al-ʿArabī, 2000), 34–35.

119. ʿAbd al-ʿAzīz b. ʿAbdallah Ibn Bāz, "Ḥukm taʿaddud al-zawjāt," n.d., at https://www.binbaz.org.sa/noor/3668.

120. Al-Qaraḍāwī, *Markaz al-mar'a*, 121–40.

121. Al-Qaraḍāwī, *Markaz al-mar'a*, 130–31; al-Qaraḍāwī, *Fiqh al-usra*, 265.

122. Al-Qaraḍāwī, *Markaz al-mar'a*, 138–41; al-Qaraḍāwī, *Fiqh al-usra*, 270–72.

123. ʿAbduh, "Taʿaddud al-zawjāt," 2:83–85.

124. G. al-Bannā, *Al-Ḥijāb*, 174–77.

125. G. al-Bannā, *Al-Ḥijāb*, 173–77.

126. G. al-Bannā, *Al-Ḥijāb*, 178–81.

127. Al-Qaraḍāwī, *Al-Ḥalāl wal-ḥarām fī al-Islām*, 151.

128. "Fiṭrat Allāh fī khalqihi."

129. "Fiṭrat Allāh fī khalqihi."

130. Shaykh Yūsuf al-Qaraḍāwī, *Mūjibāt taghayyur al-fatwā fī ʿaṣrinā* (Cairo: Dār al-Shurūq, 2008), 71–72.

131. "Fiṭrat Allāh fī khalqihi."

132. Al-Qaraḍāwī, *Mūjibāt taghayyur al-fatwā fī ʿaṣrinā*, 92–95.

133. Al-Qaraḍāwī, *Fatāwā mu'āṣira*, 1:694–96.

134. "Fiṭrat Allah fī khalqihi."

135. Islamqa, "Mā hiya 'uqūbat al-liwāṭ, wa-hal hunāka farq bayna al-fā'il wa-l-maf'ūl bihi," Mar. 13, 2006, at https://islamqa.info/ar/38622. For al-Qaraḍāwī's view on male homosexuality, see "Fiṭrat Allāh fī khalqihi."

136. Islamqa, "'Uqūbat al-siḥāq," Apr. 8, 2003, at https://islamqa.info/ar/21058.

137. Qarāmī, "Manzilat al-mithliyyīn."

138. Qarāmī, "Manzilat al-mithliyyīn."

139. Salmān al-'Awda, "Al-Mithliyya lā tuqṣī aṣḥābahā mina al-Islām raghma annahā 'amal āthim," *Ra'y al-Yawm*, May 2, 2016, at http://www.raialyoum.com/?p=433023.

140. 'Abd al-'Azīz b. 'Abdallah Ibn Bāz, "Ḥukm man fa'ala al-'āda al-sirriyya wa-'amal qawm Lūṭ wa-waṭ' al-bahīma," June 30, 1998, at https://www.binbaz.org.sa/fatawa/3181.

141. Kugle and Hunt, "Masculinity, Homosexuality, and the Defence of Islam," 258.

142. Shākir al-Nābulsī, "Al-'Ilmāniyya wa-l-dīmuqrāṭiyya janāḥāni li-ṭā'ir al-ḥurriyya," *Al-Ḥiwār al-Mutamaddin* 1195 (May 12, 2005), at http://www.ahewar.org/debat/show.art.asp?aid=37224.

143. Aḥmad al-Baghdādī, "Qarn al-mar'a," *Al-Ḥiwār al-Mutamaddin* 430 (Mar. 20, 2003), at http://www.ahewar.org/debat/show.art.asp?aid=6183.

Conclusion

1. Muḥammad Rif'at al-Sa'īd, *Al-Ta'aslum: Fikr musallaḥ* (Damascus: Dār al-Ṭālī'a, 1996), 7.

2. Muḥammad Rif'at al-Sa'īd, *Al-Tayyārāt al-siyāsiyya fī Miṣr: Al-Mārksiyyūn, al-Ikhwān al-Muslimūn, al-Nāṣiriyyūn, al-tajammu'* (Cairo: Sharikat al-Amal, 2001), 132–33.

3. Rif'at al-Sa'īd, *Al-Ta'aslum*, 7.

4. al-Anṣārī, "Thaqāfat al-karāhiya wa-intishār al-taṭarruf wa-l-tajdīd al-dīnī."

5. 'Abd al-Ḥamīd al-Anṣārī, "Mā al-sabīl ilā ansanat al-khiṭāb al-dīnī?" *Ṣawt al-Ḥurriyya al-Ikhbārī*, Jan. 19, 2010, at http://alhorya.com/arabic/?Action=Details&ID=863.

6. Al-Qaraḍāwī, *Thaqāfatunā bayna al-infitāḥ wal-inghilāq*, 79.

7. Al-Anṣārī, "Thaqāfat al-karāhiya wa-intishār al-taṭarruf wal-tajdīd al-dīnī."

8. Mas'ūd Ṣabrī, "Al-Qaraḍāwī: Ibn Taymiyyat 'aṣrihi wa-zamānihi," Mawqi' Samāḥat al-Shaykh Yūsuf al-Qaraḍāwī, May 17, 2014, at https://www.al-qaradawi.net/node/5160. For another article that likens al-Qaraḍāwī to Ibn Taymiyya, see Iḥsān al-Faqīh, "Al-Shaykh Yūsuf al-Qaraḍāwī: Ibn Taymiyyat al-'aṣr," *Turk Bris*, June 12, 2017, at http://www.turkpress.co/node/35602.

9. Al-Anṣārī uses the word *murīdūn*, which is often employed to describe the disciples of Ṣūfī shaykhs, who worship their teachers.

10. Al-Anṣārī, "Mā al-sabīl ilā ansanat al-khiṭāb al-dīnī?"

11. Al-Anṣārī, "Mā al-sabīl ilā ansanat al-khiṭāb al-dīnī?"

12. Shaykh Yūsuf al-Qaraḍāwī, "Tuhmat al-Islām al-siyāsī," Mawqiʿ Samāḥat al-Shaykh al-Qaraḍāwī, Sept. 6, 2018, at https://www.al-qaradawi.net/node/2099.

13. Al-Qaraḍāwī, *Fatāwā muʿāṣira*, 2:623–35, 195–200.

14. "Al-Fatwā wal-siyāsa."

15. S. al-Nābulsī, *Al-ʿArab bayna al-lībirāliyya*, 13, 48–49.

16. S. al-Nābulsī, *Sujūn bi-lā quḍbān*, 49, 63.

17. S. al-Nābulsī, *Sujūn bi-lā quḍbān*, 50–51, and *Al-ʿArab bayna al-lībirāliyya*, 51–52.

18. An allusion to Q13:17, which likens falsehood to foam that vanishes and truth to water that endures.

19. S. al-Nābulsī, *Al-ʿArab bayna al-lībirāliyya*, 78.

20. S. al-Nābulsī, *Al-ʿArab bayna al-lībirāliyya*, 23, 13.

21. S. al-Nābulsī, *Al-ʿArab bayna al-lībirāliyya*, 88–91.

22. Hatina, *Identity Politics in the Middle East*, 139.

23. S. al-Nābulsī, *Sujūn bi-lā quḍbān*, 44.

24. S. al-Nābulsī, *Tahāfut al-uṣūliyya*, 39.

25. S. al-Nābulsī, *Sujūn bi-lā quḍbān*, 45.

26. *Dunyā al-Waṭan*, "Ḥasan Ḥanafī yushabbihu al-Qurʾān bi-sūbir mārket wa-yaskharu mina al-asmāʾ al-ḥusnā," Aug. 31, 2006, at https://tinyurl.com/yd623v8c.

27. S. al-Nābulsī, *Sujūn bi-lā quḍbān*, 156; Shākir al-Nābulsī, "Hal satatakarraru miḥnat Abū Zayd maʿa Ḥasan Ḥanafī?" *Al-Rāya*, Oct. 10, 2006, at https://tinyurl.com/y9cudl7f.

28. S. al-Nābulsī, "Al-Qaraḍāwī wa-l-Sibāʿī wa-Bakrī."

29. S. al-Nābulsī, *Al-Lībirāliyyūn al-judud*, 22 (Art. 5).

30. Al-Akhḍar, "Iṣlāḥ al-Islām ḍarūrī wa-mumkin."

31. Gamāl al-Bannā, *Al-Islām wa-ḥurriyyat al-fikr* (Cairo: Dār al-Shurūq, 2008), 343–44.

32. Al-Qaraḍāwī, *Kayfa nataʿāmalu maʿa al-Qurʾān al-ʿaẓīm?* 249–53, and *Kayfa nataʿāmalu maʿa al-Sunna al-nabawiyya?* 145–73.

33. Al-Qaraḍāwī, *Kayfa nataʿāmalu maʿa al-Qurʾān al-ʿaẓīm?* 252, 63–65.

34. Al-ʿAshmāwī, *Al-Islām al-siyāsī*, 64.

35. G. al-Bannā, *Al-Jihād*, 4–5, 12, 50.

36. S. al-Nābulsī, *Sujūn bi-lā quḍbān*, 108.

37. Al-Qaraḍāwī, *Al-Mubashshirāt bi-intiṣār al-Islām*, 10–11.

38. Al-Qaraḍāwī, *Ummatunā bayna qarnayni*, 242.

39. Al-Qaraḍāwī, *Ummatunā bayna qarnayni*, 232–35.

40. Al-Qaraḍāwī, *Ummatunā bayna qarnayni*, 245.

41. ʿAbd al-Ḥamīd al-Anṣārī, "Tafkīk al-khiṭāb al-dīnī al-mukhātil," *Al-Ittiḥād*, Jan. 15, 2015, at http://www.alittihad.ae/wajhatdetails.php?id=83052. See also Faraj, *Al-Jihād*.

42. For the petition see *Multaqā Rābiṭat al-Wāḥa al-Thaqāfiyya*, "Naṣṣ al-Bayān al-umamī ḍidda al-irhāb," and *Arab News*, "Stop Terror Sheikhs, Muslim Academics Demand."

43. Rafīq Ṣamū'īl, "Marra wāḥid Qaraḍāwī," *Al-Ḥiwār al-Mutamaddin* 3241 (Jan. 9, 2011), at http://www.ahewar.org/debat/show.art.asp?aid=241093.

44. Al-Qaraḍāwī, *Fiqh al-jihād*, 2:1067.

45. Ṣamū'īl, "Marra wāḥid Qaraḍāwī."

46. Al-Qaraḍāwī, *Malāmiḥ al-mujtama' al-Muslim*, 87.

47. Ṣamū'īl, "Marra wāḥid Qaraḍāwī."

48. Al-Qaraḍāwī, *Khiṭābunā al-Islāmī*, 31.

49. Al-Qaraḍāwī, *Khiṭābunā al-Islāmī*, 170.

50. Al-Qaraḍāwī, *Fiqh al-jihād*, 1:583–91.

51. Al-Qaraḍāwī, *Al-Mubashshirāt bi-intiṣār al-Islām*, 30–31.

52. Al-Ṭarṭūsī, *Al-Jihād wal-siyāsa al-shar'īyya*, 34.

53. 'Abdallah b. Bajād al-'Utaybī, "Al-Islām al-musallaḥ wa-l-Islām al-siyāsī," *Al-Sharq al-Awsaṭ*, Mar. 3, 2013, at https://tinyurl.com/y8g7f3k6.

54. Al-Qaraḍāwī, *Liqā' maftūḥ ma'a al-'allāma al-Qaraḍāwī*, 14–15.

55. Al-Qaraḍāwī, "Man al-mas'ūl 'an aḥdāth al-ḥādī 'ashar min Sibtimbir," 6:89–95.

56. Al-Qaraḍāwī, "Man al-mas'ūl 'an aḥdāth al-ḥādī 'ashar min Sibtimbir."

57. Mawqi' Samāḥat al-Shaykh Yūsuf al-Qaraḍāwī, "Multaqā talāmīth al-Qaraḍāwī."

58. Al-Qaraḍāwī, *Al-Shaykh Salmān al-'Awda yuḥāwiru al-'allāma Yūsuf al-Qaraḍāwī.*

59. Shaykh Yūsuf al-Qaraḍāwī, *Kalimāt qayyima lil-Shaykh Yūsuf al-Qaraḍāwī: Multaqā al-Imām al-Qaraḍāwī ma'a al-talāmīdh wal-aṣḥāb*, video, 2007, http://www.dailymotion.com/video/xu5ejd.

Appendix A. Fundamental Principles of the *Wasaṭiyya* and Renewal Movement

1. This passage may be compared to the first of Ḥasan al-Bannā's "twenty fundamentals" (*uṣūl*) for understanding Islam: "Islam is a comprehensive system [*niẓām shāmil*] touching on every manifestation of life, for it is state and homeland or government and nation; morality and power or mercy and justice; culture and law or knowledge and judgment; matter and wealth or profit and wealth; jihad and *da'wa* or army and idea. It is also honest faith and correct worship at the same time" (al-Bannā, *Majmū'at rasā'il*, 356). Al-Qaraḍāwī interpreted and elaborated al-Bannā's principle of the all-encompassing nature of Islam (*shumūl al-Islām*).

2. This principle may be compared to al-Bannā's second principle in "Message of Teachings": "The Holy Qur'ān and the pure Sunna are the source for every Muslim to understand the laws [*aḥkām*] of Islam" (*Majmū'at rasā'il*, 356). Al-Qaraḍāwī dedicated a book to interpreting this principle: see *Al-Marji'iyya al-'ulyā fī al-Islām lil-Qur'ān wal-Sunna*.

3. This reflects the idea expressed in Q51:56: "I created jinn and mankind only to worship Me."

4. Based on Q103:3.

5. The term *'aṣaba* means heirs who do not inherit a predefined part of the estate, such as half, fourth, or third, but rather some undefined amount—for example, a brother and a nephew. *Arḥām* means relatives of the parents, such as the uncles and aunts on either side.

Appendix B. The Neoliberal Platform by Shākir al-Nābulsī

1. The translation is based in part on MEMRI, "An Arab Nationalist Attack on the Arab Progressives."

2. The requirement for the woman to cover her body—often interpreted as a requirement to cover the entire body except for the face and hands—is based in most religious rulings on two Qur'ānic verses: 24:31 and 33:59.

3. Based on Q4:11, a woman receives half the share of inheritance available to a man bearing the same degree of relation to the decedent.

4. Based on Q2:282, jurists determined that the testimony of two women is equal to that of one man.

5. Many jurists forbid women to take part in political life, based, inter alia, on Q4:34, which states that the husband has *qiwāma*—that is, responsibility for and authority over his wife—and on the *ḥadīth* that states that "a people ruled by a woman will not succeed."

6. This is an allusion to a famous medieval Islamic saying: "He who engages in logic courts heresy [*man tamanṭaqa tazandaqa*]."

7. This is a quote from medieval Arab poet Abū Firās al Ḥamadānī (d. 968). The entire line says: "We are people who do not accept half measures; we either take leadership of the worlds or choose the grave" (*Anā al-Baḥr*, "Sharḥ qaṣīdat, Arāka 'aṣī al-dam' li- Abī Firās al-Ḥamadānī," July 28, 2017, at https://tinyurl.com/y9wtzyvj).

8. In his book *Al-Mar'a al-jadīda* (Madīnat Naṣr, Egypt: Mu'assasat Hindāwī li-i-Ta'līm wa-l-Thaqāfa, 2012), Qāsim Amīn writes: "Human perfection does not necessarily have to be sought in the past. Moreover, if Allah will want to confer grace upon his servants, it will be in the far future" (89).

Bibliography

English-Language Sources

Abrahamov, Binyamin, "Ibn Taymiyya on the Agreement of Reason with Tradition." *The Muslim World* 82, nos. 3–4 (July–Oct. 1992): 256–72.

Altman, Israel Elad. *Strategies of the Muslim Brotherhood Movement 1928–2007.* Washington, DC: Hudson Institute, 2009.

Arab News. "Stop Terror Sheikhs, Muslim Academics Demand." Oct. 30, 2004. At http://www.arabnews.com/node/257332.

Baker, Raymond William. *Islam without Fear: Egypt and the New Islamists.* Cambridge, MA: Harvard Univ. Press, 2003.

Bartal, Shaul, and Nesya Rubinstein-Shemer. *Hamas and Ideology: Sheikh Yūsuf al-Qaraḍāwī on the Jews, Zionism, and Israel.* London: Routledge, 2018.

Bedford Row International. *The Egyptian Experience of the Muslim Brotherhood in Power 2012–2013.* London: Bedford Row International, June 3, 2015. At http://9bri.com/wp-content/uploads/2015/06/Report-II.9BRi.Muslim-Brotherhood-in-Power.pdf.

Bonner, Michael. *Jihad in Islamic History: Doctrines and Practice.* Princeton, NJ: Princeton Univ. Press, 2006.

Bonney, Richard. *Jihad from Qur'ān to bin Laden.* New York: Palgrave Macmillan, 2007.

Brachman, Jarret M. *Global Jihadism: Theory and Practice.* London: Routledge, 2009.

Brahimi, Alia. *Jihad and Just War in the War on Terror.* Oxford: Oxford Univ. Press, 2010.

Brisard, Jean-Charles, and Damien Martinez. *Zarqawi: The New Face of al-Qa'ida.* Cambridge: Policy Press, 2005.

Bush, George. "9/11 George Bush: This Crusade Is Gonna Take a While." Sept. 17, 2001. At https://www.youtube.com/watch?v=7TRVcnX8Vsw.

Caeiro, Alexandre, and Mahmoud al-Saify. "Qaraḍāwī in Europe, Europe in Qaraḍāwī? The Global Mufti's European Politics." In *Global Mufti: The Phenomenon of Yusuf al-Qaradawi*, edited by Bettina Gräf and Jakob Skovgaard-Petersen, 109–48. New York: Columbia Univ. Press, 2009.

Calvert, John. *Sayyid Qutb and the Origins of Radical Islamism*. New York: Columbia Univ. Press, 2013.

Cook, Michael. *Commanding Right and Forbidding Wrong in Islamic Thought*. Cambridge: Cambridge Univ. Press, 2000.

Dekmejian, R. Hrair. *Islam in Revolution: Fundamentalism in the Arab World*. 2nd ed. Syracuse, NY: Syracuse Univ. Press, 1995.

Esposito, John L. *The Islamic Threat: Myth or Reality?* New York: Oxford Univ. Press, 1992.

———. *Unholy War: Terror in the Name of Islam*. Oxford: Oxford Univ. Press, 2002.

Esposito, John L., and John O. Voll. "Introduction: Muslim Activist Intellectuals and Their Place in History." In *Makers of Contemporary Islam*, edited by John L. Esposito and John O. Voll, 3–23. Oxford: Oxford Univ. Press, 2001.

———, eds. *Makers of Contemporary Islam*. Oxford: Oxford Univ. Press, 2001.

El Fadl, Khaled Abou. "Reply." In *Islam and the Challenge of Democracy: A Boston Review Book: Khaled Abou El Fadl*, edited by Joshua Cohen and Deborah Chasman, 109–28. Princeton, NJ: Princeton Univ. Press, 2004.

Firestone, Reuven. *Jihad: The Origin of Holy War in Islam*. New York: Oxford Univ. Press, 1999.

Friedmann, Yohanan. *Tolerance and Coercion in Islam: Interfaith Relations in the Muslim Tradition*. Cambridge: Cambridge Univ. Press, 2003.

Fromherz, Allen J. *Qatar: A Modern History*. London: I. B. Tauris, 2012.

Gerges, Fawaz A. *The Far Enemy: Why Jihad Went Global*. 2nd ed. Cambridge: Cambridge Univ. Press, 2010.

———. *ISIS: A History*. Princeton, NJ: Princeton Univ. Press, 2016.

Goldziher, Ignaz. *Muslim Studies*. Translated by C. R. Barber and S. M. Stern. London: Allen & Unwin, 1890.

———. *The Ẓāhirīs: Their Doctrine and Their History*. Translated by Behn Wolfgang. 1883. Reprint. Leiden: Brill, 2008.

Govrin, David. *The Journey to the Arab Spring: The Ideological Roots of the Middle East Upheaval in Arab Liberal Thought*. London: Vallentine Mitchell, 2014.

Gräf, Bettina. "The Concept of *Wasaṭiyya* in the Work of Yūsuf al-Qaraḍāwī." In *Global Mufti: The Phenomenon of Yusuf al-Qaradawi*, edited by Bettina Gräf and Jakob Skovgaard-Petersen, 213–38. New York: Columbia Univ. Press, 2009.

———. "The International Association of Muslim Scholars: Yusuf al-Qaradawi and the Foundation of a 'Global Muslim Authority.'" *Qantara* 1 (2005). At http://en.qantara.de/wcsite.php?wc_c=6081&printmode=1.

———. "Sheikh Yūsuf al-Qaraḍāwī in Cyberspace." *Die Welt Des Islams* 47, nos. 3–4 (2007): 403–21.

Gräf, Bettina, and Jakob Skovgaard-Petersen, eds. *Global Mufti: The Phenomenon of Yūsuf al-Qaradawi*. New York: Columbia Univ. Press, 2009.

Gugart, François. *Islamism in the Shadow of al-Qaʿida*. Translated by Patrick Hutchinson. Austin: Univ. of Texas Press, 2008

Gwynne, Rosalind W. "Usama bin Laden, the Qurʿan, and Jihad." *Religion* 36 (2006): 61–90.

Haddad, Yvonne. "Muhammad Abduh: Pioneer of Islamic Reform." In *Pioneers of Islamic Revival*, edited by Ali Rahnema, 30–63. London: Zed Books, 1994.

Hallaq, Wael B. "Can the Sharīʿa Be Restored?" In *Islamic Law and the Challenge of Modernity*, edited by Yvonne Y. Haddad and Barbara F. Stowasser, 21–53. Walnut Creek, CA: Altamira Press, 2004.

———. *A History of Islamic Legal Theories: An Introduction to Sunnī Uṣūl al-Fiqh*. Cambridge: Cambridge Univ. Press, 1997.

———. "Was the Gate of *Ijtihad* Closed?" In *Law and Legal Theory in Classical and Medieval Islam*, edited by Wael B. Hallaq, 3–41. London: Variorum, 1994.

Hammoud, Mirna. "Causes for Fundamentalist Popularity in Egypt." In *Islamic Fundamentalism: Myths and Realities*, edited by Ahmad S. Moussalli, 303–36. London: Ithaca Press, 1998.

Harnisch, Chris, and Quinn Mecham. "Democratic Ideology in Islamist Opposition? The Muslim Brotherhood's Civil State." *Middle Eastern Studies* 45, no. 2 (Mar. 2009): 189–205.

Hassan, Said Fares. *Fiqh al-Aqalliyyāt: History, Development, and Progress*. New York: Palgrave Macmillan, 2013.

Hatina, Meir. "Arab Liberal Thought in Historical Perspective." In *Arab Liberal Thought after 1967: Old Dilemmas, New Perceptions*, edited by Meir Hatina and Christoph Schumann, 23–40. New York: Palgrave Macmillan, 2015.

———. "The Clerics' Betrayal? Islamists, 'Ulama', and the Polity." In *Guardians of Faith in Modern Times: 'Ulama' in the Middle East*, edited by Meir Hatina, 247–64. Leiden: Brill, 2009.

———, ed. *Guardians of Faith in Modern Times: 'Ulama' in the Middle East.* Leiden: Brill, 2009.

———. *Identity Politics in the Middle East: Liberal Thought and Islamic Challenge in Egypt.* London: I. B. Tauris, 2007.

———. *Martyrdom in Modern Islam: Piety, Power, and Politics.* New York: Cambridge Univ. Press, 2014.

———. "Redeeming Sunni Islam: Al-Qa'ida's Polemic against the Muslim Brethren." *British Journal of Middle Eastern Studies* 39, no. 1 (2012): 101–13.

Haykel, Bernard. "On the Nature of Salafi Thought and Action." In *Global Salafism: Islam's New Religious Movement,* edited by Roel Meijer, 33–57. New York: Columbia Univ. Press, 2009.

Hegghammer, Thomas. "Jihadi-Salafis or Revolutionaries? On Religion and Politics in the Study of Militant Islamism." In *Global Salafism: Islam's New Religious Movement,* edited by Roel Meijer, 244–66. New York: Columbia Univ. Press, 2009.

Helfont, Samuel. *Yusuf al-Qaradawi: Islam and Modernity.* Tel Aviv: Moshe Dayan Center, Tel Aviv Univ., 2009.

Holtmann, Philipp. *Abu Musab al Surī's Jihad Concept.* Tel Aviv: Moshe Dayan Center, Tel Aviv Univ., 2009.

International Federation for Human Rights (FIDH). "One Year into Mohamed Morsi's Term: Manifold Abuses and the Systematic Undermining of the Rule of Law." Press release by twenty rights organizations, including FIDH member organizations in Egypt, July 3, 2013. At https://tinyurl.com/y9aqv29k.

Johnston, David L. "Emerging Voices in Islamic Jurisprudence." *Humantrustees,* Oct. 8, 2012. At http://humantrustees.org/blogs/item/74-qemerging-voices.

———. "Shaykh Yusuf al-Qaradawi: Standard Bearer of the 'New Purposive Fiqh." Paper presented at the *Journal of Law and Religion* conference "Emerging Voices in Islamic Jurisprudence," Sept. 28, 2012, St. Paul, MN.

———. "Yusuf al-Qaradawi's Purposive Fiqh: Promoting or Demoting the Future Role of the 'Ulamā'." In *Maqāṣid al-Sharī'a and Contemporary Reformist Muslim Thought: An Examination,* edited by Adis Duderija, 39–71. New York: Palgrave Macmillan, 2014.

Kamali, Mohammad Hashim. *The Middle Path of Moderation in Islam: The Qur'ānic Principle of Wasaṭiyyah.* Oxford: Oxford Univ. Press, 2015.

Keddie, Nikki R. "Sayyid Jamal al-Din al-Afghani." In *Pioneers of Islamic Revival,* edited by Ali Rahnema, 11–29. London: Zed Books, 1994.

Kelsay, John. *Arguing the Just War in Islam*. Cambridge, MA: Harvard Univ. Press, 2007.

Kepel, Gilles. "Islamism Reconsidered: A Running Dialogue with Modernity." *Harvard International Review*, Summer 2000, 1–11.

———. *Jihad: The Trail of Political Islam*. Translated by Anthony F. Roberts. Cambridge, MA: Belknap Press of Harvard Univ. Press, 2002.

———. *The Prophet and Pharaoh: Muslim Extremism in Egypt*. Translated by Jon Rothschild. London: Alsaqi Books, 1985.

Kerr, Malcolm H. *Islamic Reform: The Political and Legal Theories of Muḥammad 'Abduh and Rashīd Riḍā*. Berkeley: Univ. of California Press, 1966.

Krämer, Gudrun. "Drawing Boundaries: Yūsuf al-Qaraḍāwī on Apostasy." In *Speaking for Islam: Religious Authorities in Muslim Societies*, edited by Gudrun Krämer and Sabine Schmidtke, 181–217. Leiden: Brill, 2006.

———. Preface to *Global Mufti: The Phenomenon of Yusuf al-Qaradawi*, edited by Bettina Gräf and Jakob Skovgaard Petersen, ix–xi. New York: Columbia Univ. Press, 2009.

Kramer, Martin. "Coming to Terms: Fundamentalists or Islamists." *Middle East Quarterly*, Spring 2003, 65–77.

———. "Hour of Power with an Islamist Superstar." Nov. 13, 2002. At http://www.martinkramer.org/sandbox/2002/11/hour-of-power-with-an-islamist-superstar/.

Kugle, Scott, and Stephen Hunt. "Masculinity, Homosexuality, and the Defence of Islam: A Case Study of Yusuf al-Qaradawi's Media Fatwa." *Religion and Gender* 2, no. 2 (2012): 254–79.

Lacroix, Stéphane. "Between Revolution and Apoliticism: Nasir al-Din al-Albani and His Impact on the Shaping of Contemporary Salafism." In *Global Salafism: Islam's New Religious Movement*, edited by Roel Meijer, 58–80. New York: Columbia Univ. Press, 2009.

Landau-Tasseron, Ella. "The 'Cyclical Reform': A Study of the Mujaddid Tradition." *Studia Islamica* 70 (1989): 79–117.

———. *Delegitimizing ISIS on Islamic Grounds: Criticism of Abu Bakr al-Baghdadi by Muslim Scholars*. Inquiry & Analysis Report no. 1205. Washington, DC: Middle East Media Research Institute, Nov. 19, 2015. At http://www.memri.org/publicdocs/MEMRI_IA_1205_Delegitimizing_ISIS_On_Islamic_Grounds-FINAL.pdf.

———. "Is Jihād Comparable to Just War? A Review Article." *Jerusalem Studies in Arabic and Islam* 34 (2008): 535–50.

———. "Jihād." In *EQ (Encyclopaedia of the Qur'ān)*, vol. 3, 35–43. Leiden: Brill, 2003.

———. *"Non-combatants" in Muslim Legal Thought*. Washington, DC: Hudson Institute, 2006.

———. "The Origins of the Idea of Jihad." In *War and Peace* (in Hebrew), edited by Shlomo Avineri, 99–106. Jerusalem: Zalman Shazar Center, 2010.

———. *A Self Profile of the Islamic State: The Creedal Document*. Inquiry & Analysis Report no. 1253. Washington, DC: Middle East Media Research Institute, June 1, 2016.

Lauzière, Henri. "The Construction of Salafiyya: Reconsidering Salafism from the Perspective of Conceptual History." *International Journal of Middle East Studies* 42 (2010): 369–89.

———. *The Making of Salafism: Islamic Reform in the Twentieth Century*. New York: Columbia Univ. Press, 2016.

Lav, Daniel. *Radical Islam and the Revival of Medieval Theology*. Cambridge: Cambridge Univ. Press, 2012.

Lavi, Limor. *An Examination of Egypt's Draft Constitution Part I: Religion and State: The Most Islamic Constitution in Egypt's History*. Inquiry & Analysis Report no. 904. Washington, DC: Middle East Media Research Institute, Dec. 3, 2012. At http://www.memri.org/report/en/print6846.htm.

———. *An Examination of Egypt's Draft Constitution Part II: The Egyptian Public Debate over Religion and State*. Inquiry & Analysis Report no. 906. Washington, DC: Middle East Media Research Institute, Dec. 5, 2012. At http://www.memri.org/report/en/print6851.htm.

———. *Muslim Brotherhood Efforts to Take Over Egyptian Media*. Inquiry & Analysis Report no. 875. Washington, DC: Middle East Media Research Institute, Aug. 22, 2012. At https://www.memri.org/reports/muslim-brotherhood-efforts-take-over-egyptian-media.

Layish, Aharon. "Islamic Law in the Modern World: Nationalization, Islamization, Reinstatement." *Islamic Law and Society* 21 (2014): 276–307.

Lewis, Bernard. *What Went Wrong? Western Impact and Middle Eastern Response*. Oxford: Oxford Univ. Press, 2002.

Litvak, Meir. "Islamic Democracy vs. Western Democracy: The Debate among Islamists." In *Middle Eastern Societies and the West*, edited by Meir Litvak, 199–219. Tel Aviv: Moshe Dayan Center, Tel Aviv Univ., 2006.

El Mahdy, Reem Ahmed. "The Compatibility of Yusuf al-Qaradawi's Wasateyya School of Thought with the Second Generation of the Muslim Brotherhood."

MA thesis, American Univ. in Cairo, 2014. At http://dar.aucegypt.edu/handle/10526/4298.

Maher, Shiraz. *Salafi-Jihadism: The History of an Idea*. Oxford: Oxford Univ. Press, 2016.

McCants, William. *The ISIS Apocalypse: The History, Strategy, and Doomsday Vision of the Islamic State*. New York: St. Martin's Press, 2015.

McCants, William, Jarret Brachman, and Lieutenant Colonel Joseph Felter. *Militant Ideology Atlas: Research Compendium*. West Point, NY: Combating Terrorism Center, 2006.

Meijer, Roel, ed. *Global Salafism: Islam's New Religious Movement*. New York: Columbia Univ. Press, 2009.

———. Introduction to *Global Salafism: Islam's New Religious Movement*, edited by Roel Meijer, 1–32. New York: Columbia Univ. Press, 2009.

Michot, Yahya M. "The Fatwa of Shaykh Yusuf al-Qaradawi against Gaddafi." Scribd.com, Mar. 15, 2011. At https://www.scribd.com/doc/51219918/The-fatwa-of-Shaykh-Yusuf-al-Qaradawi-against-Gaddafi.

Middle East Media Research Institute (MEMRI). "An Arab Nationalist Attack on the Arab Progressives." Special Dispatch no. 759, Aug. 6, 2004. At https://www.memri.org/reports/arab-nationalist-attack-arab-progressives.

———. "Leading Progressive Qatari Cleric: By Permitting Suicide Operations, al-Qaradhawi and His Ilk Have Caused a Moral Crisis in Islam." Special Dispatch no. 968, Aug. 25, 2005. At http://www.memri.org/report/en/print1453.htm.

———. "Reactions to Sheikh al-Qaradhaei's Fatwa Calling for the Abduction and Killing of American Civilians in Iraq." Special Dispatch no. 794, Oct. 6, 2004. At https://tinyurl.com/y9y4c4dx.

———. "Sheikh al-Qaradhawi: Permission Previously Given to Palestinians to Carry Out Suicide Attacks—No Longer Valid; They Now Have Missiles That Can Strike Deep Inside Israel." Special Dispatch no. 6116, July 28, 2015. At www.memri.org/report/en/print8678.htm.

———. "Sheikh Yousuf al-Qaradawi Calls for Resistance, Jihad, and Martyrdom Following Trump's Recognition of Jerusalem as Israel's Capital." Special Dispatch no. 7264, Jan. 4, 2018. At https://tinyurl.com/ybkzmn49.

Mitchell, Richard P. *The Society of the Muslim Brothers*. New York: Oxford Univ. Press, 1993.

Moussa, Mohammed. *Politics of the Islamic Tradition: The Thought of Mohammad al-Ghazali*. New York: Routledge, 2016.

Moustafa, Tamir. "Conflict and Cooperation between the State and Religious Institutions in Contemporary Egypt." *International Journal of Middle East Studies* 32 (2000): 3–22.

Nafi, Basheer M. "Fatwā and War: On the Allegiance of the American Muslim Soldiers in the Aftermath of September 11." *Islamic Law and Society* 2, no. 1 (2004): 78–116.

Nasr, Seyyed Vali Reza. "Mawdudi and the Jama'at-I Islami: The Origins, Theory, and Practice of Islamic Revivalism." In *Pioneers of Islamic Revival*, edited by Ali Rahnema, 98–124. London: Zed Books, 2008.

Opwis, Felicitas. *Maṣlaḥa and the Purpose of the Law: Islamic Discourse on Legal Change from the 4th/10th to the 8th/14th Century.* Leiden: Brill, 2010.

———. "Maṣlaḥa in Contemporary Islamic Legal Theory." *Islamic Law and Society* 12, no. 2 (2005): 182–223.

Pargeter, Alison. *The Muslim Brotherhood: The Burden of Tradition.* London: Saqi, 2010.

———. *The Muslim Brotherhood from Opposition to Power.* London: Saqi Books, 2013.

Peters, Rudolph. *Jihad in Classical and Modern Islam: A Reader.* Princeton, NJ: Markus Wiener, 1996.

Polka, Sagi. "Between Liberalism and Fundamentalism" (in Hebrew). PhD diss., Bar Ilan Univ., 2000.

———. "The Centrist Stream in Egypt and Its Role in the Public Discourse Surrounding the Shaping of the Country's Cultural Identity." *Middle Eastern Studies* 39, no. 3 (July 2003): 39–64.

———. "Taqrib al-Madhahib: Qaradawi's Declaration of Principles Regarding Sunni-Shi'i Ecumenism." *Middle Eastern Studies* 49, no. 3 (2013): 414–29.

Ul-Qadri, Muhammad Tahir [Muḥammad Ṭāhir al-Qadrī]. *Fatwa on Terrorism and Suicide Bombings.* Foreword by John L. Esposito. Introduction by Joel S. Hayward. London: Minhaj ul-Quran International, 2010.

———. *Introduction to the Fatwa on Suicide Bombings and Terrorism: Table of Contents, Summary, & Bibliography.* Translated by Shaykh Abdul Aziz Dabbagh. London: Minhaj ul-Quran International, 2010.

The Qur'an: A New Translation. Translated by M. A. S. Abdel Haleem Oxford: Oxford Univ. Press, 2005.

Rahnema, Ali, ed. *Pioneers of Islamic Revival.* London: Zed Books, 1994.

Reiter, Yitzhak. *War, Peace, and International Relations in Islam: Muslim Scholars on Peace Accords with Israel.* Brighton, UK: Sussex Academic Press, 2011.

Roy, Olivier. *The Failure of Political Islam*. Translated by Carol Volk. London: I. B. Tauris, 1994.

———. *Globalized Islam: The Search for a New Ummah*. New York: Columbia Univ. Press, 2004.

Safran, Nadav. *Egypt in Search of Political Community: An Analysis of the Intellectual and Political Evolution of Egypt, 1804–1952*. 2nd ed. Cambridge, MA: Harvard Univ. Press, 1981.

Salvatore, Armando. *Islam and the Political Discourse of Modernity*. London: Ithaca Press, 1997.

Shaham, Ron. "The Rhetoric of Legal Disputation: Neo–Ahl al-Ḥadīth vs. Yūsuf al-Qaraḍāwī." *Islamic Law and Society* 22 (2015): 114–41.

———. "Western Scholars on the Role of the 'Ulamā' in Adapting Sharī'a to Modernity: A Critical Review." In *Guardians of Faith in Modern Times: 'Ulamā' in the Middle East*, edited by Meir Hatina, 171–92. Leiden: Brill, 2009.

Shamir, Shimon. "Liberalism: From Monarchy to Postrevolution." In *Egypt from Monarchy to Republic: A Reassessment of Revolution and Change*, edited by Shimon Shamir, 195–212. Boulder, CO: Westview Press, 1995.

Shamni, Navit. *Egypt under Muslim Brotherhood Rule: The Constitutional Declaration, Dictatorship in the Name of the Revolution*. Inquiry & Analysis Report no. 907. Washington, DC: Middle East Media Research Institute, Dec. 7, 2012. At https://tinyurl.com/ybx3rwr7.

Shavit, Uriya. "Can Muslims Befriend Non-Muslims? Debating *al-Walā' wa-al-Barā'* (Loyalty and Disavowal) in Theory and Practice." *Islam and Christian Relations* 25, no. 1 (2014): 67–88.

———. *Islamism and the West: From "Cultural Attack" to "Missionary Migrant."* London: Routledge, 2014.

———. *Sharī'a and Muslim Minorities: The Wasaṭī and Salafī Approaches to Fiqh al-Aqalliyyāt al-Muslima*. Oxford: Oxford Univ. Press, 2015.

———. "The *Wasaṭī* and *Salafī* Approaches to the Religious Law of Muslim Minorities." *Islamic Law and Society* 19, no. 4 (2012): 416–57.

Shemesh, Menashe. *The Songs of the Islamic State: A Major Tool for Reinforcing Its Narrative, Spreading Its Message, Recruiting Supporters*. Inquiry & Analysis Report no. 1179. Washington, DC: Middle East Media Research Institute, Aug. 10, 2015. At https://tinyurl.com/y75e2bco.

Shepard, William E. "Islam and Ideology: Towards a Typology." *International Journal of Middle East Studies* 19 (1987): 307–36.

Sivan, Emmanuel. *Radical Islam, Medieval Theology, and Modern Politics*. New Haven, CT: Yale Univ. Press, 1985.

Skovgaard-Petersen, Jakob. "The Global Mufti." In *Globalization and the Muslim World: Culture, Religion, and Modernity*, edited by Birgit Schaebler and Leif Stenberg, 153–65. Syracuse, NY: Syracuse Univ. Press, 2004.

———. "In Defense of Muhammad: 'Ulama', Da'iya, and the New Islamic Internationalism." In *Guardians of Faith in Modern Times: 'Ulama' in the Middle East*, edited by Meir Hatina, 291–309. Leiden: Brill, 2009.

———. "Yūsuf al-Qaraḍāwī and al-Azhar." In *Global Mufti: The Phenomenon of Yusuf al-Qaradawi*, edited by Bettina Gräf and Jakob Skovgaard-Petersen, 27–53. New York: Columbia Univ. Press, 2009.

Soage, Ana Belén. "Rashīd Riḍā's Legacy." *The Muslim World* 98, no. 1 (Jan. 2008): 1–23.

———. "Shaykh Yusuf al-Qaradawi: Portrait of a Leading Islamic Cleric." *Middle East Review of International Affairs* 12, no. 1 (Mar. 2008). At http://www.globalpolitician.com/print.asp?id=4328.

———. "Yusuf al-Qaradawi: The Muslim Brothers' Favorite Ideological Guide." In *The Muslim Brotherhood: The Organization and Policies of a Global Islamist Movement*, edited by Barry Rubin, 19–37. New York: Palgrave Macmillan, 2010.

Stacher, Joshua A. "Post-Islamist Rumblings in Egypt: The Emergence of the Wasat Party." *Middle East Journal* 56, no. 3 (Summer 2002): 415–32.

Tamimi, Azzam. "The Origins of Arab Secularism." In *Islam and Secularism in the Middle East*, edited by John L. Esposito and Azzam Tamimi, 13–28. New York: New York Univ. Press, 2000.

Tammam, Husam. "Yūsuf al-Qaraḍāwī and the Muslim Brothers: The Nature of a Special Relationship." In *Global Mufti: The Phenomenon of Yusuf al-Qaradawi*, edited by Bettina Gräf and Jakob Skovgaard-Petersen, 55–83. New York: Columbia Univ. Press, 2009.

Tyan, E. "Djihād." *EI*² 2 (1991): 538–40.

Vatikiotis, P. J. *The History of Modern Egypt: From Muhammad Ali to Mubarak*. 4th ed. Baltimore: Johns Hopkins Univ. Press, 1991.

Vidino, Lorenzo. *The New Muslim Brotherhood in the West*. New York: Columbia Univ. Press, 2010.

Wagemakers, Joas. "Framing the 'Threat to Islam': *Al-Wala' Wa al-Bara'* in Salafi Discourse." *Arab Studies Quarterly* 30, no. 4 (Fall 2008): 1–22.

———. "'The Kāfir Religion of the West': Takfīr of Democracy and Democrats by Radical Islamists." In *Accusations of Unbelief in Islam: A Diachronic*

Perspective on Takfīr, edited by Camilla Adang, Hassan Ansari, Maribel Fierro, and Sabine Schmidke, 327–53. Leiden: Brill, 2016.

———. *A Quietist Jihadi: The Ideology and Influence of Abu Muhammad al-Maqdisi*. Cambridge: Cambridge Univ. Press, 2012.

———. "The Transformation of a Radical Concept: *Al-Wala' Wa-l-Bara'* in the Ideology of Abu Muhammad al-Maqdisi." In *Global Salafism: Islam's New Religious Movement*, edited by Roel Meijer, 81–106. New York: Columbia Univ. Press, 2009.

Warren, David H. "Qatari Support for the Muslim Brotherhood Is More Than Just Realpolitik; It Has a Long, Personal History." *Maydan Politics & Society*, July 12, 2017, 1–7. At https://tinyurl.com/yd7aou65.

———. "The 'Ulamā' and the Arab Uprisings 2011–13: Considering Yusuf al-Qaradawi, the 'Global Mufti,' between the Muslim Brotherhood, the Islamic Legal Tradition, and Qatari Foreign Policy." *New Middle Eastern Studies* 4 (2014): 2–33.

Warren, David H., and Christine Gilmore. "One Nation under God? Yusuf al-Qaradawi's Changing Fiqh of Citizenship in the Light of the Islamic Legal Tradition." *Contemporary Islam* 8, no. 3 (2014): 217–37.

Wickham, Carrie Rosefsky. *The Muslim Brotherhood: Evolution of an Islamist Movement*. Princeton, NJ: Princeton Univ. Press, 2013.

Wiktorowicz, Quintan. "Anatomy of the Salafi Movement." *Studies in Conflict and Terrorism* 29 (2006): 207–39.

Zaman, Muhammad Qasim. *Modern Islamic Thought in a Radical Age: Religious Authority and Internal Criticism*. Cambridge: Cambridge Univ. Press, 2012.

———. *The Ulama in Contemporary Islam: Custodians of Change*. Princeton, NJ: Princeton Univ. Press, 2002.

———. "The 'Ulama' of Contemporary Islam and Their Conceptions of the Common Good." In *Public Islam and the Common Good*, edited by Armando Salvatore and Dale F. Eickelma, 129–55. Leiden: Brill, 2004.

Zeghal, Malika. "Religion and Politics in Egypt: The Ulema of al-Azhar, Radical Islam, and the State (1952–94)." *International Journal of Middle East Studies* 31 (1999): 371–99.

Zelin, Aaron Y. "Jihadis and the Use of the Terms *Terror*, *Terrorist*, and *Terrorism*: A Contextual and Semantic Understanding from Islamic Tradition." 2011. At https://tinyurl.com/ydylay4p.

Zollner, Barbara H. E. *The Muslim Brotherhood: Hasan al-Hudaybi and Ideology*. London: Routledge, 2009.

Arabic Sources

ʻAbd al-ʻAzīz, Basma. *Saṭwat al-naṣṣ khiṭāb al-Azhar wa-azmat al-ḥukm*. Giza, Egypt: Dār Ṣafṣāfa, 2016.

ʻAbd al-Ghafūr, Nāṣir. "Naskh al-Qur'ān bil-Sunna." *Al-Alūka al-Sharʻiyya*, Dec. 22, 2014. At https://tinyurl.com/yblne3jg.

ʻAbd al-Karīm, ʻAmr. *Qaḍāyā al-mar'a fī fiqh al-Qaraḍāwī*. 2nd ed. Giza, Egypt: Qaṭr al-Nadā li-l-Nashr wal-Tawzīʻ, 2009.

ʻAbd al-Nasir, Gamal. "Kalimat al-ra'īs Gamāl ʻAbd al-Nāṣir fī taqdīm al-mīthāq al-waṭanī fī Jāmiʻat al-Qāhira." May 21, 1962. At http://nasser.bibalex.org/Speeches/browser.aspx?SID=1015&lang=ar.

ʻAbd al-Qādir, Ashraf. "Al-Qaraḍāwī ʻadū li-ḥiwār al-adyān." *Al-Ḥiwār al-Mutamaddin* 11507 (Apr. 1, 2006). At http://www.ahewar.org/debat/show.art.asp?aid=61121.

ʻAbd al-Quddūs, Muḥammad. "Al-Shaykh Yūsuf al-Qaraḍāwī: Imām al-wasaṭiyya." Mawqiʻ Samāḥat al-Shaykh Yūsuf al-Qaraḍāwī (website), Oct. 13, 2015. At https://www.al-qaradawi.net/node/2371.

ʻAbd al-Raḥmān b. ʻAbd al-Khāliq. "Ḥukm muʻāhadāt al-ṣulḥ wa-l-salām maʻa al-Yahūd wa-mawqif al-Muslim minhā." 2008. At http://www.ilmway.com/site/maqdis/MS_8332.html.

ʻAbd al-Raḥmān, ʻUmar. *Kalimat ḥaqq: Marāfaʻat al-Shaykh ʻUmar ʻAbd al-Raḥmān fī qaḍiyyat al-jihād*. Cairo: Dār al-Iʻtiṣām, 1987. Electronic copy at http://www.ilmway.com/site/maqdis/MS_8860.html.

ʻAbd al-Rāziq, ʻAlī. *Al-Islām wa-uṣūl al-ḥukm: Baḥth fī al-khilāfa wal-ḥukūma fī al-Islām*. Cairo: Dār al-Hilāl, 1925.

ʻAbd al-Wahhāb, ʻĪsā. "Majlis Jāmiʻat al-Azhar yuwāfiqu ʻalā tadrīs thaqāfat al-wasaṭiyya fī al-Islām." *Al-Waṭan*, June 7, 2015. At http://www.elwatannews.com/news/details/746030.

ʻAbduh, Muḥammad. *Al-Aʻmāl al-kāmila lil-Imām al-Shaykh Muḥammad ʻAbduh*. Edited by Muḥammad ʻImāra. 5 vols. Cairo: Dār al-Shurūq, 1993.

———. "Taʻaddud al-zawjāt." In *Al-Aʻmāl al-kāmila lil-imām al-Shaykh Muḥammad ʻAbduh*, 5 vols., edited by Muḥammad ʻImāra, 82–93. Cairo: Dār al-Shurūq, 1993.

Abū Dajjāna, al-Bāshā. *Ta'ammulāt fī muṣṭalaḥ al-Salafiyya al-jihādiyya*. N.p.: Shabakat al-Fidā' al-Islamiyya, Feb. 23, 2012. Electronic copy at https://tinyurl.com/y9me7v3l.

Abū al-Futūḥ, ʿAbd al-Munʿim. "Al-Qaraḍāwī nāẓir al-madrasa al-Ikhwāniyya." Mawqiʿ Samāḥat al-Shaykh Yūsuf al-Qaraḍāwī (website), Sept. 12, 2007. At https://www.al-qaradawi.net/node/3404.

Abū Muṣʿab al-Sūrī. *Daʿwat al-muqāwama al-Islāmiyya al-ʿalamiyya*. N.p.: n.p., Dec. 2004. Electronic copy at http://www.ilmway.com/site/maqdis/MS_808.html.

Abū Shaqqa, ʿAbd al-Ḥalīm Muḥammad. *Taḥrīr al-marʾa fī ʿaṣr al-risāla: Dirāsa ʿan al-marʾa jāmiʿa li-nuṣūṣ al-Qurʾān al-karīm wa-ṣaḥīḥay al-Bukhārī wa-Muslim*. 3 vols. 7th ed. Cairo: Dār al-Qalam, 2011.

Abū Zahra, Muḥammad. *Al-ʿAlāqāt al-duwaliyya fī al-Islām*. Cairo: Dār al-Fikr al-ʿArabī, 1995.

Abū Zayd, Naṣr Ḥāmid. *Naqd al-khiṭab al-dīnī*. 2nd ed. Cairo: Sīnā lil-Nashr, 1994.

———. *Al-Tafkīr fī zaman al-takfīr: Ḍidda al-jahl wal-zayf wal-khurāfa*. 2nd ed. Cairo: Maktabat Madbūlī, 1995.

———. *Al-Tajdīd wa-l-taḥrīm wa-l-taʾwīl bayna al-maʿrifa al-ʿilmiyya wa-l-khawf min al-takfīr*. Al-Dār al-Bayḍāʾ, Morocco: Al-Markaz al-Thaqāfī al-ʿArabī, 2010.

Abū Zayd, Waṣfī ʿĀshūr. *Al-Imām al-Qaraḍāwī wa-malḥamat al-Intirbūl al-duwalī*. Cairo: Dār al-Bashīr li-l-Thaqāfa wa-l-ʿUlūm, 2015.

———. *Al-Imām al-thāʾir: Dirāsa taḥlīliyya uṣūliyya . . . fī maʿālim ijtihādihi li-l-thawra al-Miṣriyya*. Britton, MI: Sulṭān li-l-Nashr, 2011.

Al-ʿAdīnī, Aḥmad b. Muḥammad b. Manṣūr. *Rafʿ al-lithām ʿan mukhālafāt al-Qaraḍāwī li-sharīʿat al-Islām*. 2nd ed. Ṣanʿāʾ, Yemen: Dār al-Āthār, 2001.

Al-ʿAdnānī, Abū Muḥammad. "Tafrīgh al-kalima al-ṣawtiyya bi-ʿunwān (yā qawmanā ajībū dāʿiya Allāh, Q46:31) lil-Shaykh Abī Muḥammad al-ʿAdnānī." June 24, 2015. At https://justpaste.it/lxzf.

Al-Akhḍar, al-ʿAfīf. "Iṣlāḥ al-Islām ḍarūrī wa-mumkin." *Al-Ḥiwār al-Mutamaddin* 5380 (Dec. 23, 2016). At http://www.ahewar.org/debat/show.art.asp?aid=336211.

———. "Kayfa nujaffifu yanābīʿ al-irhāb?" *Al-Ḥiwār al-Mutamaddin* 504 (May 31, 2003). At http://www.ahewar.org/debat/show.art.asp?aid=7812.

———. "Kayfa nuṣāliḥu al-Islām maʿa al-ʿālam?" *Al-Ḥiwār al-Mutamaddin* 1500 (Mar. 25, 2006). At http://www.ahewar.org/debat/show.art.asp?aid=60508.

———. "Min madrasat al-jihād ilā madrasat al-ijtihād." *Īlāf*, Feb. 3, 2002. At http://elaphjournal.com/Web/Archive/1012748707481471100.html.

Al-ʿAlawānī, Ṭaha Jābir. "Faqīh al-duʿāh wa-dāʿiyat al-fuqahāʾ: Al-Shaykh Yūsuf al-Qaraḍāwī." In *Al-Qaraḍāwī: Kalimāt fī takrīmihi wa-buḥūth fī fikrihi wa-fiqhihi muhdāh ilayhi bi-munāsabat bulūghihi al-aabʿīn*, 2 vols., edited by ʿAbd al-ʿAẓīm al-Dīb, 1:371–88. Cairo: Dār al-Salām, 2004.

Al-Albānī, Muḥammad Nāsir al-Dīn. *Jilbāb al-marʾa al-Muslima fī al-Kitāb wal-Sunna*. Cairo: Dār al-Salām, n.d.

Al-ʿAlyānī, ʿAlī b. Nafīʿ. *Ahamiyyat al-jihād fī nashr al-daʿwa al-Islāmiyya wal-radd ʿalā al-ṭawāʾif al-ḍālla fīhi*. 2nd ed. Riyadh: Dār Ṭayyiba, 1995.

Amīn, Qāsim. *Al-Marʾa al-jadīda*. Madīnat Naṣr, Egypt: Muʾassasat Hindāwī li-i-Taʿlīm wa-l-Thaqāfa, 2012.

Anā al-Baḥr. "Sharḥ qaṣīdat, Arāka ʿaṣī al-damʿ li- Abī Firās al Ḥamadānī." July 28, 2017. At https://tinyurl.com/y9wtzyvj.

Al-Anṣārī, ʿAbd al-Ḥamīd. "ʿAlā al-majāmiʿ al-fiqhiyya taḥrīm al-aʿmāl al-intiḥāriyya." *Al-Bayān*, Apr. 16, 2007. At https://tinyurl.com/yawt2ufl.

———. "Al-Intiḥāriyyūn abṭāl lākin fī al-jaḥīm." *Al-Waṭan*, May 21, 2016. At https://www.minhaj.org/english/oid/11082/Aljareeda.html.

———. "Limādhā yaqtulūna? Limādhā yufajjirūna? Limādhā yantaḥirūna?" *Al-Rāya al-Qaṭariyya*, July 25, 2005. At https://tinyurl.com/y7w69jv3.

———. "Mā ḥaqīqat fazaʿ al-Qaraḍāwī min al-tashayyuʿ?" Oct. 15, 2008. At http://www.siironline.org/alabwab/maqalat&mohaderat(12)/1311.htm.

———. "Mā al-sabīl ilā ansanat al-khiṭāb al-dīnī?" *Ṣawt al-Ḥurriyya al-Ikhbārī*, Jan. 19, 2010. At http://alhorya.com/arabic/?Action=Details&ID=863.

———. *Qaḍāyā al-marʾa bayna taʿālīm al-Islām wa-taqālīd al-mujtamaʿ*. Cairo: Dār al-Fikr al-ʿArabī, 2000.

———. "Tafkīk al-khiṭāb al-dīnī al-mukhātil." *Al-Ittiḥād*, Jan. 15, 2015. At http://www.alittihad.ae/wajhatdetails.php?id=83052.

———. *Thaqāfat al-karāhiya wa-mustaqbal al-tasāmuḥ al-insānī ilā ayna?* Beirut: Dār Madārik lil-Nashr, 2012. Electronic copy at https://aafaqcenter.com/post/826.8.

Al- ʿArab. "Al-Qarra Dāghī: ʿ95 alf dāʿiya wa-ʿālim bi-l-Ittiḥād aṣbaḥū irhābiyyīn!'" Nov. 24, 2017. At https://tinyurl.com/y9obwe58.

Al-Arab News. "Al-Shaykh al-Qaraḍāwī yaruddu ʿalā taṣrīḥāt shaykh al-Azhar." Dec. 7, 2001. At http://alarabnews.com/alshaab/GIF/07-12-2001/n23.htm.

Al-ʿArabī al-Jadīd. "Al-Ittiḥād al-ʿAlamī li-ʿUlamāʾ al-Muslimīn yadʿū ilā taghlīb al-ḥikma wa-rafʿ al-ḥiṣār ʿan Qaṭar." June 12, 2017. At https://tinyurl.com/ybf8m6ve.

ʿAsfūr, Jābir. *Ḍidda al-taʿaṣṣub*. Cairo: Maktabat al-Usra, 2000.

Al-ʿAshmāwī, Muḥammad Saʿīd. *Ḥaqīqat al-ḥijāb wa-ḥujjiyyat al-ḥadīth*. 2nd ed. Cairo: Maktabat Madbūlī al-Ṣaghīr, 1995.

———. *Al-Islām al-siyāsī*. 4th ed. Cairo: Maktabat Madbūlī al-Ṣaghīr, 1996.

———. *Jawhar al-Islām*. Cairo: Maktabat Madbūlī al-Ṣaghīr, 1996.

———. *Uṣūl al-sharīʿa*. 4th ed. Cairo: Maktabat Madbūlī al- Ṣaghīr, 1996.

Al-ʿAsqalānī, Ibn Ḥajar. *Fatḥ al-bārī sharḥ Ṣaḥīḥ al-Bukhārī*. 13 vols. Giza, Egypt: Dār al-Kutub al-Salafiyya, n.d. Electronic copy at https://ia801303.us.archive.org/3/items/FP2021/13_2034.pdf.

Al-ʿAwda, Salmān. "Al-Mithliyya lā tuqṣī aṣḥābahā mina al-Islām raghma annahā ʿamal āthim." *Raʾy al-Yawm*, May 2, 2016. At http://www.raialyoum.com/?p=433023.

Aʿzīz, Nūr al-Dīn b. Rābiḥ. *Al-Wasaṭiyya wal-iʿtidāl fī al-manhaj al-daʿwī ʿind al-Shaykh Muḥammad al-Ghazālī*. Damascus: Dar al-Fikr, 2010.

ʿAzzām, ʿAbdallah. *Al-ʿAqīda wa-atharuhā fī bināʾ al-jīl*. Beirut: Dār Ibn Ḥazm, 1990. Electronic copy at http://www.ilmway.com/site/maqdis/MS_161.html.

———. *Dhikrayāt Filasṭīn*. Peshawar, Pakistan: Markaz al-Shahīd ʿAzzām al-Iʿlāmī, n.d. Electronic copy at http://www.ilmway.com/site/maqdis/MS_9006.html.

———. *Al-Difāʿ ʿan arāḍī al-Muslimīn ahamm furūḍ al-aʿyān*. ʿAmmān, Jordan: Maktabat al-Risāla al-Ḥadītha, 1987. Electronic copy at http://www.ilmway.com/site/maqdis/MS_10202.html.

———. *Fī al-jihād ādāb wa-aḥkām*. N.p.: n.p., n.d. Electronic copy at http://www.ilmway.com/site/maqdis/MS_10190.html.

———. *Fī ẓilāl sūrat al-Tawba*. Peshawar, Pakistan: Markaz al-Shahīd ʿAzzām al-Iʿlāmī, n.d. Electronic copy at http://www.ilmway.com/site/maqdis/MS_9006.html.

———. *ʿIbar wa-baṣāʾir lil-jihād fī al-ʿaṣr al-ḥāḍir*. ʿAmmān, Jordan: Maktabat al-Riṣāla al-Ḥadītha, 1987. Electronic copy at http://www.ilmway.com/site/maqdis/MS_10040.html.

———. *Ilḥaq bil-qāfila*. Ṣanʿāʾ, Yemen: Maktabat al-Jīl al-Jaḍīd, 1990. Electronic copy at http://www.ilmway.com/site/maqdis/MS_10191.html.

———. "Jihād . . . lā irhāb." Jan. 1987. At http://www.ilmway.com/site/maqdis/MS_9045.html.

———. *Muqaddima fī-l-hijra wal-iʿdād*. N.p.: n.p., n.d. Electronic copy at http://www.ilmway.com/site/maqdis/MS_9006.html.

———. "Sayyid Quṭb ʿishrūna ʿāman ʿalā al-shahāda." Oct. 23, 1986. At http://www.ilmway.com/site/maqdis/MS_9077.html.

———. "Waṣiyyat al-shahīd 'Abdallah 'Azzām." *Muntadā al-Tawḥīd*, Apr. 20, 1986. At http://www.eltwhed.com/vb/showthread.php?4285.

'Azzām, 'Abd al-'Azīz Muḥammad. *Al-Qawā'id al-fiqhiyya*. Cairo: Dār al-Ḥadīth, 2005.

Badawī, Rāniyā. "Al-Duktūr Yūsuf al-Qaraḍāwī ra'īs al-Ittiḥād al-'Alamī li-'Ulamā' al-Muslimīn (2:2): Naṣīḥatī lil-ra'īs Mubārak lā tumaddid wa-lā tūrith wa-lā taẓlim ibnaka bil-ḥukm." *Al-Masrī al-Yawm*, Sept. 9, 2008. At https://tinyurl.com/y83dv8zq.

Al-Baghdādī, Abū Bakr. "Al-Dīn al-naṣīḥa [Religion Is Counsel]." Feb. 24, 2007. At http://alaqsagate.org/vb/showthread.php?t=30133.

Al-Baghdādī, Aḥmad. "Qarn al-mar'a." *Al-Ḥiwār al-Mutamaddin* 430 (Mar. 20, 2003). At http://www.ahewar.org/debat/show.art.asp?aid=6183.

———. *Tajdīd al-fikr al-dīnī: Da'wa li-istikhdām al-'aql*. Beirut: Mu'assasat al-Intishār al-'Arabī, 2008. Electronic copy at https://www.books4arab.com/2016/03/pdf_764.html.

Al-Bannā, Gamāl. *Al-Ḥijāb*. Cairo: Dār al-Fikr al-Islāmī, 2002.

———. *Al-Islām wa-ḥuriryyat al-fikr*. Cairo: Dār al-Shurūq, 2008.

———. *Al-Jihād*. Cairo: Dār al-Fikr al-Islāmī, 2002.

———. *Khitān al-banāt laysa Sunna wa-lā makruma wa-lākinna jarīma*. Cairo: Dār al-Fikr al-Islāmī, 2011. Electronic copy at https://tinyurl.com/yat6zryg.

———. *Tafnīd da'wat al-naskh fī al-Qur'ān al-karīm wa-maqālāt ukhrā*. Cairo: Dār al-Shurūq, 2004.

Al-Bannā, Ḥasan. *Majmū'at rasā'il al-imām al-shahīd Ḥasan al-Bannā*. Cairo: Dār al-Tawzī' wal-Nashr al-Islāmiyya, 1992.

———. "Risālat al-ta'ālīm." 1940. Electronic copy at https://tinyurl.com/ydxe5gtu. Also reprinted in *Majmū'at rasā'il al-imām al-shahīd Ḥasan al-Bannā*, 355–70. Cairo: Dār al-Tawzī' wal-Nashr al-Islāmiyya, 1992.

Al-Barqāwī, 'Abdallah. "Rasmiyyan, 4 duwal tuṣannifu Yūsuf al-Qaraḍāwī irhābiyyan." *Saḥīfat Sabq al-Iliktrūniyya*, June 9, 2017. At https://tinyurl.com/yavcm3st.

Baṭīsha, 'Umar. *Al-'Allāma al-Duktūr al-Qaraḍāwī: Shāhid 'alā al-'aṣr*. Giza, Egypt: Dār al-Fārūq li-l-Istithmārāt al-Thaqāfiyya, 2009.

Bawwābat al-Ahrām. "Tawṣiyāt mu'tamar al-Azhar al-'ālamī fī muwājahat al-taṭarruf wal-irhāb." Dec. 4, 2014. At http://gate.ahram.org.eg/News/568856.aspx.

Bin Laden, Osama. "I'lān al-jihād 'alā al-Amrīkān al-muḥtallīn li-Bilād al-Ḥaramayni (akhrijū al-mushrikīn min Jazīrat al-'Arab)." Aug. 23, 1996. At https://tinyurl.com/yb84rz43.

———. "Naṣṣ bayān al-Jabha al-Islāmiyya al-ʿĀlamiyya li-Jihād al-Yahūd wal-Ṣalībiyyīn," "Hal Yuʿtamadu "Bayān al-Jabha al-Islāmiyya al-ʿĀlamiyya?" Feb. 23, 1998. At https://tinyurl.com/yc66cpmo.

———. "Risāla ilā Ibn Bāz bi-buṭlān fatwāhu bi-l-ṣulḥ maʿa al-Yahūd." Rajab 27, AH 1415 [Dec. 30, 1994]. At http://www.ilmway.com/site/maqdis/MS_852.html.

Al-Bulayhid, Khālid b. Saʿūd. "Sharḥ ḥadīth ʿal-Dīn al-naṣīḥa.'" *Ṣayd al-Fawāʾid*, n.d. At https://tinyurl.com/ycbpqtem.

Al-Būṭī, Muḥammad Saʿīd Ramaḍān. *Al-Salafiyya marḥala zamaniyya mubāraka lā madhhab Islāmī*. Beirut: Dār al-Fikr al-Muʿāṣir, 2009.

CNN Arabic. "Kibār al-ʿUlamāʾ" tuḥadhdhiru min "Ulamāʾ al-Muslimīn': Tuqaddimu maṣlaḥat ḥaraka ʿalā al-Islām." Oct. 27, 2017. At https://arabic.cnn.com/middle-east/2017/10/27/saudi-muslim-scholars-union-warning.

———. "Muftī al-Suʿūdiyya: 'DĀʿSH' wal-Qāʾida min al-Khawārij yastaḥillāni al-dimāʾ wa-lā naḥsabuhumā ʿalā al-Muslimīn." Aug. 19, 2014. At https://arabic.cnn.com/middleeast/2014/08/19/saudi-mufti-isis.

Al-Ḍabʿān, ʿAlī b. Muḥammad. "Ḥukm al-anāshīd al-Islāmiyya." *Ṣayd al-Fawāʾid*, n.d. At http://www.saaid.net/fatwa/f46.htm.

Dabiq. "The Murtadd Brotherhood." No. 14 (Rajab 1437 [Sept. 2016]): 28–43. At https://www.clarionproject.org/docs/Dabiq-Issue-14.pdf.

Al-Dhāyadī, Mishārī. "Al-Qaraḍāwī wa-ḥālat al-qarḍana." *Al-Sharq al-Awsaṭ*, Jan. 15, 2018. At https://tinyurl.com/y8j5lylx.

Al-Dīb, ʿAbd al-ʿAẓīm, ed. *Al-Qaraḍāwī: Kalimāt fī takrīmihi wa-buḥūth fī fkrihi wa-fiqhihi muhdāh ilayhi bi-munāsabat bulūghihi al-sabʿīn*. 2 vols. Cairo: Dār al-Salām, 2004.

Dunyā al-Waṭan. "Ḥasan Ḥanafī yushabbihu al-Qurʾān bi-sūbir mārket wa-yaskharu mina al-asmāʾ al-ḥusnā." Aug. 31, 2006. At https://tinyurl.com/yd623v8c.

———. "Al-Ittiḥād al-ʿĀlamī lil-ʿUlamāʾ yastankiru waṣf Ḥamās bil-irhābiyya wa-yaʿtabiru al-qarār al-Miṣrī musayyasan." Mar. 2, 2015. At https://www.alwatanvoice.com/arabic/news/2015/03/02/671012.html.

Al-Fahd, Nāṣir b. Ḥamad. "Risāla fī ḥukm al-ghināʾ bil-Qurʾān." Aug. 2001. At http://www.ilmway.com/site/maqdis/MS_22514.html.

Al-Falaq, Sālim Mubārak. "Ramaḍān shahr al-jihād." *Ṣayd al-Fawaʾid*, n.d. At http://www.saaid.net/mktarat/ramadan/216.htm.

Al-Faqīh, Iḥsān. "Al-Shaykh Yūsuf al-Qaraḍāwī Ibn Taymiyyat al-ʿaṣr." *Turk Bris*, June 12, 2017. At http://www.turkpress.co/node/35602.

Faraj, ʻAbd al-Salām. *Al-Jihād: Al-Farīḍa al-ghā'iba*. N.p.: n.p., 1981. Electronic copy at http://unfulfilledduty.weebly.com/uploads/1/8/5/3/18537222/__.pdf.

Al-Fawzān, ʻAbd al-ʻAzīz b. Fawzān. "Minhaj ahl al-zaygh fī al-istidlāl." *Al-Bayān* 281 (Dec. 2010). At http://albayan.co.uk/MGZarticle2.aspx?id=509.

Al-Fawzān, Ṣāliḥ. *Al-Iʻlām bi-naqd kitāb "Al-Ḥalāl wal-ḥarām fī al-Islām*. Riyadh: Maktabat al-Maʻārif lil-Nashr wal-Tawzīʻ, 2003. Electronic copy at https://islamhouse.com/ar/books/314806/.

Al-Fazzāzī, Muḥammad b. Muḥammad. "Fatāwā mutasayyiba al-Qaraḍāwī yuḥillu al-ghinā." 1998. At http://www.ilmway.com/site/maqdis/MS_23753.html.

———. "Munāqashat al-Shaykh Yūsuf al-Qaraḍāwī fī mawḍū' al-dīmuqrāṭiyya." Dec. 24, 1996. At http://www.ilmway.com/site/maqdis/MS_23711.html.

Al-Filasṭīnī, Abū Qatāda (a.k.a. ʻUmar b. Maḥmūd Abū ʻUmar). "Jawāz al-ʻamaliyyāt al-istishhādiyya wa-innahā laysat bi-qatl li-l-nafs." Apr. 5, 1995. At http://www.ilmway.com/site/maqdis/MS_5864.html.

———. *Maʻālim al-ṭā'ifa al-manṣūra fī ʻuqr dār al-Mu'minīn (Bilād al-Shām)*. [Copenhagen]: Dār al-Nūr al-Islāmī, n.d.

France 24. "Al-Qaraḍāwī yuqāṭiʻu Mu'tamar Ḥiwār al-Adyān fī al-Dawḥa iʻtirāḍan ʻalā al-ḥuḍūr al-yahūdī." Apr. 23, 2013. At https://tinyurl.com/y85cagz2.

Al-Ghannūshī, Rāshid. "Mā al-jadīd fī *Fiqh al-jihād* lil-Qaraḍāwī?" Al-Jazeera, Sept. 20, 2009. At https://tinyurl.com/yahwk596.

Al-Ghazālī, Abū Ḥāmid. *Al-Iqtiṣād fī al-iʻtiqād*. Beirut: Qutayba li-l-Ṭibāʻa wa-l-Nashr wa-l-Tawzīʻ, 2003. Electronic copy at http://www.ghazali.org/books/iqtisad-ramadan.pdf.

———. *Al-Mustaṣfā fī ʻilm uṣūl al-fiqh*. 4 vols. Al-Madīna, Saudi Arabia: Sharikat al-Madīna al-Munawwara lil-Ṭibāʻa, n.d. Electronic copy at https://ia800509.us.archive.org/22/items/FPmustasfa/mustasfa2.pdf.

Al-Ghazālī, Muḥammad. *Dustūr al-waḥda al-thaqāfiyya bayna al-Muslimīn*. 3rd ed. Al-Manṣūra, Egypt: Dār al-Wafā', 1992.

———. *ʻIlal wa-adwiya: Dirāsāt fī amrāḍ ummatinā wa-wasā'il al-istishfā' minhā maʻa taṣḥīḥ limā wujjiha ilā al-tārīkh al-Islāmī min akhṭā'*. Alexandria, Egypt: Dār al-Daʻwa, 1991.

———. *Jihād al-Daʻwa bayna ʻajz al-dākhil wa-kayd al-khārij*. 4th ed. Giza, Egypt: Nahḍat Miṣr, 2009.

———. *Naḥwa tafsīr mawḍūʻī li-suwar al-Qur'ān al-karīm*. 2nd ed. Cairo: Dār al-Shurūq, 1996.

———. *Qaḍāyā al-mar'a bayna al-taqālīd al-rākida wal-wāfida*. 6th ed. Cairo: Dār al-Shurūq, 1996.

Al-Ghunaymī, 'Abd al-Ākhir Ḥammād. *Muṣṭalaḥāt wa-mafāhīm*. Beirut: Dār al-Bayāriq, 1999. Electronic copy at http://www.ilmway.com/site/maqdis/MS_21389.html.

———. "Waqafāt ma'a fatwā al-Qaraḍāwī ḥawla al-qawā'id al-Amrīkiyya." N.d. At http://www.ilmway.com/site/maqdis/MS_21378.html.

Gum'a, Muḥammad Mukhtār. "Ḥatmiyyat al-qaḍā' 'alā al-irhāb." Aug. 24, 2004. At http://www.awkafonline.com/portal/wp-content/uploads/2015/03/arabic.pdf.

———. "Al-Khiṭāb al-dīnī al-muftarā 'alayhi." Nov. 7, 2014. At https://tinyurl.com/y6v5mq98.

Haniyya, Ismā'īl. "Kalimat al-ustādh Ismā'īl Haniyya, ra'īs wuzarā' Filasṭīn." In *Juhūd al-Duktūr al-Qaraḍāwī fī khidmat al-Islām wa-nuṣrat al-qaḍiyy al-Filasṭīniyya*, Mu'tamar Wizārat al-Awqāf wa-l-Shu'ūn al-Dīniyya, Ghazza, Filasṭīn, edited by Ismā'īl Haniyya, Ṭālib Abū Shi'r, 'Abdallah Abū Jarbū', Wā'il Muḥyī al-Dīn al-Zirr, Yūsuf Farḥāt, Ibrāhīm Aḥmad al-Kurd, 'Iṣām al-'Abd Zuhd, et al., 15–17. Giza, Egypt: Markaz al-I'lām al-'Arabī, 2012.

Haniyya, Ismā'īl, Ṭālib Abū Shi'r, 'Abdallah Abū Jarbū', Wā'il Muḥyī al-Dīn al-Zirr, Yūsuf Farḥāt, Ibrāhīm Aḥmad al-Kurd, 'Iṣām al-'Abd Zuhd, et al., eds. *Juhūd al-Duktūr al-Qaraḍāwī fī khidmat al-Islām wa-nuṣrat al-qaḍiyy al-Filasṭīniyya*. Mu'tamar Wizārat al-Awqāf wa-l-Shu'ūn al-Dīniyya, Ghazza, Filasṭīn. Giza, Egypt: Markaz al-I'lām al-'Arabī, 2012.

Al-Huḍaybī, Ḥasan. *Du'āh lā quḍāh*. Cairo: Dār al-Tawzī' wal-Nashral-Islāmiyya, 1987.

Ḥusayn, 'Abd al-Khāliq. "Hal al-Islām dīn al-tasāmuḥ?" *Al-Ḥiwār al-Mutamaddin* 1587 (June 20, 2006). At http://www.ahewar.org/debat/show.art.asp?aid=67943.

———. "Al-Islām bayna al-tafkhīkh wa-l-tafkhīdh . . . !" *Al-Ḥiwār al-Mutamaddin* 1829 (Feb. 17, 2007). At http://www.ahewar.org/debat/show.art.asp?aid=88920.

———. "Al-Qaraḍāwī dā'iya li-l-irhāb." *Al-Ḥiwār al-Mutamaddin* 949 (Sept. 11, 2004). At http://www.ahewar.org/debat/show.art.asp?aid=23079.

Ḥusayn, Ṭaha. *Mustaqbal al-thaqāfa fī Miṣr*. Cairo: Mu'assasat al-Hindāwī, 2014.

Ibn 'Abd al-Wahhāb, Muḥammad. *Kitāb al-tawḥīd*. Al-Manṣūra, Egypt: Maktabat 'Ibād al-Raḥmān, Maktabat al-'Ulūm wal-Ḥikam, 2008. Electronic copy at http://waqfeya.com/book.php?bid=7781.

Ibn 'Āshūr, Muḥammad al-Ṭāhir. *Maqāṣid al-sharī'a al-Islāmiyya*. 5th ed. Cairo: Dār al-Salām, 2012.

Ibn Bāz, ʿAbd al-ʿAzīz b. ʿAbdallah. "Ḥukm khitān al-ināth." N.d. At https://www.binbaz.org.sa/noor/7735.

———. "Ḥukm man faʿala al-ʿāda al-sirriyya wa-ʿamal qawm Lūṭ wa-waṭʾ al-bahīma." June 30, 1998. At https://www.binbaz.org.sa/fatawa/3181.

———. "Ḥukm al-niqāb lil-marʾa." N.d. At https://tinyurl.com/y7sln8jy.

———. "Ḥukm qiyādat al-marʾa al-sayyāra." In *Al-Fatāwā al-sharʿiyya fī al-masāʾil al-ʿaṣriyya: Min fatāwā ʿulamāʾ al-Balad al-Ḥarām*, edited by Khālid b. ʿAbd al-Raḥmān al-Jeraysī. Riyadh: Muʾssasat al-Jeraysī, 1999. Electronic copy at http://waqfeya.com/book.php?bid=338.

———. *Ḥukm al-ṣulḥ maʿa al-Yahūd fī ḍawʾ al-sharīʿa al-Islāmiyya*. Riyadh: Riʾāsat Idārat al-Buḥūth al-ʿIlmiyya wa-l-Iftāʾ, 1996. Electronic copy at http://waqfeya.com/book.php?bid=2287.

———. "Ḥukm taʿaddud al-zawjāt." N.d. At https://www.binbaz.org.sa/noor/3668.

———. "Mawqif al-sharīʿa al-Islāmiyya min al-ghazw al-ʿIrāqī lil-Kuwayt." N.d. At www.binbaz.org.sa/article/177.

Ibn Kathīr, ʿImād al-Dīn Abī al-Fidāʾ. *Tafsīr al-Qurʾān al-ʿaẓīm*. 6 vols. Beirut: Dār al-Kitāb al-ʿArabī, 2004.

Ibn Rushd, Abū al-Walīd Muḥammad b. Aḥmad. *Bidāyat al-mujtahid wa-nihāyat al-muqtaṣid*. Cairo: Maktabat Ibn Taymiyya, 1994–95. Electronic copy at http://waqfeya.com/book.php?bid=9940.

Ibn Taymiyya, Taqī al-Dīn. *Al-ʿAqīda al-wāsiṭiyya: Jāmiʿ al-durūs al-ʿaqdiyya fī sharḥ al-ʿaqīda al-wāsiṭiyya li-shayk al-Islām Ibn Taymiyya*. Cairo: Dār Ibn Ḥazm, 2009.

———. *Iqtiḍāʾ al-ṣirāṭ al-mustaqīm li-mukhālafat aṣḥāb al-jaḥīm*. 2 vols. Riyadh: Maktabat al-Rushd, n.d. Electronic copy at http://waqfeya.com/book.php?bid=11466; vol. 1 also at https://ia800409.us.archive.org/4/items/FP158171/01_158171.pdf.

———. *Al-Jawāb al-ṣaḥīḥ li-man baddala dīn al-Masīḥ*. Riyadh: Dār al-ʿĀṣima, 1999. Electronic copy at https://tinyurl.com/ycdhpjky.

———. *Majmūʿat al-fatāwā*. Multiple vols. Cairo: Al-Maktaba al-Tawfīqiyya, n.d.

———. *Qāʿida mukhtaṣara fī qitāl al-kuffār wa-muhādanatihim wa-taḥrīm qatlihim li-mujarrad kufrihim*. Riyadh: n.p., 2004.

———. *Al-Siyāsa al-sharʿiyya fī iṣlāḥ al-rāʿī wal-raʿiyya*. Alexandria, Egypt: Dār al-Baṣīra, 2003.

'Īd, 'Abd al-Razzāq. *Yūsuf al-Qaraḍāwī bayna al-tasāmuḥ wal-irhāb (sadanat hayākil al-wahm/naqd al-'aql al-fiqhī)*. Beirut: Dār al-Ṭalī'a, 2005.

Imām, Imām Muḥammad. "Fatwā min al-Qaraḍāwī wal-'Awwā wal-Bishrī wa-ākharīn tujīzu lil-'askariyyīn al-Amīrikiyyīn al-Muslimīn al-mushāraka fī al-ghārāt 'alā Afghanistān." *Al-Sharq al-Awsaṭ*, Oct. 14, 2001. At http://archive.aawsat.com/details.asp?issueno=8070&article=61545#.W_CCu-hvbIU.

———. "Al-Shaykh al-Qaraḍāwī: Istihdāf al-madaniyyīn al-Isrā'īliyyīn juz' min muqāwamat al-iḥtilāl wa-mujāhadatihi." *Al-Sharq al-Awsaṭ*, Dec. 12, 2001. At http://archive.aawsat.com/details.asp?article=77264&issueno=8415#.W_PApehvbIU.

'Imāra, Muḥammad. *Al-Imām Muḥammad 'Abduh: Mujaddid al-dunyā bi-tajdīd al-dīn*. 3rd ed. Cairo: Dār al-Shurūq, 2009.

———. *Izālat al-shubuhāt 'an ma'ānī al-muṣṭalaḥāt*. Cairo: Dār al-Salām, 2010.

———. *Ma'ālim al-minhāj al-Islāmī*. 3rd ed. Cairo: Dār al-Rashād, 1997.

———. *Al-Qaraḍāwī: Al-Madrasa al-fikriyya wal-mashrū' al-fikrī*. Cairo: Nahḍat Miṣr, 1997.

———. *Al-Salafiyya wāḥida? Am salafiyyāt?* Giza, Egypt: Nahḍat Miṣr, 2008.

———. *Al-Salaf wal-Salafiyya*. Cairo: Maktabat Wahba, 2011.

———. "Al-Tajdīd fī al-mashrū' al-ḥaḍārī lil-Imām Ḥasan al-Bannā." In *Al-Mashrū' al-iṣlāḥī lil-Imām Ḥasan al-Bannā: Tasā'ulāt li-qarn jadīd: Buḥūth mu'tamar mi'awiyyat al-Imām al-Bannā*, 2nd ed., edited by Ṭāriq al-Bishrī, 13–37. Cairo: Markaz al-I'lām al-'Arabī, 2007.

Islamic State. "Bayān 'an ghazwat Bārīs al-mubāraka 'alā Faransā al-Ṣalībiyya." Nov. 14, 2015. At https://tinyurl.com/y8nvaxle.

Islamqa. "Mā hiya 'uqūbat al-liwāṭ, wa-hal hunāka farq bayna al-fā'il wa-l-maf'ūl bihi." Mar. 13, 2006. At https://islamqa.info/ar/38622.

———. "Mā huwa khabar al-āḥād?" May 4, 2013. At https://islamqa.info/ar/197554.

———. "'Uqūbat al-siḥāq." Apr. 8, 2003. At https://islamqa.info/ar/21058.

Islam.web. "Sharḥ ḥadīth Inna al-'ulamā' warathat al-anbiyā'." Oct. 5, 2005. At http://fatwa.islamweb.net/fatwa/index.php?page=showfatwa&Option=FatwaId&Id=67822.

Ittiḥād al-'Ālamī li-'Ulamā' al-Muslimīn. "Al-Ta'rīf." Mawqi' al-Ittiḥād, n.d. At http://www.iumsonline.org/ar/ContentDetails.aspx?ID=8150.

'Iyāḍ, al-Qāḍī. *Kitāb al-shifā bi-ta'rīf ḥuqūq al-Muṣṭafā*. Beirut: Dār al-Fikr, 2002. Electronic copy at https://tinyurl.com/ycc9u3gp.

Jāda al-Ḥaqq, Jāda al-Ḥaqq ʿAlī. *Bayān li-l-nās*. Cairo: Dār al-Fārūq, 2014.

Al-Jamʿiyya al-Taʾsīsiyya li-Waḍʿ Mashrūʿ Dustūr Jadīd lil-Bilād. "Mashrūʿ dustūr Jumhūriyyat Miṣr al-ʿArabiyya." Nov. 30, 2012. At https://egelections-2011.appspot.com/Referendum2012/dostor_masr_final.pdf.

Jamʿiyyat ʿUlamāʾ al-Yaman. "Naṣṣ bayān Jamʿiyyat ʿUlamāʾ al-Yaman alladhī yataḍammanu fatwā bi-taḥrīm al-muẓāharāt." Sept. 29, 2011. At https://yemen-press.com/news3298.html.

Al-Jarīsī, Khālid b. ʿAbd al-Raḥmān, ed. *Al-Fatāwā al-sharʿiyya fī al-masāʾil al-ʿaṣriyya: Min fatāwā ʿulamāʾ al-Balad al-Ḥarām*. Riyadh: n.p., 1999. Electronic copy at https://ia801404.us.archive.org/15/items/FP0402/0402.pdf.

Al-Jawziyya, Ibn Qayyim. *Aʿlām al-mūwaqqiʿīn ʿan Rabb al-ʿĀlamīn*. 2 vols. Al-Manṣūra, Egypt: Maktabat al-Īmān, 1999.

———. *Al-Rūḥ fī al-kalām ʿalā arwāḥ al-amwāt wal-aḥyāʾ bil-dalāʾil min al-Kitāb wal-Sunna wal-āthār wa-aqwāl al-ʿalamāʾ*. Beirut: Dār al-Kutub al-ʿIlmiyya, 1999.

Al-Jazeera.net. "Dustūr Miṣr 1971." Dec. 7, 2015. At https://tinyurl.com/yagox2bc.

———. "Duwal al-ḥiṣār tudriju Ittiḥād ʿUlamāʾ al-Muslimīn bi-qawāʾim al-irhāb." Nov. 23, 2017. At https://tinyurl.com/yba8dp62.

———. "Al-Iʿlān al-dustūrī li-l-raʾīs Mursī." Dec. 7, 2012. At https://tinyurl.com/y9gsf66j.

———. "Mīthāq Ḥarakat al-Muqāwama al-Islāmiyya (Ḥamās)." Aug. 1988. At https://tinyurl.com/mzbsbew.

———. "Mubādarat Jamāʿat al-Ikhwān al-Muslimīna lil-iṣlāḥ al-dākhilī fī Miṣr." May 16, 2005. At https://tinyurl.com/y8yhkolg.

———. "Naṣṣ fatwā Markaz al-Albānī bi-ḥurmat al-ʿamaliyyāt al-intiḥāriyya." Jan. 20, 2010. At https://tinyurl.com/yb8659t3.

———. "Al-Qaraḍāwī yantaqidu fatwā ʿulamāʾ bil-Yaman." Oct. 3, 2011. At https://tinyurl.com/y9xvus8t.

———. "Ṭanṭāwī: Qatl al-madaniyyīn al-isrāʾīliyyīn jāʾiz." Mar. 21, 2002. At https://tinyurl.com/ybsancf8.

Kassāb, Akram. *Al-Manhaj al-daʿwī ʿind al-Qaraḍāwī*. Cairo: Maktabat Wahba, 2008.

Khālid, Khālid Muḥammad. *Min hunā nabdaʾu*. 11th ed. Cairo: Maktabat al-Anjilū al-Miṣriyya, 1969.

Khalīl, Muḥammad. "Shaykh al-Azhar: Al-ʿAmaliyyāt al-istishhādiyya ḍidda al-muʿtadīn jāʾiza." *Al-Sharq al-Awsaṭ*, Apr. 20, 2004. At https://tinyurl.com/yaeb9etk.

Khāshuqjī, Jamāl. "Al-ʿAmaliyyāt al-intiḥāriyya akbar azma fikriyya wa-akhlāqiyya tuwājihu al-Islām." *Al-Ittiḥād*, July 19, 2005. At https://www.alittihad.ae/WejhatArticle/13358/.

Al-Khaṭīb, Muʿtazz. "Fī naqd al-qawl bi-l-wasaṭiyya wa-l-iʿtidāl." *Majallat al-Kalima: Muntadā al-Kalima li-l-Dirāsāt wa-l-Abḥāth*, Winter 2007, 113–18. At https://archive.islamonline.net/?p=50.

———. *Al-Qaraḍāwī faqīh al-ṣaḥwa al-Islāmiyya: Sīra fikriyya taḥlīliyya*. Beirut: Markaz al-Ḥaḍāra li-Tanmiyat al-Fikr al-Islāmī, 2009.

———. "Al-Wasaṭiyya al-Islāmiyya wa-fiqh al-dawla: Qirāʾa naqdiyya." *Tabayyun li-l-Dirāsāt al-Fikriyya wa-l-Thaqāfiyya* 1, no. 3 (Winter 2013): 167–92. At https://tinyurl.com/y8ofwm9t.

Mahdī, Muṣṭafā. "Al-Maʿlūm min al-dīn bil-ḍarūra." *Al-Alūka al-Sharʿiyya*, Apr. 30, 2009. At http://www.alukah.net/sharia/0/5654.

Mājid, Amānī. "Al-Qaraḍāwī: Lā ʿalāqa lī bi-tanẓīm al-Ikhwān." *Al-Ahrām*, Feb. 21, 2011. At http://www.ahram.org.eg/Archive/450/2011/2/21/12/63784.aspx.

Al-Majlis al-Islāmī al-Aʿlā fī Ustrāliyā, Dār al-Fatwā. "Al-Azhar al-sharīf ramz al-iʿtidāl wal-wasaṭiyya wa-bihimā naḥmī al-mujtamaʿ min khaṭar al-taṭarruf al-baghīḍ." Dec. 22, 2015. At https://tinyurl.com/y8q5xly6.

Al-Majlis al-Ūrūbī lil-Iftāʾ wal-Buḥūth. "Al-Bayān al-khitāmī lil-dawra al-ʿādiyya al-thāniya ʿashra lil-majlis al-ūrūbī lil-iftāʾ wal-buḥūth." Jan. 31, 2014. At https://tinyurl.com/yddfpdft.

Majmaʿ al-Lugha al-ʿArabiyya. *Muʿjam alfāẓ al-Qurʾān al-karīm*. 2 vols. Cairo: Sharikat al-Iʿlānāt al-Sharqiyya, 1990.

Al-Maqdisī, Abū Muḥammad. *Al-Dīmuqrāṭīyya dīn*. N.p.: n.p., n.d. Electronic copy at http://www.ilmway.com/site/maqdis/MS_26238.html.

———. *Hādhā mā adīnu Allāh bihi: Wujūb nuṣrat al-Muslimīn fī Afghanistān wa-kufr Man ẓāhara ʿalayhim ʿabadat al-Ṣulbān wa-kashf talbīs al-aḥbār wal-ruhbān*. N.p.: n.p., 2001. Electronic copy at http://www.ilmway.com/site/maqdis/MS_65.html.

———. *Hādhihi ʿaqīdatunā*. N.p.: n.p., 1997. Electronic copy at http://www.ilmway.com/site/maqdis/MS_35422.html.

———. "Ḥiwār maʿa al-Shaykh Abī Muḥammad al-Maqdisī sanat 1423." 1423 [2002–3]. At http://www.ilmway.com/site/maqdis/MS_121.html.

———. *Al-Jawāb al-mufīd bi-anna al-mushāraka fī al-barlamān wa-intikhābātihi munāqiḍa li-l-tawḥīd*. N.p.: n.p., 2010. Electronic copy at http://www.ilmway.com/site/maqdis/MS_65.html.

———. *Kashf al-niqāb ʿan sharīʿat al-ghāb*. N.p.: n.p., 1988. Electronic copy at http://www.ilmway.com/site/maqdis/MS_38438.html.

———. *Kashf shubuhāt al-mujādilīn ʿan ʿasākir al-shirk wa-anṣār al-qawānīn*. 2nd ed. N.p.: n.p., 1999. Electronic copy at http://www.ilmway.com/site/maqdis/MS_23039.html.

———. *Al-Kawāshif al-jaliyya fī kufr al-Dawla al-Suʿūdiyya*. 2nd ed. N.p.: n.p., 2000–2001. Electronic copy at http://www.ilmway.com/site/maqdis/MS_65.html.

———. "Mā al-farq bayna tawḥīd al-ḥākimiyya wa-tawḥīd al-ulūhiyya?" N.d. At http://www.ilmway.com/site/maqdis/MS_38161.html.

———. *Millat Ibrāhīm wa-daʿwat al-anbiyāʾ wal-mursalīn wa-asālīb al-ṭughāh fī tamyīʿihā wa-ṣarf al-duʿāh ʿanhā*. N.p.: n.p., 1984. Electronic copy at http://www.ilmway.com/site/maqdis/MS_20383.html.

———. *Al-Risāla al-thalāthīniyya fī al-taḥdhīr min al-ghulū fī al-takfīr*. N.p.: n.p., 1998. Electronic copy at http://www.ilmway.com/site/maqdis/MS_14491.html.

———. "Suʾāl ʿan ṣiḥḥat muṣṭalaḥ (al-Salafiyya al-jihādiyya)?" *Muntadā Minbar al-Tawḥīd wal-Jihād*, question no. 120 (2009). At http://www.ilmway.com/site/maqdis/FAQ/MS_3034.html.

———. "Al-Tawḥīd wal-jihād ʿunwān al-tamayyuz." Aug. 3, 2009. At http://www.ilmway.com/site/maqdis/MS_36546.html.

———. *Waqafāt maʿa thamarāt al-jihād: Bayna al-jahl fī al-sharʿ wa-l-jahl bi-l-wāqiʿ*. Nuskha mazayyada, iḍāfat al-waqfa al-tāsiʿa ʿashar (revised version with addition). N.p.: n.p., 2008. Electronic copy at http://www.ilmway.com/site/maqdis/MS_155.html.

Markaz al-Qāhira li-Dirāsāt Ḥuqūq al-Insān. "Al-Iʿlān al-dustūrī al-jadīd yamnaḥu Mursī sulutāt ilāhiyya wa-yuwajjihu ḍarba qāḍiya li-istiqlāl al-qaḍāʾ." Nov. 24, 2012. At https://tinyurl.com/ycp2ov23.

Al-Māturīdī, Abū Manṣūr. *Tafsīr al-Qurʾān al-ʿaẓīm al-musammā taʾwīlāt ahl al-Sunna*. 10 vols. Beirut: Muʾassasat al-Risāla, 2004. Electronic copy at https://tinyurl.com/yavrdjhm.

Al-Māwardī, Abū al-Ḥasan ʿAlī b. Muḥammad. *Al-Aḥkām al-sulṭāniyya wal-wilāyāt al-dīniyya*. Kuwait City: Dār Ibn Qutayba, 1989. Electronic copy at http://waqfeya.com/book.php?bid=356.

Al-Mawdūdī, Abū al-Aʿlā. *Al-Ḥukūma al-Islāmiyya*. Cairo: Al-Mukhtār al-Islāmī, 1980.

———. *Naẓariyyat al-Islām wa-hadyihi fī al-siyāsa wal-qānūn wal-dustūr*. Translated by Jalīl Ḥasan al-Iṣlāḥī. Damascus: Dār al-Fikr, 1964. Electronic copy at http://elibrary.mediu.edu.my/books/2014/MEDIU16880.pdf.

Mawqiʿ Ḥizb al-Wasaṭ. "Barnāmaj al-ḥizb." N.d. At https://tinyurl.com/yb9amq5o.

Mawqiʿ Samāḥat al-Shaykh Yūsuf al-Qaraḍāwī (al-Qaraḍāwī's website). "Bayān tawḍīḥī ḥawla ra'y al-ʿallāma al-Qaraḍāwī fī al-ʿamaliyyāt al-istishhādiyya." July 27, 2015. At https://www.al-qaradawi.net/node/433.

———. "Inṭilāq aʿmāl multaqā 'al-Imām al-Qaraḍāwī' bil-Dawḥa." July 11, 2007. At https://www.al-qaradawi.net/node/1708.

———. "Al-Islām wa-l-dīmuqrāṭiyya." Apr. 19, 2017. At https://www.al-qaradawi.net/node/3775.

———. "Istiqālat al-Qaraḍāwī min Hay'at Kibār al-ʿUlamā' bil-Azhar." Dec. 2, 2013. At https://www.al-qaradawi.net/node/4760.

———. "Al-Ittiḥād al-ʿĀlamī li-ʿUlamā' al-Muslimīn: Ittihāmunā bi-l-irhāb bāṭil lā asāsa lahu." Dec. 2, 2017. At https://www.al-qaradawi.net/node/4592.

———. "Ittiḥād 'Ulamā' al-Muslimīn yudīnu hajamāt Bārīs." Nov. 14, 2015. At https://www.al-qaradawi.net/node/4656.

———. "Al-Ittiḥād yuḥadhdhiru min zaʿzaʿat al-istiqrār fī Miṣr wa-yuṭālibu al-muʿāraḍa bi-ittibāʿ qawāʿid al-dīmuqrāṭiyya." June 26, 2013. At https://www.al-qaradawi.net/node/4788.

———. "Maktab faḍīlat al-ʿallāma yanfī mā turaddiduhu al-mawāqiʿ al-mashbūha." June 29, 2013. At https://www.al-qaradawi.net/node/928.

———. "Multaqā talāmīth al-Qaraḍāwī: Ṣināʿat qāda li-mustaqbal al-umma." June 2, 2010. At https://www.al-qaradawi.net/node/5017.

———. "Al-Qaraḍāwī: Lā uʿādī aḥadan wa-kull mā yahummunī al-Islām wal-Muslimīn." Feb. 8, 2015. At https://www.al-qaradawi.net/node/421.

———. "Al-Qaraḍāwī: Qatlā al-ṣirāʿ al-dākhilī al-Filasṭīnī laysū sawā'." Feb. 18, 2007. At https://www.al-qaradawi.net/node/4297.

———. "Al-Qaraḍāwī yanfī al-iftā' bi-qatl al-madaniyyīn fī al-ʿIrāq." Nov. 9, 2004. At https://www.al-qaradawi.net/node/4441.

———. "Al-Qaraḍāwī yuftī bi-wujūb muqāṭaʿat dustūr al-inqilābiyyīna." Aug. 1, 2014. At https://www.al-qaradawi.net/node/861.

———. "Al-Qarra Dāghī: Ittiḥād al-ʿUlamā' qāma bi-aʿmāl jalīla ḍidda al-taṭarruf wa-l-irhāb." Feb. 12, 2017. At https://www.al-qaradawi.net/node/44.

———. "Tajdīd al-īmān: Al-Taṣawwuf al-maqbūl wal-mardūd." Feb. 22, 2017. At https://www.al-qaradawi.net/node/2148.

———. "Ṭālibān dammarat al-tamāthīl al-Būdhiyya wa-wasāṭat al-ʿulamāʾ fashilat." May 8, 2001. At https://www.al-qaradawi.net/node/2035.

———. "Taʿlīq al-Shaykh al-Qaraḍāwī ʿalā al-ḥukm ʿalā al-Duktūr Muḥammad Mursī wa-Ikhwānihi." Apr. 21, 2015. At https://www.al-qaradawi.net/node/550.

Al-Mīzān al-Bawwāba al-Qānūniyya al-Qaṭariyya. "Wathīqa taʾsīsiyya li-l-Ittiḥād al-ʿĀlamī li-ʿUlamāʾ al-Muslimīn." Mar. 3, 2011. At http://www.almeezan.qa/LawPage.aspx?id=4361&language=ar.

Multaqā Rābiṭat al-Wāḥa al-Thaqāfiyya. "Naṣṣ al-Bayān al-umamī ḍidda al-irhāb." Nov. 2004. At https://tinyurl.com/yaxmjtcv.

Muntadayāt ʿĀlam Ḥawwāʾ. "Ḥukm al-muẓāharāt." Jan. 22, 2009. At https://www.hawaaworld.com/showthread.php?t=3038114.

Al-Nābulsī, Muḥammad Rātib. "Mazāyā al-Ṣaḥāba al-kirām." June 29, 1997. At http://www.nabulsi.com/green/ar/print.php?art=2973.

Al-Nābulsī, Shākir. *Al-ʿArab bayna al-lībirāliyya wal-uṣūliyya al-dīniyya.* Beirut: Al-Muʾassasa al-ʿArabiyya lil-Dirāsāt wal-Nashr, 2010.

———. "Al-ʿArab bayna taḥadiyyāt al-ʿaṣr wa-ʿawāʾiq al-taghayyur." *Al-Ḥiwār al-Mutamaddin Mūbāyil*, Apr. 13, 2005. At http://www.m.ahewar.org/s.asp?aid=35398&r=0.

———. *Bin Lādin wal-ʿaql al-ʿArabī: Kayfa fakkara al-ʿArab baʿda 11 Sibtimbir 2001.* Cologne, Germany: Manshūrāt al-Jamal, 2007.

———. "Dīmuqrāṭiyyat al-Qaraḍāwī al-Islāmawiyya al-zāʾifa." *Al-Ḥiwār al-Mutamaddin Mūbāyil*, June 15, 2004. At http://www.m.ahewar.org/s.asp?aid=19430&r=0.

———. "Fuqahāʾ safk al-dimāʾ." *Al-Ḥiwār al-Mutamaddin Mūbāyil*, Sept. 4, 2004. At http://www.m.ahewar.org/s.asp?aid=22960&r=0.

———. "Hal satatakarraru miḥnat Abū Zayd maʿa Ḥasan Ḥanafī?" *Al-Rāya*, Oct. 10, 2006. At https://tinyurl.com/y9cudl7f.

———. "Al-ʿIlmāniyya wa-l-dīmuqrāṭiyya janāḥāni li-ṭāʾir al-ḥurriyya." *Al-Ḥiwār al-Mutamaddin* 1195 (May 12, 2005). At http://www.ahewar.org/debat/show.art.asp?aid=37224.

———. *Al-Islām wa-jirāb al-ḥāwī: Limādhā ḥawwalnā al-Islām ilā ḥijāb wa-irhāb?* Beirut: Al-Muʾassasa al-ʿArabiyya lil-Dirāsāt wal-Nashr, 2011.

———. *Al-Lībirāliyyūn al-judud: Jadal fikrī.* Cologne, Germany: Manshūrāt al-Jamal, 2005.

———. "Al-Qaraḍāwī wa-l-Sibāʿī wa-Bakrī ʿalā lāʾiḥat fuqahāʾ al-irhāb." *Īlāf* interview on al-Ḥurra TV, Aug. 10, 2005. At https://tinyurl.com/yaespyja.

———. "Qaraḍāwiyyāni, lā Qaraḍāwī Wāḥid." *Al-Ḥiwār al-Mutamaddin* 894 (July 2004). At http://www.ahewar.org/debat/show.art.asp?aid=20677.

———. *Sujūn bi-lā quḍbān: Yaḥduthu fī al-'ālam al-'arabī al-'ān*. Beirut: Al-Mu'assasa al-'Arabiyya lil-Dirāsāt wal-Nashr, 2007.

———. *Tahāfut al-uṣūliyya: Naqd fikrī li-l-uṣūliyya al-Islāmiyya min khilāl wāqi'iha al-mu'āsh*. Beirut: Al-Mu'assasa al-'Arabiyya lil-Dirāsāt wal-Nashr, 2009.

Al-Nadwī, Abū al-Ḥasan. *Mādhā khasira al-'ālam bi-inḥiṭāṭ al-Muslimīn*. Al-Manṣūra, Egypt: Maktabat al-Īmān, n.d.

Al-Nawawī, Yaḥyā b. Sharaf. *Riyāḍ al-ṣāliḥīn min kalām sayyid al-mursilīn*. With interpretive commentary by al-Shaykh Muḥammad b. Ṣāliḥ al-'Uthaymīn. 3 vols. Cairo: Dār Ibn al-Haytham, n.d.

———. *Sharḥ al-Nawawī 'alā Muslim*. Al-Dammām, Saudi Arabia: Dār al-Khayr, 1996. Electronic copy at https://tinyurl.com/ya4uow25.

Al-Nawawī Yaḥyā b. Sharaf, Ibn Daqīq al-'Īd, and Shaykh Ṣāliḥ b. 'Uthaymīn. *Al-Riyāḍ al-nadiyya: Sharḥ al-Arba'īn al-Nawawiyya*. Alexandria, Egypt: Dār al-Baṣīra, 2002.

Nāẓūr 24. "Al-Su'ūdiyya tuṣdiru qarāran bi-'ḥarq' kutub al-Qaraḍāwī wa-l-Bannā." Dec. 7, 2015. At https://tinyurl.com/yd7l8ejh.

Orient Net. "Al-Intirbūl yudriju al-Qaraḍāwī 'alā qā'imat al-maṭlūbīn." Dec. 6, 2014. At https://tinyurl.com/ydxu73b7.

Al-Qaraḍāwī, Shaykh Yūsuf. *25 Yanāyir sanat 2011m: Thawrat sha'b: Al-Shaykh al-Qaraḍāwī wal-thawra al-Miṣriyya: Bayānāt wa-khuṭab wa-fatāwā wa-maqālāt wa-ṣuwar*. Cairo: Maktabat Wahba, 2012.

———. *'Ālim wa-ṭāghiya: Sa'īd b. Jubayr wal-Ḥajjāj b. Yūsuf, masraḥiyya tārīkhiyya*. 7th ed. Cairo: Maktabat Wahba, 1998.

———. *Awlawiyyāt al-ḥaraka al-Islāmiyya fī al-marḥala al-qādima*. 4th ed. Cairo: Maktabat Wahba, 1992.

———. *Al-Bābā wal-Islām: Radd 'ilmī 'alā al-babā Banadīkt al-Sādis 'Ashar fī kalimatihi fī almāniyā allatī asā'a bihā ilā al-Islām*. Cairo: Maktabat Wahba, 2007.

———. "Bayān al-Duktūr Yūsuf al-Qaraḍāwī bi-sha'n tafjīrāt Amrīkā." *Shabakat Mishkāh al-Islāmiyya*, Sept. 12, 2001. At http://www.almeshkat.net/vb/showthread.php?t=6554#gsc.tab=0.

———. "Bayān Majlis Umanā' Mu'assasat Sulṭān B. 'Alī al-'Awīs al-Thaqāfiyya ḥawla manḥ al-Shaykh al-Duktūr Yūsuf 'Abd Allāh al-Qaraḍāwī jā'izat al-Injāz al-thaqāfī wal-'ilmī 1998–1999." In *Al-Shaykh al-Qaraḍāwī: Shakhṣiyyat al-'ām al-Islāmiyya 1421/2000*, 149–51. Cairo: Maktabat Wahba, 2001.

———. "Al-Dīmuqrāṭiyya." Apr. 1, 2005. In *Khuṭab al-Shaykh al-Qaraḍāwī*, vol. 7, edited by Muḥammad Ḥūṭar and Akram 'Abd al-Sattār Kassāb, 269–86. Cairo: Maktabat Wahba, 2006.

———. *Al-Dīn wal-siyāsa: Ta'ṣīl wa-radd shubuhāt*. Cairo: Dār al-Shurūq, 2007.

———. *Al-Duktūr Muḥammad 'Imāra al-ḥāris al-yaqiẓ al-murābiṭ 'alā thughūr al-Islām*. Cairo: Dār al-Muqāṣid, 2015.

———. "Al-Durūs al-mustafāda min aḥdāth Filasṭīn wal-'Irāq." June 13, 2003. In *Khuṭab al-Shaykh al-Qaraḍāwī*, vol. 8, edited by al-Maktab al-'Ilmī li-l-Shaykh bil-Dawḥa, 99–118. Cairo: Maktabat Wahba, 2009.

———. *Fatāwā min ajli Filasṭīn*. Cairo: Maktabat Wahba, 2010.

———. *Fatāwā mu'āṣira: Min hady al-Islām*. Vols. 1, 3, 4. Cairo: Dār al-Qalam, 1990–2009.

———. *Fatāwā mu'āṣira: Min hady al-Islām*. Vol. 2. Al-Manṣūra, Egypt: Dar al-Wafā', 1993.

———. *Al-Fatāwā al-shādhdha: Ma'āyīruhā wa-taṭbīqātuhā wa-asbābuhā wa-kayfa nu'ālijuhā wa-natawaqqāhā*. Cairo: Dār al-Shurūq, 2010.

———. *Al-Fatwā bayna al-inḍibāṭ wal-tasayyub*. 2nd ed. Cairo: Dār al-Ṣaḥwa, 1994.

———. *Fī fiqh al-aqalliyyāt al-Muslima: Ḥayāt al-Muslimīn wasṭa al-mujtama'āt al-ukhrā*. Cairo: Dār al-Shurūq, 2001.

———. *Fiqh al-ghinā' wal-mūsīqā fī ḍaw' al-Qur'ān wal-Sunna*. Cairo: Maktabat Wahba, 2001.

———. *Fiqh al-jihād: Dirāsa muqārana li-aḥkāmihi wa-falsafatihi fī ḍaw' al-Qur'ān wal-Sunna*. 2 vols. Cairo: Maktabat Wahba, 2009.

———. *Fiqh al-jihād: Dirāsa muqārana li-aḥkāmihi wa-falsafatihi fī ḍaw' al-Qur'ān wal-Sunna. Ḥaẓiyat hādhihi al-ṭab'a bi-taṣḥīḥāt wa-tanqīḥāt wa-iḍāfāt bālighat al-ahamiyya*. 2 vols. 4th ed. with additions and corrections. Cairo: Maktabat Wahba, 2014.

———. *Fiqh al-usra wa-qaḍāyā al-mar'a*. Istanbul: Al-Dār al-Shāmiyya, 2017.

———. *Fiqh al-wasaṭiyya al-Islāmiyya wal-tajdīd: Ma'ālim wa-manārāt*. Cairo: Dār al-Shurūq, 2010.

———. *Fiqh al-zakāh: Dirāsa muqārana li-aḥkāmihā wa-falsafatihā fī ḍaw' al-Qur'ān wal-Sunna*. 2 vols. 21st ed. Cairo: Maktabat Wahba, 1994.

———. *Fī riḥāb al-Sunna: Sharḥ aḥādīth nabawiyya*. Cairo: Maktabat Wahba, 2010.

———. *Ghayr al-Muslimīn fī al-mujtama' al-Islāmī*. 6th ed. Beirut: Mu'assasat al-Risāla, 1994.

———. *Al-Ḥalāl wal-ḥarām fī al-Islām*. 29th ed. Cairo: Maktabat Wahba, 2007.

———. *Al-Ḥall al-Islāmī: Farīḍa wa-ḍarūra*. 5th ed. Cairo: Maktabat Wahba, 1993.

———. *Ḥaqīqat al-tawḥīd*. 8th ed. Cairo: Maktabat Wahba, 2006.

———. "Al-Ḥarb al-thaqāfiyya ʿalā al-Muslimīn." Jan. 11, 2002. In *Khuṭab al-Shaykh al-Qaraḍāwī*, 6 vols., edited by Khālid Khalīfa al-Saʿd, 6:125–37. Cairo: Maktabat Wahba, 1997–2005.

———. *Al-Ḥayāh al-rabbāniyya wal-ʿilm: Fī-l-ṭarīq ilā Allāh*. Taysīr fiqh al-sulūk *fī ḍawʾ al-Qurʾān wal-Sunna* no. 1. Cairo: Maktabat Wahba, 1995.

———. *Al-Ḥukm al-sharʿī fī khitān al-ināth*. Cairo: Maktabat Wahba, 2007.

———. *Al-Ḥulūl al-mustawrada wa-kayfa janat ʿalā ummatinā*. Cairo: Maktabat Wahba, 1993.

———. "Ḥuqūq al-insān fī al-Islām." N.d. In *Khuṭab al-Shaykh al-Qaraḍāwī*, 6 vols., edited by Khālid Khalīfa al-Saʿd, 2:178–94. Cairo: Maktabat Wahba, 1997–2005.

———. *Al-Ḥurriyya al-dīniyya wal-taʿaddudiyya fī naẓar al-Islām*. Beirut: Al-Maktab al-Islāmī, 2007.

———. *Al-ʿIbāda fī al-Islām*. 15th ed. Cairo: Maktabat Wahba, 1985.

———. *Ibn al-qarya wal-kuttāb: Malāmiḥ sīra wa-masīra*. 4 vols. Cairo: Dār al-Shurūq, 2002–11.

———. "Al-Ihdāʾ" (poem). In *Al-Muslimūn qādimūn*, 3–4. Port Said, Egypt: Dār al-Tawzīʿ wal-Nashr al-Islāmiyya, 2000.

———. *Al-Ijtihād fī al-Sharīʿa al-Islāmiyya maʿa naẓarāt taḥlīliyya fī al-ijtihād al-muʿāṣir*. 3rd ed. Kuwait City: Dār al-Qalam, 1999.

———. *Al-Ijtihād al-muʿāṣir bayna al-inḍibāṭ wal-infirāṭ*. Cairo: Dār al-Tawzīʿ wal-Nashr al-Islāmiyya, 1994.

———. *Al-Ikhwān al-Muslimūn: Sabʿūn ʿāman fī al-daʿwa wal-tarbiya wal-jihād, bi-munāsabat murūr sabʿīn ʿāman ʿalā taʾsīs Jamāʿat al-Ikhwān al-Muslimīn wa-khamsīn ʿāman ʿalā istishhād muʾassis al-Jamāʿa Ḥasan al-Bannā*. Cairo: Maktabat Wahba, 1999.

———. Introduction to *Taḥrīr al-marʾa fī ʿaṣr al-risāla: Dirāsa ʿan al-marʾa jāmiʿa li-nuṣūṣ al-Qurʾān al-karīm wa-Ṣaḥīḥay al-Bukhārī wa-Muslim*, 3 vols., 7th ed., edited by ʿAbd al-Ḥalīm Muḥammad Abū Shaqqa, 1:11–29. Cairo: Dār al-Qalam, 2011.

———. "Al-Iṣlāḥ alladhī nanshuduhu: Ahdāfuhu wa-shurūṭuhu wa-majālātuhu." Jan. 16, 2004. In *Khuṭab al-Shaykh al-Qaraḍāwī*, 6 vols., edited by Khālid Khalīfa al-Saʿd, 6:262–76. Cairo: Maktabat Wahba, 1997–2005.

———. *Al-Islām alladhī nad'ū ilayhi*. Cairo: Maktabat Wahba, 2004.

———. *Al-Islām: Ḥaḍārat al-ghad*. Cairo: Maktabat Wahba, 1995.

———. *Al-Islām wal-ʿilmāniyya wajhan li-wajhin: Radd ʿilmī ʿalā D. Fū'ad Zakariyyā wa-Jamāʿat al-ʿIlmāniyyīn*. 2nd ed. Cairo: Dār al-Ṣaḥwa, 1994.

———. *Al-Islām kamā nu'minu bihi: Ḍawābiṭ wa-malāmiḥ*. Cairo: Nahḍat Miṣr, 1999.

———. *Al-Islām wal-ʿunf naẓarāt ta'ṣīliyya*. 2nd ed. Cairo: Dār al-Shurūq, 2007.

———. *Jarīmat al-ridda wa-ʿuqūabat al-murtadd fī ḍaw' al-Qur'ān wal-Sunna*. Beirut: Mu'assasat al-Risāla, 2001.

———. *Jīl al-naṣr al-manshūd*. 6th ed. Cairo: Maktabat Wahba, 2013.

———. "Kalimat al-ʿallāma al-Qaraḍāwī bi-munāsabat al-jā'iza." Dec. 16, 2000. In *Al-Shaykh al-Qaraḍāwī: Shakhṣiyyat al-ʿām al-Islāmiyya 1421 A.H./2000*, 131–48. Cairo: Maktabat Wahba, 2001.

———. *Kalimāt fī al-wasaṭiyya al-Islāmiyya wa-maʿālimihā*. Cairo: Dār al-Shurūq, 2008.

———. *Kayfa nataʿāmalu maʿa al-Qur'ān al-ʿaẓīm?* 2nd ed. Cairo: Dār al-Shurūq, 2000.

———. *Kayfa nataʿāmalu maʿa al-Sunna al-nabawiyya?* Cairo: Dār al-Shurūq, 2000.

———. *Kayfa nataʿāmalu maʿa al-turāth wal-tamadhhub wal-ikhtilāf?* Cairo: Maktabat Wahba, 2001.

———. *Al-Khaṣā'iṣ al-ʿāmma lil-Islām*. 6th ed. Cairo: Maktabat Wahba, 2003.

———. *Khiṭābunā al-Islāmī fī ʿaṣr al-ʿawlama*. Cairo: Dār al-Shurūq, 2004.

———. *Khuṭab al-Shaykh al-Qaraḍāwī*. 6 vols. Edited by Khālid Khalīfa al-Saʿd. Cairo: Maktabat Wahba, 1997–2005.

———. *Khuṭab al-Shaykh al-Qaraḍāwī*. Vol. 7. Edited by Muḥammad Ḥūṭar and Akram ʿAbd al-Sattār Kassāb. Cairo: Maktabat Wahba, 2006.

———. *Khuṭab al-Shaykh al-Qaraḍāwī*. Vol. 8. Edited by al-Maktab al-ʿIlmī li-l-Shaykh bil-Dawḥa. Cairo: Maktabat Wahba, 2009.

———. "Lā akhāfu al-ightiyāl, bal atamannā al-shahāda." Mar. 14, 2013. In *Khuṭab al-Shaykh al-Qaraḍāwī*, 6 vols., edited by Khālid Khalīfa al-Saʿd, 6:205–17. Cairo: Maktabat Wahba, 1997–2005.

———. *Liqā'āt wa-muḥāwarāt ḥawla qaḍāyā al-Islām wal-ʿaṣr*. 2 vols. Cairo: Maktabat Wahba, 2001.

———. *Liqā' maftūḥ maʿa al-ʿallāma al-Qaraḍāwī fī l-Baḥrayn*. Cairo: Maktabat Wahba, 2011.

———. *Mabādi' fī al-ḥiwār wal-taqrīb bayna al-madhāhib al-Islāmiyya*. Cairo: Maktabat Wahba, 2005.

———. *Madkhal li-dirāsat al-sharī'a al-Islāmiyya*. 4th ed. Cairo: Maktabat Wahba, 2001.

———. *Madkhal li-ma'rifat al-Islām: Muqawwimātihi, khaṣā'iṣihi, ahdāfihi, maṣādirihi*. 3rd ed. Cairo: Maktabat Wahba, 2001.

———. *Malāmiḥ al-mujtama' al-Muslim alladhī nanshuduhu*. Cairo: Maktabat Wahba, 1993.

———. "Man al-mas'ūl 'an aḥdāth al-ḥādī 'ashar min Sibtimbir?" Sept. 21, 2001. In *Khuṭab al-Shaykh al-Qaraḍāwī*, 6 vols., edited by Khālid Khalīfa al-Sa'd, 6:82–95. Cairo: Maktabat Wahba, 1997–2005.

———. "Ma'rakat al-ḥijāb fī Faransā." Oct. 1994. In *Khuṭab al-Shaykh al-Qaraḍāwī*, 6 vols., edited by Khālid Khalīfa al-Sa'd, 2:195–210. Cairo: Maktabat Wahba, 1997–2005.

———. "Ma'rakat al-Islām wal-'ilmāniyya." June 13, 1997. In *Khuṭab al-Shaykh al-Qaraḍāwī*, vol. 7, edited by Muḥammad Ḥūṭar and 'Abd al-Sattār Kassāb, 173–91. Cairo: Maktabat Wahba, 2006.

———. *Al-Marji'iyya al-'ulyā fī al-Islām lil-Qur'ān wal-Sunna: Ḍawābiṭ wa-maḥādhīr fī al-fahm wal-tafsīr*. Cairo: Maktabat Wahba, 1992.

———. *Markaz al-mar'a fī al-ḥayāh al-Islāmiyya*. 2nd ed. Cairo: Maktabat Wahba, 2005.

———. *Mawqif al-Islām al-'aqdī min kufr al-Yahūd wal-Naṣārā*. Cairo: Maktabat Wahba, 1999.

———. *Al-Miḥna fī wāqi' al-ḥaraka al-Islāmīyya al-mu'āṣira*. Cairo: Maktabat Wahba, 2009.

———. *Min ajli ṣaḥwa rāshida: Tujaddidu al-dīn wa-tanhaḍu bil-dunyā*. 2nd ed. Cairo: Dār al-Shurūq, 2005.

———. *Min fiqh al-dawla fī al-Islām: Makānatihā, ma'ālimihā, ṭabī'atihā, mawqifihā mina al-dīmuqrāṭiyya wal-ta'addudiyya wal-mar'a wa-ghayr al-Muslimīn*. Cairo: Dār al-Shurūq, 1997.

———. "Al-Mīthāq al-Islāmī li-l-Ittiḥād al-'Ālamī li- 'Ulamā' al-Muslimīn." 2006. At http://www.iumsonline.org/uploads/books/IslamicCharter-Arabic.pdf.

———. *Al-Mubashshirāt bi-intiṣār al-Islām*. 2nd ed. Cairo: Maktabat Wahba, 1999.

———. "Muḥammad al-rasūl al-mujāhid." June. 8, 2001. In *Khuṭab al-Shaykh al-Qaraḍāwī*, vol. 8, edited by al-Maktab al-'Ilmī li-l-shaykh bil-Dawḥa, 14–31. Cairo: Maktabat Wahba, 2009.

———. *Mūjibāt taghayyur al-fatwā fī ʿaṣrinā*. Cairo: Dār al-Shurūq, 2008.

———. *Al-Muqaddimāt*. Cairo: Dār al-Rawḍa, 2015.

———. *Al-Muslimūn wal-ʿawlama*. Port Said, Egypt: Dār al-Tawzīʿ wal-Nashr al-Islāmiyya, 2000.

———. *Al-Muslimūn qādimūn*. Port Said, Egypt: Dār al-Tawzīʿ wal-Nashr al-Islāmiyya, 2000.

———. "Al-Mustaqbal lil-Islām." C. 2000–2003. In *Khuṭab al-Shaykh al-Qaraḍāwī*, 6 vols., edited by Khālid Khalīfa al-Saʿd, X:280–97. Cairo: Maktabat Wahba, 1997–2005.

———. *Mustaqbal al-uṣūliyya al-Islāmiyya*. Cairo: Maktabat Wahba, 1997.

———. "Naḥnu al-Ikhwān" (poem). In *Al-Muslimūn qādimūn*, 53–54. Port Said, Egypt: Dār al-Tawzīʿ wal-Nashr al-Islāmiyya, 2000.

———. *Naḥnu wal-gharb: As'ila shā'ika wa-ajwiba ḥāsima*. Cairo: Dār al-Tawzīʿ wal-Nashr al-Islāmiyya, 2006.

———. "Naṣṣ bayān al-Qaraḍāwī ḥawla mawqifihi min al-Shīʿa." Sept. 2008. At https://archive.islamonline.net/?p=9502.

———. *Al-Niqāb lil-mar'a bayna al-qawl bi-bidʿiyyatihi wal-qawl bi-wujūbihi*. 2nd ed. Cairo: Maktabat Wahba, 1999.

———. "Nuṣrat al-nabī." Feb. 3, 2006. In *Khuṭab al-Shaykh al-Qaraḍāwī*, vol. 8, edited by al-Maktab al-ʿIlmī li-l-Shaykh bil-Dawḥa, 349–67. Cairo: Maktabat Wahba, 2009.

———. "Qaḍiyyat al-ʿIrāq." Mar. 7, 2003. In *Khuṭab al-Shaykh al-Qaraḍāwī*, 6 vols., edited by Khālid Khalīfa al-Saʿd, 6:188–204. Cairo: Maktabat Wahba, 1997–2005.

———. "Qaḍiyyat al-murtadd Salmān Rushdī." Mar. 1989. In *Khuṭab al-Shaykh al-Qaraḍāwī*, 6 vols., edited by Khālid Khalīfa al-Saʿd, 1:163–75. Cairo: Maktabat Wahba, 1997–2005.

———. "Al-Qaraḍāwī: Ḥizb Allāh Ḥizb al-Ṭāghūt wal-Shayṭān . . . wal-jihād bi-Sūriyā maṭlūb." June 9, 2013. At https://mz-mz.net/158239.

———. *Al-Qawāʿid al-ḥākima li-fiqh al-muʿāmalāt*. Cairo: Dār al-Shurūq, 2010.

———. "Al-Qimma al-Islāmiyya al-Masīḥiyya al-ūlā fī Rūmā ḥawla al-irhāb wa-asbābihi." Oct. 12, 2001. In *Khuṭab al-Shaykh al-Qaraḍāwī*, 6 vols., edited by Khālid Khalīfa al-Saʿd, 6:96–109. Cairo: Maktabat Wahba, 1997–2005.

———. *Al-Quds: Qaḍiyyat kull Muslim*. Beirut: Al-Maktab al-Islāmī, 2002.

———. *Al-Rabbāniyya abraz khaṣā'iṣ al-tarbiya al-Islāmiyya*. Cairo: Maktabat Wahba, 2009.

———. "Risāla ilā al-mu'tamar al-Islāmī al-tāsi'." Nov. 10, 2000. In *Khuṭab al-Shaykh al-Qaraḍāwī*, 6 vols., edited by Khālid Khalīfa al-Sa'd, 5:191–204. Cairo: Maktabat Wahba, 1997–2005.

———. *Risālat al-Azhar bayna al-ams wal-yawm wal-ghad*. 3rd ed. Cairo: Maktabat Wahba, 2009.

———. "Rudūd 'ilmiyya 'alā al-shaykh aw al-jinirāl 'Alī Gum'a." Mawqi' Samāḥat al-Shaykh Yūsuf al-Qaraḍāwī (website), Sept. 17, 2013. At https://www.al-qaradawi.net/node/2849.

———. *Al-Ṣaḥwa al-Islāmiyya bayna al-ikhtilāf al-mashrū' wal-tafarruq al-madhmūm*. Cairo: Dār al-Shurūq, 2001.

———. *Al-Ṣaḥwa al-Islāmiyya bayna al-juḥūd wal-taṭarruf*. 12th ed. Al-Manṣūra, Egypt: Dār al-Wafā', 1992.

———. *Al-Ṣaḥwa al-Islāmiyya bayna al-jumūd wal-taṭarruf*. Cairo: Dār al-Shurūq, 2001.

———. *Al-Saḥwa al-Islāmiyya wa-humūm al-waṭan al-'arabī wal-Islāmī*. 2nd ed. Cairo: Maktabat Wahba, 1997.

———. *Al-Ṣaḥwa al-Islāmiyya min al-murāhaqa ilā al-rushd*. 3rd ed. Cairo: Dār al-Shurūq, 2008.

———. *Sharī'at al-Islām ṣāliḥa lil-taṭbīq fī kull zamān wa-makān*. Cairo: Maktabat Wahba, 1997.

———. *Al-Shaykh al-Ghazālī kamā 'araftuhu: Riḥlat niṣf qarn*. Cairo: Dār al-Shurūq, 2000.

———. *Shumūl al-Islām fī ḍaw' sharḥ mufaṣṣal li-l-usūl al-'Ishrīn li-l-Imām Ḥasan al-Bannā*. 3rd ed. Cairo: Maktabat Wahba, 2003.

———. *Al-Siyāsa al-shar'iyya fī ḍaw' nuṣūṣ al-sharī'a wa-maqāṣidihā*. Beirut: Mu'assasat al-Risāla, 2001.

———. *Al-Sunna maṣdaran lil-ma'rifa wal-ḥaḍāra*. 3rd ed. Cairo: Dār al-Shurūq, 2002.

———. "Tafjīrāt masraḥ Qaṭar 'amal mustankar." Mar. 25, 2005. In *Khuṭab al-Shaykh al-Qaraḍāwī*, vol. 7, edited by Muḥammad Ḥūṭar and 'Abd al-Sattār Kassāb, 256–68. Cairo: Maktabat Wahba, 2006.

———. *Al-Taḥdhīr min al-'urf al-khāṭi' wal-khidā' al-lafẓī wal-tarkīz 'alā al-'aqīda wa-ta'thīrihā fī al-'amal*. Cairo: Maktabat Wahba, 2013.

———. *Tajdīd al-dīn alladhī nanshuduhu*. Cairo: Maktabat Wahba, 2011.

———. *Al-Taṭarruf al-'ilmānī fī muwājahat al-Islām*. Al-Manṣūra, Egypt: Andalūsiyā li-l-Nashr wa-l-Tawzī', 2000.

———. *Thaqāfat al-dā'iya*. 10th ed. Cairo: Maktabat Wahba, 1996.

———. "Thaqāfat al-tasāmuḥ 'inda al-Muslimīn." Mawqi' Samāḥat al-Shaykh Yūsuf al-Qaraḍāwī (website), Nov. 23, 2015. At https://www.al-qaradawi.net/node/2293.

———. *Thaqāfatunā bayna al-infitāḥ wal-inghilāq*. Cairo: Dār al-Shurūq, 2000.

———. "Tuhmat al-Islām al-siyāsī." Mawqi' Samāḥat al-Shaykh Yūsuf al-Qaraḍāwī (website), Sept. 6, 2018. At https://www.al-qaradawi.net/node/2099.

———. *Al-Umma al-Islāmiyya: Ḥaqīqa lā wahm*. Cairo: Maktabat Wahba, 1995.

———. "Al-Umma al-Islāmiyya taḥta wiṣayat al-gharb." Jan. 18, 2002. In *Khuṭab al-Shaykh al-Qaraḍāwī*, 6 vols., edited by Khālid Khalīfa al-Sa'd, 6:152–64. Cairo: Maktabat Wahba, 1997–2005.

———. *Ummatunā bayna qarnayni*. Cairo: Dār al-Shurūq, 2000.

———. "Wā Islāmāh." N.d. In *Khuṭab al-Shaykh al-Qaraḍāwī*, edited by Khālid Khalīfa al-Sa'd, 5:242–54. Cairo: Maktabat Wahba, 1997–2005.

———. "Waqafāt ma'a Shaykh al-Azhar wa-qaḍiyyat al-inqilāb 'alā al-shar'iyya." Sept. 4, 2013. At https://tinyurl.com/y79sfua8.

———. "Waqfa ma'a al-shahīd Sayyid Quṭb." In *Sayyid Quṭb wal-'unf wa-takfīr: Azmat afkār am mushkilat qurrā'?* edited by Mu'tazz al-Khaṭīb, 49–62. Cairo: Maktabat Madbūlī, 2009.

———. "Al-Wasaṭiyya wa-dawr al-i'lām fī ibrāzihā." Mawqi' Samāḥat al-Shaykh Yūsuf al-Qaraḍāwī, Oct. 15, 2006. At https://www.al-qaradawi.net/new/304-2014-01-26-18 . . . /4783.

———. *Al-Waṭan wal-muwāṭana fī ḍaw' al-uṣūl al-'aqdiyya wal-maqāṣid al-sharī'iyya*. Cairo: Dār al-Shurūq, 2010.

———. *Ẓāhirat al-ghulū fī al-takfīr*. 5th ed. Cairo: Maktabat Wahba, 2010.

Qarāmī, Āmāl. "Manzilat al-mithliyyīn fī khiṭāb al-Islāmiyyīn: Al-Qaraḍāwī namūdhajan." *Al-Ḥiwār al-Mutamaddin*, June 29, 2006. At http://www.ahewar.org/debat/show.art.asp?aid=68755.

Al-Qimnī, Sayyid. *Ahl al-dīn wa-l-dīmuqrāṭiyya*. Cairo: Dār Miṣr al-Maḥrūsa, 2005.

Al-Quds al-'Arabī. "Al-Intirbūl yaḥdhifu ism al-Qaraḍāwī min al- maṭlūbīn wa-Miṣr tasta'limu 'an al-asbāb." Sept. 11, 2017. At http://www.alquds.co.uk/?p=787587.

———. "Ramatni bi-dā'ihā wa-insallat: Al-Qaraḍāwī yaruddu 'alā duwal al-ḥiṣār wa-ittihāmihi bi-l-irhāb." Nov. 25, 2017. At http://www.alquds.co.uk/?p=833102.

Al-Qurṭubī, Shams al-Dīn. *Al-Jāmiʿ li-aḥkām al-Qur'ān*. 24 vols. Beirut: Mu'assasat al-Risāla, 2006. Electronic copy at https://ia801406.us.archive.org/13/items/waq73651/03_73653.pdf.

Quṭb, Sayyid. *Fī ẓilāl al-Qur'ān*. 6 vols. 25th ed. Cairo: Dār al-Shurūq, 1996.

———. *Maʿālim fī al-ṭarīq*. Cairo: Dār al-Shurūq, n.d. Electronic copy at http://www.ilmway.com/site/maqdis/MS_705.html.

Rābiṭat ʿUlamā' Filasṭīn. "Al-ʿAmaliyyāt al-istishhādiyya jihād fī sabīl Allāh . . . ḥalāl sharʿan." N.d. At http://www.ilmway.com/site/maqdis/MS_5833.

al-Rāfiʿī, Muṣṭafā Ṣādiq. *Taḥta Rāyat al-Qur'ān—Al-Maʿraka bayna al-Qadīm wal-ḥadīth*. 7th ed. Beirut: Dār al-Kitāb al-ʿArabī, 1974. At https://ia600603.us.archive.org/29/items/FP11523/11523.pdf.

Al-Rā'id Ittiḥād al-Munaẓẓamāt al-Ijtimāʿiyya fī Ūkrāniyā. "Al-Bayān al-khitāmī al-ṣādir ʿan al-Mu'tamar al-Islāmī al-ʿĀlamī ʿal-Islām wa-muḥārabat al-irhāb.'" Feb. 26, 2015. At http://www.arraid.org/ar/node/4352.

Ramaḍān, Bassām. "Wazīr khārijiyyat Qaṭar: Isā'at ʿal-Qaraḍāwī' lil-Imārāt Lā tuʿabbiru ʿan siyāsatina al-khārijiyya." *Al-Maṣrī al-Yawm*, Feb. 1, 2014. At http://www.almasryalyoum.com/news/details/386434.

Al-Rāshid, ʿAbd al-Raḥmān. "Al-Qaraḍāwī mutasāmiḥ wa-mutaʿaṣṣib." *Al-Sharq al-Awsaṭ*, July 10, 2004. At https://tinyurl.com/ya33mjc6.

Riḍā, [Muḥammad] Rashīd. *Tafsīr al-manār*. 12 vols. 2nd ed. Cairo: Dār al-Manār, 1948. Electronic copy at http://waqfeya.com/book.php?bid=786.

Rifʿat al-Saʿīd, Muḥammad. *Al-Ta'aslum: Fikr musallaḥ*. Damascus: Dār al-Ṭālīʿa, 1996.

———. *Al-Tayyārāt al-siyāsiyya fī Miṣr: Al-Mārksiyyūn, al-Ikhwān al-Muslimūn, al-Nāṣiriyyūn, al-tajammuʿ*. Cairo: Sharikat al-Amal, 2001.

"Risāla maftūḥa ilā Abī Bakr al-Baghdādī." Letter to Abū Bakr al-Baghdādī by several persons, Sept. 19, 2014. At http://lettertobaghdadi.com/14/arabic-v14.pdf.

Al-Rīsūnī, Aḥmad. "Al-Qaraḍāwī: Faqīh al-maqāṣid." In *Al-Qaraḍāwī: Kalimāt fī takrīmihi wa-buḥūth fī fikrihi wa-fiqhihi muhdāh ilayhi bi-munāsabat bulūghihi al-sabʿīn*, 2 vols., edited by ʿAbd al-ʿAẓīm al-Dīb, 1:111–27. Cairo: Dār al-Salām, 2004.

RTonline. "Qaṭar tatasallamu maṭālib al-duwal al-muqāṭiʿa." June 23, 2017. At https://tinyurl.com/yd5xu35f.

Sābiq, al-Sayyid. *Fiqh al-Sunna*. 3 vols. Cairo: Dār al-Fatḥ lil-Iʿlām al-ʿArabī, 2000.

Ṣabrī, Mas'ūd. "Al-Qaraḍāwī: Ibn Taymiyyat 'aṣrihi wa-zamānihi." Mawqi' Samāḥat al-Shaykh Yūsuf al-Qaraḍāwī (website), May 17, 2014. At https://www.al-qaradawi.net/node/5160.

Al-Ṣalābī, 'Alī Muḥammad. *Al-Wasaṭiyya fī al-Qur'ān al-karīm*. Cairo: Dār Ibn al-Jawzī, 2007.

Salqīnī, Ibrāhīm 'Abdallāh. *Sharḥ ḥadīth lā tazālu ṭā'ifa min ummatī*. Beirut: Dār al-Muqtabis, 2014.

Ṣamū'īl, Rafīq. "Marra wāḥid Qaraḍāwī." *Al-Ḥiwār al-Mutamaddin* 3241 (Jan. 9, 2011). At http://www.ahewar.org/debat/show.art.asp?aid=241093.

Al-Ṣan'ānī, Muḥammad b. Ismā'īl al-Amīr. *Al-Tanwīr sharḥ al-jāmi' al-ṣaghīr*. Riyadh: Maktabat Dār al-Salām, 2011. Electronic copy at http://shamela.ws/browse.php/book-122096/page-3630.

Al-Ṣāwī, Ṣalāḥ. *Al-Wasaṭiyya: Al-'Aqīda, al-'ilm, al-'ibādāt, al-mu'āsharāt, al-mu'āmalāt, al-akhlāq*. Cairo: Dār al-Kitāb al-Ḥadīth, 2010.

Al-Sayyid, Usāma. *Al-Qaraḍāwī fī al-'arā': Dirāsa naqdiyya manhajiyya mu-waththaqa tubayyinu mukhālafāt al-Qaraḍāwī li-ṣaḥīḥ al-naql wa-ṣarīḥ al-'aql*. Beirut: Sharikat Dār al-Mashārī', 2002. Electronic copy at https://tinyurl.com/y9ldahv6.

Shabakat al-Da'wa al-Salafiyya mina al-Aqṣā al-Mubārak. "Ḥukm al-muẓāharāt fī al-Islām." Jan. 26, 2011. At http://vb.alaqsasalafi.com/showthread.php?2500.

Shabakat Saḥāb al-Salafiyya. "Fatāwā 'ulamā' al-Sunna fīmā yussamā bi-l-anāshīd al-Islāmiyya." Oct. 26, 2009. At https://tinyurl.com/y7s8rob2.

———. "Ilā al-'uqalā': Ḥukm al-muẓāharāt bayna al-Shaykh al-Albānī wal-Ḥawīnī." Aug. 30, 2010. At http://www.sahab.net/forums/index.php?showtopic=113495.

———. "Kalām al-'ulamā' wa-sharḥuhum 'alā ḥadīth inna al-'ulamā' warathat al-anbiyā'." Aug. 26, 2010. At https://www.sahab.net/forums/index.php?app=forums&module=forums&controller=topic&id=113380.

Shaltūt, Maḥmūd. *Al-Fatāwā: Dirāsa li-mushkilāt al-Muslim al-mu'āṣir fī ḥayātihi al-yawmiyya al-'āmma*. 18th ed. Cairo: Dār al-Shurūq, 2004.

Al-Sharq. "Al-Qarra Dāghī li-al-Sharq: 'Muḥāṣarat sha'b Muslim lā tajūzu shar'an fī kull al-ẓurūf.'" Sept. 22, 2017. At https://tinyurl.com/yak65y3q.

Al-Sharq al-Awsaṭ. "Al-Azhar yudīnu al-i'tidā' 'alā al-madaniyyīn min ayy jiha." Dec. 4, 2001. At https://tinyurl.com/y88mwulz.

———. "Al-Yūnīskū tad'ū al-wafd al-Islāmī li-badhl dawr yunqidhu mā tabaqqā min tamāthīl Bāmiyān." Mar. 12, 2001. At https://tinyurl.com/yd8yq3ss.

Al-Shāṭibī, Abū Isḥāq Ibrāhīm b. Mūsā. *Al-Muwāfaqāt.* 2 vols. Cairo: Dār al-Faḍīla, 2010.

Al-Shawkānī, Muḥammad b. ʻAlī b. Muḥammad. *Nayl al-awṭār: Sharḥ muntaqā al-Akhbār min aḥādīth Sayyid al-akhyār.* 4 vols. Cairo: Dār al-Ḥadīth, 2000.

Al-Shaykh al-Qaraḍāwī: Shakhṣiyyat al-ʻām al-Islāmiyya 1421 A.H./2000. Cairo: Maktabat Wahba, 2001.

Shorouk News. "Muntadā al-Samāḥa wal-Wasaṭiyya bil-awqāf yuṭālibu bi-taʻāwun mukhtalif al-mu'assasāt li-intāj khiṭāb dīnī muttazin." May 26, 2015. At http://www.shorouknews.com/news/view.aspx?cdate=26052015&id=5e0f8692-b6ca-4fc7-bdcl-ele72e445dla.

Al-Shuʻaybī, Ḥamūd b. ʻUqalā'. "Ḥukm al-ʻamaliyyāt al-istishhādiyya." Apr. 2001. At http://www.ilmway.com/site/maqdis/MS_5788.html.

———. "Ḥukm al-daʻwa ilā waḥdat al-adyān." Sept. 17, 2000. At http://www.ilmway.com/site/maqdis/MS_22437.html.

———. *Ḥukm mā jarā fī Amrīkā min aḥdāth.* N.p.: n.p., 2001. Electronic copy at http://www.al-oglaa.com/?section=subject&SubjectID=176.

———. "Maʻnā al-irhāb wa-ḥaqīqatuhu." Nov. 20, 2001. At http://www.ilmway.com/site/maqdis/MS_516.html.

———. *Al-Qawl al-mukhtār fī ḥukm al-istiʻāna bil-kuffār.* N.p.: n.p., 1999. Electronic copy at http://www.ilmway.com/site/maqdis/MS_15136.html.

Al-Sūrī, Abū Muṣʻab. *Daʻwat al-muqāwama al-Islāmiyya al-ʻālamiyya.* 2 vols. N.p.: n.p., Dec. 2004. Electronic copy at http://www.ilmway.com/site/maqdis/MS_808.html.

Al-Takrūrī, Nawāf Hāyil. *Al-ʻAmaliyyāt al-istishhādiyya fī al-mīzān al-fiqhī.* Cairo: Dār al-Fikr, 1997. Electronic copy at https://www.goodreads.com/book/show/18306943.

Talīma, ʻIṣām. "Al-Mufakkir wal-tanẓīm fī al-ḥaraka al-Islāmiyya . . . ʻalāqa mutawattira." Mar. 17, 2017. At https://www.facebook.com/ikhwanturk/posts/1918540955045808:0.

———. *Al-Qaraḍāwī: Faqīh al-duʻāh wa-dāʻiyat al-fuqahā'.* Damascus: Dār al-Qalam, 2001.

———. *Al-Qaraḍāwī faqīhan.* Cairo: Dār al-Tawzīʻ wal-Nashr al-Islāmiyya, 2000.

Tammām, Ḥusām. "Qaraḍāwī wal-Ikhwān: Qirā'a fī jadaliyyat al-shaykh wal-ḥaraka." *Islamism Scope*, July 2008. At https://tinyurl.com/y9he4ul4.

Al-Ṭarṭūsī, Abū Baṣīr ʻAbd al-Munʻim Muṣṭafā Ḥalīma. *Aʻmāl tukhriju ṣāḥibahā mina al-milla.* N.p.: n.p., 2001. Electronic copy at http://www.abubaseer.bizland.com/books/read/b10.doc.

———. "Bayān ḥawla al-tafjīrāt allatī ḥaṣalat fī Madīnat Landan." July 10, 2005. At http://tartosi.blogspot.co.il/2005/07/blog-post_09.html.

———. "Faṣl al-kalām fī mas'alat al-khurūj 'alā al-ḥukkām." Apr. 11, 2001. At http://www.ilmway.com/site/maqdis/MS_8756.html.

———. *Fiqh al-ikhtilāf 'ind ahl al-Sunna wa-ahl al-bida'*. N.p.: n.p., Dec. 2006. Electronic copy at http://www.ilmway.com/site/maqdis/MS_145.html.

———. "Al-Ghulām wal-malik." Dec. 1, 2004. At http://www.ilmway.com/site/maqdis/MS_35815.html.

———. *Hādhihi 'aqīdatunā wa-hādhā alladhī nad'ū ilayhi*. N.p.: n.p., 2002. Electronic copy at http://www.ilmway.com/site/maqdis/MS_35310.html.

———. *Hādhihi hiya khiṣāl al-Khawārij fa-Iḥdharūhā*. N.p.: n.p., 2013. Electronic copy at http://www.abubaseer.bizland.com/books/read/b%2047.doc.

———. "Ḥubb al-tashaffī am al-ḥukm al-shar'ī." July 11, 2005. At http://tartosi.blogspot.co.il/2005/07/blog-post_11.html.

———. *Ḥukm al-Islām fī al-dīmuqrāṭiyya wa-l-ta'addudiyya al-ḥizbiyya*. 2nd ed. N.p.: n.p., 1999. Electronic copy at http://www.abubaseer.bizland.com/books/read/b11.pdf.

———. "Al-Irhāb ma'nāhu wa-wāqi'uhu min manẓūr Islāmī." N.d. At http://www.ilmway.com/site/maqdis/MS_28456.html.

———. *Al-Jihād wal-siyāsa al-shar'īyya: Munāṣaḥa wa-mukāshafa lil-jamā'āt al-jihādiyya al-mu'āṣira*. Nuskha mazayyada, iḍāfat al-waqfa al-tāsi'a 'ashar (revised version with addition). N.p.: n.p., 2008. Electronic copy at http://www.abubaseer.bizland.com/books/read/b%2025.doc.

———. "Limādhā kaffartu Yūsuf al-Qaraḍāwī . . . ?" Nov. 1, 2008. At http://www.abubaseer.bizland.com/articles/read/a%20118.doc.

———. "Maḥādhīr al-'amaliyyāt al-istishhādiyya aw al-intiḥāriyya." Aug. 2005. At http://tartosi.blogspot.co.il/2005/08/blog-post_24.html.

———. *Al-Mawqif al-shar'ī mina al-Qaraḍāwī*. N.p.: n.p., n.d. Electronic copy at http://www.ilmway.com/site/maqdis/MS_23692.html.

———. "Munāqashat adillat wa-i'tirāḍāt al-mukhālifīn ḥawla al-'amaliyyāt al-intiḥāriyya." Sept. 23, 2005. At http://tartosi.blogspot.com/2005/09/blog-post_23.html.

———. *Muṣṭalaḥāt wa-mafāhīm shar'iyya 'alāhā ghubār ta'wīlāt al-mubṭilīn yajibu taṣḥīḥuhā*. N.p.: n.p., 2007. Electronic copy at http://www.ilmway.com/site/maqdis/MS_145.html.

———. *Qawā'id fī al-takfīr*. N.p.: n.p., 1994. Electronic copy at http://www.abubaseer.bizland.com/books/read/b16.pdf.

———. *Rasā'il fī al-i'dād wal-jihād*. N.p.: n.p., n.d. Electronic copy at https://tinyurl.com/y7kucd6j.

———. *Al-Shī'a al-Rawāfiḍ ṭā'ifat shirk wa-ridda*. N.p.: n.p., Aug. 2002. Electronic copy at http://www.abubaseer.bizland.com/books/read/b%2044.pdf.

———. *Ṣifat al-ṭā'ifa al-manṣūra allatī yajibu an tukaththira sawādahā*. N.p.: n.p., 1993. Electronic copy at http://www.abubaseer.bizland.com/books/read/b12.doc.

———. *Al-Ṭāghūt*. N.p.: n.p., Jan. 1996. Electronic copy at http://www.abubaseer.bizland.com/books.htm.

———. "Ta'rīf al-irhāb." Feb. 10, 2005. At http://www.ilmway.com/site/maqdis/MS_28487.html.

Al-'Utaybī, 'Abdallah b. Bajād. "Al-Islām al-musallaḥ wa-l-Islām al-siyāsī." *Al-Sharq al-Awsaṭ*, Mar. 3, 2013. At https://tinyurl.com/y8g7f3k6.

Al-'Uthaymīn, Muḥammad b. Ṣāliḥ. "Mā ḥukm al-khitān fī ḥaqq al-rijāl wa-l-nisā'?" *Ṭarīq al-Islām*, Dec. 1, 2006. At https://tinyurl.com/y7u78y95.

———. *Majmū' fatāwā wa-rasā'il faḍīlat al-Shaykh Muḥammad b. Ṣāliḥ al-'Uthaymīn*. 26 vols. Edited by Fahd b. Nāṣir b. Ibrāhīm al-Sulaimān. Riyadh: Dār al-Thurayyā, 2008.

Al-Wāḥidī, Abū al-Ḥasan 'Alī b. Aḥmad. *Sharḥ Dīwān al-Mutanabbī*. N.p.: n.p., n.d. Electronic copy at http://islamport.com/w/adb/Web/754/124.htm.

Al-Yawm al-Sābi'. "'Abd al-Raḥmān Yūsuf al-Qaraḍāwī yaktubu: 'Afwan abī al-ḥabīb . . . Mursī lā shar'iyya lahu." July 7, 2013. At https://tinyurl.com/ya8gpkuq.

Zakariyyā, Fu'ād. *Al-Ṣaḥwa al-Islāmiyya fī mīzān al-'aql*. Alexandria, Egypt: Dār al-Wafā', 2006.

Al-Zarqā, Aḥmad b. Shaykh Muḥammad. *Sharḥ al-qawā'id al-fiqhiyya*. 6th ed. Damascus: Dār al-Qalam, 2001.

Al-Zarqā, Muṣṭafa Aḥmad. "Yūsuf al-Qaraḍāwī: Ḥujjat al-'aṣr wa-huwa min ni'am Allāh 'alā al-Muslimīn." In *Al-Qaraḍāwī: Kalimāt fī takrīmihi wa-buḥūth fī fikrihi wa-fiqhihi muhdāh ilayhi bi-munāsabat bulūghihi al-sab'īn*, 2 vols., edited by 'Abd al-'Aẓīm al-Dīb, 1:41–44. Cairo: Dār al-Salām, 2004.

Al-Zarqāwī, Abū Muṣ'ab. *Hal atāka ḥadīth al-Rāfiḍa?!* [Baghdad]: Warshat 'Amal al-Burāq, no. 2, June 2006. Electronic copy at http://www.ilmway.com/site/maqdis/MS_26057.html.

Al-Ẓawāhirī, Ayman. *Fursān taḥta rāyat al-Nabī*. 2nd ed. N.p.: Mu'assasat al-Saḥāb lil-Intāj al-I'lāmī, 1431 [2010]. Electronic copy at http://www.ilmway.com/site/maqdis/MS_874.html.

———. *Al-Ḥiṣād al-murr: Al-Ikhwān al-Muslimīn fī sittīn ʿāman.* 2nd ed. N.p.: Markaz al-Fajr lil-Iʿlām, 2005. Electronic copy at http://www.ilmway.com/site/maqdis/MS_25064.html.

———. *Tawjīhāt ʿāmma lil-ʿamal al-jihādī.* N.p.: Muʾassasat al-Saḥāb, 1434 [2013]. Electronic copy at http://www.ilmway.com/site/maqdis/MS_10765.html.

———. *Al-Walāʾ wal-barāʾ: ʿAqīda manqūla wa-wāqiʿ mafqūd.* N.p.: n.p., 2002. Electronic copy at http://www.ilmway.com/site/maqdis/MS_20361.html.

Al-Zuḥaylī, Wahba. *Āthār al-ḥarb: Dirāsa fiqhiyya muqārana.* Damascus: Dār al-Fikr, 2009.

Audio and Video Recordings

Al-Albānī, Muḥammad Nāsir al-Dīn. "Mā ḥukm al-ʿamaliyyāt al-intiḥāriyya?" Audio recording, no. 533 of *Silsilat al-Hudā wal-l-Nūr,* Aug. 16, 2004. At http://alathar.net/home/esound/index.php?op=tadevi&id=424&coid=4893.

Al-ʿAdnānī, Abū Muḥammad. "Al-Silmiyya dīn man?" Video, Aug. 2013. At https://justpaste.it/6151.

———. *Walayumakkinanna lahum dīnahum alladhī irtaḍā lahum: He Will Empower the Religion He Has Chosen for Them (Q24:55).* Video, Apr. 3, 2014. At https://archive.org/details/al_adnani2.

———. "Wa-yaḥyā man ḥayya ʿan bayyina" ("Those who were to live might live after seeing a clear proof" [Q8:42]). Audio recording, May 23, 2016. At https://archive.org/details/ntheer14_mail.

Al-Anṣārī, ʿAbd al-Ḥamīd. "Judhūr al-irhāb." *Al-ʿArabiyya,* video, May 11, 2007. At https://www.youtube.com/watch?v=urvxEFTszjs&t=17s.

———. "Thaqāfat al-karāhiya wa-intishār al-taṭarruf wa-l-tajdīd al-dīnī." Interview on *Ḥadīth al-ʿArab,* program on Sky News, Aug. 5, 2016. At https://www.youtube.com/watch?v=fA0edaPSCvU&t=792s.

Al-Baghdādī, Abū Bakr. *Infirū khifāfan wa-thiqālan* [So Go Out, No Matter Whether You Are Lightly or Heavily Armed (the first words of Q9:41)]. Muʾassasat al-Furqān, video, Apr. 15, 2015. At https://tawhid.website/?video=3059.

Gumʿa, ʿAlī. "Al-Ḥiwār al-kāmil lil-Shaykh ʿAlī Gumʿa maʿa Khayrī Ramaḍān." Episode of *Mumkin,* CBC, Aug. 23, 2013. At https://www.youtube.com/watch?v=DcAoD8FttnU.

Islamic State. "Risāla bi-shaʾn ghazwat Bārīs al-mubāraka." Audio recording, Nov. 14, 2015. At https://archive.org/details/mksnd73iu4.

———. *ʿUmalāʾ, lā ʿulamāʾ.* Video, May 26, 2017. At https://www.youtube.com/watch?v=HJeVOsSA9qI.

Al-Qaraḍāwī, Shaykh Yūsuf. *Ḥiwār al-adyān al-Shaykh Yūsuf al-Qaraḍāwī*. Video, Dec. 30, 2014. At https://www.youtube.com/watch?v=sCTN9qpQ QPU.

———. *Kalimāt qayyima lil-Shaykh Yūsuf al-Qaraḍāwī: Multaqā al-Imām al-Qaraḍāwī ma'a al-talāmīdh wal-aṣḥāb*. Video, 2007. At http://www.daily motion.com/video/xu5ejd.

———. *Khuṭbat al-Jum'a lil-Duktūr al-Qaraḍāwī*. Video, June 21, 2013. At https://www.youtube.com/watch?v=iKb8048QjLQ.

———. *Khuṭbat al-Jum'a lil-Duktūr Yūsuf al-Qaraḍāwī*. Video, Nov. 23, 2012. At https://www.youtube.com/watch?v=nJrImaCkxo4&t=35s.

———. *Khuṭbat al-Jum'a lil-Shaykh al-Qaraḍāwī 'an dhikrā thawrat 25 Yanāyir*. Video, Jan. 24, 2014. At https://www.youtube.com/watch?v=7KtfIQyT6cw.

———. *Khuṭbat Yūsuf al-Qaraḍāwī bi-Jāmi' al-Azhar*. Video, Nov. 16, 2012. At https://www.youtube.com/watch?v=M8lVhA2nzGY.

———. *Al-Qaraḍāwī yaṣifu Ḥizb Allāh bi-Ḥizb al-Shayṭān wa-yad'ū duwal al-Nātū li-mazīd al-tadakhkhul fī Sūriyā*. Video, May 2013. At https://www .youtube.com/watch?v=-2d0LBXsYFg.

———. *Al-Qaraḍāwī yuftī bi-qatl Mu'ammar al-Qadhdhāfī*. Video, Feb. 21, 2011. At https://www.youtube.com/watch?v=QrXN1FVIhio.

———. *Al-Shaykh al-Qaraḍāwī yuftī bi-jawāz qatl al-Qadhdhāfī*. Video, Feb. 21, 2011. At https://www.youtube.com/watch?v=X8fpg8_hR2Q.

———. *Al-Shaykh Salmān al-'Awda yuḥāwiru al-'allāma Yūsuf al-Qaraḍāwī fī liqā' khāṣṣ 'alā qanāt al-ḥiwār*. Video, Nov. 18, 2016. At https://www.youtube .com/watch?v=C825fzdDm6A&t=28s.

———. "Sheikh Al-Qaradhawi Retracts Fatwā Permitting Palestinian Suicide Bombings: No Need for Them Anymore." *MEMRI TV* Clip no. 5760, Nov. 18, 2016. http://www.memritv.org/clip_transcript/en/5760.htm.

———. "Al-Wasaṭiyya 1." Episode of the program *Fiqh al-ḥayāh*, Anā TV, Sept. 15. 2009. At https://www.youtube.com/watch?v=oHSzIM6SqlQ.

———. *Yūsuf al-Qaraḍāwī yaqūlu innahu yuqātilu fī sabīl al-dīmuqrāṭiyya*. Video, May 5, 2012. At https://www.youtube.com/watch?v=6O1Abw6JG3k.

Al-Sisi, 'Abd al-Fattah. *Al-Sīsī fī iḥtifāl al-Mawlid al-Nabawī*. Video, Jan. 2015. At https://www.youtube.com/watch?v=OPoIJEDcPEo.

Episodes of *Al-Sharī'a wal-Ḥayāh*

The episodes of Shaykh Yūsuf al-Qaraḍāwī's al-Jazeera program *Al-Sharī'a wal-ḥayāh* (Sharī'a and Life) given here are listed chronologically.

"Al-Wasaṭiyya fī al-Islām." Al-Jazeera, Oct. 26, 1997. At https://tinyurl.com/y7agxjsr.

"Ru'yat al-Islām lil-ta'addudiyya al-siyāsiyya." Al-Jazeera, Apr. 4, 1999. At https://tinyurl.com/kdemb4b.

"Al-Jāliyāt al-Islāmiyya fī bilād al-gharb." Part 2. Al-Jazeera, May 9, 1999. At https://tinyurl.com/y7w49ywz.

"Fiqh al-jāliyāt al-Islāmiyya fī al-gharb." Part 2. Al-Jazeera, May 16, 1999. At https://tinyurl.com/lm6nem3.

"Al-Irhāb wa-ḥamalāt al-karāhiya ḍidda al-'Arab wal-Muslimīn." Al-Jazeera, Sept. 16, 2001. At https://tinyurl.com/yb2vfl5a.

"Ḥiwār al-adyān." Al-Jazeera, Nov. 4, 2001. At https://tinyurl.com/y9lg3vpu.

"Al-Intifāḍa al-Filasṭīniyya wal-'amaliyyāt al-fidā'iyya." Al-Jazeera, Dec. 9, 2001. At https://tinyurl.com/y7mfrvnu.

"Dalālāt wa-rasā'il al-muẓāharāt fī al-gharb li-ṣāliḥ al-'Irāq." Al-Jazeera, Feb. 16, 2003. At https://tinyurl.com/ybf44ze9.

"Al-Islām wa-'alāqatuhu bi-l-dīmuqrāṭiyya." Al-Jazeera, June 6, 2004. At https://tinyurl.com/y9qwbecv.

"Fiṭrat Allāh fī khalqihi." Al-Jazeera, June 7, 2006. At https://tinyurl.com/yac86hus.

"Libās al-mar'a al-Muslima." Al-Jazeera, July 8, 2007. At https://tinyurl.com/ycegfzbp.

"Al-Fatwā wal-siyāsa." Al-Jazeera, Jan. 13, 2010. At https://www.youtube.com/watch?v=VKLOsxSLDAU.

"Al-Khawārij bayna al-dīn wa-l-tārīkh wa-l-siyāsa." Al-Jazeera, Aug. 25, 2011. At https://tinyurl.com/y955zsax.

"Al-Thawra: Fitna am raḥma." Al-Jazeera, Sept. 15, 2011. At https://tinyurl.com/ybjo8w54.

"Ḥalqa khāṣṣa ḥawla al-sha'n al-'āmm li-l-umma." Al-Jazeera, Nov. 25, 2012. At https://tinyurl.com/y9awubsb.

"Ḥalqa khāṣṣa ḥawla al-sha'n al-'āmm li-l-umma." Al-Jazeera, Dec. 2, 2012. At https://tinyurl.com/y9vxo5zc.

"Ḥalqa khāṣṣa lil-ijāba 'alā istifsārāt al-mushāhidīn." Al-Jazeera, Mar. 17, 2013. At https://tinyurl.com/y7shufdl.

"Al-Radd 'alā istifsārāt al-mushāhidīn ḥawla al-sha'n al-'āmm." Al-Jazeera, Apr. 21, 2013. At https://tinyurl.com/yay59hlk.

Index

Photos, figures and tables are indicated by italicized pages numbers.

Sagi Polka is a guest researcher at the Nehemia Levtzion Center for Islamic Studies in the Hebrew University of Jerusalem. He wrote his PhD dissertation at Bar-Ilan University on the *wasaṭiyya*. For many years, he has taught text-based courses on various aspects of al-Qaraḍāwī's teachings at the Hebrew University of Jerusalem and at the Ben-Gurion University of the Negev. He has also published a number of fundamental papers on aspects of the *wasaṭiyya* and contemporary Islamic thought.